CINEMA AND *Sorcery*

THE COMPREHENSIVE GUIDE TO FANTASY FILM

**BY ARNOLD T. BLUMBERG &
SCOTT ALAN WOODARD**

Cinema and Sorcery: The Comprehensive Guide to Fantasy Film

Authors: Arnold T. Blumberg and Scott A. Woodard

Editor: Jessica Kristine

Publisher: Chris Pramas

Graphic Design: Hal Mangold

Cover Art: Ozan Art & Christophe Swal

Green Ronin Staff: Joseph D. Carriker, Steve Kenson, Jon Leitheusser, Nicole Lindroos, Hal Mangold, Jack Norris, Chris Pramas, Donna Prior, Evan Sass, Marc Schmalz, Owen K.C. Stephens, and Barry Wilson

Cinema and Sorcery: The Comprehensive Guide to Fantasy Film is published by Green Ronin Publishing, LLC.

Cinema and Sorcery: The Comprehensive Guide to Fantasy Film © 2016 by Arnold T. Blumberg and Scott A. Woodard. All rights reserved.

Any discussion of trademarked, service marked, or copyrighted material or entities in this book should not be construed as a challenge to their legal owners. The owners of these trademarks, service marks, and copyrights have not authorized or endorsed this book.

Reproduction of material from within this book for any purposes, by photographic, digital, or other methods of electronic storage and retrieval, is prohibited.

Green Ronin Publishing

3815 South Othello Street

Suite 100, #304

Seattle, WA 98118

Visit us online at greenronin.com.

10 9 8 7 6 5 4 3 2 1

Stock number GRR4003, May 2016.

ISBN: 978-1-934547-71-7

Printed in the United States.

CINEMA AND *Sorcery*

THE COMPREHENSIVE GUIDE TO FANTASY FILM

DEDICATION

During the writing of this book, a surprising number of key people involved in many of the films covered here left this plane of existence for realms unknown. We'd like to dedicate this guide to all the fantastic fantasy filmmakers, actors, and other individuals without whom these journeys to lands of wonder and adventure would never have happened. We don't think any of the other people listed here would blame us, however, if we dedicate this book primarily to one man: someone who shaped our childhoods and the childhoods of millions of others (including, no doubt, many of our readers), a genius who gave life to inanimate objects and not only crafted movies and memories that would last well beyond him but also taught us about the pure beauty and power of imagination.

Farewell, Ray Harryhausen (1920-2013), the guiding force behind many of the films covered in this book. Even if he himself is abandoned or forgotten, his work will never fade. Never. It will stand until the end of time.

ACKNOWLEDGEMENTS

The authors wish to thank the following for their encouragement and contributions to this book:

First and foremost, our "third author," Rochelle Blumberg. Without her, this book would not exist. She put together the main list of titles with which we started, kept it updated throughout the project, researched countless movies whenever we had annoying questions ("It has swords, but is there magic in it?" or "There's tons of magic, but does anyone ever use a sword?"), and wrote the majority of the blurbs for the titles in the index.

Green Ronin and Chris Pramas, for agreeing to take on this project. We're grateful for the chance to pontificate on one of our favorite genres.

The filmmakers and other creators who provided personal insight into some of the films: Michael J. Bassett, Andrew Belling, Greg Costikyan, Luigi Cozzi, Bert I. Gordon, Albert Pyun, William Stout, John Terlesky, Chris Walas, Jim Wynorski, and many more.

Keith Topping, one of the pioneers of a format for delving into the rich history of genre film and television in guides like these; David J. Howe and Stephen James Walker, the men behind Telos Publishing, the publishers of Arnold's *Zombiemania: 80 Movies to Die For* (co-authored with Andrew Hershberger) and long-time supporters of Arnold's publishing efforts in a variety of capacities; Andy Hershberger; and Marvin A. Blumberg.

Scott wishes to thank TaMara for tolerating the many months of obsessive sword-and-sorcery movie-watching and all the subsequent late nights (and ungodly early mornings) at the computer. As promised to you, we included *The Dark Crystal*.

TABLE of CONTENTS

Dedication v
Acknowledgements vi
Introduction: Taking Up The Sword ix
The Movies xiii
    The Thief of Bagdad 1
    The 7Th Voyage of Sinbad 9
    The Magic Sword 16
    Jason and the Argonauts 23
    The Golden Voyage Of Sinbad 30
    Monty Python and the Holy Grail 36
    Wizards 45
    Star Wars 52
    Sinbad and the Eye of the Tiger 62
    Hawk The Slayer 69
    Excalibur 77
    Clash Of The Titans 85
    Dragonslayer 93
    The Sword and the Sorcerer 100
    Conan The Barbarian 109
    The Beastmaster 122
    The Last Unicorn 130
    The Dark Crystal 137
    Ator, The Fighting Eagle 146
    Krull 152
    Hercules 159
    Conquest 166
    The Neverending Story 171
    The Warrior and the Sorceress 177
    Red Sonja 183

The Black Cauldron	190
Wizards of the Lost Kingdom	198
Highlander	204
Legend	211
Labyrinth	220
Big Trouble In Little China	229
The Barbarians	237
The Princess Bride	243
Deathstalker II	252
Willow	259
Barbarian Queen II: The Empress Strikes Back	267
Army Of Darkness	272
Dragonheart	279
Dungeons & Dragons	286
The Lord of the Rings: The Fellowship of the Ring	294
Versus	307
The Lord of the Rings: The Two Towers	312
Pirates of the Caribbean: The Curse of the Black Pearl	322
The Lord of the Rings: The Return of the King	330
The Chronicles of Narnia: The Lion, the Witch and the Wardrobe	340
Solomon Kane	347
How to Train Your Dragon	354
Your Highness	361
Brave	369
The Hobbit: An Unexpected Journey	376
A Concordance of Sword-And-Sorcery Movies 1924-2015	387
Index of Main Films	480
The Authors	481

INTRODUCTION: TAKING UP THE SWORD

"What is best in life?"
"To crush your enemies—see them driven before you—and to hear the lamentation of their women."

—Conan the Barbarian (Arnold Schwarzenegger), *Conan the Barbarian*

"The closer we are to danger, the farther we are from harm."

—Peregrin "Pippin" Took (Billy Boyd), *The Lord of the Rings: The Two Towers*

A sword-and-sorcery story begins like a mythological tale: with a need for a hero, a quest for power or fame or perhaps a damsel in distress, a call to arms.... It ends with victory against the forces of evil and the chance to forge a new and brighter future. As children, we found a lot to enthrall us in these tales of adventure, and we never lost the sense of wonder that rose with every sword held aloft, every monster vanquished, every kingdom restored to peace and prosperity.

We—Arnold and Scott—met thanks to a mutual appreciation or *Doctor Who*, comics, cheesy horror, and a tendency for both of us to turn up at conventions celebrating those and other aspects of pop culture. During a visit together to Dark Delicacies, a Southern California boutique that specializes in the horror genre, we discovered and purchased a signed copy of the soundtrack to *Deathstalker II* and germinated the seed of an idea for this book. The quest began: to revisit and discover the best and worst sword-and-sorcery movies ever made and record our opinions for generations to come. We wrote this guide as fans for fans.

At the time of this writing, over 400 feature-length sword-and-sorcery movies exist. You'll find them in the index, which we compiled by researching from the present day all the way back to the first cinematic treatments in the silent-film era. (We cut off the project in mid-2015 on a case-by-case basis.) We counted only feature-length presentations—theatrical films and made-for-TV movies of 59 minutes or longer—so no miniseries, single or multiple episodes of a TV series, documentaries, fan-made works, or short films.

WHAT IS SWORD AND SORCERY?

The most important question we had to ask was, "What *is* a sword-and-sorcery movie?" With what definition would most people agree?

There's a hero, often from an unspecified ancient time of magic and monsters. There's a "princess" or land (or both) in peril and an evil wizard or king threatening the good and innocent. Protagonists must undertake a quest to gather allies, locate an enchanted artifact, or perhaps just test their own heroic hearts. Classical Greek and Roman mythology and folklore from around the world influence and even directly adapt to sword-and-sorcery cinema. (Joseph Campbell understood this very well.) This loose framework allows for a lot of variation.

The term "sword and sorcery" arose in 1961, in a fanzine exchange between writers Michael Moorcock (Elric) and Fritz Leiber (Fafhrd and the Gray Mouser), who sought to label Robert E. Howard stories that we will discuss later in this book. Leiber felt that "sword and sorcery" conveyed the right blend of setting, supernatural elements, and adventure. He might have borrowed the structure of the term from Italian "sword-and-sandal" movies prevalent at the time.

We painstakingly established criteria for deciding what films to include in the comprehensive index. From them, we then selected fifty to highlight in their own chapters. Although we all have a general idea of what sword and sorcery is, the genre has many offshoots and cul-de-sacs, like those sword-and-sandal films, which feature no fantasy elements like magic or monsters but merely take place in historic or quasi-historic ancient times. Such a film might feature a lead character who has a fantastical origin, like Hercules and Samson. (Hercules is the son of Zeus and a human woman, and Samson is a biblical figure granted great power by God.) If we considered a hero's origin enough to warrant inclusion, we would have to catalogue all those sword-and-sandal films as well as countless biblical epics. We decided that for a movie to merit the label "sword and sorcery," it needed to reach a "critical mass" of fantasy elements and other factors. Godlike being? No. Godlike being fighting a griffin with a magic sword? Yes.

Then there were movies like *Reign of Fire*, which features dragons as real creatures that existed at the time of the dinosaurs and are therefore not magical. This film turns up on many fans' sword-and-sorcery lists, presumably because, for most people, the presence of dragons in any form qualifies it. But was that enough for us? Hmm. . . .

In addition to establishing criteria that qualified movies as sword and sorcery, we wanted to reflect consensus forged over the years by the fan community. What films did fans embrace as sword and sorcery? That approach, though, could be a—forgive us—double-edged sword.

Ultimately, we accepted that we couldn't nail things down neatly and logically every time. We left out some movies and included others based on what *felt* right. The heart of the warrior is often a better guide than the mind.

Readers might disagree with some of our choices, so here's to the debate! Our shopping list went something like this:

1. The movie had to include swords or sword-like weapons.
2. The movie had to have a critical mass of fantasy elements: world/setting, magic wielders, and/or mythological or supernatural creatures. We considered a period setting important, either throughout or for a significant portion of the movie, but rather than focus on movies set in the sort of loincloth-laden barbaric era in which Conan and the Beastmaster roam, we included fantasy-tinged Arthurian epics and even a few hybrids, like the fairytale/sci-fi adventure *Krull*. A few of our choices might raise the eyebrows of even a lenient fan, but we stand behind—for example—the first *Star Wars* as a quintessential sword-and-sorcery film. It has magic (the Force), swordplay (lightsabers), and an ancient setting ("a long time ago . . .").
3. Magic had to appear as an external force that characters could draw upon, manipulate, or apply to other people or things. If magical powers appeared in the story only as (super)natural abilities inherent to a particular type of creature—say, vampires—then they didn't qualify as magic or sorcery for our purposes.

4. Dragons counted. We decided that above all other criteria, if a dragon showed up, it satisfied the magical side of the equation, on the basis that dragons are one of the most ubiquitous and identifiable monsters of this category of storytelling. They derive from source material that inspired and defined the genre. Be a dragon Vermithrax or Toothless, it trumped every other consideration for the "sorcery" designation. Swords or sword-like weapons would still need to fulfill the "sword" part; therefore, children's movies like *Pete's Dragon* do not appear in our index. We decided to include *Reign of Fire*, because although it's a science-fiction film in which the dragons are actual ancient creatures, it includes harpoon-like weapons.

See how tough this was? We're glad you appreciate it.

THE 50 FILMS

So how did we pick the fifty movies that inspired this book's chapters? Even the most dyed-in-the-wool sword-and-sorcery fan has to admit that some of these movies are really bad. And not "so bad they're good"—just plain awful.

Celebrating a genre means acknowledging the full range of fare under its banner, so we decided to spotlight movies that represent the best and worst that sword and sorcery has to offer, from true classics and award-winning blockbusters to horrific misfires and cheesy-fun films best shared with friends.

We also tried to focus on films that in some way, shape, or form enhance the gaming experience, either with material directly familiar to gamers or because characters, settings, or storylines inspire gaming scenarios. *Dungeons & Dragons* co-creator Gary Gygax himself cited fantasy films as sources of inspiration in the earliest versions of that game's rules (and *D&D* just celebrated its 40th anniversary in January 2014!).

We did our best to select easily obtainable films, but we couldn't help but put a small number of films on the list that are out of print or awaiting commercial release. We hope that your favorites are here—and perhaps even a few you never saw and might want to check out. If we skipped anything that you think is a glaring oversight, well, we might cover it in Volume 2!

We list the fifty films by their English titles. The index cross-references them with any alternate titles. In each chapter, after the title, we list the U.S. year of release, which sometimes differs from the first release in the film's country of origin or another country. If a gap between domestic and U.S. releases is insanely long—such as between a local release in the 1970s and a U.S. DVD release in the 2000s—we fall back on the earlier date. In some cases, we couldn't locate an official U.S. release date, so we used the dates of earliest release in the countries of origin for those as well. (These rules also apply to the dates in the index.)

After the release date, we list the country or countries of origin/production. The company or companies responsible for production follow, as well as running time, whether the movie is black-and-white or color, and Motion Picture Association of America (MPAA) ratings. We took cast-and-crew credits from the films themselves and compared them with several online and print references, including the Internet Movie Database (IMDb). Wherever we encountered a conflict, we deferred to the screen credits.

xii • CINEMA AND SORCERY

Finally, some of these movies have more titles than we've had hot dinners, including working titles used only during development and/or production, and planned release titles changed at the last minute. We've included these here if they exist.

After all those nuts and bolts, we list the following:

ON THE MAP: The location(s) in which the story takes place.

OUR STORY SO FAR: The plot. Easy one.

ALTERNATE VERSIONS: If different cuts of the film float around out there on TV, DVD, or elsewhere, we describe them here.

IT'S MAGIC: How do the powers of good and evil manifest themselves in this film? How does magic operate in this reality? We discuss it in detail.

THE QUEST FOR MEANING: Here we explore deeper thoughts about events and issues in the film, especially where they evoke a gaming experience or touch on meaningful themes in fantasy and adventure.

WHO GOES THERE?: You've seen those actors somewhere but can't place them. We tell you where they have appeared. If a familiar face appears in more than one of our fifty films, we cover that person's career and credits in the first appearance and not in subsequent chapters.

6 DEGREES OF SORCERY: Here we list deliberate or tenuous ways we think the film connects with other movies in this book or in the wider world of pop culture—visual, verbal, or other. You might come up with connections of your own.

SHATTERING THE ILLUSION: The making of the movie.

MUSIC OF THE MINSTRELS: Music plays such a large role in this genre (often bleeding over into the gaming experience) that we feel it deserves its own section. Songs featured in the film—and information from the soundtrack—appear here.

THE SAGA CONTINUES: We examine the larger legacy of the movie, including sequels, remakes, games, and other merchandise that tie in with the film.

TAKE UP THY SWORD!: In this section, something *very* similar to a selected hero, villain, monster, or artifact from the film gets a roleplaying-game treatment, with information to help you incorporate it into your campaigns.

THE FILM'S DESTINY: Our review.

THIS YEAR IN GAMING: Events in the history of gaming that took place in the year of the film's release.

TAGLINES: These are the things on the movie poster that tell you not to see the film if you have a heart condition or that proclaim it's "the greatest adventure of all time!" We tried to stick with taglines from posters, lobby cards, and other advertisements contemporary with the release, not those made up years later for video and other home releases—though some of those might have slipped in. You'll find these scattered through the entries on each movie.

And now it's time to begin our journey. The prophecy must be fulfilled, the world must be saved, and many days and nights lie between us and victory in our quest. Raise your sword and join us, for glory and adventure await!

Arnold and Scott
Last seen heading into the desert with plastic swords and a 2-liter bottle of Mountain Dew...
2015

THE MOVIES

THE THIEF OF BAGDAD

1940 • UK • LONDON FILMS / UNITED ARTISTS • 106M • COLOR • NR

SCREENPLAY AND DIALOGUE: Miles Malleson
SCENARIO: Lajos Biro
DIRECTORS: Ludwig Berger, Michael Powell, Tim Whelan, Alexander Korda (uncredited), Zoltan Korda (uncredited), and William Cameron Menzies (uncredited)
PRODUCER: Alexander Korda
MUSIC: Miklos Rozsa. Lyrics to "I Want to be a Sailor" by Robert Vansittart and William Kernell. Lyrics to "Hungarian Lullabye" by Zoltan Korda; performed by Adelaide Hall.
MAKEUP: Stuart Freeborn (uncredited)
SPECIAL EFFECTS DIRECTED BY: Lawrence Butler
PRODUCTION DESIGNED IN COLOR BY: Vincent Korda
CHIEF PHOTOGRAPHER: George Perinal
ART DIRECTOR: Vincent Korda (uncredited)
COSTUMES DESIGNED BY: Oliver Messel, John Armstrong, and Marcel Vertes
FIGHT CHOREOGRAPHER: Ralph Faulkner (uncredited)
DANCE INSTRUCTOR: Wendy Toye (uncredited)
CAST: Conrad Veidt (Jaffar), Sabu (Abu), June Duprez (Princess), John Justin (Ahmad), Rex Ingram (Djinn), Miles Malleson (Sultan), Morton Selten (The Old King), Mary Morris (Halima/Silver Maid), Bruce Winston (The Merchant), Hay Petrie (The Astrologer), Adelaide Hall (The Singer), Roy Emerton (The Jailer), Allan Jeayes (The Story Teller), Joseph Cozier (Man Selling Fish, uncredited), Alexander Laine, Cleo Laine, Sylvia Laine, and Leslie Phillips (Urchins in Bagdad Market, uncredited)
ALTERNATE TITLE: *The Thief of Bagdad: An Arabian Fantasy in Technicolor* (UK title)

ON THE MAP

The journey begins and ends in Bagdad, with trips to the city of Basra, a remote island, Mount Everest in Tibet (the presumed location of the Temple of the Dawn), and the mysterious Land of Legend.

OUR STORY SO FAR

King Ahmad's grand vizier, the wizard Jaffar, ousts him, with designs on a beautiful princess from Basra whom Ahmad would make his bride. Allied with a clever young thief named Abu, Ahmad must brave blindness and other trials to save the princess from Jaffar's clutches, while Abu finds magical aid in the form of a deranged genie and a kindly old man dwelling in a mystical land.

IT'S MAGIC

This is definitely a reality filled with fantasy. If the genie is telling the truth, this "roof of the world" perches in succession on another genie, an eagle, a boar, and a fish swimming in the Sea of Eternity.... Right, and it's also turtles all the way down.

While this world has plenty of magic, a lot of it manifests itself as luck and convenience. The mad genie's bottle washes up on shore at just the time when Abu most needs magical intervention. Then, when rescuing Ahmad and the princess proves beyond his ability, Abu spontaneously appears in the Land of Legend, some form of extra-dimensional encampment of old men (or perhaps gods), where he obtains magical weapons and the means to make it back to Bagdad in record time. True, his arrival there appears to be facilitated by smashing the All-Seeing Eye, but why exactly would that be the method of reaching the Land of Legend? Ah, magic: so illogical.

Speaking of that genie, he's quite a piece of work. While adhering to the oft-seen trope of three wishes, he is also a lunatic with a murderous streak and a bone-chilling laugh. Apparently imprisoned by King Solomon—there's a story we'd like to hear—he spent 1,000 years planning to reward anyone who rescued him and then another 1,000 scheming deadly revenge on that person, whomever it would be. Abu's luck is formidable.

As for Jaffar's powers, including mesmerism, transmogrification, and the blooming of flowers that leech memory, they all demonstrate dark manipulation used by an unscrupulous magician to curse and doom his foes. Jaffar also builds enchanted clockwork devices like his flying horse, suggesting a foreboding melding of magic and machinery that we'll see reflected time and again. (See **The Quest for Meaning** for more.)

After the princess's enchantment, upon which she might never remember her past, merely one syllable uttered by Ahmad breaks the spell. Even Jaffar is not immune, because his genuine love for the princess stays his hand from manipulating her more directly and seals his fate. As we'll also see more than once, love is more powerful than any other magic. Aww.

THE QUEST FOR MEANING

While the theme of true love drives much of the plot as Ahmad quests to win the heart of the princess and save her from the dark and lustful desires of the evil magician, he doesn't really come across a hero. He fulfills the romantic leading role, weathers a variety of challenges (such as the curse of blindness), and travels far and wide before at last uniting with his love, and he fights for her hand in a near-climactic battle, but he also loses that battle and finds himself imprisoned with her, awaiting execution. Not exactly Conan or Hercules, is he?

On the other hand, the plucky little thief, who seems more like a sidekick by his stature and his disregard for little things like the rules of law, ethics, or honor, proves a loyal and capable

---

An Arabian Fantasy in TECHNICOLOR (on screen)

GIGANTIC! The Wonder Picture of All Time! Dwarfing anything ever seen ... A Mountainous Genie piercing the clouds ... Flying Horses winging over jewelled cities ... A Magic Carpet that spans the world like the swiftest bird. All the glories, romance, adventure of the Thousand and One Nights-woven into a thrilling triumph of motion picture magic!

Thousand and One Sights From the Thousand and One Nights!

companion to Ahmad and in fact turns out to be the hero of the tale. He does all the legwork, completes all the magical quests, receives gifts from the gods (or near enough, anyway), and sweeps in during the film's final moments to kill the villain and save the lovers from their doom. Like in *Big Trouble in Little China* after it, the inversion of the hero-sidekick dynamic is central to this movie.

> THE WONDER OF THE ENCHANTED PRINCESS. WHOEVER LOOKS UPON HER BEAUTY DIES-BUT AHMAD DARES TO WIN HER LOVE!

The film is highly charged sexually, but in ways that abide by the Hays code—apart from the footage completed in the UK with the princess's "excessive" décolletage. The true intent is still obvious. Jaffar's curse that can only be lifted when he holds the princess in his arms, and the scene in which that takes place, feels like a metaphorical placeholder for a greater violation of her purity. There's even a subtle and perhaps inadvertent undercurrent in Abu's devotion to Ahmad. When the former king expresses his desire to win the princess at all costs, Abu sadly inquires if there is truly nothing for Ahmad but the princess . . . ? Is he offering . . . an alternative?

Jaffar's blending of technology with magic ties in with many other films in this book, in which the villain introduces the cold influence of modern machinery to a world of fantasy and magic and is hoist by his own petard when his mechanical contrivances fail him. He's also like world leaders today who want to deprive people of access to knowledge (like a clock) because it makes them easier to control. Still, he's doomed. In love and in technology, nothing works out for the grand vizier.

We could discuss the color-coding of cities throughout the movie (Bagdad in white, Basra in pink), the interweaving of stories within stories, and prophecies that prove true in the end, but perhaps most relevant to the scope of this book, we see modern-day gaming attitudes at play. Jaffar and the sultan relax with a game of chess at one point, but the sultan's single-minded obsession with acquiring clockwork toys should especially resonate with those who fill their homes with collectibles and roleplaying accessories. Just don't give up your daughter for that limited-edition poseable flying horse, and the evil blue fake multi-limbed sex doll won't kill you.

WHO GOES THERE?

Conrad Veidt became one of the early icons in horror cinema with his role in *The Cabinet of Dr. Caligari* and almost played the titular vampire eventually portrayed by Bela Lugosi in *Dracula*. Veidt also appeared in *The Man Who Laughs*, *Casablanca*, and *Above Suspicion*. He died in 1943 at age 50.

Sabu debuted in *Elephant Boy* and had roles in *Jungle Book*, *Arabian Nights*, *Cobra Woman*, *Black Narcissus*, *Jungle Hell*, and *Sabu and the Magic Ring*. He died in 1963 at age 39.

June Duprez also appeared in *The Spy in Black*, *The Four Feathers*, *Don Winslow of the Coast Guard*, and *And Then There Were None*. She died in 1984 at age 66.

Rex Ingram started his career in silent films such as *Tarzan of the Apes* and *The Ten Commandments* and later appeared in movies like *A Thousand and One Nights* and *Tarzan's Hidden Jungle*, and TV shows like *I Spy*, *Daktari*, and *The Bill Cosby Show*. He died in 1969 at age 73.

> THE WONDER OF THE MASKED MAGICIAN WHO TRANSFORMS A PRINCE INTO A BEGGAR ... A BOY INTO A BARKING DOG!

Writer and actor Miles Malleson also appeared in *Dead of Night*, *Horror of Dracula*, *The Hound of the Baskervilles*, *The Brides of Dracula*, *The Phantom of the Opera*, and *First Men in the Moon*. He died in 1969 at age 80.

Mary Morris made memorable television appearances in *The Terrible Choice (Macbeth)*, *A for Andromeda*, *The Prisoner*, and the *Doctor Who* story "Kinda." She died in 1988 at age 72.

Allan Jeayes appeared in the legendary sci-fi film *Things to Come* and the seminal horror anthology *Dead of Night*. He died in 1963 at age 78.

Leslie Phillips is best known to British comedy fans as Dr. Tony Burke in *Doctor in Love* and *Doctor in Trouble* and for multiple roles in the raunchy *Carry On* movies. He also had several roles in the TV series *The Adventures of Robin Hood*; was the voice of Mr. Tumnus in the TV movie *The Lion, the Witch & the Wardrobe*; and was the voice of the Sorting Hat in the *Harry Potter* films.

6 DEGREES OF SORCERY

Although the source material of *One Thousand and One Nights* dates centuries earlier—and many cite the 1924 Fairbanks version of the tale as equally if not more influential in the scheme of things—this version ripples most powerfully through pop culture, especially with other films in this book made long after its release. The visuals in particular weave connective threads throughout the genre, from the works of Ray Harryhausen to traditionally animated adventures to the latest CGI-laden fantasy spectacles. Yet this movie also owes a debt, ironically enough, to the creator of *Conan*! In Robert E. Howard's much-praised 1933 story, "The Tower of the Elephant," the Cimmerian teams up with a "prince of thieves" to retrieve a gem much like the All-Seeing Eye. The story even features a battle with a giant spider, although unlike with Abu, that arachnid defeats the thief.

The evil-eye motif turns up in *Sinbad and the Eye of the Tiger*, *The Beastmaster*, and *The Lord of the Rings* films, among others. Ahmad asking for alms might elicit a chuckle if you recall Monty Python's *Life of Brian*. A scene in which someone observes a sleeping princess turns up in *Clash of the Titans*. The women who tempt Ahmad to remain are like the ladies of Castle Anthrax with Galahad in *Monty Python and the Holy Grail*. Abu gives to the poor like Robin Hood, and a later execution-rescue also feels like a rescue in that classic tale. Sabu hides from pursuers in a basket, as Marion does in *Raiders of the Lost Ark*. The princess's sequestered life and the threat of death for looking upon her turn up in many other fantasy tales, including (in some ways) *Clash of the Titans*. The princess's entourage giggles and gathers around a pool much like the ladies of the palace in *The Ten Commandments*. The princess asks Ahmad if he's a good genie, just as Dorothy asks if Glinda is a good witch in *The Wizard of Oz*. The theme of true love's transcendence over all other powers appears in *The Princess Bride*. In a fleeting reference to Sinbad, Abu tells Ahmad they have passage on the famous sailor's ship. In *Pirates of the Caribbean: The Curse of the Black Pearl*—another film in which temporary stranding on an island plays a part—Elizabeth also finds herself held aboard a ship. Jaffar's attempted hypnosis of the princess echoes Bela Lugosi's iconic Murder Legendre in *White Zombie* and inspires later scenes, such as Ming controlling Dale in *Flash Gordon* (which also mirrors a later scene in which Ahmad becomes chained and imprisoned).

The statue of Kali in *The Golden Voyage of Sinbad* and Ann Magnuson's Calli in the largely execrable *Cabin Boy* clearly owe their look to the multi-armed, blue-skinned "robot" Silver Maid. The Temple of the Dawn looks like similar structures in movies like *Clash of the Titans*, as does the huge statue within. The green natives are just like Kali's protectors in *Golden Voyage*, with faces that resemble Calibos from *Clash*. Some of the temple ruins have the same atmosphere as the Mines of Moria from *The Lord of the Rings: The Fellowship of the Ring*, and the chasm-spanning pathway is like the one in that film and also the one in *The 7th Voyage of Sinbad*.

Giant spider? You know we're going to bring up Shelob, right?

The octopus didn't necessarily inspire Harryhausen's use of one in *It Came from Beneath the Sea*, but who knows? The All-Seeing Eye is like the Palantír in *The Lord of the Rings* films as well as many other visual or verbal magical transmitters appearing in other films in this book. Blue roses figure in David Lynch's *Twin Peaks: Fire Walk with Me*. The notion that the imagination of youth can reinvigorate the Land of Legend sounds a bit like the way of overcoming the Nothing in *The NeverEnding Story*. Although not winged like in the 1924 version, the flying white horse here resembles Pegasus in *Clash*. Jaffar's clockwork horse shattering and his fall resemble Saruman's final fall in *The Lord of the Rings: The Return of the King* and the failure of his own technology. A wheel of progress, indeed.

SHATTERING THE ILLUSION

As some of the credits at the beginning of this chapter might suggest, this film, despite a good reception, had a tortured production and might never have seen the light of day were it not for the dedication and perseverance of producer Alexander Korda. Korda had already worked with young Indian actor and former stable boy Sabu after another filmmaker, Robert Flaherty, had discovered Sabu. Deciding to feature Sabu in an epic based upon the *Arabian Nights* stories, Korda faced one potential stumbling block easily resolved with a single conversation: star Douglas Fairbanks had retained the rights to the title *The Thief of Bagdad* from when he had starred in the 1924 silent adaptation that would serve only partially as an inspiration for this film. Korda met Fairbanks and convinced him to sell the rights. He also made the decision to split Fairbanks' hero in the first movie into two characters, one for the romance with the princess and one for the thieving and most of the derring-do.

Conrad Veidt was the only choice for the villain. The world just missed seeing Scarlett O'Hara as the princess. Vivien Leigh was Korda's first choice, but that other complicated production called *Gone with the Wind* interceded and Korda cast June Duprez instead. Stepping in as an obvious Douglas Fairbanks and Error Flynn substitute for the romantic lead was the similarly mustached John Justin.

Initially, Korda planned this film in black and white, but he decided to shoot in Technicolor to take full advantage of the extraordinary design

> THE WONDER OF THE SPIDER KING . . . TEN TIMES HUMAN SIZE-YET ABU DARES HIM TO BATTLE!

work his brother Vincent was generating. The scale of the project also grew with that choice, and it now required someone else at the helm. Korda had made his first choice of director, Ludwig Berger, on the assumption of a black-and-white film. Although Korda still considered Berger's input valuable, he turned over active shooting of the movie to Michael Powell, who began working with Sabu on location in Cornwall.

Korda's piecemeal approach to the making of the movie, assigning various men to helm different aspects of the story, led to the hiring of another director, Tim Whelan, for sequences that featured action or comedy. Korda's producer partners also directed parts of the movie, with William Cameron Menzies bringing his experience as art director for Fairbanks' 1924 version to the mix.

As if all this weren't complex enough, the UK-based production journeyed thousands of miles after World War II began. Wearing gas masks for a short time while still reporting to work in England, some of the crew switched over to work on an RAF propaganda film, *The Lion Has Wings*, that Korda promised to Prime Minister Winston Churchill. Then the entire *Thief of Bagdad* company relocated to the United States to complete the film, with some location work in the Grand Canyon. The move also necessitated changes, including reshooting some scenes with Sabu, because the boy had grown taller in the time between UK and US production. The Hays Code also affected the film, requiring the princess's costumes to cover more of her skin.

The special-effects team used an array of cutting-edge techniques, including matte paintings and scale-shifting sleight-of-hand camera shots of the type later used by Peter Jackson's team in *The Lord of the Rings* movies. This movie, lauded for its breathtaking color imagery, won Oscars for cinematography, art direction, and special effects at the 13th Academy Awards, the most wins that night. Although the Academy also nominated the film for original music score, it lost that honor to Disney's *Pinocchio*.

For many critics, the movie was a huge hit. Audiences agreed, perhaps for no other reason than its time-capsule–like preservation of an innocent kind of escapist entertainment that was fading as the world plunged deeper into World War II.

MUSIC OF THE MINSTRELS

Miklos Rozsa's score for this film is "a symphony accompanied by a movie," to borrow musician Oscar Levant's description of Max Steiner's work on *King Kong*, but originally the film might have featured not the rousing melodies and occasional vocals that Rozsa wrote but Viennese waltzes from another Oscar: original composer Oscar Straus. First director Berger advocated the use of Straus, a friend and colleague, but Korda went with Rozsa supposedly after hearing his music coming from an office next to Berger's. While much of the score lacks the more ethnically tinged tunes that later films like the *Sinbad* cycle favored, this somewhat strange blend of orchestral composition and Hollywood musical-style singing sometimes veers into a more "Arabian" sound.

> NEVER BEFORE SUCH A SCREEN THRILL! . . . TWO YEARS TO FILM, A FORTUNE TO PRODUCE . . . ALEXANDER KORDA'S GREATEST ACHIEVEMENT! AN ARABIAN FANTASY IN TECHNICOLOR (ON SCREEN)

As with many of the soundtracks in this book, you'll have to look to find copies of this for your collection. A German LP from Celine Records in 1983 mixed music from this movie with *Jungle Book*. A Varese Sarabande CD release that same year and a 1990 German CD from the Colosseum label both brought the same vinyl tracks over to the newer format. In all cases, the albums feature re-recordings and not material from the original film soundtrack.

> THE WONDER OF THE ALL-SEEING EYE, GUARDED BY FIERCE "GREEN MEN"; A 1000-TENTACLED OCTOPUS; A MIRACLE ECHO HALL!
>
> IN MAGIC TECHNICOLOR!

THE SAGA CONTINUES

This was not the first version of *The Thief of Bagdad*, nor was it the last. The 1924 silent version is in its own right a historic piece of cinema, while other versions—often using the spelling *Baghdad*—include a 1961 Italian epic with Hercules himself, Steve Reeves, in the lead, and a 1978 TV-movie version. (Go look in the index; we'll wait.)

Saalfield published an illustrated children's book adaptation and a coloring book the same year as the film. In 1948, Selchow & Righter released a board game with a spinner and simple cardboard tokens.

Disney's 1992 animated feature film *Aladdin* borrowed heavily from both the plot and visual design of this film, combining aspects of Abu and Ahmad into their titular hero and giving Abu's thieving skills to a monkey of the same name. In 2004, Hypostyle Hall Publishers released an entire book on the film, written by Philip Leibfried and Malcolm Willits: *Alexander Korda's The Thief of Bagdad: An Arabian Fantasy*. The movie's legacy continues today, in places as varied as the *Prince of Persia* franchise and the cover of the Grip Weeds' album *Giant on the Beach*, which features a modified image from the beach scene, with the genie gazing down on the band members rather than Abu.

TAKE UP THY SWORD!

The Magic Carpet (Magical Artifact): Originally designed to carry its owner to "Paradise," this exquisitely woven 5' x 7' carpet, constructed in the Land of Legend, has the mystical power of unlimited flight. It can carry weight equivalent to that of three grown men across great distances. Additional weight slows the carpet and decreases its altitude.

To use the carpet, one stands upon it and commands it to fly. It obeys additional instructions during flight, but barring those, it takes the most direct route to a destination given, such as a city or even an individual.

While inactive, the carpet looks and feels like a normal carpet and can be rolled and carried. If the carpet takes damage beyond a minor hole or tear, it ceases to function until repaired by a master's hand guided by a mage capable of enchanting items.

The carpet possesses no defenses. Any attack that would normally affect a mundane rug, such as fire or a swift blade, can damage it.

> GIGANTIC! THE WONDER PICTURE OF ALL TIME! DWARFING ANYTHING EVER SEEN . . . A MOUNTAINOUS GENIE PIERCING THE CLOUDS . . . FLYING HORSES WINGING OVER JEWELLED CITIES . . . A MAGIC CARPET THAT SPANS THE WORLD LIKE THE SWIFTEST BIRD. ALL THE GLORIES, ROMANCE, ADVENTURE OF THE THOUSAND AND ONE NIGHTS--WOVEN INTO A THRILLING TRIUMPH OF MOTION PICTURE MAGIC!
>
> THOUSAND AND ONE SIGHTS FROM THE THOUSAND AND ONE NIGHTS!

THE FILM'S DESTINY

Not just a classic fantasy adventure film but a historic cinematic event in general, *The Thief of Bagdad* is a lush, enchanting experience that transcends its age and delights audiences on just about every level. Although this film is a romantic kaleidoscope for all ages, modern viewing audiences might find its pace unfamiliar. It's worth the effort to look past that for the treasures the movie holds.

Many have likened this film to its contemporary, *The Wizard of Oz*. It inspired fantasy films that followed, including a great many of Ray Harryhausen's memorable works, and influences our entertainment today. Fans of Disney's *Aladdin* are watching a redrawn, animated version of this classic feature, leavened with modernistic additions.

The Thief of Bagdad is a landmark technical achievement in terms of special effects—one that other films rarely if ever surpassed for decades after its release—even if not all those moments look as good to us today. Cutting-edge filmmakers still employ some of the same tricks.

This film's romantic leads aren't the most scintillating performers, but they fulfill the basic roles of lovers we want to see united by the movie's end. The mesmerizing Conrad Veidt as the oily yet occasionally almost sympathetic magician doomed by his love for the princess, Sabu in his earnest and engaging heroic performance as the thief with a heart of gold, and Rex Ingram, whose painfully visible bald cap might be the movie's worst effect but whose maniacal laugh makes him one of the most terrifying yet enchanting genies in any fantasy film, handle most of the heavy lifting in character development.

With all the matte paintings, brightly garbed characters, and fanciful settings, *The Thief of Bagdad* approaches the level of a painting brought to life. For 106 minutes you are in another world, one you might be reluctant to leave when "THE END" appears as if by magic on the screen.

THIS YEAR IN GAMING

Science-fiction and fantasy writer Fletcher Pratt—co-author of the *Enchanter* series with L. Sprague de Camp, to which the *Dungeons & Dragons* magic system owes much—published a set of naval wargaming rules titled *Fletcher Pratt's Naval War Game,* originally released by Lake Shore Press. Many consider it one of the most successful naval wargames of the twentieth century. Upwards of sixty people at a time on each side played the game on ballroom floors using handmade wooden ships in roughly 1/600 to 1/1200 scales, with referees officiating. Unlike with many other wargames—even modern ones—each player controlled a single ship, similar to the way each player in a roleplaying game runs a single character. A young Gary Gygax became aware of this set of rules, as well as H. G. Wells' *Little Wars,* and cited their influence throughout his career.

THE 7TH VOYAGE OF SINBAD

1958 • US/Spain • Columbia Pictures • 88m • Color • G

Screenplay: Kenneth Kolb
Story: Ray Harryhausen (uncredited)
Director: Nathan Juran
Producers: Charles H. Schneer and Ray Harryhausen (uncredited)
Music: Bernard Herrmann
Director of Photography: Wilkie Cooper
Special Visual Effects Created By: Ray Harryhausen
Art Director: Gil Parrendo
Stunt Supervisor: Enzo Musumeci-Greco

IN DYNAMATION THE NEW MIRACLE OF THE SCREEN

Cast: Kerwin Mathews (Sinbad), Kathryn Grant (Princess Parisa), Richard Eyer (Barani the Genie), Torin Thatcher (Sokurah), Alec Mango (Caliph of Bagdad), Danny Green (Karim), Harold Kasket (Sultan of Chandra), Alfred Brown (Harufa), Nana de Herrera (Sadi), Nino Falanga (Sailor), Luis Guedes (Crewman), and Virgilio Teixeira (Ali)
Alternate Titles: *Sinbad the Sailor* and *The Adventures of Sinbad* (development titles)

ON THE MAP

Apart from a brief stopover in Bagdad, the entire film takes place on the island of Colossa and in the surrounding waters.

OUR STORY SO FAR

Returning home to Bagdad to marry Princess Parisa of Chandra, thus averting war and uniting his land with hers, Sinbad must first battle the manipulative magician Sokurah, cure the princess of a curse that shrank her, and save a boyish genie from eternal imprisonment.

ALTERNATE VERSIONS

Although the UK theatrical release suffered heavy editing, video versions reverted to the complete cut of the film.

IT'S MAGIC

Sokurah might call on dark forces for his magic, similar to those of his film-series successors Koura *(Golden Voyage)* and Zenobia *(Eye of the Tiger),* but he has a much easier time of it than they do. He suffers no ill effects for accessing the powers of evil. Fate does catch up with him, however.

10 • CINEMA AND SORCERY

> 8TH WONDER OF THE SCREEN!
>
> OUT OF THE AGE OF WONDERS--ONE OF THE MOST WONDERFUL MOTION PICTURES OF OUR TIME!

Although Sokurah accomplishes much of his work through his own arts, he strongly desires to retain access to the genie's lamp. Barani doesn't use his abilities to cause harm directly, but presumably a sharp fellow like Sokurah can figure out ways to make the most of the boy's protective powers.

THE QUEST FOR MEANING

This is the least of the three Schneer/Harryhausen *Sinbad* movies in terms of a physical journey, because almost all the action takes place in one location. Despite a primary goal—reversing the curse on the princess—and the bonus of great treasure that Sinbad reaches via a series of secondary goals, it's frustrating that Sokurah so easily plays our hero, the caliph of Bagdad, and the sultan of Chandra, when none of them are supposed to be stupid and Sokurah couldn't be more transparently evil and manipulative.

Similarly disturbing is Parisa's behavior. She never seems the least bit concerned about her sudden diminutive stature or whether she can be restored.

The story subtly implies that those who dabble in technology carry an air of corruption about them. Sokurah proposes to build a mechanical crossbow to defeat the Cyclops, but in a clever ironic twist, that very invention costs him his own life. The next two films revisit the theme of modern technological thinking infiltrating the mystical world. Not always is technology a sign of darkness . . . but this exploration belongs more in the "6 Degrees" section, so we'll stop here. As in many quest stories, we have items to collect, monsters to fight, and a princess to save. All in a day's work for the greatest sailor of all time! Let's just hope that crimson ball in Sokurah's lair isn't "red matter."

WHO GOES THERE?

Ray Harryhausen, one of the undisputed masters of special visual effects and an architect of wondrous flights of imagination and menageries of monsters that paraded through countless childhoods, does not often get acting credits, but behind every one of his characters is a performance nonetheless. He saw *King Kong* in 1933 and thrilled to the story and the techniques that brought the giant ape to life. As the years passed, he honed his skills in stop-motion animation and forged a lifelong friendship with another *Kong* aficionado and future fantasist: Ray Bradbury.

Harryhausen began his career working with producer George Pal on a series of fairytale short features called *Puppetoons*. In 1949 he achieved the goal of working with his hero, *King Kong* animator Willis O'Brien, on the award-winning *Mighty Joe Young*. When *Kong* proved a big hit in a 1952 re-release, it inspired the production of a new "monster on the loose" movie based on a *Saturday Evening Post* story penned by none other than Harryhausen's friend, Ray Bradbury. *The Beast from 20,000 Fathoms* was a huge success.

When Harryhausen met producer Charles H. Schneer through a mutual friend, the two men formed a partnership that led to twelve films that continuously pushed the limits of Harryhausen's "Dynamation" process while garnering accolades from audiences worldwide. More than just a special-effects technician, Harryhausen directed live-action sequences that relied on his post-production work, shaped stories from development to final script in collaboration with Schneer and the screenwriters, and "acted" in the films through his emotive puppetry.

Since his retirement in 1981 (after the release of *Clash of the Titans*), Harryhausen settled into a role as an elder statesman of fantasy film and passed the baton to a full industry of professional creators inspired by the decades of dreams and nightmares that he had brought to life. He died in 2013 at age 92.

Kerwin Mathews became one of the era's most reliable clean-cut cinematic heroes in this film, *The 3 Worlds of Gulliver*, and *Jack the Giant Killer*, but made only a small number of other film and television appearances before retiring to become an antiques dealer in San Francisco. He died in 2007 at age 81.

Kathryn Grant appeared in the groundbreaking *Anatomy of a Murder* and provided the voice of Princess Yasminda in the Mr. Magoo–led animated version of *1001 Arabian Nights*, but her biggest claim to fame was marrying Bing Crosby in 1957, after which she retired from acting, apart from involvement in some of Crosby's specials.

Richard Eyer was *The Invisible Boy*, starring alongside Robby the Robot.

Torin Thatcher made suspicious, sinister types his stock in trade through many film, television, and stage appearances, starring opposite Kerwin Mathews again in *Jack the Giant Killer* and appearing in both *Lost in Space* and *Star Trek*. He died in 1981 at age 76.

6 DEGREES OF SORCERY

The island of Colossa recalls Skull Island from *King Kong* in a number of ways. Given Ray Harryhausen's lifelong devotion to that film and its effect on his psyche, that's no big surprise. The stone face resembles a similar edifice in *The Time Machine*.

The Cyclops has a segmented chest that presages the look of the similarly orange-skinned Thing from the *Fantastic Four* comic books. Although not one of his best creations, Harryhausen's serpentine Sadi looks a little like an early version of his design for Medusa in *Clash of the Titans*. *Sinbad and the Eye of the Tiger* returns to the notion of shrinking a woman, except in that film, the evil witch Zenobia does it to herself.

Getting the words just right to invoke a magical force turns up in other films in this book, like *Army of Darkness*. Sokurah's destruction of the bridge is a bit like the crumbling-bridge sequence in *The Lord of the Rings: The Fellowship of the Ring*, and tossing the lamp into lava to release the genie—as well as the poetic prophecy that instructs Parisa to do it—is like returning the ring to the fires of Mount Doom in *The Lord of the Rings: The Return of the King*. (Sorry, can't think of a *Two Towers* link. Can you?) The subsequent swing across the chasm after the bridge is destroyed is virtually identical to Luke and Leia's Death Star escape . . . although Parisa doesn't kiss Sinbad for luck first. The battle between the dragon and the Cyclops is another *King Kong* echo.

> ADVENTURE OF THE AGES—
> FOR ALL AGES
>
> NEWEST MOVIE-MAKING
> MIRACLE . . . DYNAMATION

Sinbad intends to marry Parisa, but he's determined to do the same with Farah in *Eye of the Tiger*. Is it a matter of a girl in every port, a bigamist sailor, a broken engagement, or each *Sinbad* movie existing in its own universe, like variations on a theme?

SHATTERING THE ILLUSION

Having crafted some of the most memorable "monster on the loose" and alien-invasion movies of the 1950s, including *The Beast from 20,000 Fathoms, It Came from Beneath the Sea, Earth Vs. the Flying Saucers,* and *20 Million Miles to Earth,* Ray Harryhausen grew tired of laying waste to cities and turned instead toward more fanciful adventures inspired by mythology and folklore. With partner Charles H. Schneer, he turned to the tales of the *Arabian Nights* (or *One Thousand and One Nights*) for source material—although translators added some of the most famous stories from that cycle, including "The Seven Voyages of Sinbad the Sailor," over the years.

The first concept-drawing Harryhausen ever made concerning a *Sinbad* adventure featured the sailor battling a sword-wielding skeleton on a spiral staircase, borrowing the dramatic potential of staircase-based action made popular in Errol Flynn movies. Such sequences appear in future installments in this saga as well.

With several other sketches and an outline, Schneer and Harryhausen began work on *Sinbad the Sailor*. A variety of story points and creatures never made the final script, such as a monstrous toad, rats of unusual size (hmm), bat devils (which would later turn up as the harpies in *Jason and the Argonauts*), a valley of diamonds, and a scheming daughter of the caliph eager to capture Sinbad for herself.

20 Million Miles to Earth writer Bob Williams originally scripted the film, but his dark take on the story was not "family-friendly." Kenneth Kolb replaced him and drafted a version called *The Adventures of Sinbad*. With a choice of number that would recur throughout Harryhausen's career, the title finally became *The 7th Voyage of Sinbad*. At this point, Harryhausen cut a sequence involving two Cyclops arguing over cooking the human sailors, a scene similar to an event in J. R. R. Tolkien's *The Hobbit*.

Principal photography took place in Spain, where illness plagued the cast and crew. Mathews had to film one of the more physically stressful scenes—Sinbad at the wheel of his ship as a tumultuous storm lashed him with water—while running a high fever. The water thrown over him was harbor sewage, which did little for his condition. The photo cover of the soundtrack album immortalizes the moment.

Communication with the Spanish-speaking crew caused a number of problems, but the production team overcame such obstacles. When crewmembers forgot to bring the prop swords to a location for shooting one day, Harryhausen and others raided a pile of logs nearby, quickly whittled replacements, and painted them silver. The need to shoot at night to avoid interference from tourists meant that the production had to shoot a lot of material "night for day," lighting scenes brightly against natural darkness.

> THE SCREEN'S MOST FANTASTIC ADVENTURE!

This film was Harryhausen's first in color, a challenge to which he had to adjust after perfecting his techniques for black-and-white effects. Reducing the amount of contrast where live-action footage joined model work involved a great deal of experimentation. Scenes required longer hours per night, because temperature changes from night to night might result in noticeable shifts in color quality. This film's promotion introduced the term "Dynamation" for Harryhausen's stop-motion process.

> THE SHEER MAGIC OF DYNAMATION NOW RE-CREATES THE MOST SPECTACULAR ADVENTURES EVER FILMED!

Harryhausen made the Cyclops a much larger creature than in the original mythology, designing it as a hybrid of Pan and his own Ymir from *20 Million Miles to Earth*. In fact, he built the Cyclops on the Ymir armature. He based the dragon partly on the work of French artist Gustav Doré.

Mathews and Olympic fencing master Enzo Musumeci-Greco choreographed Sinbad's fight with Sokurah's skeleton servant in counts of eight, like a dance. Perhaps Harryhausen found this especially challenging, because this was the first time he animated one of his creatures in a direct-contact battle with a live actor. Harryhausen took lessons to get a better understanding of fencing technique for the skeleton's performance, and Mathews proved adept at shadowboxing with his absent opponent. The animation for the fight took three months; Harryhausen finished his work on the movie within a year.

Costing $650,000, *7th Voyage* was a huge hit, but Schneer and Harryhausen didn't make the obvious choice of continuing Sinbad's adventures at that time. They turned instead to a completely different mythological tradition for their next production. (See the chapter on *Jason and the Argonauts*.) As of 2008, the United States Library of Congress has preserved *The 7th Voyage of Sinbad* through the auspices of the National Film Registry.

MUSIC OF THE MINSTRELS

Collectors sought after Bernard Herrmann's rousing score for many years due to the rarity of the original Columbia Records release. In 2009, a CD edition of the entire score came out, including material not featured on the record.

This was the first of Herrman's four scores for Ray Harryhausen movies. His attention to detail in crafting an authentic-sounding main title impressed Harryhausen, who had initially wanted either Max Steiner or Miklos Rozsa to score the film.

THE SAGA CONTINUES

Although plans to follow up *7th Voyage* already began to take shape in the 1960s, Schneer and Harryhausen moved onto other projects, like *Jason and the Argonauts, First Men in the Moon*, and *The Valley of Gwangi*, before returning to Sinbad with *The Golden Voyage of Sinbad*. (See that chapter for more.) Dell published a comic-book adaptation of *7th Voyage* in *Four Color Comics* #944. Strangely, the comic omits the iconic battle with the skeleton, but a one-panel reference to the battle appears on a back-page look at "Sinbad's Other Voyages."

Columbia released four now much-prized 8mm film reels titled *The Cyclops, Strange Voyage, Evil Magician,* and *Dragon's Lair,* and a promotional record that featured pop songs with no real connection to the film or to Herrmann's musical score apart from oblique references to Sinbad. The success of *Golden Voyage* even led to a theatrical re-release of *7th Voyage* in 1975, spawning not one but two new comic-book adaptations. In the US, Marvel featured one version in *Marvel Spotlight* #25, while in the UK a poster magazine titled *Legend Horror Classics* featured an oddly spot-colored black-and-white adaptation in its third issue.

TAKE UP THY SWORD!

THE BOY GENIE

ATTACKS/DEFENSES: This genie, like most of his kind, avoids combat except in self-defense. Even then, he works to disarm or intimidate rather than to inflict injury.

POWERS: The boy genie has spell-like abilities, including various defensive powers, such as a heat barrier. He can conjure items like rope to assist those in danger and magically transport objects (such as treasure).

DETAILS: This boy is one of the Djinn, dwellers in the elemental plane of air and beings of great insight and intelligence (though compared to others of his kind, this particular genie is young, inexperienced, and somewhat unsure of his abilities). He appears physically like a normal human boy. Trapped for an unknown period of time within a magic lamp, the boy genie must obey anyone who possesses said lamp. He can never use his power to inflict harm upon a mortal being.

Like most of his kind, the boy genie ultimately desires to obtain his freedom from the lamp and his master. The promise of freedom and a somewhat cryptic description of the process by which he can accomplish it appear on the interior walls of the lamp: the lamp must be tossed into a lake of fire in order to destroy it and free its prisoner.

THE FILM'S DESTINY

From the moment the enthralling score begins to the final *King Kong*-like battle royale between the Cyclops and the dragon, *The 7th Voyage of Sinbad* is one of the most stirring adventure sagas ever committed to celluloid, beloved by those who saw it first as children and enthralling new generations with every passing year. This is not to say that the film isn't dated in some respects. Although it takes place in a fanciful world with colorful costumes, storybook settings, and amazing creatures that transcend time and place, its primary weakness is part of its period charm: the lead actors.

> SEE THESE INCREDIBLE SCENES BEFORE YOUR UNBELIEVING EYES!
> SEE THE SORCERY OF COLOSSA'S MOST EVIL MAGICIAN!
> SEE THE ATTACK OF THE TWO-HEADED GIANT ROC!
> SEE THE BATTLE OF THE CYCLOPS AND THE DRAGON!
> SEE SINBAD IN HIS BREATHTAKING FIGHT FOR SURVIVAL!

Mathews and Grant are clearly not the best choices to play characters of their supposed heritage. Neither do they sport appropriate hairstyles. But that's how movies were back then. Even the later installments in this series rarely achieve much verisimilitude on that score, so just look past the clean-cut American good looks and get caught up in the adventure.

It's hard not to get swept away when even the film itself can't seem to wait long enough to provide plot set-up before whisking us to that first frightening encounter with the Cyclops. The story fills in eventually—in fact, we drop into the adventure at what amounts to the end of the voyage—but the pace never lets up and the enthusiasm of everyone involved pours from the screen like all the dazzling magic that swirls through Sinbad's world.

Minor quibbles, like the fact that Sokurah is so clearly a conniving rat hell-bent on heading back to Colossa (yet no one sees through the obvious tactic of cursing the princess to get his way), and like the odd siren sequence that seems a perfect spot for another Harryhausen creation but never delivers, aren't deal-breakers. Like pages torn from favorite childhood books with lush illustrations and timeless tales of heroic adventure, *7th Voyage* is what escapist entertainment is all about.

THIS YEAR IN GAMING

Following the success of what many consider the first commercial wargame, *Tactics*, the founder and designer of The Avalon Game Company, Charles S. Roberts, renamed it Avalon Hill. The first game released by the company under the new name was the second edition of *Tactics*, titled *Tactics II*, also published in 1958.

THE MAGIC SWORD

1962 • United States • Bert I. Gordon Productions / United Artists
80 min • Color • Rated G

Screenplay: Bernard Schoenfeld
Story: Bert I. Gordon
Director: Bert I. Gordon
Producer: Bert I. Gordon
Music: Richard Markowitz
Director of Photography: Paul Vogel
Production Designer: Franz Bachelin
Special Effects: Milt Rice
Special Visual Effects: Bert I. Gordon and Flora Gordon
Make-Up: Dan Striepeke
Dragon Trainer: Ross Wheat
Cast: Basil Rathbone (Lodac), Estelle Winwood (Sybil), Gary Lockwood (Sir George), Anne Helm (Princess Helene), Liam Sullivan (Sir Branton), Danielle De Metz (Mignonette), Merritt Stone (King), Jacques Gallo (Sir Dennis of France), David Cross (Sir Pedro of Spain), John Mauldin (Sir Patrick of Ireland), Taldo Kenyon (Sir Anthony of Italy), Angus Duncan (Sir James of Scotland), Leroy Johnson (Sir Ulrich of Germany), Marlene Callahan (Princess Grace), Nick Bon Tempi (Left Siamese Twin), Paul Bon Tempi (Right Siamese Twin), Ann Graves (Princess Laura), Lorrie Richards (Anne), Jack Kosslyn (The Ogre), Maila Nurmi (The Hag / The Sorceress), Ted Finn (First Dwarf, uncredited), Paul Frees (Voice of Sir Ulrich of Germany, uncredited), Angelo Rossitto (Second Dwarf, uncredited), and Richard Kiel (Pinhead, uncredited)
Alternate Titles: *The Seven Curses of Lodac*, *The Sorcerer's Curse*, *St. George and the Dragon*, and *St. George and the Seven Curses* (Bert I. Gordon's original title)

ON THE MAP

The story takes place in a fantastical and unspecified area of Europe during the Dark Ages, with action focused on the lands between the castle of a king and the evil Lodac. A range of diverse and nonspecific terrain includes rolling hills, bubbling swamps, forests, mountains, and caves.

OUR STORY SO FAR

Evil wizard Lodac kidnaps the beautiful Princess Helene in an act of revenge for the death of his sister. Sir George, adopted son of an elderly sorceress, steps up to rescue the princess before Lodac sacrifices her to his dragon in seven days' time. Along the road, Sir George and his company of knights face a series of seven "curses," including a savage ogre, a deadly swamp, the restless spirits of the dead, and a fire-breathing, two-headed dragon. All in a day's work for an errant knight!

IT'S MAGIC

Sybil, Sir George, and Lodac can all use magic in one form or another, including the abilities to far-see, teleport, and transform into animals. While Sybil and Lodac are powerful and apparently ancient wizards, Sir George can cast only the simplest of spells, seemingly due to the fact that he is a "mere human." Although both Lodac and Sybil wield comparatively awesome power, Lodac exhibits more control over his abilities. Sybil clumsily and explosively miscasts an essential spell, which almost spells doom for George and his companion knights. Magic is also present in items wielded by Sir George—his armor, shield, and sword—and in Lodac's ring of power, which protects the one who wears it from undefined threats, such as—perhaps—large, man-eating felines.

THE QUEST FOR MEANING

The Magic Sword explores selfishness from a few different angles. For one thing, Sir George's infatuation with Helene motivates him to imprison his aunt in an ancient cellar and set off on the quest to rescue the damsel from Lodac's clutches. For another, Sybil's motherly desire to prevent George from leaving the roost and becoming a man gives the young man no choice but to deceive her. Lodac, meanwhile, desires revenge against the king, which is why he kidnaps the fair maiden and sets the wheels of the entire adventure in motion. Branton's desire to possess Helene spurs him at first to mount a rescue mission and later to sabotage George and his men, resulting in some of their deaths. Branton also manipulates almost everything that transpires, having promised Lodac the return of his magical ring, which Branton somehow acquired after Lodac misplaced it prior to the events depicted in the film. With all this personal desire and the clouded judgment that goes along with it, you could derive a bit of nuanced rumination on ethics—surprising, given something as simple and seemingly straightforward as a Bert I. Gordon production. Who says Mr. BIG couldn't provoke some deeper contemplation? Think about it, won't you? Thank you.

WHO GOES THERE?

Basil Rathbone (born Philip St. John Basil Rathbone), most famous for portraying Sherlock Holmes in fourteen feature films, also wielded swords in a number of period pieces, including *Captain Blood*, *The Adventures of Robin Hood*, *Tower of London*, and *The Court Jester*. His lengthy career also included appearances in films like *Son of Frankenstein*, *The Mark of Zorro*, *The Black Cat*, *Tales of Terror*, and *Hillbillys in a Haunted House*. He died in 1967 at age 75.

Estelle Winwood (born Estelle Ruth Goodwin) was a young 79 years of age when she played Sybil. Her few forays into fantasy included *Darby O'Gill and the Little People* (alongside Sean Connery), the big-screen adaptation of *Camelot*, and an episode of TV's *Bewitched*, in which she played Enchantra. She also played Lucretia in *The Producers* and appeared in episodes of multiple television series: *Alfred Hitchcock Presents*, *The Twilight Zone*, *Thriller*, and *Batman* (in which she played yet another witch). One of the oldest actors to have a major role in a

> THE MOST INCREDIBLE WEAPON EVER WIELDED!

18 • Cinema and Sorcery

feature film, she played Nurse Withers in *Murder by Death*. She was 93 at the time. She died in 1984 at the ripe old age of 101!

Most who remember Gary Lockwood (born John Gary Yurosek) know him best as either Gary Mitchell on *Star Trek* or Frank Poole in *2001: A Space Odyssey*. He also appeared in TV movies *The Girl, the Gold Watch & Dynamite* and *The Return of the Six Million Dollar Man and the Bionic Woman*, and TV series like *Perry Mason, Rod Serling's Night Gallery, Mission: Impossible, The Six Million Dollar Man, MacGyver*, and *Dark Skies*.

For Anne Helm, *The Magic Sword* was her only big-screen fantasy appearance. She has had a long career on the small screen in *Sea Hunt, Perry Mason, The Fugitive, Gunsmoke, Hawaii Five-O, Airwolf*, and *Amazing Stories*. She also turned up in a strange remake of *House of Wax* titled *Nightmare in Wax*.

Liam Sullivan worked almost exclusively in television for five decades, appearing in *Lights Out, Alfred Hitchcock Presents, The Twilight Zone, Voyage to the Bottom of the Sea, Lost in Space, Star Trek, The A-Team*, and *Dallas*. He died in 1998 at age 74.

French beauty Danielle De Metz had an impressive run on the big and small screens throughout the '60s. Her first role was in the film *Return of the Fly*. She also appeared in *Valley of the Dragons* and TV shows *Alfred Hitchcock Presents, Voyage to the Bottom of the Sea, I Spy, I Dream of Jeannie*, and *The Man from U.N.C.L.E.* (in a role that earned her an Emmy nomination).

Merritt Stone appeared in four of Bert I. Gordon's films, including *War of the Colossal Beast, Earth vs. the Spider*, and *Tormented*. His last film credit was *The Magic Sword*. Rumor has it that he eventually went on to manage a small movie theater in Culver City, California. An episode of *Mystery Science Theater 3000* featured a sketch in which characters attempted to determine if Stone worked under pseudonyms in other films, but before the truth came out, Tom Servo's head exploded. Stone died in 1985 at age 70.

The '50s and early '60s were rather kind to actor Jacques Gallo, who appeared in a variety of often uncredited roles in movies such as *The Buccaneer* and *The Honors of War*, and an episode of the TV series *Men into Space*. He died in 2005 at age 81.

David Cross (no relation to the *Mr. Show* and *Arrested Development* actor of the same name) squeezed in a surprising number of small and uncredited roles on TV and in movies between the years 1955 and 1962, including films like *The Night Holds Terror, Cry Terror!*, and *The Creation of the Humanoids*, and TV shows like *Peter Gunn, 77 Sunset Strip*, and *Thriller*. He died in 1990 at age 57.

Taldo Kenyon's first role was in the TV show *Sea Hunt*, and his last was in the film *Frame Up*. He also appeared in episodes of *Alfred Hitchcock Presents, Men into Space*, and *Mission: Impossible*.

Accomplished actor of stage and screen Angus Duncan had a respectable career of more than four decades. He appeared in the TV series *The Twilight Zone, Mission: Impossible, The Incredible*

> Feats beyond description ... Spectacle beyond imagination!
> The story of the bold adventurer who held a fantastic sword ... and faced the most fearsome black magic that ever gripped the screen!

Hulk, *The Phoenix, Airwolf,* and *Starman,* as well as movies like *Simon, King of the Witches;* and . . . *And Justice for All.* Though he had no sorcerous connections, many people remember Duncan best as the boyfriend who drove Mary Richards off to Minneapolis to start her career on WJM-TV in the pilot episode of *The Mary Tyler Moore Show.* He died in 2007 at age 70.

Jack Kosslyn wore a few different hats during his long career in Hollywood, including that of drama and dialogue coach, casting director, and actor. He appeared in a few other Bert I. Gordon films, including *The Amazing Colossal Man, Attack of the Puppet People, War of the Colossal Beast, Earth vs. the Spider,* and *Empire of the Ants.* He also had a long-running relationship with Clint Eastwood, for whom he worked as his production company's casting director and an actor in films like *Play Misty for Me, High Plains Drifter, Magnum Force,* and *The Eiger Sanction.* He died in 2005 at the age of 84.

You might remember Maila Nurmi (born Maila Elizabeth Syrjäniemi) more for her alter ego Vampira, whom she based on Morticia from the Charles Addams cartoons made (in)famous in *The New Yorker.* She was television's very first late-night horror host and starred in Ed Wood's *Plan 9 from Outer Space* as well as *I Woke Up Early the Day I Died.* She died in 2008 at age 85.

Paul Frees is a voice-acting legend with credits too numerous to list, for short and feature-length films, radio, and television—especially because much of his work involved looping other actors and providing dubbed voices for foreign films. Purely from a fantasy perspective, he played roles in Rankin/Bass's *The Hobbit, The Return of the King,* and *The Flight of Dragons,* as well as films like *Son of Sinbad, The Sword and the Dragon,* and *The Sword of Ali Baba.* Really, we're not even going to try to go further; look him up. He died in 1986 at age 66.

Angelo Rossitto co-founded the Little People of America with Billy Barty and ran Bartertown in *Mad Max Beyond Thunderdome.* He also appeared in more than eighty other movies and television shows going all the way back to the late 1920s, including movies like *Freaks, Hellzapoppin', The Corpse Vanishes, Invasion of the Saucer Men, The Wonderful World of the Brothers Grimm, Dracula vs. Frankenstein,* Ralph Bakshi's rotoscoped *The Lord of the Rings* (in the live-action footage), *Galaxina,* and *Something Wicked This Way Comes,* and TV series such as *H. R. Pufnstuf, Lidsville, Baretta, Jason of Star Command,* and *The Incredible Hulk.* He died in 1991 at age 83.

Richard Kiel is a towering (literally) pop-culture icon known to generations as James Bond's foe Jaws in *The Spy Who Loved Me* and *Moonraker,* as well as in two videogames (voice only). Kiel also made his mark in movies like *Eegah, The Human Duplicators* (both of which *Mystery Science Theater 3000* ribbed), *Silver Streak, So Fine, Happy Gilmore,* and *Tangled,* and television series such as *Thriller, The Twilight Zone, The Monkees, The Wild Wild West, Kolchak: The Night Stalker,* and *Land of the Lost.* He died in 2014 at age 74.

6 DEGREES OF SORCERY

The story loosely follows the medieval legend of St. George and the dragon. Sybil looks and even acts a bit like Agnes Moorehead's Endora from TV's *Bewitched;* it's fitting, then, that Winwood played Endora's sister, Enchantra, in a 1966 episode. Lodac's appearance, complete with turban, is likely a nod to Conrad Veidt's Jaffar from *The Thief of Bagdad.* He might also have inspired the look of Tom Baker's Koura in *The Golden Voyage of Sinbad* more than a decade later.

The group of mismatched knights resembles the knights of the Round Table from *Monty Python and the Holy Grail,* although these adventurers at least have real horses and not empty halves of coconuts. The knights also derive from mythology, likely Richard Johnson's late sixteenth-century work, *The Seven Champions of Christendom.*

The ogre (curse number one) is a cross between the Hunchback of Notre Dame, particularly Lon Chaney's version, and the Wolfman of Lon Chaney, Jr. The burbling swamp looks and sounds like the Bog of Eternal Stench from *Labyrinth,* or the Swamps of Sadness from *The NeverEnding Story,* and maybe even the Fire Swamp in *The Princess Bride.*

Sybil consults a mirror of magic similar to that of *Snow White*'s evil queen and even Queen Gedren in *Red Sonja.* The hag looks like one of the witches in the original *Star Trek* episode "Cat's Paw," and the appearance of the ghosts in the haunted cave resembles the scene featuring the witches' appearance in the same episode. The haunted cave looks like Merlin's cavern in *Excalibur,* complete with oddly lit stalactites and stalagmites.

When Helene kisses George as he's chained up, it feels like the scene in *Star Wars: The Empire Strikes Back* in which Princess Leia kisses Han Solo goodbye before he's lowered into the carbonite chamber. It also resembles a scene in *Flash Gordon.*

Helene gets tied up and offered to the dragon just as Ann Darrow becomes an offering for Kong in *King Kong,* as Elinore gets presented to the fairies in *Wizards,* and as Andromeda, restrained, awaits the arrival of the Kraken. The design of the dragon harkens back to a similar (though three-headed) beast in the 1939 Russian film, *Vasilisa the Beautiful,* and might well have inspired the Eborsisk that appears some years later in *Willow.*

SHATTERING THE ILLUSION

Director Bert I. Gordon (a.k.a. Mr. BIG) was one of the kings of B-grade horror and science fiction for decades, writing and directing films like *The Amazing Colossal Man, Earth vs. the Spider, Attack of the Puppet People,* and *Tormented,* all before lensing this film in 1962. *Mystery Science Theater 3000* featured eight of his twenty-plus movies. (See **The Saga Continues** for more on the episode featuring *The Magic Sword.*)

This was Gordon's first color motion-picture and the second film he did with United Artists (the first being another fantasy adventure titled *The Boy and the Pirates*). Mr. Gordon shot it in 1961 using his own "Super-Percepto-Vision," a combination of split-screen and traveling-matte techniques. Shooting took place on 20th Century Fox and MGM studio lots as well as in and around the famous Bronson Caves, home of the entrance to the Batcave as seen in the 1960s television cult classic *Batman.*

Choosing to avoid the use of miniatures, the art department fabricated a large-scale dragon puppet that accommodated two operators. The post-production team optically enlarged the puppet so that it dwarfed actors Gary Lockwood and Anne Helm.

Makeup artist Dan Striepeke handled a reported twenty-five gallons of latex as well as a variety of cosmetic products and paints, not to mention about four pounds of feathers supposedly sourced from turkeys, to craft all the creatures seen in the film . . . especially actress Maila Nurmi's alter ego, the hag. According to a contemporary article about Striepeke's work on the film,

> SEE THE BATTLE WAGED BY THE MAGIC SWORD
> AGAINST THE DREAD SEVEN CURSES!
> SEE THE TWO-HEADED FLAME BREATHING DRAGON!
> SEE THE BEAUTIFUL VAMPIRE WOMAN!
> SEE THE GREEN FIRE DEMONS!
> SEE THE SCORCHING FIREBALL!
> SEE THE BOILING CRATER OF DEATH!
> SEE THE 25-FOOT TALL OGRE!
> SEE THE UNNAMABLE—MOST FANTASTIC CURSE OF ALL!

he modeled Nurmi's ugly guise on an impression taken of her face, which then required sixty-six hours of work and six different versions to arrive at the design used in the film. Put those sixes together, and you might wonder if the film's PR department was pulling someone's leg. . . .

MUSIC OF THE MINSTRELS

Richard Markowitz was thirty-five when hired to score *The Magic Sword*. Prior to that, he had collaborated on three films with Irvin Kershner, the man who would later direct *Star Wars: The Empire Strikes Back*. After *The Magic Sword*, Markowitz made his mark in television on series such as *The Invaders*, *The Wild, Wild West*, and *Mission: Impossible*.

As for the music itself, the score is pretty standard fare for adventure films of the time, although a few themes stand out, such as those linked to the various curses. To date, despite interest among soundtrack collectors, the original recordings have not surfaced. The search continues.

THE SAGA CONTINUES

The film didn't generate much peripheral activity, then or now. Dell Publishing released a *Movie Classic* comic-book adaptation in September 1962 under the title *The Magic Sword*. *Mystery Science Theater 3000* had their way with the film in episode #411, in which Crow admitted his new and altogether bizarre infatuation—through music—with Estelle Winwood, who beat out Kim Cattrall.

Many years later, this movie (along with *Star Wars*, also featured in this book) shared the dubious honor of having footage lifted from it for a Turkish concoction often referred to as *Turkish Star Wars*. Music from sci-fi and fantasy films like *Planet of the Apes*, *Flash Gordon*, and *Raiders of the Lost Ark* also grace that unique curio.

TAKE UP THY SWORD!

ASCALON: THE BLADE (MAGIC WEAPON)

Ascalon grants the wielder significant attack and defense bonuses. It can dispel any resident magic of an evil nature, including that of cursed items, diabolical traps, and demonic presences.

With but a touch, Ascalon grants access through all doorways, including those secured magically. It can also shut and seal—with the appropriate locking spell—these selfsame portals.

If Ascalon's wielder ever faces imminent death—such as drowning in a pit of bubbling acid—the sword can telekinetically lift its owner to safety. It might be able to do this only a finite number of times (at the game master's discretion).

Despite Ascalon's impressive abilities, a highly experienced user of magic can permanently dispel its powers. If divested of its magical abilities, Ascalon retains its attack bonus, because it is a masterfully forged weapon in its own right.

THE FILM'S DESTINY

Considering the source, this film could be a whole lot worse. It's a mildly entertaining mixed bag of corny, almost childlike adventure with genuinely horrific and downright creepy moments. When you compare the rather comedic opening sequence—complete with head-scratching chimpanzee and synchronized conjoined twins—with later scenes of people being boiled, burned, murdered, and possessed, one wonders which audience the film targeted, or if it had been two different movies spliced together.

This was Bert I. Gordon's only true sword-and-sorcery film, so perhaps that motivated him to pull out all the stops and feature all the clichés, including knights in shining armor, dueling wizards, a twenty-five-foot-tall, boulder-chucking ogre, and of course, a fire-breathing dragon. Although touted as great challenges to test even the hardiest of knights, the "curses" technically range only from actors sporting simple pullover masks to what must have been a rather complicated, two-headed dragon puppet presented in "Super-Percepto-Vision." Just what *is* Super-Percepto-Vision, anyway?

Undoubtedly this movie, an admirable attempt given the obvious budgetary limitations, was Mr. BIG's answer to Nathan Juran's highly successful release (and another of our featured films), *The 7th Voyage of Sinbad,* which had come out just four years earlier. It earns merit for the effort alone and is a decent although somewhat juvenile adventure. It's certainly one of the better Bert I. Gordon films. If even Joel Hodgson of *Mystery Science Theater 3000* proclaimed it to be so, you can't argue with that!

THIS YEAR IN GAMING

Publisher Stanley Paul released *War Games,* written by gaming guru Donald F. Featherstone. Many believe that book more than any other launched the modern tabletop wargaming hobby into the civilian market.

The first issue of Featherstone's *Wargamer's Newsletter* came out this same year. A decade later, Gary Gygax would contribute an article titled "Fantasy Battles" to that journal to discuss *Chainmail,* the medieval wargame from which *Dungeons & Dragons* rules would eventually derive.

JASON AND THE ARGONAUTS

1963 • US/UK • COLUMBIA PICTURES • 104M • COLOR • G

SCREENPLAY: Jan Read and Beverley Cross
DIRECTOR: Don Chaffey
PRODUCER: Charles H. Schneer
ASSOCIATE PRODUCER AND CREATOR OF SPECIAL VISUAL EFFECTS: Ray Harryhausen
MUSIC: Bernard Herrmann
CINEMATOGRAPHER: Wilkie Cooper
PRODUCTION DESIGNER: Geoffrey Drake
ART DIRECTORS: Herbert Smith, Jack Maxsted, and Tony Sarzi Braga
SWORDFIGHT ARRANGER: Ferdinando Poggi (uncredited)
CAST: Todd Armstrong (Jason), Nancy Kovack (Medea), Gary Raymond (Acastus), Laurence Naismith (Argos), Niall MacGinnis (Zeus), Michael Gwynn (Hermes), Douglas Wilmer (Pelias), Jack Gwillim (King Aeetes), Honor Blackman (Hera), John Cairney (Hylas), Patrick Troughton (Phineas), Andrew Faulds (Phalerus), Nigel Green (Hercules), Ennio Antonelli (Argo Drummer Dmitrius, uncredited), John Crawford (Polydeuces, uncredited), Aldo Cristiani (Lynceus, uncredited), Ferdinando Poggi (Castor, uncredited), Doug Robinson (Eupaemus, uncredited), Davina Taylor (Briseis, uncredited), Tim Turner (voice of Jason, uncredited), and Eva Haddon (voice of Medea, uncredited)
ALTERNATE TITLE: *Jason and the Golden Fleece* (working title)

ON THE MAP

The Argonauts travel the known world from Thessaly to Colchis, with stops along the way at the Isle of Bronze and Phrygia.

OUR STORY SO FAR

Determined to reclaim his kingdom after the evil King Pelias murders his family and seizes control, Jason assembles a crew of heroes and sails the known—and unknown—world, facing fanciful creatures and challenges, in hopes to retrieve the fabled Golden Fleece and bring peace and prosperity back to his father's land.

ALTERNATE VERSIONS

UK theatrical and VHS releases omitted the creepy shriek that signaled the skeleton army's advance. The UK DVDs include it.

IT'S MAGIC

All the magical elements of this movie derive from ancient Greek mythology. It's not clear whether certain enchanted objects possess their own power or merely extend the power of the Olympian gods.

> GREATEST ODYSSEY OF
> THE AGES!

The Golden Fleece can heal in addition to possessing the more nebulous powers of somehow creating an atmosphere of peace and prosperity and eliminating plague and famine for the nation that possesses it. The hydra's teeth can reanimate the remains of the creature's victims; the skeletons arise when called upon, once their caller throws the teeth to the ground.

THE QUEST FOR MEANING

As with *Clash of the Titans* after it, one of the central themes of this movie is humanity discovering its independence and emerging from the shadows of the gods. A pretty strong anti-religious statement comes through metaphorically, but the basic lesson is that heroes like Jason can forge their own paths and make their own choices. They sometimes require divine intervention, but the time might come when they no longer do. The gods seem bemused by that notion but also resigned to the possibility that they might one day be obsolete. Harryhausen's other main cycle—the *Sinbad* films—also features a lead hero who expresses skepticism about the true value or power of the gods. This film shares another theme with the *Sinbad* films: the encroachment of technology into an ancient world, from the robotic, steam- or fluid-driven Talos of this film to Bubo in *Clash* and the Minaton of *Sinbad and the Eye of the Tiger*.

Another theme, appropriately enough, concerns the "game of life." As the gods look down from Olympus, they play with the destinies of men and women via a tabletop wargame complete with figurines. Reminiscent of scenes of military leaders planning campaigns in other films, this type of scene evolves as Harryhausen and his team revisit Olympus in *Clash of the Titans*. The entire film is awash with references to the structure of gaming. Jason must adhere to various rules (obtain help from Hera no more than five times, leave the treasure of the gods alone . . .) in his quest to steal the Golden Fleece.

The Olympic Games evaluate candidates for the crew of the *Argo*. Note that Hylas wins a position on board not by being the strongest, but by being the smartest, so these contests don't necessarily revolve around brawn.

WHO GOES THERE?

Todd Armstrong attended acting classes with the likes of Gene Hackman and Dustin Hoffman. He appeared in the TV series *Manhunt* before *Jason*, but apart from a few other films and later guest roles in shows like *Gunsmoke, Hawaii Five-O,* and *The Greatest American Hero,* Armstrong had a short career and took his own life in 1992 at the age of 55.

Nancy Kovack was a ubiquitous presence in '60s television, appearing on *Voyage to the Bottom of the Sea, I Dream of Jeannie, Honey West, Batman, The Man from U.N.C.L.E., The Invaders, Star Trek,* and *Bewitched.* She made her last film appearance in *Marooned* and is still married to Zubin Mehta, world-famous musical director and conductor for multiple orchestras in the United States and Israel.

Laurence Naismith was a merchant marine and a black belt in karate and judo, but he best made a name for himself as a prolific character-actor in film, on television, and onstage. He appeared in movies like *Village of the Damned, Cleopatra, Camelot,* the Schneer/Harryhausen-produced *The Valley of Gwangi,* and *Diamonds Are Forever.* He died in 1992 at age 83.

Niall MacGinnis had an extensive film and stage career. He became most famous for *Jason* and the horror classic *Curse of the Demon.* He died in 1977 at age 63.

Michael Gwynn was a ubiquitous presence in British films and television shows, with appearances in movies like *The Revenge of Frankenstein, Village of the Damned, Cleopatra,* and *The Scars of Dracula,* and television series like *Secret Agent, The Saint, The Avengers,* and *Fawlty Towers.* He died in 1976 at age 59.

Another Shakespearean stalwart, Douglas Wilmer also appeared in *Cleopatra, A Shot in the Dark, The Vampire Lovers,* and *Revenge of the Pink Panther,* and reappeared in the Schneer/Harryhausen film *The Golden Voyage of Sinbad.*

Jack Gwillim returned as Poseidon in *Clash of the Titans.* He died in 2001 at age 91.

Honor Blackman will forever be Pussy Galore from *Goldfinger* and Catherine Gale from *The Avengers* television series.

John Cairney is yet another *Jason* cast member who also appeared in *Cleopatra.* (Did they get a group rate?)

Patrick Troughton was the second Doctor in the long-running BBC television series *Doctor Who,* from 1966-1969. He returned for special appearances in the series' tenth, twentieth, and twenty-first anniversary years. He also turned up as Klove in *Scars of Dracula* and as the ill-fated Father Brennan in *The Omen.* Like some of his costars, he returned to the Schneer/Harryhausen fold, as Melanthius in *Sinbad and the Eye of the Tiger.* He died in 1987 at age 67.

Nigel Green made his final screen appearance as the titular knight in *Gawain and the Green Knight* (1973), released one year after he died at the age of 47 from a possibly intentional overdose of sleeping pills.

6 DEGREES OF SORCERY

Clash of the Titans also begins with an evil leader attempting to assert his authority over fate or the will of the gods, and in that film we also leap forward in time to rejoin a young boy in adulthood as he seeks his destiny. The temple of Thetis and similar architecture in *Clash* echo this film's Hera statue and temple, as well as this film's temple of Hecate in Colchis ... which makes sense, considering the filmmakers. Pelias seeks the one-sandaled man, as Richard Kimble keeps an eye out for the one-armed man in *The Fugitive.* (Okay, that one's a stretch.)

Hermes' dramatic transformation into a towering deity looks like the final appearance of Apollo in the mythologically themed *Star Trek* episode "Who Mourns for Adonis?" Talos's "Colossus of Rhodes" routine presages that of similar statues seen in *The Lord of the Rings* trilogy and the *Clash of the Titans* remake. Talos's death is like that of the Kraken in *Clash.* Both creatures crack across their "skin."

Phrygia was a real place located in what is now Turkey. It also gets a brief mention in *Sinbad and the Eye of the Tiger* (although the captioning there spells it "Phyrgia").

Medea's gold-green dancing makeup and the accompanying music gives her more than a passing resemblance to *Star Trek*'s iconic Orion slave girl played by Susan Oliver in the show's unaired 1965 pilot, "The Cage" (later re-edited and aired as a two-parter, "The Menagerie"). Medea pleads with the statue of Hecate, as Calibos will one day implore the statue of Thetis in *Clash*. Skeletons (or dead soldiers) brought back to do battle recur as a theme in many other movies, including *Army of Darkness* and *The Lord of the Rings: The Return of the King*.

SHATTERING THE ILLUSION

The film began as scribbled notes on the back of Harryhausen's script pages for *Mysterious Island* and initially called for a meeting of heroes. *Sinbad in the Age of the Muses* would have teamed Jason with Sinbad as they searched together for the Golden Fleece. A gryphon appeared among the creatures and sequences to which those early notes referred but did not, in the final cut, join its harpy and skeleton colleagues. It had to wait until *The Golden Voyage of Sinbad*. Medusa would have to wait her turn in *Clash of the Titans*.

In the concept, Jason replaced Perseus, who was Harryhausen and Schneer's first choice of hero. Perseus, like Medusa, would have to wait for his chance at the spotlight.

Jan Read's first screenplay featured a modern framing sequence with present-day tourists—quickly discarded. The script was also too faithful to mythology for the film's purposes, so Beverley Cross came in to prepare future drafts. She worked on dialogue and other adjustments throughout production.

The film was to shoot in Yugoslavia, but financial issues arose concerning inappropriate padding of costs. Schneer, angry, moved the production to Italy. Much of the shooting took place around the seaside village of Palinuro. The 2,500-year-old ruins of the temple of Hera at Paestum served as the setting for Phineas's struggle against the harpies. Crewmembers even had permission to climb the ancient stones.

Excessive rainfall hampered the filming at times, and food supplies became a problem for the crew. At one point, vehicles from the production ran over some of a local farmer's fallen olives. Schneer paid him off rather than risk excessive attention from, shall we say, "good family men."

Famously, the *Argo* met the *Golden Hinde* when a British crew shooting footage for the television series *Sir Francis Drake* happened upon the same location, creating a unique clash of eras. A trio of Mercedes-Benz engines enabled the $250,000 *Argo*—essentially one of the film's principle sets—to move into position anywhere. (To defray some of the cost, *Cleopatra* used the same boat.) Segments of the ship's hull and a smaller model version allowed for camera angles and sequences for which the full boat did not suffice.

Harryhausen's father built the metal armatures for the creatures in the film and shipped them from America to Italy. Although Talos was only slightly taller than human-size in the original myth and killed sailors by embracing them after heating himself in fire, Harryhausen—partly inspired by the Colossus of Rhodes—reinvented him as a towering bronze automaton. The creature's home almost moved from Crete to the Valley of the Titans on the Isle of Bronze. Harryhausen commented that animating the creature went against years of honing his skills, because it required movements that appeared jerky to suggest a stiff, metallic body. The ichor that pours from Talos's "Achilles heel" was a mixture of colored water and oatmeal in the live-action shots, and animated cellophane in the model shots.

Harryhausen cast Triton as an actor rather than a creature. To create the illusion of massiveness, Harryhausen shot that footage at ninety-six frames a second. With film hurtling at such high speed, one camera exploded during shooting.

> FOR THE FIRST TIME ON THE SCREEN ... THE GLORY THAT WAS GREECE ... THE LEGEND THAT WAS JASON!

Because the original myth of Jason included a dragon akin to the one already created for *The 7th Voyage of Sinbad,* Harryhausen reinvented it as a multi-headed serpent of one of Hercules' labors. Myths describe the dragon as having anything from nine to a hundred heads; Harryhausen settled on a more manageable seven.

That number cropped up again with the skeletons (rotting zombies in the myth) that fight Jason and his crew. One of them survived from the *7th Voyage* shoot; its six colleagues debut in this film. Cuts included a comedic shot in which a skeleton searches for its severed skull on the ground, and in the UK, the bone-chilling moment when the skeletons rush forward, shrieking. The latter reappeared in later releases.

The entire skeleton fight, still one of Harryhausen's most complex and celebrated sequences, took four and a half months to complete, with Harryhausen marrying exhaustively rehearsed live-action footage—shot with the actors fighting stuntmen wearing numbered sweatshirts—with movements of the model skeletons on a duplicate set. Designs of the skeleton's shields stand for previous Harryhausen creations, like the octopus from *It Came from Beneath the Sea.*

After $3 million and two years of production, the film came out to mixed reviews but eventually became a classic of the genre. Plans to continue the story with Jason confronting Pelias, and perhaps even a spin-off film focusing on Hercules' other labors, never came to fruition.

Just after the film wrapped, Harryhausen married Diana Livingstone Bruce, one of seven—hmm—members of the team who tied the knot during or after production of the movie. (The couple remained together until he died.)

Jason was both Harryhausen's and Schneer's personal favorite of the films they made. They aren't alone; when Tom Hanks presented Harryhausen with his special Academy Award, he cited *Jason* and not *Casablanca* or *Citizen Kane* as the "greatest film ever made."

MUSIC OF THE MINSTRELS

This was Bernard Herrmann's fourth and final score for a Harryhausen movie, after *The 7th Voyage of Sinbad* and the non–sword-and-sorcery films *The Three Worlds of Gulliver* and *Mysterious Island*. Herrmann recycled a lot of his themes from scores originally written for Hitchcock films like *North by Northwest* and the sci-fi classic *The Day the Earth Stood Still.* Although he achieved fame for using strings for terrifying effect in *Psycho,* he composed this soundtrack with no string section at all.

THE SAGA CONTINUES

None of the dangling plot threads or characters from *Jason and the Argonauts* reappear in movies later, but *Clash of the Titans* is effectively a sequel to this film because it maintains the

> THE EPIC STORY THAT WAS DESTINED TO STAND AS A COLOSSUS OF ADVENTURE!

style Harryhausen and Schneer established in *Jason*, including the depiction of Olympus and the gods' penchant for playing miniatures-driven games that affect their human subjects.

Jason's underlying theme of humanity progressing toward a deeper understanding of itself and its world (leaving the guidance and domination of the gods behind as it marches toward the modern world) continues in *Clash*.

Hallmark Entertainment produced an unrelated miniseries that adapted much of the mythology of Jason and the quest for the Fleece, and aired it in 2000. It starred Jason London as his namesake, Jolene Blalock as Medea, Brian Thompson as Hercules, Dennis Hopper as Pelias, Frank Langella as King Aeetes, and Derek Jacobi as Phineas.

Dell Publishing released a comic-book adaptation of the film. Columbia also released four 8mm film reels titled *Battle with Talos, Triton—Lord of the Deep, Hydra of Hades,* and *The Golden Fleece*. In 2007, Bluewater Productions began publishing *Ray Harryhausen Presents*, a series of sequels to classic Harryhausen films, in cooperation with the legendary filmmaker. *Jason and the Argonauts: The Kingdom of Hades* debuted in 2008 and ran for five issues, picking up where the film left off and continuing Jason's adventures.

TAKE UP THY SWORD!

TALOS (DIVINE CONSTRUCT)

SPECIAL ATTACKS/DEFENSE:
SHORT SWORD: Talos's "short" sword is more than a hundred feet long and can deliver lethal crushing damage with each successful strike.
ROCK-THROWING: Talos can hurl boulders several hundred feet, potentially inflicting massive damage.
BRONZE ARMOR: As an artificial construct, Talos's thick bronze "skin" is impenetrable to all but magical spells and weapons. Transmutation spells (those able to convert metal into another material) have reduced (and localized) effects against Talos.
VULNERABILITY: Talos's only weakness is his simple circulatory system: a vein running from head to ankles. One can access this vein via threaded ports at his heels. Removing the plugs requires great strength. Success drains Talos's molten ichor, rendering him immobile and—if the plugs remain open—emptied and lifeless.
DETAILS: Mistaken for a Titan (due to his colossal size), Talos is actually a giant living statue forged by the divine smith Hephaestus and placed upon the Isle of Bronze as a guardian against pirates and invaders. He cannot reason or communicate, being little more than a programmed automaton.

THE FILM'S DESTINY

Anchored by a likable lead, the reliable assortment of Harryhausen creations (including one of his most technically incredible achievements, the complex battle between the men of the *Argo* and the seven skeletons), and what might be cinema's most interesting incarnation of

Hercules, *Jason and the Argonauts* is a delightful episodic journey that adapts the mythological source material into a colorful, well-paced action-adventure that never slows down. Some of the details differ from the original tales for dramatic reasons, and even though the story ends before everything goes bad in the Jason-Medea relationship, Harryhausen and company never intended to touch the darker side of that dynamic. That's understandable. After all, it's escapist entertainment for all ages.

Nigel Green is a revelation, imbuing his gray-haired Hercules with such humor, hubris, and honor that he commands attention every moment he's on screen, which is all too brief. In fact, the film's only real flaw is that it rolls along at such a breakneck pace, it runs out of steam abruptly, ending just after the spectacular reanimated-skeleton battle and leaving the entire driving purpose of the quest unresolved. Having acquired the Golden Fleece (like you didn't know he'd get it), Jason kisses Medea, and the gods turn off the show. Wait a minute.... What about Pelias? What about the kingdom awaiting Jason? Those were supposed to be subjects of the next film, which never happened. Harryhausen and Schneer moved onto other projects, other ideas.

Still, what we have remains one of the best mythology-based movies ever made, with iconic monsters, lavish costumes and locations, and thematic ruminations on free will and humankind's need to strive for individual achievement.

THIS YEAR IN GAMING

Richard Channing Garfield, a direct descendant of President James A. Garfield, was born on June 26, 1963, in Philadelphia, Pennsylvania. He grew up in Oregon, became a passionate gamer when he discovered *Dungeons & Dragons*, and by the age of 13 was already designing his own games.

As a graduate student in mathematics, he began to develop the game that would become *Magic: The Gathering*, which debuted in 1993. Garfield became a full-time employee of Wizards of the Coast a year later. Still working as an independent designer today, Garfield has designed many other games, such as *Android: Netrunner* and *Vampire: The Eternal Struggle*. He designed special *Magic* cards to propose to his wife and to mark the births of their two children.

THE GOLDEN VOYAGE OF SINBAD

1974 • US/UK • COLUMBIA PICTURES • 105M • COLOR • G

SCREENPLAY: Brian Clemens
STORY: Brian Clemens and Ray Harryhausen
DIRECTOR: Gordon Hessler
PRODUCERS: Charles H. Schneer and Ray Harryhausen
MUSIC: Miklos Rozsa
DIRECTOR OF PHOTOGRAPHY: Ted Moore
CREATOR OF SPECIAL VISUAL EFFECTS: Ray Harryhausen
PRODUCTION DESIGNER: John Stoll
ART DIRECTOR: Fernando Gonzalez
MAKE-UP: Jose Antonio Sanchez
COSTUMES: Verena Coleman and Gabriella Falk
SPECIAL MASKS: Colin Arthur

FILMED IN DYNARAMA

CAST: John Phillip Law (Sinbad), Caroline Munro (Margiana), Tom Baker (Koura), Douglas Wilmer (Vizier), Martin Shaw (Rachid), Gregoire Aslan (Hakim), Kurt Christian (Haroun), Takis Emmanuel (Achmed), John D. Garfield (Abdul), Fernando Poggi, Aldo Sambrell (Omar), Robert Rietty (various character voices), and Robert Shaw (The Oracle of All Knowledge, uncredited)
ALTERNATE TITLES: *Sinbad's 8th Voyage*, *Sinbad in India*, and *Sinbad's Golden Voyage* (working titles)

ON THE MAP

Sinbad and his crew journey from the seaside city of Marabia to the legendary island of Lemuria.

OUR STORY SO FAR

Koura the Black Prince threatens the safety and security of Marabia, whose grand vizier calls on Sinbad to undertake a voyage to the island of Lemuria. There he must prevent Koura from accessing the Fountain of Destiny and obtaining its gifts of youth, a shield of darkness, and a crown of untold riches.

ALTERNATE VERSIONS

A videotape release of the film featured captions for Koura's unintelligible intonations that were television cereal-ads written backward. Recent DVD releases have added digital hair to a scene in which Sinbad helps Margiana out of a boat, thus censoring a brief costume malfunction.

IT'S MAGIC

Koura dabbles in black arts that take quite a toll on the user. For every spell he intones, he suffers physical aging that threatens his very life. The Fountain of Destiny and the golden tablets that access its gifts contain power of their own.

Sinbad receives mystical visions of unknown origin at the beginning of the film. Perhaps Allah? Speaking of which . . . .

THE QUEST FOR MEANING

Undercurrents throughout the movie cast doubt about whether the gods are reliable or even present; for example, when the vizier prays for Koura not to hear their plans, the audience sees that Koura is already finding everything out. Although Sinbad receives what might be divine visions, he is skeptical about religion and faith and eschews some of the common practices of his culture, such as slavery, preferring a pragmatic approach summed up in the film's most memorable proverb: "Trust in Allah . . . but tie up your camel."

Some have noted that Sinbad's boat has a figurehead, something not allowed by devout Muslims. Considering Sinbad's attitude, the figurehead might be a deliberate show of defiance that illustrates independent thinking.

Sinbad is not only the best choice to undertake a quest based around a nautical chase. He's also the best equipped to win a game that involves assembling a map and capturing a magical prize at the end of a perilous journey.

The gryphon and the centaur represent the battle between good and evil: the gryphon evidently good, because Koura wounds it, thus aiding the centaur's cause. Probably the silliest aspect of the final prize is the "shield of darkness," which is just invisibility. When Koura wields a sword while cloaked, Sinbad can still see where he must be standing and can still stab him—so what good is the "shield"?

WHO GOES THERE?

Brian Clemens wrote and directed the 1974 cult adventure *Captain Kronos—Vampire Hunter* and wrote the story for the poorly received *Highlander II*. He died in 2015 at age 83.

John Phillip Law was the good-hearted Alexei in *The Russians Are Coming, the Russians Are Coming*; but firmly established his cult credentials as the titular thief in *Danger: Diabolik* and as Pygar the angel in *Barbarella*. He died in 2008 at age 70.

Caroline Munro is one of the most iconic female cult-figures of sci-fi, horror, and fantasy cinema, with cleavage-baring roles in films like *Dracula A.D. 1972, Captain Kronos—Vampire Hunter, At the Earth's Core, The Spy Who Loved Me*, and *Starcrash*. She turned up in '80s slashers *Maniac, The Last Horror Film*, and *Slaughter High*. She also appeared as little more than set dressing in *The Abominable Dr. Phibes* and *Dr. Phibes Rises Again* as the mad scientist's preserved wife, never uttering a word.

> DYNARAMA MEANS SUPREME ADVENTURE!

A NEW DIMENSION IN MOTION PICTURE ENTERTAINMENT

Legions of fans worldwide know Tom Baker as arguably the most recognizable incarnation of the Doctor in the long-running BBC television series *Doctor Who*. His landmark seven-year run on the series as the fourth man to play the role began when BBC reps saw him in *The Golden Voyage of Sinbad*. He also appeared in *Nicholas and Alexandra*, *The Vault of Horror*, and *The Mutations*. He played Sherlock Holmes and Puddleglum in TV adaptations of *The Hound of the Baskervilles* and *The Silver Chair*, and turns up as Halvarth in *Dungeons & Dragons*. Many modern UK television watchers know him best as the voice of the sketch-comedy series *Little Britain*.

Douglas Wilmer previously appeared as Pelias in *Jason and the Argonauts*.

Kurt Christian appeared next as Rafi in *Sinbad and the Eye of the Tiger*.

By the time Robert Shaw appeared in this movie, he had already appeared as the blond assassin in *From Russia with Love* and as Henry VIII in *A Man for All Seasons*. After this film, he made memorable appearances in *The Sting*, *The Taking of Pelham One Two Three*, and *Force 10 from Navarone*. Perhaps audiences remember him best as grizzled seafarer Quint in *Jaws*. He died in 1978 at age 51.

6 DEGREES OF SORCERY

This film shares a composer with the 1940 film *The Thief of Bagdad*, as well as similarities in its presentation of Kali, who moves like her earlier counterpart and has an identical number of limbs. The island of Lemuria takes its name from a mythical lost continent or land in the Indian or Pacific Ocean that has inspired other pop-culture phenomena, such as a rival seaborne nation battling Atlantis in Marvel Comics and the remnants of Mu in Robert E. Howard's *Kull* tales.

Sinbad strategically heads into a misty region of the sea, similar to the way Kirk took the *Enterprise* into the Mutara Nebula in *Star Trek II: The Wrath of Khan*. Another ship in pursuit spied at night and at daybreak is "inconceivable" in *The Princess Bride*. Cliffs of giant faces turn up in the other two *Sinbad* films in the series.

Koura's use of chemical explosive presages Zenobia's reliance on semi-modern technology in *Sinbad and the Eye of the Tiger*. The green-skinned natives are virtually identical to those who appear in one of Tom Baker's *Doctor Who* stories, "The Power of Kroll," and recall those in *The Thief of Bagdad*. The vizier's unmasked face vaguely resembles Vincent Price's scarred visage in *House of Wax*.

Koura's superimposed eyes bear similarity to Bela Lugosi's in *White Zombie* and *Revolt of the Zombies*. This series uses that gimmick again with Zenobia in *Sinbad and the Eye of the Tiger*.

The centaur-gryphon match recalls the battle between the dragon and the Cyclops in *7th Voyage*. Another monster mash-up finale turns up in *Sinbad and the Eye of the Tiger*.

SHATTERING THE ILLUSION

Most filming took place in Spain—Madrid and Majorca—after the threat of bureaucratic and other difficulties on location in India forced the production to return to familiar territory.

Only the inclusion of Kali remains of that plan. After eight weeks of principal photography and two years of post-production effects work, the movie cost a little under $1 million.

Harryhausen's earliest sketches for the film date to 1964, when *7th Voyage* was still fresh in his mind and plans abounded for another *Sinbad* adventure. In the early '70s, he drafted an outline that drew on Conrad Veidt's performance in *The Thief of Bagdad* to shape his villain, then named Jaffa. Schneer cut a planned, illustrated "Valley of the Vipers" sequence, oddly suggesting that it would disturb pregnant women.

Writer Brian Clemens' first draft of a script, *Sinbad in India*, featured a story-point originated by Harryhausen involving a character transformed into a baboon. It did not, in the end, appear in this film but later turned up as a major thread in *Sinbad and the Eye of the Tiger*.

The Golden Voyage of Sinbad significantly shifted stylistically from the first *Sinbad* film. A hired advisor crafted some authentic-sounding proverbs to lend the film a more Eastern quality. The production team left behind the storybook quality and created an adventure that grounded the fantasy in reality and appealed to an older audience. The color palette became more muted and some of the themes more mature.

Writer Brian Clemens brought Munro into the production, having just worked with her as writer and director of the Hammer film, *Captain Kronos—Vampire Hunter*. Christopher Lee was an early favorite for Koura. Orson Welles was first choice for the oracle, but Robert Shaw, who had wanted to play Sinbad, got that role. Welles later provided a tongue-in-cheek narration for a contemporary behind-the-scenes short feature on the making of the film.

Harryhausen drew on the distinctive image of the Bride of Frankenstein for the animated figurehead, and on his own previous work on the birth of the Ymir in *20 Million Miles to Earth* for the awakening of the homunculus.

The cyclopean centaur combined two mythological creatures into one unique monster. Harryhausen took inspiration from his recollection of an opera tenor for its dramatic death.

He added two additional arms to the traditionally four-armed Kali. Choreography used stand-ins belted together for the dance and fight sequences—an Indian dancer and her student for one, and three stuntmen for the other—to provide reference for the multiple limbs Harryhausen would animate. Unfortunately, a fabricator contracted to construct the full-size Kali statue that would stand on set in live-action shots did not match Harryhausen's model, so he obscured it in its few, fleeting appearances.

The runaway success of the film upon its release all but guaranteed that Schneer and Harryhausen would follow it with another *Sinbad* adventure, but they did not invite Law, though he wanted to return. The studio and producers wanted to avoid labeling the next film as a mere sequel. Law later said that of all his films, this one was closest to his heart.

MUSIC OF THE MINSTRELS

Ever since *7th Voyage*, Harryhausen had wanted Miklos Rozsa to score a *Sinbad* adventure. Although this is Rozsa's one and only score for the series, his themes are satisfyingly

Sinbad Battles the Creatures of Legend in the Miracle of Dynarama!

distinctive and bombastic. They also sound familiar to anyone who has heard his later work in *Time After Time* and *Dead Men Don't Wear Plaid*.

THE SAGA CONTINUES

The film series concluded with *Sinbad and the Eye of the Tiger* in 1977. (See that chapter for more.) The final two issues (7 and 8) of Marvel Comics' short-lived sci-fi anthology series *Worlds Unknown* adapted the movie as "The Golden Voyage of Sinbad: Land of the Lost," and Warner published a paperback novelization by Steve Hart. Columbia released two different sets of edited 8mm film reels, the first set subtitled *Sinbad Duels the Idol of Many Arms, Sinbad Challenges the Monster, Sinbad and the Magic Sword,* and *Sinbad and the Oracle,* and the second set subtitled *Sinbad's Mystical Adventure, Sinbad and the Mysterious Amulet, Sinbad Battles Koura's Evil Magic,* and *Sinbad's Triumph.*

TAKE UP THY SWORD!
HOMUNCULI (SORCEROUS FAMILIARS)

These tiny, winged creatures (appearing as diminutive gargoyles) are a sorcerous combination of mandrake root, mysterious chemicals, a couple drops of the summoner's blood, and of course a hint of dark magic. While summoning them, the caster binds them to obedience. Though roughly the same size as common bats, homunculi can fly at twice the speed of a bat and can hover.

The greatest benefit from these creatures is that their caster can see through their eyes and hear through their ears even from miles away. Because of this, homunculi are perfect scouts. If captured by anyone other than their creator, these creatures self-destruct in flashes of light, disintegrating to ash.

THE FILM'S DESTINY

Although this is perhaps the weakest of the three *Sinbad* films in this series, with slightly sluggish pacing and some of the lesser creature set-pieces of Harryhausen's career (though only in comparison to the extraordinary heights of his very best), it has four major assets: John Phillip Law's definitive Sinbad, Tom Baker's magnetic magician Koura, and of course Caroline Munro. Yes, we said four; we went there.

Law is the best Sinbad of the three, with an appropriate look and an actual attempt at an accent, unlike Mathews before him and Wayne after him. His more subdued approach to the role, coupled with a bemused twinkle in his eye, makes him a believable hero capable of facing and defeating all manner of mythical dangers.

Comic relief comes from the inept antics of Haroun. Though he never quite learns the ropes of sailing, he exhibits great courage by the film's end and even dispatches Kali.

As for all the creatures, plenty of them delight, from the almost cute homunculus to the fuzzy-headed centaur with one eye to Munro's delectable form. Even the sameness of the figurehead and Kali-statue designs don't detract from the technical brilliance of their realization.

While this film might not keep up the pace and dynamic of *7th Voyage,* it feels more *real,* thanks to more naturalistic shooting and acting styles. Following the basic framework of the first film, with Sinbad first encountering a similarly-named magician and finding himself on a quest with equal parts romance and adventure, backed by another beautiful score, a wittier script, and another two-monster mash-up at the end, *Golden Voyage* is great fun throughout.

THIS YEAR IN GAMING

In January, fledgling game publisher Tactical Studies Rules, Inc. commercially released *Dungeons & Dragons,* credited to Gary Gygax and Dave Arneson. In 1974, the initial print run of 1,000 hand-assembled copies quickly sold out, requiring an additional 2,000 by year's end. A wood-grain cardboard box contained the initial set, including three digest-sized booklets: *Book 1: Men & Magic, Book 2: Monsters & Treasure,* and *Book 3: The Underworld & Wilderness Adventures.* The first printing also "required" a copy of the *Outdoor Survival* simulation game published by Avalon Hill. Now highly prized, near-mint–condition copies of this original set have sold for more than $4,000 each at auction.

MONTY PYTHON AND THE HOLY GRAIL

1975 • UK
EMI Films / Python (Monty) Pictures /
Michael White Productions / National Film Trustee Company
87m • Color • PG

Writers: Graham Chapman, John Cleese, Eric Idle, Terry Gilliam, Terry Jones, and Michael Palin
Directors: Terry Gilliam and Terry Jones
Producer: Mark Forstater
Songs: Neil Innes
Additional Music: DeWolfe (library tracks)
Make-Up: Pearl Rashbass and Pam Luke
Production Designer: Roy Smith
Costume Designer: Hazel Pethig
Special Effects: John Horton And Julian Doyle
Animation Assistance: Lucinda Cowell and Kate Hepburn
Fight Director & Period Consultant: John Waller
Cast: Graham Chapman (King Arthur / Voice of God / Middle Head / Hiccoughing Guard); John Cleese (Sir Lancelot the Brave / Second Swallow-Savvy Guard / Man with Not Dead Body / The Black Knight / Peasant #3 / Taunting French Guard / Tim the Enchanter); Eric Idle (Sir Robin the-Not-Quite-So-Brave-as-Sir-Lancelot / Dead Collector / Peasant #1 / Confused Swamp Castle Guard / Concorde / Roger the Shrubber / Brother Maynard); Terry Gilliam (Patsy / Green Knight / Old Man from Scene 24 / Sir Bors / Animator / Gorilla Hand); Terry Jones (Sir Bedevere / Dennis' Mother / Left Head / Cartoon Scribe / Prince Herbert / French Knight); Michael Palin (Sir Galahad the Pure / First Swallow-Savvy Guard / Dennis / Peasant #2 / Right Head / Narrator / King of Swamp Castle / Brother Maynard's Brother / Leader of the Knights Who Say Ni / French Knight / Guest at Swamp Castle / Mud-Eater); Connie Booth (The Witch); Carol Cleveland (Zoot/Dingo); Neil Innes (First Monk / Singing Minstrel / Page Crushed by the Rabbit / Peasant #4); Bee Duffell (Old Crone);, John Young (Not Dead Body / Historian); Rita Davies (Historian's Wife); Avril Stewart (Dr. Piglet); Sally Kinghorn (Dr. Winston); Mark Zycon (Prisoner); Sandy Johnson (Knight of Ni / Villager at Witch Burning / Musician at Wedding / Monk / Knight in Battle); Romilly Squire (Musician at Wedding / Villager at Witch Burning); Elspeth Cameron, Mitsuko Forstater, Sandy Rose, Joni Flynn, Alison Walker, Loraine Ward, Anna Lanski, Sally Coombe, Vivienne Macdonald, Yvonne Dick, Daphne Darling, Fiona Gordon, Gloria Graham, Judy Lams, Tracy Sneddon, Sylvia Taylor, Joyce Pollner, and Mary Allen (Girls in Castle Anthrax); Julian Doyle (Police Sergeant, uncredited); Margarita Doyle (Peasant, uncredited); Charles Knode (Camp Guard / Robin's Minstrel, uncredited); Zack Matalon (Guard Who Falls into Barrels, uncredited); William Palin (Sir Not-Appearing-in-This-Film, uncredited); Tom Raeburn (Guard Eating Apple, uncredited); Roy Forge Smith (Inspector End of Film, uncredited); and Maggie Weston (Page Turner, uncredited).

ON THE MAP

Can't you read? It says right there in the beginning that we're in England, 932 A.D.! The knights visit a variety of castles controlled by rude French soldiers, oversexed maidens, and a

> And Now! At Last! Another Film Completely Different From Some of the Other Films Which Aren't Quite the Same as This One Is

doomed wedding party; dangerous forests inhabited by insistent and occasionally multi-headed knights; deadly caverns; and of course the Bridge of Death spanning the Gorge of Eternal Peril.

OUR STORY SO FAR

Arthur, King of the Britons, assembles an impressive band of courageous—well, mostly courageous—knights because God charges him to quest for the Holy Grail. As Arthur and his companions seek that most exalted of prizes, they have a variety of violent and perverse adventures and face a greater truth: that perhaps the quest was not about the goal, but the journey. At the very least, it gave them all something to do.

ALTERNATE VERSIONS

For a movie that so many fans have committed to memory, some might find it annoying how many minor (and some not so minor) alterations it has undergone in its various home-video releases, including alternate scenes, additional or altered dialogue, and a variety of small cuts. Perhaps most irksome, in recent years the only version of the film available on DVD features entirely new narration links rerecorded by Michael Palin, supposedly to improve upon the sound quality of the originals. Besides clearly being performed by a much older Palin, the current links lack the energy and inflection of his original efforts. You cannot hear the film as first released unless you have an older copy. It's enough to make dedicated Python fans want to chew their own feet off.

IT'S MAGIC

Magic permeates this Arthurian world. Who knows—perhaps even the Black Knight is enchanted. That would explain how he can carry on a coherent conversation while bleeding profusely from all four limbless stumps.

We never discover from where the powers of the Old Man from Scene 24 truly derive. Because he is subject to the same force that dooms anyone answering a question dishonestly, the magic must come from the gorge locale and not from him.

Tim, a formidable if irritating enchanter, has a real knack for translocating, and an animated monster can give live-action knights a run for their money, but surely nothing possesses the sheer ferocious magical might of the killer rabbit that defies gravity and common sense in the pursuit of a meal. This is also a world in which God exists. Like many of the other folks in the story, he's as short-tempered as he is powerful.

Is time travel involved as well? That might explain the presence of a twentieth-century historian throughout the film, as well as the shocking, sudden conclusion in which a modern-day movie crew shuts down the quest once and for all . . . but it's probably just a joke.

THE QUEST FOR MEANING

Should we really do this? Wouldn't this be a case of ruining comedy by analyzing too much? Sure, we could talk about how this film demonstrates familiar genre themes like the heroic ideals of loyalty, devotion to a higher calling, chastity, and the random bloodletting that goes with being a rampaging lunatic with a sharp sword, but that's what the *Excalibur* chapter is for. When you really dig deep down, this movie has one and only one true meaning, one purpose from which everything else in the film is mere distraction, preventing the full weight of truth from crushing lesser intellects and leaving them cowering in a corner, cold and alone in an uncaring universe. At long last, we reveal that truth to you.

An unladen swallow can achieve an airspeed velocity of approximately twenty-four miles an hour (eleven meters a second) and beats its wings an average of seven to nine times each second. While it's true that a bird weighing five ounces could never hope to carry a coconut weighing a pound, it's an impossible scenario, anyway, because a common barn-swallow weighs only about two-thirds of an ounce.

African or European? Oh, go look it up.

WHO GOES THERE?

Together, the Monty Python troupe wrote and performed in three seasons of *Monty Python's Flying Circus*, with a shorter fourth season re-titled simply *Monty Python*, to reflect the departure of John Cleese. The entire group also made the movies *And Now for Something Completely Different*, *Life of Brian*, *Live at the Hollywood Bowl*, and *The Meaning of Life*; recorded a number of albums; performed in stage productions in the UK and the US; and produced books, video games, and reunion specials, among a plethora of other merchandise.

Graham Chapman worked on *At Last the 1948 Show*, appeared in John Cleese's *How to Irritate People*, and had roles in *The Magic Christian*, *The Rise and Rise of Michael Rimmer*, *The Odd Job*, and *Yellowbeard*. He died in 1989 at age 48.

John Cleese's elongated form and biting wit made him one of the world's most recognizable and celebrated funny men for decades, beginning with early work on television shows like *That Was the Week That Was*, *At Last the 1948 Show*, *The Frost Report*, and his own special, *How to Irritate People*. He also made early appearances in films like *The Magic Christian* and *The Rise and Rise of Michael Rimmer*. Post-Python, Cleese co-created one of the most celebrated sitcoms ever, *Fawlty Towers*, with then (and then not) wife Connie Booth. He had roles in films like *The Great Muppet Caper*, *Time Bandits*, *Yellowbeard*, *Silverado*, *Clockwise*, *A Fish Called Wanda* (which he co-wrote), *Erik the Viking*, *An American Tail: Fievel Goes West*, *Frankenstein*, *Mr. Toad's Wild Ride*, *Fierce Creatures* (which he unfortunately also co-wrote), *The World Is Not Enough*, *Die Another Day*, *Charlie's Angels: Full Throttle*, *The Day the Earth Stood Still*, and the first two *Harry Potter* films, and TV shows like *Doctor Who* ("City of Death"), *Cheers*, *3rd Rock from the Sun*, and *Will & Grace*. He was the voice of the king in the latter three *Shrek* animated movies and remains a busy and still sometimes funny man.

> NOMINATED FOR 26 OSCARS
> 3 BRIANS A MAUREEN &
> 1 SERGIO

Eric Idle began his television career with writing for *The Frost Report* and *Do Not Adjust Your Set*. He created *Rutland Weekend Television* and its TV-movie follow-up, *All You Need Is Cash*, and appeared in films like *Yellowbeard, European Vacation, The Adventures of Baron Munchausen, Nuns on the Run, Mom and Dad Save the World, Splitting Heirs, Casper, Mr. Toad's Wild Ride*, and *An Alan Smithee Film: Burn Hollywood Burn*, as well as television series and miniseries like *Laverne & Shirley, Faerie Tale Theatre, Around the World in 80 Days*, and *Nearly Departed*. In recent years, Idle has become the steward of the Monty Python brand via an online presence, video game and other projects, and the successful adaptation of *Holy Grail* into a Broadway musical, *Spamalot*.

Terry Gilliam left behind the animation that made such a mark on the *Monty Python* projects and distinguished himself as a fantasy filmmaker in his own right, directing movies such as *Jabberwocky, Time Bandits, Brazil, The Adventures of Baron Munchausen, The Fisher King, Twelve Monkeys, The Brothers Grimm, The Imaginarium of Doctor Parnassus*, and *The Zero Theorem*.

Terry Jones worked on *Complete and Utter History of Britain* and *Do Not Adjust Your Set*, appeared in *Jabberwocky* and *Mr. Toad's Wild Ride* as well as an episode of Michael Palin's anthology television series *Ripping Yarns* (for which he co-wrote all the episodes), and lent his voice to the TV miniseries *Dinotopia*. He directed *Personal Services, Erik the Viking* (which he also wrote), and the "Barcelona, May 1917" episode of *The Young Indiana Jones Chronicles*. He did voice work and wrote the tie-in novel for Douglas Adams' game *Starship Titanic*, and in recent years he has become a prolific writer and presenter of television documentaries on ancient and medieval culture. Also recently, he directed and co-wrote the Simon Pegg film *Absolutely Anything*, to which the remaining Pythons lent their voices as aliens.

Michael Palin is legendarily "the nicest Python," and he's too polite to debate anyone on that point. He worked as writer and/or performer on *How to Irritate People, Complete and Utter History of Britain*, and *Do Not Adjust Your Set*, and appeared in *Jabberwocky*, the TV movie *All You Need Is Cash, Time Bandits, The Missionary* (which he also wrote), *A Private Function, Brazil, A Fish Called Wanda, American Friends* (again, which he also wrote), *Mr. Toad's Wild Ride*, and *Fierce Creatures*. He created and co-wrote *Ripping Yarns* and appeared in all nine episodes, did voice work in *The Wind in the Willows* TV movie and *Arthur Christmas*, and worked on two episodes of the travel series *Great Railway Journeys*. Starting with the television miniseries *Around the World in 80 Days* in 1989, Palin reinvented himself as the world's most beloved travel presenter, circling the globe multiple times in follow-up series *Pole to Pole, Full Circle with Michael Palin, Hemingway Adventure, Sahara with Michael Palin, Himalaya with Michael Palin, New Europe*, and *Brazil with Michael Palin*. He also served as president of the Royal Geographical Society from 2009–2012.

During and after Connie Booth's marriage to John Cleese, she co-wrote and costarred in the legendary sitcom *Fawlty Towers* with him. She also appeared in *Monty Python's Flying Circus* and *And Now for Something Completely Different*, as well as *High Spirits* and the Palin-scripted *American Friends*.

Carol Cleveland, "the female Python," made numerous appearances on the show, in Python stage productions, and in every Python feature film. She also appeared in *The Return of the Pink Panther*.

Neil Innes was a frequent Python collaborator, especially where music was concerned, and was dubbed "the seventh Python." Co-founder of the Bonzo Dog Doo-Dah Band, Innes also worked on *Do Not Adjust Your Set* and Eric Idle's *Rutland Weekend Television* and made appearances in *Jabberwocky*, the Palin-scripted *The Missionary*, and Terry Jones' *Erik the Viking*.

Bee Duffell was also in *Fahrenheit 451* and *Five Million Years to Earth*. *Holy Grail* was her last film. She died in 1974 at age 60.

John Young appeared in *The Wicker Man, Life of Brian, Chariots of Fire,* and *Time Bandits*. He died in 1996 at age 80.

Rita Davies was in *The Last Horror Movie, The Da Vinci Code, Children of Men,* and the 2010 BBC series *Sherlock*.

Sally Kinghorn was one of two actresses to voice Maudie in *Brave*.

Joni Flynn also appeared in *Octopussy*.

6 DEGREES OF SORCERY

Credit that superb classical British education, because despite their satirical approach to the material, the Pythons drew liberally from well-established sources when constructing their version of Arthur's legend, so this film links many times to our other main Arthurian adaptation, *Excalibur*. It references other mythologies, too, not least the tale of the Trojan horse. As with *The NeverEnding Story* and *The Princess Bride*, one could interpret this movie's reality as existing within a book.

Another group of mismatched knights turns up in *The Magic Sword*. In *The Sword and the Sorcerer*, Talon echoes God's order not to grovel. If you're a cricket enthusiast, you might identify the visage of God as none other than famous player W. G. Grace.

The triumphant music that accompanies the appearance of Camelot also serves as Rediffusion Television's identifying music. Rediffusion produced shows previously worked on by several Pythons: *At Last the 1948 Show* and *Do Not Adjust Your Set*.

The Marx Brothers' comedy *Duck Soup* also features a sequence in which Harpo bangs on soldier's helmets like a musical instrument. The recurring refrain of "Get on with it!" refers to a 1961 UK comedy film by that title, also known as *Dentist on the Job* (see **The Saga Continues**).

A feminine trap similar to the one endured by Galahad here befalls Ahmad in *The Thief of Bagdad*. John Cleese's genuinely death-defying appearance as Tim standing at the top of a high mountain presages a similar life-threatening shot that concludes *The Beastmaster*. The Black Knight's death scene resembles one seen in *Lancelot of the Lake*. Lancelot's horse has the same name as the mount used by Cleese's television-sketch character, confused Robin Hood wannabe Dennis Moore.

The greatest influences, however, run from this film to other types of media, especially gaming, which long ago embraced it as an endlessly quotable *I Ching*. Games that make direct references to characters, settings, dialogue, or other elements of this movie include the tabletop game *Warhammer 40,000;* computer and console games like *Baldur's Gate, Destroy All Humans!, The Elder Scrolls IV: Oblivion, Fallout 2, The Secret of Monkey Island: Special Edition, SimCity 2000,* and *Warcraft III: Reign of Chaos;* and the MMORPGs *Guild Wars, Runescape,* and of course *World of Warcraft* ("Bring me a shrubbery!"). The *Mortal Kombat* series also frequently invokes the killer rabbit. As for other media, if it weren't for this movie, the rapid-fire ribbing machine known as *Mystery Science Theater 3000* would have lacked a good third of its gags.

SHATTERING THE ILLUSION

The Monty Python comedy group was riding the crest of a wave of popularity and working on their third series of television episodes when member John Cleese expressed an interest in leaving, citing repetitive material and increasing creative boredom. An abbreviated fourth series would eventually go on without him, but between the third and fourth year, the entire group—Cleese included—embarked on their first all-new feature film. They had filmed a compilation of television sketches titled *And Now for Something Completely Different*, but this time the movie would feature a single main storyline with a period setting.

Terry Jones and Terry Gilliam shared directorial duties, both directing for the first time. The relationship was not always harmonious; they differed drastically at times in their approach to the material. Apparently, most of the rest of the group favored Jones, because he focused more on the actors. Gilliam thought more about the technical side of things, given his animation background. This would be the last time two Pythons directed together; Jones took the reins for future Python films.

Part of the film's budget came from the band Pink Floyd, the members of which were Python fans and provided money from sales of their *Dark Side of the Moon* album. Conditions on the set were primitive. The local hotel didn't offer many amenities, and it limited hot-water use. In one of the most famous innovations borne of desperation, the use of coconuts in the film to mimic the sound of horse hooves came about not merely as a joke, but because the production couldn't afford to hire horses.

The team faced a serious challenge when the Scottish Department of the Environment blocked the use of many previously selected locations just two weeks before production began. It claimed the script lacked respect for the castles' historic standing. Most of the castles in the completed film, therefore, were a single location—the privately owned Doune Castle—re-dressed for the various sequences.

As befits a king, Chapman's chainmail was authentic and weighed nearly twenty-five pounds. The others didn't shoulder that burden; they wore wool pullovers covered with metallic paint.

Covered head to toe and thus unidentifiable, Cleese and Gilliam performed the duel between the Black and Green Knights; it was too much fun to turn the action over to stuntmen. Depending on who you believe, the final shot of the legless Black Knight was either John Cleese standing in a hole (according to Cleese), or a partial amputee who was hired to appear in the shot in which Arthur slices off one leg, and then buried in a hole that accommodated his remaining leg (according to Gilliam).

The bridge sequence offered its share of real-world perils, not least that Chapman was undergoing serious withdrawal. A heavy drinker, he could not find alcohol on location and had a physical breakdown. Ironically, he knew how to rock-climb and so went across, anyway. (A qualified mountaineer had built the very real bridge, but Cleese demanded a stunt double.) Chapman's harrowing experience on the set contributed to his decision to reform his lifestyle and give up alcohol. Friends and colleagues noted that he had become a changed man by the time the troupe was making *Life of Brian* a few years later.

> SETS THE CINEMA BACK
> 900 YEARS!

> MAKES BEN HUR LOOK
> LIKE AN EPIC!

In the original plan, Arthur and the knights would find the Holy Grail at Harrods, the modern-day London department store. *Monty Python's Flying Circus* featured some of the material developed for that time-bending finale, including parts with Cleese's participation, in the fourth-season "Michael Ellis" episode, with Cleese's blessing.

When *Holy Grail* made a heavily edited American debut on the CBS television network in 1977, the Pythons did not at all like the alterations to their work and rescinded the right to air the movie. They allowed it to air on PBS stations, and later, in the cable era, on several other stations, but only unedited.

MUSIC OF THE MINSTRELS

The soundtrack includes songs contributed by "seventh Python" Neil Innes, who also played several roles and later took part in some of the troupe's live performances. The rest of the score comprised stock music, often employed in direct opposition to its apparent mood, from the famous DeWolfe library. Charisma/Arista released *The Album of the Soundtrack of the Trailer of the Film of Monty Python and the Holy Grail*, which featured extensive sections of dialogue in addition to all-new linking sketch material. Cassette and CD versions featured a sketch called "A Foul-Tempered Rabbit" that had been edited on vinyl and 8-track editions. One extended CD version came out in 1997, and another, *The Special Edition of the Executive Version of the Album of the Soundtrack of the Trailer of the Film of Monty Python and the Holy Grail*, in 2006, with additional tracks and a few edits. The DVD box set (referenced in **The Saga Continues**) included yet another version, with a different mix of additions and cuts. Clearly, the quest to obtain the most complete version of the soundtrack CD, like the search for the Holy Grail, is an exercise in futility.

THE SAGA CONTINUES

You might not have thought the Python troupe ever considered a sequel to this movie, but strangely enough, Eric Idle briefly championed the idea in 1990. He proposed to make it a meta-commentary on their careers, with the knights gathering together as older men for one more adventure. Graham Chapman (Arthur) had died the previous year, and none of the other Pythons were interested, but that wasn't the end of Idle's crusade. Thanks to the success of other comedy-films-turned-Broadway-musicals, like Mel Brooks' *The Producers*, Idle secured the permission of the other Pythons to transform the quest into a song-and-dance extravaganza called *Spamalot*. It debuted on Broadway in 2005. Still running today in a variety of international regional productions, despite less than positive comments from Terry Jones, it racked up some Tony Award wins and nominations under the stewardship of director Mike Nichols. One UK version of the production featured *Doctor Who*'s fifth incarnation, Peter Davison, in the role of King Arthur. On the first anniversary of the play's opening (in March 2006) and again a little more than a year later, *Guinness World Records* declared that the show had assembled the world's largest-ever coconut orchestra.

As we noted in "**Alternate Versions**," the film has had several home-video releases. A bare-bones 1999 DVD preceded a 2001 "Extraordinarily Deluxe" edition, which includes multiple audio-commentary tracks, funny optional subtitles drawn from Shakespeare, and a new opening for the movie that tries to trick viewers by starting with the title sequence and first scene from the UK comedy film *Dentist of the Job* (or *Get on with It*). This version of *Holy Grail* restores a previously cut scene in which Dingo briefly talks to the audience about whether to cut the scene. Other extras include "The Camelot Song," with stop-motion LEGO mini-figures performing a re-creation of the sequence that accompanied the original audio track—and very cute they are, too! A box set of this release, which included some limited-edition extras like a film cel, cards, and a CD of the soundtrack, omitted a few of the disc's features. When the thirty-fifth anniversary rolled around in 2012, the film came to the Blu-ray format and digital media.

Not a great deal of merchandising coincided with the original release of the film. Methuen published a script book in 1977; it offered fans a glimpse of Terry Jones' shooting script supplemented with a variety of other bits and bobs. In later years, the movie inspired quite a few products, including trading cards, a line of action figures, bobblehead dolls, plush dolls (your own puffy disassembling Black Knight, Black Beast of Arrrggghhh, Holy Hand Grenade, and killer rabbit!), killer-rabbit slippers, a Tim the Enchanter hat, and much more.

Games? You want games? It's no surprise that this movie, so embraced by gaming culture, has seen more than a few game adaptations over the years. Perhaps the most extensive application of the Grrrrrrail theme in gaming to date was during the heyday of the CCG (collectible card game) era in the 1990s. Kenzer and Company launched the *Monty Python and the Holy Grail* game in 1996 and then released a *Taunt You a Second Time!* expansion in 2000 with more than 150 additional cards. The expansion could stand alone or combine with the original edition.

7th Level released a computer game for both the Windows and Mac platforms in 1996 that incorporated film clips. The company re-released the game in a stripped-down (steady now) version in 2002.

In 2008, Looney Labs added *Monty Python* to its growing stable of *Fluxxx* card games, with plenty of *Holy Grail*–themed cards and references in the Python deck. A 2009 *Castle Expansion* added eight more cards.

Toy Vault released a licensed board game in 2008 called *Python-opoly* that mimicked the classic *Monopoly* game. Despite its generic-Python title, the entire game centered on *Holy Grail*.

TAKE UP THY SWORD!

KILLER RABBIT (MONSTER)

SPECIAL ATTACK: *Horrible Decapitating Strike*. When the killer rabbit attacks, a critical result decapitates any foe of up to medium (human) size, regardless of type or quality of armor. Even the rabbit's regular attack inflicts twice as much damage as that of a typical longsword.

POWER: Due to its diminutive size (and its lightning-fast speed), the rabbit is a difficult target to hit.

DETAILS: The killer rabbit is not worth screwing with. Employed by various madmen and ill-tempered beasts throughout the ages, the rabbit is quite possibly the greatest guardian that ever lived. It's fast. It's vicious. It's cute as a wee little button. Know this: if ye be brave enough to challenge it, you'll need a spare suit of armor—unless, of course, you lose your head!

> ENJOY A GOOD KNIGHT OUT WITH A PILOT? PREPARE YOURSELF
> FOR THE FUNNIEST DOUBLE BILL OF THE YEAR.
> (1982 RE-RELEASE POSTER PAIRING HOLY GRAIL WITH AIRPLANE II: THE SEQUEL)

THE FILM'S DESTINY

For decades, this film has been one of the "secret handshakes" of the genre's fan community. Learning to quote *Holy Grail* dialogue verbatim is not only a rite of passage for many fans but also an ongoing exercise that binds friends and communities and excludes the rest of the world. The movie's endless quotability reaches such a point that some call themselves Python fans even if this is the only Python production they ever see. (Ah, but some of us know better.)

As with its namesake, *The Holy Grail* inspires, entices, and holds considerable power over those who seek its wisdom. It's one of the greatest comedy films of all time, immersing audiences realistically in its setting and then letting the lunacy fly.

As we mentioned, the Python team—already a finely honed machine—was concluding its television series when it made this film. If nothing else, this movie demonstrates that the group still had plenty of energy. The time was right to take on long-form projects. Even if this weren't a minor comic masterpiece—which it is—it's the stepping stone to *Life of Brian*, which is no small achievement.

Perhaps one aspect of this movie that might irk some is the way in which it shatters its own reality by merging with the present, running out the clock, and stopping . . . after interminable, insipid exit music (which is itself rather funny). For one segment of fans, the film's meta-heavy non-ending is the final touch of brilliance that caps the zaniest Arthurian adaptation ever made, while for another, it might suggest a missed opportunity to provide a better and more satisfying conclusion to the foregone story. If you are one of the people who feel *Holy Grail* is nearly but not entirely perfect, don't worry. *Life of Brian* is better.

THIS YEAR IN GAMING

Just as *Dungeons & Dragons* was celebrating its first official birthday, Flying Buffalo Games released a simplified answer to TSR's flagship roleplaying game, titled *Tunnels & Trolls*. Designed by Ken St. Andre *(Stormbringer; Monsters! Monsters!;* and the award-winning computer game *Wasteland)* as a more accessible alternative to *D&D*, *Tunnels & Trolls* emphasized solitaire play. Since its release, the game has remained in print. A few noteworthy *Tunnels & Trolls* adventure authors include Larry Ditillio (who went on to be a lead writer and story editor on *Babylon 5*), Michael A. Stackpole (author of several *Star Wars* and *BattleTech* novels), and "Lee" Russell, author of *Labyrinth,* notable as the first woman to independently write a published RPG adventure module.

WIZARDS

1977 • US • Bakshi Productions / 20th Century Fox • 80m • Color • PG

Writer: Ralph Bakshi
Director: Ralph Bakshi
Producer: Ralph Bakshi
Music: Andrew Belling
Animation Production Manager: William Orcutt
Illustrated Histories: Mike Ploog
Cast: Bob Holt (Avatar), Jesse Welles (Elinore), Richard Romanus (Weehawk), David Proval (Peace), James Connell (President), Steve Gravers (Blackwolf), Barbara Sloane (Fairy), Angelo Grisanti (Frog), Hyman Wien (Priest), Christopher Tayback (Peewhittle), Mark Hamil (Sean), Peter Hobbs (General), Tina Bowman (Prostitute), Ralph Bakshi (Fritz/Stormtrooper, uncredited), Victoria Bakshi (Fairy Girl, uncredited), and Susan Tyrrell (Narrator, uncredited)
Alternate Title: *War Wizards* (working title)

ON THE MAP

The action takes place across two lands, Montagar and the dark land of Scortch, which is blighted by radiation and mutation. At one point, a map actually appears onscreen, showing Scortch in the southeast and Montagar in the northwest, separated by what appears to be a bomb-blasted wasteland.

OUR STORY SO FAR

In the distant future, long after a nuclear holocaust divides the land, two brothers must face one another to determine the fate of all life on Earth. One is a peaceful wizard named Avatar, in tune with the world of magic alongside elves, dwarves, and fairies, and the other is his sadistic brother Blackwolf, who believes that technology will enable him to reclaim the planet for mutants.

ALTERNATE VERSIONS

A cut of the film (Bakshi's personal print) that screened in Los Angeles in 2005 as part of a Bakshi retrospective lacked the title of the book at the top of the opening narration and lacked the introductory narration for Necron 99.

IT'S MAGIC

Avatar and Blackwolf wield magic and have it inherent within them, but for completely different purposes. While Avatar typically uses his magic for good, he can be selfish, manifesting cigars or food. Blackwolf slings his spells to enact his will over a dark army of mutants and demons. Avatar is

THE ULTIMATE FUTURISTIC FANTASTIC EPIC.

an old-school mage who acknowledges the existence of magic within everyone and everything, while Blackwolf looks at magic as a threat to his plan for world domination and employs assassins to slaughter users of magic who might oppose him. He recognizes the power of sorcery but wishes to be the only one capable of using it. In the end, Avatar turns to technology, not magic, in the conflict with his brother (although the sudden appearance of the offending weapon might have resulted from a cunning act of off-camera prestidigitation). The film presents the art of spellcasting in stereotypical fashion, complete with magic words, hand waving, and both lighting and sound effects.

THE QUEST FOR MEANING

In many modern—and even not so modern—tales of the fantastic, the worlds of magic and machines are often at odds. Tolkien addresses this in *The Lord of the Rings* as a personal commentary about industry and the devastating power of modern warfare. *Wizards* advances the story millions of years, past wars that bring all life on Earth to the brink of extinction. While one scarred and irradiated aspect of humankind sluggishly continues down the path we walk today, with its almost religious worship of guns and bombs, the other turns its back on cogs, wheels, and engines to re-attune itself with nature and evolve—or perhaps devolve—into the stuff of myth and legend: faeries, elves, and wizards.

Avatar walks a fine line between the two worlds, even with science and technology having been outlawed epochs before. He surveys the lands from his tower through a telescope, he transforms caged pets into a working jukebox, and he defeats his brother with a firearm. In a way, as good triumphs over evil through the use of technology, we conclude with the understanding that neither path is ideal. For humankind to advance, the two worlds must blend in harmony.

A second theme regards fascism and its potential for return at the hands of a cunning leader. As described through narration, the inhabitants of Scortch could easily work up into frenzies, but they lacked focused and competent leadership. Blackwolf, through his analysis of unearthed artifacts from Nazi Germany, learns how to use propaganda and fear to motivate the mutants and demons and drive them into war with the peaceful peoples of Montagar. Ultimately, as Bakshi freely admits, the story is a fantasized take on the life of a Jew living in Nazi Germany with the growing threat of the Holocaust, and the eventual establishment of the state of Israel.

WHO GOES THERE?

Bob Holt was in huge demand as a voice actor throughout the 1970s and '80s. Some of his more memorable cartoon characters included Hoot Kloot, Dogfather, The Hulk, and Cop-Tur (from *Challenge of the GoBots*). He died in 1985 at age 56.

Jesse Welles appeared on the big screen in *The Return of Count Yorga* (her first and one of her only films, unless you want to remember *Rhinestone*) and also showed up in guest-starring roles on television throughout the '70s and '80s on shows like *McCloud, Kojak, The Rockford Files, Soap, T.J. Hooker,* and *Newhart*.

Another accomplished veteran of the big and small screens, Richard Romanus has appeared in TV series such as *Mod Squad, Charlie's Angels, Strike Force, Tales from the Darkside, MacGyver,*

The A-Team, and *The Sopranos,* as well as films like *The Ghastly Ones, Mean Streets, Murphy's Law, Oscar,* and *Point of No Return.* He was the voice of Harry Canyon in *Heavy Metal.*

David Proval's first role was that of Tony DeVienazo in Martin Scorsese's *Mean Streets. Wizards* marked his first voice-acting role in a feature film. Since then he has become a reliable character actor, especially in gangster roles, in films like *The Monster Squad, UHF, Innocent Blood, The Shawshank Redemption, The Phantom,* and *Balls of Fury,* as well as on TV shows such as *Kojak, Police Story, Knight Rider, The Equalizer, Quantum Leap,* and *The Sopranos.*

James Connell appeared in the fondly remembered horror TV-movie, *Gargoyles.*

Steve Gravers lost his battle with lung cancer a year after the release of *Wizards,* at age 56. He appeared on television in *Peter Gunn, Alfred Hitchcock Presents, Combat!, Rawhide, Bonanza, Gunsmoke, I Spy, Get Smart, The Wild Wild West, Columbo, Ironside, Kojak,* and *Cannon* (so basically every western and detective show you can think of), and in films such as *Al Capone, Hell Bent for Leather, Blood Sabbath,* and *The Car.*

Mark Hamill (or "Hamil," as it reads in the credits) started acting with early television appearances on *The Partridge Family* and *General Hospital.* While working on a little something called *Star Wars* (see that chapter), Hamill broke away to record for the part of Sean. He appeared in the next two *Star Wars* movies as well as films like *Corvette Summer, The Big Red One, Slipstream, The Guyver,* and *Village of the Damned.* He did voice work for television early in his career, but beginning in the '90s he became a prolific voice artist in cartoon series and films. For fans of the animated *Batman* series of the 1990s, Hamill's deranged, cackling vocal interpretation of the Joker remains the definitive portrayal of the Dark Knight's ultimate archfoe, a part to which he returned in the *Batman: Arkham Asylum* and *Arkham City* video games. Hamill played the villainous Trickster in two different incarnations of *The Flash* television series, poked fun at his *Star Wars* association on *The Simpsons* and in *Jay and Silent Bob Strike Back,* and returns to that galaxy far, far away in *Star Wars: Episode VII—The Force Awakens.*

Peter Hobbs fought in the Battle of the Bulge (yes, for real) and later enjoyed a fifty-year career in film and television, appearing in movies like *The Killers, The Andromeda Strain,* Woody Allen's *Sleeper,* and *The Man with Two Brains.* On television, nary a popular series from the '60s, '70s, or '80s could go by without an appearance by Hobbs, including *Perry Mason; The Dick Van Dyke Show; The Andy Griffith Show; Marcus Welby, M.D.; The Odd Couple; The Streets of San Francisco; Barney Miller; M*A*S*H;* and numerous others. He also lent his voice to *Heavy Traffic* and *The Nine Lives of Fritz the Cat.* He died in 2011 at age 92.

Tina Bowman (Tina Romanus) worked with Bakshi again on *Hey Good Lookin'* and also provided the voice of Aunt Bella in *Starchaser: The Legend of Orin.*

Annie Award–winner Ralph Bakshi had already achieved notoriety for his adult—even pornographic—animated films, including *Fritz the Cat, Heavy Traffic,* and *Coonskin.* He also worked on a number of shorts and television cartoons, including *Spider-Man* (1967-1970). After *Wizards,* Bakshi returned to fantasy a few more times in films like the loved/hated 1978 *Lord of the Rings* and like *Fire and Ice,* co-produced with legendary artist Frank Frazetta.

Susan Tyrrell carved a niche for herself as a bit of a real-life, over-the-top "character," appearing in avant-garde

A FANTASY VISION OF THE FUTURE.

films like Andy Warhol's *Bad* and *Forbidden Zone, Avenging Angel, Flesh+Blood, Tapeheads, Big Top Pee-Wee, Rockula,* and *Cry-Baby*. She also worked as a voice actor in a few other films and television projects, including *The Chipmunk Adventure, Cow and Chicken,* and *Extreme Ghostbusters,* as well as *Fire and Ice*. She died in 2012 at age 67.

6 DEGREES OF SORCERY

The work of the late Vaughn Bodē clearly inspired many of the character designs. Of particular note are the similarities between Avatar and Cheech Wizard, and Necron 99 and Cobalt-60 (even down to similar names). Necron 99's design, in turn, might well have inspired the design of Boba Fett—especially the latter's original, animated appearance in the infamous *Star Wars Holiday Special* that aired in 1978.

The design of Weehawk and his kind clearly inspired Wendy Pini's *Elfquest* character designs. Some people have even speculated (albeit falsely) that she worked on the film.

The chase involving Necron 99 and Weehawk resembles the famous chase sequence depicted in Disney's 1949 production *The Adventures of Ichabod and Mr. Toad* (later released in 1958 as *The Legend of Sleepy Hollow*), even down to Necron 99's "horse" being black with red eyes, just like the Headless Horseman's. Blackwolf's demonic army resembles Saruman's Uruk-hai from *The Lords of the Rings* trilogy, with pretty apparent similarity between Blackwolf and Saruman. Blackwolf's design also owes much to the look of Czar Ivan IV featured in Sergei Eisenstein's *Ivan the Terrible* films, brought to life by actor Nikolai Cherkasov. Avatar's tower stands at the shore like those of many other wizards of fantasy, even Leezar's tower in *Your Highness*.

When deactivated, Necron 99 transmits a signal back to Scortch. The Borg of *Star Trek: The Next Generation* possess a similar ability.

Necron 99's conversion into Peace has him secured to a table akin to Frankenstein's monster. When the ground collapses under Weehawk and he plunges into a pit, Avatar mutters some words, one of which is "Frazetta," a reference to legendary fantasy artist Frank Frazetta (who would later collaborate with Bakshi on 1983's *Fire and Ice*). The restraints holding Elinore in her presentation to the fairies in their sanctuary are like Ann Darrow's in *King Kong*. The journey through the snowy mountains is similar to the Fellowship's journey over Caradhras in *The Lord of the Rings: The Fellowship of the Ring*. The first edition of TSR's *Gamma World* roleplaying game, released in 1978, cites *Wizards,* among other sources, as inspiration.

SHATTERING THE ILLUSION

Although many of the ideas and even the design of the film began as Bakshi's high-school sketches, he fleshed out other details for a series he pitched to CBS in 1967, titled *Tee-Witt*. A character in *Wizards* possesses the similar name "Peewhittle."

> SCIENCE AGAINST SORCERY.
> MAGIC AGAINST TECHNOLOGY.
> BROTHER AGAINST BROTHER.

Bakshi presented the concept of his feature *War Wizards* (the original working title) to 20th Century Fox decisionmakers in 1976, in hopes of convincing them that he could produce a more "family-friendly" animated feature film than his previous body of mature animated work. Bakshi wrote the first draft of the script in a single week while he and his wife were on vacation in the Grand Tetons.

> AN EPIC FANTASY OF PEACE AND MAGIC.

Bakshi chose Bob Holt as the voice of Avatar based almost exclusively on Holt's ability to impersonate Peter Falk. (Bakshi was a fan.) Other voice actors, including Jesse Welles, Richard Romanus, and David Proval, had collaborated with Bakshi on *Hey Good Lookin'* (produced in 1975 but not released until 1982).

Bakshi had always wanted a female narrator for the picture and was a fan of Susan Tyrrell. Though Tyrrell accepted the gig and delivered a memorable performance, she requested not to be credited on the film. Amusingly, her narration helped her land several gigs, and she has since regretted requesting anonymity.

The title *War Wizards* held for most of the production, until George Lucas requested a change to avoid any confusion with his little science-fiction project, *Star Wars*. Because Lucas had allowed Mark Hamill to break away from principal photography on that project a long time ago in a galaxy far, far away, Bakshi agreed to the request and dropped *War* from the title.

The entire film cost roughly $1 million, a budget so low that the animators had to skip the pencil-test step of the animation process. The film employed several veteran animators from Disney, MGM, and Warner Bros., including Irven Spence, Martin B. Taras, and John Vita. In addition to Mike Ploog, who focused on concepts for Montagar, British artist Ian Miller provided material for Scortch.

Bakshi had requested a budget increase to help complete the large battle sequences, but Fox declined, forcing him to investigate other options. By rotoscoping footage—hiring painters to modify live-action scenes frame by frame—from films like *Alexander Nevsky, Battle of the Bulge, El Cid, Patton,* and *Zulu*, Bakshi created sprawling battle scenes under budget, thanks to tireless animators.

Until 2012, questions persisted as to whether Bakshi lifted concepts from Vaughn Bodē's work. Then Bodē's son Mark reported that Bakshi had called him and apologized, offering to send back Vaughn Bodē artwork in his possession as well as signed cels from *Wizards*.

Wizards was 20th Century Fox's first animated feature film. William Stout, original screenwriter of *The Warrior and the Sorceress* (covered later in this volume), designed the film's original teaser poster, one that *Iron Man* director Jon Favreau considers his favorite movie poster of all time.

MUSIC OF THE MINSTRELS

Andrew Belling began his career as a musician and arranger for acts like Linda Ronstadt, Glen Campbell, and The Eagles. Prior to *Wizards,* he had composed the scores for a handful of films and TV movies, including *The Killing Kind* and *Deliver Us from Evil*. The *Wizards* soundtrack blends styles ranging from standard score material to jazz, funk, and even progressive rock.

The soundtrack also features a haunting track called "Time Will Tell," with words and music by Belling—but long after the film's release, the performer's identity was in question: some attributed the vocals to Jesse Welles (the voice of Elinore) and others to former Miss California and *Goldengirl* actress Susan Anton. Only recently did Belling add a comment to a fan-produced YouTube music video of the song, assuring fans that the vocalist was Anton. Originally, he had composed the song with Judy Collins in mind. Belling pushed Fox to release the track as a single or to put it up for an Academy Award nomination, but it expressed zero interest at the time.

Bakshi, normally an outspoken critic of film music, is a big fan of Belling's score and considers it one of his favorite scores of any film. He has stated that Belling came up with the music entirely on his own, although he might have suggested that Belling listen to the work of German electronic group Tangerine Dream for inspiration—and he did insist that the individual pieces have a "Jewishness" about them.

Belling returned to feature animation with 1985's *Starchaser: The Legend of Orin* and continues to work as a composer and arranger for film, TV, and even theme-park attractions. In late 2012, LaLaLand Records finally released the complete remastered score to *Wizards,* featuring exclusive liner notes by Randall D. Larson.

THE SAGA CONTINUES

A DVD finally came out in 2004, and a remastered deluxe Blu-ray edition coincided with the film's 35th anniversary. According to Bakshi, he always meant the film to be the first of a trilogy. He had already worked out the story of the second film during production of the first. A graphic novel, announced in 2004, would have picked up where the first film left off, but that stalled while Bakshi began work on the now-abandoned animated film, *The Last Days of Coney Island.* In 2008, rumors began circulating that Main Street Pictures was considering a sequel, but no further developments with that have materialized, either.

In 1992, fifteen years after the film's release, Whit Publications released the officially licensed *Wizards* roleplaying game. Designed by Edward Bolme, the game spawned four expansions, including sourcebooks for Montagar and Scortch as well as a gamemaster screen and a pack of specialized character sheets.

Artists like Cypress Hill and Vanilla Ice have audio-sampled the movie on their albums. Don't hold that against the movie, though.

TAKE UP THY SWORD!

LIFE UNTO STONE (MAGIC SPELL)

By touching a single, qualified stone-carving and successfully casting this spell, a wizard imbues the statue with temporary corporeal mortality for a number of minutes equal to the wizard's experience level, and grants the statue a will of its own. A qualified statue has the form of a creature known to the magic user. The spell does not work on stone that does not bear an intentional resemblance to a living creature that the caster recognizes—so it does not work on naturally occurring rock, on an architectural column (unless suitably sculpted), or on a structural wall unless said wall features sculpted reliefs.

Once a statue comes to life in this way, it assumes all aspects of the creature it resembles, effectively becoming that creature. Note that damage to a statue—bad cracks or missing digits or limbs—translates into that damage in flesh. While one might bring "life" to a statue missing its head, that life lasts but an instant, because the animated creature immediately perishes. Statues in the form of normally intelligent creatures—humanoids, for example—come to life possess-

> From Ralph Bakshi, master of animation, comes an epic fantasy in wondrous colour. A vision of the world, 10 million years in the future, where Wizards rule the earth. And the powers of magic prevail over the forces of technology in the final battle for world supremacy.

ing minimal, instinctual survival skills and no means of discourse beyond animalistic reactions. Once a caster brings something to life, that same caster can return it to stone.

THE FILM'S DESTINY

[Personal disclosure by SAW]: When I was nine years old, my parents took my older brother and me to see a double feature of *Watership Down* and *Wizards* at the Stutson Street Theater in Rochester, New York, sometime in late 1978—a year after *Wizards'* initial release. It moved me then as it still moves me today. I had never seen such scenes of violence in my nine years on this planet, and they remain with me. Some viewers might have criticized the violence and brightly colored flowing blood in a PG-rated animated feature, but the message behind those graphic images was clear: violence is not something to be celebrated. It is grotesque and traumatic. Of course Blackwolf positively thrives on it.

Avatar's resorting to a violent act in order to defeat his brother is equally grotesque, but it works, giving him a Hammurabian taste of his own medicine. He does not take pride in stooping to that level. You get the feeling that he will likely never do it again.

Wizards also stands as one of Bakshi's greatest and most accessible films. Most genre fans have already seen it. Those who haven't might look forward to a pleasant surprise when they do. The heroes all have their own charms—even Avatar at his most irascible. Elinore shines as one of the sexiest animated characters of all time.

The film's images alone influence artists and filmmakers to this day. A quick Google search for "Necron 99" leads to a number of impressive interpretations of the iconic character.

Ultimately, the film might owe its lasting popularity to its applicability to modern audiences. Empires with silos full of nuclear missiles do not cast the most fear around the globe; that honor typically goes to those who turn away from the advancement of science and industry and resort to cunning appropriation of others' technology. If the proposed sequel to *Wizards* should ever see the light of day, it could deal with that timely issue veiled behind the primitive innocence of Montagar.

THIS YEAR IN GAMING

Just four months after the US theatrical release of *Wizards*, Games Workshop launched *White Dwarf*, subtitled *The Science Fiction and Fantasy Games Magazine*, with an initial run of just 4,000 copies. Edited by Ian Livingstone and devoted almost exclusively to *Dungeons & Dragons*, the twenty-page glossy publication had a cover price of $1.50 (50p). The magazine celebrated its thirty-fifth anniversary in 2012 and continues to this day, although the content has shifted to focus entirely on tabletop miniature games produced by parent company Games Workshop. When asked to explain the name, Livingstone pointed out that, due to widespread interest in fantasy and science-fiction gaming at that time, audiences would recognize a white dwarf as either a fantasy character or a type of star.

STAR WARS

1977 • US • LUCASFILM / 20TH CENTURY FOX • 121M • COLOR • PG

WRITER: George Lucas
DIRECTOR: George Lucas
PRODUCER: Gary Kurtz
MUSIC: John Williams
DIRECTOR OF PHOTOGRAPHY: Gilbert Taylor
PRODUCTION DESIGNER: John Barry
SPECIAL PHOTOGRAPHIC EFFECTS SUPERVISOR: John Dykstra
SPECIAL PRODUCTION AND MECHANICAL EFFECTS SUPERVISOR: John Stears
SPECIAL DIALOGUE AND SOUND EFFECTS: Ben Burtt
MAKE-UP SUPERVISOR: Stuart Freeborn
PRODUCTION ILLUSTRATOR: Ralph McQuarrie
ART DIRECTORS: Norman Reynolds and Leslie Dilley
COSTUME DESIGNER: John Mollo
STUNT COORDINATOR: Peter Diamond
FIGHT ARRANGER: Bob Anderson (uncredited)
CAST: Mark Hamill (Luke Skywalker), Harrison Ford (Han Solo), Carrie Fisher (Princess Leia Organa), Peter Cushing (Grand Moff Tarkin), Alec Guinness (Ben "Obi-Wan" Kenobi), Anthony Daniels (C-3PO), Kenny Baker (R2-D2), Peter Mayhew (Chewbacca), David Prowse (Darth Vader), James Earl Jones (Voice of Darth Vader, uncredited), Phil Brown (Uncle Owen), Shelagh Fraser (Aunt Beru), Jack Purvis (Chief Jawa), Alex McCrindle (General Dodonna), Eddie Byrne (General Willard), Drewe Hemley (Red Leader), Dennis Lawson (Wedge, Red Two), Garrick Hagon (Biggs, Red Three), Jack Klaff (John D., Red Four), William Hootkins (Porkins, Red Six), Angus McInnis (Gold Leader), Jeremy Sinden (Gold Two), Graham Ashley (Gold Five), Don Henderson (General Taggi), Richard Le Parmentier (General Motti), and Leslie Schofield (Commander #1)
ALTERNATE TITLES: *Adventures of Luke Starkiller, as Taken from the Journal of the Whills; Saga I: The Star Wars;* and *The Star Wars* (all early working titles); *A New Hope, Star Wars Episode IV: A New Hope,* and *Star Wars Special Edition*

CAST NOTE

More than with any other film described in this book, performers whose names do not appear in the film credits (but which appear in various places on the Internet) far outnumber the credited primary cast. Rather than include all of them, we leave it to you to discover all those unsung actors at one of the online *Star Wars* or general movie databases of your choice. Some of the cast also turn up in some of our other chapters' cast sections.

ON THE MAP

This planet-hopping adventure takes us from the desert world of Tatooine to the world-sized weapon known as the Death Star and finally to the forest world of Yavin where the Rebellion plans its desperate assault on that devastating floating fortress in space.

OUR STORY SO FAR

A young farm boy loses his family but discovers his destiny with the help of an aging wizard and mentor. With two droids, a rogue smuggler, and the smuggler's hairy sidekick as companions, the boy must learn the truth of his family heritage and save a captured princess from the clutches of the evil Empire and its ebon-clad, sword-wielding sorcerer.

ALTERNATE VERSIONS

Oh, don't get us started. While most people know of the massive amounts of tinkering that took place beginning in 1997, which saw the release of the first special edition, changes took place as early as the film's early-release schedule. By now, so many altered editions of this movie exist—from its theatrical days to multiple home-video releases featuring ever-increasing numbers of CGI sequences plastered all over it—that our dwindling reserves of energy do not extend to even an attempt at cataloguing them all.

Suffice to say, if you want to enjoy the closest possible version to the original film in the twenty-first century, you have to spring for either the last pre–special-edition VHS release and a player (if you can find one that still works) or the 2006 DVD release that offered the original version as a non-anamorphic "bonus feature" sourced from a 1993 laserdisc release and paired with the 2004 version of the special edition. Thanks ever so much, Lucasfilm. With more alterations turning up in recent Blu-ray editions of the films, we can only say . . . so where's that VHS copy again?

IT'S MAGIC

What else is the Force but an intangible energy field that adept practitioners can access to achieve all manner of amazing things? None of that midichlorian talk now; remember, this is B.P. ("before prequels"). The Force is a spiritual thing, pre–*Phantom Menace*. This film goes to lengths to establish that, by contrasting those with a deeper understanding of the Force and an appreciation for the mystical side of existence with those who favor a more secular approach—that "good blaster" at one's side. A symbiotic relationship with observable nano-creatures measurable in the blood and defined in scientific terms doesn't generate the Force of the original trilogy. Back in the '70s and '80s, the Force was magic.

THE QUEST FOR MEANING

"Wait a minute . . . *Star Wars*? Are you kidding?" No, we're serious here. Think about it: prior to the existence of the prequel trilogy, and with what we just outlined in **It's Magic**, the original *Star Wars* and its two sequels are sword-and-sorcery films. For all its space-age trappings, *Star Wars* represents one of the most classic expressions of the heroic journey seen in this book, from swordplay and sorcery (deal with it) to the premise of a boy losing his family and leaving his simple life behind to save a princess and strike back against an empire, with the help of a party of companions and the guidance of an aging wizard.

> COMING TO YOUR GALAXY
> THIS SUMMER.
> (TEASER PRE-RELEASE POSTER)

So far, so good, but perhaps the most compelling evidence is in that opening caption. That's right: no matter how many people out there think of these movies as "futuristic" science-fiction adventures, they take place long ago and far away. Long before *The Sword and the Sorcerer* snapped up the title *Tales of an Ancient Empire* for its semi-awaited sequel, those words could just as easily have described *Star Wars*.

The color-coding alone is about as straightforward as can be: our pure young lead wears white, as does the noble princess, while the villains wear black. (Okay, and olive green, but let's not get crazy here. And no, we don't want to hear about the white-armored Stormtroopers; just go with us on this one. Sigh.) Obi-Wan is a sort of fallen wizard wearing the brown of his desert home, with perhaps a nod to a gray-clad kinsman from another franchise. And what of our roguish anti-hero, the smuggler extraordinaire? He wears a white shirt with a black vest on top, confidently melding both philosophies: a scoundrel with a heart of gold . . . and we don't mean money.

WHO GOES THERE?

Through his work in the first three *Star Wars* movies as well as all three *Indiana Jones* adventures (yes, yes, those didn't come until much later), Harrison Ford established himself as one of the quintessential heroic leads of '80s fantasy film. Other film roles include *American Graffiti*, *The Conversation*, *Heroes*, *Force 10 from Navarone*, *Apocalypse Now*, *Hanover Street*, *The Frisco Kid*, *More American Graffiti*, *Blade Runner*, *Witness*, *Frantic*, *Working Girl*, *Regarding Henry*, *Patriot Games*, *The Fugitive*, *Clear and Present Danger*, *Air Force One*, *What Lies Beneath*, *Cowboys & Aliens*, *Ender's Game*, *Anchorman 2: The Legend Continues*, and *The Expendables 3*. He retained most of his dignity in *The Star Wars Holiday Special*, comes home to the Millennium Falcon in *Star Wars: Episode VII—The Force Awakens*, and makes a brief appearance as a bearded fifty-year-old Indy in the "Mystery of the Blues" episode of *The Young Indiana Jones Chronicles* . . . and we think that's where he should have stopped. (Let's not even get into the upcoming *Blade Runner* sequel.)

Carrie Fisher was born into Hollywood royalty as the daughter of Debbie Reynolds and Eddie Fisher. Much of her writing and stage performance in the latter part of her career have focused on her tumultuous personal life, but as a film actress she appeared in *Shampoo*, *The Blues Brothers*, *Under the Rainbow*, *Hannah and Her Sisters*, *Hollywood Vice Squad*, *Amazon Women on the Moon*, *The Time Guardian*, *The 'Burbs*, *When Harry Met Sally . . .*, *Drop Dead Fred*, *Soapdish*, *Scream 3*, *Jay and Silent Bob Strike Back*, *Charlie's Angels: Full Throttle*, *Fanboys*, and *Sorority Row*, as well as in the first two *Star Wars* sequels. She sleepwalked (let's be charitable) through *The Star Wars Holiday Special*, jump-started an entire male generation's sexuality with a simple gold bikini in *Return of the Jedi*, lent her voice to *Family Guy*, wrote novels such as *Postcards from the Edge*, and has also become one of the industry's most sought-after script doctors. She returns sans buns for *Star Wars: Episode VII—The Force Awakens*.

With his cadaverous but distinguished features, Peter Cushing became an icon of horror cinema beginning in the 1950s. He first appeared in Hammer Films' *The Curse of Frankenstein* as Victor Frankenstein and in *Horror of Dracula* as Doctor Van Helsing. He played both parts several more times and appeared as Sherlock Holmes in *The Hound of the Baskervilles*, in a '60s TV series, and in a 1984 TV-movie (even playing Sir Arthur Conan Doyle in a 1970s TV-movie). He was the sheriff of Nottingham in *Sword of Sherwood Forest* and the time-traveling Dr. Who in *Dr. Who and the Daleks* and *Daleks' Invasion Earth: 2150 A.D.* He also had roles in *The Gorgon, Dr. Terror's House of Horrors, She, The Skull, Scream and Scream Again, The Vampire Lovers, The House That Dripped Blood, Twins of Evil, Tales from the Crypt, Dr. Phibes Rises Again, Asylum, Horror Express, The Creeping Flesh, —And Now the Screaming Starts!, From Beyond the Grave, Madhouse, The Beast Must Die, The Ghoul, At the Earth's Core, Shock Waves, House of the Long Shadows, Top Secret!,* and *Sword of the Valiant: The Legend of Sir Gawain and the Green Knight*. In many of those productions he costarred with best friend and cohort-in-horror Christopher Lee. After his last role, in *Biggles: Adventures in Time,* Cushing segued into a quiet retirement. He died in 1994 at age 81.

> A LONG TIME AGO IN A GALAXY FAR, FAR AWAY . . .

Alec Guinness might have had a low opinion of this saga's popularity, but for him it arrived toward the end of a long and distinguished career that began on stage and moved into film and occasionally television. In movies he appeared in Dickens adaptations *Great Expectations* and *Oliver Twist* and in Ealing Studios comedies *The Lavender Hill Mob* and *The Ladykillers*. He earned an Academy Award for Best Actor for his role in *The Bridge on the River Kwai*. He also had roles in *Lawrence of Arabia, Doctor Zhivago, Scrooge, Hitler: The Last Ten Days* (as the dictator himself), *Murder by Death, Raise the Titanic,* and *A Passage to India.* He played George Smiley in the *Tinker, Tailor, Soldier, Spy* TV miniseries, returned to Dickens with one of his last film roles—in *Little Dorrit*—and yes, made ghostly reappearances in the two original *Star Wars* sequels. He died in 2000 at age 86.

Anthony Daniels was the voice of Legolas in Ralph Bakshi's *The Lord of the Rings* animated film, but otherwise he made a career out of playing C-3PO in six other *Star Wars* theatrical releases, *The Star Wars Holiday Special,* the *Droids* cartoon TV-show, the *Clone Wars* and *Star Wars Rebels* animated TV-series, *The New Yoda Chronicles* TV movies, and video games.

Kenny Baker has played R2-D2 in six other *Star Wars* films and appeared in *Flash Gordon, The Elephant Man, Time Bandits, Amadeus, Labyrinth,* and *Willow.*

Peter Mayhew appeared uncredited as the towering Minaton in *Sinbad and the Eye of the Tiger* and returned to the fur suit for *The Star Wars Holiday Special* and four more *Star Wars* films.

David Prowse began his career as a weightlifter alongside competitors and friends Arnold Schwarzenegger and Lou Ferrigno. He made early film appearances in *Casino Royale* and *The Horror of Frankenstein,* both times as creatures made by Dr. Frankenstein. He played a minotaur in "The Time Monster" episodes of *Doctor Who* and a mob bodyguard in *The Hitchhiker's Guide to the Galaxy* TV adaptation and also appeared in *A Clockwork Orange, Vampire Circus, Jabberwocky,* and *The People That Time Forgot.* He wore the Vader costume for the other two films in the original *Star Wars* trilogy.

James Earl Jones' stentorian tones resulted from years of study to overcome a childhood stutter. Remembered most by genre fans for his uncredited voice work as Darth Vader in this and the other two original *Star Wars* films—as well as brief returns in the final film in the prequel trilogy, *Star Wars: Episode III—Revenge of the Sith,* and the *Star Wars Rebels* animated TV series—Jones also played roles in films like *Dr. Strangelove, Exorcist II: The Heretic, The Last Remake of Beau Geste, Conan the Barbarian* (as Thulsa Doom), *Allan Quatermain and the Lost City of Gold, Coming to America, Field of Dreams, The Hunt for Red October, Patriot Games, Sneakers,* and *Clear and Present Danger.* He also voiced Mufasa in *The Lion King* and its sequel. He either appeared in or provided his voice for television series and miniseries like *The Defenders, Roots, Roots: The Next Generations* (as writer Alex Haley), *Jesus of Nazareth, Highway to Heaven, L.A. Law, Gabriel's Fire, Pros and Cons, Law & Order, Lois & Clark: The New Adventures of Superman, Frasier, Stargate SG-1, Homicide: Life on the Street, The Simpsons, House M.D.,* and *The Big Bang Theory* (as himself, in an episode that also featured Carrie Fisher as herself).

Phil Brown moved from the US to the UK when blacklisted during the Communist scare of the 1950s. He worked in film, television, and theater. He appeared in *The Pink Panther Strikes Again* and *Superman,* and last played a role in a *Battlestar Galactica* short feature written and directed by Richard Hatch. He died in 2006 at age 89.

Shelagh Fraser racked up 500-plus roles in radio and appeared regularly on British television throughout the '60s and '70s. She died in 2000 at age 79.

Jack Purvis appeared in different roles in the next two *Star Wars* movies and also had roles in *Time Bandits, The Dark Crystal, Brazil, Labyrinth, Willow,* and *The Adventures of Baron Munchausen.* He died in 1997 at age 59.

Dennis (Denis) Lawson is Ewan McGregor's uncle. Obi Wan is Wedge's nephew? Not in our universe, but Lawson did return as Wedge in the next two *Star Wars* films and appeared in *Local Hero.*

Although a good portion of Garrick Hagon's work in this movie initially ended up on the cutting-room floor, it was just a footnote in a long career largely in television. He also appeared in films like *The Spy Who Loved Me, Batman,* and *Mission: Impossible.* He played roles in two *Doctor Who* stories forty years apart, "The Mutants" and "A Town Called Mercy."

William Hootkins was another ubiquitous American presence in '80s films shot in the UK, appearing in *Flash Gordon, Raiders of the Lost Ark, Trail of the Pink Panther, Curse of the Pink Panther, Superman IV: The Quest for Peace,* and *Batman.* He was also the voice of Falkor in *The NeverEnding Story III.* He died in 2005 at age 57.

Angus Mcinnis also turned up in *Rollerball, Force 10 from Navarone, Superman II, Outland, Witness, Hellbound: Hellraiser II, Eyes Wide Shut,* and *Hellboy.*

Don Henderson also appeared in *Brazil* and *The Adventures of Baron Munchausen,* as well as the *Doctor Who* story "Delta and the Bannermen." He died in 1997 at age 64.

Richard LeParmentier, of the preternaturally square mouth, also appeared in *The People That Time Forgot, Superman II, Octopussy,* and *Who Framed Roger Rabbit.* He died in 2013 at age 66.

Leslie Schofield unfortunately appeared in *The Star Wars Holiday Special.* Otherwise, he has had a prolific career on UK television.

6 DEGREES OF SORCERY

The film owes a lot to the history of World War II movies, with its adaptation of classic dogfight cinema choreography, as well as to legendary director Akira Kurosawa's *Yojimbo* and *The Hidden Fortress,* which tell the same basic story without the spaceships and glow effect on the swords. (You'll see these Kurosawa movies referenced in a number of our other chapters.) *The Magic Serpent* (listed in our index), itself an adaptation of the Japanese folktale *The Tale of the Gallant Jiraiya*, might also have inspired much of this movie. Give credit to Lucas: when he takes, he takes from solid sources.

This movie also parallels the Arthurian legend cycle, Tolkien's *The Lord of the Rings* saga, and any number of mythological heroic journeys. Besides another Lucas inspiration—the classic *Flash Gordon* movie serials he originally wanted to adapt—the film owes more than a little to *The Wizard of Oz*, with a farm boy replacing a farm girl, a protocol droid doubling as both the Tin Man and the Cowardly Lion (although Chewbacca covers the furry part), and R2-D2, with his apparent extensive knowledge, perhaps as a Scarecrow stand-in. The Jawas also resemble the Munchkins, something that gets a satirical twist when Mel Brooks spoofs *Star Wars* in *Spaceballs*: "Dink dink!"

Recurring references to "spice" freighters and smuggling, as well as the desert planet of Tatooine, recall a similar world named Arrakis and the "spice" found on its surface in Frank Herbert's *Dune* series. Herbert bemoaned the similarities, commenting that he found adapting *Dune* to film more difficult because of Lucas's use of so much *Dune*-like material in *Star Wars*.

C-3PO's design might be a direct evolution of the robot Maria in the seminal 1927 science-fiction classic *Metropolis*. A great deal of the spaceship (exterior and interior) and technology design work clearly owes a debt to Stanley Kubrick's *2001: A Space Odyssey* from nine years earlier.

SHATTERING THE ILLUSION

This one isn't easy. As one of the most documented film sagas in history (another being *The Lord of the Rings* trilogy—but let's complain about that in those chapters), precious few insights remain unearthed in the making of this movie, and even fewer facts that a casual viewer might not already know. Still, in the interest of providing at least some information about how this modern blockbuster classic came into being, let's go back to the beginning, a long, long . . . never mind.

Blending his love of World War II combat cinema, the work of Japanese director Akira Kurosawa, and heroic fantasy storytelling, Lucas—having already made his first film, *THX-1138*, and the nostalgic *American Graffiti*—conceived a generational saga that superseded his desire to bring *Flash Gordon* back to the screen, when the cost of obtaining the rights to that property proved prohibitive. The degree to which he had already drafted or planned the story for this and the subsequent films is impossible to tell, because Lucas has shifted details about the real-life story behind *Star Wars* many times.

According to most accounts, Lucas first set down many elements of the saga—including recognizable names and elements from the prequels made decades later—in the early 1970s as part of "The Journal of the Whills." Simplifying his sprawling tale by using Kurosawa's *The Hidden Fortress* template as his main narrative, Lucas renamed his primary hero from Annikin Starkiller to Luke Skywalker by the time of the first chapter's production.

Thinking that the opportunity might be his only chance to bring the story to the screen, Lucas largely planned *Star Wars* as a standalone adventure. The trick was to get a studio to back the project. Universal, which had produced *American Graffiti*, turned it down, as did United Artists, but 20th Century Fox head Alan Ladd took a chance on the young filmmaker. Multiple drafts and countless character changes, additions, deletions, and story changes later, Lucas zeroed in on the tale he wanted to tell, with conceptual artist Ralph McQuarrie providing visual input.

> MAY THE FORCE BE WITH YOU

As principal photography began, difficulty on the unforgiving Tunisian locations that stood in for the desert world of Tatooine led to schedule delays and problems with equipment. Once relocated to Elstree Studios in the UK, Lucas faced a more complex problem: his cast and crew were less than committed to the project, at times believing they were working on something that would appeal only to children, if that, and that it might be doomed to failure. Harrison Ford took Lucas to task for writing dialogue that the actors found hard to say naturally. Director of photography Gilbert Taylor fought with Lucas over the writer-director's aesthetic choices until Lucas was so distraught that he detached from much of the process, leading to many of the legendary stories of him directing with one-word notes like "faster." Lucas suffered from exhaustion. The production spread efforts across three separate units to wrap photography in time.

To handle the elaborate post-production effects work, Lucas envisioned a dedicated company—devoted to creating movie magic—that would become a powerhouse in its own right: Industrial Light & Magic (ILM). The by-now famous description of the *Star Wars* universe as "used" or "lived in" was key to the look Lucas wanted to achieve in the ships and other fanciful technology: not a gleaming, brand-new reality but one that looked as if it actually functioned on a daily basis. The work wasn't easy, with the beleaguered team creating models and shots and other effects in six months rather than the year the process ideally would have taken, inventing a variety of techniques along the way.

An early edit of the film didn't please Lucas at all, leading to additional work by several editors, including his wife Marcia. He used action footage from movies like 1955's *The Dam Busters* (which director of photography Gilbert Taylor had also shot) and 1964's *633 Squadron* to assemble a rough cut of what he wanted for the final attack on the Death Star and to inspire the effects team to create the appropriate material.

When *Star Wars* finally came out on May 25, 1977 (moved from Christmas 1976 and then shifted again to avoid competition with *Smokey and the Bandit*), it earned almost $775 million worldwide, far in excess of its $11 million budget, and won six out of the ten Academy Awards for which it was nominated. Theaters across the country ran the movie for more than a year, an unheard-of occurrence today (when a movie barely lasts a weekend even if it's successful). By the time of its first re-release in 1978, *Star Wars* was well on the way to becoming a lasting pop-culture phenomenon, a status that the arrival of two sequels cemented over the next five years. For more about that, we suggest you look at **The Saga Continues**...

MUSIC OF THE MINSTRELS

John Williams has written the soundtrack for childhoods of several generations. Sweeping adventure themes defined the worlds of Superman, Indiana Jones, Harry Potter, and even a plucky white shark named Bruce. (Gotcha! After all, *Jaws* wasn't his name!)

The *Star Wars* suite of music might be Williams' greatest lasting contribution to pop culture. From the crisp, triumphant main-title tune to the romantic yearning of the Force theme, Williams' compositions in the first film established a timeless tone upon which he elaborated in subsequent films.

Having sat near the record player and stared endlessly at the photos on the gatefold sleeve of *The Empire Strikes Back* soundtrack LP while listening to those themes again and again, this author [ATB] can safely say that Williams' scores didn't feel like just music, but like the Force incarnate. It drew me into that other world as surely as any of the spectacular visual effects.

As with so many aspects of this series, the soundtrack came out in a plethora of versions, including the original double-LP vinyl version (which included a poster by painter John Berkey); 8-track, cassette, and CD editions; extended re-releases; compilations; box sets; digital copies via iTunes and Amazon; and much more. Unlike with many of the films in this book, just about any format you can imagine offers the *Star Wars* music, be it online, in stores, or in the collectors' aftermarket.

THE SAGA CONTINUES

Do we really need to go into this? All right, then, the short version....

Following the success of the first film, Lucas and company produced two sequels, *The Empire Strikes Back* and *Return of the Jedi*, completing the first triad of one of the most extraordinary worldwide pop-culture phenomena in entertainment history. Spawning massive amounts of merchandise in every conceivable category and expanding into every other medium, the *Star Wars* story became a modern mythology that captivated a generation. This was no fluke, either. Lucas had hired a marketing director, Charles Lippincott, who not only arranged many of the licensing deals that made the film so visible in stores everywhere but also planned its promotion at the San Diego Comic-Con.

After briefly fading somewhat in the years following the release of the third film, *Star Wars* resurged in novels and in the re-release of the trilogy beginning in 1997, now labeled "Special Editions" and enhanced with an array of new, computer-generated effects not possible in the films' initial production. That revision was the first step in a major re-launch of the brand that culminated with the release of an all-new trio of movies: prequels set decades before the first *Star Wars*.

The new movies severely divided fandom. Many older fans were disappointed (to put it charitably) in various aspects of the new trilogy, while young moviegoers found as much to enjoy as their parents had with the original films. For some, *Star Wars* became an indivisible six-film saga.

The saga continued with a cartoon television series, multiple video games, countless toys and books and comics, and of course, a vast array of traditional game products. We can't possibly catalogue all the material, even if we were just to list what is widely available as we go to print, so we'll leave it at the fact that as a brand, *Star Wars* is one of most ubiquitous presences in pop culture and shows no sign of fading again anytime soon.

As we wrapped work on this volume, we received all the stunning news that followed the acquisition of Lucasfilm by Disney, including details (and trailers!) for the first installment in a new, post–*Return of the Jedi* trilogy. Directed by J.J. Abrams and scheduled to arrive in December 2015, *Star Wars: Episode VII—The Force Awakens* reunites original stars Mark Hamill, Carrie Fisher, and Harrison Ford, in addition to a number of other familiar and new cast members. Announcements have also arrived to herald "anthology" films set in different time periods, so it seems the Force is with us . . . for good.

... You still want a list of some merchandise, don't you? Fine. Alan Dean Foster ghostwrote the novelization for Lucas and also wrote the original *Star Wars* novel *Splinter of the Mind's Eye.* Marvel Comics published an adaptation of the film in several formats, including an oversize tabloid "Treasury Edition" and six issues of a regular-format comic book. The comic continued with original stories approved by Lucasfilm, becoming one of the longest-running comic-book tie-ins ever published. The series expertly wove its continuity around the subsequent movie sequels, benefiting from a close relationship with Lucasfilm when it came time to move the ongoing comic story toward the debut of the original trilogy's last installment, *Return of the Jedi.* The comic-book series continued until 1986, years beyond the third movie's release. In the 1990s, Dark Horse Comics acquired the license and published a variety of series, miniseries, one-shots, and other specials spanning the history of the saga, but recently Marvel—now another Disney subsidiary—has reacquired the *Star Wars* license.

We covered the snarl of home-video releases in "**Alternate Versions.**" If you think we're going to catalogue all the Kenner, Hasbro, LEGO, and other *Star Wars* toys—even just those related to this first film—then you have midichlorians clogging your brain. We could note a few early game releases, however.

You could gather around the kitchen table to play the Parker Brothers board game *Escape from Death Star,* which neatly dovetailed with another PB release, *Destroy Death Star.* (Palitoy released a completely different game also called *Destroy Death Star* for the UK/European market.) If you wanted a less intense board-game experience, Parker Brothers also released *The Adventures of R2-D2* children's game.

Kenner joined the home-electronic game party with a two-header: the *Electronic Laser Battle Game* and the *Battleship*-esque *Electronic Battle Command Game,* the latter of which looked like every computer console from sci-fi TV shows of the '70s and '80s. [ATB: I still have mine!] As for that fondly remembered vector-graphics *Death Star* coin-op from Atari, surprise! That didn't come out until 1983.

Along with many other tie-in items that followed the films, roleplaying in the *Star Wars* universe didn't arrive until years later. West End Games published *Star Wars: The Roleplaying Game* from 1987 to 1998. The license then passed to Wizards of the Coast and, most recently, Fantasy Flight Games.

TAKE UP THY SWORD!

THE SABER (MAGIC WEAPON)

While inactive, this rare weapon resembles a bladeless hilt. When energized (a standard-use magic-item action for unskilled wielders), it appears as a sword-shaped beam of light. Depending on which crystals the wielder employs to focus mystical energies, the generated "blade" of the weapon can vary in hue. Emerald green and sapphire blue are common within one order. Antagonistic sects typically wield ruby red.

In the hands of wielder not specifically trained in its use, the Saber behaves as a longsword. In the hands of a skilled knight of a dedicated order, it behaves as a rapier in regard to weight and speed, with a damage rating twice that of an ordinary rapier.

A knight with particular sensitivity to the relevant magical forces can wield the Saber without penalties for weight or speed, because the weapon becomes a supernatural extension of mind and body. The knight can also energize or deactivate the weapon as a free action. Such sensitivity also negates the potential for critical fumbles and personal injury. If crafted by the wielder—a feat best left to those with significant experience—the Saber gains slight bonuses to both attacks and damage.

When the weapon is in its active state, its glow provides light akin to that of a torch and thus betrays the presence of a wielder attempting a stealthy approach. The weapon's constant emission of a low, otherworldly hum also jeopardizes such clandestine operations. Lastly, the blade generates incredible heat, so it can ignite flammable materials and instantly cauterizes any wound it causes.

THE FILM'S DESTINY

It's hard to review something so hard-wired into one's consciousness. For the authors and anyone else who experienced *Star Wars* when it first arrived on the global pop-culture scene, there is no easy way to look at it as anything other than a landmark achievement, not only in the mechanics of moviemaking, but in the capturing of childhood dreams.

Of course the film consists of familiar archetypes and narrative elements; frankly, it doesn't have anything all that original in those regards. The sum of all its parts is what makes it so powerful: the appeal of a great cast, the exhilarating visuals that seamlessly (at least for the time) drew audiences into a complete world unlike any that had come to movies before, the timeless theme of good versus evil, and the warmth of the human heart and spirit triumphing over cold technology and imperialism. All this and more made *Star Wars* a flashpoint: a moment when everything converged just right and the results entertained and affected all the moviegoers in the '70s who sat in a theater, watched that Star Destroyer fill the screen, and became children again (if they weren't children already).

The years have been kind in some ways and unkind in others to the original movie's legacy. *Star Wars* has evolved. Its creator has made revisiting the original film, as it first appeared, almost impossible without significant effort: a profoundly sad notion. Nevertheless, we have done precisely that for this book: used the last VHS videotape release of the original trilogy. That original version retains all the charm that made it the foundation of an enduring brand that continues to enthrall new fans today. Whether you're a devotee from the days when this movie played in theaters or someone who first discovered the saga with six films already out in various home-video formats, *Star Wars* isn't just science fantasy. It's pure magic.

THIS YEAR IN GAMING

Game Designers' Workshop (GDW) released the first edition of *Traveller*, a highly detailed science-fiction roleplaying game designed by Marc Miller. The format of the initial release mirrored that of the earlier editions of *Dungeons & Dragons*, with three booklets—*Characters and Combat, Starships and Worlds,* and *Adventures*—packed inside a small black box. GDW supported the game for almost twenty years, with additional booklets, box sets, and revisions, until the company folded in 1996. In 2008, Mongoose Publishing released an edition of the game with very few changes to the original's innovative game mechanics. In 2013, Far Future Enterprises published a fifth edition in the form of a colossal 656-page book.

SINBAD AND THE EYE OF THE TIGER

1977 • US/UK • Columbia Pictures • 113m • Color • G

Screenplay: Beverley Cross
Story: Beverley Cross and Ray Harryhausen
Director: Sam Wanamaker
Producers: Charles H. Schneer and Ray Harryhausen
Music: Roy Budd
Director of Photography: Ted Moore
Creator of Special Visual Effects: Ray Harryhausen
Production Designer: Geoffrey Drake
Art Directors: Fernando Gonzalez and Fred Carter
Make-Up: Colin Arthur
Costume Designer: Cynthia Tingey
  FILMED IN DYNARAMA
Cast: Patrick Wayne (Sinbad), Taryn Power (Dione), Margaret Whiting (Zenobia), Jane Seymour (Farah), Patrick Troughton (Melanthius), Kurt Christian (Rafi), Nadim Sawalha (Hassan), Damien Thomas (Kassim), Bruno Barnabe (Balsora), Bernard Kay (Zabid), Salami Coker (Maroof), David Sterne (Aboo-Seer), and Peter Mayhew (Minaton, uncredited)
Alternate Titles: *Sinbad in Hyperborea—An Adventure Fantasy, Sinbad Beyond the North Wind, Sinbad at the World's End,* and *Sinbad III* (development titles)

ON THE MAP

Sinbad travels from the city of Charak to the haunted island of Casgar off the coast of Phrygia. From there, it's onto the Shrine of the Four Elements in the ancient realm of the Arimaspi under the Aurora Borealis, Hyperborea.

OUR STORY SO FAR

Sinbad arrives at Charak intending to end his days at sea and marry the Princess Farah, but first he must undertake one last voyage to find a cure for Farah's stricken brother, Kassim. Before Kassim could be crowned caliph, his evil stepmother Zenobia transformed him into a baboon. Sinbad must travel to the very ends of the Earth to enlist the aid of a brilliant hermit and rediscover an ancient power that could restore Kassim, stop Zenobia's bid for power, and ensure a happy ending for Sinbad and Farah.

IT'S MAGIC

Zenobia's magic requires her to call upon the spirits of the underworld, although not in the unintelligible language spoken by Koura in *The Golden Voyage*. She uses plain English. (Of course, the characters probably don't actually speak English, but never mind.) Her eyes sometimes become green, catlike orbs while she practices her arts. She can even transform herself into a green mist and insert her soul or life essence into another creature with no visible spell or physical aid. She also has chemical explosive like Koura, and her transmogrifying potion can change humans into other animals and alter size—but a critical mass of potion must result in undesired side-effects.

The robotic golem called the Minaton operates via a hybrid of internal clockwork and dark magic, showing an intriguing reliance on modern technology. It's not just the dark side that needs to ask for help: Melanthius operates the Shrine of the Arimaspi by calling on the gods.

THE QUEST FOR MEANING

Following up on *The Golden Voyage* theme that questions the gods' trustworthiness and even presence, *Eye of the Tiger* suggests that Sinbad's world of magic and superstition is evolving toward a more modern sensibility, with technological additions to the adventure coming not just from the evil Zenobia via her Minaton and her Nautilus-like mechanical iron vessel but from the good magician-scientist Melanthius, whose makeshift, candle-powered laser and ability to use "telepathia" that reaches to the stars indicates that science is quickly gaining ground. Even his reaction to the troglodyte is not that of a man to a monster but rather of a fascinated explorer recognizing a scientifically proven ancestor and wishing to reach out in peace and friendship.

For *Doctor Who* fans, this movie offers a whole other layer of enjoyment if you imagine that Melanthius is a version of the Second Doctor, who has retired to Earth for a while before returning to face his sentence of regeneration and exile. Some of you know what we're talking about—especially because Melanthius seems rather Merlin-esque, with knowledge beyond his time and years.

As for the Arimaspi, the more ancient culture is the more "advanced." They lived a long time ago in a land far, far away, after all, but their self-destruction is surely a meta-commentary on our present-day tendencies.

Sinbad's compatriots haven't learned much more, though. Farah and Melanthius seem to go out of their way to give Zenobia information she needs to defeat them. The contest to reach the shrine is a months-long race that depends on fortitude and secrecy, but Zenobia keeps pace with Sinbad all the way.

As with all good villains, Zenobia's defeat in this particular game might not mean the vanquishing of her evil. Watch to the end of the credits, and ask yourself: do those eerie eyes imply she still lives?

WHO GOES THERE?

Although Sam Wanamaker achieved the most fame as an actor, with television and film roles in the *Holocaust* TV miniseries, *Private Benjamin*, and *Superman IV: The Quest for Peace*, as well as extensive theatrical work, he also directed, mainly in television, including episodes of *The Defenders*, *Hart to Hart*, and *Columbo*. He supported the Globe Theatre restoration but died in 1993 at age 74 and never saw the facility's 1997 opening.

Patrick Wayne, son of American icon John Wayne, lingered under his father's shadow for

> SINBAD! THE GREATEST OF ALL ADVENTURERS IN HIS BIGGEST ADVENTURE OF ALL!

many years and appeared in many films with him, all of them directed by John Ford. Finding new independence in his role as Sinbad, Wayne went on to another heroic role in *The People That Time Forgot* and settled into regular appearances on popular '70s television series, game shows, and variety programs. He played hilariously against type and spoofed his father's most famous genre in the Western comedy, *Rustlers' Rhapsody*.

The daughter of another Hollywood legend, Tyrone Power, Taryn Power has made few other film and television appearances, though she participated in events related to her father's career.

Margaret Whiting appeared in episodes of *The Count of Monte Cristo*, *The Avengers,* and appropriately enough, *C.A.T.S. Eyes*.

Cult-film appearances defined Jane Seymour's early career: movies like this one, *Live and Let Die,* and *Somewhere in Time*. She has also appeared on television, most famously as the star of *Dr. Quinn, Medicine Woman*.

Nadim Sawalha is the father of actresses Julia and Nadia Sawalha. He made appearances in *The Return of the Pink Panther, Young Sherlock Holmes, The Living Daylights, Son of the Pink Panther,* and a television production of *Arabian Nights*.

Damien Thomas was Count Karnstein in *Twins of Evil*.

Bernard Kay made a number of cult-film and TV appearances in *They Came from Beyond Space;* the TV miniseries version of *The Lion, The Witch and the Wardrobe; The Witchfinder General; Doctor Who;* and *Space: 1999*. He died in 2014 at age 86.

David Sterne also turned up in *Pirates of the Caribbean: Dead Man's Chest* and *Harry Potter and the Goblet of Fire*.

6 DEGREES OF SORCERY

The number seven often plays a role in Harryhausen's *Sinbad* films. Here the characters must cure Kassim's condition in seven moons, or he will be doomed.

A misty region in this film resembles the one in *Golden Voyage*. For the third time, a *Sinbad* adventure features a large rock-hewn face, this time with a King Kong–like gate set into its mouth.

Hyperborea is northeast of Cimmeria in the *Conan* universe, and it turns up in Greek mythology as a legendary place where long-lived people dwelled in peace and contentment. The green valley of Hyperborea surrounded by an icy wasteland resembles the oasis-like plateau of *The Lost World* (based on the novel by Sir Arthur Conan Doyle) and its cousin in *The Land That Time Forgot* and *The People That Time Forgot* (the latter of which starred Sinbad himself, Patrick Wayne), based on the work of Edgar Rice Burroughs.

Melanthius mentions Zeus and Apollo, tying Sinbad's world however briefly and tenuously to the *Jason/Clash* mythos. The Minaton recalls another robotic Harryhausen creature, Talos from *Jason and the Argonauts*. Zenobia's superimposed cat-eyes resemble the eyes of Koura in *Golden Voyage* and their mutual ancestor, Bela Lugosi's eyes in *White Zombie* and *Revolt of the Zombies*.

The requisite monster-battle finale established in *7th Voyage* with the dragon-Cyclops showdown and continued in *Golden Voyage* with the centaur-gryphon contest reappears in this third and final installment with the fight between the Zenobia-inhabited tiger and poor Trog.

SHATTERING THE ILLUSION

Schneer and Harryhausen, encouraged by the success of *The Golden Voyage of Sinbad*, immediately planned a follow-up with the same character, although they did not want to make it a sequel. Their aversion to a "sequel" label might have contributed to the reasons they did not ask John Phillip Law to return as Sinbad.

Returning to the concept of a prince transformed into a baboon that Harryhausen had dropped from *Golden Voyage*, he prepared an outline and drawings for Schneer to review. As usual, many concepts suggested for the film did not make the script, including a mammoth trapped in ice, the same "Valley of the Vipers" sequence dropped during the development of *Golden Voyage*, a shipboard attack by wood-eating worms, and a battle between Trog and the Minaton (which might explain why the robotic creature, referred to as Zenobia's "army," gets a chance to perform that function only briefly and "dies" rather expediently, something Harryhausen later regretted).

Writer Beverley Cross shaped the script through several drafts while consideration of a long list of actors proceeded for the lead role, including Michael York, Timothy Dalton, and Michael Douglas. Harryhausen had intended the role of Melanthius for long-time collaborator Laurence Naismith. When Naismith proved unavailable, *Jason and the Argonauts* veteran Patrick Troughton stepped up. Actor Sam Wanamaker, an odd choice for director, did not prove ideal for such a unique production, which involved collaborating with Harryhausen to achieve the myriad effects.

Potential Zenobias included Patricia Neal, Anne Baxter, and Mercedes McCambridge. Bette Davis rose to first choice, but the budget didn't allow for her; hence Margaret Whiting became Zenobia. Post-production saw Margaret dub in her entire vocal performance, to give Zenobia a more pronounced, exotic accent.

The home of Melanthius is the famous Petra in Jordan, a very real and very impressive ancient façade that appears in films like the 1942 *Arabian Nights*, *Indiana Jones and the Last Crusade*, and *Transformers: Revenge of the Fallen*. *Eye of the Tiger* was the first production to shoot there since *Lawrence of Arabia*. King Hussein even visited the set and supplied one of his wife's hairdressers to replace a member of the crew who suffered from the heat.

Most of the rest of the shooting occurred in Spain and on the island of Malta. A 400-foot-long tank holding more than 3 million gallons of water, dubbed "the biggest bathtub in the world," simulated stormy waters. Malta also played host to the walrus sequence. An ice-floe set accommodated the fur-swathed actors as they pretended to battle the creature in what were often 110°F-degree temperatures, thanks to the reflection of the hot summer sun on all the artificial white surfaces. A centuries-old synagogue in Toledo, Spain doubled as the palace for the coronation.

The "zomboids," a variation on the skeletons of past Harryhausen films, were horned ghouls with insect-like eyes. Creepy chittering noises accompanied their attacks. Harryhausen would employ the technique of lighting the ghouls to mimic the glow of nearby fire to even greater effect in the Medusa sequence in *Clash of the Titans.*

Drawing on an image of a monkey and a man playing chess from an illustrated copy of *Arabian Nights,* and devoting lots of time to research at the London zoo in order to painstakingly create the illusion of realistic animal behavior for the baboon Kassim (as well as the tiger), Harryhausen made this one of his most accomplished single-character performances.

He later admitted what sharp-eyed viewers noted: the transformation of a live-action bee into an animated wasp or hornet (referred to in the scene as a mosquito) during that sequence. That minor bit of discontinuity did not adversely affect the scene.

On the other hand, Harryhausen has expressed dismay that while the Kassim baboon often draws praise, relatively few people note the equally meticulous and subtle performance that he created for Trog. Trog's rushed death was another of Harryhausen's regrets.

Nearly tripling the budget of its predecessor *Golden Voyage* and taking three years to wrap all production, *Eye of the Tiger* did not fare as well, in an environment shifting toward more high-tech sci-fi fare. Promotion for the film often focused on the "Hollywood royalty" angle because stars because of the lineage of Patrick Wayne and Taryn Power. When the time came to contemplate another follow-up, Schneer and Harryhausen decided to leave Sinbad at sea and return to a source that had served them well in the past. It was time to rejoin the gods of Olympus and see what they were up to....

MUSIC OF THE MINSTRELS

While not boasting a reputation like those of former *Sinbad* score composers Bernard Herrmann and Miklos Rozsa, jazz musician and film composer Roy Budd—who also worked on *Get Carter* and composed a score for the silent *Phantom of the Opera* starring Lon Chaney—follows nicely in their tradition. His ethnically tinged sweep of adventurous melodies might not rival his predecessors' work, but at least it maintains the proper mood, with romantic themes for the heroes and menacing motifs for Zenobia and her creations. Music from the film has turned up in numerous compilations. Cinephile released a CD of the entire score in 2000.

THE SAGA CONTINUES

John Ryder Hall wrote the Pocket Books novelization of the film. Cadaco released a board game that not only featured photos from *Eye of the Tiger* and a huge illustration of the two-headed roc from *7th Voyage* on the box lid, but included artwork paying tribute to Harryhausen's creations from all three *Sinbad* films on the game board. A special magazine included a UK black-and-white comic-book adaptation and featured color photos and behind-the-scenes information from the film. Columbia released a single 8mm film reel with an edited version of the story.

Although the *Sinbad* series did not continue, discussions about further adventures might have resulted in our hero visiting the Seven Wonders of the World or perhaps even Mars! Following up on the science-fiction flavor so tangible in *Eye of the Tiger,* and in the wake of the post–*Star Wars* sci-fi explosion, *Sinbad Goes to Mars,* shelved in the late '70s as too silly and unworkable, would have sent the intrepid sailor to the red planet and revealed links between Martian and Egyptian civilizations. After those discussions fizzled, Sinbad's voyages under the Schneer/Harryhausen partnership officially ended.

In 2007, comic-book publisher Bluewater Productions released a miniseries titled *Sinbad: Rogue of Mars*, continuing the saga under license from Harryhausen and using the discarded premise. Early in 2011, Morningside Entertainment optioned the comic to produce a "fourth" Sinbad film, but no further information has come forth as of this writing.

TAKE UP THY SWORD!
ELIXIR OF SPECIAL TRANSMUTATION (MAGIC POTION)

One who drinks this draught chooses an animal and transforms into that animal's form: flesh, muscle, and bone. This polymorphic potion is so powerful, it affects all aspects of the user, including clothing, jewelry, weapons, and armor worn or carried. All such accoutrements become animal tissue.

If the person undergoing the transformation holds the phial containing the potion, it (along with everything else) scales accordingly. In other words, a cup of the liquid in the hands of a human-size character magically shrinks to a vessel holding but a spoonful, should the user transform into something like a bird or snake. This could mean that the user would not have enough elixir to return completely to the original form and would become trapped in a horrific state of partial transformation. Because of this, a wise user relinquishes the phial at the beginning of the transmutation process.

An individual in animal form assumes the natural abilities of that form, such as flight (as a bird) or water-breathing (as a fish). Any damage taken while in an animal aspect translates and scales when the user returns to the original form. For example, a nick on the paw of a rat could become a significant gash on a human hand, requiring immediate medical attention.

THE FILM'S DESTINY

A rousing finale to the series that incorporates timely science-fiction elements into Sinbad's otherwise pseudo-historical, magical world, *Sinbad and the Eye of the Tiger* features some extraordinary location work and set pieces as well as some of the most emotionally moving performances by stop-motion creatures in Harryhausen's career. The double act of Trog—a sort of inarticulate, horned Tommy Lee Jones—and Kassim as baboon is a good pairing. Both characters are delightfully endearing, with subtle facial expressions and vocalizations that breathe life into fur and foam.

Harryhausen also seamlessly mixes realistic animal designs like the baboon, walrus, and sabertooth tiger with the robotic Minaton and creepy demon ghouls in all their skin-crawling, fire-lit wonder. Most of the live-action cast attacks its roles with gusto, especially Margaret Whiting as Zenobia, but the real star of the movie is Patrick Troughton, whose curious and enthusiastic Melanthius steals every scene. Sadly, the weakest link in the cast is Patrick Wayne,

> NEW!! SINBAD'S BOLDEST AND MOST DARING ADVENTURE!

who does the best he can and cuts the right action figure but can't bend his flat American accent around the embellished dialogue that the others manage.

The *Sinbad* movies are bigger than any one part—even the part of lead actor. With Harryhausen at the peak of his powers, an epic finale in a cavernous temple setting, and the offbeat addition of icy environs in a usually temperate series, *Eye of the Tiger* bids farewell to the world of Sinbad in style.

THIS YEAR IN GAMING

TSR released the *Monster Manual*—the very first hardcover rulebook for *Advanced Dungeons & Dragons*—with the early "lizardman" TSR logo and catalog number 2009. Written by Gary Gygax and featuring a foreword by editor Mike Carr, the book contained stats, descriptions, and illustrations of more than 350 monsters, demons, and races. To produce a sturdy tome and handle the requested-order volume of 50,000 copies, TSR turned to a publisher of school textbooks.

Using the *Monster Manual*, a Dungeon Master could pull together stats for almost every monster that appears in *Sinbad and the Eye of the Tiger*, including a baboon, a metallic golem, a giant wasp, and a troglodyte (with obviously a number of cosmetic differences between the properties). The *Monster Manual* in name and content has remained a core rulebook with every published edition of *Dungeons & Dragons* and an inspiration for game bestiaries produced by other publishers.

HAWK THE SLAYER

1980 • UK • ITC Entertainment / Chips Productions • 90m • Color • PG

WRITERS: Terry Marcel and Harry Robertson
DIRECTOR: Terry Marcel
PRODUCER: Harry Robertson
MUSIC: Harry Robinson
CINEMATOGRAPHER: Paul Beeson
ART DIRECTOR: Michael Pickwoad
MAKE-UP SUPERVISOR: Michael Morris
SPECIAL EFFECTS SUPERVISOR: Martin Gutteridge
SPECIAL PHOTOGRAPHIC EFFECTS: Paul Beeson
COSTUME SUPERVISOR: Ken Lewington
STUNT COORDINATOR: Eddie Stacey
MASTER AT ARMS: John Waller
CAST: Jack Palance (Voltan), John Terry (Hawk), Bernard Bresslaw (Gort), Ray Charleson (Crow), Peter O'Farrell (Baldin), Patricia Quinn (Woman), Morgan Sheppard (Ranulf), Christopher Benjamin (Fitzwalter), Shane Briant (Drogo), Cheryl Campbell (Sister Monica), Harry Andrews (High Abbot), Annette Crosbie (Abbess), Roy Kinnear (Innkeeper), Catriona MacColl (Eliane), Patrick Magee (Priest), Ferdy Mayne (Old Man), Graham Stark (Sparrow), Warren Clarke (Scar), Declan Mulholland (Sped), Derrick O'Connor (Ralf), Peter Benson (Black Wizard), Maurice Colbourne (Axe Man 1), Barry Stokes (Axe Man 2), Anthony Milner (Ferret), John J. Carney (Soldier), Robert Putt (1st Rough in Tavern), Stephen Rayne (Brother Peter), Ken Parry (Thomas), Lindsey Brook (Little Nun), Eddie Stacey (Chak), Jo England (1st Nun), Frankie Cosgrave (2nd Nun), Melissa Wiltsie (3rd Nun), Mark Cooper (2nd Rough in Tavern), Andy Bradford (Voltan Man, uncredited), Michael Crane (Drago Man, uncredited), Michael G. Jones (Guard, uncredited), Ryan Orwig (Notnoah, uncredited), and Robert Rietty (Narrator, uncredited)

ON THE MAP

The story takes place in an undefined fantasy world. According to the back of the DVD, it happens "once upon a time, long ago, but perhaps not far away." We have references to an abbey located in Caddonbury and to the Holy Fortress at Danesford (both less-than-convincing matte paintings). Other settings include the Forest of Weyr, a supernaturally dark place of cobwebs, screams, and rubber monsters; the Iron Hills (the dwarf's former home); and the River Shale.

OUR STORY SO FAR

Following the death of his beloved and his father at the hands of his older brother Voltan, the warrior known as Hawk journeys forth to exact revenge with the help of his old friends, a party of adventurers including a witch, an elven archer, a giant, a dwarf, and a one-handed mercenary.

IT'S MAGIC

Magic manifests in a variety of traditional ways here, including in weapons, in people, and of course, in magical eggs, Superballs, and silly string. (Well, why wouldn't there be?) Hawk's world is akin to your stereotypical fantasy setting, in which magical races (elves, dwarves, and giants) co-exist with humans, and rangers, fighters, and acrobats battle shoulder to shoulder with sorcerers.

The Elfin Mind Sword, an artifact from a bygone age, relocates into the hands of its bonded owner with but a thought. The sorcerous blind woman can teleport people—more than one on a few occasions—encase enemies in webs, and blast locked doors open with a hail of Technicolor rubber balls. Voltan serves a dark, mysterious enemy known as the Black Wizard, who can relieve the pain from his burns using glowing crystals. Let's face it: the whole place is lousy with magic.

THE QUEST FOR MEANING

While so many of our tales focus on relationships between fathers and sons, sibling relationships are by no means absent from heroic lore. Even as Voltan's brother, Hawk steps up to do what's right, while Voltan allies himself with the forces of darkness and desires nothing but conquest and power. Granted, prophecy foretells of his evil polluting the land, so he really doesn't have much choice, does he? Fate can be a harsh mistress. In short, Voltan embodies selfishness while Hawk covers the flip side, selflessness.

Another familiar force motivates Hawk: desire to avenge the deaths of his loved ones. To secure that vengeance, Hawk calls on a band of friends from his off-screen past, knowing that even with a weapon as powerful as the Mind Sword, taking on Voltan single-handed would be suicide. Having lost people close to him, and being doomed to lose a brother, too, Hawk has found a surrogate family.

WHO GOES THERE?

Jack Palance was a boxer under the name Jack Brazzo as well as a wounded and decorated World War II veteran before he became an easily recognizable film villain, with his broad, bony visage and breathy delivery. He appeared in *Panic in the Streets, Shane, The Silver Chalice, The Barbarians* (the 1960 release, not the 1987 film covered later in this volume), *Sword of the Conqueror, Young Guns, Gor II, Batman, Tango & Cash, City Slickers, City Slickers II: The Legend of Curly's Gold,* and *Treasure Island*. He also made several memorable television appearances in *Lights Out,* the "Requiem for a Heavyweight" episode of *Playhouse 90* written by Rod Serling, *The Greatest Show on Earth, Convoy, The Man from U.N.C.L.E.,* and *Buck Rogers in the 25th Century*. He played the title roles in the television-movie versions of *The Strange Case of Dr. Jekyll and Mr. Hyde* and *Bram Stoker's Dracula*. He died in 2006 at age 87.

Many readers know John Terry for one of his most recent roles, that of Jack Shephard's father Christian on the TV series *Lost,* but he's

> BEYOND THE EDGE OF DARKNESS THERE IS A WORLD OF SWORD AND SORCERY.

also appeared in a number of other productions since his first television role in an episode of *Soap* in 1978. His films include *Full Metal Jacket*, *The Living Daylights* (in which he played long-time James Bond ally Felix Leiter), and *Zodiac*. Other TV appearances include *E.R.*, *24*, and *Trauma*.

A fixture in several of the British *Carry On* comedies, Bernard Bresslaw—at a towering 6' 7"—often played in sight gags about his height. In 1958, he appeared in his first genre film, *Blood of the Vampire*. In 1968, he played Varga in the *Doctor Who* story "The Ice Warriors." He also appeared in films like *Old Drac*, *Jabberwocky*, and *Krull*, as well as an episode of *The Young Indiana Jones Chronicles* (his final role). He died in 1993 at age 59.

Ray Charleson worked with Terry Marcel a second time in *Prisoners of the Lost Universe*. He also appeared in *Shock Treatment*, *Empire of the Sun*, *United 93*, and *Dark Corners*.

Peter O'Farrell has made a career of appearing in fantasy and adventure films and TV series, starting with his first credited role in the 1972 production of *Alice's Adventures in Wonderland*. You can also find him in *Crossed Swords*, *Prisoners of the Lost Universe* (alongside *Hawk the Slayer* costar Ray Charleson), *Legend*, *Santa Claus*, and *Harry Potter and the Chamber of Secrets*.

In 1975, Patricia Quinn took on the role that would make her forever famous around the world: that of Magenta in *The Rocky Horror Picture Show*. (She is also the actress behind the singing lips in the title sequence.) She has appeared on the small screen in *I, Claudius*; *Tales of the Unexpected*; *The Box of Delights*; and *Doctor Who*. She played in a few other notable movies, including *Shock Treatment* (with Ray Charleson), *Monty Python's The Meaning of Life*, and *The Lords of Salem*.

Morgan Sheppard (a.k.a. William Morgan Sheppard) is a true king of genre films, with more than 170 acting roles to his name! He is one of the few actors who have appeared in both *Doctor Who* and *Star Trek*. He also appeared in two other cult science-fiction series, *Max Headroom* (as aging punk-rocker Blank Reg) and *Babylon 5*. On the big screen, he appears in *The Duellists*, *The Elephant Man*, *The Keep*, *The Doctor and the Devils*, *Elvira: Mistress of the Dark*, *Star Trek VI: The Undiscovered Country*, *Needful Things*, *The Prestige*, and the 2009 *Star Trek*.

Christopher Benjamin appeared in a number of British TV series familiar to genre fans, including multiple episodes of *Doctor Who*: he was Henry Gordon Jago in the classic series' "The Talons of Weng-Chiang." Other series of note include *Secret Agent* (a.k.a. *Danger Man*), *The Prisoner*, *The Avengers*, *The Saint*, *Thriller*, *She-Wolf of London*, *The Tomorrow People*, and the TV movie *The Magical Legend of the Leprechauns*.

Shane Briant shows no sign of slowing in a career that has included acting on stage and screen, penning five best-selling novels, and writing an award-winning short film. Though critics referred to him as a "pretty boy" early in his career, he transcended that image and turned in impressive dramatic performances for films like *Demons of the Mind*, *Frankenstein and the Monster from Hell*, *Captain Kronos—Vampire Hunter*, and *Lady Chatterly's Lover*. He also appeared on the small screen in *Mission: Impossible*, *Time Trax*, *Search for Treasure Island*, *Farscape*, and the long-running series *All Saints*, all of which saw production in his adopted home of Australia, to where he emigrated in 1983.

Cheryl Campbell has had a long and respectable career primarily in British television on series such as *Pennies from Heaven*, *Waking the Dead*, *MI-5*, and *The Sarah Jane Adventures*, although she also appeared on the big screen in *Chariots of Fire* and *Greystoke: The Legend of Tarzan, Lord of the Apes*.

Gruff-looking (and -acting) Harry Andrews, typecast in tough military roles for much of his long and distinguished career, played more than a hundred film and television roles. Some of the more notable titles include *Moby Dick*, *The Devil's Disciple*, *The Hill* (for which he was nominated for a BAFTA), *Battle of Britain*, *Man of La Mancha*, *Theatre of Blood*, *Watership Down*, and *Superman*. He died in 1989 at age 77.

Annette Crosbie was the voice of Galadriel in Ralph Bakshi's animated version of *The Lord of the Rings* and also voiced Granny Weatherwax in the miniseries *Wyrd Sisters*, based on Terry Pratchett's *Discworld* novels. She made an appearance in Matt Smith's premiere *Doctor Who* adventure, "The Eleventh Hour," but she became perhaps most famous for her starring role in the long-running British sitcom *One Foot in the Grave*.

Round-faced Roy Kinnear, perhaps best known as the father of spoiled brat Veruca Salt in *Willy Wonka & the Chocolate Factory*, was a close friend of director Richard Lester. He performed in eight of Lester's films, including *Help!* (with the Beatles), *A Funny Thing Happened On the Way to the Forum*, *The Three Musketeers*, and *Juggernaut*. He also appeared in *The Hill* along with fellow *Hawk* alumnus Harry Andrews, in a few episodes of *The Avengers*, and in *Scrooge*, *Alice's Adventures in Wonderland*, and *Blake's 7*. He provided voices for *The Plague Dogs* and *The Princess and the Goblin*. Tragically, he died while filming *The Return of the Musketeers* in 1988 at age 54.

The lovely Catriona MacColl found her characters terrorized through the camera of notorious Italian horror director Lucio Fulci, in the films *The Beyond*, *The House by the Cemetery*, and *City of the Living Dead* . . . in which she almost took a pickaxe to the face. The things actors do for their art! She currently lives in France and has enjoyed a bit of resurgence in her acting career over the past few years.

Patrick Magee, assaulted by Malcolm McDowell in *A Clockwork Orange*, also played the madman in Lucio Fulci's *The Black Cat*. A staple of horror films and thrillers, he appeared in *Dementia 13* (Francis Ford Coppola's directorial debut); *The Masque of the Red Death*; *The Skull*; *Die, Monster, Die!*; *Tales from the Crypt*; *Asylum*; *—And Now the Screaming Starts!*; and *The Monster Club*. He died in 1982 at age 60.

Ferdy Mayne (born Ferdinand Philip Mayer-Horckel) dabbled in practically every genre over his long career. He was among the casts of *The Fearless Vampire Killers*, *The Vampire Lovers*, *Barry Lyndon*, *Frightmare*, *Yellowbeard*, *Conan the Destroyer*, *Howling II: Your Sister Is a Werewolf*, and *Warlock: The Armageddon*. He also appeared in the 1962 children's serial *Masters of Venus*, in which he played a character named Votan (no relation to Voltan). His daughter Belinda Mayne appeared in *Krull*. He died in 1998 at age 81.

Close friend of the late Peter Sellers, British comic actor Graham Stark appeared in most of the *Pink Panther* films, beginning with *A Shot in the Dark* in 1964, although his credited acting career began more than ten years prior. He also played in *Sword of Lancelot*, *Alfie*, *Casino Royale* (the 1967 one), *The Magic Christian*, *Crossed Swords*, *The Prisoner of Zenda*, *Victor Victoria*, and *Superman III*. He died in 2013 at age 91.

Warren Clarke was Dim in *A Clockwork Orange*. (No, that was his character's name.) He also appeared in the films *Antony and Cleopatra*, *O Lucky Man!*, *Firefox*, *Enigma*, *Top Secret!*, and *Crusoe*, as well as in numerous TV series, including *The Avengers*, *Hammer House of Horror*, the miniseries *Masada*, and *Black Adder the Third*. He died in 2014 at age 67.

Character actor Declan Mulholland probably garnered the most fame for a role that never made it to theaters (at least officially): that of the original Jabba the Hutt in *Star Wars*. Lucas cut Mulholland's Jabba completely from the original theatrical release

> TWO BROTHERS LOCKED IN DEADLY COMBAT TO THE END OF TIME!

and, in the special-edition re-releases, replaced him with a CGI creation. Mulholland appeared in a number of other genre roles over the years in both films and TV shows, like *Theatre of Blood*, *The Land That Time Forgot*, *Time Bandits*, and a few episodes of *Doctor Who*. He died in 1999 at age 66.

Derrick O'Connor has been a member of both the Scottish National Theatre and the Royal Shakespeare Company. Among his many roles, he appeared in the films *The Blood on Satan's Claw*, *Jabberwocky*, *Time Bandits*, *Brazil*, *Deep Rising*, *Daredevil*, and *Pirates of the Caribbean: Dead Man's Chest*.

Doctor Who fans know Maurice Colbourne as Lytton, a mercenary who appeared in '80s stories "Resurrection of the Daleks" and "Attack of the Cybermen." He also appeared in the impressive BBC miniseries adaptation of *The Day of the Triffids* and the movies *Cry of the Banshee*, *The Duellists*, and *Venom*. He died far too young in 1989 at age 49.

You can find actor Barry Stokes in such movies as *Alien Prey*, *Spaced Out*, and *Enemy Mine*. He also pops up in TV shows like *UFO*, *Space: 1999*, *Survivors*, and *Hammer House of Horror*.

John J. Carney appeared alongside fellow *Hawk* actors Patrick Magee and Warren Clark in *A Clockwork Orange*. He also appeared in *Burke & Hare*, *Top Secret!*, and *Sword of the Valiant: The Legend of Sir Gawain and the Green Knight*, as well as in the TV series *Doctor Who* ("The Time Warrior") and *Blake's 7*. He died in 1995 at age 55.

Melissa Wiltsie was also a nun in *Superman II*.

Andy Bradford was a Hawkman in *Flash Gordon*, 009 in *Octopussy*, and Darro in *Krull*.

Michael Crane was the giant in *Gawain and the Green Knight*. He died in 2009 at age 72.

6 DEGREES OF SORCERY

Voltan's appearance mirrors that of Darth Vader from *Star Wars*, down to the shape of his helmet and his black cloak. If you look at the poster art and not so much the film itself, Hawk even seems to sport Han Solo's vest. The green glow of the Mind Sword has almost the same color and intensity as Luke Skywalker's lightsaber in *Return of the Jedi*.

The musical sting that accompanies many of Hawk's appearances is an homage to Ennio Morricone's theme from *The Good, The Bad and The Ugly*, and Hawk's encounter with the thieves while rescuing Ranulf is staged like the final three-way duel in the same film. The oscillating, multicolored rings surrounding Hawk when he visits with the woman are like those spinning around Kryptonian criminals Zod, Ursa, and Non in the *Superman* films. The cremation of Drogo occurs in the same fashion as the cremation of Darth Vader / Anakin Skywalker, only here the father sets the son alight. The scene also presages a pyre scene in *Conan the Barbarian* and joins the countless ranks of other pyre scenes in fantasy films and television shows.

The fogging of Voltan's camp resembles what Merlin does to Mordred's camp in *Excalibur*— though Merlin has no need of glowing eggs—and the subsequent battle bears some similarity to *Excalibur*'s final Battle of Camlann. The nuns with nooses around their necks are like the hanged Sister Jeanne in Ken Russell's *The Devils*. If we were to try to catalogue all the similarities to Tolkien's *The Lord of the Rings* books, we'd be here all day.

SHATTERING THE ILLUSION

Terry Marcel was a childhood fan of sword and sorcery, particularly the works of Edgar Rice Burroughs. While directing the feature-film comedy *There Goes the Bride,* Marcel met Harry Robertson, and the two began hashing out the idea for *Hawk the Slayer*. During work on that same film, Marcel also met actor John Terry and knew then that should his fantasy adventure go forward, Terry would be the perfect hero.

Marcel intended from the start for *Hawk* to be family-friendly fare, with no nudity or excessive violence—mainly to help make it a commercial success. He initially approached Roger Corman to produce, offering him $750,000, or roughly three-fourths of their desired budget. Fortunately, Lew Grade of ITC offered complete funding. The film's principal photography started one month later.

Ferdy Mayne, only three years older than Jack Palance, played Voltan's father. Catriona MacColl, apparently one of the few actors who got along well with Palance, had broken the ice by chatting with him about the scene in which she was meant to thrust a burning torch into his face. According to her, a discussion of Scotland and Palance's desire to buy a castle there smoothed everything out between them. Marcel and Robertson both admired Palance, going all the way back to his Oscar-nominated performance in *Shane*. While many considered him standoffish, he enjoyed himself so much on the film that when talk of a sequel came up, he was one of the first to express interest.

Interior shoots took place at Pinewood Studios in Buckinghamshire, England, and several exteriors in nearby Black Park Country Park and around Blackpark Lake (sites of earlier Hammer film shoots), as well as Mansfield in Nottinghamshire.

Quite a few cast members sustained injuries during shooting, including Bernard Bresslaw, whose head and neck weathered some damage in two scenes, and Patricia Quinn, who burned her hand. Terry's sword skewered Palance, but the dedicated actor kept going!

From the outset, Marcel wanted sword combat to be less Errol Flynn and more *Yojimbo*—quick and short versus long and dramatic. Fight-arranger John Waller based the resulting choreography on the ancient Chinese martial art of tai chi to give it fluid, almost dance-like movement.

Waller also provided the hero versions of Hawk's and Voltan's swords, which had authentic sixteenth-century blades. Marcel still owns the Mind Sword, despite an offer of $15,000 for it, but Voltan's sword went missing after production.

While *Hawk* performed well in UK cinemas, ITC collapsed and sold out just prior to the film's release in the US, thus killing any possibility of US theatrical distribution. Still bitten by the fantasy bug, Marcel and Robertson later attempted to acquire the rights to *The Chronicles of Thomas Covenant* novel series by author Stephen R. Donaldson for adaptation into films, but they discovered that someone else already owned the rights. Some quests end before they begin.

> TWO BROTHERS LOCKED IN DEADLY COMBAT TILL THE END OF TIME!

MUSIC OF THE MINSTRELS

Composed by Harry Robertson (a.k.a. Harry MacLeod or Harry Robinson), the score is rather infamous among fans for its funky, disco-like electronics and dance beats, complete with burbling synthesizers and twangy electric guitars. Some people love it, and others consider it one of many problems with the film. Despite its unique qualities, the score is as intrinsic to the films as the characters. One can't imagine the movie without it.

Robertson was an active composer throughout the '60s, '70s, and '80s, responsible for a number of Hammer film scores including *The Vampire Lovers, Lust for a Vampire, Twins of Evil,* and *The Ghoul.* He used typical orchestration for most of his scores, but he treaded new ground for his work on *Hawk the Slayer.* Some elements of the score bear similarities to pieces from Jeff Wayne's *War of the Worlds* concept-album released two years earlier, though whether he did that intentionally is debatable.

In 1980, Chips Records released a soundtrack on vinyl, now quite collectible. In December 2012, BSX Records released a limited-edition CD featuring a remastered score, liner notes by Randall D. Larson, and a new performance of the legendary theme by orchestrator Dominik Hauser *(Freddy vs. Jason, The Chronicles of Riddick,* and *Æon Flux).*

THE SAGA CONTINUES

In 1981, New English Library published a 128-page novelization of the movie, co-written by Marcel and Robertson. The British behind-the-scenes TV show *Clapperboard* devoted an episode to the film and featured interviews with cast and crew.

Marcel and Robertson kicked around the idea of a feature-film sequel and even a TV-series spin-off early on, even going so far as to scout locations in New Zealand. As of this writing, Marcel is attempting to launch two sequels to the film, entitled *Hawk the Hunter* and *Hawk the Destroyer. Hawk the Hunter* supposedly deals with the return of Voltan, resurrected by the Black Wizard, lord of the undead—an idea teased at the end of the first film.

The legacy of the original film continued, often in music. Metal band Griffin, formed in 1982, opened their first full-length album, *Flight of the Griffin,* with a track titled "Hawk the Slayer." The song featured lyrics clearly inspired by the film. Another band, the UK group The Darkness, included a quote from the film at the top of their track "Nothin's Gonna Stop Us" from their 2012 album *Hot Cakes.* TV's *Spaced* (written by and starring Simon Pegg and Jessica Stevenson and directed by Edgar Wright) has an oft-quoted mention of the film, in which Tim's (Pegg's) boss Bilbo Bagshot (Bill Bailey) states that he "once punched a bloke in the face for saying *Hawk the Slayer* was rubbish."

TAKE UP THY SWORD!

THE SWORD OF LEGEND (MAGIC WEAPON)

To bring this two-handed greatsword to life, one must join the expertly forged blade with a mysterious green elven stone: a magical, glowing jewel that grants the weapon three unique properties. First, the sword performs as a good-aligned magical weapon with an above-average bonus to hit. Second, the stone, bonded with the sword, generates an aura of evil-repelling green light with brightness equivalent to that of a standard lantern. Third, the sword becomes psychically bonded with its wielder and, with but a thought, can fly through the air of its own accord or instantaneously teleport into the wielder's hands. A dark-aligned counterpart to this weapon exists, but its abilities remain a mystery.

THE FILM'S DESTINY

This film is an unapologetic pastiche of elements from *The Lord of the Rings* novels and *Star Wars*, among other things, arriving smack-dab in the era of *Dungeons & Dragons*. There is no denying the intended audience here. It's hard not to side with *Spaced*'s Bilbo Bagshot.

The film never attempts to be anything more than an entertaining fantasy romp that could well have leapt from someone's game table right onto the screen. The elements are all there: the Darth Vader–like villain (heck, he even has the same silhouette), the variety of fantasy races (elves, dwarves, giants, and so on), the sorcery, the magic items, and the grand quest. In fact, this feels like the sort of fantasy film a group of gamers might have produced on their own between sessions ... and that's not necessarily a bad thing.

If you go into this one expecting anything more than a rollicking good time, you will be sorely disappointed. The film is hardly a work of art and certainly won't win any awards, but despite all its flaws, it's still lots of fun. Performance-wise, the legendary Jack Palance chews up and spits out the scenery, the script, the costumes, and the rest of the cast but still makes a formidable villain opposite young and handsome John Terry. Ray Charleson's performance as Crow the elf also stands out. He speaks in a strange, stilted manner as if to project an otherworldly quality, but unfortunately it comes across as clunky. Morgan Sheppard's Ranulf goes through a lot of shit (losing a hand, taking a dagger in the shoulder, getting mugged ...) before he joins up with Hawk, making him a gritty and likeable character. When he spoke with this author [SAW] in 2012, he seemed to have enjoyed his time working on the film but knew full well that it wasn't an award-winning production. His attitude suggests just the right approach for prospective viewers.

THIS YEAR IN GAMING

The RPGA (Role Playing Game Association) formed in November 1980 to help coordinate tournaments at gaming conventions. At its start, the organization focused exclusively on products published by TSR, including *Advanced Dungeons & Dragons*, *Top Secret*, and *Gamma World*. In the mid-'80s, it recognized and supported names from other publishers, but that did not last long. In recent years, a community organization called the Wizards Play Network has more or less absorbed the RPGA, with almost all mention of the original name purged from the Wizards of the Coast website. The Wizards Play Network focuses on sanctioned *Dungeons & Dragons* events (including "living" campaign events) and events featuring other games (including trading card games) published by Wizards of the Coast.

EXCALIBUR

1981 • UK/US • ORION PICTURES CORPORATION / WARNER BROS. • 140M • COLOR • R

SCREENPLAY: Rospo Pallenberg and John Boorman
BASED ON: *Le Morte d'Arthur* by Thomas Malory
DIRECTOR: John Boorman
PRODUCER: John Boorman
MUSIC: Trevor Jones
CINEMATOGRAPHER: Alex Thomson
PRODUCTION DESIGNER: Anthony Pratt
ART DIRECTOR: Tim Hutchinson
MAKE-UP: Anna Dryhurst and Basil Newall
COSTUME DESIGNER: Bob Ringwood
SPECIAL EFFECTS: Michael Doyle, Peter Hutchinson, Gerry Johnston, and Alan Whibley
SPECIAL OPTICAL EFFECTS: Wally Veevers
ARMORERS: Terry English, Nick Fitzpatrick, Peter Leicht, and Steve Tidiman
FIGHT ARRANGER: William Hobbs
HORSE MASTER: Michael Rowland
CAST: Nigel Terry (King Arthur), Helen Mirren (Morgana), Nicholas Clay (Lancelot), Cherie Lunghi (Guenevere), Paul Geoffrey (Perceval), Nicol Williamson (Merlin), Robert Addie (Mordred), Gabriel Byrne (Uther Pendragon), Keith Buckley (Uryens), Katrine Boorman (Igrayne), Liam Neeson (Gawain), Corin Redgrave (Cornwall), Niall O'Brien (Kay), Patrick Stewart (Leondegrance), Clive Swift (Sir Hector), Ciaran Hinds (Lot), Liam O'Callaghan (Sadok), Michael Muldoon (Astamor), Charley Boorman (Boy Mordred), Mannix Flynn (Mordred's Lieutenant), Garrett Keogh (Mador), Emmet Bergin (Ulfus), Barbara Byrne (Young Morgana), Brid Brennan (Lady in Waiting), Kay McLaren (Aged Morgana), Eamonn Kelly (Abbot), Hilary Joyalle (Lady of the Lake, uncredited), and Prudence Wright Holmes (Sunshine, uncredited)
ALTERNATE TITLES: *The Knights and Merlin* (working titles)

ON THE MAP

Much of the story takes place in and around Cornwall, with the conception of Arthur and the birth of Mordred taking place within the walls of Tintagel Castle, overlooking the Celtic Sea. Camelot lies upon rolling hills nearby. The film does not specify the geographical location of Arthur's final battle—the legendary Battle of Camlann. The battle takes place on a cliff overlooking the sea, which links it to Cornwall and perhaps even Tintagel. Don't try to nail down the time frame, which the film gives as the Dark Ages despite armor dating much later: a deliberate anachronism that enhances the story's mythic qualities.

OUR STORY SO FAR

Excalibur tells the tale of King Arthur from his conception to his death at the hands of his son, Mordred. We don't really have to give you details, surely? You know this stuff.

ALTERNATE VERSIONS

Excalibur initially had an R rating. Demand for a more accessible version resulted in a PG-rated cut released theatrically but not to all markets. For the American network television premiere in 1985, CBS edited about twenty minutes from the film. An edited version still airs on commercial stations and even some movie channels.

IT'S MAGIC

Merlin is an ancient and powerful being who has walked the Earth since the dawn of time. Like others of his kind, he can wield great magic, although the casting of a spell can exhaust even him. It takes him "nine moons" to recover from the spell that allows Uther to lie with Igrayne. Merlin also exhibits direct, mystical links to the animal kingdom: crows often announce his appearances, and he can whisper a command to a horse that it clearly understands. Morgana, in her lust for power, learns the Charm of Making and imprisons Merlin's physical form in crystal forever—she thinks—but not even that prison can keep Merlin contained.

The sword Excalibur is an ancient blade from another time ... and perhaps even another world. (*Doctor Who* fans might know a thing or two about this from the 1989 story "Battlefield.") At first the Lady of the Lake gives the sword to Man. Later, with Uther's dying breath, it is driven into a stone, where it waits for the man who would draw it forth and become king.

Characters have one foot in the pagan world and one foot in the shadow of the Christian God, so we see ancient mystical and more modern spiritual traditions vying for supremacy. The Holy Grail is less the cup used by Christ than a magical chalice somehow linked to Arthur's life force, a magical power we've seen in several other films. (More on that in the "Quest for Meaning" and "6 Degrees" sections.)

THE QUEST FOR MEANING

The Arthurian legend comes with an array of thematic elements, from honor and courage to sacrifice and even immortality. As one of the best-known adaptations of the lore into film, *Excalibur* covers a wide range of the stories and tropes that define that legend for many modern fantasy fans. It owes its depiction of this fictional but seemingly historic tale to numerous literary works that we'll mention in **Shattering the Illusion**.

All the sorcery comes from a time before humans. With the vanishing of Merlin—who states that there are "other worlds" for him—and perhaps of others like him, already departed, the time of magic and legends is drawing to a close. As with other films in this book, this movie teeters on the verge of leaving behind an ancient, more mysterious world for a more modern, familiar one ... and one heavily influenced by the emergence of a new spiritual tradition. Even Arthur cannot stand against the growing tide of Christianity, though he does a fair job at least for a while as a Christ figure himself.

By the conclusion of the film, we have witnessed the last gasp of a land where magic is taken for granted. The dragon's grasp on the world has ended.

Upon his farewell, Merlin tells Arthur that the gods are gone and it is the time for Men. Now what other departing magical figure in another story said something like that while preparing to sail away into the west . . . ?

WHO GOES THERE?

Nigel Terry, while perhaps best known for his role as King Arthur, is a veteran actor of stage and screen both big and small. He appeared in *The Lion in Winter*, reunited with his Guenevere in the short-lived medieval television series *Covington Cross*, played Archeptolemus in *Troy*, and guest-starred in a 2008 episode of *Doctor Who*. He died in 2015 at age 69.

Dame Helen Mirren has won numerous awards for her work in film and television, including a 2007 Oscar for *The Queen*, three BAFTA TV Awards for the series *Prime Suspect*, and more than sixty additional awards. For her performance as Morgana, she was nominated for the 1982 Best Supporting Actress Saturn Award. She has also appeared in *O Lucky Man!, Caligula, 2010*, and *Red*.

Best known for his portrayal of Lancelot, Nicholas Clay worked on stage (as a member of Sir Laurence Olivier's National Theatre Company for a time), screen *(Terror of Frankenstein, Zulu Dawn,* and *Lionheart: The Children's Crusade)*, and television *(The New Adventures of Robin Hood, Highlander,* and *Merlin)*. He died in 2000 at age 53.

Cherie Lunghi was the leading ingénue at the Royal Shakespeare Company in the 1970s. After leaving the company to do *Excalibur*, she became successful though her appearances in *The Mission, Mary Shelley's Frankenstein, Horatio Hornblower: The Duchess and the Devil*, and of course, *Covington Cross* alongside Nigel Terry in 1992.

Paul Geoffrey also appeared in *Greystoke: The Legend of Tarzan, Lord of the Apes; A Flame to the Phoenix;* and *The Thomas Crown Affair*.

Often referred to as one of the truly great actors of the '60s and '70s, Nicol Williamson starred in Tony Richardson's exquisite 1969 production of *Hamlet*. He also costarred with Sean Connery in *Robin and Marian*, portrayed a cocaine-addicted Sherlock Holmes in *The Seven-Per-Cent Solution*, matched wits with *Columbo* on television, appeared in *Return to Oz* and *The Exorcist III*, and played Cogliostro in *Spawn*. That was his last role. He died in 2011 at age 75.

Robert Addie secured the role of Mordred due to his uncanny resemblance to Charley Boorman. Many remember him for his recurring role as Sir Guy of Gisburne in the *Robin of Sherwood* TV series. He also showed up in *Crossbow*—yet another TV series about a bow-wielding hero—*Red Dwarf*, the *Merlin* miniseries, *Bugs*, and the TV movie *A Knight in Camelot*. He died in 2003 at age 43.

This was Gabriel Byrne's first big film, but many moviegoers know him best for *The Usual Suspects* or *Miller's Crossing*. He also appeared in films like *The Keep, Lionheart: The Children's Crusade, Gothic*, and *Ghost Ship*, and TV shows like *Vikings*. He lent his voice to the animated feature *Quest for Camelot*.

Keith Buckley started acting on the small screen in his late teens, a career choice that would occupy him for decades in shows like *Out of the Unknown, The Avengers, Red Dwarf*, and *Jake and the Fatman*. He also landed a number of interesting big-screen roles, in films like *King & Country, Alfred the Great, Dr. Phibes Rises Again*, and *The Spy Who Loved Me*.

Katrine Boorman appeared in three of her father's films: *Zardoz* (an uncredited role), *Excalibur*, and *Hope and Glory*. In 2011 she produced and directed a documentary about her father titled *Me and Me Dad*.

As with a number of other cast members, this was Liam Neeson's first feature film, but he would become another well-liked and respected actor over the years, from his work in *Krull, Darkman, Schindler's List, Rob Roy,* and of course, *Star Wars: Episode I—The Phantom Menace*. In more recent years, he has been cast in more and more genre films, including *The Haunting, Batman Begins, The Chronicles of Narnia* series (as the voice of Aslan), the remake of *Clash of the Titans* as well as its sequel *Wrath of the Titans* (both times as Zeus), *Battleship,* and *The Dark Knight Rises*. He also turns up in *Gangs of New York, Love Actually, Kinsey, Kingdom of Heaven,* all three *Taken* films, *The A-Team,* and (in voice only) *The Lego Movie*. Clearly he has a particular set of skills acquired over a very long career that make him a nightmare for writers like us ... but he's worth the effort.

Corin Redgrave (brother of Vanessa and Lynn) had a long and respectable career on the big and small screens from 1964 through 2010, when he died at age 70, less than a month before the passing of his sister Lynn. He appeared in *A Man for All Seasons, Four Weddings and a Funeral,* and *To Kill a King,* as well as the vampire TV-series *Ultraviolet, The Forsyte Saga,* and *Waking the Dead*.

Niall O'Brien also appeared in films like *Gorky Park, Rawhead Rex, Braveheart,* and *Vanity Fair*. He died in 2009 at age 63.

Patrick Stewart has been acting since he was a young boy. Through an extensive career that has also made him one of the most distinguished Shakespearean actors alive today, he's also been lucky to have landed some long-lasting, memorable characters in genre entertainment, including Captain Jean-Luc Picard in the *Star Trek: The Next Generation* television series and films, and Professor Charles Xavier in the *X-Men* movies. He also appeared in *Dune, Lifeforce,* and *Robin Hood: Men in Tights* and lent his voice to animated features like *The Pagemaster, The Prince of Egypt,* and *Sinbad: The Fifth Voyage*.

Beloved comedic actor, songwriter, and Liverpudlian Clive Swift has been performing on stage and screen for much of his life. He is perhaps most noted for his role as the long-suffering husband of Hyacinth Bucket on *Keeping Up Appearances*. He also appears in the films *Frenzy* (directed by Alfred Hitchcock), *Raw Meat,* and *A Passage to India,* and TV series like *Doctor Who,* where he has appeared twice in different roles ... twenty-two years apart!

Ciaran Hinds has *Excalibur* to thank for launching his long film and television career. He also appears in *Mary Reilly,* the six-part *Ivanhoe* miniseries, *Road to Perdition, Lara Croft Tomb Raider: The Cradle of Life,* the HBO series *Rome, Harry Potter and the Deathly Hallows: Part 2, Ghost Rider: Spirit of Vengeance, John Carter,* and HBO's *Game of Thrones*.

Motorcycle fan and documentary-series producer Charley Boorman, son of director John, was only fifteen when cast as Mordred in *Excalibur*. He appeared in several other films that his father produced and directed, including *Hope and Glory, The Emerald Forest, In My Country,* and *Beyond Rangoon*.

> FORGED BY A GOD·
> FORETOLD BY A WIZARD·
> FOUND BY A KING·

Barbara Byrne was the voice of Urgl in the short-lived *Neverending Story* animated television-series.

Brid Brennan began her career acting on the Dublin stage. Since then she has appeared in a number of notable TV-movies and series, including the BBC Halloween "mockumentary" *Ghostwatch*, *Guinevere*, *Cracker*, and *Doctor Who*.

6 DEGREES OF SORCERY

We can take as read that one might make many connections between this and our other featured Arthurian film, *Monty Python and the Holy Grail*, but only because they both draw from the same source material. The shot of the magically repaired Excalibur rising from the pool of water in the hands of the Lady of Lake is a deliberate visual homage to the image of the shotgun rising from the water (used for some of the original poster art) in John Boorman's earlier film, *Deliverance*. Boorman has acknowledged that the scene where Perceval approaches the desiccated knight is a reference to *The Seventh Seal*. Over the years, footage from *Excalibur* has found its way into a number of other places, including PBS documentaries on Arthurian legends and the short-lived fantasy-comedy TV-series *Wizards & Warriors* from 1983, which frequently used *Excalibur* battle footage. In *Star Trek: Nemesis*, the fight between Captain Picard (he looks familiar) and Shinzon mirrors the gruesome final battle between Arthur and Mordred. Arthur's introductions to Excalibur (his father's "lightsaber") and the Dragon ("the Force") are no doubt nods to *Star Wars*, despite the fact that the tales of Arthur and Merlin predate the birth of George Lucas by a few hundred years. And let's not forget that J. R. R. Tolkien's mythological text, which led to *The Lord of the Rings* and *The Hobbit* cinematic series, harkens back to many elements of this adventure: Merlin's magical abilities and affinity for animals are traits that later turn up in Middle-earth wizards Gandalf and Radagast, Merlin's departure and acceptance of a time for Men is like that of the wizards and elves into the west at the end of *The Lord of the Rings: The Return of the King*, and the Grail's link to Arthur's life force is similar to the One Ring's connection to Sauron and—in those films and in some interpretations of the dialogue—perhaps to Arwen. Other fantasy films in this book feature artifacts or objects tied to a person's life or fate, from *Barbarian Queen II: The Empress Strikes Back* to the *Harry Potter* movies.

Merlin's metal skullcap—at least one of them, anyway—also makes an appearance in the low-budget horror-fantasy film *Guardian of the Realm*. Mordred appears among the villains of Imaginationland in *South Park*. A 2010 episode of Nickelodeon's *iCarly* series, "iStart a FanWar," uses the Charm of Making. A scene similar to Merlin's imprisonment appears in *Iron Warrior* (the third of the *Ator* films).

Finally, Excalibur's design appears to be based on an heirloom sword of the Scottish Lindsay clan, believed to have been forged in 1072. Prior to its burial with a family member in 1683, it appeared in a painting, on which the film's designers likely based the prop.

SHATTERING THE ILLUSION

Drawing largely from the work of Sir Thomas Malory and his take on the Arthurian legend in *Le Morte d'Arthur*, and weaving in some thematic material from other sources like Chrétien de Troyes' Arthurian writing and *The Golden Bough*, this film includes some of its own twists. Shot in Ireland, it was the culmination of a longstanding plan by director John Boorman to adapt the story of Arthur and Merlin to the big screen.

United Artists turned down his original pitch in 1969. In a development that would have altered our understanding of fantasy film forever, he received a counter-proposal: make *The Lord of the Rings* instead! Boorman and co-writer Rospo Pallenberg created a one-film version that was then considered too expensive to pursue. The project failed at other studios as well. A Boorman version of Middle-earth was not to be, but some set designs and imagery now associated with *Excalibur* came from that abandoned *Rings* project.

When an adaptation of Malory's Arthurian text finally clicked, Boorman cast Helen Mirren and Nicol Williamson, fully aware that the actors were not speaking to one another after a less-than-enjoyable professional relationship several years earlier in *Macbeth*. Boorman hoped that the bad blood might enhance the chemistry of their performances. Boorman originally chose Max Von Sydow for Merlin.

Known as "the Boorman family project," this film involved four of that family's members: John at the helm, daughter Katrine as Igrayne, son Charley as Mordred, and daughter Telsche as the Lady of the Lake (uncredited). Originally written and planned as a three-hour epic, the film suffered cuts, including a sequence with Lancelot and Guenevere fending off bandits that appears in the trailer.

Terry English designed the elaborate suits of armor out of aluminum. (English also designed the Colonial Marine armor for *Aliens* and handled armor for *Jabberwocky, Sword of the Valiant*, and *King Arthur*.) He even had a brief cameo as, appropriately enough, a blacksmith.

The horses in the film were polo ponies, which allowed the actors to ride one-handed and wield their weaponry. Camelot, when seen from a distance, is . . . yes, wait for it . . . only a model. Filming a big fight sequence at night proved hazardous, but not for the obvious reasons. Underexposed film, blamed on a faulty exposure meter, led to not one but two reshoots to capture a usable version of the sequence and led to the departure of the cameraman, who broke down as a result of the experience and could not continue.

When released in Australia, screenings of the film often met with laughter, not because of issues with performances, story, or design, but due to unfortunate timing. Just a few months prior to the film's release, Nescafé aired a TV commercial that featured Carl Orff's *"O Fortuna."* Audiences couldn't help but connect the triumphant music played during charges into battle with instant coffee!

MUSIC OF THE MINSTRELS

Excalibur features a combined score of fifty-five minutes of original music by Trevor Jones (*The Dark Crystal, Labyrinth*), a number of classical pieces by Richard Wagner drawn from his *Tristan und Isolde* and *Ring* works, among others, and of course, "O Fortuna" from the cantata *Carmina Burana* composed by Carl Orff. The musical selections made such an impression on Hollywood that for years you couldn't see an action film promoted without the musical accompaniment of "O Fortuna"! Obtaining a copy of the soundtrack is surprisingly difficult. Island

Records released a compilation in 1981 that contained the classical tracks from *Excalibur*, but the only complete scores released to date have been little more than bootlegs of varying quality and content. Why no love for the musical accompaniment to one of cinema's greatest Arthurian adaptations?

> NO MORTAL COULD POSSESS IT!
> NO KINGDOM COULD COMMAND IT!

THE SAGA CONTINUES

Having covered the tale of Arthur from birth to death, what more was there to say? For collectors, a few different manufacturers have made replicas of Excalibur available across the years. Quality varies. Some are little more than cheaply made wall-displays, while others are high-priced "battle-ready" weapons with sharp blades!

In late 2009, Warner Bros. and Legendary Pictures had a remake in the works, with Bryan Singer of *X-Men* and *Superman Returns* fame slated to direct. In 2011, though, Warner Bros. canceled that project to pursue another project, *Arthur & Lancelot*, which has also faced numerous challenges, including the loss of original lead actor Colin Farrell. As of this writing, the film is still a possibility.

TAKE UP THY SWORD!

THE CHARM (MAGIC SPELL)

The power of summoning, the true names of the charms of Doing and Undoing: this is *the* Charm, ancient and mysterious. Only Merlin and his ilk, the nonhuman walkers of the Earth, know the origins of the words.

With this charm, a caster can summon and control fogs and mists and even make them solid enough to hold up a man on his horse or encase an ancient and powerful wizard in stone and crystal. It is with the aid of the Dragon that those walking the Earth can craft such powerful magic.

THE FILM'S DESTINY

[personal disclosure by SAW]: As a boy, I was lucky enough to have parents willing to take me to see the occasional R-rated film as long as it was a genre picture. Somehow, spacesuits or armor made violence and nudity okay. I will never forget the call my father made to the local cinema to ask about the content of *Excalibur*, to see if it was suitable for a 12-year-old. Whatever the minimum-wage-earning employee told him wasn't enough to keep us away, for which I am truly thankful. *Excalibur* defined how I perceived a lot of my fantasy, growing up. Whether it was the design of the armor, or the battles imagined in my RPG sessions, or the random sketches I made in art class, the imagery from Boorman's movie affected me and remains with me today. I loved this film when I first saw it, and despite a few technical issues—mainly special effects that show their age—I routinely revisit this one and will surely never grow weary of its majesty.

At the end of 2011, we lost Nicol Williamson. Despite his extensive career, to many of us he will always be remembered as Merlin. In fact, I often judge Arthurian adaptations by the quality of their Merlins, and no one has yet come close to Williamson's charismatic portrayal. But let us not forget the gorgeous and young Helen Mirren and the terrific supporting cast, many of whom went on to iconic careers in film and television.

There's the aforementioned amazing score. How many of us invested in copies of Carl Orff's *Carmina Burana* after seeing this movie, and how many trailers and ads has "O Fortuna" graced since its use in *Excalibur*?

Some films transcend their performances or technical flaws. *Excalibur* is one of them. Of all the films in this volume, this one hovers at the top of my list.

THIS YEAR IN GAMING

In November 1981, seven months after the theatrical release of *Excalibur*, Chaosium Games unleashed the first edition of *Call of Cthulhu*, designed by Sandy Petersen (known by many as the most prolific level-designer on the hugely popular *Doom* videogame series). Though originally pitched as a supplement for Chaosium's *RuneQuest* RPG, *Call of Cthulhu* was a self-contained roleplaying game using a simplified version of Chaosium's percentile skill-based system known as Basic Role-Playing (BRP). It received the Origins Award for Best Role Playing Game of 1981 as well as the Game Designer's Guild Select Award. Since then, *Call of Cthulhu* has spawned hundreds of expansions, variant rules using other game systems, and seven unique editions. The brand has also appeared in boardgames, card games, and even videogames. In 1985, using a variation of the BRP system, Chaosium finally visited the world of King Arthur via its *Pendragon* roleplaying game, written by Greg Stafford.

CLASH OF THE TITANS

1981 • US/UK • METRO-GOLDWYN-MAYER (MGM) • 118M • COLOR • PG

SCREENPLAY: Beverley Cross
DIRECTOR: Desmond Davis
PRODUCERS: Charles H. Schneer and Ray Harryhausen
MUSIC: Laurence Rosenthal
DIRECTOR OF PHOTOGRAPHY: Ted Moore
PRODUCTION DESIGNER: Frank White
ART DIRECTION: Giorgio Desideri, Fernando Gonzalez, Peter Howitt, and Don Picton
COSTUME DESIGN: Emma Porteous
MAKE-UP: Basil Newall and Connie Reeve
MASKS: Colin Arthur
CREATOR OF SPECIAL VISUAL EFFECTS: Ray Harryhausen
VISUAL EFFECTS: Steven Archer and Jim Danforth
SPECIAL OPTICALS: Frank Van Der Veer and Frank Field
STUNT COORDINATOR: Ferdinando Poggi
CAST: The Immortals: Laurence Olivier (Zeus), Claire Bloom (Hera), Maggie Smith (Thetis), Ursula Andress (Aphrodite), Jack Gwillim (Poseidon), Susan Fleetwood (Athena), and Pat Roach (Hephaestus). The Mortals: Harry Hamlin (Perseus); Judi Bowker (Andromeda); Burgess Meredith (Ammon); Siân Phillips (Cassiopeia); Flora Robson, Anna Manahan, and Freda Jackson (The Stygian Witches); Tim Pigott-Smith (Thallo); Neil McCarthy (Calibos); Donald Houston (Acrisius); Vida Taylor (Danae); Harry Jones (Huntsman); Ferdinando Poggi (Guard, uncredited); and Ellie Nicol-Hilton (Aura).
ALTERNATE TITLE: *Perseus and the Gorgon's Head* (early development title)

ON THE MAP

Cast into the sea on the shores of Argos, Perseus grows up on the island of Seriphos and later gets whisked away to Joppa in the kingdom of Phoenicia by "chance." His adventures take him to Calibos's marsh, the Wells of the Moon, the shrine of the Stygian witches in the mountains north of Joppa, and finally to the Isle of the Dead.

OUR STORY SO FAR

Perseus, son of Zeus by a human woman, must face a series of magical and mythological challenges in his quest to reclaim his heritage and save his love, Andromeda, from the clutches of the dreaded Kraken.

ALTERNATE VERSIONS

The theatrical release in the UK had a few minor cuts to scenes involving characters being stabbed. All home video versions are intact.

IT'S MAGIC

As with its stylistic and spiritual predecessor, *Jason and the Argonauts*, this film's magical elements almost all derive from the influence of the gods of Olympus, though some objects might be enchanted independently, or perhaps Zeus and his kin remotely empower the "gifts of the gods" bestowed upon Perseus. Zeus' two-way shield communication supports the latter interpretation. Whether it's a helmet or a sword or a spherical "eye," nearly every object with which Perseus comes into contact has an extraordinary ability or two.

The ultimate magical construct is Bubo, a robotic creature who seems sentient but whose true nature never really becomes apparent. He's darn cute, though.

THE QUEST FOR MEANING

Beyond the basic tropes common to many of these movies—the hero collecting items and knowledge to aid him in a quest to save a princess, and the young man coming of age and discovering his inner hero as he crusades to restore his honor and heritage—an almost irresistible melancholy invites a look beyond the movie to the man shaping the myth. The idea of the Olympians contemplating the growing independence of humankind and the gods' decreasing relevance is another common motif, one that also turned up in *Jason and the Argonauts*, but it seems particularly profound here, with good reason. The end of Ray Harryhausen's career infuses this film with the man's weary resignation and acknowledgement that all things must pass and that perhaps even the gods are ultimately transitory. (The 2010 remake takes this one step further by giving us a Perseus who actively rejects the influence of the gods, refuses to take his place among them, and chooses the open sea and the mortal world over the Olympian heights.)

As for Zeus's penchant for playing with the fates of humans, the chief deity's gaming supplies have evolved since *Jason and the Argonauts*. Rather than a simple mapped table, he now uses a detailed amphitheater model and an extensive selection of clay figurines stored in alcoves built into a wall. On the surface, Perseus has the passion and brawn, but he's the "tank" in the scenario, with faithful Ammon always chiming in with the right strategy to win the game. In some ways, Perseus, who has all the gifts, is also locked in a rivalry with an almost-brother, because Calibos also carries divine blood but suffers all the setbacks. Perhaps the greatest realization of Calibos's curse is his artful off-camera transformation via figurine, as if the event is so horrific that even though Harryhausen could animate it onscreen, it's best left in shadow.

WHO GOES THERE?

Laurence Olivier is an acting legend with a gift for Shakespearean theater and a lifetime of accomplishment stretching across all media. He appeared in film adaptations of classic plays and novels like *As You Like It, Wuthering Heights, Rebecca, Pride and Prejudice, Henry V, Hamlet, Richard III,* and *Othello*. Later in his career

EXPERIENCE THE FANTASTIC

(and life), he experienced a surge in exposure through roles in films like *Sleuth, Marathon Man, The Boys from Brazil, Dracula,* and *The Jazz Singer.* He died in 1989 at age 82. Infamously, in 2004 his likeness—via archival clips—appeared in a genre-busting flop: *Sky Captain and the World of Tomorrow.*

Claire Bloom also has a career that spans film, television, and stage in the UK and US, appearing in *Richard III, The Haunting, The Spy Who Came in from the Cold, The Illustrated Man* (with husband Rod Steiger), *Mighty Aphrodite,* and *The King's Speech.* She also appeared on television as the Doctor's mother in David Tennant's swan song from the BBC science fiction series *Doctor Who,* "The End of Time."

To an entire generation of moviegoers, Maggie Smith will always be Professor Minerva McGonagall from the *Harry Potter* series. Another generation of TV viewers knows her from *Downton Abbey,* but her career stretches back decades through film, television, and stage, including plenty of Shakespearean productions. (See a pattern building here?) Films include *Othello, Murder by Death, Death on the Nile, California Suite, Evil Under the Sun, A Room with a View, Hook, Sister Act, Sister Act 2: Back in the Habit,* and *Nanny McPhee Returns.* She was married to *Clash of the Titans* writer Beverley Cross for many years, until his death in 1998.

Blink and you miss her as Aphrodite, but Ursula Andress had long before established herself as a pop-culture icon when she emerged from the surf in her white bikini in the first James Bond feature film starring Sean Connery, *Dr. No.* She also appeared in *She, What's New Pussycat, Casino Royale* (the one with David Niven), and *The Mountain of the Cannibal God.* Famously married to John Derek for nearly ten years, she lived with *Clash* costar Harry Hamlin during production; the two had a son in 1980.

Jack Gwillim first worked with Schneer and Harryhausen as King Aeetes in *Jason and the Argonauts* and also played Van Helsing in *The Monster Squad.* He died in 2001 at age 91.

Susan Fleetwood, whose older brother Mick helped found the band Fleetwood Mac, is another classically trained stage actress. She also appeared in *Young Sherlock Holmes, The Krays,* and *Persuasion.* She died in 1995 at age 51.

Pat Roach was a competitive wrestler who shaped a career as a memorable antagonist, threatening film heroes like Indiana Jones, Conan, and James Bond with his imposing physique. Just missing the chance to be Darth Vader in *Star Wars,* he nevertheless became a part of pop-culture history with appearances in *A Clockwork Orange, Unidentified Flying Oddball, Raiders of the Lost Ark, Never Say Never Again, Indiana Jones and the Temple of Doom, Conan the Destroyer, Red Sonja, Willow, Indiana Jones and the Last Crusade, Robin Hood: Prince of Thieves,* and *Kull the Conqueror.* He died in 2004 at age 67.

Harry Hamlin's biggest role was as one of the founding regular cast members on the long-running drama *L.A. Law,* in which he played lawyer Michael Kusak. He also had a recurring role in *Mad Men.*

Judi Bowker was in the television series *The Adventures of Black Beauty* and played a handful of other film and TV roles, only recently returning to acting after taking a break for most of the 1990s.

Burgess Meredith's long career, broken by a stint in the Air Force during WWII, generated a number of memorable characters who endeared him to different generations of fans—through multiple appearances in Rod Serling's landmark television anthology, *Twilight Zone*, his recurring role as the Penguin in the 1960s *Batman* TV-show and its film spinoff, the gruff trainer Mickey in the *Rocky* films, or Grandpa Gustafson in *Grumpy Old Men* and its sequel. Other film appearances included *Of Mice and Men, Story of G.I. Joe, A Big Hand for the Little Lady, The Sentinel, Foul Play,* and *The Last Chase*. He died in 1997 at age 89.

Siân Phillips is mainly known as Livia from the BBC series *I, Claudius* and as the Reverend Mother in David Lynch's *Dune*. For twenty years, she was married to Peter O'Toole, and late in her career began to work in musical productions.

Dame Flora Robson's career in film and theater spanned a lifetime, with notable appearances in *Essex and Elizabeth* and *Black Narcissus*. She died in 1984 at age 82.

Anna Manahan mainly worked in television and died in 2009 at age 84.

Freda Jackson worked with Olivier in his film adaptation of *Henry V* and also appeared in *The Brides of Dracula* and the Schneer-Harryhausen western-dinosaur hybrid, *The Valley of Gwangi*. Her role in *Clash of the Titans* was her last. She died in 1990 at age 82.

Tim Pigott-Smith has a rich background in Shakespearean and other stage acting. He made his television debut in a 1971 *Doctor Who* story, "The Claws of Axos," and returned for another appearance in 1976. He has also appeared in films like *The Remains of the Day, Johnny English, V for Vendetta,* and *Quantum of Solace,* and has lent his cultured voice to a number of audio productions.

Neil McCarthy was a ubiquitous presence on British television with appearances in *Danger Man, The Saint, Dixon of Dock Green, The Avengers, Jason King,* and *Doctor Who* (twice), as well as films like *Where Eagles Dare* and *Time Bandits*. He died in 1985 at age 52.

6 DEGREES OF SORCERY

Clash has plenty of visual, verbal, and thematic references to *Jason and the Argonauts*, including the general look of Olympus and the Earth-bound cities. Thetis's communication via statue is similar to Hera's figurehead conversations with Jason. The freedom with which so many characters launch into detailed synopses of mythological stories recalls the enthusiastic historical accounts provided by the partygoers in the Monty Python sketch, "Dennis Moore." Zeus's disembodied appearance in the shield resembles the Oracle in *The Golden Voyage of Sinbad* as well as the many holographic transmissions in the *Star Wars* films. "Help me, Perseus. You're my only hope!"

The Kraken is an obvious design descendant of the Ymir from *20 Million Miles to Earth* and sports the same mustache-like structure, which Harryhausen once explained as an indication of an enhanced olfactory sense. Capping a career inspired by *King Kong*, Harryhausen designed the Kraken sequence as a nod to Kong menacing Fay Wray. The creature's death echoes that of Talos in *Jason and the Argonauts*, with the spidery cracks stretching across its skin.

The film includes many alterations and additions to the mythology from which it derives its story. (See **Shattering the Illusion**.) Neither the Kraken nor Medusa are even Titans, despite the Stygian witches claiming they are (in an effort to justify the film's title). Pegasus' triumphant return at the end of the movie—emerging from the same spot in the ocean where Medusa's head fell—is an acknowledgment of the actual myth, in which Pegasus is an offspring of the Gorgon.

SHATTERING THE ILLUSION

Looking for a change of pace after the last *Sinbad* movie, Schneer and Harryhausen turned back to *Jason and the Argonauts* and one of its screenwriters, Beverley Cross, to craft what would be their final feature film together, still showcasing Harryhausen's Dynamation process. The team first considered adapting the Perseus myth in the '50s. Cross even drafted an outline for *Perseus and the Gorgon's Head* in 1969, but concern over the complexity of the story and the hero's name—similar to "Percy," which Harryhausen thought might draw ridicule—halted plans until the end of the '70s.

Columbia passed on the project due to its scale. MGM not only supported the idea but also provided a larger budget to attract bigger-name stars: $16 million, greater than the total of every previous film produced from Schneer and Harryhausen's partnership.

Actors as diverse as Arnold Schwarzenegger, Malcolm McDowell, and Michael York were either suggested for considered for Perseus before Harry Hamlin. Burgess Meredith won out over the likes of Peter Ustinov, because MGM worried that American audiences would resist the film without at least a couple recognizable faces. Laurence Olivier took the role of Zeus over Orson Welles, Ralph Richardson, and John Gielgud, while Maggie Smith presumably secured her part through her impressive stage and film work and not by virtue of her marriage to Cross.

The team returned to familiar territory for some of the location shooting, including the temples at Paestum first used in *Jason* for the sequence outside Medusa's lair. In addition to Italy, the production made use of locations in Spain and Malta, while interiors and much of Harryhausen's work took place at Pinewood Studios in England. Given the scope of the project, his advancing age, and the threat of running over time and budget, Harryhausen recruited assistants for some of the model work, including Janet Stevens, who returned from *Sinbad and the Eye of the Tiger* to sculpt some of the model studies, and animators Steve Archer and Jim Danforth.

Some of the stock footage used in the initial engulfment of the *Argos* came from unused material for *Jason and the Argonauts*, further strengthening the decades-wide link between the two films. The model of Calibos cannibalized Trog from *Sinbad and the Eye of the Tiger*.

Although the film adapts the Perseus myth, many creatures and elements of the story came from other sources and took new shapes to suit the narrative. Calibos is a rough approximation of Caliban from Shakespeare's *The Tempest* and was to remain mute. When dialogue became essential, the character morphed into a complicated combination of live-action footage with actor Neil McCarthy in makeup, and Harryhausen's stop-motion model.

The Kraken, a Scandinavian creature, replaced Leviathan from the original myth,

An Epic Entertainment Spectacular!

90 • CINEMA AND SORCERY

> YOU WILL FEEL THE POWER.
> LIVE THE ADVENTURE.
> EXPERIENCE THE FANTASTIC.

and the two-headed dog Dioskilos was an alteration of Cerberus, the guard dog of Hades, described as having three or even fifty heads. (A three-headed version turns up in another film, *Harry Potter and the Sorcerer's Stone*!) The Stygian witches are a composite of nymphs consulted by Perseus and the Gorgon's sisters. As for the lovable Bubo, Harryhausen insists that R2-D2 of *Star Wars* fame could not have influenced the robotic owl, because the creation of Bubo predated that film.

One of Harryhausen's main inspirations for taking on the Perseus myth was to realize the vision of the hero's battle with Medusa, which remains a landmark achievement not just in Harryhausen's career but also in fantasy cinema in general. Discovering that classical artists had often depicted Medusa as beautiful despite her monstrous powers, Harryhausen decided to create a version that externalized the horror of the character, with twelve snakes as hair and a serpent-like body to match. Harryhausen highlighted her eyes with a technique he referred to as "Joan Crawford lighting." A sequence in Tod Browning's *Freaks* inspired her creepy way of dragging herself along the ground. A rare injury that left Harryhausen with what might have been a broken finger cut short his work on the final-sacrifice sequence. Steve Archer completed the scene.

Some of the film's poster art clearly aped the look and composition of the famous posters for *Star Wars*. Although Schneer and Harryhausen discussed a follow-up film—either another *Sinbad* adventure or a tale titled *Force of the* Trojans—this was not only the final collaboration in their extraordinary partnership, which spanned four decades: it was also the last film for both men.

MUSIC OF THE MINSTRELS

Laurence Rosenthal provided a grander, more romantic score than had accompanied many of the previous Schneer-Harryhausen films. His melodic approach to the material lifts the movie above its predecessors. Combined with the star names in the cast, Rosenthal's hummable themes lend a classic Hollywood feel to the proceedings.

THE SAGA CONTINUES

Warner Books published a novelization by Alan Dean Foster. Mattel made a short-lived line of action figures, and Whitman released a boardgame featuring a colorful game board, spinner, and character cards that sent players on a quest to collect the items necessary to obtain Medusa's head, show it to the Kraken, and save the day. Golden Press published a full-color graphic novel of the movie, and a serialized adaptation in the form of black-and-white strip advertisements appeared in the UK under titles like *2000 AD* and *Starburst*. MGM also released one of their last sets of three 8mm film-reels featuring edited highlights from the movie.

In 2010, Warner Bros. produced a remake with Sam Worthington as Perseus. The less said about that movie, the better, especially because it took pains to feature Bubo in a cameo only to make a joke about leaving him behind . . . along with all the heart and charm that made the original film so memorable and beloved. A disquieting tendency in modern culture derides things once beloved in childhood, as if that lends some sort of credibility to an adult. The fact remains that despite the desire of some to insult the memory of that brave little brass owl, Bubo is one of the most delightful aspects of *Clash*. He can fly rings around any of the characters in the remake.

When a sequel, titled *Wrath of the Titans*, entered development, a legal issue arose: comic-book publisher Bluewater Productions had already used the title *Wrath of the Titans* in 2007 when it released two five-issue sequels to *Clash* as part of its licensed *Ray Harryhausen Presents* imprint. A settlement enabled both Bluewater and the film sequel to use the name. The *Wrath of the Titans* film sequel came out in March 2012, with some critics noting that it was at least better than its 2010 predecessor Faint praise aside, the success of *Wrath* led to plans for a third film titled *Revenge of the Titans*, which producer Basil Iwanyk quickly placed on hold, pending a "fresh" take.

TAKE UP THY SWORD!

THE MECHANICAL OWL (DIVINE CONSTRUCT AND MECHANICAL FAMILIAR)

Constructed by Hephaestus as a mechanical replacement for the goddess Athena's flesh-and-blood owl, this device is an all-seeing and all-knowing divine automaton. As a gift of the gods, the owl can communicate with anyone to whom it is bound, as if hearing and speaking the same language. (To all others, the automaton sounds as if it emits a series of whirs, buzzes, and clanks.) The owl can provide information (transmitted directly from the gods) and can scout when stealth (or a diminutive reconnoiterer) is required. The owl is either a familiar or a companion.

THE FILM'S DESTINY

An enthusiastic, delightful ode to classical mythology and to the spirit of heroism and romance, enhanced by a master craftsman working at the peak of his powers, *Clash of the Titans* is an epic episodic journey that rarely flags in excitement and provides the perfect finale to Harryhausen's incredible career. Although some of the acting might seem hammy by today's standards—all right, even by 1981 standards—and a few effects-shots have aged poorly due to differentiating film stocks, those minor flaws cannot dampen the exuberance of the production. Years of repeated cable showings assured its popularity. [The "taming of Pegasus" scene was, like the *Star Wars* "trash masher" scene, the one that would invariably be showing whenever I turned it on. –ATB] A real sense of heart permeates every aspect of the sprawling saga. Like many of the previous Schneer-Harryhausen films, it feels like we are glimpsing a complete world from another era.

Despite his unmistakable stubbly adulthood, Harry Hamlin imbues Perseus with an endearing youth and innocence. He even initially wears an actor's cloak and sword as if playing at being a man. Judi Bowker is equally innocent and about as beautiful as any princess could hope to be. The adventure culminates in a tour-de-force sequence set in Medusa's fire-lit lair and an exhilarating daylight rescue.

> No adventure in space . . . No battle on Earth . . .
> No dream of glory . . . can ever match the experience.

Like many '80s movie heroes—Indiana Jones being a prime example—Perseus succeeds almost in spite of himself, with those around him facilitating his triumph more than he does. Hell, without Bubo, this would have ended in tears!

Exploring themes of hubris, revenge, loyalty, and the reliable old notion that love conquers all, *Clash* also has a bittersweet atmosphere as it signals the end of a particular kind of filmmaking at the dawn of a more technologically driven age of science-fiction blockbusters. Burgess Meredith's Ammon provides much of the melancholy meta-commentary, but Laurence Olivier's Zeus delivers the most poignant observation at movie's end. Speaking of the inevitable passing of the gods, he might as well be talking about Harryhausen himself and those who will take their place among the stars with the heroes and monsters they brought to life.

THIS YEAR IN GAMING

Primarily known at the time for its *Star Trek*-like starship combat game, *Star Fleet Battles* (released in a boxed edition just two years prior), Task Force Games stepped up to the RPG table with *Heroes of Olympus,* designed by B. Dennis Sustare *(Bunnies & Burrows)*. An interesting roleplaying-wargame hybrid set in ancient Greece, the game originally came in a boxed set that contained rules, hex maps, dice (a d6 and a d20), and several die-cut counters, and it used skill-based game mechanics and a point-based character-creation system. The rulebook featured background on the gods, magic, races, and pre-generated characters. While the game contained much to link it to *Jason and the Argonauts,* its publisher likely timed it to coincide with the release of *Clash of the Titans.* A few magazine articles supported the game, and a second edition came out in 1983.

DRAGONSLAYER

1981 • US • PARAMOUNT PICTURES / WALT DISNEY PRODUCTIONS • 108M • COLOR • PG

WRITERS: Hal Barwood and Matthew Robbins
DIRECTOR: Matthew Robbins
PRODUCER: Hal Barwood
MUSIC: Alex North
PERIOD MUSIC BY: Christopher Page
DIRECTOR OF PHOTOGRAPHY: Derek Vanlint
MAKE-UP: Graham Freeborn, Jane Royle, and Nick Dudman
PRODUCTION DESIGNER: Elliot Scott
DRAGON DESIGN, GRAPHICS, AND TITLES: David Bunnett
ART DIRECTOR: Alan Cassie
MAGIC ADVISOR: Harold Taylor
LATIN ADVISOR: Eric Watts
COSTUME DESIGNER: Anthony Mendleson
SUPERVISOR OF SPECIAL MECHANICAL EFFECTS: Brian Johnson
PHOTOGRAPHIC EFFECTS PRODUCED BY: Industrial Light & Magic, Inc.
SUPERVISOR OF SPECIAL VISUAL EFFECTS: Dennis Muren
DRAGON SUPERVISORS: Phil Tippett and Ken Ralston
CLOSE-UP DRAGON: Christopher Walas
DRAGON CONSULTANT: Jon Berg
CAST: Peter MacNicol (Galen Bradwarden); Caitlin Clarke (Valerian); Ralph Richardson (Ulrich); John Hallam (Tyrian); Peter Eyre (Casiodorus Rex); Albert Salmi (Greil); Sydney Bromley (Hodge); Chloe Salaman (Princess Elspeth); Emrys James (Simon, Valerian's Father); Roger Kemp (Horsrik); Ian McDiarmid (Brother Jacopus); Ken Shorter and Jason White (Henchmen); Yolande Palfrey (Victim); and Douglas Cooper, Alf Mangan, David Mount, James Payne, and Chris Twinn (Urlanders)

ON THE MAP

The majority of the story takes place in the sixth-century country of Urland, a land beyond Valvasia.

OUR STORY SO FAR

When his mentor dies before undertaking one last quest, a young apprentice sorcerer must face the devastating power of an aging dragon, Vermithrax Pejorative, defy the will of a self-absorbed king and his sadistic guardsman, and prove his worth to the people of Urland, to the girl he loves, and to himself.

ALTERNATE VERSIONS

Television viewers would be forgiven for having a hard time figuring out when Galen twigs to Valerian's true gender or what everyone is talking about when Galen first claims to take care of

> IN THE DARK AGES,
> DRAGONS WERE REAL.
>
> NOT A FANTASY.

Vermithrax, because TV showings omitted the crucial lake and avalanche sequences. We understand the omission of the first, because of brief nudity ... but the falling rocks?

In the UK, censors edited out most of the gore in the admittedly shocking scene with Elspeth and baby dragon. It remains missing from the most recent Region 2 DVD release. Everything is intact on the 2003 US DVD.

IT'S MAGIC

This film has one of the more intriguing and arguably realistic depictions of magic, as implemented by the wizards of its realm, than most of the other movies in this book. A blend of Latin intonation, reagents, and other physical components, plus a focusing amulet, creates the illusion—appropriately enough—of a system that works within some restrictions and physical laws. This is also one of the rare movies that blends fantasy magic with the more mundane prestidigitation with which we're familiar in the real world. After all, apart from slaying dragons, what would sorcerers most likely do except use their extraordinary abilities to perform cheap conjuring tricks for kings and rich people? Ulrich's implication that sorcerers were responsible for dragons, and his destruction along with Vermithrax's, suggests that an inextricable bond exists between both sides of the magical equation: one cannot exist without the other.

THE QUEST FOR MEANING

It's fascinating how many of these films depict a world of genuine magic not in its heyday but on the cusp of being left behind for modern, more secular sensibilities. Here again we have a culture that has seen wonders—fire-breathing dragons and accomplished wizards—but is weary, as though the weight of the knowledge it possesses has become too much for it to bear.

As if that isn't enough of a theme, this film also deals with the rise of Christianity, and not in a flattering light. Whether it's the use of magic to create monsters, religious manipulation to control people, or the deceitful arrogance of the ruling class, every single organized system in this movie is corrupt and unworthy of trust. Yet, despite this excessive cynicism, a glimmer of hope at the end suggests that the times to come might still have room for magic. Does Galen still have the gift?

WHO GOES THERE?

Peter MacNicol reportedly isn't too proud of his debut role in this film (we don't see why not), but that doesn't matter, because his career has encompassed a great many respectable credits in films like *Sophie's Choice, Ghostbusters II, Addams Family Values, Dracula: Dead and Loving It, Bean, Baby Geniuses*, and television series like *Chicago Hope, Ally McBeal, 24, Numb3rs, Grey's Anatomy*, and *CSI: Cyber*. He's also written and directed for *Ally McBeal, Boston Public*, and *Numb3rs*.

This was Caitlin Clarke's first role as well. She also appeared in *"Crocodile" Dundee*, on TV shows like *Moonlighting* and *Law & Order*, and on Broadway in a '90s production of *Titanic*. She spent most of the rest of her career teaching in Pittsburgh and acting in regional theater. She died in 2004 at age 52.

Sir Ralph Richardson was one of the most accomplished theater actors of his generation (or indeed any other), but he also had an extensive film career, with early appearances in *The Ghoul* and *Things to Come*. Later in life he began to rack up an impressive number of cult roles in films like *Doctor Zhivago, Tales from the Crypt, Whoever Slew Auntie Roo?, Alice's Adventures in Wonderland, O Lucky Man!, Rollerball, Time Bandits*, and *Greystoke: The Legend of Tarzan, Lord of the Apes*. He also appeared in TV movies like *Frankenstein: The True Story* and *The Man in the Iron Mask* and was the voice of the chief rabbit in *Watership Down*. He died in 1983 at age 80.

John Hallam appeared in *The Wicker Man, The People That Time Forgot, Flash Gordon*, and the *Doctor Who* story "Ghost Light." He also played Mandara in *Kull the Conqueror* and made his final appearance in a 2000 television version of *Arabian Nights*. He died in 2006 at age 65.

Peter Eyre appeared in dozens of television shows and miniseries, including *The Young Indiana Jones Chronicles*, the 1998 *Merlin*, and *Friends*. He also appeared in *From Hell*.

Albert Salmi, a prolific character-actor, appeared in film and television from the '50s to the '80s, after starting out on stage. Known as "Finland's Favorite Son," he had memorable roles in *Twilight Zone, Lost in Space*, and dozens of westerns, in addition to appearing in films like *Escape from the Planet of the Apes, Empire of the Ants*, and *Caddyshack*. He died in 1990 at age 62, in tragic circumstances: he was found shot to death in his home along with his estranged wife, in what might have been a murder-suicide.

Sydney Bromley carved out a unique niche for himself later in life, often portraying eccentric, toothless old men in films such as *Candleshoe, An American Werewolf in London*, and *The Never-Ending Story*. He died in 1987 at age 78.

Ian McDiarmid will forever be known as the evil Emperor Palpatine from the *Star Wars* films, although his career has also encompassed appearances in films like *The Awakening, Dirty Rotten Scoundrels*, and *Sleepy Hollow*, as well as work as a theater director.

Yolande Palfrey turned up in *Blake's 7* and *Doctor Who*. She died in 2011 at age 54.

6 DEGREES OF SORCERY

Much of the movie's story is a loose adaptation of the classic tale of Saint George and the dragon: an adventurous narrative from the East (introduced to the West via the Crusades) that covered things like sacrifices, lotteries, princesses in peril, and a powerful lance. Many people have noted this film's multiple similarities to *Star Wars*, and they're not wrong, although arguably most of the resemblances are not unique to *Star Wars*, either, because that film was itself a collection of heroic-narrative clichés. But to be specific: Ulrich is Obi Wan and similarly dies in a strategic gambit, Galen is

> IN THE DARK AGES,
> MAGIC WAS A WEAPON.
> LOVE WAS A MYSTERY.
> ADVENTURE WAS EVERYWHERE ...
> AND DRAGONS WERE REAL.

Luke, the amulet stands in for the lightsaber, and Galen's journey into the dragon's lair looks like that of Luke's surreal experience on Dagobah in *The Empire Strikes Back*.

Ulrich's story arc also resembles that of Gandalf in *The Lord of the Rings: The Two Towers*, in that he dies and then returns in white to play a role in the resolution. He even stares down the dragon and braves the flames while holding his staff aloft, as Gandalf does with the Balrog in *The Lord of the Rings: The Fellowship of the Ring*. His ashes are thrown into the lake of fire, an action similar to those taken in *7th Voyage of Sinbad* and *The Lord of the Rings: The Return of the King*. The forging of the Dragonslayer is also like the reforging of the shards of Narsil or the opening sequence of *Conan the Barbarian*.

The chained damsel echoes Andromeda from *Clash of the Titans*. Magical fire is green, perhaps influencing the use of blue fire for magic in *Beastmaster*. Galen attends the lottery in a cloak just as Robin Hood shows up for that archery contest in disguise.

The baby dragons look a bit like giant versions of the Ceti eels from *Star Trek II: The Wrath of Khan*. A battle with one of those creatures resembles the struggle with the R.O.U.S. in *The Princess Bride*, while Galen's leap onto Vermithrax's back has a Harryhausen feel. The dragon alights on a mountaintop in an homage to *Fantasia*. Vermithrax's design and behavior has influenced decades of dragons in other movies, television shows, and especially games, as recently as his scaly cousins that appear in *The Elder Scrolls V: Skyrim*.

SHATTERING THE ILLUSION

After working on their first collaborative effort, *Corvette Summer*, and finding their second film project stalling due to actor issues, Hal Barwood and Matthew Robbins decided to turn to fantasy, because they could control every aspect of production by creating their lead character from "rubber and plastic." Inspired by the tale of St. George, as well as the "Sorcerer's Apprentice" segment of Walt Disney's *Fantasia*, they set out to craft a story that would ground the adventure in realism and eschew many familiar fairytale elements, such as chivalric knights questing for veiled damsels.

Barwood and Robbins began the outline for what would become *Dragonslayer* in June of 1979 and by summer's end were shopping it all over the movie industry. Their inexperience with the financial side of the business put them at a serious disadvantage, leading to a string of disappointments until Paramount expressed interest and set it up as their second co-production with Walt Disney, after *Popeye*.

MacNicol wasn't a fan of magic as a kid, but he gained some appreciation for the art while studying to perform some of Galen's tricks with Harold Taylor, a British magician who had entertained the royal family and who served as this film's "magic advisor." MacNicol even performed for cast and crew between takes. He suppressed his natural Texas twang while delivering his lines and endured horse training to ride bareback. When MacNicol's double proved too hesitant to make usable scenes, MacNicol even wound up performing most of his

> ITS TALONS TEAR.
> ITS BREATH BURNS.
> IT IS TERROR.
> AND ONLY SORCERY CAN DESTROY IT.

own stunts, including a leap onto the back of the full-size Vermithrax, which ended with him falling to the ground and bending the supposedly indestructible Dragonslayer spear.

> **WHEN DRAGONS WERE REAL.**

Caitlin Clarke nearly passed up her film debut to perform in a Chicago stage production, but she was grateful later, claiming that even just rehearsing with Ralph Richardson taught her more about acting than classes ever could. The star of the film, however, is undoubtedly the 400-year-old dragon Vermithrax Pejorative. About a quarter of the movie's total budget of $16 million went toward making him a reality. David Bunnett was the principal designer of the dragon's look—all the more impressive given that he had no experience in film prior to this production. Sixteen different puppets each performed a specific movement or action, in concert with full-size radio- and cable-controlled versions of the head, neck, tail, grasping claws, and wings.

For some of the creepiest shots of the dragon—of Vermithrax crawling over the rocky terrain of his lair—ILM's Phil Tippett helped pioneer a new variation on an old technique. Established by the likes of Ray Harryhausen in many of the films covered elsewhere in this book, stop-motion animation became "go-motion" via a "dragon-mover." A programmer could direct the motor-driven dragon model to complete a series of moves while the camera ran, thus eliminating much of the halting movement associated with traditional stop-motion animation. Chris Walas joined the team later to give Vermithrax a more expressive personality in some of the close-up sequences, for which he operated a puppet head that he created. He handled molding and fabrication and also assembled the baby dragons that Ken Ralston not only designed, but operated during shooting.

Location shooting in North Wales and Scotland immensely enhanced the historic look of the film, including the use of the 13th-century Dolwyddelan Castle as Ulrich's home. As with many other films in the genre, the production team researched historic architecture and clothing to create a convincing 6th-century setting for the adventure. One of the film's biggest triumphs, however, might be the deceptively simple hellish lair of the dragon, with its natural-looking rock formations and burning lake. Although the environs look real enough, builders created the entire setting as a huge interior set, with a combination of Welsh rock and polystyrene. Costumers limited their color palette to what might have been available in the era and kept stitching inexact and visible, as if sewn by hand.

The film was not a commercial success in its initial release, but its cult status grew through video and cable. Controversy over its violent content might have influenced Disney in its decision to develop its Touchstone division. In 2011, Guillermo del Toro attended a 30th-anniversary screening of *Dragonslayer*—one of his favorite movies—and spoke about campaigning for Paramount to release a Blu-ray special edition that would do justice to the film.

MUSIC OF THE MINSTRELS

Alex North's inventive, discordant score with its cavernous lows and sprightly highs is as much a character in the movie as the rest of the cast; indeed, Vermithrax exists in the music whenever those brash horns shatter the soundscape and trumpet his influence or herald his appearance. No less an authority than famous film-critic Pauline Kael praised North's work and noted the synchronicity between the dragon and the instruments that accompanied him. As with several other movies in this book, however, the well-regarded soundtrack to *Dragonslayer* remained elusive for decades and arrived in an official release only in 2010, from La-La Land Records. The album included some supplementary tracks. In the '80s and '90s, an Australian bootleg version turned up on LP and CD. A 1996 Alex North compilation featured music from this film and from *Cheyenne Autumn* and *South Seas Adventure*.

THE SAGA CONTINUES

A novelization by Wayland Drew featured some intriguing additions to the story, filling in background details on many characters and further delving into Ulrich's fleeting assertion in the film that sorcerers were responsible for the existence of dragons. Marvel Comics published a comic-book adaptation as both a two-issue miniseries and a one-shot magazine, *Marvel Super Special* #20, which included a full-color behind-the-scenes section about the film. SPI released two editions of an elaborately designed, beautifully illustrated *Dragonslayer* boardgame; this "Fantastic Game of Quest and Adventure" sent players across a map of Urland to collect companions and items, while dodging the king's men, on the way to fight Vermithrax.

TAKE UP THY SWORD!
SLAYER SHIELD (MAGIC ARMOR)

Constructed from over thirty individual molted dragon scales collected from the lair of a 400-year-old great dragon, this heavy, oval-shaped dragonscale shield grants cover against fire breath attacks. The shield absorbs the first third of total damage per successful attack. Fabricating one of these shields requires the ability to craft unique arms and armor as well as unparalleled courage to penetrate the dragon's lair, avoid the many dragonets, and collect the discarded scales undetected.

THE FILM'S DESTINY

It's always nice when something lives up to the almost impossible-to-match promise of childhood memories. Apart from some aging matte effects desperately in need of digital cleaning (where is a special edition of this, anyway?), *Dragonslayer* is a great-looking, well-made fantasy adventure with a surprising amount of philosophical depth to reward returning viewers, striking a difficult balance between more mature elements like stomach-turning gore and its fairytale roots.

Some criticize the movie for its similarities to *Star Wars*, and it's hard not to see the parallels. The very DNA of that sci-fi series runs through this film's veins, with Phil Tippett and ILM providing the special effects. Even the Emperor himself turns up ... and he wouldn't appear in *Return of the Jedi* for another two years!

If you can dismiss the film on that score, you still cannot dismiss Vermithrax. One of cinema's greatest creature designs, the impressive and terrifying apparition, so expertly introduced slowly over the course of the film, underscores just how far CGI has to go before it can conjure the feeling of palpable menace so perfectly achieved in *Dragonslayer*. A child of the '80s could be forgiven for believing, if only for a moment, that perhaps there was such a time when winged nightmares took to the skies.

The neat subversion of some genre clichés—principally the fact that the princess is not the love interest and doesn't even survive the story—gives the film a fresh approach to an otherwise traditional coming-of-age heroic journey. The only real flaw is that the movie never spawned a sequel. The prospect of seeing a powerful, older Galen and Valerian traveling further into a transforming world of Christianity and modern sensibilities is enticing, but it was not to be. Ah, well, we'll always have Urland.

THIS YEAR IN GAMING

The first edition of one of the longest-lasting and most influential superhero roleplaying games, *Champions,* came out this year. Designed by Steve Peterson and George MacDonald, and featuring a unique point-based character-creation system, the initial handmade edition sold surprisingly well at Pacific Origins. A thousand out of 1,500 copies sold, and thanks to distributor orders, the remaining 500 were gone within a month. Though Hero Games recently succumbed to downsizing, *Champions* remains a strong IP even today, several editions later; the *Hero System* that evolved from the initial release continues to be a fan favorite. *Champions* also exists as a popular massively multiplayer online game, and for a while it enjoyed life as a comic-book series from Eclipse Comics and Hero Comics/Graphics. (The 1970s Marvel Comics *Champions* series that preceded these was entirely unrelated.)

THE SWORD AND THE SORCERER

1982 • US • SORCERER PRODUCTIONS • 99M • COLOR • R

SCREENPLAY: Tom Karnowski, John Stuckmeyer, and Albert Pyun
DIRECTOR: Albert Pyun
PRODUCERS: Brandon Chase and Marianne Chase
MUSIC: David Whitaker
DIRECTOR OF PHOTOGRAPHY: Joseph Mangine
ART DIRECTOR: George Costello
COSTUME DESIGNER: Christine Boyar
HEAD MAKE-UP ARTIST: Ve Neill
SPECIAL-EFFECTS SUPERVISOR: John Carter
SPECIAL MAKE-UP EFFECTS: Gregory Cannom, Douglas White, Allan Apone, And Frank Carrisosa
CHAIN MAIL: Fred Lieberman
WEAPONS MASTER: John Spencer
TRI-BLADED SWORD CONSTRUCTION: Elroy Payne
SWORD TRAINER: Anthony De Longis
FENCING TUTOR: Reggie Parton
CAST: Lee Horsley (Talon), Kathleen Beller (Alana), Simon Mac Corkindale (Mikah), George Maharis (Machelli), Richard Lynch (Cromwell), Richard Moll (Xusia), Anthony De Longis (Rodrigo), Robert Tessier (Verdugo), Nina Van Pallandt (Malia), Anna Bjorn (Elizabeth), Jeff Corey (Craccus), Joseph Ruskin (Malcolm), Joe Regalbuto (Darius), Russ Marin (Mogullen), Earl Maynard (Morgan), George Murdock (Quade), John Davis Chandler (Guard 1), Emily Yancy (Ban Urlu), Christopher Cary (King Richard), Peter Breck (King Leonidas), Alan Caillou (King Sancho), Michael Evans (King Ludwig), Jay Robinson (King Charles), Simmy Bow (The Cardinal), Reb Brown (Phillip), Eric Cord (Eric), Jo-Jo D'Amore (A Drunk), Steve Davis (Thogan), Anthony Farrar (Young Mikah), Greg Finley (Rumbolt), George Fisher (Ninshu), Tammi Furness (Myra), Hubie Kerns (Renquo), Lennie Geer (Cornellus), Michael Hoit (Red Dragon Archer 1), James Jarnigan (Young Talon), Edgy Lee (Acolyte), Charlie Messenger (Pablo), Shelley Taylor Morgan (Bar-Bro), Christina Nigra (Young Elizabeth), Buckley Norris (Bartender), Patrick O'Moore (Devereux), Thomas Rosales (Kabal), Gina Smika (Young Alana), Alvah Stanley (Sades), Mark Steffan (Sades Aide), William Watson (Karak), Barry Chase (Tavis), Corinne Calvet ("special appearance"), and Corey Burton (voice, uncredited)

ON THE MAP

The story opens on a remote rocky crag known as Tomb Island. Elysium is the seaside capital of rival kingdom Ehdan; upon its fog-shrouded cliffs, Cromwell defeats Richard, and the rest of the film takes place within, above, and even below it in sewers, dungeons, and caves.

OUR STORY SO FAR

In a war-torn world of swords and magic—well, that sounds familiar—a mercenary with a royal lineage agrees to help a princess defeat a vicious tyrant in control of the city of Ehdan, as well as a powerful and ancient sorcerer resurrected as a weapon and driven by vengeance.

ALTERNATE VERSIONS

Various scenes required multiple shoots to allow for PG-rated versions, mainly for eventual television broadcast. The DVD, released in 2001, features two trailers, one of which contains at least one of these more "family-friendly" alternate takes. In the R-rated version (Trailer 1) of a shot of Talon falling atop a woman in a harem, the woman is topless, but she sports a Princess Leia-style brassiere in Trailer 2.

IT'S MAGIC

The first magic-user we see is a sorceress, Ban Urlu, hired to help summon Xusia from his hellish slumber. While her abilities appear significant, she is no match for Xusia's power. The sorcerer slays her to make an example of her.

Xusia can control minds. His claws and his victims' eyes glow red when he uses this power. He also has telekinetic powers: he can rip a heart from a chest cavity or throw a person across a room. Exactly what he does against Cromwell's foes is unknown, but whatever it is, it clearly turns the tide in the mad king's favor.

THE QUEST FOR MEANING

This is a tale of *reluctant* revenge. Talon, after witnessing the brutal slaughter of his family, has gone through life hating Cromwell, but apparently never considered striking back face-to-face. His successful life as a mercenary, however, coincidentally draws him into the events that lead up to Cromwell's downfall. Unlike with many sword-and-sorcery films in this book, in which solely revenge motivates the hero, here an offer of a night with a sexy girl gets the hero to re-enter a world ripped away by Cromwell's savagery. When Talon finally manages to free the kingdom and has the crown rightfully in his hands, he tosses it to a friend and rides off to be a hero somewhere else. His destiny was chosen when his family was slain, but it was not to become the crowned head of Ehdan. That Talon: what a guy.

WHO GOES THERE?

Texas native Lee Horsley is probably best known for *Matt Houston,* a 1980s TV series about a Texas millionaire-cum-private-detective living in Los Angeles. He also starred in a few other series, including *Nero Wolfe, Guns of Paradise, Bodies of Evidence,* and *Hawkeye.* In film, he returned as Talon in *Abelar: Tales of an Ancient Empire* and appeared in Quentin Tarantino westerns *Django Unchained* and *The Hateful Eight.*

Kathleen Beller made her biggest impressions in her many successful TV roles, including as Kirby Anders-Colby in *Dynasty.* She also appeared in a number of films—including a brief but memorable appearance in *The Godfather: Part II.* Her last onscreen role was in 1992's *Life after Sex.* For fans of '80s music, we'd be remiss not to mention that Beller is married to Thomas Dolby (yes, the "She Blinded Me With Science" guy).

Simon MacCorkindale bounced back and forth from the big screen to the small screen and from America to Britain, popping up on TV in *Manimal* (as the lead), *Falcon Crest, Counter-*

strike, *Poltergeist: The Legacy,* and *Casualty,* as well as in films like *Death on the Nile, The Riddle of the Sands, Jaws 3,* and *Wing Commander.* He died in 2010 at age 58.

Another veteran of the small screen who made few forays into features, George Maharis starred in *Route 66, The Most Deadly Game, Rod Serling's Night Gallery,* and *Fantasy Island,* as well as in the TV-movie sequel *Look What's Happened to Rosemary's Baby* and the films *The Satan Bug* and *Doppelganger.*

Fans of science fiction or horror know Richard Lynch. His notable sharp features and imposing presence have appeared on the big and small screens since the early 1970s, when he almost cornered the market on villainy. He appeared in films such as *Deathsport, Bad Dreams, Alligator II: The Mutation, Scanner Cop,* and the 2007 *Halloween.* He also guest-starred in several television productions (series and movies) including *The Bionic Woman, The Vampire* (one of his favorite roles), *Star Trek: The Next Generation,* and *Highlander.* His final film was Rob Zombie's *The Lords of Salem.* He died in 2012 at age 72.

Fans of *Night Court* will forever know Richard Moll as that show's kind-hearted though somewhat simple-minded bailiff, Nostradamus "Bull" Shannon, but considering his more than 150 acting credits, other audiences might know his name, face, deep voice, and stature—a whopping 6′ 8″—for plenty of other reasons. Among his many films, Moll appears with and without makeup in *Caveman, Evilspeak, Metalstorm: The Destruction of Jared-Syn, Ragewar* (a.k.a. *The Dungeonmaster), House, Galaxis, Evolution, Scary Movie 2,* and *Sorority Party Massacre.* On TV he plays animated characters in *Buck Rogers in the 25th Century, Fantasy Island, Highlander, Batman: The Animated Series* (as Harvey Dent / Two-Face), *Hercules: The Legendary Journeys, Babylon 5,* and *Spider-Man* (as Mac Gargan / Scorpion).

Anthony De Longis holds a black belt and is a master fencer, knife-thrower, and bullwhip handler. He appeared in the films *Circle of Iron* and *The Warrior and the Sorceress* (both with David Carradine), *Masters of the Universe* (in which he appeared as Blade and worked as Frank Langella's stunt double), *Wild Bill, Sinbad: The Battle of the Dark Knights,* and *Nightcomer,* as well as TV series such as *Logan's Run, Battlestar Galactica, The A-Team, V, MacGyver, Star Trek: Voyager,* and *Grimm.* He also worked as a sword master, fight choreographer, and horse-action consultant on a number of film and television projects, including *Batman Returns, Indiana Jones and the Kingdom of the Crystal Skull,* and the reality-TV series *Deadliest Warrior.*

Of Algonquin descent, Robert Tessier—nicknamed "Cueball"—got his start in the low-budget 1967 motorcycle film *The Born Losers* (the first of the *Billy Jack* series). He became typecast as thugs, bouncers, and gang members in numerous films and TV shows from the '70 to the '90s, including movies like *The Velvet Vampire, Doc Savage: The Man of Bronze, The Deep, Starcrash, The Cannonball Run, The Lost Empire,* and *Nightwish,* and TV shows such as *Buck Rogers in the 25th Century, The Incredible Hulk, Manimal, The A-Team, The Fall Guy,* and *Amazing Stories.* He also played Mr. Clean in a commercial that had him thrusting his head through a bathroom wall. He died in 1990 at age 56 (but not from that).

Danish actress and singer Nina van Pallandt has led one of the most interesting and downright bizarre lives of anyone in this volume. Born Nina Magdelene Møller, she married Baron Frederik van Pallandt in 1960 (becoming a baroness). Not long after their wedding, they formed the musical duo Nina & Frederik. After they divorced in 1975, Nina's now ex-husband relocated to the Philippines, remarried, and got involved with a notorious Australian crime syndicate, an affiliation that might have led to his homicide some years later. Nina, on the other hand, became the mistress of Clifford Irving, the man jailed for forging a biography of Howard Hughes. Got all that? As for her acting career, Nina appeared in the films *The Long Goodbye*, *Cloud Dancer*, and *Jungle Warriors*, as well as TV series such as *Ellery Queen*, *Bring 'Em Back Alive*, and *Tales of the Unexpected*.

> A LUSTY EPIC OF REVENGE AND MAGIC, DUNGEONS AND DRAGONS, WIZARDS AND WITCHES, DAMSELS AND DESIRE, AND A WARRIOR CAUGHT BETWEEN.

Prolific character-actor and occasional TV-director Jeff Corey was blacklisted in 1951 as a member of the Communist Party. It took years for him to recover from that. He became a well-known acting coach and also appeared in films like *Frankenstein Meets the Wolf Man*, *Beneath the Planet of the Apes*, *The Premonition*, *Battle beyond the Stars*, and *Conan the Destroyer*, as well as in TV series like *The Outer Limits*, *The Wild Wild West*, *Star Trek*, *Rod Serling's Night Gallery*, *The Six Million Dollar Man*, *Babylon 5*, and the animated *Spider-Man* (as Silvermane). He died in 2002 at age 88.

Joseph Ruskin held the honor of appearing onscreen alongside every televised *Star Trek* crew through the early 21st century. He also appeared on TV in *The Twilight Zone*, *The Outer Limits*, *Voyage to the Bottom of the Sea*, *Get Smart*, *Rod Serling's Night Gallery*, *Mission: Impossible*, and *Max Headroom*. His last appearance was on an episode of *Bones*. He died in 2013 at age 89.

Probably best known for his role as Frank Fontana on TV's *Murphy Brown*, actor-director Joe Regalbuto also appeared on *Mork & Mindy*, *Street Hawk*, *Amazing Stories*, *Night Court*, *Magnum P.I.*, and *Ghost Whisperer*.

Another actor who spent most of his time on the small screen, Russ Marin popped up on *Planet of the Apes*, *Isis*, *The New Adventures of Wonder Woman*, *Battlestar Galactica*, *The Greatest American Hero*, and *Beauty and the Beast*. He also appeared in *The Dark*, *Body Double*, *Stitches*, and *Deadly Friend*. He died in 2005 at age 70.

Barbados native Earl Maynard worked as a bodybuilder, professional wrestler, actor, director, and film producer. He appeared in the movies *Black Belt Jones*, *The Deep*, *Circle of Iron*, and *The Nude Bomb*.

George Murdock appeared in more than 180 TV and film projects, including as recurring characters Lt. Scanlon on *Barney Miller* and Dr. Salik on *Battlestar Galactica*, as well as *The Twilight Zone*, *The Six Million Dollar Man*, *Knight Rider*, *Star Trek: The Next Generation*, *The X-Files*, and *Torchwood: Miracle Day*. He also appeared in the films *Earthquake*, *Star Trek V: The Final Frontier* (where he portrayed "God" ... or did he?), *The American President*, and *Looney Tunes: Back in Action*. He died in 2012 at age 81.

Known for a number of villainous roles, especially in westerns, John Davis Chandler appeared in *Shoot Out*, *Walking Tall Part II*, *The Outlaw Josey Wales*, *Adventures in Babysitting*, *Phantasm III: Lord of the Dead*, and *Carnosaur 2*. He died in 2010 at age 75.

Emily Yancy was in *Blacula*, which is almost awesome enough cred on its own, but she also popped up in TV series, including *Starsky and Hutch* and *MacGyver*, as well as in movies like *The Abyss*.

Christopher Cary started as a dancer but opted for acting after moving to LA from England in 1955. He landed a series of TV roles on *The Man from U.N.C.L.E.*, *Batman*, and *Garrison's*

Gorillas, in which he was a series regular. He also appeared in the films *Marlowe, Raid on Rommel, The White Buffalo, Lifepod,* and *Watchers.* He died in 2000 at age 69.

Another longtime veteran of American TV, Peter Breck wore a number of cowboy hats through the '60s in *Have Gun—Will Travel, Wagon Train, Black Saddle,* and *Maverick.* He continued to work on television and in films, including Canadian-produced avant-garde fare like *Terminal City Ricochet* and *Highway 61,* as well as B-grade horror and action films like *The Unnamable II: The Statement of Randolph Carter* and *Enemy Action.* He died in early 2012 at age 82.

Alan Caillou (born Alan Lyle-Smythe) had supporting roles in *Pirates of Tortuga, Five Weeks in a Balloon, The Devil's Brigade, Beyond Evil,* and *The Ice Pirates.* He also appeared in several TV series, including *Thriller, The Man from U.N.C.L.E., Daniel Boone,* and science-fiction spoof *Quark,* in which he played "the Head." He even wrote a number of paperback novels, most of them thrillers, under pseudonyms, including the name "Alex Webb." He died in 2006 at age 91.

For those of us who grew up in the 1970s, Jay Robinson was Dr. Shrinker on *The Krofft Supershow,* but he had already built up quite a career, appearing as Caligula in the films *The Robe* and *Demetrius and the Gladiators* and playing in *The Virgin Queen,* an episode of *Star Trek,* and *Everything You Always Wanted to Know About Sex* (*But Were Afraid to Ask).* He continued to work in television in *Buck Rogers in the 25th Century, Voyagers!,* and *Tales of the Gold Monkey,* and in movies like *Shampoo* and *Bram Stoker's Dracula.* He died in 2013 at age 83.

Simmy Bow appeared in *Mansion of the Doomed, Rocky, End of the World, Laserblast,* and *Pee-wee's Big Adventure.* He died in 1987 at age 66, just a few months before the theatrical release of *Beetlejuice,* his final film.

Some—or maybe just one or two—of you best remember Reb Brown as Steve Rogers, a.k.a. Captain America, in two made-for-TV-movies from the late '70s. His first role was in the serpentine thriller *Ssssss.* He later went on to appear in television shows like *Kolchak: The Night Stalker, The Six Million Dollar Man,* and *Hercules: The Legendary Journeys,* as well as the TV movie *Brave New World* and films such as *Yor, the Hunter from the Future* (in which he played the lead); *Howling II: Your Sister is a Werewolf; Space Mutiny;* and *Night Claws.*

Lennie Geer appeared in tons of TV westerns as well as movies like *Zombie of Mora Tau* and Ralph Bakshi's *The Lord of the Rings.* He died in 1989 at age 74.

Charlie Messenger appears in *Under the Rainbow, Friday the 13th Part III,* and *Chained Heat.*

Christina Nigra appeared in *Twilight Zone: The Movie* and *Cloak & Dagger.*

Buckley Norris first guest-starred in an episode of *Project U.F.O.* and then went on to appear in *Alligator* and *Alligator II: The Mutation, Highlander* and *Highlander: The Source,* and *Waxwork* and *Waxwork II: Lost in Time.*

Gina Smika also turned up in *The Slumber Party Massacre.*

Corey Burton's voiceover career is way too extensive. Look him up.

6 DEGREES OF SORCERY

Director Albert Pyun has acknowledged the influence of Richard Lester's *The Three Musketeers* on *The Sword and the Sorcerer,* as well as Japanese *chambara* movies like the *Zatoichi* and *Lone Wolf and Cub* films. The blades of Talon's sword launch and even sound like model rockets.

Ban Urlu looks a bit like Calypso from the *Pirates of the Caribbean* films, with just a hint of Grace Jones. When Xusia rises from his goop-filled casket, the music is reminiscent of John Williams' "Well of Souls" composition featured in *Raiders of the Lost Ark*. A recurring piece of music heard throughout the film and often accompanying Talon also sounds rather similar to the *Indiana Jones* theme.

Ban Urlu's cry, "It lives," clearly echoes, "It's alive," as said by Victor Frankenstein (Colin Clive) in the 1931 *Frankenstein*. The dying, plague-ridden messenger wears blood-soaked armor like many of the dying and dead in *Excalibur*. The establishing shot of Ehdan looks remarkably like stock footage of Istanbul (not Constantinople), probably because it is.

When Talon and his band of mercenaries enter the tavern, they epitomize a fantasy roleplaying-game adventure-party seeking adventure at the local inn. Talon himself is Conan-meets-Indiana-Jones-meets-Han-Solo. Craccus the innkeeper looks a bit like writer-director Garry Marshall. He also offers Talon and Alana dates: another reference to *Raiders*, perhaps?

The camera dollying across the faces of the Red Dragon Archers is similar to a move in *Excalibur* at the start of the Battle of Camlann. Rodrigo bears an undeniable resemblance to a young Viggo Mortensen of *The Lord of the Rings* films. When Rodrigo examines the room beyond the crumbling wall in the sewer, he speaks yet another line from *Raiders* in saying to Talon, "You go first."

Talon's order to the prisoners to get up and not grovel harkens back to God's same order to King Arthur and his men in *Monty Python and the Holy Grail*. Talon rushes up a flight of stairs in the dungeons and quickly retreats with a group of soldiers in pursuit, just like Han Solo fleeing from the squad of Stormtroopers aboard the Death Star in *Star Wars*.

Phillip looks a bit like Will Ferrell, even down to the curly golden locks. Alas, Captain Morgan looks *nothing* like his rum-hawking namesake. Perhaps it's the hair!

Talon's crucifixion harkens back to Conan's. The image of Cromwell in his elaborate costume and tall-spiked crown has inspired images in fantasy and gaming artwork for years, especially images of liches, for some reason. Alana's wedding veil is very similar to the one worn by Guenevere in *Excalibur*. Like Dar in *The Beastmaster*, Talon also gives up a crown to seek pastures new.

SHATTERING THE ILLUSION

For five years, no one took an interest in the script, not even producer Brandon Chase *(Alligator)*, but all that changed with the release of *Excalibur* in April of 1981. Albert Pyun was only 26 when, encouraged to direct the film despite never having directed a feature before, he storyboarded the entire movie, resulting in several thousand illustrations.

The film had a budget of $4 million. Shooting took place in the summer of 1981 around the Los Angeles area, including Bronson Canyon in Griffith Park for exteriors and Laird International Studios in Culver City. Several major studios offered to distribute it, but in fear of losing control, the producers opted to handle distribution themselves via Group 1 International Distribution Organization Ltd.

The movie opened in April and made almost $2 million that weekend. The June 16th issue of *Variety* reported that the movie had already grossed $14 million by the time of publication.

In the end, the adventure that no one wanted to produce took in almost $37 million in the US alone, making it the 18th most successful film released in 1982 and the most profitable independent film of the year.

The film credits a crew of ninety stunt actors. The most notorious tale to rise out of the production regards the horrifying death of stuntman Jack Tyree. The scene in question—Cromwell pushing Xusia over the cliff—appears in the film. Tyree took the fairly routine fall incorrectly and plummeted to his death—or perhaps the edge of the cliff gave way slightly when he leapt, altering his trajectory. A dedication to Tyree appears at the end of the credits. Pyun has said that after this incident, he found directing stunt action incredibly difficult and even, at times, overwhelming.

Sword trainer and actor Anthony De Longis refers to his portrayal as Rodrigo as his final "ingénue" role. He was in his mid-30s at the time of filming.

MUSIC OF THE MINSTRELS

Prior to *The Sword and the Sorcerer*, David Whitaker took responsibility for the scores for *Scream and Scream Again*, *Dr. Jekyll & Sister Hyde*, *Vampire Circus*, and *Death Wish II*. His *Sword* score brazenly harkens back to the work of Erich Wolfgang Korngold (*The Prince and the Pauper*, *The Adventures of Robin Hood*, and *The Sea Hawk*, to name a few), and at times has a twinge of classic Western as well as more than a few nods to *Raiders of the Lost Ark*. It received a nomination for a Saturn Award in 1983 for Best Music but lost to John Williams' music for *E.T.: The Extra-Terrestrial*.

In 1982, Varese Sarabande released an official soundtrack on vinyl containing fifteen tracks. A limited, extended CD release came out in 1999 from Super Tracks Music Group and contained twenty-three tracks. Expect to pay through the nose for a copy, but it is exciting stuff that makes for great background music at your game table.

THE SAGA CONTINUES

In March 1982, Pinnacle Books—publisher of a short-lived line of American editions of *Doctor Who* novelizations—published the official novelization of the film. Written by Norman Winski and based on the original screenplay by Tom Karnowski, John Stuckmeyer, and Albert Pyun, the book remains pretty faithful to the film, although it occasionally goes into oddly graphic detail in certain sexual situations. You might want to keep this one out of the hands of the kiddos. The novelization also contains additional material, including Talon's sibling rivalry with his brother, the fact that King Richard not only designed the sword himself but also created it as a blessed artifact capable of healing injuries (including Talon's hands, post-crucifixion), and Talon and Mikah's childhood together in Ehdan. This last element seems to have been shot as well, the film has a credit for young Mikah (Anthony Farrar).

> THE GREATEST DUEL EVER FOUGHT BETWEEN DEATHLESS COURAGE AND ENDLESS EVIL!

This R-rated movie also, perhaps surprisingly, spawned a line of cheap toys—produced by Fleetwood in 1983—like the kind of stuff you would find on the racks at your local pharmacy. The line included figure packs featuring heroes and bizarre monsters, and playsets.

Several attempts to bring a sequel to the screen began with an announcement in May 1982, which claimed that the second part of the story had a $12 million budget, that it world shoot in Germany, and that it would be on screens in time for Christmas 1983. Titled *The Serpent's Orb*, it would have dealt with dragon creatures unleashed by a villainous sorceress, but ultimately Pyun wasn't too eager to rush back into the genre, because the first film had taken so much time and effort.

In 1994, Pyun attempted to mount a "loose" sequel, titled *City of Blood*, set in ancient Rome, but it proved too expensive, because he wanted to shoot in Tunisia or Morocco. The following year, Walter Manley's new company Palisades Communications teased "Brandon Chase's" *The Sword and the Sorcerer Part II* in promotional materials distributed at Cannes, but nothing came of that, either. *City of Blood*, or at least a project possessing the same title, floated back onto Pyun's radar in 2002. This time it was to star Dolph Lundgren and introduce vampires into the mix. Again, the idea never got off the ground.

Finally, in 2007, *Tales of an Ancient Empire* received a green light. It went in front of cameras in 2008. In 2010, the long-awaited sequel—announced as "coming soon" in the original film's credits—went direct to DVD with a slightly different title: *Abelar: Tales of an Ancient Empire* (instead of *Tales of the Ancient Empire*). Written by long-time Pyun collaborator Cynthia Curnan, directed by Pyun, and starring Kevin Sorbo (TV's *Hercules: The Legendary Journeys, Kull the Conqueror*), Michael Paré *(Eddie and the Cruisers, The Philadelphia Experiment)*, and Ralf Moeller (TV's *Conan, The Scorpion King*), the film returned to the fantasy world of the original but with a shoestring budget, a few mediocre performances, and some lackluster imagery all lovingly shot on digital video. The brief appearance of Lee Horsley as Talon does make it a proper sequel, however. As if all that weren't convoluted enough, a sequel to the 2010 film, teased as *Red Moon*, is in discussion, with some footage for it already shot on location during production of *Abelar: Tales of an Ancient Empire*.

As of this writing, the Region 1 DVD of the original film is out of print, although an Australian (Region 4) "Collector's Edition" came out in 2012, featuring exclusive commentary by Pyun and film critic Chris Gore.

TAKE UP THY SWORD!

THE TRI-BLADED SWORD (MAGIC WEAPON)

In the hands of someone of lesser strength or skill, the tri-bladed sword is an unwieldy beast, weighing as much as a two-handed sword when all three blades are present. Thus, a median penalty applies to all melee attacks. Someone with the skill—and superior strength—can use it to deal damage equivalent to that of a broadsword.

Two spring-loaded flanking blades are what make the tri-bladed sword special. The wielder activates them by depressing release catches positioned on the grip just below the cross-guard. When launched, the blades rocket through the air and can strike targets up to fifty feet away, each inflicting damage equivalent to that of a two-handed spear. Once both blades fire, the remaining center blade functions as a standard longsword. Lastly, the wielder can withdraw the grip from the base of the central blade, revealing a short sword... ideal for sneak attacks!

As for the weapon's enchantments, it magically regenerates its missing blades... over a significant period of time: hours or even days. Also, this regenerative force expands into the body of the weapon's owner, with a healing energy capable of curing minor wounds per the game system's equivalent healing spell.

THE FILM'S DESTINY

No question, *The Sword and the Sorcerer* is Albert Pyun's best film, which is shocking, considering it's his first. Sure, *Cyborg* and *Nemesis* have their fans, but for some reason all the elements coalesced back in 1982 to produce a glossy, entertaining romp that, in this author's opinion [SAW], ranks right up there with *Conan the Barbarian*. I remember watching it on a Beta videocassette with my family shortly after its video release and finding myself creeped out by Xusia's rise from his casket of bubbling slop, but what 14-year-old (the ideal target age) at the time wouldn't have been thoroughly fascinated and entertained by such a film, especially if he also had a collection of *AD&D* books sitting on modular brown-plastic bookshelves, along with a few boxes of Grenadier miniatures (lovingly painted with Testors™ enamels), a yellow velvet pouch of dice, and a constant desire to ignore homework in favor of preparing for roleplaying game sessions? *The Sword and the Sorcerer* is a pulpy, genuinely fun blend of action, magic, and boobies. (Sorry, had to go there.) It is not to be taken seriously—the unwieldy and rather ridiculous tri-bladed sword should help in this regard—but treated as exactly what it was intended to be: a light-hearted romp. At that modest goal, the film absolutely succeeds and will leave you wanting more adventures featuring Talon and his band of mercenaries. Speaking of which, we already covered the realization of those desires in **The Saga Continues** section: a great example of why you should "be careful what you wish for."

THIS YEAR IN GAMING

TSR terminated the license for Judges' Guild—a publishing company founded on July 4, 1976—so that all existing and future products could no longer feature *Dungeons & Dragons* stats or even references. Because Judges' Guild was more or less founded on a publishing arrangement with TSR, this proved a significant blow. The company was out of business within three years.

Also noteworthy this year, anti-*Dungeons & Dragons* furor from religious-right organizations around the country reached a pop-culture fever peak, in some ways best signified by the network television premiere of CBS's TV-movie adaptation of Rona Jaffe's 1981 novel, *Mazes & Monsters*. (The network originally planned to title the movie *Dungeons & Dragons* but wisely avoided that legal wrangle.) It starred a young Tom Hanks. Despite its campiness and wild inaccuracies, it is actually surprisingly enjoyable even today. Hanks gives an impressive and memorable performance.

CONAN THE BARBARIAN

1982 • US • UNIVERSAL PICTURES • 129M • COLOR • R

WRITERS: John Milius And Oliver Stone
BASED ON THE CHARACTER CREATED BY: Robert E. Howard
DIRECTOR: John Milius
PRODUCERS: Dino De Laurentiis, Buzz Feitshans, and Raffaella De Laurentiis
MUSIC: Basil Poledouris
DIRECTOR OF PHOTOGRAPHY: Duke Callaghan
SPECIAL EFFECTS SUPERVISOR: Nick Allder
SPECIAL EFFECTS MAKE-UP SUPERVISOR: Frank Van Der Veer
SPECIAL VISUAL EFFECTS: Frank Van Der Veer
SPECIAL EFFECTS MAKE-UP: Colin Arthur
PRODUCTION DESIGNER: Ron Cobb
PRODUCTION ARTIST: William Stout
ART DIRECTORS: Pierluigi Basile And Benjamin Fernandez
COSTUME DESIGNER: John Bloomfield
TECHNICAL ADVISOR: L. Sprague De Camp
SPIRITUAL ADVISOR: Doctor Fred L. Rexer
ANIMAL HANDLER: Franciso Ardura
SNAKE TRAINER: Dr. Yves De Vestel Tiva
SERPENTS EXPERT: I.T.I. Ophiology
MASTER OF THE SWORD: Kiyoshi Yamazaki
SWORD MAKER: Jody Samson
STUNT COORDINATORS: Terry J. Leonard and Juan Majan
CAST: Arnold Schwarzenegger (Conan), James Earl Jones (Thulsa Doom), Max Von Sydow (King Osric), Sandahl Bergman (Valeria), Ben Davidson (Rexor), Cassandra Gaviola (The Witch), Gerry Lopez (Subotai), Mako (The Wizard), Valerie Quennessen (The Princess), William Smith (Conan's Father), Luis Barboo (Red Hair), Franco Columbu (Pictish Scout), Leslie Folduary (Sacrificial Snake Girl), Gary Herman (Osric's Guard), Erick Holmey (Turanian War Officer), Akio Mitamura (Mongol General), Nadiuska (Conan's Mother), Jorge Sanz (Young Conan), Jack Taylor (Priest), Sven Ole Thorsen (Thorgrim), Kiyoshi Yamazaki (Sword Master), Pilar Alcón (Orgy Slave Girl, uncredited), Florencio Amarilla (Man, uncredited), John Milius (Lizard-on-a-Stick Vendor, uncredited), Ron Cobb (Black Lotus Street Peddler, uncredited), Dragon Dronet (Pit Fighter, uncredited), Donald Gibb (Osric's Guard, uncredited), Andrea Guzon (Breeding Woman, uncredited), and Corrie Jansen (Beautiful Woman Jumping to her Death, uncredited)

ON THE MAP

The story takes place in Robert E. Howard's fictional Hyboria, in roughly 10,000 B.C. We begin in Conan's homeland, Cimmeria, as he sets out on a journey that ultimately takes him to Shadizar in Zamora and then Thulsa Doom's temple stronghold in his Mountain of Power. One day Conan will reign over Aquilonia . . . but we're not there yet.

OUR STORY SO FAR

With his village destroyed and his family slaughtered, a young barbarian goes through great hardship in slavery, becomes an accomplished pit fighter, meets friends and an equally capable female warrior and lover, and seeks revenge on the evil wizard who placed him on the path to becoming a man.

ALTERNATE VERSIONS

Some of the multiple cuts of the movie result from censorship in the UK that trimmed out scenes of animal-related violence and sexual content. The 1980s broadcast-network airing naturally trimmed the movie as well. On VHS videotape, Universal released two cuts of the movie running 115 and 123 minutes—neither as long as the theatrical version. An extended cut, available on DVD since 2000, includes additional character moments and an epilogue narration; this version also restores director John Milius's cameo appearance as a lizard-on-a-stick vendor and runs 131 minutes. Some dialogue and other variations pop up in European releases of the film. If you get the US Blu-ray, you're in for more surprises, because that cut differs yet again from the US DVD and the original theatrical version. It's confusing, all right. If you're a dedicated fan, you might just have to collect them all.

IT'S MAGIC

While much of this movie tends toward a more realistic depiction of an ancient time than many other films in this book, plenty of magic and supernatural influences point not only to the existence of sorcery but to the gods (like Crom) worshiped by the characters. In fact, one might wonder if Thulsa Doom is actually an incarnation of Set and not merely a warlock of some kind, because he can transform into a huge snake and is a thousand years old.

Other gods—which might or might not exist—range from the steel-obsessed Crom to Subotai's sky god and appear to derive from the elements and other parts of nature. Magic seems to hold sway over these beings, because you can fight back against the forces of Death itself, as Conan's companions do when he dies (for all intents and purposes) and specters set upon him, determined to drag him to an afterlife (presumably). The process of resurrecting him, which includes writing incantations all over his body and leaving him to bake for a night (kidding), is complex and difficult... but it works.

The witch who beds Conan seems to derive at least some of her magical energy from sex, which is nice work if you can get it. As with so many of our movies, blue appears to be the default color for this energy, although she also becomes a fireball that flies away into the distance.

THE QUEST FOR MEANING

As with many of this genre's movies, we witness the crumbling of old ways, the prospect of restoring them, or perhaps the dawn of an era with the glories of the past receding into the distance, marked by monuments and entombed artifacts like the ages of Middle-earth in a certain other fantasy saga. The film hangs its shingle early with the quote from Friedrich Nietzsche, "That which does not kill us makes us stronger." As we watch the forging of the sword—and as Milius and Schwarzenegger confirm on the DVD audio commentary—the entire film becomes a metaphor for crafting a perfect weapon, whether in a sword or of a man. Conan's experience tempers him like steel, but only because of Doom's actions, so the villain creates the hero and his own eventual demise, as

> THIEF
> WARRIOR
> GLADIATOR
> KING

in many other fantasy and superhero stories. Thulsa even refers to their relationship as one of a son and a surrogate father. In fact, this culture seems determined to create someone who will take it all down: training him in combat, building a perfect fighter, and instilling all the seething resentment in him that will one day turn against the establishment. Its members even teach him writing and make him smarter! The wheel serves as a form of natural selection, leaving only the strongest warrior alive, but even for those destined for greatness like the Cimmerian, his fall into the Atlantean tomb where sits another ancient king (which mirrors the shot at the end of the film) foreshadows his fate: Conan will one day be another discarded weapon of a bygone age.

Scourging, crucifixion, and resurrection create obvious parallels with Christ. Sadly, though, despite this film's revered status, it has disturbing thematic currents—not just in subtext but in text. In the aforementioned audio commentary, director and star hold court throughout, making misogynistic and homophobic jokes that lend further distaste to Milius's oft-stated main message of the film: that might makes right, especially when you're holding cold blue steel. Indeed, this movie and its "Riddle of Steel" are nothing more than a fantasy epic wrapped around an NRA pro-gun commercial . . . and guess which director is a board member of that organization? Perhaps not surprisingly, the runes on the sword declare that its wielder suffers no guilt when using it in the service of Crom, so the implication is that killing in the service of one's deity is A-OK. Symbols of civilization and social structure are condemned as corrupt or wicked in comparison to the anarchy of a barbarian's existence. Time to load up on canned goods and ammo? It's also no surprise, then, that the movie attacks anyone devoted to the cause of peace. Milius calls out the worshippers of Doom in the mock Woodstock sequence as "hippies," as though the word is poison. Doom, the only black character in the film, is a cult leader and monster. Is there a racial angle here, too?

As for women, we make plenty of jokes in this book about the often sexist nature of some of these films, but rarely does it seem quite as intentional and mean-spirited as it does here. Valeria might be a strong and independent warrior . . . but only until she falls in love with the hero, gives up that independence, and then dies. Although Conan's "lamentation of the women" quote remains one of the genre's most memorable, it seems to sum up what both he and Milius thought truly *was* best in life. In the commentary, Milius goes so far as to say that when male viewers hear Conan wax eloquent about women mourning, they're thinking, "I want to be like him." Count these two authors out, thanks.

WHO GOES THERE?

Arnold Schwarzenegger is a living legend whose iconic stature as one of the greatest film action-heroes of all time makes it difficult to summarize his career in a few lines. With a dubious beginning in acting after making the transition from bodybuilding—including multiple reigns as Mr. Universe and Mr. Olympia—he made the infamous *Hercules in New York,* an "official" debut in *Stay Hungry,* and an appearance as Mickey Hargitay in the TV-movie *The Jayne Mansfield Story. Conan the Barbarian* set him on the path to true and lasting Hollywood heroics, which continued with roles in *Conan the Destroyer, The Terminator, Red Sonja, Commando, Raw Deal, Predator, The Running Man, Red Heat, Twins, Total Recall, Kindergarten Cop, Terminator 2: Judgment Day, Last Action Hero, True Lies, Eraser, Batman & Robin, The 6th Day,* and *Terminator 3: Rise of the Machines.*

Following his third *Terminator* film and after years of diminishing returns on many projects, Schwarzenegger reinvented himself once again as "the Governator," serving as the governor of California from 2003-2011. Now that he's "bahk"... to acting (like we weren't going to make that joke?), Schwarzenegger is picking up where he left off, with roles in *The Expendables* and its sequels, the zombie film *Maggie, Terminator Genisys,* and a planned sequel to *Twins* called *Triplets* (introducing Eddie Murphy as another sibling for Schwarzenegger's and Danny DeVito's characters), not to mention taking up the steel once more... but we'll talk more about that in **The Saga Continues**.

Max Von Sydow is a film institution, known to generations of cinema fans for a variety of projects that include everything from esteemed productions by Ingmar Bergman *(The Seventh Seal)* to gleefully camp comic-strip adaptations *(Flash Gordon)*. Other film credits include *Wild Strawberries, The Greatest Story Ever Told* (in which he played Jesus), *The Exorcist, Three Days of the Condor, Voyage of the Damned, Exorcist II: The Heretic, The Adventures of Bob & Doug McKenzie: Strange Brew, Never Say Never Again* (as James Bond's nemesis Blofeld), *The Ice Pirates, Dreamscape, Dune, Hannah and Her Sisters, Ghostbusters II* (as the uncredited voice of Vigo), *Needful Things, Citizen X, Judge Dredd, What Dreams May Come, Minority Report, Rush Hour 3, Solomon Kane, Shutter Island, Robin Hood,* and *Star Wars: Episode VII—The Force Awakens.* He's also appeared on television in *The Diary of Anne Frank, Samson and Delilah, The Young Indiana Jones Chronicles,* and *The Tudors,* and was the voice of Esbern in the videogame *The Elder Scrolls V: Skyrim.*

Sandahl Bergman is the first in our cast who would return in a different role in the not-quite-*Conan* follow-up, *Red Sonja.* She also appeared in *Xanadu, She, Airplane II: The Sequel, Hell Comes to Frogtown,* and *Sorceress II: The Temptress,* and turned up on television in *Moonlighting, Cheers, Hard Time on Planet Earth, Swamp Thing,* and *Sliders,* and as the same character in two creepy episodes of the horror anthology TV series, *Freddy's Nightmares.*

Ben Davidson was a football player for three teams during his career and moved into acting with appearances in TV shows like *Banacek, CHIPs, Charlie's Angels, Fantasy Island, The Dukes of Hazzard, B.J. and the Bear,* and *Simon & Simon,* as well as the film *Necessary Roughness.* He died in 2012 at age 72.

Cassandra Gaviola was a regular on the TV series spinoff of *M*A*S*H,* was in *Trapper John, M.D.,* and also appeared on *Fantasy Island, Taxi,* and *General Hospital,* as well as in the movies *Night Shift* and *Dead by Dawn.*

Gerry Lopez is revered in the surfing world for his accomplishments and contemplative approach to the lifestyle. He made only a few other film appearances, including *Storm Riders* and *Farewell to the King.*

Mako was a ubiquitous presence on film and in television, appearing in movies like *Under the Rainbow, Conan the Destroyer, RoboCop 3, Highlander: The Final Dimension,* and *Pearl Harbor,* and TV series such as *I Dream of Jeannie, I Spy, The Time Tunnel, Kung Fu, Ironside, Mannix, Columbo, Wonder Woman, The Incredible Hulk, M*A*S*H, Fantasy Island, Bring 'Em Back Alive, Voyagers!, Quincy M.E., The Greatest American Hero, Kung Fu: The Legend Continues,* and *Charmed.* He was also the narrator of the animated series *Dexter's Laboratory* and lent his voice to the cartoon shows *Samurai Jack, Duck Dodgers,* and *Avatar: The Last Airbender.* He died in 2006 at age 72.

Valerie Quennessen was an acrobat as a child and started acting as a therapeutic attempt to overcome shyness. Her brief career included appearances in *Bolero* and *Summer Lovers.* She died in 1989 at age 31, due to a car accident.

William Smith has had a prolific career as one of those instantly identifiable faces on television and in film, often as a menacing figure. He started as a child actor, making an appearance in Universal's *The Ghost of Frankenstein,* but throughout the 1960s, '70s, and '80s, he turned up in western, action, and science-fiction series, also playing Falconetti in the *Rich Man, Poor Man* miniseries (both of them) and appearing in films like *Piranha, The Thing with Two Heads, Invasion of the Bee Girls, The Frisco Kid, Any Which Way You Can, Red Dawn, Hell Comes to Frogtown, Maniac Cop, Manosaurus,* and *Warriors of the Apocalypse.*

Luis Barboo began his career in westerns like *A Fistful of Dollars* and also appeared in *Where Time Began, Mystery on Monster Island,* and *Night of the Werewolf.* He died in 2001 at age 74.

Franco Columbu has shared a long friendship with Arnold Schwarzenegger, training alongside him as a bodybuilder and even standing as best man at the big man's wedding. He also appeared in *The Terminator, The Running Man,* and *Big Top Pee-wee.*

Erick Holmey returned (uncredited) in *Conan the Destroyer* and *Red Sonja.*

Akio Mitamura's few other film credits include *1941, Indiana Jones and the Temple of Doom,* and *Flight of the Intruder.*

Nadiuska spent most of her career prior to this movie in softcore fare.

Jack Taylor started his career on the classic television series *The Jack Benny Program* and later segued into Mexican horror films, the Jess Franco-directed *Count Dracula* starring Christopher Lee, *Female Vampire, The Ghost Galleon* (one of the *Blind Dead* movies), *Exorcismo, Where Time Began, Pieces,* and *The Ninth Gate.*

Sven Ole Thorsen spent years in the bodybuilding world and holds the record as Schwarzenegger's most frequent costar. After this movie and roles in *Conan the Destroyer* and *Red Sonja,* he continued to appear in action epics and cult hits, such as *Raw Deal; Lethal Weapon* and its second sequel; *Predator; The Running Man; Overboard; Red Heat; Twins; The Hunt for Red October; Last Action Hero; The Quick and the Dead; Mallrats; Eraser; Kull the Conqueror; The 13th Warrior;* and *Gladiator.* He also had a regular part on the TV series *Captain Power and the Soldiers of the Future* and lent his voice to the Danish animated parody *Ronal the Barbarian.*

Kiyoshi Yamasaki's only other acting credit came in *Red Sonja,* although he also served as sword master again for *Conan the Destroyer* as well as fight coordinator for *Dune.*

Revenge of the Nerds fans might best know Donald Gibb for yelling "Nerds!" at the top of his lungs, as the jock Ogre in the '80s cult classic and two of its sequels, but he also played in films like *Any Which Way You Can, Stripes, Meatballs Part II, Lost in America, Transylvania 6-5000,*

> OUT OF AN AGE UNDREAMED OF COMES THE BRUTE FORCE OF CONAN THE BARBARIAN.

Amazon Women on the Moon, Bloodsport, Bloodsport 2, and *Hancock,* TV shows such as *The A-Team, Knight Rider, Otherworld, Night Court, MacGyver, Quantum Leap, The X-Files,* and *Seinfeld,* and the *Zork: Grand Inquisitor* videogame. Now lots of television viewers know him as one of the gray-bearded "pillagers" from the Capital One credit-card commercial series.

6 DEGREES OF SORCERY

The Nietzsche quote comes from *Twilight of the Idols.* The forging-of-the-rings sequence at the start of *The Lord of the Rings: The Fellowship of the Ring* echoes the title sequence of this movie. The tale of Conan's father about Crom has some passing similarity to the tale of Prometheus. Conan's gladiatorial days mirror those of other heroes created by their enemies in games of violence, such as in the science-fiction film *Rollerball.*

Conan's legendary line about "the lamentations of the women" is a paraphrase from Genghis Khan. Several other elements of Conan's character and story also parallel aspects of that historic figure's life. Subotai was even the name of his general.

The Atlantean tomb resembles the later Egyptian crypt seen in *Raiders of the Lost Ark.* Another witch's cottage appears in *Brave* . . . but it sure does have a different occupant. Her diabolical laughter is a bit like that of the Deadites of the *Evil Dead* series.

Quite a few visual sequences honor the work of fantasy artist Frank Frazetta. Look for notable similarities in the orgy chamber, for example.

The Eye of the Serpent is one of many familiar "MacGuffins" in fantasy films, like the All-Seeing Eye in *The Thief of Bagdad* (which, as we note in that chapter, owes much to *Conan* and Robert E. Howard) and the Arkenstone in *The Hobbit: An Unexpected Journey.* The big snake might remind *Doctor Who* fans of the Mara, while a similar scene to the close-up shot of its eye opening turns up in the final moments of *The Hobbit: An Unexpected Journey.* Its keeper is also sad about its demise, as is the rancor-keeper in *Star Wars: Return of the Jedi.*

King Osric's difficulty with his daughter mirrors that of another Von Sydow monarch and his female offspring: Ming and Aura in *Flash Gordon* . . . prints of which carried trailers for this movie! Conan tries to spare Valeria from danger at one point, as Perseus does with Andromeda in *Clash of the Titans.*

We've seen plenty of heroes trudge through the snow, including *Superman.* The Tree of Woe is a none-too-subtle crucifixion followed by a magical resurrection. The spirits that try to collect Conan's soul resemble spirits in *Fantasia* and *Ghost.* Schwarzenegger dons similar war paint in his action romp *Commando.*

Maax's ziggurat in *The Beastmaster* echoes Thulsa's high-staired headquarters. Milius has said that the set, with its speech-ready parapet, puts Thulsa in the position of Hitler *a la* the work of Leni Reifenstahl.

Thulsa himself shares a name with Robert E. Howard's nemesis for Kull, but he's a very different character, more reminiscent of *Conan* antagonist Thoth-Amon. He has a cult status similar to that of the infamous Jim Jones. His following was partially based on the same Thuggee cult that inspired the villains in *Indiana Jones and the Temple of Doom*. (That word seems so familiar....)

The imprisoned princess sits at Thulsa's feet like Princess Leia in *Star Wars: Return of the Jedi* and is later chained as bait like Andromeda in *Clash of the Titans*. Columns fall like they do in the tale of Samson and in the Well of Souls in *Raiders of the Lost Ark*. Thulsa fires snake-arrows made rigid, like Moses transforming a snake into a staff in *The Ten Commandments*. How many times have we seen the funeral pyre scene in these films and others? The sword of Conan's father shatters like Narsil in *The Lord of the Rings: The Fellowship of the Ring*. Our hero holds up the villain's severed head like Perseus with the Medusa in *Clash of the Titans*. If you want to see Conan's Atlantean sword again, check out Schwarzenegger's recent comeback film *The Last Stand*, where it is briefly wielded not by him but by actor Luiz Guzman!

SHATTERING THE ILLUSION

Author Robert E. Howard followed the creation of his character Kull with the debut of this heroic Cimmerian in 1932 via short stories published in the pulp magazine *Weird Tales*. Partially inspired by Thomas Bulfinch's *The Outline of Mythology*, as well as the Cthulhu stories of H. P. Lovecraft, Howard crafted a fictional ancient world in which his barbarian could have adventures and introduced a character who would become a multimedia hero for decades. Other authors, like L. Sprague de Camp and Lin Carter, carried on with new *Conan* stories, but it took some time for the warrior to fight his way into film—and not before a defeat or two along the way.

Edward Summer was the first to try to bring Conan to the big screen, in the 1970s, hoping to spark a James Bond-style series, with at least six adventures planned in advance. Roy Thomas (Marvel Comics writer, responsible for that publisher's *Conan* comic-book adaptation) co-scripted a very faithful version of the Howard mythos, but it was shelved.

Then Oliver Stone drafted a screenplay, and Dino De Laurentiis entered the picture as primary financier. Early on in development, they hoped that legendary illustrator Frank Frazetta would serve as a designer or consultant, but when they could not make a deal with him, Rob Cobb became production designer, with the intention of avoiding the style of many previous movies of the genre by creating more of a Dark Age look than Greco-Roman. He also employed a number of Frazetta-style tableaux.

When John Milius came in as director (over other possible helmers who included Ridley Scott), he extensively reworked Stone's script, which would have set the movie in a post-apocalyptic timeframe instead of the Howard-faithful ancient one. From Stone's version of the tale, he also dropped a variety of creatures more akin to those in Ray Harryhausen's *Sinbad* adventures. Milius's vision combined elements of adventures written by past *Conan* authors and borrowed from previous films, such as *Seven Samurai*.

Sterling Hayden of *Dr. Strangelove* and *The Godfather* fame was cast as King Osric but had to drop out due to medical reasons, leaving the role open for Max Von Sydow. Such talented thespians among the cast, including James Earl Jones, were to provide support for less-experienced lead actors, such as dancer Sandahl Bergman and professional surfer Gerry Lopez (whose dialogue Sab Shimono ultimately re-dubbed).

And who else could be Conan? Although it's hard to imagine now, other choices included future Arnold Schwarzenegger action-hero rival Sylvester Stallone, Charles Bronson, and even Conan's dad, William Smith, whom Schwarzenegger knew as a child following Smith's bodybuilding career. But Schwarzenegger, as he appeared in *Pumping Iron,* attracted the production's attention and made the choice obvious.

Schwarzenegger signed for four films with a salary that would rise with every subsequent sequel and a percentage of profits. Schwarzenegger's relationship with De Laurentiis might not have gotten off on the right foot, though, due to a comment Schwarzenegger made about the producer's height, but the actor did bond with costar Jones as hoped, with Schwarzenegger helping Jones to stay fit during the production while Jones provided coaching on Schwarzenegger's performance.

The first filming took place in the UK at Shepperton Studios with the shot of an older Conan on his throne. It appears only briefly at the end of the film, but the scene originally ran longer and included Conan reading to the audience. Schwarzenegger was supposed to narrate the film beginning with this scene, but the powers that be had concerns about his accent. Even speech training with voice coach Robert Easton and Milius himself couldn't eliminate it. Schwarzenegger did, however, train to slim down and become a bit more athletic (beyond simple weightlifting), learned a variety of fighting styles, did his own stunts, and wielded multiple copies of two specially forged (unsharpened) swords that cost $10,000 each to fabricate. In fighting scenes, he used lighter-weight versions, saving the expensive, detailed ones for use as "hero" props in close-ups.

As with many of these movies, actors didn't escape unscathed. In addition to Schwarzenegger, Bergman also performed her own stunts, with both actors often in danger. Schwarzenegger hurt his back falling ten feet during the dog-chase scene, and a sword chopped off a piece of Bergman's finger!

Injuries among actors might be one thing, but the film also attracted the attention of the American Humane Association, which labeled the movie "unacceptable" when news of cruelty to animals such as horses, camels, and dogs filtered out during production. Environmentalists also took exception to the crew's alterations to the local landscape and required the production to pledge that it would return everything to its original state.

Most of the principal photography took place in Almeria, Spain, after production canceled initial plans to shoot in Yugoslavia due to concerns about the local political climate. Ironically, an attempted coup in Spain still plagued rthe filming, but cameras rolled on. A Madrid warehouse served as the local headquarters for the filmmakers and also as a soundstage for interiors, along with one other warehouse and an airplane hangar.

While the locale worked out well, the stunt performers tended to pad their parts by dying in overly dramatic ways. Milius eventually offered bonus pay if they would keep it simple and die quickly.

The movie made use of sets from other productions as well as historic locations, with marble shavings standing in for snow and eight large miniatures taking the place of buildings, with clever camera angles creating the illusion of scale. Not everything was small: builders constructed forty feet of the tower scaled by Conan's party in full size, as well as a $350,000 temple structure with 120 steps. When shooting wrapped, the production team burned the temple to the ground. Conan would have been proud.

Special-effects supervisor Nick Allder, a crane operator from *Dragonslayer*, utilized a motorized mounted camera system he had created on that film to shoot some of this movie's action sequences. Practical effects included body parts and beheadings partly overseen by make-up man Colin Arthur, who had previously worked at Madame Tussauds.

Only the front of the thirty-six-foot-long mechanical snake appeared in the film, because the rest of the construct didn't fit on the set. Schwarzenegger had to hit the right spot on the snake to explode it and release the blood for the beheading scene.

Doom's transformation employed a number of effects to create the illusion of his human form shifting into—eventually—that of a real live snake shot on a miniature set.

Milius kept a tight reign on optical effects, believing that they would add more of a note of fantasy to the film than he intended. For Conan's near-death experience with ghostly beings from beyond, however, a company called VCE—which had previously provided similar apparitions for *Raiders of the Lost Ark* and had also worked on *Dragonslayer*—and ILM teamed up to create the otherworldly struggle to save the barbarian's soul.

The studio delayed the film's release, originally planned for Christmas 1981, when censors balked at an edited version that they felt needed further trimming: more than ten minutes' worth. Audiences therefore missed seeing Conan's decapitated mother in close-up, for example, and the cuts required adjustments to the musical score. When previews began, though, audiences responded effusively. The studio even moved up the US opening to take advantage of the positive buzz.

The film made over $100 million and cemented Schwarzenegger as a rising action star, leading him one day to credit the role as "God's gift" to his Hollywood career. Conan conquered cinema, by Crom!

MUSIC OF THE MINSTRELS

Few other scores in this genre can compete with Basil Poledouris's bombastic, foreboding, propulsive, operatic, and ultimately triumphant soundtrack for *Conan the Barbarian*. So confident was Milius in Poledouris—they had worked together before—that he brought the composer in to develop the score purely from pre-production storyboards. Poledouris would continue refining it during shooting, visiting the set and finalizing his work based on a temp-tracked, edited version of the movie that Milius prepared by inserting a variety of classical pieces to provide Poledouris with the appropriate mood for each sequence. *Excalibur* nixed Milius's plans to base some choral elements on Carl Orff's *Carmina Burana* by beating him to the punch, so Poledouris employed a twenty-four-member chorus to create an original piece loosely translated into partially nonsensical Latin and based on *Dies Irae*, a Gregorian hymn from the 1200s. He completed the soundtrack in mono rather than stereo, the last such score to accompany a studio release of that caliber. The score had so powerful an impact that the music often appeared in other movies' trailers and temp tracks. Even negative critics of the film praised Poledouris's work, which stands the test of time. Varese Sarabande expanded upon the original soundtrack release, adding four tracks and nearly twenty minutes of music to the preceding twelve-track version.

THE SAGA CONTINUES

Although Schwarzenegger had signed for four movies, some discussion ensued of making a trilogy of films that would follow Conan's heroic journey: the first to illustrate his strength, the second to focus on the use of his sword, and the third to dwell on the consequences of his actions and life. A sequel did come out; you can read about it in the index. It didn't do well enough to allow for the third chapter . . . yet. (More on this later.)

Bantam published a novelization of the film in May 1982, co-authored by Lin Carter, L. Sprague, and Catherine de Camp. As for comics, Conan had beaten his film incarnation to that medium when Marvel brought the barbarian to its pages in 1970; its success certainly didn't hurt the eventual development of the film and Conan's more prominent place in pop culture. Initially written by Roy Thomas, with art by Barry Windsor-Smith, a color comic-book series titled *Conan the Barbarian* later gained the supplement of a more mature black-and-white magazine called *Savage Sword of Conan*, also written by Thomas, with art by John Buscema, among others. The comic books also spawned a newspaper strip that ran until about a year before the release of this film. When the time came, Marvel released an adaptation of this movie and later its sequel in two issues of its *Marvel Comics Super Special* series. (Two earlier issues had featured unrelated *Savage Sword of Conan* stories.) The same adaptation—scripted by Michael Fleisher and illustrated by John Buscema—also appeared as one of the publisher's Marvel Illustrated Books paperback volumes and is now one of the rarest releases in that line.

A $5 million, twenty-minute live stage attraction at Universal Studios Hollywood, *The Adventures of Conan: A Sword and Sorcery Spectacular,* ran for ten years, starting in 1983. It made use of Poledouris's music and treated audiences to an animatronic dragon that actually spewed flames and towered eighteen feet high!

Merchandise includes decades' worth of Conan-related memorabilia, but if we look specifically at tie-ins to this film (and its sequel) and not just material featuring the Conan character in general, we can narrow the range a bit and save our sanity at the same time. While there have been a number of Conan-themed videogames, the 1984 Datasoft release, *Conan: Hall of Volta*, most closely associated with this film (actually, its sequel). The box art showcased Schwarzenegger as seen in *Conan the Destroyer,* but it wasn't the most faithful tie-in, seeing as it featured a character who threw a "boomerang sword." Designers had first planned it as an unrelated game called *Visigoth*. The game, such as it was, was available for the Apple II and Commodore 64 as well as the Atari 400/800.

When one of Howard's characters finally made his way to tabletop gaming in 1984, it was Conan, thanks to a licensing deal made by TSR to release movie tie-in modules for their *Advanced Dungeons & Dragons* line. David Cook's *Conan Unchained* and Ken Rolston's *Conan Against Darkness!* featured Schwarzenegger photo covers and gained enough popularity to inspire an entire game built around the character. TSR followed up its 1985 release of the *Conan Role-Playing Game* with three more modules: Kim Eastland's *Conan the Buccaneer* and *Conan the Mercenary*, and William Carlson's *Conan Triumphant*. In addition, TSR published James M. Ward's *Conan the Undaunted* and Roger E. Moore's *Conan and the Prophecy* and *Conan the Outlaw*, which were *Endless Quest* books similar to the *Choose Your Own Adventure* series. Steve Jackson Games brought Conan over to the GURPs system in 1986 with an initial release, followed by four supplements.

Many later *Conan*-related games have returned to the original source material and might not have a direct connection to this movie, but but the legacy of the film looms large in almost every adaptation of the character, if only in the minds of fans and gamers. Recent examples of games include 2004's d20-based *Conan: The Roleplaying Game* from Mongoose Publishing, a 2006 collectible card game designed by Jason Robinette and released by Comic Images, a 2008 MMORPG from Funcom and Eidos Interactive called *Age of Conan: Hyborian Adventures*, and a 2009 *Age of Conan* boardgame from Fantasy Flight Games.

In one of the murkier stories related to the film, the Mattel toy company supposedly entered into a licensing agreement to produce a *Conan*-themed toy line in conjunction with the movie's release. Mattel then requested the agreement's termination in early 1982 after seeing the movie and realizing its violent tone did not suit their usual market. Immediately after that, however, Mattel debuted its *He-Man and the Masters of the Universe* action figures and playsets, sparking a lawsuit that Mattel won. *He-Man* lead designer Roger Sweet has gone on record as saying he devised the character and his cohorts in 1980 with partial inspiration from the work of Frank Frazetta (then again, Conan as a character certainly predates this), and some sources say that the *He-Man* line clearly moved into production parallel with the film and that there never was any such licensing agreement. This story seems to have evolved from fans speculating on the origins of a mysterious Wonder Bread promotion that offered a brown-haired prototype He-Man, later resurrected in the line under the name Wun-Dar. Meanwhile, who produced the *Masters of the Universe* feature film adaptation five years later? *Conan* executive producer Edward R. Pressman, the man who, as rumors claim, negotiated the toy deal in the first place: hmm. A short-lived *Conan* action-figure line did briefly turn up in 1984 from Remco. It was "compatible" with the *Masters of the Universe* toys and borrowed designs from some of Remco's other products.

So . . . about that third *Conan* movie . . . .

A long-awaited *King Conan* project reared its weary, crowned head from time to time, involving filmmakers like Milius, the Wachowski brothers, and Robert Rodriguez, but all seemed completely sunk to the depths of Atlantis by Schwarzenegger's transition to political life as governor of California in 2003. Through a convoluted series of rights and financial deals, a *Conan* project finally started up at Nu Image / Millennium Films, with Marcus Nispel directing and Jason Momoa *(Game of Thrones)* in the title role. The results of this "reboot" were less than spectacular. The film suffered post-release controversy when script doctor Sean Hood took to the web and candidly discussed the plagued production and its box-office failure.

> HE CONQUERED AN EMPIRE WITH HIS SWORD.
> SHE CONQUERED HIM WITH HER BARE HANDS.

Meanwhile, fans watched as Schwarzenegger left office and began plans to segue back into the world of movie making....

Writer-director Frank Darabont commented on his own proposal for a *Conan* film, which would return to the Howard material and feature his former *Walking Dead* star, Jon Bernthal, as a wittier, smarter barbarian, but let's face it: for fans there's only one Conan, and there can be no greater quest than the journey to a third and final *Conan* film, at long last fulfilling the promise of the older warrior sitting heavily on his throne, as teased at the ends of both films. One can complete even the most miraculous quests if one is courageous—and patient—enough.

Soon enough, everyone learned that Schwarzenegger's Hollywood comeback included revisiting the Cimmerian who helped make him an action star. Unlike the "reboot," the new project, titled *The Legend of Conan,* is a full-fledged studio production backed by Universal that will ignore both that 2011 movie and the 1984 sequel that so irked Schwarzenegger. Currently Chris Morgan is co-producing and co-writing the film, which one interview characterizes as "Conan's *Unforgiven.*" Morgan drew the actor back to the fold by promising that this project would be like catching up with an old friend. Further news revealed that at least three other original *Conan the Barbarian* actors will return alongside Schwarzenegger and that production will start in the fall of 2015. Co-producer Frederik Malmberg also expressed interest in involving the WETA team from the *Lord of the* Rings and *Hobbit* films. We'd recommend a thematic connection to Osric's speech about jewels ceasing to sparkle, gold losing its luster, the throne room becoming a prison, and the only thing left being a father's love for his child. Pair Conan with a son or daughter, and roll camera!

And so the one, the only, the original cinematic Conan will take up the sword again. (We do know that Schwarzenegger still has the Fangs of the Serpent dagger.) Speaking of which ....

TAKE UP THY SWORD!

THE SERPENT'S FANGS (WEAPON)

The dual, kris-like blades of this nasty-looking dagger contain vials of heart-seeking snake venom. A successful strike yields better-than-average damage (per a standard dagger), but a critical strike shatters the vials, envenoming the victim with a deadly toxin. In a very short time, the venom reaches the heart, causing death unless the victim successfully saves versus poison. Even with a save, the venom still inflicts devastating damage. While fanatical members of a well-known snake cult typically wield these daggers, assassins also highly prize them.

THE FILM'S DESTINY

This is the one, a film so revered, so cherished by the sword-and-sorcery and gaming fan communities that it is almost review-proof. Sure, we could talk about how some of the acting isn't exactly perfect (not including Schwarzenegger, who was, after all, born to play this part and acquits himself very well so early in his film career) or about how some of the effects haven't aged so well, but there's really no point in doing that. Although this book illustrates that the genre has a history stretching back much earlier than 1982, with several crucial films arriving in theaters in just the two years prior to *Conan the Barbarian,* this is the moment that sets in stone nearly everything about the modern conception of a sword-and-sorcery film. All the tropes of the hero journey, though in existence throughout the history of storytelling, take shape cinematically here, forged and tempered into the forms they bring to the present day.

This isn't to ignore the troubling thematic elements (for which we took the movie to task in the "Quest for Meaning" section), but if we review the film purely as an entertainment experience, and within the context of the genre we're celebrating, there really are few finer examples than this one. The creation of a hero has rarely been as directly drawn, exhilarating, and memorable, and few human beings on Earth could have embodied the essence of adventure and sheer strength in the face of unspeakable evil as Schwarzenegger. It's now hard, looking back at what we can see in the movie, to be as forgiving as perhaps we want to be, but we'll try: *Conan the Barbarian* is, flaws and all, a classic with truly artful imagery and is the benchmark for every pretender (and a few worthy successors) that followed.

THIS YEAR IN GAMING

The Warlock of Firetop Mountain, by authors Steve Jackson and Ian Livingstone, began development as *The Magic Quest*. Puffin Books—the children's division of Penguin—published it in 1982, with an impressive cover by illustrator Peter Andrew Jones, poster artist for *The Sword and the Sorcerer* and cover artist for the *Kult* RPG (Metropolis Ltd.), *Stormbringer* RPG (Chaosium), and the *Dungeonquest* boardgame (Games Workshop). This was the first of more than sixty solitaire roleplaying-game books in the *Fighting Fantasy* series. The plot had the player-reader take on the role of an adventurer on a quest to find the treasure of the warlock buried deep within Firetop Mountain. The initial volume spawned two book sequels, videogames, and a boardgame from Games Workshop. In late 2012, to celebrate the 30th anniversary of the series, Australian videogame studio Tin Man Games produced iPhone and Android versions of the *Fighting Fantasy* series, with Livingstone's blessing.

THE BEASTMASTER

1982 • US / WEST GERMANY • METRO-GOLDWYN-MAYER (MGM) • 118M • COLOR • PG

WRITERS: Don Coscarelli and Paul Pepperman
DIRECTOR: Don Coscarelli
PRODUCERS: Paul Pepperman and Sylvio Tabet
MUSIC: Lee Holdridge
PHOTOGRAPHED BY: John Alcott
SPECIAL MAKE-UP EFFECTS DESIGNED BY: William Munns
SPECIAL EFFECTS: Roger George And Frank Demarco
CONSULTANT SPECIAL VISUAL EFFECTS: Mike Minor
STUNT COORDINATOR: Steve Boyum
PRODUCTION DESIGNER: Conrad E. Angone
COSTUME DESIGNER: Betty Pecha Madden
DAR'S SWORD BY: Victor Anselmo
HEAD ANIMAL TRAINER: Boone Naar
CAST: Marc Singer (Dar); Tanya Roberts (Kiri); Rip Torn (Maax); John Amos (Seth); Josh Milrad (Tal); Rod Loomis (King Zed); Ben Hammer (Young Dar's Father); Ralph Strait (Sacco); Billy Jacoby (Young Dar); Janet DeMay (Witchwoman #1); Chrissy Kellogg (Witchwoman #2); Janet Jones (Witchwoman #3); Tony Epper (Jun Leader); Vanna Bonta (Zed's Wife); Kim Tabet (Sacco's Daughter); Daniel Zormeier (Winged Creature Leader); Jim Driggers and Mick Thibodeau (Hanging Priests); Paul Reynolds (Tiis); Monty Simons (Zed's Guard); Bruce Barbour and Diamond Farnsworth (Marauders); Linda Smith (Kiri's Friend); Henry Carbo (Man in Cage); Jonathan Gravish and Don Heyn (Death Guard Priests); Larry Randles (Death Guard Rider); Vince Deadrick, Sr. (Guard on Parapet); Tim Dunlavey (Young Villager); Jeremy Whelan, George Scott, Dale Shawver, Hugh Armstrong, Eddie Donno, Eddie Hice, Freddie Hice, Hank Hooker, Tom Huff, Richard Humphreys, Mike Kirton, Gary McLarty, and Fess Reynolds (Jun Priests); Blake Bolger (Infant Dar, uncredited); Derek Elmore (Baby Dar, uncredited); and Chuck Hicks (Boatman, uncredited)

ON THE MAP

Born in Aruk, Dar grows up in the village of Emir some distance away before returning to his homeland, with a stop along the way to an inviting waterfall and the lair of some seriously creepy winged creatures.

OUR STORY SO FAR

Dar, last of the Emirites, possessed of the incredible ability to communicate with animals, returns to his ancestral home of Aruk with his "eyes" (Sharak the eagle), his cunning (ferrets Kodo and Podo), and his strength (panther Ruh) to save the people from a fanatical high priest who has seized power. He must also defend them from the Jun horde with the help of trusted friend Seth, half-brother Tal, and new love (and possibly cousin) Kiri.

ALTERNATE VERSIONS

For its first release, the film was cut down to a running time of less than ninety minutes, seriously affecting the coherence of the story and eliminating vital explanatory material. That version is no longer in circulation. All home releases and cable airings derive from the superior "Director's Cut."

IT'S MAGIC

An intriguing dichotomy exists with the magic in this film, in that the forces of good have power via natural means—Dar's two-way communication with animals—and the forces of evil manipulate magic via unnatural methods, such as the creation of the Death Guards and stirring up trouble in a good old-fashioned cauldron. In fact, although Maax is our central evil wizard, he never really demonstrates abilities of his own. For the magical heavy-lifting, he relies on his witchwomen, who do their dastardly work with a combination of intonations and mystical substances like glowing blue liquid and eyeball rings. Blue fire accompanies many of their feats. When the eye ring takes damage, at least one of the witches recoils in pain as though it is somehow tied to her.

Maax also commands extraordinary loyalty from his priests and follows a program of regular child sacrifice to the god Ar, but it's unclear whether that accomplishes anything—refueling the witches' magical storehouse of energy, perhaps?—or if it's merely a tactic for keeping the people of Aruk frightened and defeated. He has unusual facial features that suggest he might have some affinity for animals himself, specifically birds, but he doesn't appear to share Dar's telepathic powers.

THE QUEST FOR MEANING

Not for the first or last time, this movie subverts the familiar theme of a hero returning to reclaim his birthright, when our lead character decides that he prefers the freedom of the road and the promise of greater challenges beyond the walls of his birthplace. The Beastmaster's affinity for animals also makes him the embodiment of ecological and environmental forces. His treatment at the hands of his father symbolizes humanity's fears of what it doesn't understand while it damns itself to destruction.

In the midst of all this high-minded thinking, the movie is a straightforward contest of wills between Dar and the manipulative Maax, presaged by the usual prophecies concerning a first-born son and a long-standing quest for revenge. Not one but two "boss" fights conclude the struggle and free the people of Aruk from subjugation. It's ironic that the act of stealing Dar from his mother and placing him in the belly of a cow, a crime perpetrated on Maax's orders, most likely gives him the powers that enable him to defeat Maax.

WHO GOES THERE?

Part of a creative family that includes actor Lori Singer (sister) and director Bryan Singer (cousin), Marc Singer made early appearances on the *Planet of the Apes* television show and the

> BORN IN THE FORM OF A MAN HE POSSESSED THE COURAGE OF A PANTHER THE CUNNING OF AN EAGLE THE POWER THAT MADE HIM MORE THAN A HERO OR LOVER. HE WAS LORD AND MASTER OVER ALL BEASTS.

miniseries *Roots: The Next Generations*. He garnered positive critical attention for his portrayal of blind musician Tom Sullivan in *If You Could See What I Hear* and became a genre icon via this film and his role as Mark Donovan, rebel leader, in the two 1980s *V* television miniseries and its one-season TV-series follow-up. He returned to the *Beastmaster* saga several times (more on that later) and also appeared in the recent *V* series remake (but not as Donovan) and in *Arrow*.

Tanya Roberts was the last of the Angels in the TV show *Charlie's Angels*. She went on to star in *Sheena: Queen of the Jungle* and *A View to a Kill*, and later had a recurring role on *That '70s Show*.

John Amos is best remembered as the long-suffering father in the TV series *Good Times*, a role to which he came after many other television appearances. He earned an Emmy nomination as the older Kunta Kinte in the miniseries *Roots* and went on to many more television roles, as well as appearances in films like *Coming to America* and *Die Hard 2*.

Rip Torn is a Hollywood legend as much for his real-life exploits as for his acting career, in which he quickly became known as an "actor's actor" through extensive television, film, and stage experience. Recent generations might know him best for his appearances in *Summer Rental*, *Defending Your Life*, *Freddy Got Fingered*, and the *Men in Black* movies, as well as the cable-TV series *The Larry Sanders Show*. He was also the voice of Zeus in the Disney animated film *Hercules*.

Rod Loomis was Paul Manheim in *Star Trek: The Next Generation* and turned up on *Jason of Star Command*, *Dynasty*, *Quantum Leap*, and *Stargate SG-1*. He also played Sigmund Freud in *Bill & Ted's Excellent Adventure*.

Ben Hammer appeared in the cult classic *Invasion of the Bee Girls* and is one of many recurring judges on the original *Law & Order* television series. He has a long list of other TV and Broadway roles stretching back to the 1950s, including *Mission: Impossible, Dragnet 1967, Police Woman, Police Story, The Six Million Dollar Man, Gemini Man, Charlie's Angels, The Incredible Hulk*, and *The A-Team*.

Ralph Strait turned up in a few '80s television shows, like *The Incredible Hulk* and *The Dukes of Hazard*, but horror fans recognize him as Buddy Kupfer from *Halloween III: Season of the Witch*. He died in 1992 at age 56.

Billy Jacoby comes from another prolific acting family and appeared in an *ABC Afterschool Special* as well as series like *Lou Grant, Galactica 1980, The Bad News Bears, Silver Spoons*, and *Parker Lewis*.

The most famous of the witchwomen, Janet Jones is married to hockey player Wayne Gretzky.

6 DEGREES OF SORCERY

The three witchwomen echo the classic image of the three witches toiling and troubling away in Shakespeare's *Macbeth*, as well as the Norns and Fates of folklore and mythology. A similar triad appears in *Clash of the Titans* and its remake.

Maax's ability to compel his priests to commit suicide is similar to the power Thulsa Doom wields over his people in *Conan the Barbarian*. Some of the scenes involving the witchwomen utilize POV shots that resemble camera work in the *Evil Dead* films. Dar's father makes a speech about Dar's abilities and destiny, reminiscent of Pa Kent's speech in *Superman*. Some of the sweeping landscape shots in Dar's journey resemble those in many other sword-and-sorcery epics, like *The Lord of the Rings* films. The sacs that hang in the lair of the winged creatures resemble the eggs in the *Alien* films.

The Death Guards are vaguely zombie-like. When they reach through the grating, they borrow that behavior from numerous zombie-themed films like the classic *Night of the Living Dead*. The same year that this movie depicted the placement of a slug/leech in the ear of a Death Guard in the making, *Star Trek II: The Wrath of Khan* had another earwig creature that controlled two Starfleet officers.

The witchwomen die, teleport, or transform themselves into white doves, leaving empty cloaks behind, like several Jedi in the *Star Wars* movies. Dar takes out one of Maax's priests with a backward sword thrust in much the same way as Ash fires his "boomstick" at a witch in *Army of Darkness*. Another fiery-gate confrontation takes place in *The Princess Bride*.

SHATTERING THE ILLUSION

Filmmaker Don Coscarelli planned to follow up his ultra-low-budget horror film, *Phantasm*, with a bigger-scale fantasy project very loosely based on Andre Norton's novel, *The Beast Master*. Norton's book and its sequels were set in a post-apocalyptic western world; the film bears virtually no resemblance to the source material apart from the notion of a central character as a wanderer with an affinity for animals. Inspired by their love of Ray Harryhausen's films and sword-and-sandal epics starring Steve Reeves, Coscarelli and company transplanted the Norton premise to a Bronze Age setting. Displeased with the dramatic departure from her work, Norton had her name removed from the film.

Coscarelli chose Klaus Kinski for Maax, but when the producers had a disagreement concerning Kinski's fee, the search went on. When Rip Torn met with Coscarelli, he informed the filmmaker that he was going to play the part as a "turkey vulture" and even oversaw the makeup artist's creation of the hawkish wax nose. Demi Moore tried out several times for the role of Kiri, but once again one of the producers overrode Coscarelli, and cast Tanya Roberts instead. That same producer also replaced the original animal trainer with a personal friend.

One of the great boons of the production was obtaining the services of cinematographer John Alcott, who had worked with Stanley Kubrick on *A Clockwork Orange, Barry Lyndon*, and *The Shining*, and as an additional photographer on *2001: A Space Odyssey*. His work on *Barry Lyndon* had involved a great deal of shooting by natural firelight, and he employed the same technique for much of this film's production to achieve the orange tones he wanted.

Vic Anselmo fashioned all of the film's bladed weapons, particularly the unique katana-scimitar hybrid that served as Dar's sword. A functional sword and not merely a prop, the weapon took Anselmo three weeks to craft, with some of the components ground out of solid brass. Sadly, the sword went missing during post-production, presumed stolen. More than thirty years later, its whereabouts are still unknown. Anselmo fashioned one copy of the original for Marc Singer's personal collection and would revisit the design in the 21st century. (See **The Saga Continues**.)

After more than twelve weeks of pre-production, shooting took place on a punishing six-day-a-week schedule, mostly in Simi Valley, California. Builders constructed the city of Aruk just off the freeway. A few sequences were filmed at Pyramid Lake a short distance from Los Angeles, and several shots of massive rocky landscapes—including the film's final scene—took the production to the Valley of Fire State Park in Nevada.

Conrad Angone based most of his designs on research into ancient cultures, including the distinctive thatching between dwellings that characterizes the city of Aruk. While the ziggurat-like temple mimicked the pyramids of Tikal and consisted of a foreshortened construction on location surrounded by a very small number of actual huts shot to create the illusion of a more extensive town, many other seemingly exterior sequences were shot indoors, like those of the winged creatures' lair.

Most of the film's greatest challenges stemmed from the use of animals. The sequence involving young Dar, played by Billy Jacoby, and the bear was originally planned for the tiger and might have been Dar's first encounter with Ruh. Jacoby's safety was in question when the tiger was brought in for the scene, however, so his on-set teacher removed him for the day. Josh Milrad wasn't allowed on set with the animals at all, requiring the production to use a stunt double in shots featuring the beasts and Tal in the same scene.

The golden eagle that played Sharak was so unwilling to fly that it had to be lifted into the air via a radio-controlled balloon and then released, forcing it to soar down. But the most infamous animal-related aspect of the production was the tiger painted black, as Dar's panther, Ruh. Tigers were supposedly more trainable than panthers, but the dye would wear off easily, especially around the tiger's face whenever it would drink, requiring them to spray touch-up paint throughout shooting. A long-standing story that the tiger later died from poisoning due to toxic paint is belied by the fact that it was a water-soluble dye. The Humane Society was also present during the making of the movie, so we can probably file the death of the tiger under "urban legend."

When some of the special-effects makeup proved too challenging for the existing crew, William Munns came in to fix the problem. Ironically, several years later he would be replaced on the crew of *The Return of the Living Dead* for a similar reason.

The final battle at the moat took seven cameras, more than a dozen special-effects technicians, and about sixty horses. A low-flying helicopter captured the last shot, of Dar and Kiri embracing at the top of a mountain. Watch closely, and you'll see that the two actors are actually holding each other close for fear of being blown off their perch.

The disagreements with one of the producers that affected early decision-making on the film also impacted its completion. Coscarelli and Pepperman were excluded from the editing process and were not involved in the selection of some of the less-successful optical effects.

As a marketing ploy for the film, the production team arranged for Roberts to appear in the October 1982 issue of *Playboy*, but due to a miscalculation in lead times between the release of the film and the magazine, that issue hit the stands months after the movie appeared in theaters.

> BORN WITH THE COURAGE OF AN EAGLE, THE STRENGTH OF A BLACK TIGER, AND THE POWER OF A GOD.

Accusations that the film was a rip-off of *Conan the Barbarian* are ludicrous, because *Conan* was released in May 1982 and *The Beastmaster* was already complete in August, giving the production team no time at all to have seen the competition in advance. Coscarelli and Pepperman also claim never to have read a thing about *Conan*, apart from the fact that a movie of that title was being made.

Although the film was not particularly successful in its initial release, it became a phenomenon in the early days of cable television. In fact, it became so ubiquitous that almost any time of the day or night you could turn on channels like HBO ("Hey, *Beastmaster*'s On") or TBS ("The *Beastmaster* Station") and catch a showing, hence the running gags about the network acronyms.

Coscarelli has attributed the enduring popularity of *The Beastmaster* to its extensive presence on cable and its plentiful supply of "beefcake." More surprising is Coscarelli's assertion that he was making a film for children, and that—despite its substantial quotient of partial nudity, violence, and extreme subject matter like child sacrifice—he believes it's a movie the entire family can enjoy.

Dino De Laurentiis certainly enjoyed *The Beastmaster*: he asked Coscarelli to helm *Conan the Destroyer*. Coscarelli refused the job, however, citing the sequel's bad script.

MUSIC OF THE MINSTRELS

Despite being one of the most melodic, majestic scores in this genre's history, with a tender romantic side as well as an epic heroic central theme, music from *The Beastmaster* is elusive on CD. A 2000 album appended some of composer Lee Holdridge's music for the TV series *Beauty and the Beast* to a complete soundtrack from this film, but the 1995 Italian CD titled *Kaan Principe Guerriero*, also featuring the complete released score, is easier to find today and worth the price. You can also find a suite of music from the movie on a Varese Sarabande collection of Holdridge compositions, including *Wizards and Warriors, Splash!*, and the *East of Eden* TV miniseries. Just picture yourself up on a high rocky peak, swinging your sword, as the orchestra swells to a crescendo. That is the spirit of adventure, my friend.

THE SAGA CONTINUES

Despite its cult status, nearly ten years passed before *The Beastmaster* saw a sequel. The 1991 follow-up, *Beastmaster 2: Through the Portal of Time*, paired Dar with a present-day LA sidekick played by Kari Wuhrer, turned Ruh into a regular striped tiger, and lacked any of the original movie's period feel and intriguing mythology. A third, TV-movie installment, *Beastmaster: The Eye of Braxus* (1996) tried to recapture some of that atmosphere, and even brought back Seth and Tal (played by different actors), but lacked the first film's production values. Ruh had also inexplicably become a lion. A 1999-2002 TV series, *BeastMaster*, started from scratch and gained a fan following. In a nod to the films, Marc Singer appeared in the third season as Dartanus, Dar's spirit-warrior guide.

A unique tie-in to the original film came along twenty years later, when Albion Swords made an arrangement with swordmaker Vic Anselmo to craft exact replicas of Dar's sword for purchase by collectors. He even replicated the scabbard with the circular symbol of Emir in precise detail.

TAKE UP THY SWORD!

BAT CREATURES (MONSTERS)

Attacks/Defenses: In the wild, bat creatures (also known as bat people) spend much of their time in a daily torpor state, their metabolic rates greatly reduced but their awareness as sharp as if they were fully conscious. Should prey draw near, a bat creature lashes out, requiring a check for surprise. With a successful attack, it engulfs its victim in curtain-like leathery wings. Only a successful opposed strength test frees the prey from this vice-like grip. Failure means horrific injury or death, as the creature quickly digests victim to bone with extremely corrosive acid.

Power: The creatures' corrosive digestive acid dissolves most organic materials, leaving behind nothing but slime-coated piles of metal and bone.

Details: Little is known about these mysterious creatures. Some researchers believe that they are sorcerous abominations summoned from the Abyss, while others suggest that they are the product of a hybridization between bats and humans. A certain level of intelligence and sophistication behind the creatures' animal-like exterior makes them capable of constructing objects (cages and so on) as well as worshipping a bird god. Though their methods of attack and consumption are swift and brutal, ultimately they are nonaggressive and content to be left alone, at peace, and in silence.

THE FILM'S DESTINY

Given this film's omnipresence on cable for so many years, rare is the fan of genre entertainment who hasn't seen it. One could even argue that because of this, the film's influence on subsequent sword-and-sorcery movies, as well as gaming and pop culture in general, might be more widespread than more exalted films like the original *Conan the Barbarian*. Part of the movie's charm—of which it has much—is that it does an excellent job not only in creating a sense of an entire ancient world of which we're getting merely a glimpse, but also in shaping a unique, macabre mythology with magical powers, creatures, and cultures that all fit together into a seamless whole. An almost dreamscape quality to the proceedings makes sense, because Coscarelli's previous work was the surreal nightmare known as *Phantasm*.

> THE EPIC ADVENTURE OF A NEW KIND OF HERO.

Another endearing aspect of the film is its enthusiastic and childlike lead. Marc Singer's Dar is almost unlikeable at times, especially in his treatment of Kiri, but besides the too-easy answer that this is a man behaving within the limits of his culture and time, he's also a kid who never had a chance to grow up. As a child playing at being a man—one who has been shunned by many, including his own father—he is a lonely and confused outcast. His real heroism lies in rising above all that to do what's right, no matter what.

And does he have style! Whether he's racing up those steep steps, wooing a Trov warrior with the help of his panther pal, or rolling over the back of an opponent during a sword fight, his soul, though tortured, finds joy in adventure and irresistibly draws an audience's admiration. He has ample support in the comely and capable charms of Tanya Roberts and the coiled anger and ferocity beneath a good-humored surface embodied by John Amos—and opposition in the loathsome villainy of Rip Torn's avian antagonist. There's also no underestimating the contribution of the majestic musical score, which lifts a seemingly low-budget affair to near-epic grandeur. With extreme and almost comic-book-like violence, and dialogue that blends heightened language with a few contemporary, casual turns of phrase, *The Beastmaster* is just about the perfect package.

THIS YEAR IN GAMING

Iron Crown Enterprises (I.C.E.) released a boxed *Rolemaster* set collecting *Arms Law, Character Law, Claw Law,* and *Spell Law* together in one kit. The box contained seven booklets (including *Spell Law, Spell Law—Of Channeling Book I, Spell Law—Of the Essence Book II,* and *Spell Law—Of Mentalism Book III*): a set of supplemental material for use with *Advanced Dungeons & Dragons,* promoted on the box as "A complete set of Fantasy Role Playing Guidelines." It offered alternative options for character creation, combat, and magic, and included a set of percentile dice. It retailed for $38 US.

THE LAST UNICORN

1982 • US / UK / Japan / West Germany • Rankin/Bass Productions / ITC Films
92m • Color • G

Screenplay By: Peter S. Beagle (based on his novel)
Directors: Arthur Rankin, Jr., and Jules Bass
Producers: Arthur Rankin, Jr., and Jules Bass
Music And Lyrics: Jimmy Webb
Songs Performed By: America. Additional vocals by Jeff Bridges and Mia Farrow.
Director of Photography: Omoto Hiroyasu
Production Designer: Arthur Rankin, Jr.
Character Design: Lester Abrams
Cast: Alan Arkin (Schmendrick), Jeff Bridges (Prince Lir), Mia Farrow (Last Unicorn / Lady Amalthea), Tammy Grimes (Molly Grue), Robert Klein (The Butterfly), Angela Lansbury (Mommy Fortuna), Christopher Lee (King Haggard), Keenan Wynn (Captain Cully / Harpy), Paul Frees (Mabruk), Rene Auberjonois (The Speaking Skull), Brother Theodore (Ruhk), Don Messick (The Pirate Cat), Jack Lester (Hunter #1 / Old Farmer / Cully's Man), Nellie Bellflower (The Tree), Edward Peck (Jack Jingley / Cully's Man), and Kenneth Jennings (Hunter #2 / Cully's Man)

ON THE MAP

Starting in an enchanted forest where it's always spring, the last unicorn's adventures take her to a distant seaside tower ruled by King Haggard after an encounter with a traveling magical menagerie.

OUR STORY SO FAR

When a unicorn discovers she might be the last of her kind, she embarks on a quest, with the help of a nebbishy magician, to find out what happened to the other unicorns. Her mission becomes a journey of self-discovery when she takes on human form, learns the meaning of love, and faces the possibility of permanently shedding her equine identity forever.

ALTERNATE VERSIONS

Two distinctly different versions of the film each omit and include material that the other version does not. The home-video/DVD version cut a handful of "damns" and "hells" in an apparent effort to "clean up" the film, but you get the original audio as well as the altered version on the Blu-ray release.

IT'S MAGIC

You'd think that magic could get you anything you desire, but it's not that easy. For one thing, much of the magical world of *The Last Unicorn* is shielded from those who would abuse its powers. For example, most people cannot see the immortal unicorns as anything other than ordinary mares. Only those who search and trust can penetrate that illusory cloak and see the amazing creatures within.

Unicorns who change into human form also face great risk, in that experiencing mortal emotions—especially sorrow and its physical manifestation, crying—can trap them in that dying form and cause them to go mad. Some humans, like Schmendrick, can achieve great things with faith and a pure heart, but others use magic for corrupt purposes—like Haggard, who calls upon the elemental Red Bull, or Mommy Fortuna, who disguises animals and imprisons them for profit. The real beauty is in nature and its purity . . . except for those annoying butterflies. What is with them, anyway?

THE QUEST FOR MEANING

This film follows the same basic quest structure as so many of its genre companions, but with a twist. Because the unicorn is not seeking an object but her fellow creatures and knowledge of their fate, her search is more profound than the usual "collect an item, complete the task" mission. In fact, because her transformation introduces her to love and a deeper understanding of humanity, the *real* quest in *The Last Unicorn* is about identity and what makes us all who we are. This third-person narrative therefore tells a story with a distinctly first-person focus.

As for the message in this picture, while some find spiritual or religious symbolism in the story (the unicorn as Christ, the bull as Mithras), the more apparent theme is environmental: destruction of the natural ecological balance by industrialization. The unicorn's purity and her harmonious existence with nature stand for all that is good and Gaia-friendly, while the Red Bull, relentlessly chasing down the poor creatures, belching steam and glowing like the embers of a coal furnace, is as direct an embodiment of mechanized factories poisoning the atmosphere and raping the land as any in this book. (See *The Lord of the Rings* films for more on this theme.) Mommy Fortuna's bewitched zoo is also a commentary on the evils of imprisoning animals for the amusement of humans. This film features a twist on the common theme of magic passing from existence, because its conclusion restores the unicorns to the world and staves off the transition to the modern era.

WHO GOES THERE?

By the time Alan Arkin became familiar to filmgoers with roles in *The Russians Are Coming, the Russians are Coming* and *Wait Until Dark*, he had already made his mark in improv comedy, on stage, and as the co-writer (with the Tarriers) of one version of "The Banana Boat Song." He also appeared in *Inspector Clouseau, Catch-22, The Seven-Per-Cent Solution, The In-Laws, Simon, Chu Chu and the Philly Flash, Bad Medicine, Edward Scissorhands, The Rocketeer, Glengarry Glen Ross, Gattaca, Little Miss Sunshine, Get Smart, The Muppets,* and *Argo*.

Part of a Hollywood acting family, Jeff Bridges first appeared in his father Lloyd Bridges' TV series, *Seahunt*, and later established himself as a reliable film presence in *The Last Picture Show, King Kong, Heaven's Gate* (well, maybe not this one), *Against All Odds, Starman, Jagged Edge, Tucker: The Man and His Dream, The Fabulous Baker Boys, The Fisher King, The Vanishing, Wild*

Bill, The Big Lebowski, Iron Man, True Grit, and *Seventh Son.* Many fans remember him best as Kevin Flynn / Clu in *TRON* and *TRON: Legacy.*

Mia Farrow is one of those actors known as much for her private life as for her career. The daughter of director John Farrow and actress Maureen O'Sullivan, and romantically linked or married at one time or another to Frank Sinatra, André Previn, and Woody Allen, Farrow has occupied tabloid covers as often as cinema screens. She appeared in *Rosemary's Baby, The Great Gatsby, The Haunting of Julia, Death on the Nile, A Midsummer Night's Sex Comedy, Zelig, Broadway Danny Rose, Supergirl, Radio Days, Crimes and Misdemeanors,* and the remake of *The Omen.*

Tammy Grimes was the original Molly Brown, coincidentally, on Broadway, and has had an extensive stage career. She also made appearances on a variety of TV series during the '50s and '60s and voiced Albert in the Rankin/Bass Christmas special, *'Twas the Night Before Christmas.*

Robert Klein is mostly known as a comedian and stage performer, although he has made appearances in films like *The Owl and the Pussycat, Hooper, Radioland Murders,* and *Sharknado 2: The Second One,* as well as television shows like *Murder, She Wrote; Law & Order;* and *Sisters.*

Angela Lansbury kicked off a massive media career with an Oscar-nominated film debut in *Gaslight* and went on to appear in *National Velvet, The Picture of Dorian Gray, Samson and Delilah, The Court Jester, The Manchurian Candidate, Bedknobs and Broomsticks, Death on the Nile, The Pirates of Penzance, The Company of Wolves, Nanny McPhee,* and *Mr. Popper's Penguins.* TV viewers know her best as Jessica Fletcher from *Murder, She Wrote.* Some might recognize her voice as that of Mrs. Potts in Disney's *Beauty and the Beast.*

We feel confident stating that Christopher Lee was one of the greatest actors who ever lived, with a career of such weight and scope that attempting to encapsulate it here would be lunacy. Generations of fans came to know him by a variety of iconic genre roles, including Hammer's bloodthirsty Count Dracula, James Bond's golden gun-wielding foe Scaramanga, the *Star Wars* prequels' suspiciously named Count Dooku, and—of course—Saruman in *The Lord of the Rings* film trilogy and two of the subsequent *Hobbit* movies. A frequent collaborator with director Tim Burton as well, with roles in *Sleepy Hollow, Corpse Bride, Charlie and the Chocolate Factory,* and *Dark Shadows,* Lee was an elegant, literate man with a deep respect for his craft and for fantasy in general: one of the greats in every sense. He died in 2015 at age 93 ... far too soon.

Son of legendary comic actor Ed Wynn, Keenan Wynn distinguished himself as a character-actor and voice performer in film and television. His often brusque demeanor enlivened films like *Dr. Strangelove or: How I Learned to Stop Worrying and Love the Bomb, Stagecoach, Finian's Rainbow, The Devil's Rain, Orca, Laserblast, Piranha,* and *The Clonus Horror,* and television shows like *Twilight Zone, Kolchak: The Night Stalker,* and *The Bionic Woman.* He also voiced the Winter Warlock in Rankin/Bass's *Santa Claus Is Comin' to Town.* He died in 1986 at age 70.

Star Trek fans know Rene Auberjonois best as Odo in *Star Trek: Deep Space Nine* and as

A TREASURED FANTASY CLASSIC OF INCOMPARABLE CHARM! THE MAGICAL FANTASY ADVENTURE BASED ON THE BESTSELLING BOOK.

Colonel West in the extended cut of *Star Trek VI: The Undiscovered Country*, but his career has spanned the stage as well as television and film, with notable roles in films like *MASH*, *King Kong*, *Eyes of Laura Mars*, *Where the Buffalo Roam*, and *Batman Forever*, and TV shows such as *The Bionic Woman*, *Man from Atlantis*, *The New Adventures of Wonder Woman*, *Charlie's Angels*, *Benson*, *Judging Amy*, and *The Librarians*. In recent years he has also done extensive voice work, for *Justice League*, *The Looney Tunes Show*, *Pound Puppies*, and many more.

Brother Theodore was the bizarre stage persona of Theodore Gottlieb, whose talk-show appearances were legendary for their surreal blend of comedy and confusion, but for a certain generation he was the voice of Gollum for the Rankin/Bass productions of *The Hobbit* and *The Return of the King*. His last film appearance was in *The 'Burbs*. He died in 2001 at age 94.

Don Messick is another prolific voice-actor with countless credits that helped shape childhoods for generations. During his decades in the business, he voiced the likes of Droopy, Boo Boo Bear, and Ranger Smith from *Yogi Bear;* Astro from *The Jetsons;* Scooby-Doo; Papa Smurf; and Ratchet and other Transformers. He died in 1997 at age 71.

Jack Lester was radio's *Sky King* and also worked on Rankin/Bass's *The Flight of Dragons*. He died in 2004 at age 89.

Nellie Bellflower lent her voice to two other Rankin/Bass fantasy features: as Eowyn in *The Return of the King* and as Danielle in *The Flight of Dragons*. She also worked on the *Thundarr the Barbarian* TV show.

6 DEGREES OF SORCERY

The Amalthea of Greek myth was a goat that fed Zeus when he was on the run from his father Kronos. In gratitude, the Olympian made one of her horns into the Horn of Abundance.

Ruhk's riddle is from *Alice in Wonderland*. The Robin Hood legend is directly referenced as a myth, with Schmendrick conjuring images of the outlaw and his Merry Men. That tree sure does remind us of Divine from the rather more adult-themed films of John Waters.

It's interesting that Haggard makes special note of Amalthea's throat; after all, he *is* Dracula. Much of Haggard's part of the plot mirrors that of another Lee character, Saruman from *The Lord of the Rings* trilogy, including his imposing tower, his penchant for raping the natural world, and his fatal fall.

The unicorns riding back on the crests of ocean waves resemble the river taking the shape of horses when Arwen rides with an injured Frodo in *The Lord of the Rings: The Fellowship of the Ring*. Listen closely, and you'll hear Godzilla's roar in the dragon scene. This doesn't count as a pop-culture connection in the same vein, but just try to watch this movie today without thinking, "Red Bull gives you wings."

SHATTERING THE ILLUSION

Peter S. Beagle had always wanted to write an original fairytale. His central idea was as simple as a unicorn going on a quest with some kind of companion, and the story evolved from there. A painting of unicorns and a crimson bull created by his cousin's spouse, a Spanish artist, inspired him to include the Red Bull as an antagonist.

Beagle long resisted a film adaptation of this 1968 novel, even turning down *Peanuts* television-special veterans Lee Mendelson and Bill Melendez. He didn't want to work with the Rankin/Bass company, either, but when he spoke with their negotiators, they won him over.

Rankin/Bass remains one of the most beloved production companies for its incomparable contribution to pop culture via three decades of holiday classics like *Rudolph the Red-Nosed Reindeer* and *Santa Claus Is Comin' to Town*. Although it accomplished many of its best-known television specials via a form of stop-motion puppetry dubbed "Animagic," *The Last Unicorn* was one of many traditional two-dimensional animated projects. This film was, perhaps appropriately, the company's last theatrical release.

Many of the voice artists featured in the film worked with Rankin/Bass on other productions, but for the principal roles, the goal was to cast well-known actors whose names could help sell the movie: a practice known to fans of Disney's animated features. In the case of Christopher Lee, he was already as much an aficionado of Beagle's work as he was of J. R. R. Tolkien's. (More on that in *The Lord of the Rings* chapters.) While recording his role as King Haggard, Lee kept a personal copy of the book at hand, with passages marked that he felt must be included in the film.

Perhaps the easiest casting process was for the role of Prince Lir. Jeff Bridges contacted the producers and offered to take part for no fee at all, although they did pay him. Bridges also suggested that his friend Jimmy Webb might be the right man to handle the musical score. Rankin and Bass were thrilled to get Webb and had no criticism to offer when he played them his entire composition for the movie.

The participation of the band America is one of the most distinctive elements in the shaping of the final film, but it wouldn't have happened had Beagle been involved in the decision. (There's a pattern emerging here.) His memory of America consisted of his daughter playing their hit song, "A Horse with No Name," over and over until he despised it. Although he would not have agreed to letting them sing in the movie, he has admitted that he was glad he wasn't consulted, because he thought their contribution worked very well.

Japan-based Topcraft, later known for its work on *Nausicaä of the Valley of the Wind* and now called Studio Ghibli, handled the animation. This accounts for the hybrid nature of the film, which features character designs familiar from other Rankin/Bass productions but Amalthea herself drawn in an anime-influenced style. Don Duga designed the rather aggressive tree after a cherry tree near his home in Long Island, and Irra Verbitsky styled the beginning of the film on a tapestry she had seen at the Cloisters in New York. According to Rankin, the movie garnered Rankin/Bass's most positive critical response in the studio's history.

MUSIC OF THE MINSTRELS

One of the most memorable—and for fans, most cherished—aspects of *The Last Unicorn* is the melancholy, contemplative score provided by Jimmy Webb and America. German fans made it the best-selling album of 1983 there, but so far the US has never seen a release. The German album features original vocalist Katie Irving instead of Mia Farrow. What is it about the lack of fantasy-film soundtracks in the States, anyway?

THE SAGA CONTINUES

Of course the novel preceded the film. Although no games came out in association with the movie, a game company called Last Unicorn operated for a little while at the turn of the most recent century, developing collectible card and roleplaying games based on properties like *Dune* and *Star Trek* before Wizards of the Coast acquired it . . . thus finishing the Red Bull's job and removing the last unicorn from the world.

Beagle has written several short stories that serve as partial sequels or as prequels to the original novel, with various characters returning. One such story, titled "Two Hearts," won Hugo and Nebula awards for Best Novelette in 2006. IDW Publishing adapted the film into a six-issue comic book in 2010 and published a collected edition in early 2012. Christopher Lee had long supported developing a live-action adaptation and had offered to play Haggard again in such a production.

For many years, Beagle became embroiled in a legal scuffle concerning unpaid royalties on sales of DVDs, settling the matter in 2011. He and his business partner followed that with a relaunch of *The Last Unicorn* brand via a "Screening Tour" involving a re-release of the original film in a 2K digital print with in-person Q&A appearances, running through 2015. Who knows: thanks to revitalized interest and possibilities for new merchandising, you might be able to get your very own plush Last Unicorns and Red Bulls to hang from your rearview mirror any day now.

TAKE UP THY SWORD!

THE RED BULL (MONSTER)

DEADLY CHARGE: This, the Red Bull's favored attack, requires enough space between the bull and the target for the bull to get up to charging speed. A successful attack knocks the target prone and inflicts crushing and fire damage.

FLAMING GORE: The Red Bull can attack multiple targets with its massive, flaming horns. A blow from these horns causes damage equal to a large club and might also set the target afire.

DRIVE: No creature can herd another like the Red Bull. A chosen target simply cannot escape the Red Bull's pursuit, no matter how hard it might try, except by sorcerous means. The Red Bull can match the ground speed of any target and does not tire until it delivers the target to the bull's chosen destination.

DETAILS: The origins of the Red Bull are lost to time. Because it appears very rarely, most people believe it to be a legend. Likely, a person or demon summoned it from its plane and bound it to service.

THE FILM'S DESTINY

A palpable scent of patchouli—and perhaps a few other herbs—suffuses *The Last Unicorn*, a modern fairytale crafted in the 1960s and bearing the imprint of that decade in more ways than one. While there's no denying the movie's

> THERE'S MAGIC IN BELIEVING!

all-ages appeal, it suffers from poor choices, mainly in areas of character and casting. For one thing, strange, random entrances by characters resist any explanation, like the cat who inexplicably talks, acts, and dresses like a pirate, and the incredibly annoying butterfly who flits in for anachronistic exposition and then departs, never to return . . . mercifully. For another thing, although Rankin/Bass had a great track record with casting superb voice talent in many of its other television and film productions, this movie suffers from serious miscasting of several main characters. Mia Farrow's thin, ethereal tones rarely waver in emotional temperature, but she still pretty well suits the creature she's playing. Her two male costars, however, are out of their depth. Alan Arkin gives it everything he's got, but he's really perfect only for characters with deeply imbedded cynicism or weariness about the world. As Schmendrick, he never convincingly captures the youthful wizard's exuberance. The worst offender, though, is Jeff Bridges, whose monotone delivery suggests he didn't have the slightest understanding of how to convey emotion using his voice alone. For this we'd also have to blame the directors for being unable to coax anything like an actual performance out of their romantic lead. Despite these missteps, *The Last Unicorn* has a melancholy, dreamlike charm that is hard to resist if you're willing to get caught up in the occasionally disjointed story, forget understanding all of the plot, and just let the visuals and music sweep over your consciousness . . . man.

THIS YEAR IN GAMING

The *Dungeons & Dragons* brand began to spread like wildfire, with the game's core elements, logo, and images appearing on tie-in merchandise beyond the gaming table. For the Intellivision game console, Mattel released the *ADVANCED DUNGEONS & DRAGONS Cartridge (*TSR Hobbies contractually required the inclusion of the word "Cartridge" and the capitalization), developed by APh Technological Consulting in Pasadena, California. Henry Thomas (Elliott from *E.T.: The Extraterrestrial*) and a very young Andrea Barber (Kimmy Gibler from TV's *Full House*) appeared in a 1982 TV commercial promoting the game. A second game, titled *Treasure of Tarmin, followed* in 1983.

In another development, toy company LJN beat rival Mego in securing the rights to produce a line of officially licensed *Dungeons & Dragons* action figures . . . or "Poseable Player Characters" and "Bendable Monster Adventure Figures." The line didn't launch until the following year.

THE DARK CRYSTAL

1982 • US/UK • ITC Entertainment / Jim Henson Productions / Henson Associates
93M • Color • PG

Screenplay: David Odell
Story: Jim Henson
Directors: Jim Henson and Frank Oz
Producers: Jim Henson and Gary Kurtz
Music: Trevor Jones
Director of Photography: Oswald Morris
Production Designer: Harry Lange
Art Directors: Brian Ackland-Snow, Terry Ackland-Snow, Charles Bishop, and Malcolm Stone
Conceptual Designer: Brian Froud
Makeup Department: Stuart Artingstall
Cast: Stephen Garlick (Voice of Jen); Jim Henson, Kathryn Mullen, and Kiran Shah (Jen Performers); Lisa Maxwell (Voice of Kira); Kathryn Mulle, Stephen Whitmire, and Kiran Shah—uncredited (Kira Performers); Billie Whitelaw (Voice of Aughra); Frank Oz, Dave Greenaway, and Kiran Shah—uncredited (Aughra Performers); Percy Edwards (Voice of Fizzgig); Dave Goelz (Fizzgig Performer); Steve Whitmire (Voice and Performer of Scientist); Brian Muehl (Voice and Performer of Ornamentalist / Dying Master); Barry Dennen (Voice of Chamberlain); Frank Oz (Chamberlain Performer); Michael Kilgarriff (Voice of General); Dave Goelz (General Performer); Jerry Nelson (Voice of High Priest); Jim Henson (High Priest Performer); Jerry Nelson (Voice of Dying Emperor); Dave Goelz (Dying Emperor Performer); Thick Wilson (Voice of Gourmand); Louise Gold (Gourmand Performer); John Baddeley (Voice of Historian); Bob Payne (Historian Performer); David Buck (Voice of Slave Master); Mike Quinn (Slave Master Performer); Charles Collingwood (Voice of Treasurer); Tim Rose (Treasurer Performer); Sean Barrett (Voice of Urzah); Brian Muehl (Urzah Performer); Barry Dennen, Patrick Monckton, and Sue Westerby (Voices of Podlings); Jim Henson, Frank Oz, and Dave Goelz (Podling Performers); Joseph O'Conor (Narrator / Voice of Urskeks); Jean Pierre Amiel (Performer of Weaver); Hugh Spight (Performer of Cook / Landstrider); Robbie Barnett (Performer of Numerologist / Landstrider); Swee Lim (Performer of Hunter / Landstrider); Simon Williamson (Performer of Ursol the Chanter); Hus Levant (Performer of Scribe); Toby Philpott (Performer of Alchemist); Richard Slaughter (Performer of Healer); Mike Edmonds, Peter Burroughs, Malcolm Dixon, Sadie Corre, Deep Roy, Jack Purvis, Gerald Stadden, Mike Cottrell, John Ghavan, Abbie Jones, Natasha Knight, and Lisa Esson (Additional Performers)
Alternate Title: *The Dark Chrysalis* (working title). The final title actually came about because of a misunderstanding. Conceptual designer Brian Froud thought Jim Henson had said "Crystal" instead of "Chrysalis" in one of their early conversations, so Froud's resulting logo design reflected that.

ON THE MAP

As the tagline states, it is another world in another time. Thra, a planet with three suns, is a world divided by a cracked crystal where a grotesque race—the Skeksis—rules with savage brutality, and the other race—a quiet and gentle race known as the Mystics—bides its time in the pursuit of peace and harmony with nature. The film depicts a number of diverse environments, including expansive deserts, rocky cliffs, serene rivers, and forests populated by all manner of strange creatures.

OUR STORY SO FAR

A thousand years ago, a great crystal cracked, splitting the world asunder. Now in a ravaged world ruled by a group of ten vicious Skeksis, two of the last surviving Gelflings, named Jen and Kira, must embark on a quest to recover the missing shard of the Dark Crystal and restore balance to their planet. The clock is ticking as all the elements come into position in time for the imminent conjunction of Thra's three suns.

ALTERNATE VERSIONS

The only officially released variation of note is the original home-video release of the film, which for some reason presents different end credits, placing them over a still of Aughra's face, versus the theatrical credits that rolled over the final shot in the film. In late 2013, a fan by the name of Christopher Orgeron presented a "new" and dramatically different cut of the film that he intended to be closer to the makers' original version. Drawing together material from a poor-quality work print on VHS tape originally assembled by Jim Henson and Frank Oz in 1981, several infamous deleted scenes previously presented on DVD, the original Skeksis dialogue, and alternate music composed by Vangelis, the resulting fan edit is a bit shaky but required viewing for hardcore fans.

IT'S MAGIC

The Mystics embrace some sort of ancient path in a shamanic way, with nods to Buddhism and even hints of the Force from *Star Wars,* while the Skeksis have embraced a form of warped technology that draws its power from the suns and the Dark Crystal. Aughra, Keeper of Secrets, remains neutral in her allegiances and also in her science, using it simply to monitor the world and the heavens and to help maintain balance.

THE QUEST FOR MEANING

The Dark Crystal, like most fantasy films or novels, tackles a number of real-world issues, from the Tolkien-esque struggle between nature and technology—especially the advance of industrialism—to racism, classism, and intolerance. All but the Skeksis are linked to the environment in such a way as to be an extension of it. Though the Skeksis and the Mystics are aspects of a whole called the Urskeks, the hippie-like Mystics reache back and within to peacefully coexist with nature, while the grotesque, lizard-bird Skeksis pushed all that away to become the walking definition of decadence and excess. The Skeksis exploit those linked to the world of Thra by perverting the natural order and forcibly drawing out the life force of others to arrest the aging process.

WHO GOES THERE?

The late Jim Henson really needs no introduction. He created the friggin' Muppets, for heaven's sake! To fans of the sword-and-sorcery genre, however, we should note that he also wrote and directed *Labyrinth* and was the executive producer of *The Witches* and the creator of the *Storyteller* television series. He died in 1990 at age 53.

Most know Frank Oz via his work with Yoda (as well as Miss Piggy, Fozzie Bear, Animal, and so on). He also directed *Little Shop of Horrors*, *The Indian in the Cupboard*, and the 2004 version of *The Stepford Wives*.

Stephen Whitmire is one of only two Muppeteers who have been involved in all the Muppet feature films. Though primarily known for his character Rizzo the Rat, since Henson's passing Whitmire has been the official voice of both Kermit the Frog and Ernie *(Sesame Street)*.

Welsh actor Stephen Garlick got his start as a child actor, appearing in films like *Carry on Doctor* and *Scrooge*. Some of you might remember him as Hippo Ibbotson from the 1983 *Doctor Who* adventure "Mawdryn Undead."

Since 2003, Kiran Shah has held the Guinness World Record as the "shortest professional stuntman currently working in films." He auditioned for the role of R2-D2 but lost out to Kenny Baker. His first role was in *The People That Time Forgot* in 1977. Since then, he has worked as an actor, stunt performer, and published poet. You can see him with and without practical and/or digital makeup in *Raiders of the Lost Ark; Star Wars: Return of the Jedi; Legend; Gothic; The Adventures of Baron Munchausen; The Lord of the Rings* trilogy (as a hobbit-scale double for Frodo and Bilbo); *The Chronicles of Narnia: The Lion, the Witch and the Wardrobe; Your Highness; The Hobbit: An Unexpected Journey* (as the goblin scribe and Bilbo's scale double once again); and *Doctor Who*.

Billie Whitelaw had been a performer since the early 1950s. Many recall her award-winning performance as Mrs. Blaylock in the original 1976 version of *The Omen*, but she had other impressive credits as well, including *The Flesh and the Fiends, Twisted Nerve, Frenzy, Quills*, and *Hot Fuzz*, her last film. She died in 2014 at age 82.

Percy Edwards contributed voice work to live-action and animated films like *The Plague Dogs* and *Labyrinth*. Though uncredited, he was also the voice of the xenomorph in the original *Alien*. He died in 1996 at age 88.

Barry Dennen has more than a hundred credits to his name as both a voice actor and an on-camera performer. He appears in *Jesus Christ Superstar, Madhouse, The Shining, Superman III*, and *Titanic*. His voice can be heard in numerous animated films and TV series, as well as a number of popular videogames.

The imposing (both in stature and voice) Michael Kilgarriff has played several towering characters on television, including four different roles in *Doctor Who* over three decades and with four different Doctors.

Jerry Nelson, another veteran Muppeteer, performed various iconic Muppets on the small and big screens, such as the Count *(Sesame Street)* and Statler *(The Muppet Show)*. He also took a few turns in front of the camera sans puppet, in films like *Nail Gun Massacre* and *Robocop 2*. He died in 2012 at age 78.

Portly character-actor Thick Wilson (not to be confused with Flip Wilson) appeared in *The Dirty Dozen, The Mirror Crack'd*, and *The Adventures of Bob & Doug McKenzie: Strange Brew*.

David Buck appeared in *The Mummy's Shroud, Deadfall*, and *Mosquito Squadron* and provided the voice of Gimli in Ralph Bakshi's animated take on *The Lord of the Rings*. He died in 1989 at age 52.

Accomplished actor and playwright Joseph O'Conor appears in *Gorgo, The Gorgon, Oliver!, Doomwatch, The Black Windmill, Elizabeth,* and *The Messenger: The Story of Joan of Arc.* He died in 2001 at age 90.

6 DEGREES OF SORCERY

The dying Master Mystic is akin to Yoda, and the sequence itself mirrors that of Yoda's passing in Luke's presence in *Star Wars: Return of the Jedi.* Even more obvious is the way that the deceased Mystic fades away, leaving his empty robes in much the same way as a Jedi. There are three suns in the sky versus Tatooine's two from *Star Wars.*

Your Highness would later intentionally echo Jen's flute-playing. Aughra uses her eye in much the same way as the Stygian witches from *Clash of the Titans,* as do Mr. and Mrs. Potato Head in the *Toy Story* films.

Speaking of Aughra, she speaks and imparts wisdom in a fashion similar to Yoda. Is it catching?

The flaming destruction of Aughra's home high atop a mountain peak harkens back to the burning windmill at the conclusion of the 1931 *Frankenstein.* The Skeksis' over-the-top dinner is reminiscent of the equally grotesque display in *Indiana Jones and the Temple of Doom,* sans monkey brains, chilled or otherwise. The Podling band, particularly certain examples of the puppeteering, resembles the Max Rebo Band from Jabba's palace in—again—*Return of the Jedi.*

When Jen first wanders into the ruins near the houses of the Old Ones, the music sounds like the score that accompanies appearances of the Lady of the Lake in *Excalibur.* No surprise there, however, because Trevor Jones did both scores!

The Landstriders are much like the fire mares of *Krull,* carrying the heroes on their backs and traveling great distances at high speed. The extraction of the Podling life essence via the crystal fragment seems reminiscent of Zarkov's treatment at the hands of General Kala in *Flash Gordon.* The Castle of the Crystal looks like, and is filmed similarly to, the Black Fortress in *Krull.* The walls of the pit above which the crystal is suspended have a similar appearance to the sets of Krypton and the Fortress of Solitude in *Superman* and the exterior walls of the aforementioned Black Fortress in *Krull.*

Kira can communicate with animals in the same way as Dar in *The Beastmaster.* The universe of *The Dark Crystal* is high fantasy in its purest sense, akin to roleplaying-game settings such as *Tékumel* (1975), *Jorune* (1984), and *Talislanta* (1987). A ritual designed to take place at the precise alignment of heavenly bodies mirrors that of the unfortunately named ritual in *Your Highness*... although in that film, it is the conjunction of moons versus suns.

The Halosians, an alien race appearing in the TV series *Farscape,* bear a striking similarity to the Skeksis—not all that surprising considering that the Jim Henson Company's Creature Shop handled them. The Arakkoa, a race of birdlike humanoids that dwells in Outland in the massively multiplayer online game *World of Warcraft,* also strongly resemble the Skeksis.

SHATTERING THE ILLUSION

From 1975 to 1976, Jim Henson, Frank Oz, Jerry Nelson, and a few others built and puppeteered characters for a series of rather odd sketches for *Saturday Night Live.* Known as *The Land of Gorch,* the sketches—although never particularly successful—allowed Henson and company to stray from the usual felt-and-ping-pong-eye creations of *Sesame Street* and create a gang of more realistic- and organic-looking monsters with

> ANOTHER WORLD,
> ANOTHER TIME . . .
> IN THE AGE OF WONDER.

scales, scraggly hair, taxidermy eyes, and a tad more character. Around this time, illustrations by Leonard B. Lubin that appeared in a 1975 edition of Lewis Carroll's *The Pig-Tale* also inspired Henson, especially those depicting crocodiles dressed in elaborate period costumes.

Thanks to Henson's licensing vice-president, Jerry Houle, Henson also discovered the fantastic art of Brian Froud. He soon contacted Froud to discuss a possible feature-film collaboration. Everyone gathered in New York and began to design a new world and construct prototypes to populate it.

Henson wanted to build a whole multi-tiered world in an organic fashion, from the rocks and plants up to the most intelligent races, and then tell a myth set in that unfamiliar landscape. The team even sketched out strange religions, some lost to this fabricated past, and realized them in the form of sculptures and carvings shown in the final film.

Froud sculpted a number of maquettes and models, often drawing from his previously produced and published work, including his unique and noteworthy trolls, which clearly inspired the look of the Mystics. The easy way to tell a Froud troll from a Mystic is to count the number of arms: Froud trolls have two arms, Mystics four.

Conceptual inspiration for the individual Skeksis designs came from the Seven Deadly Sins: lust, gluttony, greed, and so on. Before the team settled on the name Skeksis, other possibilities included "Reptus" and "Karackt." Initially, Henson considered having the Skeksis communicate via unique sounds, but that idea eventually evolved into a complicated language combining ancient Greek and Egyptian, developed by linguist Alan Garner, who receives special thanks for his work in the end credits. Test audiences did not respond well to the unusual tongue, however, so all the dialogue was rerecorded in English. Much of the original language made it to the film's novelization and a 2013 fan-edit of the movie.

Early designs and sculpts of the Skeksis resembled fish creatures with a slight *Creature from the Black Lagoon* vibe, more than the eventual lizards or birds. It was Froud who initially suggested or even insisted on a larger size for the Skeksis, although Henson disagreed. In the end, Henson deferred to the team, because everyone else agreed with Froud. Ancient Canterbury cathedral banners somewhat inspired the fabrics of the Skeksis' elaborate costumes.

The mechanized puppet of the Chamberlain included twenty-one unique cable-controlled parts, including brows, eyes, eyelids, and beak. The Gelflings were troublesome from the start, because Henson insisted they be classical puppets. Wendy Froud (nee Midener), hot off *Star Wars: The Empire Strikes Back,* where she helped bring Yoda to life, came in exclusively to help fabricate them. At one point, Academy Award-winning makeup expert Dick Smith instructed Midener and others in the use of foam latex. In the end, the production team used an estimated 3,300 gallons of it. Aughra was sculpted by Henson veteran Lyle Conway and puppeteered by Frank Oz. She began her life as a wise "Earth mother" with one eye that looked outward and one that looked inward.

The work of Flemish Renaissance painter Pieter Bruegel the Elder inspired the Podlings—their appearance, costume, and environment—although the designers looked at naturally occurring objects, like potatoes, for additional ideas. The Podlings' language was based on elements of Serbo-Croatian.

Lobster dinners inspired the hulking Garthim; Froud often saved the cast-off lobster shells from their meals to use a trick similar to one Ray Harryhausen once used on a project. Designers rebuilt the suits several times to make them lighter for the performers.

While a number of somewhat complicated puppets represented the various background creatures and animated plants, when it came to living "food" for the Skeksis, production opted for dressing up small wind-up toys and releasing them once cameras rolled.

Filming began on May 4, 1981, at Elstree Studios in London, with Academy Award-winning cinematographer Oswald "Ossie" Morris, known for his live-action work in films such as *Moby Dick, A Farewell to Arms, The Guns of Navarone, Lolita, Oliver!,* and *Fiddler on the Roof* (for which he won an Oscar). Using a system called "light flex," which allowed for in-camera tinting of footage during shooting, he could adjust the tone of scenes to match the look of Froud's artwork. This was Morris's final film before he retired from the industry.

The film took roughly five years to complete, from early concept and pre-production to final cut. Its cast and crew grew from the nine people who first gathered in New York to a crowd of more than 500 by show's end. Many members of the company divided their time with the final season of *The Muppet Show*. Fortunately, both productions were being shot in London.

The film won the 1983 Saturn Award for Best Fantasy Film, beating *Conan the Barbarian, The Sword and the Sorcerer, The Secret of NIMH,* and *Zapped!,* and also received a Hugo nomination for Best Dramatic Presentation (but lost to *Blade Runner*) and a BAFTA nomination for Best Special Visual Effects (that went to *Star Wars: Return of the Jedi*).

MUSIC OF THE MINSTRELS

The Dark Crystal features a sweeping score by veteran composer Trevor Jones *(Excalibur, Labyrinth),* with the London Symphony Orchestra. Henson approached Jones, who was in his early 30s, after hearing Jones' work on *Excalibur*. Jones took the opportunity to experiment with the score and combined traditional orchestral arrangements with unusual period instruments like recorders, a double-flageolet (a side-by-side woodwind that allows for harmonies), and crumhorns (cane-shaped, capped reed instruments somewhat similar to bagpipes that emit a characteristic buzzing sound), as well as generous use of both Fairlight and Synclavier synthesizers.

Each group of characters in the film has its own sound. Fittingly, the themes of the Mystics and Skeksis combine into one at the end of the movie. Jones composed the Landstrider theme in celebration of the birth of his eldest daughter.

The soundtrack first came out on vinyl and cassette in 1982 on the Warner Brothers Records / HUM! label. That version included an exclusive poster featuring liner notes on one side and art by conceptual designer Brian Froud on the other, and it remains collectible.

Despite high demand and a handful of inevitable bootlegs, an authorized version of the score took eleven years to come out on CD, eventually seeing the light of day from Numenorean Music in 2003. The two-disc limited edition of 5,000 copies featured almost two hours of music—some of varying quality—and a twelve-page book of liner notes. In 2007, La-La Land Records released a single-disc "25th Anniversary Edition" with far superior sound. It has since gone out of print.

THE SAGA CONTINUES

The Dark Crystal was enough of a success—the highest-grossing release of 1983 in both France and Japan—that it merited a significant amount of tie-in merchandise. Marvel Comics published a sixty-page magazine-size adaptation as *Marvel Comics Super Special* #24, as well as a two-issue comic-book miniseries. David Anthony Kraft scripted the comic, with cover and interior art by Bret Blevins.

Owl Books / Henry Holt & Co. published a paperback novelization of the film, written by A. C. H. Smith, with a cover by Brian Froud. It featured eight pages of color stills.

Despite Henson dividing his time between *The Dark Crystal, Fraggle Rock, Sesame Street,* and *The Muppet Show*, he still managed to read the novelization manuscript and provide the author with twenty pages of notes. The notes appear in the deluxe hardcover reprint of the novelization from Archaia Entertainment. In 1983, Owl Books / Henry Holt also published a ninety-six-page behind-the-scenes book, *The Making of the Dark Crystal: Creating a Unique Film*, with text by Christopher Finch.

Perhaps the most memorable tie-in product was another book, *The World of The Dark Crystal*, a large-format, lavishly illustrated volume released in 1982, featuring full-color art by Brian Froud, complete with transparent vellum overlays and text by J. J. Llewellyn. It was a finalist for the 1983 Hugo Award for Best Non-Fiction Book, but it lost to a book about science-fiction author Isaac Asimov and soon went out of print . . . until 2003—during which time, collectors were buying copies for hundreds of dollars!

Two tie-in games came out in 1982, both published by Milton Bradley. The first was *The Dark Crystal Game*, a roll-and-move-style boardgame for two to four players that featured a brightly illustrated game board, several cards featuring items and characters from the film, pawns, and dice. The second was *The Dark Crystal Card Game* for three to four players, a hand-management style game featuring an unusual board and a deck of attractive cards, again depicting characters and items from the film.

In 1983, Sierra On-Line released *The Dark Crystal* computer game, designed by Roberta Williams (the *King's Quest* series, *Phantasmagoria*) for Apple, Atari, and home PCs. A simplified version of this game, titled *Gelfling Adventure* and designed by Al Lowe *(Leisure Suit Larry)*, came out the following year for younger audiences.

Grenadier Models, Inc., producers of several lines of metal gaming miniatures, including licensed lines for *Advanced Dungeons & Dragons, Call of Cthulhu, and Traveller*, released *The Dark Crystal Adventure Collection* under the brand name Pinnacle Products. Two boxed sets contained models of characters and items in the film.

Don Post Studios produced three latex pullover masks—Aughra, a "Pod peasant," and a Skeksis—all released in 1982. There were also lunchboxes, patches, posters, puzzles, trading cards, View-Master reels, a Read-Along Book and Record set, stickers, and more.

In 1997, electronic music duo The Crystal Method featured dialogue samples from the film's narration in the track "Trip Like I Do" on their debut album, *Vegas*. Canadian metal band Strapping Young Lad featured a track called "Skeksis" on their 2005 album, *Alien*. Even today, tie-in merchandise continues: new graphic novels, a limited manga series from Tokyopop, apparel, plush toys, action figures, collectible resin-statues, and even an announced *Dark Crystal Roleplaying Game* from Archaia.

As for a film sequel, the years have seen plans drawn up and scrapped numerous times. Brian Froud has provided consultation on more than one occasion, and a number of techniques from traditional puppetry to CGI have been considered. Most recently, The Jim Henson Company, along with publisher Grosset & Dunlap, launched a writing competition to find the author of a new *Dark Crystal* prequel novel that could lead to a new film. They selected J. M. Lee's "The Ring of Dreams" as the winner. As of this writing, IMDb still has *The Power of the Dark Crystal* marked as "in development." Some speculate that the film will tell the story of how the crystal cracked.

TAKE UP THY SWORD!
CRYSTAL CRUSTACEANS (MONSTER)

These monstrous black isopods—a large hybrid of crab and rhinoceros beetle—often become guards, raiders, or battlefield warriors. Their thick, spiky carapaces give them almost impenetrable defenses against most mundane edged and blunt weapons, but they do appear to be especially vulnerable to magical attacks made by artifacts from the time of the ancients.

Though the monsters have little intelligence, they can obey simple orders to go forth and raid, kidnap, or destroy. If defeated, they fall to pieces, revealing nothing within their hollow shells. Perhaps they are animated constructs like golems and not living beings at all.

THE FILM'S DESTINY

The Dark Crystal is unique among sword-and-sorcery films in a number of ways. From its amazing—and *total*—cast of nonhuman characters to its alien world design, it remains embedded in the public consciousness to this day. It was the introduction for many to the incredible art of Brian Froud, which in turn has fueled Froud's own commercial endeavors, including art books, calendars, and oracle card decks. Audience admiration has also ensured the success of various spinoffs, like the ongoing comic-book series, numerous fan sites, and perhaps a sequel or prequel on the big screen at some point. For some, the fantastic world of *The Dark Crystal* helped inspire careers in art, literature, or motion pictures. Author and critic Harlan Ellison once referred to the film as "the only fantasy that has worked." I [SAW] will never forget the first brief teaser that appeared in theaters almost a year prior to the release of the film, which made my family eager to see what sort of world was about to be unleashed. While that tantalizing teaser didn't show much except a view of the Skeksis around the crystal, an approaching Mystic, and a final image of the Skeksis castle illuminated by flashes of lightning, it was enough to have us and others talking about it for months.

For some, the film is still endearing, magical, and a childhood favorite, but for others it's a dark, disturbing, or frightening adventure that diverges from the larger Henson canon. Ultimately, its creators accept both sentiments all these years later. It remains a unique masterpiece among the creations of Brian Froud and the late Jim Henson.

THIS YEAR IN GAMING

Already dominating the tabletop roleplaying-game industry, thanks to the ongoing success of *Dungeons & Dragons*, TSR was investigating and continuing to support other genres with new and existing boxed games, like their popular espionage title *Top Secret* (1980), their foray into the Old West called *Boot Hill* (1981), the 1930s-era organized-crime adventure *Gang Busters*, and their outer-space exploration game *Star Frontiers* (1982).

Using an easy-to-learn and fast-moving percentile-based core game mechanic, *Star Frontiers* introduced gamers to new spacefaring races, including the insectoid Vrusk, the amorphous Dralasites, and the winged, simian Yazirians, all allied under the banner of the United Planetary Federation. The game was a 180-degree alternative to *Traveller* (published by Game Designers' Workshop), emphasizing fun space adventure over hard science. The initial boxed set contained two rulebooks, a pair of ten-sided dice with a crayon to color in the numbers, a map, cardboard counters, and an adventure titled *Crash on Volturnus*. The following year, TSR released a second boxed set bearing the subtitle *Knight Hawks* (after the first boxed set's subtitle *Alpha Dawn*), this time covering spacecraft and space travel and offering a set of starship wargaming rules for use with a line of officially licensed miniatures. Sadly, despite support materials, official RPGA-sanctioned events, a couple licensed products (including adventures based on the films *2001: A Space Odyssey* and *2010: The Year We Make Contact*), and fan interest, the game didn't stick around long. TSR officially pulled the plug following the release of the rule-tweaking sourcebook *Zebulon's Guide to Frontier Space* in 1985. A few of the core races appeared in the now out-of-print *d20 Future* (1984, Wizards of the Coast) supplement for the defunct *d20 Modern* line. Today, *Star Frontiers* thrives in the hands of its fans, who continue to support it with new supplemental material and adventures.

ATOR, THE FIGHTING EAGLE

1983 • ITALY • FILMIRAGE / METAXA CORPORATION • 98M • COLOR • PG

WRITER: David Hills (Joe D'Amato) and Michele Soavi (uncredited)
DIRECTOR: David Hills (Joe D'Amato)
PRODUCER: Alex Susmann
MUSIC: Carlo Maria Cordio
DIRECTOR OF PHOTOGRAPHY: Frederick Slonisco (Joe D'Amato)
ART DIRECTOR: John Gregory
WARDROBE: Kim Dascovitz
MAKE-UP: Pat Russel
STUNT COORDINATOR: James Hadley
CAST: Miles O'Keeffe (Ator), Sabrina Siani (Roon), Ritza Brown (Sunya), Dakkar (Dakkar, High Priest of the Spider), Laura Gemser (Indun), Edmund Purdom (Griba), Chandra Vazzoler (Woman in the Tavern), Nat Williams (Bardak), Jean Lopez (Nordya), and Olivia Goods (Queen)
ALTERNATE TITLES: *Ator* and *Ator the Invincible*

ON THE MAP

The tale is set at the end of the Age of Darkness, when the Kingdom of the Spider ruled over the land and the people lived in bondage in the Valley of the Shadows ... which also contains the Volcano of Shadows. You try to figure out where that is.

OUR STORY SO FAR

Ator, reluctant warrior son of Thoren, embarks on a quest to rescue his bride (and sister—yup, same person) from the clutches of the high priest of the spider cult. Along the way he meets a beautiful Amazon named Roon. Together with a precocious little bear cub named Keog, they face undead warriors, a seductive witch, betrayal, and the spider god itself.

ALTERNATE VERSIONS

A scene of a beheading, missing from English language releases, appears in some foreign trailers. When the film originally came out on UK video, it had lost just under thirty seconds of fight-scene material. Considering the type of material normally seen in D'Amato films up to this point, US censors might have deleted even more content. A few baby dolls do get ripped from actors and chopped up in silhouette or off-camera during the attack on Ator's village, but that must have been A-OK.

IT'S MAGIC

Magic, though present in Ator's world, is fairly understated. World-altering supernatural signs of prophecy link to Ator's birth, such as lightning, thunder, tremors, a flame-colored sky, and the cry of animals, as well as an enormous bird statue that cries tears of blood.

> A MAGICAL POWER WAS DESTINED TO FIGHT AT HIS SIDE.

The witch, Indun, is an ancient illusionist in the purest *Dungeons & Dragons* sense of the word and possesses much power. She lures Ator into her cave by projecting a false Sunya, and she generates false images of a smiling Sunya picnicking with Dakkar. Indun also claims to possess the ability to transform unwilling captors into animals, although we never actually see her do this. While she says she is immortal—and tells Ator that he will also become immortal should he remain with her in her dirt hole—her beauty is arrested by the large mirror kept under wraps within her lair. Why she doesn't pack that thing away somewhere so that she doesn't accidentally knock the curtain aside, exposing her grotesque countenance, is beyond us. Despite her powers, her curse upon Ator—which, by the way, is for not really doing anything at all, because knocking the curtain aside was all Roon's doing—is an empty one. Roon loses her life in the end, but Ator and Sunya live happily ever after.

THE QUEST FOR MEANING

Mirrors, both literally and figuratively, feature significantly throughout the film. When the witch passes in front of one, her true, hideous self reflects back. After Ator looks into the Shield of Mordor [sic] and sees his reflection, he must battle a living shadow of himself. When the high priest of the Spider looks into the shield, he inexplicably explodes! Finally, the Shield of Mordor reflects the sun's light into darkness and into the eyes of the spider god, which defeats it and in turn destroys the shield.

Griba's true reflection is that of a selfish, power-hungry betrayer, while Roon is a more barbaric reflection of Sunya. In fact, the Ator we first meet is hardly the character we witness defeating evil at the end of the story. One could even surmise that the bright, idyllic world of Ator and Sunya is the reflection of the dark world of the spider god, where zombies walk in shadow, and pain and suffering rule.

Ator joins a number of films and literary works that feature mirrors as narrative and thematic devices, including *Snow White* by the Brothers Grimm (the queen's magic mirror), *Through the Looking Glass* by Lewis Carroll (the mirror through which Alice passes to enter another world), and even *Dracula* by Bram Stoker (the mirror that reveals the count's true, supernatural nature to Jonathan Harker). Other mirrors of note include the mirror of Galadriel in *The Lord of the Rings*, which can reveal the past, the present, and the future . . . but now we're getting into "6 Degrees" territory.

WHO GOES THERE?

Miles O'Keeffe got his big break playing *Tarzan, the Ape Man* alongside Bo Derek's breasts. He also returned as Ator in *The Blade Master* and *Iron Warrior* and had roles in *Sword of the Valiant: The Legend of Sir Gawain and the Green Knight*, *Waxwork*, and *The Unknown* (known by the far cheesier title, *Clawed: The Legend of Sasquatch*).

> ATOR MUST RESCUE SUNYA AND FULFILL THE PROPHECY BY
> KILLING THE HUGE, MONSTROUS ANIMAL THAT IS THE SPIDER.

Sabrina Siani graced our screens in only a handful of films over the course of ten short years. She lived among the flesh eaters in *White Cannibal Queen* and *Cannibal Terror*, donned armor and wielded swords in *Gunan, King of the Barbarians*; *Barbarian Master*; and *The Throne of Fire*; and survived the holocaust in *2020 Texas Gladiators* (also directed by Joe D'Amato). She appeared topless in more than a few titles, including Lucio Fulci's sword-and-sorcery misstep, *Conquest*. (See our chapter on that film for more.)

Ritza Brown portrayed a young Sophia Loren in the 1980 TV-movie, *Sophia Loren: Her Own Story*. She also appeared in *Beyond Good and Evil, Monsignor, Tuareg: The Desert Warrior,* and *Grand Larceny*.

This was Dakkar's final film, although he lived for many years afterward. Formerly a wrestler from Peru, he made an impression in a few films directed by Federico Fellini, including *Spirits of the Dead* and *Fellini Satyricon*, before finding his way into Lucio Fulci's *Zombi 2* (a.k.a. *Zombie*) and *Zombie Holocaust* (a.k.a. *Dr. Butcher M.D.*). He died in 2004 at age 83.

Exotic Laura Gemser appeared in a number of skin flicks, including a flood of *Emanuelle* films, many of which Joe D'Amato directed. You can also find her in *Erotic Nights of the Living Dead, Invaders of the Lost Gold, Endgame,* and *Metamorphosis*. She even worked as a costume designer on a few movies, including the infamous *Troll 2*!

British actor Edmund Purdom built up a respectable resume in films like *Julius Caesar* (with Marlon Brando), *The Egyptian, The Prodigal, Malaga, The Night Child,* and *Pieces*. He died in 2009 at age 84.

Nat Williams (a.k.a. Nello Pazzafini) appears in almost 200 films, including a pile of Italian sword-and-sandal epics of the 1960s, numerous spaghetti westerns, and movies like *Yor, the Hunter from the Future; Endgame; The Blade Master;* and *The Barbarians*. He died in 1997 at age 63.

6 DEGREES OF SORCERY

The high priest of the spider god and Herod "the Great" both gave the order to massacre innocents in order to slay a child of prophecy. Griba's entrusting someone else to raise baby Ator is akin to Merlin having young Arthur raised by Sir Hector, or Obi-Wan Kenobi passing Luke off to Owen and Beru in *Star Wars*. Ator's village is razed in similar—okay, identical—fashion to that of young Conan's village or the village of Dar, the Beastmaster, and others in this book.

If Ator is Luke, then Griba—looking like a medieval Charles Bronson—is his Ben Kenobi, with a twist. Roon is clearly modeled after Valeria from *Conan*, although one can't help but see a bit of Han Solo and a little Leela from *Doctor Who* in there as well. Sabrina Siani and Louise Jameson do look a bit alike. Dakkar's high priest is practically a carbon copy of James Earl Jones' Thulsa Doom, even down to the quality of the dubbed English voice.

Deathstalker II in 1987 parodies the village of the Amazons and the events that transpire there. The exotic witch Indun is a knockoff variant of Cassandra Gava's witch from *Conan the Barbarian* and a number of similar figures in other films. When Indun shows Ator what Sunya is up to with Dakkar, even if it is an illusion, we're reminded of the mirror of Galadriel in *The Lord of the Rings*. When the mirror reveals Indun's true self, she looks a lot like the hag from *The Magic Sword*, but when you've seen one hag, you've seen them all, right? The spider god is a cheap-looking puppet that resembles the abomination seen in 1975's *The Giant Spider Invasion*, but at least you see more of it than 1986's *Robot Holocaust* shows.

SHATTERING THE ILLUSION

There's not much to tell. *Ator, The Fighting Eagle* came out quickly and on the cheap to cash in on the phenomenal success of *Conan the Barbarian*. (As a side note, the Monte Gelato waterfalls located in the Valle del Treja park make yet another appearance in it, having been used in countless films over the years.) Given its motivation and rapid production schedule, one cannot help but be impressed by the almost magical speed at which it all transpired. *Conan the Barbarian* came out in the United States in May of 1982 and didn't arrive on Italian screens until September of that year. Triple-threat writer-director-cinematographer (and we do mean "threat") Joe D'Amato and his team wrote, casted, shot, and distributed this first *Ator* film in time to have it pop up in Italian cinemas in October of that same year, likely while *Conan* was still enjoying its box-office success. Now *that's* heroic. And this quest didn't end there, because then D'Amato and O'Keeffe were at it again, substantially ad-libbing a two-week sequel-shoot so that they could release the first follow-up, *The Blade Master*, to compete with *Conan*'s sequel, *Conan the Destroyer*, in 1984.

MUSIC OF THE MINSTRELS

Carlo Maria Cordio did well with the genuinely heroic score. For soundtrack collectors: Fulltime, out of Italy, released a 45 vinyl record featuring the tracks "Runn" [sic], performed by Simona Prione, and "Sanda" in 1983.

Let's talk a little about that Prione track, shall we? There is no denying that at first it sounds similar to "For Your Eyes Only" as performed by Sheena Easton for the James Bond film of the same name, released just a year before production on *Ator* began. There is, however, one slight difference: Sheena Easton's track is actually good—worthy of its number-four position on the US Billboard Hot 100 at the time. I [SAW] had never believed that auto-tune was a good idea until I heard "Runn" by Simona Prione; ouch.

THE SAGA CONTINUES

Three additional *Ator* films followed: *The Blade Master* (a.k.a. *Ator The Invincible* or *Cave Dwellers*), *Iron Warrior* (written and directed by Alfonso Brescia), and finally *Quest for the Mighty Sword* (a.k.a. *The Hobgoblin* or *Troll 3*—seriously!) with D'Amato back at the helm, sans O'Keeffe in the lead role. Joel, Mike, and the robotic gang of *Mystery Science Theater* gave the first sequel the *MST3K* treatment under its alternate title, *Cave Dwellers*. For more on that, check out the entry on *The Blade Master* in our index, and consider the world safer today that this saga never begat any further sequels, reboots, or peripheral merchandise.

TAKE UP THY SWORD!
THE SHIELD OF SHADOWS (MAGIC ARMOR)

SHADOW WARRIOR ATTACK: Should anyone peer into the mirrored surface of the Shield of Shadows while it lies in state in its chambers (for as long as the shield remains uncovered and exposed to a source of illumination) the shadow of that person metamorphoses into a living shadow from the negative material plane and attacks. The shadow-creature has the abilities of its counterpart, with offensive and defensive abilities halved.

RAY OF OBLIVION ATTACK: When wielded, the shield emits a beam of light that extends out several hundred feet. Anyone or anything caught in the beam takes significant heat damage, with a slight chance of catching on fire. Creatures accustomed to dwelling in darkness are especially vulnerable, suffering twice the normal level of damage. Three or more successful attacks with the beam result in a one-in-six chance per successful attack of the target overheating and exploding. Because the beam can be as bright as the sun, it can also blind opponents, resulting in appropriate penalties for blindness and distraction. Should the shield defeat a spider god, it shatters and renders itself useless, its divine mission fulfilled.

DETAILS: This shield, hidden in the Volcano of Shadows, wards off death: it grants immortality as long as it remains in the wielder's keeping . . . or so the legend states. A special-purpose item, it appears as a large, ornate, circular mirror but possesses a number of mystical abilities, including the ability to protect itself.

THE FILM'S DESTINY

Okay, so it's an obvious *Conan* knockoff, but it really could have been a hell of a lot worse. See our chapter on *Conquest* if you don't believe that. O'Keeffe is a charismatic hero despite the rather outrageous '80s metal hair and frilly costume, Siani is a sexy and competent sidekick, Dakkar plays a menacing villain who actually refers to himself as "Dakkar" in a reality-melting but amusing way, and then you've got that damned-adorable little bear!

This otherwise very shaky production has some other things going for it. For one thing, Cordio's score, as noted above, is pretty good. Just be sure to mute the audio when the credits roll. For another, you can easily adapt elements featured in this film for your game table: the blind warriors are kind of cool, and the Shield of Mordor is pretty rad as well. Finally, despite the movie's rather mundane technical aspects—being that D'Amato shot this whole thing quickly as a money-grab—a few nicely composed scenes, especially in regard to lighting, prove that D'Amato wasn't completely without talent.

HE WAS BORN TO WIELD THE MIGHTY SWORD OF THOREN.

No matter what positive elements we highlight or how many factors we forgive, however, it's unavoidable that the movie has plenty of laughable moments as well. The wedding-day dance number alone is pretty cringe-worthy. For that reason, *Ator* still might make for fun viewing with friends and a few drinks.

THIS YEAR IN GAMING

Victory Games, a subsidiary of Avalon Hill, released the officially licensed *James Bond 007* roleplaying game to great fanfare. Crafted by Gerard Christopher Klug, Robert Kern, Greg Gorden, and Neil Randall, it was a well-designed cinematic system and an instant hit, proving the most popular espionage RPG for its five years of publication. Victory Games supported it with eleven adventures and five supplements before losing the license in 1987. *James Bond* fan Raymond Benson, who wrote the adventure *You Only Live Twice II: Back of Beyond* for the roleplaying game, later went on to become the official author of some *James Bond* novels, including the novelizations of *Tomorrow Never Dies*, *The World Is Not Enough*, and *Die Another Day*.

KRULL

1983 • UK/US • COLUMBIA PICTURES • 121M • COLOR • PG

WRITER: Stanford Sherman
DIRECTOR: Peter Yates
PRODUCER: Ron Silverman
MUSIC: James Horner
DIRECTOR OF PHOTOGRAPHY: Peter Suschitzky
PRODUCTION DESIGNER: Stephen Grimes
ART DIRECTORS: Tony Curtis, Norman Dorme, Colin Grimes, and Tony Reading
COSTUME DESIGNER: Anthony Mendleson
SPECIAL MAKEUP DESIGNER: Nick Maley
VISUAL EFFECTS SUPERVISOR: Derek Meddings
STUNT COORDINATOR: Vic Armstrong
ANIMATOR: Steven Archer
CAST: Ken Marshall (Colwyn); Lysette Anthony (Lyssa); Freddie Jones (Ynyr); Francesca Annis (Widow of the Web); Alun Armstrong (Torquil); David Battley (Ergo); Bernard Bresslaw (Cyclops); Liam Neeson (Kegan); John Welsh (Seer); Graham McGrath (Titch); Tony Church (Turold); Bernard Archard (Eirig); Belinda Mayne (Vella); Dicken Ashworth (Bardolph); Todd Carty (Oswyn); Robbie Coltrane (Rhun); Clare McIntyre (Merith); Bronco McLoughlin (Nennog); Andy Bradford (Darro); Gerard Naprous (Quain); Bill Weston (Menno); Michael Elphick (Voice of Rhun); Trevor Martin (Voice of the Beast); Lindsay Crouse (Voice of Princess Lyssa, uncredited); Derek Lyons (White Slayer with Tiger, uncredited); Dinny Powell and Nosher Powell (Slayers in the Swamp, uncredited); and Tom Rumpf (Sword Fighter, uncredited)
ALTERNATE TITLES: *Dragons of Krull*, *Dungeons and Dragons*, *The Dungeons of Krull*, and *Krull: Invaders of the Black Fortress*

ON THE MAP

Krull is a planet in an unidentified binary star system. Due to the unusual teleportation powers of the Beast's Black Fortress, Colwyn and his companions must journey far and wide across the surface of the world to catch up to it, through dense forests, flowering fields, and burbling swamps, and among snow-capped peaks.

OUR STORY SO FAR

Lyssa and Colwyn, grown heirs to two kingdoms, are marrying to unite their people. To ensure that a prophecy foretelling that their child will one day rule the galaxy does not come to pass, the Beast within the Black Fortress kidnaps Lyssa on the wedding day and leaves everyone—including her husband—for dead. Our hero survives the attack and embarks on a quest to rescue his wife and destroy the Beast.

> A WORLD LIGHT-YEARS BEYOND YOUR IMAGINATION.

IT'S MAGIC

More science-fantasy than strict fantasy, *Krull* presents us with a world of swords and sorcery alongside technology like laser guns and spaceships . . . well, one big, chunky spaceship, anyway. The Seer and Ergo are the film's typical magic users, though Ergo is a bit of a novice in his control over his abilities. Magic manifests in several other ways as well, including during the flame ritual in the wedding ceremony, in Colwyn's ability to plunge his hand into magma without injury, in the Widow of the Web's control over the spider, and in the remote manipulation of the Glaive, akin to *Star Wars'* all-pervasive Force (more on that later). One might say that in Krull, magic harmonizes with technology, though the civilization of the Beast and his army of Slayers has not made the transition gracefully.

THE QUEST FOR MEANING

Krull is a straightforward, almost stereotypical fantasy adventure. It has all the usual tropes, right down to the rescue of a princess from a terrifying "dragon," a wise older fellow guiding an emerging young hero as he discovers his destiny, and so on. Underneath it all, the film is about sacrifice and the simple notion that the love of two people is stronger than any weapon—another oldie, but a goodie.

Regret, old age, forgiveness, redemption—the tragic figure of the Widow of the Web embodies all these things. Furious over the loss of her beloved Ynyr, she killed the child she had from him, and as a result became consigned to the web for the rest of her life. Her story echoes similar tales from mythology and folklore and offers more substance than does the love of our central characters. You could argue that the older couple's story is a cautionary parallel to our young leads: they didn't get the storybook happy ending and failed at romance, while Colwyn and Lyssa have a chance to succeed.

One nice innovation is that the elusive quality of the Black Fortress undercuts the usual quest structure that entails reaching a fixed location. And the concept of the cyclops having traded an eye for the curse of future-sight adds poignancy to a creature traditionally seen as a threatening rather than a tragic figure.

Perhaps most importantly, unlike many of the movies in our book, which feature a world leaving behind an era of superstition or magical energy (read: innocence) for one of technology (read: greater wisdom or greater corruption), *Krull* seems to have achieved a balance between the two, showing no signs of leaving any of it behind. Maybe Krullians could teach a thing or two to some of those other cultures.

WHO GOES THERE?

Ken Marshall was a relative newcomer when cast and has appeared in productions on both the big and small screen. Genre fans might know him as Lt. Commander Michael Eddington on *Star Trek: Deep Space Nine*.

Born Lysette Chodzko, Lysette Anthony is the daughter of actors Michael Anthony *(Becket, Khartoum)* and Bernadette Milnes *(The Elephant Man)*. Prior to *Krull*, she worked almost

> BEYOND OUR TIME, BEYOND OUR UNIVERSE THERE IS A PLANET BESIEGED BY ALIEN INVADERS, WHERE A YOUNG KING MUST RESCUE HIS LOVE FROM THE CLUTCHES OF THE BEAST. OR RISK THE DEATH OF HIS WORLD.

exclusively in television movies, like *Ivanhoe* and *Beauty and the Beast*. Since this film, she has appeared in a number of other productions, including *Without A Clue*, the 1990 television remake of the series *Dark Shadows* (as Angelique), *Dracula: Dead and Loving It*, *Trilogy of Terror II*, the TV spinoff *Highlander: The Raven*, and *Strippers vs. Werewolves*.

Freddie Jones is no stranger to genre films and television, having appeared in movies like *Frankenstein Must Be Destroyed*, *The Satanic Rites of Dracula*, *Son of Dracula*, *The Elephant Man*, *Firestarter*, *Dune*, *Black Cauldron*, *Young Sherlock Holmes*, and *The NeverEnding Story III*. He has also made several televised journeys into horror and science fiction, including *Space: 1999*, *Children of the Stones*, and *Neverwhere*.

Francesca Annis has a long and impressive filmography going back to her early teens. One of her first big Hollywood roles was alongside Elizabeth Taylor in *Cleopatra*. Immediately following this film, she appeared with *Krull* costar Freddie Jones in David Lynch's *Dune*.

Like most people in this cast, Alun Armstrong has racked up an impressive number of British TV appearances and has also had roles in films like *Braveheart*, *The Saint*, *Sleepy Hollow*, *The Mummy Returns*, *Van Helsing*, and *Eragon*.

David Battley was the befuddled and befuddling teacher in *Willy Wonka & the Chocolate Factory*. He died in 2003 at age 67.

Bernard Archard's chiseled features also turned up in movies like *Village of the Damned* and *The Horror of Frankenstein* and in television series like *Doctor Who* ("Pyramids of Mars"). He died in 2008 at age 91.

Belinda Mayne was Delta in the 1987 *Doctor Who* story "Delta and the Bannermen."

Robbie Coltrane had a successful film and television career long before he donned the enormous coat and bushy beard of Rubeus Hagrid in the *Harry Potter* film series (the first to be cast in the films, selected by J. K. Rowling herself). For UK TV watchers, he was the lead in *Cracker*, a popular police series that also jumpstarted the career of future *Doctor Who* star Christopher Eccleston. Blink and you'll miss him, but in one of his first film roles he's at the door of the plane that takes Flash and Dale into the eye of the storm in the early moments of *Flash Gordon*! He also appeared in movies like *Nuns on the Run*, James Bond installments *GoldenEye* and *The World Is Not Enough* as Valentin Zukovsky, *From Hell*, *Van Helsing* (we forgive him), and *Ocean's Twelve*, and lent his voice to Pixar's *Brave*.

Michael Elphick was best known for a TV show called *Boon* but also appeared in movies such as *Quadrophenia*, *The Elephant Man*, *Curse of the Pink Panther*, *Pirates*, and *Withnail & I*. He died in 2002 at age 55.

In some circles, Trevor Martin is best known as the Doctor in a stage production of *Doctor Who* titled "Doctor Who and the Seven Keys to Doomsday."

Lindsay Crouse also appeared in films like *Slap Shot* and *Iceman*, and TV shows like *Hill Street Blues*, *Buffy the Vampire Slayer*, and *Law & Order: Special Victims Unit*.

Derek Lyons also had uncredited stints in *Star Wars, The Shining, Flash Gordon, Superman II, Victor Victoria, Gandhi, Octopussy, Superman III, Greystoke: The Legend of Tarzan, Lord of the Apes, Supergirl, A View to a Kill, Superman IV: The Quest for Peace, Who Framed Roger Rabbit, Indiana Jones and the Last Crusade,* and *GoldenEye.* (That's a lot of credits for an uncredited actor.)

Stuntman and actor Nosher Powell had a number of credited and uncredited roles over the years on both the big and small screens starting in the late '40s. You'll find him in the films *Demetrius and the Gladiators, A Fistful of Dollars, She, Willow,* and *Legionnaire.* He died in 2013 at age 84.

6 DEGREES OF SORCERY

Since *Star Wars* clearly inspired *Krull,* the many parallels are no surprise. *Krull* has a number of thematic connections with Arthurian legend and Tolkien's *The Lord of the Rings.*

Ynyr is very much in the mold of Obi-Wan Kenobi, with hot-headed Colwyn acting the part of Luke Skywalker. Both similarities by extension continue the grand Merlin-Arthur tradition. Toward the end of the film, Colwyn trying to extract the Glaive from the chest of the Beast is reminiscent of the scene in *The Empire Strikes Back* in which Luke uses the Force to pull his lightsaber from the snow in the Wampa's ice cave, as well as Arthur pulling Excalibur from the stone.

Krull, like Tatooine, has two suns, and the moving menace of the Black Fortress is a bit like the Death Star. The design of the fortress also resembles the design in *Zardoz* and of Sauron's tower in *The Lord of the Rings* films. The run across a chasm-spanning path is similar to sequences in a number of our other movies, including *The 7th Voyage of Sinbad* and *The Lord of the Rings: The Fellowship of the Ring.*

The Slayers are akin to the Nazgul in *The Lord of the Rings,* as well as guards in *Flash Gordon,* which also features a seer and quicksand like in the swamp here. Quicksand also turns up in *The Beastmaster* and *The Princess Bride.*

The Wizard of Oz also makes its influence felt in everything from the design of ornate doors to the Emerald Temple. The capture of the fire mares recalls Perseus's efforts to enlist the aid of Pegasus in *Clash of the Titans.* The Beast's attempt to woo Lyssa is very similar to the efforts of Darkness in *Legend,* even down to presenting her with a "bridal gown."

The giant spider, very Harryhausen-like in design and action, has cousins in movies like *The Thief of Bagdad* and *The Lord of the Rings: The Return of the King.* The room with the extending spears is an old trope from serials, also resurrected in *Indiana Jones and the Temple of Doom.* Listen for one of the famous "Wilhelm screams" that can be heard in every *Star Wars* and *Lord of the Rings* movie. The way the Beast is filmed is reminiscent of the titular creature in *Alien* ... where less is most definitely more.

SHATTERING THE ILLUSION

At the time, *Krull* was one of the most expensive films ever produced, with a budget of $27 million. Location-filming took the production to Italy, Spain, and areas around the UK, but most of the work took place at Pinewood Studios and spread over ten soundstages, including, for the expansive swamp set, the James Bond 007 stage. Peter Yates, excited to work on a film without boundaries, which would allow him to try almost anything, brought together the entire company for a table read-through of the complete script as a means to rehearse and bond the team.

According to a persistent rumor, *Krull* was, for a time, intended to be the official *Dungeons & Dragons* tie-in movie, but when asked about this in 2007, Gary Gygax replied that to the best of his knowledge, the film's producers had never inquired about obtaining a license from TSR and therefore were unlikely to have planned a *Dungeons & Dragons* connection. While it is possible, perhaps even probable, that negotiations bypassed Gygax, there is no conclusive evidence either way. The potential origins of *Krull* as a lost *Dungeons & Dragons* adaptation might just be the stuff of legends . . . which is rather appropriate.

As with many lead actors in this book, Ken Marshall followed a regimen that included courses in fighting, fencing, and riding. In addition to the human members of the cast undergoing physical preparation for their roles, a group of sixteen Clydesdale horses also required special attention to become the fire mares. No one had ever ridden them, so they required months of training to get ready for their film debut.

To create the planet Krull, production designer Stephen Grimes blended past and futuristic styles. Some interiors invoke an organic feel.

Lysette Anthony was taken by surprise when she found out that the voice of American actress Lindsay Crouse had replaced hers, on the basis that—according to Columbia Pictures president Frank Price—an American-accented lead character would help sell tickets. She wasn't the only one subjected to post-production alteration: Michael Elphick's voice replaced Robbie Coltrane's. Even the Slayers underwent dubbing treatment, with library sounds of screams from *At the Earth's Core* looped in for their death throes. The film did not start a franchise as did its inspiration, *Star Wars*, although it gathered more of a following in later years via cable and home video.

MUSIC OF THE MINSTRELS

A young James Horner *(Willow, Titanic, Avatar),* not yet 30 years old at the time, took responsibility for the heroic-sounding score, performed by the London Symphony Orchestra and the Ambrosian Singers. Composed in just seven weeks, the music typifies many of Horner's other scores from that period, with elements particularly reminiscent of his work in *Star Trek II: The Wrath of Khan*. Horner later won two Oscars for his work on *Titanic* and continues to produce memorable scores for big Hollywood blockbusters, having left *Krull* far, far behind.

In 1987, Southern Cross Records released a forty-five-minute record album, which contained all the essential tracks, and later expanded it to seventy-five minutes, with limited-edition pressings, in the early '90s. Since then, the soundtrack has remained in demand and has been expanded and released in additional collectible variations.

THE SAGA CONTINUES

Believing they had the next *Star Wars* on their hands, Columbia Pictures licensed the property to publishers as well as toy and videogame companies. The plan did *not* launch consumers to another galaxy far, far away, however. As for sequels . . . are you kidding?

Alan Dean Foster, who ghostwrote the original *Star Wars* novelization attributed to George Lucas, penned the *Krull* novelization released by Warner Books in July 1983. Marvel Comics published a two-issue comic-book adaptation written by David Michelinie, with art by Bret Blevins, and also released the material in the magazine-format *Marvel Super Special* #28, which added behind-the-scenes articles. The DVD features an animated version of the entire Marvel adaptation, with motion and sound—one of the coolest bonus features we have seen!

Parker Bros. handled the boardgame and card game, while Gottlieb took charge of videogames, releasing a stand-up, dual-joystick controlled arcade game and a home version for the Atari 2600 console. Originally planned for Atari's 5200 console, the game is still widely regarded as one of the better early film-to-videogame adaptations. Gottlieb also designed a pinball machine, but that never made it past the prototype stage. Knickerbocker Toy Company had a line of action figures in the works, hiring *G.I. Joe* sculptor Bill Merklein to produce the masters, but canceled the line before the film even came out.

To this day, prop-collectors seek the Glaive. A quick search online reveals a number of producers of unlicensed non-working and working—yes, with retractable blades—versions for you to purchase and quickly put away.

TAKE UP THY SWORD!

THE STAR (MAGIC WEAPON)

An ancient item of unknown origin, this artifact is a formidable magical weapon in the hands of the right person. Weighing roughly two pounds, it possesses the power to strike an enemy or enemies and return to its wielder.

In its neutral state, it appears as a bejeweled, five-pointed star: a sort of golden starfish. When activated, two-inch blades spring out from the end of each spoke. The star's wielder throws it at the target in a spinning motion—a ranged missile attack. It returns after each throw unless the attack roll is a critical success or a critical failure, in which case the weapon either remains stuck in the target, inflicting significant damage, or falls to the floor, unmoving. The wielder can then recover and reuse it as usual.

THE FILM'S DESTINY

A lot of bad feeling and bitterness surround this movie. For one thing, director Peter Yates insists it isn't sword and sorcery. Sorry, Peter, we beg to differ.

For another, actress Lysette Anthony has publicly disparaged the film, warning people—perhaps with tongue in cheek—not to mention "the 'K' word." Nevertheless, she returned to contribute to the commentary on the DVD.

> SOMEWHERE BEYOND OUR UNIVERSE THERE IS A DISTANT WORLD. A WORLD WHERE TWIN SUNS RISE, GOOD TRIUMPHS OVER EVIL AND LOVE PREVAILS. A WORLD CALLED … KRULL.

Her attitude is within reason. Despite its pedigree and its rather large budget, the movie is a mishmash of good and bad elements. On the one hand, you have gorgeous exteriors beautifully photographed, thanks to the talented Peter Suschitzky, but when the film returns to some of the soundstages, the sets look a bit cheap (with a few exceptions). The swamp in particular is sparse and flatly lit, while the exterior of the Black Fortress appears to be little more than repurposed and repainted hexagonal spires lifted from the Fortress of Solitude in *Superman*—which is quite possible, considering that both *Superman* and *Krull* used the 007 soundstage at Pinewood.

The Glaive, despite appearing in the main titles and on every tie-in product ever released, gets very little screen time, which is disappointing. It makes its appearance in a scene reminiscent of Arthur yanking Excalibur from the stone, and then moments later, right as Colwyn attempts to give it a toss on the mountainside, Ynyr tells him to put it away. We really don't see it return until the film's end, at which point we learn that it is pretty useless against the main villain because it requires some sort of combined "love-fire" to defeat the Beast.

One of your authors [SAW] really enjoyed this movie as a 14-year-old. It likely influenced his gaming at that age in a variety of ways. All these years later, though, it's hard to overlook the film's shortcomings. Perhaps they're the natural consequence of the movie's hollow origin: from a studio's desire for a franchise rather than as an inspired endeavor to create a magical new adventure. While there are a lot of nice elements here—the Widow of the Web's sequence is still terrific, the Slayers have a great look, and both the cyclops and Ergo are exceptional characters—overall, *Krull* is a bit of a mess.

THIS YEAR IN GAMING

Less than two months after the release of *Krull* in theaters (on Saturday, September 17th), an animated *Dungeons & Dragons* television series premiered on the CBS network. A number of well-known animation writers, comic writers, and novelists scripted it, including Michael Reaves, Paul Dini, and Mark Evanier. Gary Gygax received a co-producer credit. It ran for twenty-seven episodes, with the final episode airing on December 7th, 1985. A booklet accompanying the complete DVD collection (released in 2006) featured profiles and stats of the series characters for *Dungeons & Dragons 3.5*, as well as a prequel adventure that acted as a prelude to the controversial episode "The Dragon's Graveyard." (In that episode, the main characters contemplate killing their nemesis Venger, something unheard of in Saturday morning cartoons.)

HERCULES

1983 • US/Italy • Cannon Italia Srl / Golan-Globus Productions • 98m • Color • PG

Writer: Lewis Coates (Luigi Cozzi)
Director: Lewis Coates (Luigi Cozzi)
Producers: Menahem Golan and Yoram Globus
Music: Pino Donaggio
Director of Photography: Alberto Spagnoli
Production Designer: M. A. Geleng
Special Visual Effects: Armando Valcauda
Special Effects: Herman Nathan and Jeffrey Unger
Makeup: Freddy Spinks
Costume Designer: Adriana Spadaro
Costumes: Russo
Stunt Coordinator: Edward L. Greco
Cast: Lou Ferrigno (Hercules), Sybil Danning (Adriana), Brad Harris (King Augeias), Rossana Podestà (Hera), Ingrid Anderson (Cassiopeia), William Berger (King Minos), John Garko (Valcheus), Mirella D'Angelo (Circe), Bobby Rhodes (King Xenodama), Yehuda Efroni (Dorcon), Delia Boccardo (Athena), Claudio Cassinelli (Zeus), Frank Garland (The Thief), Gabriella George (Mother), Steven Candell (Father), Ralph Baldassar (Sostratos), Valerie Montanari (Chambermaid), Roger Larry (The Friend), and Eva Robbins (Daedalus)

ON THE MAP

Events occur concurrently on the moon (Olympus), across Earth in places like Thebes (Hercules' birthplace), in Thera and its "capital" Atlantis, and even in hell.

OUR STORY SO FAR

Zeus creates Hercules and sends him among humans to be their champion. After one of Daedalus's mechanical creations kills Hercules' adoptive parents, Hercules sets out on a series of adventures across the world. In Thera, he falls in love with Cassiopeia, but she is soon whisked away to be a sacrifice at the hands of King Minos. Hercules—with the help of the sorceress Circe—must rescue Cassiopeia before she meets her tragic end in the heart of a volcano.

IT'S MAGIC

Magic is a given in the world of Hercules, even though Minos and Daedalus turn away from sorcery in favor of "science." As Arthur C. Clarke once said, "Any sufficiently advanced technology is indistinguishable from magic," and in this film Minos's infatuation with science and, by extension, the mechanical creations of Daedalus are prime examples. From the perspective of primitive mortals, Daedalus's machines, though manipulated by the gods and colossal in size, are as much living beings as the dangerous predators that prowl the surrounding forests.

Circe, dropped into the adventure by Athena, is a sorceress in every stereotypical sense of the word, even appearing in a couple traditional guises of the triple-goddess motif: those of the Crone and the (rather sexy) Maiden. Her ability to weave spells places her, like Hercules, somewhere between mortal and god.

THE QUEST FOR MEANING

Hercules displays a number of themes similar to those already discussed in other mythological big-screen adventures, like *Jason and the Argonauts* and *Clash of the Titans*. Once again we see those wily, competitive Olympian gods manipulating humanity like pieces on a game board.

Hercules, though descended from the gods, remains mostly unaware of this link, apart from the fact that he possesses powers unlike anyone else on Earth. Zeus "inserts" him into an innocent newborn's body, apparently usurping control and pushing out the previous occupant to who-knows-where, like a demonic possession. As an orphan, Hercules grows up with Ma and Pa Kent in Smallville ... or was it Aunt Beru and Uncle Owen on that moisture farm on Tatooine?

As the chosen—or crafted—champion of humankind in its time of trial, Hercules must stand against the forces of darkness and either defeat them (allowing human beings to advance) or lose (allowing evil to control all life on Earth). Though the gods know of Hercules' role in these proceedings, he must make his own way through a series of labors, including a few lifted from myth and several straight from the mind of writer-director Luigi Cozzi. (Yes, classical mythology really doesn't mention clockwork robots that look remarkably like relatives of Ideal's Mr. Machine toy from 1960—look it up—even if Harryhausen himself also gave us robotic automatons; those, too, went far afield of the source material.)

As with so many other films in our book, we also have a struggle between, on the one hand, the forces of magic and an older tradition, and on the other hand, the mechanized science of the future ... and guess which one is evil? As Hercules learns about his abilities by tossing bears into space and splitting continents asunder (as you do), he uses these powers not only to defeat evil per the initial divine quest, but also to rescue the woman he loves. So "love conquers all" plays its thematic part in this veritable soup of sword-and-sorcery subjects.

WHO GOES THERE?

Lou Ferrigno made his mark under a layer of green greasepaint, a bulbous rubber nose, a yak-hair fright-wig, and purple pants as primetime television's *The Incredible Hulk*. A lifelong bodybuilder, he has appeared in numerous films and television series, including *Desert Warrior*, *Sinbad of the Seven Seas* (written and co-directed by Luigi Cozzi), *Cage*, *Hulk* and *The Incredible Hulk* (cameos in both), *Liberator*, the fan-produced *Star Trek Continues*, and *The Scorpion King 4: Quest for Power*. Although his voice didn't make the cut for Hercules, he speaks as the Hulk in the 1996-97 animated TV series

> THE STRONGEST MAN ON EARTH

and in the aforementioned feature film *The Incredible Hulk*, *The Avengers*, and *Avengers: Age of Ultron*.

Austrian-born Sybil Danning might still be the reigning queen of the B-movies. She made her big-screen debut in the 1968 West German sex farce *Komm nur, mein liebstes Vögelein*. She soon began appearing in English-language pictures such as *Bluebeard*, *The Three Musketeers*, *Crossed Swords*, and *Meteor*, but her work in films like *Battle Beyond the Stars*, *Chained Heat*, *Howling II*, *Reform School Girls*, and *Amazon Women on the Moon* truly secured her cult status. She was an obvious choice for Rob Zombie to toss into his faux-trailer contribution to *Grindhouse*, titled *Werewolf Women of the S.S.*, and his remake of *Halloween*.

Muscle-bound Brad Harris is a member of the Stuntman's Hall of Fame. He started in films as a stand-in and occasional stuntman and eventually landed roles in *Li'l Abner* and Stanley Kubrick's *Spartacus* (an uncredited role as a gladiator). While working in Italy, Harris found opportunities in European sword-and-sandal and spaghetti-western movies, including *Goliath Against the Giants*, *The Fury of Hercules*, *Durango Is Coming*, *Pay or Die*, and *Three Giants of the Roman Empire*. He also appeared in a few horror and science-fiction films, including *The Mad Butcher*, *The Mutations*, *Lady Dracula*, and *Shiver*.

Rossana Podestà had a long career in sword-and-sandal films, including *Ulysses*, *Helen of Troy*, *Fury of the Pagans*, and *Sodom and Gomorrah*. She also starred with Christopher Lee in *Horror Castle*. She died in 2013 at age 79.

William Berger guest-starred in a number of television series prior to his long string of appearances in spaghetti westerns like *Face to Face*, *Sabata*, *A Bullet for a Stranger*, and *Keoma*. He also appeared in *Von Ryan's Express*, *Island of Terror*, *The Sinister Eyes of Dr. Orloff*, and *The Spider Labyrinth*. He died in 1993 at age 65.

Fans of spaghetti westerns perhaps know John Garko (a.k.a. Gianni Garko) best for his Derringer-wielding character Sartana, who appeared in several films, including *$1,000 on the Black* (a.k.a. *Blood at Sundown*), *If You Meet Sartana Pray for Your Death*, *Sartana the Gravedigger*, and *Light the Fuse . . . Sartana Is Coming*. Garko also appeared in *Waterloo*, *Night of the Devils*, *The Psychic* (written and directed by Lucio Fulci), *Encounters in the Deep*, *Star Odyssey*, and *Devil Fish*.

The lovely Mirella D'Angelo portrayed Livia Orestilla in the notoriously over-the-top production of *Caligula* starring Malcolm McDowell. She also appeared in *The Return of Casanova*, Dario Argento's *Tenebre* (where she met a predictably grisly end), *Apartment Zero*, and *Maya*.

Large and imposing Bobby Rhodes was Tony the Pimp in Lamberto Bava's *Demons* and returned for the sequel in a different role. He also appeared in *Screamers*, *The Great Alligator*, *Hearts and Armour*, *Flight from Paradise*, and *Circle of Fear*.

Israeli actor Yehuda Efroni had his first mainstream success with *Diamonds* in 1975 and quickly became a fixture in films produced by Golan and Globus. He appears in *The Delta Force*, *Braddock: Missing in Action III*, *Sinbad of the Seven Seas*, a 1989 version of *The Phantom of the Opera*, *The Omega Code*, and *Children of Wax*.

Many remember the beautiful Delia Boccardo for her comedic role alongside Alan Arkin in *Inspector Clouseau*. Her other films include *The Adventurers*, *Snow Job*, *Massacre in Rome*, and *Tentacles*.

Claudio Cassinelli bounced from one genre to the next in films such as *Lion of the Desert, Murder Rock, The Mountain of the Cannibal God, Screamers,* and *The Great Alligator.* In 1985, at age 46, he met an untimely end in a helicopter accident while shooting the science-fiction adventure *Hands of Steel* (a.k.a. *Atomic Cyborg*) in Arizona.

Frank Garland (Franco Garofalo) appeared in *Hell of the Living Dead* (no, he isn't the one in the tutu) under the name Frank Garfield. He also starred in *Guardian of Hell, The Scorpion with Two Tails,* and *The Violent Breed.*

Gabriella George (Gabriella Giorgelli) first appeared on the big screen in *The Grim Reaper.* Other notable films include *The Crook, Women in Cell Block 7, The Beast,* Fellini's *City of Women,* and *The Wax Mask.*

Steven Candell (Stelio Candelli) appears in *War Gods of Babylon, Planet of the Vampires,* and *Demons.*

Ralph Baldassar (Raf Baldassarre) was yet another veteran of the spaghetti-western and sword-and-sandal genres, appearing in films like *Hercules in the Haunted World, Erik the Conqueror, A Fistful of Dollars, Web of the Spider,* and *Thor the Conqueror.* He died in 1995 at age 63.

Roger Larry (Rocco Lerro) had several small roles over the years, in films like *High Rollers, The Inglorious Bastards, 1990: The Bronx Warriors,* and *The Raiders of Atlantis.* He succumbed to Parkinson's disease in 2005.

Eva Robbins (Roberto Coatti) is a transsexual model and recording artist who occasionally wanders before the cameras, appearing in *Tenebre, Mascara,* and *Massacre Play.*

6 DEGREES OF SORCERY

The Olympian gods stand about, stare into a gazing pool, and converse about and manipulate events on Earth much like they do in *Jason and the Argonauts* and *Clash of the Titans.* Some of the sets have an original-TV-series *Star Trek* quality to them. A few stock images in montages clearly come from from old epics. The dubbed voice of Valcheus sounds a little like Adam West (no, chum, it's not him). Hercules at the grinding wheel is like Conan at the "wheel of pain," although the brief scene here is far more benign.

Daedalus sports a costume that makes her look like she just walked off the set of *Buck Rogers in the 25th Century.* A similar costume, designed by Elizabeth Waller, appeared on a character in the 1977 *Doctor Who* story "The Robots of Death."

The stop-motion beasties are all less-polished but well-intentioned nods to the work of Ray Harryhausen. Hercules questions his abilities as does a young Clark Kent. The hag version of Circe is much like Yoda … apart from the whole creepy blood-drinking thing, but then again, who knows what Yoda does in his spare time? There are also nods to Aughra from *The Dark Crystal.*

The presentation of a shield and sword to Hercules is again like the gifts of the gods in *Clash of the Titans* and other films. When Hercules becomes a giant and pushes the continents apart, the scene mirrors the actions of Triton in *Jason and the Argonauts.* King Minos appears to be modeled after Hitler. He embraces the pure magic of science and seeks perfect order; he even proposes the creation of a race of supermen. Minos's flaming sword stands in for a *Star Wars* saga lightsaber.

SHATTERING THE ILLUSION

Legendary writer-director Bruno Mattei—who had just directed Ferrigno and Danning in *The Seven Magnificent Gladiators*—originally conceived the film as an R-rated, mythological, and decidedly Italian response to *Conan the Barbarian*, complete with sex, nudity, and violence. The casting of Ferrigno led to the dumping of the first script and the revision of the production as a more family-friendly *peplum*, likely at Ferrigno's insistence. In a 1982 interview, the actor described the film as something for kids and a good adventure for the whole family to enjoy.

Fresh off his television series *The Incredible Hulk*, Ferrigno was thrilled to work on this production, following in the footsteps of his idol Steve Reeves. Menahem Golan was also eager to produce a *Hercules* project, especially with "The Incredible Lou Ferrigno" (as promoted in the trailer).

In preparation for the role, Ferrigno trained for three months straight to get into the best physical shape of his life. He learned how to sword-fight from master-of-arms Enzo Musumeci Greco (credited as Edward L. Greco), who had previously taught fencing to the likes of Errol Flynn, Tyrone Power, Charlton Heston, and Steve Reeves. Unfortunately for Ferrigno, audiences would not hear his unique voice—the result of being eighty percent deaf from a series of severe childhood ear infections—in the film or its sequel. (More on that at the end of this section.)

Many of the scenes were shot on location among ancient ruins around Italy, with elaborate interior sets contained in soundstages at the De Paolis INCIR Studios and R.P.A. Elios Studios, both in Rome. Tension between Sybil Danning and Lou Ferrigno existed even beyond the set, having started beforehand during *The Seven Magnificent Gladiators* and reared its head in print and even television interviews. According to Danning, her original role in *Hercules* was as a love interest, but this quickly changed when the two actors would not even speak to each other at the start of production. In more recent interviews, Ferrigno has downplayed this conflict and looks back on the films he did with Danning—and on Danning herself—with great fondness.

Two performers went uncredited on the film: the narrator and the somewhat over-the-top dubbed voice of Hercules. According to director Luigi Cozzi, the legendary dialogue and dubbing director Gene Luotto likely performed narration in his studio in Rome. (Luotto died in 2011.) As for Hercules, the film's executive producer (and occasional actor) John Thompson provided his voice and did the same double duty on the sequel.

MUSIC OF THE MINSTRELS

This was Pino Donaggio's first collaboration with director Luigi Cozzi and his first of six films for Cannon. Prior to *Hercules*, Donaggio had composed music for *Don't Look Now, Carrie, Piranha, The Howling, The Black Cat,* and *Beyond the Door*. His contributions to this film are rich, symphonic associates to contemporary adventure films, especially John Williams' score for *Superman,* that still reflect the style of scores

> FROM OUT OF THE HEAVENS COMES THE STRONGEST MAN ON EARTH.

THE LEGEND LIVES! of sword-and-sandal/*peplum* epics of the 1960s. It has its bombastic highs but also softer, melodic moments. The film's sequel, *The Adventures of Hercules,* would reuse the bulk of the score. Oddly, the films *Gor* and its sequel *Outlaw of Gor* would also later recycle much of it—without credit.

Intrada released a 1,000-copy, limited-edition, thirty-track CD soundtrack in 2007. It expanded on the 1983 Varèse Sarabande LP release, with the inclusion of thirteen additional tracks. Overall, Donaggio's exciting score is worthy of a place on the shelf alongside the likes of Rosenthal *(Clash of the Titans)*, Poledouris *(Conan the Barbarian)*, Holdridge *(The Beastmaster)*, and Whitaker *(The Sword and the Sorcerer)*.

THE SAGA CONTINUES

Lou Ferrigno returned to the role in the slightly more gruesome and psychedelic 1985 follow-up, *Hercules II* (a.k.a. *The Adventures of Hercules*), released in 1985. Although we cover that film in the index, it's worth noting here that its title sequence blatantly rips off *Superman*, right down to the pale blue glowing names rushing toward the screen before a swiftly moving field of stars. The sequel also features a couple of creature cameos, including one by a cut-rate version of Harryhausen's Medusa from *Clash of the Titans* and another by the Id Monster from *Forbidden Planet* . . . or rather, the Id's lesser-known, poorly-rendered Italian cousin. (Do I dare insert a "Cousin Id" joke here?) A single DVD contains both films, should you wish to indulge in this epic double-feature.

TAKE UP THY SWORD!
THE SACRED SWORD OF THEBES (MAGIC SWORD)

Ancient makers of weapons forged the Sacred Sword of Thebes from fragments of a fallen star that possessed the ability to control fire. The sword is not only a dangerous blade in the hands of its wielder; it is also a key to a special lock. While installed in its stand of pure gold, it contains a captured phoenix (or *the* Phoenix, depending on your campaign) in the heart of an active volcano. Due to its ability to control flame, it also prevents that volcano from erupting. Should the sword vacate its stand, the volcano unleashes its suppressed force and releases the phoenix.

In combat, the sword grants bonuses to puncturing attacks and damage. Those slain by it immediately turn to ash.

THE FILM'S DESTINY

A Technicolor '80s spin on the mythological Labors of Hercules—ignoring some and completely butchering others—*Hercules* is an overly ambitious adventure filled with cheesy monsters of both the live-action and stop-motion variety, poorly photographed models, and completely wacky visual effects. There's a laser-beam-spewing mechanical hydra, a guy in a tacky bear-suit who gets chucked into outer space, and a cast of semi-competent actors all doing their best to make heads or tails of it all.

Yet this film—and others of its ilk—is a bright, bold, fun adventure-comic-book-in-motion from the neon decade. Look upon it as nothing more than that. Sometimes the plot wanders a bit and the special-effects budget isn't up to task, leaving you scratching your head and wondering what you've just witnessed, but in the imagery, in Ferrigno's perfectly Hulkish physique, and in the bevy of beautiful women, plenty is here for you to sit back and enjoy.

The film received nominations for a pile of Razzie Awards in 1983 (and won two) for several reasons, so don't get your hopes up too much, but it was the fourth-highest-grossing film in the US for its opening weekend, beaten out only by *Easy Money* (in its second week), *Risky Business* (in its fourth week), and *Mr. Mom* (which enjoyed the top slot six weeks after its release)! Now that's a slice of pop-culture history right there.

THIS YEAR IN GAMING

In 1983, the first of five boxed sets of Frank Mentzer's revised and expanded edition of *Dungeons & Dragons* came out. The initial *Basic Rules* set, affectionately referred to as "the Red Box," featured an iconic cover by artist Larry Elmore and contained a *Players Manual,* a *Dungeon Masters Rulebook,* six polyhedral dice, and a crayon. The next few years saw releases of the other four linked boxed sets, including *Expert Rules, Companion Rules, Master Rules,* and *Immortal Rules.* Material from the first four sets (excluding the *Immortal Rules*) later became the 304-page hardcover *Rules Cyclopedia* released in 1991. Wizards of the Coast acknowledged the importance of the *Basic Rules* set in 2011 with the release of a new "Red Box"—sporting the same cover art—that contained similar booklets and used Fourth Edition *Dungeons & Dragons* rules.

CONQUEST

1984 • Italy/Spain/Mexico
Clemi Cinematografica / Golden Sun / Producciones Esme S.A. • 88m • Color • R

Story: Giovanni Di Clemente
Screenplay: Gino Capone, Josè A. de la Loma Sr., and Carlos Vasallo
Director: Lucio Fulci
Producer: Giovanni Di Clemente
Music: Claudio Simonetti
Director of Photography: Alejandro Alonso Garcia
Art Director: Massimo Lentini
Make-Up Masks: Franco Rufini
Wardrobe: Alvaro Grassi and Costumi Sat
Equipment: Rodolfo Ruzza
Cast: George Rivero (Mace), Andrea Occhipinti (Ilias), Conrado San Martin (Zora), Violeta Cela (Sacrificial Victim), Jose Gras Palau (Fado), Maria Escola (Girl Ilias Saves from Snake), Sabrina Sellers (Ocron), Steven Luotto (Voice of Ilias, English language dub), and Robert Sommer (Voice of Mace, English language dub)
Alternate Title: *Conquest of the Lost Land*

ON THE MAP

This film takes place in a prehistoric, nameless world where the concept of a bow—even a nonmagical one—is alien. Ilias and Mace journey across the savage land, braving sea, swamps, mountains, and caves. Basically, it's hard to nail down where it is; use your imagination.

OUR STORY SO FAR

Ilias, a young warrior armed with a magical bow, sets out on a journey to defeat the forces of evil, while Ocron, a sorceress with some sort of control over the sun, seeks the weapon for her own nefarious purposes. Along the way, Ilias befriends a man who possesses a supernatural bond with the animal kingdom, and together they find themselves beset by wave after wave of deadly obstacles and opponents.

ALTERNATE VERSIONS

The Blue Underground DVD release is uncut (the first time since the film's original European theatrical release), but early videotape releases of the film suffered from numerous edits. Censors removed more than four minutes of material from the 1983 UK release, including shots of nudity, close-ups of Ilias's oozing pustules, and the slaughter of the poor sacrificial victim, her head hacked open and her brains consumed (barf!). As late as 2006, the British Board of Film Classification insisted on additional edits. They might not have been wrong to do so.

IT'S MAGIC

Magic has an odd way of manifesting in this film. To begin with, at first the bow behaves like a normal bow, but suddenly, when its wielder needs the most help, it launches glowing blue arrows that can split apart and strike multiple targets.

Ocron seems to possess magical powers—she can summon Zora—but her abilities might be limited and her displays of solar control a drug-induced sham. Who knows, maybe the entire *movie* is a drug-induced sham.

THE QUEST FOR MEANING

As the chosen hand of the gods (at least, gods are what they appear to be), Ilias receives the magical bow. Presumably he possesses some special trait, that such high forces would select him. Based on all our preconceptions from similar heroic sagas, viewers would be forgiven for assuming that in the end, evil is vanquished and Ilias not only grows and becomes a hero in those dark times but take his rightful place as a representative of the divine forces, *a la* Perseus in *Clash of the Titans*.

It's all the more surprising, then, when Ilias meets a shockingly untimely end—oh, sorry, spoiler!—leaving companion Mace to finish things off as an act of revenge. Sure, Ocron meets her defeat, but the world appears to remain plagued with creatures intent on wishboning innocent girls as our new hero strolls off into the sunset. The gods work in mysterious ways . . . or perhaps they really just don't give a crap. Sometimes a bow is just a bow.

All this aside, Fulci believed he was directing a film about the enduring bond of friendship between Ilias and Mace. Did you get that part?

WHO GOES THERE?

George Rivers—sometimes credited as Jorge Rivero—appeared in a number of Mexican productions and was for many years a box-office draw as a ruggedly handsome leading man. In his first American production, he appeared alongside the great John Wayne in *Rio Lobo*. He also appeared in *Soldier Blue*, *The Last Hard Men*, and *Day of the Assassin*.

Andrea Occhipinti hails from Milan and worked with Lucio Fulci on *The New York Ripper*. You can also find him in *A Blade in the Dark*, *Bolero* (with Bo Derek), and *The Sea Inside*.

Conrado San Martin appeared in *King of Kings* and *The Awful Dr. Orlof*, and in uncredited roles in Sergio Leone's *Once Upon a Time in the West* and *Duck, You Sucker*.

Jose Gras Palau appeared in *Hell of the Living Dead* (credited as Robert O'Neil) as Lt. Mike London, leader of the main commando unit.

Maria Scola, credited as Marie Fields in the US release, starred in *The Raiders of Atlantis*, also known as *Atlantis Interceptors*.

6 DEGREES OF SORCERY

The music occasionally sounds like a cross between a Dario Argento score and the soundtrack to *Flash Gordon* by Queen. The natives with their white makeup and mud-encrust-

> IN A PLACE BEYOND TIME,
> COMES A TERRIFYING
> CHALLENGE BEYOND
> IMAGINATION!

ed hair bear a striking similarity to natives depicted in many of the Italian cannibal films of the time. The young girl saved by Ilias from the snake looks like a cast member from *Quest for Fire* who has wandered onto the wrong set; poor girl. The wolfman soldiers of Ocron look like a cross between Chewbacca from the *Star Wars* films and the apes from the *Planet of the Apes* movies and television series.

Mace is clearly modeled after Dar from *The Beastmaster*. Ocron—especially with her mask off—looks similar to the witches in that film. Her escape by transforming into a dog mimics the transformation of *The Beastmaster* witch who "dies" and flies away in the form of a bird. The mark on Mace's forehead is remarkably similar to the Mark of Eibon in Fulci's 1981 film, *The Beyond*, itself inspired by *The Book of Eibon* created by H. P. Lovecraft contemporary Clark Ashton Smith.

In another *Star Wars* parallel, Ilias is to Mace as Luke Skywalker is to Han Solo. The amusingly fake-looking bird puppets have appeared in other Fulci films, including *Manhattan Baby*. The following of the snake out of the cave came from *Raiders of the Lost Ark*.

Ilias is remarkably similar to Perseus in *Clash of the Titans*, from his bow—a gift from the gods—to his coiffure. Sadly, he does not share Perseus's happier fate.

SHATTERING THE ILLUSION

Producer Giovanni Di Clemente was determined to make *Conquest* after securing the services of actor Jorge Rivero, who at the time was a top box-office draw all over Mexico. Director Lucio Fulci came onto the project with the understanding that he would direct a prehistoric *peplum* (sword-and-sandal film).

Fulci later sang the praises of camera operator Alexandro Ulloa, but the rather confusing decision to shoot everything backlit by the sun and in a perpetual foggy haze did not help the overall look of the picture. This was Fulci's first film after the end of his long-time relationship with cinematographer Sergio Salvati, and it absolutely shows.

Fulci had also recently severed ties with screenwriter Dardano Sarchetti *(Zombie, City of the Living Dead, The Beyond)* and producer Fabrizio De Angelis *(Zombie, The Beyond, The House by the Cemetery)*, all of which might have caused him to tire of the production before completing filming. He left all post-production duties in the hands of his crew and decided not to shoot a second picture, though bound by contract. Di Clemente filed a lawsuit.

Whether in reference to an early concept for what became *Conquest,* or for an entirely different film, an ad promoting an upcoming sword-and-sorcery epic titled *The Sword of Siegfried* appeared in film marketing materials around the time of this film's production. The ad claimed that Fulci was to direct, and principal photography to begin in October 1982. Obviously *The Sword of Siegfried* was never completed . . . or even started, for that matter.

Conquest was a box-office flop in Italy, but thanks to Jorge Rivero's popularity, people lined up to buy tickets throughout Mexico. It had a very limited theatrical release in the United States, with little accompanying fanfare.

MUSIC OF THE MINSTRELS

Keyboardist Claudio Simonetti *(Warriors of the Wasteland, Demons, Opera)* of the group Goblin composed the inconsistent and at times positively cacophonic score. If you're masochistic and so must own a copy: Beat Records released a CD compilation featuring some of Simonetti's music from the films *Aenigma, Morirai A Mezzanotte,* and *Conquest* in 1998.

THE SAGA CONTINUES

Alas, no sequels, spinoffs, tie-ins, or toys based on *Conquest* ever came out, apart from the CD soundtrack sampler mentioned above, despite the incredible marketing potential. Just imagine a little bisectable cave-girl action figure, complete with realistic "intestini"! Someone really missed an opportunity there.

TAKE UP THY SWORD!

THE BOW OF TIME (MAGIC WEAPON)

At first glance, this magical weapon appears to be an ordinary short bow. It offers a moderate bonus when used to shoot standard arrows; however, due to its divine nature, it manifests mystical arrow-shaped bolts of blue energy if, during combat, the user pulls back on the bowstring without notching an arrow. Once such a bolt leaves the bow, it splits into identical shafts of energy that strike all targets within a range equal to twice that of a standard short bow, and it inflicts total damage equal to that of a longbow. These divinely guided beams of light can bypass and even pass through barriers standing between the attacker and the target, with no reduction in damage. The bow can also teleport its owner up to five miles, once per day.

THE FILM'S DESTINY

A true appreciation of Fulci's work is somewhat of an acquired taste, but one cultivated by many in the horror-fan community. If anything, Fulci was a master of mood and, of course, over-the-top gore. Though *Conquest* indeed has some pretty hellacious examples of the grotesque—see poor Violeta Cela getting ripped in two, decapitated, and eaten—the film is nevertheless an overall disaster.

It's also surprising that Fulci skips pulling his almost traditional attacks on eyeballs out of his bag of tricks: usually guaranteed to gross out audiences. (See *Zombie* for a definitive example.) One could point out, however, that Ocron takes an arrow to the eye when Mace shoots her dead, so maybe we can give Fulci that one to maintain his ocular average.

Although the movie pulls off an almost admirable twist that completely undercuts viewer expectations, turning the traditional adventure plot structure on its head (and other limbs), and though Rivero winds up being a strong "lead" (see the latter part of the film to understand this), he struggles behind what appears to be a filter of gauze to the accompaniment of a score that incessantly assaults the ears. For a

> HE IS A HUNTER FROM A FUTURE WORLD TRAPPED IN PREHISTORIC TIMES.

> PART ALIEN...
> PART HUMAN...
> ALL NIGHTMARE

screenplay that apparently needed four people to write it, it doesn't have much of a story, apart from a tale of two dudes wandering around a strange prehistoric world, constantly doing battle with pretty much any living (or unliving) thing that crosses their path. These guys can't even catch a nap! As noted earlier, Fulci himself had major problems with the production of *Conquest*, and it shows.

This film is only for die-hard Fulci fans. It represents the low end of the quality range among the films we showcase in this book.

THIS YEAR IN GAMING

The "final frontier" opened to roleplaying gamers worldwide with the release of the officially licensed *Star Trek: The Role Playing Game* from FASA. Guy McLimore, Jr.; Greg Poehlein; and David F. Tepool—a freelance group of designers who referred to themselves as the Fantasimulations Association—made this RPG accessible to new gamers while still offering an exciting experience for veterans. For the next six years, FASA continued to support the game, with dozens of well-produced supplements and adventures, and even a line of miniatures, before losing the license in 1989.

THE NEVERENDING STORY

1984 • US / West Germany
Neue Constantin Film / Bavaria Studios / WDR / Warner Bros. / Producers Sales Organization
102M • Color • PG

Screenplay: Wolfgang Petersen and Herman Weigel
Based On The Book By: Michael Ende
Additional Dialogue: Robert Easton
Director: Wolfgang Petersen
Producers: Bernd Eichinger and Dieter Geissler
Director of Photography: Jost Vacano
Production Designer and Set Decorator: Rolf Zehetbauer
Art Directors: Johann Kott, Herbert Strabel, and Götz Weidner
Conceptual Artist, Scenery, Creature and Costume Designer: Ul De Rico
Music: Klaus Doldinger and Giorgio Moroder
Director Of Special and Visual Effects: Brian Johnson
Special Effects Make-Up And Sculpture Supervisor: Colin Arthur
Costume Designer: Diemut Remy
Horse Groom: Gaby Richter
Stunt Coordinator: Tony Smart
Cast: Noah Hathaway (Atreyu), Barret Oliver (Bastian), Tami Stronach (The Childlike Empress), Moses Gunn (Cairon), Patricia Hayes (Urgl), Sydney Bromley (Engywook), Gerald McRaney (Bastian's Father), Drum Garrett (1st Bully), Darryl Cooksey (2nd Bully), Nicholas Gilbert (3rd Bully), Thomas Hill (Koreander), Deep Roy (Teeny Weeny), Frank Lenart (Voice of Teeny Weeny), Tilo Prückner (Night Hob), and Alan Oppenheimer (Rockbiter / Falkor / G'mork / Voice of Narrator)

ON THE MAP

The story begins in a real-world town in a generic American city (actually Vancouver, B.C.). From there, the action switches to Fantasia, a strange world of diverse climates and terrain where the fantastic exists alongside the mundane. Atreyu's initial journey in search of a cure for the empress takes him several days on horseback; he travels 10,000 miles, with Falkor's help, to visit the Southern Oracle. G'mork reveals to Atreyu that Fantasia is as limitless as a child's imagination . . . so this is a big place.

OUR STORY SO FAR

An imaginative boy with a love of books comes into the possession of (i.e., steals) a special volume that magically binds him with the fantastical world described within its pages. There its inhabitants fight against the encroaching menace of an empty force known as the Nothing.

ALTERNATE VERSIONS

The German cut of the film runs a few minutes longer than the US release and lacks Limahl's theme song as well as all the other synth-pop tracks from the score. Instead—echoing a similar situation with the two distinct cuts of *Legend*—it features an orchestral score by Klaus Doldinger of Passport, a German jazz band. Numerous other differences include a simplified title sequence with white text on a black background, a scene in which Bastian hides in the attic from the school janitor, and several shots of some of the more unusual characters of Fantasia as Cairon addresses them within the Ivory Tower. The Region A Blu-ray edition of the film features a 5.1 surround-sound track and marks the first time a US release has included a 5.1 track.

IT'S MAGIC

Magic in *The NeverEnding Story* permeates Fantasia, a world created by the hopes, dreams, and limitless imagination of humanity. Belief in the fantastic holds together the very fabric of this realm of strange creatures, beautiful landscapes, and diverse peoples; therefore, magic is basically synonymous with unwavering faith. Shake that faith, and worlds collapse.

This particular world contains magical items, beings, and elements that present themselves throughout the film. The fact that Falkor, a wingless dragon, can soar through the sky implies some sort of enchantment. The talisman called AURYN—yes, always to be written out in caps and with no preceding "the"—guides Atreyu through Fantasia and somehow directly links to the empress: it can grant its magical advantages only through her will. It echoes the look of another famous serpent symbol, the Ouroboros.

THE QUEST FOR MEANING

Because the world of Fantasia is a manifestation of humanity's hopes and dreams—imagination made reality—it theoretically can have no limits. Unfortunately, in these modern times, with people telling each other to take their heads out of the clouds and keep their feet on the ground—to stop daydreaming and face their problems—Fantasia is fading into the Nothing.

The message behind this film is not lost on this generation and likely will remain as relevant to future generations. The sad state of affairs in which children lose interest in books and in the glorious tales contained therein is a hot topic even today. The bookshop owner played by Thomas Hill grumbles about how children don't like books because they require a little effort and don't beep. A writer at the time commented that *The NeverEnding Story* was essentially a 60,000,000-deutschmark ad for books. At the time of writing in 2013, kids continue to turn away from the printed page and toward the illuminated screen.

The film is also one of few examples of a "high fantasy" movie. Atreyu, Bastian, and the empress are the only humans in Fantasia. All the other characters exhibit unusual features and characteristics right out of the pages of a roleplaying-game bestiary.

Speaking of roleplaying games, this film—perhaps more than any other covered in this volume—is most akin to the roleplaying experience. The book is the campaign world as well as the game master, with Bastian and the audience as the players. When Atreyu looks into the mirror, he sees Bastian, implying that from an RPG standpoint, Atreyu is Bastian's player character. When the fourth wall collapses near the end of the film, the empress actually addresses Bastian—and us—begging him to save the world. Roll for success!

> BOY WHO NEEDS A FRIEND FINDS A WORLD THAT NEEDS A HERO.

WHO GOES THERE?

Noah Hathaway started on television. Most know him as Boxey from the original *Battlestar Galactica*. He also appeared in the movie *Troll*, in which he played a character named Harry Potter, Jr.!

Barret Oliver got his start as a young boy in series like *The Incredible Hulk* and *Knight Rider* and appeared in a few memorable films, such as *Uncommon Valor*, *D.A.R.Y.L.* (in which he had the title role), *Cocoon*, and *Cocoon: The Return*. He also starred in the original Tim Burton short *Frankenweenie* as Victor Frankenstein. He now teaches photography, having long ago left acting behind.

Tami Stronach became a dancer and to date has only a couple additional acting credits.

We can forgive Moses Gunn's appearance in Bill Cosby's disastrous *Leonard Part 6* because he starred in so many other damned-cool projects over the years, including the original *Shaft* and its first sequel, *Shaft's Big Score!*, as well as the 1975 *Rollerball*, *The Ninth Configuration*, *Firestarter*, and *Heartbreak Ridge*. He died in 1993 at age 64.

A staple of British television for six decades, Patricia Hayes had several successful ventures on the big screen as well, including *The Terrornauts; Goodbye, Mr. Chips; Willow;* and *A Fish Called Wanda*. She died in 1998 at age 88.

Most associate Gerald McRaney with his long-running TV roles on *Simon & Simon* and *Major Dad*, although his career has spanned decades and includes more than a hundred other credits, including the films *Comanche*, *The A-Team*, *Red Tails*, and *Django Unchained*.

Thomas Hill had recurring roles in TV's *Newhart* and *Wizards & Warriors*. He also appeared in the miniseries *V: The Final Battle* and the films *The Nude Bomb* and *Firefox*. He died in 2009 at age 81.

Seemingly ageless Deep Roy is no stranger to genre films and television, with roles in *Doctor Who*, *Blake's 7*, *The Dark Crystal*, *Star Wars: The Return of the Jedi*, *Return to Oz*, *Freaked*, the 2001 remake of *Planet of the Apes*, *Big Fish*, *Charlie and the Chocolate Factory*, the 2009 *Star Trek*, and its 2013 sequel, *Star Trek into Darkness*.

Alan Oppenheimer is one of those rare actors who has had a successful acting career both on- and offscreen as a voice actor, with almost 300 credits to his name. Perhaps audiences know him best as the second man to play Dr. Rudy Wells on *The Six Million Dollar Man* and as the voice of Skeletor in *He-Man and the Masters of the Universe*. He also voiced characters in *Transformers*, *Bionic Six*, *BraveStarr*, *Rambo*, and *DuckTales*.

6 DEGREES OF SORCERY

A book, a young boy, and a journey into a world of fantasy have since shown up in *The Pagemaster*. As in *Alice in Wonderland*, *Time Bandits*, *Labyrinth*, *The Princess Bride*, and even *Pan's Labyrinth*, events in the real world link to events in a realm of fiction. Taking it a step further, the connec-

> BEGIN A JOURNEY INTO A LIMITLESS UNIVERSE OF ENTERTAINMENT.

tion between film and viewers is reminiscent of John Carpenter's *In the Mouth of Madness*. *South Park* also explored this in its epic *Imaginationland* miniseries, with Falkor making an appearance in the third episode. *The Last Action Hero* explores a similar theme.

The gnomes Engywook and Urgl are remarkably similar to Miracle Max and Valerie from *The Princess Bride*. They also resemble fairly stereotypical tinkerer gnomes in certain roleplaying games and in MMORPGs such as *World of WarCraft*.

The Ivory Tower is very much like the Emerald City, with the Childlike Empress standing in for the Wizard of Oz. The Swamps of Sadness look a lot like Dagobah from *The Empire Strikes Back* or even the Bog of Eternal Stench from *Labyrinth*. A 2005 episode of *Doctor Who*, "The End of the World," mirrors the gathering of various races for Cairon's address; you might also see connections with the classic *Star Trek* episode "Journey to Babel" and the sequence in Ming's palace in *Flash Gordon*.

SHATTERING THE ILLUSION

This was Wolfgang Petersen's first English-language film, following the global success of *Das Boot*. He came in after the firing of the first director, well before filming began. Legendary special-effects artist Jim Danforth provided some of the matte paintings for the film, and future director David Fincher *(Alien³, Se7en, Fight Club, The Social Network, The Girl with the Dragon Tattoo)*, credited as Dave Fincher, assisted with matte photography.

Principal photography began in Germany in 1983—the hottest summer to date!—with much of the production accomplished at Bavaria Studios in Munich. At the time, it was the highest-budgeted film in German history and the most expensive non-US and non-USSR movie, coming in at approximately $27 million.

Rumors have persisted that a horse died in the filming of the Swamps of Sadness sequence, despite cast and crew repeatedly insisting that no animal—nor Noah Hathaway, for that matter—was harmed in the filming. It is possible, however, that a horse or two was distressed a bit by being lowered into a fake swamp on a mechanical platform: the price of fame.

Production wrapped in May of 1984. Steven Spielberg now owns the original AURYN prop, which makes a lot of sense if you think about it.

Michael Ende, the author of the novel, was so displeased with the changes made to his story that he tried to block the making of the movie and then sued the production. The studio won. This film based its plot on half of Ende's book, with the second half waiting until the sequel for adaptation.

The film won the Bavarian Film Award for Best Production in 1985. Noah Hathaway took home the Saturn Award for Best Performance by a Younger Actor.

MUSIC OF THE MINSTRELS

Limahl, lead singer of Kajagoogoo, created quite the ear worm in 1984 with his poppy theme tune for this film, which features music by Giorgio Moroder and lyrics by Keith Forsey. Released as a single, it hit #4 on the UK singles chart and also made the US *Billboard* Adult

Contemporary and Hot 100 lists. Over the years, a number of bands have covered the track, including Dragonland and Kenji Haga.

As with the film *Legend*, two unique soundtracks exist for the film. On the one hand is the Klaus Doldinger orchestral score found exclusively in the German cut of the movie, and then there is the Giorgio Moroder synth-pop score—along with some Doldinger tracks—in the English-language version. Both scores are commercially available, although you might need to check European importers to obtain a copy of the Doldinger-exclusive score.

THE SAGA CONTINUES

The film spawned less-successful sequels in the hands of different directors and actors, as well as live-action and animated television spinoffs. A few computer games came out over the years, including a text adventure in 1985 by Ocean Software for a number of home computer platforms, *The NeverEnding Story II* by LinEL in 1990, and a first-person PC adventure game titled *The NeverEnding Story: Auryn Quest* from DreamCatcher Interactive in 2002.

Rumors of a remake/reboot from Warner Bros. have flown around for a few years now, associated with the Kennedy/Marshall Co. and Appian Way (Leonardo DiCaprio's production company). By 2015, no significant developments have surfaced.

As for the film's enduring legacy, *Robot Chicken* has parodied elements of it a few times, even crafting one sketch titled "The Neverending Party," featuring a bored Atreyu throwing a wild party on a Friday night. Peter Griffin took a brief ride on Falkor's back in an episode of *Family Guy*. There is a metal band from Southern California called *Atreyu*. A short audio sketch called "Falcor vs. Atreyu—Classy Skit #1" appeared on the second studio album, *Turtleneck & Chain*, of comedy/hip-hop group The Lonely Island, in 2011. And if you ever get to Munich, visit the Bavaria Filmstadt, where you can ride a replica of Falkor, complete with blowing fans and a blue screen to transport you into Fantasia!

TAKE UP THY SWORD!

FEATHERED DRAGON (BENEVOLENT MONSTER)

ATTACKS/DEFENSES: Though a non-aggressive creature, the feathered dragon stands his ground if anything threatens him or his friends. Typically, he does his best to slip away from danger unharmed, but he is never cowardly.

POWER/VULNERABILITIES:

FLIGHT: A feathered dragon can travel at great speeds in the air and under the sea. With his incredible stamina, he can traverse fantastic distances without pausing to rest, instead recharging after arriving at his destination.

WATER-BREATHING: He can breathe freely under water.

SUPERNATURAL LUCK: Feathered dragons are in tune with the forces of fate and chance. Whenever the odds seem against one, he has a twenty-five-percent chance of escaping or finding precisely the right clue, answer, or object.

> EXPERIENCE THE ENCHANTED WORLD OF A YOUNG BOY'S IMAGINATION AND BEHOLD THE REMARKABLE ADVENTURE THAT UNFOLDS BEFORE YOUR EYES.

DETAILS: A feathered dragon has a long, serpentine body covered in white fur, feathers, and scales. His facial features resemble those of a canine. Although he has no wings to speak of, he can fly at incredible speeds for long durations. Wise, insightful, and wholly benevolent, he makes for a reliable and compassionate companion. His optimism alone can help him and his companions survive even the onslaught of the forces of darkness.

THE FILM'S DESTINY

Despite a few technical issues and an occasional bit of stilted dialogue, *The NeverEnding Story* is a adventure film with grand artistry and scale, especially for the time in which it was made. Even if you just watch it for the numerous large-scale animatronic puppets, creative makeup, or elaborate costumes, it is something to behold. Today, with an industry dedicated to playing it safe, filmmakers would render ninety percent of of the movie digitally and shoot on green-screen, with the actors—if they're even real themselves—staring at tennis balls on the ends of sticks. But back in the early '80s, the creatures were right there on set, with actors sweating inside suits of thick foam latex and wearing mechanical heads buzzing and whirring in their ears to the manipulations of puppeteers off-camera. Material tossed into fans created environmental effects, and explosions were real. By 2012, the organic qualities of a film like this were extinct, but in 1984, when this screenplay slid across the producers' desks, they didn't scoff at the scope but gathered their funds, found the best physical-FX people in the industry, and told them to build it. The results are not only impressive but also emblematic of the kind of creativity and imagination this movie embraces and celebrates.

There might be fantasy epics more beloved, adventures better remembered, or films more respected, but as a unique ride that not only fascinates and entertains but deals with deep ideas and inspirational themes, *The NeverEnding Story* is something special. Share it with the people you love and pass the tale on to the generations that follow. If you do, the Nothing will never win.

THIS YEAR IN GAMING

Despite securing the Middle-earth license from Tolkien Enterprises two years earlier and releasing supplemental material for the *Rolemaster* line in that time, Iron Crown Enterprises (I.C.E.) didn't launch the first edition of *Middle-Earth Roleplaying*, or *MERP*, until the year *The NeverEnding Story* came out. A simplified version of the *Rolemaster* system, *MERP* proved hugely successful for Iron Crown, spawning dozens of highly detailed sourcebooks, adventure modules, and tie-in boardgames. The company released a second edition of the game in 1993, and the last published *MERP* tie-in product four years after that. The company finally lost the license in 1999.

THE WARRIOR AND THE SORCERESS

1984 • ARGENTINA/US
ARIES CINEMATOGRÁFICA ARGENTINA / NEW HORIZON PICTURE CORP • 81M • COLOR • R

STORY: William Stout and John Broderick
SCREENPLAY: John Broderick
DIRECTOR: John Broderick
PRODUCERS: Hector Olivera, Alex Sessa, Frank Isaac, and John Broderick
MUSIC: Louis Saunders
DIRECTOR OF PHOTOGRAPHY: Leonard Solis
MAKE-UP SPECIAL EFFECTS: Chris Biggs and William Smith
MAKE-UP: George Barry
ART DIRECTOR: Emmett Baldwin
COSTUME DESIGNER: Mary Bertram
SPECIAL EFFECTS: Richard Lennon
STUNT COORDINATOR AND SWORDPLAY CHOREOGRAPHER: Anthony DeLongis
ORIGINAL ART: William Stout
CAST: David Carradine (Kain); Luke Askew (Zeg); Maria Socas (Naja); Anthony DeLongis (Kief); Harry Townes (Prelate Bludge); William Marin (Bal Caz); Arthur Clark (Burgo); Daniel March (Blather); John Overby (Gabble); Richard Paley (Scar-face); Mark Welles (Burgo's Captain); Cecilia North (Exotic Dancer); Dylan Willias, Joe Cass, Michael Zane, Herman Cass, Arthur Neal, Herman Gere, and Gus Parker (Zeg's Guards); Ned Ivers (Slave); Lilian Cameron (Drowning Slave); and Eve Adams (Woman at Well)
ALTERNATE TITLE: *Kain of Dark Planet* (working title)

ON THE MAP

The story takes place on the planet Ura (or "Vra," if you believe the back of the box), in the divided city of Yam-A-Tar.

OUR STORY SO FAR

On the planet Ura, two rival warlords vie for control of a single source of water, positioned between their gates. Kain, a.k.a. "the Dark One," is a highly skilled mercenary from the wastelands who sells his sword to the highest bidder, often shifting his allegiance depending on the situation.

ALTERNATE VERSIONS

The running time varies between the US (81 minutes) and UK versions (74 minutes), but as we go to print, we cannot confirm details about variations between these two cuts of the film.

IT'S MAGIC

The princess and titular (heh) sorceress, Naja, possesses some sort of arcane knowledge linked to an ancient religious order. She uses it to forge the Sacred Sword of Ura. While overseeing the sword's creation, she states that it has been "forged from our blood," implying an off-screen ritual as well as a variation on that old blood magic. Once forged, the sword can pass through stone and anvil—and let's not forget flesh—like a hot knife through butter. Didn't we once see some infomercials for knives that were as magical as that?

THE QUEST FOR MEANING

Yet another tale of a once-enlightened world that has since descended into barbarism, this movie offers us a world that has gone to waste. The old order—particularly the religious one—might once have kept such chaos at bay, but at some point might won out over reason. Naja, a priestess of the squelched order, is now prisoner of a warlord keen on crushing his enemy with the aid of a legendary sword that only she can craft—so those who represent the spiritual order of days gone by are now to bring about the end of everything they knew. Prelate Bludge, also of the order, lives in hiding between the warlords—and Kain is a Homerac: a holy warrior of a forgotten time. Together they rally a movement to strike back, crush this new world, and perhaps return things to the way they once were—one corrupt, shoddily built town at a time. But will it work?

The movie isn't necessarily as deep as all that, but perhaps it's an attack on anti-intellectualism and militarism, both issues the real world has dealt with for some time now. Who knew *The Warrior and the Sorceress* would become so relevant all over again?

WHO GOES THERE?

David Carradine appeared in hundreds of films and television shows, leaving behind a legacy of cool that will last a very long time. He began his onscreen acting career in his late 20s, despite the influence of father and legendary actor John Carradine, with a number of TV roles in programs like *Wagon Train*, *The Alfred Hitchcock Hour*, and *Shane*. He achieved incredible success in the role of Shaolin monk Kwai Chang Caine (a.k.a. Grasshopper) on the TV series *Kung Fu*, a role he would revisit several times via TV movies and the sequel series *Kung Fu: The Legend Continues* in the 1990s. His second collaboration with Roger Corman (his first was *Boxcar Bertha* in 1972) was *Death Race 2000*; it would not be his last. Carradine also starred in *Deathsport*, *Circle of Iron*, *Q*, *Warlords*, *Wizards of the Lost Kingdom II*, *Future Force*, *Evil Toons*, *Waxwork II: Lost in Time*, *Light Speed*, *Kill Bill: Vol. 1* and *Vol. 2*, *Hell Ride*, and *Crank: High Voltage*. He died in 2009 at age 72.

Known for his many villainous roles, character-actor Luke Askew made his big start in *Cool Hand Luke* alongside Paul Newman, but for many, the role that really got him noticed was that of "the stranger on the highway" in *Easy Rider*. He also appeared in films like *The Beast Within*, *Dune Warriors* (again alongside David Carradine), and *Frailty*, but the majority of his roles were on the small screen, in series like *Mission: Impossible*, *S.W.A.T.*, *The Six Million Dollar Man*, *How the West Was Won*, *Fantasy Island*, *The Greatest American Hero*, *Tales of the Gold Monkey*, *Knight Rider*, *Matt*

Houston, Automan, Kung Fu: The Legend Continues (with guess-who), and more recently, *Big Love*. He died in 2012 at age 80.

Maria Socas also appeared in *Wizards of the Lost Kingdom, Deathstalker II,* and *Hollywood Boulevard II,* in which she played an Amazon queen.

Harry Townes worked almost exclusively in television through the 1950s, '60s, and '70s, appearing in *Alfred Hitchcock Presents, Men into Space, Twilight Zone, Thriller, The Wild Wild West, Star Trek, Kung Fu, Planet of the Apes, Ark II, Buck Rogers in the 25th Century,* and a memorable two-part *The Incredible Hulk,* in which he played a character afflicted by a condition similar to that of Dr. David Banner. Later in life, he more-or-less retired and became an Episcopal priest in his hometown of Huntsville, Alabama, where he died in 2001 at age 86.

William Marin (Guillermo Marin) was a fixture of the Spanish stage and also had over seventy-five credits in film and television productions. He died in 1988 at age 82.

Arthur Clark, otherwise known as Armando Capo, also had roles in *Barbarian Queen* and *Amazons*. Richard Paley's only other credit was in *Wizards of the Lost Kingdom*.

Mark Welles (Marcos Woinsky) was a fixture in several sword-and-sorcery films—especially those linked with Roger Corman—throughout the '80s. Look for his familiar face under hoods, behind masks, or with eye patches in the first *Deathstalker, Wizards of the Lost Kingdom, Barbarian Queen, Amazons, Stormquest,* and *Deathstalker II*.

Arthur Neal (Arturo Noal) is another sword-and-sorcery veteran. He worked as an actor and stunt coordinator in films like *Wizards of the Lost Kingdom, Barbarian Queen, Amazons, Stormquest, Deathstalker II,* and *Highlander II: The Quickening*.

6 DEGREES OF SORCERY

It all begins with Dashiell Hammett's 1929 novel, *Red Harvest*, which bears more than a few similarities to Akira Kurosawa's 1961 film, *Yojimbo*. Sergio Leone transplanted that story into the Old West for 1964's *A Fistful of Dollars* starring Clint Eastwood. Twenty years after that, the core elements of the plot found their way to the fantasy world known as Ura.

From the first frame, this movie feels and sounds like a spaghetti western, obviously drawing a lot of its inspiration from Leone's work, with its dry and rocky desert backdrop, a solitary stranger, and a musical score reminiscent of the work of Ennio Morricone. In fact, in a few moments later in the film, Morricone's spirit most *definitely* makes its presence known.

Ura's twin suns are a nod to Tatooine from *Star Wars*, while the rocky, angled crags above which they rise in the opening shot look like the outcroppings of Vasquez Rocks, a Los Angeles-area formation seen in countless genre productions but most famously used as the site of Captain Kirk's battle with the Gorn in the "Arena" episode of *Star Trek*. The gratuitous nudity mirrors popular fantasy art of the time by artists like Frank Frazetta and Boris Vallejo. The large, spiked skull in Zeg's throne room also appears in the *Deathstalker* films, as do a number of the sets. The lizard advisor to Bal Caz is reminiscent of Salacious Crumb of Jabba's palace in *Return of the Jedi,* and Bal Caz himself is very much in

> AN AGE UNDREAMED OF. AN AGE OF MYSTERY AND MAGIC. OF SWORDS AND SORCERY.

> HE WAS THE WARRIOR SHE HAD BEEN WAITING FOR ... WAITING WITH A SWORD AND A SACRED VOW!

the mold of Jabba the Hutt, although one can see similarities to Baron Harkonnen of *Dune* as well. When this same reptilian creature walks upright, he looks a bit like a Skeksis from *The Dark Crystal*.

The Protector in the dungeons is one-half Audrey II *(Little Shop of Horrors)* and one-half Roper from *Dungeons & Dragons* (the RPG, not the film). A few bits of music sound like ripoffs of James Horner's score from *Krull* (which of course Horner lifted from his own *Star Trek II* score). The slavers behave similarly to the Orcs and Uruk-hai later depicted in *The Lord of the Rings* films. Incidentally, the basic plot returns in Walter Hill's 1996 Bruce Willis vehicle, *Last Man Standing*.

SHATTERING THE ILLUSION

What became *The Warrior and the Sorceress* was originally *Kain of Dark Planet*, a title that even made it to the February 1981 issue of *Fangoria* magazine and came up again in the May 1981 issue of *Starlog*, which then announced its cancellation. The project was based on a screenplay by writer and artist William Stout, who has contributed to numerous genre projects, including *Conan the Barbarian*, *The Return of the Living Dead*, *Masters of the Universe*, *Pan's Labyrinth*, and *The Mist*.

The *Gor* novels by John Norman provided the original inspiration. Stout was not pleased with the large number of changes director and cowriter John Broderick made to his script, many of which helped transform Stout's original story into little more than a fantasy-themed copy of *Yojimbo* (a situation further detailed earlier, in the "6 Degrees" section).

Shooting took place back-to-back with *Deathstalker* and thus shares many of the same sets. Director John Broderick wanted his friend, actor Gary Lockwood *(The Magic Sword, 2001: A Space Odyssey)*, in the role of Kain, but Stout's first choice was David Carradine.

Carradine might not have been so happy to win the role, after all, when on the third day of production, he broke his right hand. To hide the cast, he wore a black leather gauntlet.

Broderick couldn't adequately handle the difficult shooting schedule, so the production ran longer than planned. This infuriated executive producer Roger Corman. Broderick never directed another picture for Corman.

On Corman's insistence, an American replaced all of Argentinean actress Maria Socos's dialogue. This was the last Corman production released by New World Pictures before he launched New Horizons.

MUSIC OF THE MINSTRELS

Sharing a few uncredited cues with Óscar Cardozo Ocampo's score to *Deathstalker*, *The Warrior and the Sorceress* music of Argentinean composer Luis María Serra (billed here as Louis Saunders) delivers a varied experience. Drawing inspiration from both Ennio Morricone and James Horner, Serra made the score an inconsistent mishmash of styles. From the early whine of analog synthesizers to the twang of electric guitars and a few dramatic orchestral movements, there is a surprising lack of focus. This is not to say that Serra is an incompetent composer—his fifty-some film credits suggest otherwise—but *The Warrior and the Sorceress* likely does not rank highly on the list.

THE SAGA CONTINUES

Apart from the appearance of some sets, costumes, weapons, footage, and music in a few other films following the release of *The Warrior and the Sorceress* (see the *Deathstalker* series and *Wizards of the Lost Kingdom* for a few examples), the story of Kain and the world of Ura would never again be revisited; however, William Stout has stated that at one point David Carradine asked him to pen a sequel.

TAKE UP THY SWORD!

THE SACRED SWORD (MAGIC WEAPON)

This weapon, a dangerously sharp two-handed greatsword in anyone's hands, becomes even more lethal when wielded by a holy warrior. This magical blade grants significant bonuses to attacks and damage—double for holy warriors.

The weapon can sever a limb or even a head with a critical hit. Roll 1d8 and consult the accompanying table to determine the location of the severance.

A skilled smith working under the guidance of a priestess of the holy order can forge a sacred sword. The ritual and forging must take place at night, with the steel anointed by blood freely given by those within the order. The price for the creation of such a weapon is difficult to determine, because the priestess usually selects the weapon's wielder prior to its forging.

d8 Roll	Severs At
1	Left wrist
2	Right wrist
3	Left shoulder
4	Right shoulder
5	Left thigh
6	Right thigh
7	Torso
8	Neck

THE FILM'S DESTINY

This was one of those many films we all saw on the "Action" shelf at our local video stores in the mid-'80s and begged our parents to rent. What teenager could resist the faux-Boris painting—actually created by Joann Daley—on the cover of that box, featuring all the elements we had seen between the covers of our *D&D* books: a ripped warrior (with David Carradine's face), a lethal-looking serpent about to strike, an approaching horde of shadowy figures, and a scantily dressed sorceress weaving some sort of smoky magic spell? Let's not ignore the fact that she has four breasts; surely that's twice as interesting! Of course, the cover is a completely inaccurate representation of the film, apart from two elements: David Carradine (sans the muscular physique), and those four breasts... although even those are misrepresented on the box, shown as fully covered. This might have been a lesson in false advertising just waiting to happen... but maybe it was the way Carradine was holding his "sword" on that cover or the mention of "exotic women" on the back of the box: for many of us the desire to see the film would burn in our brains until the fateful day we were old enough to rent it on our own. After all that anticipation, once we did set eyes on it, all we came away with was a poorly acted, poorly produced fantasy with—admittedly—a hundred percent more boobs than normal. Hell, for some, that was probably enough.

No, this is not a great film by any stretch of the imagination. A lot of the other movies covered in this volume have left us believing that repeated viewings would entertain just as much, but *The Warrior and the Sorceress*—a cold, poor entry—is not one of them. Carradine clearly walks through this one to pick up a check, and most of the supporting cast either is equally disinterested or simply lacks in acting ability. You do get to see a fair number of bare breasts for your eighty-one minutes, but trust us: after ten minutes of that, you grow a bit numb to the whole deal.

THIS YEAR IN GAMING

West End Games, a company already known for its tactical wargames, released the first edition of *Paranoia* at GenCon in August of 1984. Written by Greg Costikyan, Dan Gelber, Eric Goldberg, and Ken Rolston, the game took the RPG industry by storm, receiving loads of critical acclaim and winning the Origins Award for Best Roleplaying Rules of 1984. The dystopian science-fiction setting and free-for-all (fun-over-rules) approach proved a winner for West End for three editions, until the company dissolved in 1998. In 2004, Mongoose Publishing released a new edition of the game; a 25th Anniversary Edition followed in 2009.

RED SONJA

1985 • Netherlands/US • MGM / Dino De Laurentiis Company
89m • Color • PG-13

Writers: Clive Exton and George MacDonald Fraser
Based On The Character Created By: Robert E. Howard
Director: Richard Fleischer
Producer: Christian Ferry
Music: Ennio Morricone
Director of Photography: Giuseppe Rotunno
Production Designer: Danilo Donati
Art Director: Gianni Giovagnoni
Costume Designer: Danilo Donati
Creative Makeup: Rino Carboni
Special Effects: John Stirber
Special Visual Effects: Universal City Studios
Armorer: Giuseppe Cancellara
Martial Arts: Kiyoshi Yamasaki
Martial Arts Consultant: Ernie Reyes, Sr.
Stunt Coordinator: Sergio Mioni
Fish Machine And Spider Designed And Built By: Colin Arthur and Giuseppe Tortora
Cast: Arnold Schwarzenegger (Kalidor), Brigitte Nielsen (Red Sonja), Sandahl Bergman (Queen Gedren), Paul Smith (Falkon), Ernie Reyes, Jr. (Tarn), Ronald Lacey (Ikol), Pat Roach (Brytag), Terry Richards (Djart), Janet Agren (Varna, Red Sonja's Sister), Donna Osterbuhr (Kendra the High Priestess), Lara Naszinsky (Gedren's Handmaid), Hans Meyer (Red Sonja's Father), Francesca Romana Coluzzi (Red Sonja's Mother), Stefano Mioni (Barlok, Red Sonja's Brother), Tutte Lemkow (Wizard), Kiyoshi Yamasaki (Kyobo), Tad Horino (Swordmaster), Erik Holmey (Brytag's Warrior, uncredited), and Sven-Ole Thorsen (Brytag's Bodyguard, uncredited)

ON THE MAP

In the Hyborian Kingdom, we journey from Red Sonja's unnamed birthplace to a temple housing the Talisman, then the ruined city of Hablock, before ending the quest at the fortress of Queen Gedren in Berkubane, the Land of Eternal Night.

OUR STORY SO FAR

A flame-tressed warrior named Sonja joins forces with a mysterious wanderer, an aggravating young prince, and the prince's oafish but dedicated bodyguard to seek vengeance against an evil monarch who murdered her family and took her honor. The malevolent Queen Gedren also holds a magical power that could doom the entire world. The unlikely companions are the only ones who can stop Gedren and destroy the object before all is lost.

ALTERNATE VERSIONS

In the UK, a very slightly edited version made it to theaters and home video, but later releases restored the full cut of the film. Because the opening sequence seems painfully edited from a much longer prologue that would have set up Sonja's origin in more detail, one wonders if another, unrated cut of this film might exist in the archives somewhere.

IT'S MAGIC

The primary manifestation of otherworldly forces is the glowing green globe known as the Talisman, about which not much is known. Of divine origins, it supposedly played a part in creating the world. It can also destroy the world in a nuclear metaphor that "rings" familiar to *Lord of the Rings* fans. Its power appears gender-specific: it vaporizes men, but women can manipulate it. Is this a play on the argument of hunter-gatherer versus nurturer?

Between that and the queen's apparent use of a steampunk-like magical imaging apparatus, which seems more like technology, we are back in Tolkien territory and might even wonder: Where *did* the Talisman come from? If the characters think it's from the gods, did it come from the sky? Doesn't that suggest a more sci-fi, extraterrestrial explanation? Hmm....

There *is* magic afoot in Sonja's world, or at least some kind of supernatural force, if the blue spirit that appears to her in the movie's opening moments is any indication. We never learn what sort of specter it is, apart from the fact that its sole purpose seems to be to sum up a scene savagely cut down to a brief montage in order to garner a PG-13 rating. Perhaps the spirit is from the MPAA? Now that's *truly* frightening!

THE QUEST FOR MEANING

Red Sonja is a paradoxical figure, because she's supposed to be a strong woman in a male-dominated ancient world, but her most famous incarnation in Marvel Comics is also as eye candy in a scale-mail bikini for fanboys. Though Neilsen wears a far more sensible outfit for the film, the script undercuts the potential to make a leap ahead in the genre by placing Sonja in situations in which she regularly needs help and even rescue; sorry, Kalidor. She can handle herself in battle, but she often makes critical strategic mistakes that require her to rely on support from a guy who just looks *so* familiar.

Sexuality is also a subject of debate for critics of this film, because from the start Queen Gedren's interest in Sonja is very personal. Sonja's reaction is one of utter revulsion. Let's be fair here: Gedren's people did kill Sonja's family and rape her—but the subtext suggested by Sonja's disgust is that homosexuality is evil. Maybe Sonja doth protest too much, because the Grandmaster does ask her not to hate men so much. She also has that rule about not allowing a man to "take" her who has not bested her in combat, which not only keeps men at arm's length but might in fact be a vow of chastity ... or is it? After all, it doesn't say anything about other women. Maybe Sonja is just confused.

> A WOMAN AND A WARRIOR WHO BECAME A LEGEND.

WHO GOES THERE?

Statuesque model Brigitte Nielsen was a fantasy figure of the '80s and '90s before her marriage to Sylvester Stallone and before other aspects of her personal life made her a regular feature of supermarket tabloids and reality television shows. After her debut in this film, she went on to roles in *Rocky IV, Cobra, Beverly Hills Cop II, Chained Heat II,* and *Galaxis*. She also provided the voice of the Amazon queen in *Ronal the Barbarian*.

Paul L. Smith's formidable presence also graced films like *Midnight Express, The In-Laws, Popeye, Dune, Haunted Honeymoon,* and *Gor*. He appeared in the television series *Emergency* and the miniseries *Masada*. He died in 2012 at age 75.

Ernie Reyes, Jr., also appeared in films like *The Last Dragon, Teenage Mutant Ninja Turtles II: The Secret of the Ooze, Surf Ninjas,* and *Indiana Jones and the Kingdom of the Crystal Skull,* as well as in TV shows *Highway to Heaven, Sidekicks, Kung Fu: The Legend Continues,* and *Charmed*.

Ronald Lacey was one of film's slimiest toadies, a latter-day Peter Lorre who most famously played Toht in *Raiders of the Lost Ark*. He also appeared in films like *The Fearless Vampire Killers, Gawain and the Green Knight, Firefox, Yellowbeard, Sahara, Sword of the Valiant: The Legend of Sir Gawain and the Green Knight, The Adventures of Buckaroo Banzai Across the 8th Dimension, Flesh+Blood,* and *Valmont,* and on television series such as *Z Cars, The Avengers, Jason King, Thriller, The New Avengers, Blake's 7, Hart to Hart, Magnum P.I., Blackadder II,* and *The Ray Bradbury Theater*. He died in 1991 at age 55.

Terry Richards achieved cinema immortality as the swordsman taken down by Indiana Jones with a single shot in *Raiders of the Lost Ark*, but he also appeared in *The Pink Panther Strikes Again, Flash Gordon,* and *Tomorrow Never Dies*. He died in 2014 at age 81.

Janet Agren also appeared in infamous cult-horror fare like *Eaten Alive!* and *City of the Living Dead,* as well as *Hands of Steel* and a very different version of *Aladdin*.

This was Tutte Lemkow's final role in a career that included dance as well as acting and often intersected with pop-culture icons. He choreographed sequences for an episode of the *Doctor Who* story "The Celestial Toymaker" and for films like *Casino Royale, The Fearless Vampire Killers,* and *Theatre of Blood*. He also appeared in the *Doctor Who* stories "Marco Polo," "The Crusade," and "The Myth Makers," was a dancing Cossack in *A Shot in the Dark*, played the title character in the feature-film adaptation of *Fiddler on the Roof*, wooed Diane Keaton in *Love and Death*, and told Indy how to use the headpiece of the Staff of Ra in *Raiders of the Lost Ark*. He died in 1991 at age 73.

Tad Horino appeared on television in *I Spy, Ironside, M*A*S*H, Kung Fu,* and *Columbo,* and in films such as *Galaxina; Oh, God! Book II; Bachelor Party; Eliminators; Bill & Ted's Bogus Journey; Teenage Mutant Ninja Turtles III; Surf Ninjas;* and *Mulholland Dr.* He died in 2002 at age 81.

6 DEGREES OF SORCERY

The film begins with a text crawl, a common device famously used in *Star Wars*. The blue specter that illuminates Sonja's fate is akin to the similarly colored wisps that guide Merida in *Brave*. Sonja also receives a sword, perhaps a gift from the gods like Perseus's gifts in *Clash of the Titans*. The green glowing ball of a Talisman looks very much like the evil Loc Nar from *Heavy Metal*; perhaps this was one of its unrecorded journeys? The careful handling of the Talisman recalls the tentative lifting and transport of the Ark of the Covenant—another object imbued with divine power—in *Raiders of the Lost Ark*. Although the statue in the Swordmaster's amphitheater never moves, it has a Ray Harryhausen-esque look.

Sonja's selection of a sword echoes the drawing of Excalibur from the stone in the Arthurian legend. Choosing the sword from among a variety of other weapons also presages the choosing of the Grail in *Indiana Jones and the Last Crusade*. Sonja's sister burns on a pyre like Darth Vader at the end of *Star Wars: Return of the Jedi* (and like characters in a thousand other fantasy films: let's be fair). Continuing the consistent links to that galaxy far, far away, the use of the Talisman against Hablock recalls the destruction of Alderaan by the eerie green beam of the Death Star.

Queen Gedren's golden half-mask resembles that of the Phantom of the Opera and Klytus's mask in *Flash Gordon*. (No shock there, because Danilo Donati also worked on the designs for that film.) Gedren's towered domain and the molten rock that divides its Land of Eternal/Perpetual Night is like Sauron's tower and the shadowy realm of Mordor in *The Lord of the Rings* series. In the same vein, the Talisman, which could represent corrupting technology in a natural world, is also interchangeable with the One Ring. The Talisman's fate, the same as Queen Gedren's—plunging into a river of lava—is identical to that of the "Precious" and its would-be keeper, Gollum. Similar falls also turn up in *The Dark Crystal* and *Your Highness*.

The enormous skeleton that spans the chasm is similar to the mysterious, huge bones half-buried in the desert of Tatooine in *Star Wars*. The robot sea-monster poses a threat not unlike the shrieking eels in *The Princess Bride*. Sonja and Kalidor's lengthy battle, ending with both of them collapsing with fatigue, foretells the legendary knock-down, drag-out fight between Roddy Piper and Keith David in *They Live*. Queen Gedren's spider pet might suggest an affinity for those creatures that links her with the High Priest of the Spider in *Ator, the Fighting Eagle*.

SHATTERING THE ILLUSION

Although Robert E. Howard receives credit as the character's creator, his Red Sonya of Rogatino from the 1934 story "The Shadow of the Vulture" bears little resemblance to the Red Sonja seen here. The film takes more cues from the Marvel Comics version (also spelled with a "j") created by writer Roy Thomas and artist Barry Windsor-Smith; for example, the film incorporates comic-book Sonja's vow to which we referred earlier. Thomas had adapted the 1934 tale for comics in 1973's *Conan the Barbarian* #23, hybridizing Sonya with a character in another Howard creation (published posthumously): 16th-century French swordswoman Dark Agnes de Chastillon. A series of six novels by David C. Smith and Richard L. Tierney—one of which Thomas also adapted into comics form—came out in the early 1980s. It was time to introduce movie audiences to Sonja once Howard's Conan achieved iconic status through Arnold Schwarzenegger's portrayal in those two films.

Dino De Laurentiis had a harder job finding the right actress to carry the film than expected. Only two months before shooting began did he bring in 21-year-old Danish model Brigitte Neilsen for a screen test, after he saw her on a magazine cover.

The opening sequence, not a full-fledged opening, reeks of the severe editing down to the brief montage. Trailers for the movie feature footage that would have appeared in a lengthier version of that sequence.

Although the film saw the reunion of Schwarzenegger and Bergman (sort of) from *Conan the Barbarian*, it did not achieve the significance it could have, because of two factors. First: Bergman, initially offered the lead role, decided it was too similar to Valeria and wanted to play the villainess. Second, Schwarzenegger's character was Conan in all but name, because despite De Laurentiis's involvement in the *Conan* movies, the rights to the name remained with Universal Pictures.

Whether the character was named Conan or not, Schwarzenegger's fate was sealed, because under his contract to De Laurentiis, he had to appear in a third *Conan* installment. With the poor performance of *Conan the Destroyer*, Schwarzenegger fulfilled his contractual commitment to the producer in two parts: with the movie *Raw Deal*, and by reuniting with *Destroyer* director Richard Fleischer—an odd decision in itself—to play a supporting role in this film . . . but not as "Conan"—oh, no.

Shooting in Italy provided the production with the opportunity to recruit legendary composer Ennio Morricone for the soundtrack. Having already written similar music for 1983's *Hundra* (one of many *Conan* clones, which offers a feisty female lead and is well-regarded by many but not listed in this book due to lack of sorcery), Morricone borrowed from that work and Basil Poledouris's Hyborian themes from the *Conan* movies to craft the sound of this one. (More on that later.) William Stout did uncredited creature design work on the film.

Following this film's release, Schwarzenegger's growing discontent with its existence became well known. He was angered at having prominent billing despite his small role, a move the producers made to cash in on his growing star-power. His then-wife Maria Shriver supposedly told him at the film's premiere that if *Red Sonja* didn't ruin his career, nothing would. Many years afterward, he called it one of the worst movies he'd ever done and said that he kept his children in line by threatening to make them rewatch it.

The movie garnered no accolades from critics or the Academy and was a bonafide box-office flop, but it did receive an impressive three Golden Raspberry Award nominations in the categories of Worst Actress and Worst New Star, both for Nielsen, and Worst Supporting Actress for Bergman. Nielsen actually won the Worst New Star award: not Red Sonja's finest victory.

MUSIC OF THE MINSTRELS

How is it possible that a man who had composed many amazing, iconic scores turned in this lackluster, sleep-inducing stuff? Ennio Morricone, who had defined the sound of the spaghetti western and made body-horror palpable with his heartbeat-driven soundscape for John Carpenter's *The Thing*, apparently turned on autopilot, perhaps due to lack of inspiration, and churned out a forgettable, passionless score.

Though it sounds epic and sweeping only during the end titles, you can obtain a copy . . . if you must. JMP Records in Germany released a contemporary vinyl soundtrack, and Varese Sarabande released both an LP and a limited, 1,000-copy CD version in 1990, featuring suites of music pulled from the vinyl album that don't follow the order in which the music played in the film. The CD also included Morricone's work on the film *Bloodline*.

Collectors disappointed by this lackluster presentation and accompanying sound issues gravitated to a cassette version that marginally improved the quality. In 2010, long after the

> A WOMAN AND A WARRIOR
> THAT BECAME A LEGEND.

Varese Sarabande version went out of print, Perseverance Records picked up the gauntlet and put out a 2,000-copy soundtrack with properly ordered tracks and detailed critical liner notes on the music cues and their legacy. (There was a legacy?)

At a quick glance, the excellent album cover art, taken from the release poster created by the prolific Renato Casaro (whose work includes the *Conan* movies and others covered in this book), could confuse you. It features the looming presence of Schwarzenegger's Kalidor holding his sword aloft, dwarfing the figure of Red Sonja with her sword lowered (subtle), but rest assured you're not buying a *Conan* album.

THE SAGA CONTINUES

The unengaging production that led a legend like Morricone to falter also meant that little peripheral activity occurred around the release of this would-be franchise starter. *Marvel Comics Super Special* #38 did offer a comic-book adaptation of the film, also published in a two-issue miniseries. The writer and artist were both women: Louise Simonson and Mary Wilshire. The only other live-action appearance of the character to date came in an episode of the 1997-1998 *Conan* TV show, in which Angelica Bridges played the redheaded warrior.

In 2008, enticing ad-art featuring Rose McGowan as Sonja in her comic-book scale-mail outfit made the Internet rounds, heartening fans around the world: perhaps a really good—or at least really good-looking—adaptation of the character was on its way. Spearheaded by McGowan's then-boyfriend, filmmaker Robert Rodriguez, the production began development through Rodriguez's Troublemaker Studios but then halted; McGowan said that a previous car accident had left her with an arm injury that sword-handling would worsen.

In 2011, *Conan the Barbarian* remake producer Avi Lerner announced that director Simon West was involved in a new effort to bring Sonja back to the big screen, with actress Amber Heard a favorite for the lead role. Since then, though, production has not yet begun.

TAKE UP THY SWORD!

THE TALISMAN (MAGICAL ARTIFACT)

The Talisman is an ancient artifact linked to the origins of the world, now in the care of a religious order. Appearing as a large (roughly eighteen inches in diameter) green glowing sphere of unknown composition held within an ornate golden lattice, it can create in the hands of the divine, or focus destruction via raging storms and earthquakes. It draws its power from light; thus, if banished into shadow, it can deactivate. Its fate lies in its eventual and inevitable annihilation at the hands of its guardians.

As a source of life generation, the Talisman aligns with females, regardless of species, so they may touch it without harm. It instantly wipes from existence any male who lays a hand upon its surface. If anyone uses the Talisman as a force of destruction, its power can target any number of creatures ranging from an individual (a lethal bolt of lightning) to an entire kingdom (a tremendous earthquake).

Alas, the lifespan of the Talisman is limited if it remains in the light. According to prophecy, on a particular day known only to those of the holy order, the sphere will self-destruct and split the world asunder.

THE FILM'S DESTINY

This film has so much going for it, but almost all of it has to do with its visuals, in particular the beautifully shot landscapes and the elaborate, colorful costume and set designs. Sadly, this wonderful milieu is woefully underpopulated, as if the Hyborian Kingdom had been evacuated just before shooting began—and the characters who do show up are cardboard cutouts often acted by performers with limited range.

The plot offers very little motivation for anyone's behavior beyond the fact that they all are who they are. Gedren, for example, is evil, but we receive little explanation; she just fills the "big bad" slot and gives Bergman a chance to squander any goodwill she gained from her far better performance in *Conan the Barbarian*. To be fair, Schwarzenegger's Kalidor gets some explanatory backstory.

At first glance, Neilsen seems a good choice to play Sonja. She gives it more effort than some people might credit her for, but she doesn't have the chops to convey any emotional depth in her character between battle sequences.

Even the battles—essential for success in the genre—have no flair, with flat choreography and filming. Neilsen can handle a sword well enough, but the movie doesn't take advantage of her skill or make her look as heroic as it should.

As with many other entries in this genre, this film links to Frank Frazetta artwork, but the imagery never leaps off the canvas to come alive. That, along with the aforementioned throwaway score by Morricone, leaves us with a very disappointing product that is less than the sum of its parts. Though *Red Sonja* is often pretty to look at, unlike far worse films that are fun because they're so bad, this one just aggravates because it suggests a possibility of something much better and never delivers. Still, if one approaches the movie with low expectations, it is an acceptable if mediocre way to pass the time . . . once.

THIS YEAR IN GAMING

Created in 1984 by a group of former TSR alums, including Mark Acres, Troy Denning, Andria Hayday, Gali Sanchez, Stephen D. Sullivan, and Michael Williams, Pacesetter Ltd. entered its second year with a number of successful RPGs and support products already in circulation, including *Chill* (gothic horror), *Star Ace* (science fiction), and *Timemaster* (time travel). In the summer of 1985, the company introduced the concept of an "instant adventure roleplaying game" with *Sandman: Map of Halaal*. (The originally advertised title was *The Bard's Legacy*, but the release of *The Bard's Tale* computer game from Electronic Arts that year likely put the kibosh on that plan.) The boxed set, intended as the first in a series, contained everything a game master and three players needed to begin a collaborative investigation into a mystery that offered a real-life $10,000 cash prize! Unfortunately, although Pacesetter had already advertised the second set, *Key to the Inland Sea*, financial issues led to the company's dissolution in 1986, prior to the release of further sets. The mystery of the "Sandman," as well as the identities of the player characters, would forever go unrevealed.

THE BLACK CAULDRON

1985 • US • WALT DISNEY PICTURES / SILVER SCREEN PARTNERS II • 80M • COLOR • PG

STORY: David Jonas, Vance Gerry, Ted Berman, Richard Rich, Al Wilson, Roy Morita, Peter Young, Art Stevens, and Joe Hale (based on The Chronicles of Prydain series by Lloyd Alexander)
DIRECTORS: Ted Berman and Richard Rich
PRODUCER: Joe Hale
MUSIC: Elmer Bernstein
CHARACTER DESIGNERS: Andreas Deja, Mike Ploog, Phil Nibbelink, Al Wilson, David Jonas, and Milt Kahl (uncredited)
TITLE GRAPHICS: Ed Garbert
END TITLE DESIGN: David Jonas
CAST: Grant Bardsley (Taran); Susan Sheridan (Eilonwy); Freddie Jones (Dallben); Nigel Hawthorne (Fflewddur Fflam); Arthur Malet (King Eidilleg); John Byner (Gurgi/Doli); Lindsay Rich, Brandon Call, and Gregory Levinson (Fairfolk); Eda Reiss Merin (Orddu); Adele Malis-Morey (Orwen); Billie Hayes (Orgoch); Phil Fondacaro (Creeper/Henchman); Peter Renaday, James Almanzar, Wayne Allwine, Steve Hale, Phil Nibbelink, and Jack Laing (Henchmen); John Hurt (The Horned King); and John Huston (Prologue Narrator)
ALTERNATE TITLE: *Taran and the Magic Cauldron*

ON THE MAP

The adventure begins and ends on a small farm, Caer Dallben, owned by an enchanter in the mystic land of Prydain. The journey takes us from the castle of the Horned King and the Fairfolk's underground kingdom to the Marshes of Morva.

OUR STORY SO FAR

The evil Horned King seeks an ancient black cauldron said to possess the power to raise an army of deathless warriors. To find his prize, he seeks a magical, oracular pig named Hen Wen, and tasks a young assistant pig-farmer named Taran with taking the pig to safety. Along the way, Taran meets several friends, including furry little Gurgi, beautiful and headstrong Princess Eilonwy, and the bard Fflewddur Fflam. Together they must evade the forces of the Horned King and find and destroy the Black Cauldron before its powers can doom the world.

ALTERNATE VERSIONS

Prior to this film's release, Disney studio chairman Jeffrey Katzenberg demanded edits of approximately twelve minutes of footage, including scenes deemed too shocking or violent, particularly in regard to the zombielike Cauldron-Born and some of their acts of violence against innocent people. Rumors of additional edits—including a scene of Taran using his sword to slay enemies during his escape, as well as a scene depicting the Cauldron's mist dissolving a man—have also circulated over the years. A cut with all of these original scenes intact has never come out; however, versions of the film with additional edits have aired on television. The "25th Anniversary Edition," released on DVD in September 2010, includes one deleted scene, "The Fair Folk," as a bonus feature.

IT'S MAGIC

The porcine Hen Wen has clairvoyant powers considered highly unusual, but other types of magic are not so strange in the world of *The Black Cauldron*. Dallben performs a ritual complete with magic words before Hen Wen's abilities come to light, the Horned King can harness the powers of darkness and anxiously longs for the day when the shadowy powers of the cauldron will course through his veins, the three godlike witches cast spells with ease, transforming people into frogs and back with flicks of the wrist, and the Fairfolk are magical creatures through and through.

Taran, however, possesses no magical talents; nevertheless, he's the hero of the tale. He even acknowledges being little more than a pig-farmer. Furthermore, the "self-sacrifice" of Gurgi, another non-magical character, leads to the salvation of the world and the destruction of the Horned King. Speaking of which . . . .

THE QUEST FOR MEANING

Like so many other tales of young, brash heroes—see *Star Wars*, for example—the story told here is about the transition of boy into man, of child into adult. While most of us ease into that stage of our lives, characters in tales like these get kicked into the deep end of the swimming pool and told to mind the sharks. Apart from Eilonwy and Taran, pretty much everyone else in the film is well into adulthood, many of them even elderly and feeble. It's as if Prydain itself has grown old and weary. The actions of the Horned King—despite his diabolical aims of destruction, domination, and death—actually help bring about the world's rebirth.

Sacrifice plays a huge part in the story, as when Gurgi gives his life to save his friends and the world, stepping into the cauldron in Taran's place. Even after that, Taran stands and fights, risking his own life to try to save his furry little friend. This entire thematic thread, however, somewhat loses its impact when the witches simply bring Gurgi back from the dead and give the story a happy ending.

WHO GOES THERE?

The Black Cauldron was the big Hollywood project that should have made Grant Bardsley a household name. As a boy, he starred alongside Elizabeth Taylor, Jane Fonda, Ava Gardner, and Cicely Tyson in the George Cukor-directed fantasy *The Blue Bird*. The bulk of his other credits are on the small screen, in *The Famous Five*, *Tales of the Unexpected*, and *The Jim Henson Hour*.

Genre fans might best know Susan Sheridan for her vocal performance in the role of Trillian in the original BBC4 radio production of *The Hitchhiker's Guide to the Galaxy*, a role to which she returned in 2012 for a live touring production of the original saga.

Larger-than-life Oscar-winning writer/actor/director John Huston left an impressive legacy spanning several decades. With dozens of writing and directing credits to his name, including such classics as *The Maltese Falcon, The African Queen, Moby Dick* (cowritten by Ray Bradbury), *The Man Who Would Be King,* and *Prizzi's Honor,* as well as numerous acting roles, including *Battle for the Planet of the Apes, Chinatown,* and the Rankin/Bass animated specials *The Hobbit* and *The Return of the King* (as Gandalf), Huston was already a respected force in Hollywood when he read the prologue for *The Black Cauldron.* He died in 1987 at age 81.

Another John worthy of note and critical praise is John Hurt. A lot of us remember him as Kane, the unfortunate crewmember of the *Nostromo* who met a gruesome end at breakfast in *Alien,* but it's pretty much guaranteed that you all have seen him in other films over the years. Some of his notable live and voice performances include contributions to *I, Claudius; Midnight Express; Watership Down;* Ralph Bakshi's *The Lord of the Rings; The Elephant Man; History of the World: Part I; 1984; Spaceballs* (parodying his *Alien* role); *Rob Roy; Contact;* the first and final two *Harry Potter* films; both *Hellboy* movies; *V for Vendetta; Indiana Jones and the Kingdom of the Crystal Skull* (sigh); and *Immortals*. He's also the voice of the Dragon on the TV show *Merlin* and the War Doctor in the 50th-anniversary *Doctor Who* story "Day of the Doctor."

Legendary actor Nigel Hawthorne had a long, award-winning career both in front of the camera—in film and television roles in *Firefox, Gandhi, Demolition Man, The Madness of King George,* and *Amistad*—and at the microphone, lending his voice to animated projects such as *Watership Down, The Plague Dogs,* and Disney's *Tarzan*. He died in 2001 at age 72.

Yet another talented British actor with a widely diverse resume is Arthur Malet. With more than 120 credits to his name, stretching back to the 1950s, he has appeared in TV series like *Alfred Hitchcock Presents, Perry Mason, My Favorite Martian,* and *Dallas,* as well as a wide selection of animated and live-action films, including *Mary Poppins, Young Frankenstein, Halloween, The Secret of NIMH, Beastmaster 2: Through the Portal of Time, Hook,* and *Anastasia*. He died in 2013 at age 85.

If you grew up in the 1980s, you might remember John Byner as the star and host of the irreverent Canadian sketch-comedy show, *Bizarre*. A master impressionist, Byner has had a long voice-acting career, with roles in *The Pink Panther Show, Garfield and Friends, Aaahh!!! Real Monsters,* and *Duckman.*

Brandon Call was 8 years old when cast in his first motion picture as the voice of one of the Fairfolk. He also appeared in the films *Jagged Edge, Warlock,* and *Blind Fury,* as well as the TV show *The Charmings,* although audiences probably know him best for his role as J.T. on the long-running sitcom *Step by Step.* While working on that series, he was involved in a violent traffic dispute and wound up shot in both arms. Fortunately he made a full recovery, but he dropped out of showbiz after *Step by Step* went off the air.

A veteran of stage and screen, Eda Reiss Merin was already in her 70s when she took the role of Orddu. Most of us remember her for roles that came after that: on TV in *Amazing Stories,*

> HIDDEN BY DARKNESS. GUARDED BY WITCHES.
> DISCOVERED BY A BOY. STOLEN BY A KING.
> WHOEVER OWNS IT WILL RULE THE WORLD. OR DESTROY IT.

Misfits of Science, and *Beauty and the Beast,* and in movies like *Ghostbusters, Turner & Hooch,* and *Don't Tell Mom the Babysitter's Dead.* She died in 1998 at age 84.

Adele Malis-Morey also appeared in *Kingdom of the Spiders, Critters,* and *Doc Hollywood.* She died in 2000 at age 72.

Audiences will forever remember Billie Hayes as the long-nosed, red-haired, wildly made-up comedic villain Witchiepoo on TV's *H. R. Pufnstuf,* and she is perfectly fine with that despite a long and varied career. Her first big role was in 1959's *Li'l Abner,* in which she played "Mammy" Yokum. After appearing in a number of TV shows throughout the '60s, '70s, and '80s, Hayes began working as a voice actor, contributing to *Aaahh!!! Real Monsters, Duckman, Rugrats, Johnny Bravo, Teen Titans,* and *Transformers: Rescue Bots.*

Phil Fondacaro is no stranger to genre films, thanks to being a little person working in Hollywood. His first role was in 1981's *Under the Rainbow,* but he also appeared in *Something Wicked This Way Comes, Star Wars: Return of the Jedi, Ragewar* (a.k.a. *The Dungeonmaster), Hard Rock Zombies, Troll, Willow, Phantasm II,* and *Land of the Dead.*

Peter Renaday has more than 130 credits to his name, most as a voice actor; however, some of his most recognizable roles don't occur onscreen: he has provided a number of memorable voices for attractions in various Disney theme parks. As for animation, Renaday provided voices for *Challenge of the GoBots, The Transformers, Defenders of the Earth, Teenage Mutant Ninja Turtles, Gargoyles, Justice League,* and *Ben 10: Ultimate Alien.* He also voiced a number of characters in videogames and appeared on camera in films like *The Love Bug* and *The Devil and Max Devlin,* as well as television shows like *Dallas, Night Court,* and *Angel.*

James Almanzar—apart from having an awesome last name suitable for any sword-and-sorcery character—made his first film appearance in 1963's *The Quick and the Dead* and his last in 2000's *The Harvesters.* He also appeared alongside Elvis Presley in *Charro!* and appeared in TV series, including *The Man from U.N.C.L.E., The Wild Wild West, Mission: Impossible, Gunsmoke,* and *Columbo.* He died in 2002 at age 67.

Up until the death of Wayne Allwine in 2009 at age 62, only three actors had performed the voice of Mickey Mouse: Walt Disney, James MacDonald, and Allwine. That role alone kept him working steadily for more than twenty years, in everything from *Mickey's Christmas Carol* and *Who Framed Roger Rabbit* to *Toontown Online* and *Kingdom Hearts* videogames.

6 DEGREES OF SORCERY

Elements of the story come from the collection of Welsh tales called the *Mabinogion,* which also inspired the novels from which this film derives. The narration at the top of the film, read by John Huston over a vista of swirling dark clouds, is mighty similar to the opening narration from *Evil Dead II,* even down to the opening words: "Legend has it . . . ." Huston's voice also links it to similar narration provided by him in the Rankin/Bass Tolkien adaptations and even in *Battle for the Planet of the Apes.* Much of the score sounds like music from *Ghostbusters,* and with good reason. (See **Music of the Minstrels**.)

The look of Dallben's farmstead is reminiscent of idyllic images of the Shire from the films based Tolkien's work. Taran is eager to go off to war much like Luke Skywalker in *Star Wars.*

Dallben readying Hen Wen for a vision works like the readying of the Palantír in *The Lord of the Rings*, even down to the villain then sensing those using it. Dallben interrupts the visions in the same way that Gandalf covers the Palantír. The initial apparitions viewed in the water appear to have come directly from the "Night on Bald Mountain" sequence in *Fantasia* and might be an intentional homage. Dallben is very much in the mold of Gandalf and Obi-Wan Kenobi; he even sends Taran off on his quest in the same way Gandalf sends Frodo out of the Shire and Kenobi takes Skywalker off Tatooine.

Dragons circle the Horned King's fortress as the mounted Nazgul circle Barad-dûr in *The Lord of the Rings*. When Taran envisions himself as an armored and celebrated warrior, he bears some similarities to Dirk the Daring in the Don Bluth-animated *Dragon's Lair* arcade games. Some elements of the sequence in which Taran looks for Hen-Wen in the Forbidden Forest came from from *The Sword in the Stone*. Gurgi sounds a bit like Andy Serkis's interpretation of Gollum—or vice-versa—and even refers to the hero as "master." The dragon designs are reminiscent of Maleficent's dragon form from *Sleeping Beauty*.

Creeper, the Horned King's froglike lackey, is quite similar to Larry, the bouncy lizard-mutant servitor of Blackwolf in Ralph Bakshi's *Wizards*, or even Bartok in Don Bluth's *Anastasia*. He's also akin to another Gollum, the one voiced by Brother Theodore in the Rankin/Bass *Lord of the Rings* specials. The Horned King sounds a bit like the villainous Mok from Nelvana's *Rock & Rule*, as voiced by Don Francks.

Eilonwy's magical bauble appears to glow blue much like Bilbo's magical sword, Sting, when in the presence of evil, and it bobs around following its companions like Tinkerbell *(Peter Pan)*, Bit *(Tron)*, and Oona *(Legend)*. Speaking of Tinkerbell, she—or at least a character remarkably similar to her—appears among the Fairfolk, even down to her hair and fringed skirt. Eilonwy bears some resemblance to Princess Odette from the animated version of *The Swan Princess*, also directed by Richard Rich.

The Black Cauldron's wrath visited upon the Horned King, his minions, and his entire fortress is reminiscent of the chaos spewed forth from the Ark of the Covenant at the end of *Raiders of the Lost Ark*. Of course, raising an army of the dead can have bad consequences *(Army of Darkness)* and good results, too *(The Lord of the Rings: The Return of the King)*.

SHATTERING THE ILLUSION

Disney first optioned Lloyd Alexander's *Chronicles of Prydain* book series in 1971, but not until the end of the decade did it begin adapting the first two volumes in the series, *The Book of Three* and *The Black Cauldron*, taking the title of the second book for the film adaptation. At the time, *The Black Cauldron* was Disney's most ambitious animated feature film, as well as its most expensive, coming in at $25 million. Shot in 70mm, it boasted more special visual effects than any Disney film of the previous forty-five years. As the company's twenty-fifth animated feature, it also marked a number of historical "firsts": it was Disney's first PG-rated animated feature, first animated feature not to include any musical numbers, first animated feature to use CGI, and (surprisingly) first animated feature to have a full end-credits sequence. All of Disney's previous films had opted for the old-school extended title sequences instead, up to and including 1981's *Fox & The Hound*.

Disney artists Mel Shaw and James Coleman contributed to the overall look of the film, with more than 2.5 million illustrations rendered in preproduction. Uncredited, Tim Burton worked as a concept artist on the film, but Disney rejected his designs as decidedly unlike anything it was producing at the time. Sharing cubicle space in the studio with Burton was animator Andreas Deja, who designed the Horned King and later went on to design Gaston *(Beauty and the Beast)*, Jafar *(Aladdin)*, and Scar *(The Lion King)*. This was Deja's first film with Disney.

In 1979, with preproduction well underway, animator Don Bluth left Disney and took thirteen colleagues with him. This delayed production, as did a ten-week-long animators' strike in 1982. Plans were drawn up and even tested to add a "holographic" sequence in theaters during the scenes featuring the Cauldron-Born, but the concept proved too expensive. Hayley Mills was originally cast as the voice of Eilonwy, and even mentioned having the role at the start of a 1981 episode of *Walt Disney's Wonderful World of Color*, titled "The Illusion of Life."

When Jeffrey Katzenberg took charge as studio chairman, he not only hated *The Black Cauldron*; he also discussed eliminating feature animation altogether. As discussed earlier in "**Alternate Versions**," Katzenberg caused yet another delay in the production and release of the film when he demanded edits to remove some of the darker content. At one point, he went into the editing room and physically began cutting the movie until Disney CEO Michael Eisner interceded.

The movie's release, originally planned for the 1984 holiday season, had moved to the summer of 1985 when all was said and done, and it went to theaters with parts of the completed animation removed. It was a critical and commercial failure that sullied the grand tradition of Disney feature animation and sent it into dormancy until the success of *The Little Mermaid* in 1989.

MUSIC OF THE MINSTRELS

Undeniable similarities exist between Elmer Bernstein's score for this film and his work on *Ghostbusters*. Production for the movies happened within a couple years of each another, and both feature extensive use of the ondes Martenot, a keyboard variant of the theremin, invented in France in 1928. Its iconic sound—the result of varying oscillation frequency within vacuum tubes—plays in numerous films, including *Lawrence of Arabia* (Maurice Jarre) and *Amélie* (Yann Tiersen), as well as television series such as *The Outer Limits* (Dominic Frontiere) and *The Thunderbirds* (Barry Gray). The sounds of *The Black Cauldron* also share a number of similarities with Leonard Rosenman's adventurous score for Ralph Bakshi's animated version of *The Lord of the Rings*, released a few years earlier.

The score was about as under-appreciated as the film, but Varèse Sarabande did release a re-recorded thirty-minute sampler, performed by Bernstein and the Utah Symphony Orchestra, on vinyl and CD in 1985. That release went out of print in the early '90s but csame back to lifeonline in 2007. In 1996, a bootleg known as "the Taran release" leaked, featuring more than seventy minutes of music of varying quality. Thankfully, in April 2012, Disney and Intrada teamed up to release the ultimate version of the score, remastered by Randy Thornton and containing liner notes by Jeff Bond. This new version features more than seventy-five minutes of original music across thirty-two tracks. For the completist: one of the tracks from the score also appears alongside tracks from *The Magnificent Seven, True Grit, Wild Wild West*, and *The Great Escape* on the compilation *Elmer Bernstein: Great Composers*, released by Varèse Sarabande in 1999.

> STOLEN BY A KING … DISCOVERED BY A BOY …
> IT CAN EITHER RULE THE WORLD … OR DESTROY IT!

THE SAGA CONTINUES

For those wishing to learn more of Taran and the world of Prydain, the Newbery Award-winning source material upon which the film is based (*The Chronicles of Prydain* series by Lloyd Alexander) is still very much in print. For the initial release of the film, the cover of the second volume in the series in both the Yearling and Dell Books editions featured the movie-poster artwork, along with the caption, "Now a major motion picture from Walt Disney Pictures."

In 1986, Sierra On-Line released a computer game based on the film for a number of platforms, including the Apple II, PC, Atari ST, and Amiga. Author Roberta Williams based it somewhat on the company's hugely successful *King's Quest* series of games, simplifying it for children.

Tie-in children's books, plush characters, collectible enamel pins, and McDonald's Happy Meal toys—including at least one of Gurgi—came out over the years. For tabletop gaming stats (specifically for *Dungeons & Dragons 3.5*) for both the Black Cauldron and the unliving Cauldron-Born, get yourself a copy of *Dragon Magazine* #340, originally published in February 2006.

A VHS of the film came out in response to the insistence of fans in 1998, followed two years later by a DVD released as part of Disney's "Gold Collection." This disc, though relatively light on content, offered a few gems in the rough, including a fun interactive trivia game featuring clips from the film, an original Halloween-themed Donald Duck short entitled "Trick or Treat," and a still-frame gallery that is actually nothing to scoff at! Delve into the gallery for an impressive collection of images illustrating everything from initial project development, including photos of cast and crew, to promotional artwork and even a selection of preproduction and final images from an impressive-looking Tokyo Disney attraction based on the film. In 2010, the "25th Anniversary Edition" DVD, which contained even more fascinating content, superseded that edition. It included a deleted scene and a second interactive game, along with all the previously released material.

Surprisingly, Disney still holds the rights to the *Prydain* series. Perhaps one day it will return to Lloyd Alexander's fantastic world … but don't hold your breath.

TAKE UP THY SWORD!

GOLDEN BAUBLE (MAGICAL ARTIFACT)

The golden bauble is an ancient artifact that bonds with its user for as long as the user lives or continues to command it. While dormant, it appears as a perfect sphere of gold or brass roughly the size of an orange, but when activated it floats above the user and glows with a golden light equivalent to that of a standard torch. The user can command it to brighten or darken. It glows blue in the presence of evil creatures within a twenty-foot radius.

A semi-sentient artifact, it can move on its own, usually directly above or slightly ahead of its owner. For some inexplicable reason, it chases off small creatures, particularly rodents. Some dark forces believe the bauble possesses a talent for sniffing out certain magical items, thus making it a highly prized artifact.

THE FILM'S DESTINY

In an interview conducted for Scholastic, author Lloyd Alexander admitted to enjoying the movie despite the minimal connection between his work and the finished product. He added that the book was more emotionally complex and might offer readers a deeper experience. To be fair, Alexander was probably being a tad gracious . . . and thankful for what had likely been a profitable movie deal.

The film was a failure at the box office, earning only $21.3 million, and was widely regarded—at least within Walt Disney Pictures—as a failure of its makers in general, forcing the animation department to undergo radical changes over the next few years. Disney essentially disowned the movie, even suppressing mention of it in publicity. Eventually, succumbing to pressure from fans, it released the film on VHS in 1998, thirteen years after the initial theatrical release. Maybe the company was right in its judgment; overall, the movie is an uneven and disappointing entry in both its genre and Disney's lavish legacy of animated classics. The plot moves quickly—Taran arrives at the Horned King's castle no less than fifteen minutes into the film—and somewhat sloppily, with several things happening without any forewarning whatsoever. There's an odd infatuation with large-breasted women—including a dancing gypsy in the castle and Orwen (into whose expansive cleavage Fflewddur Fflam ventures in the form of a frog)—but that's a bit of a tradition in Disney films, emphasized slightly here thanks to the more liberal PG rating. We recommend this one only for Disney enthusiasts or for those who want to take a look at one damned-frightening animated villain: the Horned King. Eek!

THIS YEAR IN GAMING

Using a core-rules system similar to that employed by the hugely popular *Star Trek: The Role Playing Game* published in 1983, FASA released *The Doctor Who Role Playing Game*. Though the company supported it with three two-book sourcebook sets covering the Daleks, the Cybermen, and the Master, along with seven adventure modules, a line of miniatures, and even two solo-play paperback adventure books, it discontinued the line the following year due to mediocre reviews and disappointing sales figures. Though it existed only for a year, the boxed set underwent content and cosmetic changes, including revised box art, the removal of publicity images of Colin Baker (the Sixth Doctor), and three variant covers for the rulebooks within.

WIZARDS OF THE LOST KINGDOM

1985 • ARGENTINA/US • TRINITY PRODUCTIONS • 72M • COLOR • PG

SCREENPLAY: Tom Edwards (a.k.a. Ed Naha)
DIRECTOR: Hector Olivera
PRODUCERS: Frank Isaac and Alex Sessa
MUSIC: Chris Young and James Horner
DIRECTOR OF PHOTOGRAPHY: Leonard Solis
PRODUCTION DESIGNER: Mary Bertram
MAKE-UP SPECIAL EFFECTS: Mike Jones
MAKE-UP: Mary Laura
SPECIAL EFFECTS: Richard Lennox
COSTUMERS: Gloria Hartwell And Beatrice Rowe
STUNT COORDINATORS: Arthur Neal and Guy Reed
CAST: Bo Svenson (Kor); Vidal Peterson (Simon); Thom Christopher (Shurka); Barbara Stock (Udea); Maria Socas (Acrasia); Dolores Michaels (Aura); Edward Morrow (Wulfrick / Old Simon / Gulfax); August Larreta (King Tylor); Michael Fontaine (Hurla); Mark Welles (Rongar); Mary Gale (Linnea); Norton Freeman (Sipra); Arch Gallo (Bobino); Mark Peters (Timmon); Rick Gallo (Malkon); Patrick Duggan (Advisor); Art Tass (Warrior I); Carl Fountain (Warrior II); Ernie Smith (Friar); Nick Cord (Bat Creature); Carl Garcia (Lizardtaur); Helen Grant (Rongar's Sister); and J. C. Topper, Richard Paley, and Guy Reed (Rongar's Warriors)
ALTERNATE TITLE: *Wizard Wars* (working title)

ON THE MAP

We start in the peaceful kingdom of Axholm. When Shurka—with some help from Queen Udea—usurps control, Wulfrick teleports Simon and Gulfax to safety in a forest somewhere beyond the edge of the kingdom. From there, they must journey back to the kingdom, passing through haunted caverns and traversing raging waterfalls.

OUR STORY SO FAR

When villainous sorcerer Shurka assassinates King Tylor, Simon—son of the court wizard Wulfrick (who also died at Shurka's hands)—must go on a quest to help restore the kingdom and recover a lost magical ring. Along the way, he is joined by furry companion Gulfax and alcoholic mercenary Kor the Conqueror.

ALTERNATE VERSIONS

This is another case of varying running times. The American VHS release even has different lengths listed between the box and the tape! The UK tape says "85 minutes," which, if true, would mean thirteen more minutes of Bo Svenson to enjoy in that edition. That's probably only because it feels longer, but don't say we didn't warn you.

IT'S MAGIC

The wizards in this realm can sling bolts of energy, disintegrate enemies from a distance, and mutter incantations capable of distorting the others' perceptions. Wulfrick's ring gives Simon his most powerful abilities, and Shurka can observe Simon from afar via Wulfrick's Knowledge Pool. Simon believes that his magic won't work beyond the walls of the castle, but he proves this untrue, first by disrupting the Knowledge Pool.

Simon can also manifest images in water with a wave of his hands. He even indulges in a little necromancy when he raises the dead Foxfire warriors.

Shurka transforms three advisors into mice. On Hurla's property, Simon casts a powerful spell capable of disintegrating or teleporting the lizardtaur. Linnea creates a rainbow bridge across the falls for Simon and Kor to cross. Shurka murders Udea and Bobino with the gentlest waving of his hand. The final battle between Shurka and Simon features fireballs, swirling blue vortexes, and hellfire. With the ring in his possession and Shurka defeated, Simon appears able to use powerful magic, teleporting himself from a castle tower to the ground with but a thought. So there's lot of crazy magic in this one, but that's the point.

THE QUEST FOR MEANING

This isn't the most profound film in the book. We're probably working too hard to try to find some thematic meaning here, but let's indulge for a minute, shall we?

The film focuses on a quest for vengeance but also spends a fair amount of time dwelling on the concept of belonging. Young Simon knows that he belongs in the castle. Prior to Shurka's insurgency, he was in a good place with his father under the rule of a benevolent king. Kor, however, doesn't know where he belongs, but when given the chance to join with others he opts for that instead of going off on his own, so clearly he has a desire for connection and companionship. Ultimately, though, Kor belongs alone and on the road. Shurka believes that he belongs on the throne and has clearly spent time contemplating this: not only does he find flaws with the kingdom's leadership; he also holds contempt for it. Udea stands in the way of Shurka's plans, because though she plays his games, she seems to believe that she belongs on the throne. (Ah, the game of thrones: you win or . . . you've heard it?)

Lastly, although for the most part we just see Aura stoically standing up to Shurka's rather gross advances, her heart clearly belongs to Simon. The movie doesn't explore the relationship as much as it deserves. Vengeance, strength in belonging and forging bonds, and true love conquering all: it's a familiar trifecta of fantasy tropes.

WHO GOES THERE?

Horribly miscast actor Bo Svenson started his career on television in shows like *Mission: Impossible*, *Daniel Boone*, *Ironside*, and *Kung Fu*. For some who grew up in the '70s, his version of the Creature in the 1973 TV-movie adaptation of *Frankenstein* remains a unique and memorable performance. Later that decade, he broke into feature films and appeared in movies like

Walking Tall Part II (along with its sequel, *Final Chapter: Walking Tall,* and the subsequent TV series), *The Son of the Sheik, The Inglorious Bastards, North Dallas Forty, The Delta Force, Heartbreak Ridge, Speed 2: Cruise Control, Kill Bill: Vol. 2,* and *Inglourious Basterds*. He also lent his voice to *The 7 Adventures of Sinbad*.

Vidal Peterson (born Vidal Palacios) also started his acting career on television, appearing in sitcoms like *Mork & Mindy* and miniseries like *The Thorn Birds*. He also appeared as a Romulan in an episode of *Star Trek: The Next Generation* and a Cardassian in *Star Trek: Deep Space Nine*. His only other credited feature-film appearance—and the role for which audiences probably know him best—is as Will Halloway in the adaptation of Ray Bradbury's dark fairytale, *Something Wicked This Way Comes*.

Thom Christopher has inserted himself into a few different corners of fandom, ranging from a long run in the daytime soap opera *One Life to Live* (for which he won an Emmy), to appearing as feather-topped Hawk in the second season of *Buck Rogers in the 25th Century,* to playing his two sword-and-sorcery roles under Roger Corman's banner in this film and *Deathstalker and the Warriors from Hell* (a.k.a. *Deathstalker III*).

Another veteran of the small screen, Barbara Stock appeared in *CHiPs, Fantasy Island, Remington Steele, The A-Team, Knight Rider, Otherworld, Spenser: For Hire, MacGyver, Dallas,* and *Charmed*.

6 DEGREES OF SORCERY

Amusingly, the working title for Ralph Bakshi's *Wizards*, covered elsewhere in this volume, had the working title *War Wizards* through much of its production, while this film's working title was originally *Wizard Wars*! Well, it might seem amusing if you look at it from a certain angle.

The cover art for the UK videotape release features imagery lifted from a variety of other well-known sources. In the upper left we see a Skeksis from *The Dark Crystal*. Riding atop the dragon in the middle of the montage is none other than Luke Skywalker from *Star Wars*! Talk about truth in advertising. Meanwhile, the image of Simon astride the chimera that appears with the US box art is clearly meant to attract fans of *The NeverEnding Story*.

The film includes recycled footage from both *Deathstalker* and *Sorceress*, including a couple scenes of violence that don't fit the tone of the rest of the movie. Due to this footage, as well as actors and even costumes from the *Deathstalker* films (one of the dwarf actors appears in both *Deathstalker II* and this film in the exact same outfit), *Wizards of the Lost Kingdom* comes across as a sort of sequel to some of those films—although more kid-friendly, with only one relatively innocent flash of boob.

Further *Star Wars* connections include Gulfax, who is the white, '70s shag-carpet answer to Chewbacca. The line, "Are you talkin' to me, furball?" further emphasizes the homage (or parody).

Wulfrick's Knowledge Pool is a variant of the Mirror of Galadriel from *The Lord of the Rings: The Fellowship of the Ring*. Shurka bears a striking resemblance to Leezar from *Your Highness*. The wizard duel between Wul-

ON THE FAR EDGE OF FANTASY
THE ULTIMATE CONFLICT IS
DRAWING NEAR . . .

frick and Shurka comes off as an homage to elements of the duel between Craven (Vincent Price) and Scarabus (Boris Karloff) in *The Raven*.

> A BOY MAGICIAN ON A
> FABULOUS ADVENTURE
> THROUGH A WORLD BEYOND
> FANTASY!

Kor has apparently borrowed Kain's sword (the Sacred Sword of Ura) from *The Warrior and the Sorceress*. Does this mean that Kor is a Homerac as well? Wulfrick's communication with his son from beyond the grave is much like Obi-Wan's posthumous guidance in *Star Wars* (again), and his telling Simon to draw the sword from the tree alludes to the drawing of Excalibur from the stone in every Arthurian story you've ever read or seen.

Simon's desire to raise the four fallen warriors to help in battle is much like Aragorn seeking the aid of the armies of the dead in *The Lord of the Rings: The Return of the King*. The raised dead warriors themselves resemble the blind Templar Knights from the *Blind Dead* series of films that also inspired Peter Jackson's take on the Nazgul in the *Rings* movies. A few of them lean up out of a thin layer of soil in a fashion similar to that of the notorious "Ol' Worm-Eye" zombie from Lucio Fulci's *Zombi 2*. They also ask Simon to join them in much the same way as the demons do in *The Evil Dead*. Lastly, as they return to their graves, they quote the Monster from *The Bride of Frankenstein* in saying, ". . . We belong dead."

The diminutive lizardmen bear some resemblance to the disappointingly redesigned Sleestaks of the 1991 *Land of the Lost* TV series. The end credits roll over a shot of Kor wandering off through a daylit field while bombastic James Horner music plays; alas, *Krull* ends in much the same way.

SHATTERING THE ILLUSION

Tom Edwards is a pseudonym for screenwriter Ed Naha *(Troll; Dolls; Honey, I Shrunk the Kids)*. *Wizards of the Lost Kingdom* was Naha's second and last script for executive producer Roger Corman, his first being the summer camp comedy *Oddballs* starring Foster Brooks.

Argentine writer, director, and producer Hector Olivera helmed the film, having already directed *Barbarian Queen* and *Cocaine Wars* for Corman. Because this film used footage from other films, particularly *Sorceress* and *Deathstalker,* some fans desperately eager to make sense of this sprawling epic saga (yes, we're kidding) have retconned the films and grouped them together as part of a series all set on the same world.

MUSIC OF THE MINSTRELS

The movie features a veritable feast of heroic-sounding James Horner music, much of which sounds like it came from one of his other scores . . . because it did. In fact, all of Horner's music featured in this film is in the soundtrack for *Battle Beyond the Stars*, released in 1980. Still, even if it is secondhand Horner, it's a decent score, sharing more than a few similarities with his work from films prior to *Wizards of the Lost Kingdom*. He also reused that original score for several Roger Corman productions; one wonders what sort of contract he

> A BRAVE BOY AND A GREAT WARRIOR SEEK THE RING OF ULTIMATE POWER.

signed to allow for that. For those interested in obtaining a copy: as of this writing, BSX Records still offers the limited-edition score for *Battle Beyond the Stars,* originally released in the summer of 2011. If you're a completist, check out the scores for *Space Raiders* and *Barbarian Queen* as well.

THE SAGA CONTINUES

A 1989 sequel bears little or no relation to the first film other than in name. It also borrows liberally from a lot of the same sources. Recycled movies: now there's an ecologically friendly way to craft fantasy films.

The creators of the 1988 *Andy Colby's Incredible Adventure* (also known as *Andy Colby's Incredible Video Adventure, Andy Colby's Incredibly Awesome Adventure,* and *Andy and the Airwave Rangers* . . . just in case you needed to track it down) crudely inserted several scenes from this movie into that film, including a few scenes cut from the final version, such as one of Kor besting someone in a sword fight and stealing his wine, which then leads to Kor staggering around the forest, drunk. Or maybe it just used outtakes of Svenson knocking back a few between takes; who knows?

TAKE UP THY SWORD!
LIZARDTAUR (MONSTER)

Reptile people and their relations often employ these hulking, slow-moving reptilian humanoids—no relation to either minotaurs or centaurs, despite the similar-sounding name—in the same way that orcs and goblins employ ogres. Though of low intelligence, lizardtaurs can obey orders and can train to become skilled fighters with melee weapons and to wear clothing and armor. Unarmed, lizardtaurs are still fearsome foes, attacking with their claws and wide mouths of sharp teeth. That said, they are vulnerable to offensive magic—possibly a side effect of their sorcerous conception—granting casting bonuses to attacking magic users.

THE FILM'S DESTINY

How can you *not* love a movie that features a "lizardtaur"? Seriously! Apart from a few scenes of violence, many of which came from other films, anyway, and one brief and rather surprising flash of a bare breast, *Wizards of the Lost Kingdom* is bloodless, family-friendly—one might even say kid-friendly—fare. The animation team did a surprisingly good job with some of the wizard duels (given the source material and people behind the scenes), especially the demonic swirling red fire summoned by Shurka in the final battle with Simon. So there are definitely highlights to watch out for. Svenson walks through the film (quite literally—and perhaps tall?), apparently believing that showing up and reading his lines aloud is enough effort. It's hard to argue with that approach in this case.

Overall, the film is a pile of finely shredded Colby (Andy Colby?) cheese, but for the young gamer looking for adventure, it isn't a *total* disappointment—a *partial* one, sure, but then again, you're asking for it as soon as you decide to watch a fantasy-adventure starring—*starring*, mind you—Bo Svenson. We can only show you the door; you're the one who has to . . . oh, wait, that's a whole other series and genre entirely.

THIS YEAR IN GAMING

After George Lucas copyrighted the term "droid" because of its use in his *Star Wars* films, FASA renamed the game *BattleDroids*, which had already existed for a year, to *BattleTech* and re-launched it in a revised second edition in June 1985. Jordan Weisman, the eventual founder of WizKids (the company behind several collectible miniatures games, including *MageKnight* and *HeroClix*), and L. Ross Babcock III, editor-in-chief at FASA, designed *BattleTech* as a hybrid of roleplaying and tabletop wargaming. The game inspired several expansions, a number of bestselling novels, videogames, and a healthy fan base, and has achieved longevity via a couple different publishers. A specialized RPG titled *MechWarrior: The BattleTech Role Playing Game* came out in 1986.

HIGHLANDER

1986 • US/UK
THORN EMI SCREEN ENTERTAINMENT / HIGHLANDER PRODUCTIONS LIMITED
116M • COLOR • R

WRITERS: Gregory Widen, Peter Bellwood, and Larry Ferguson
DIRECTOR: Russell Mulcahy
PRODUCERS: Peter S. Davis and William N. Panzer
MUSIC: Michael Kamen and Queen (John Deacon, Brian May, Freddie Mercury, and Roger Taylor)
CINEMATOGRAPHY: Gerry Fisher
ART DIRECTORS: Martin Atkinson and Tim Hutchinson
COSTUME DESIGNER: James Acheson
SWORD MASTER: Bob Anderson
MAKEUP SUPERVISOR: Lois Burwell
SPECIAL EFFECTS SUPERVISOR: Martin Gutteridge
CAST: Christopher Lambert (Connor MacLeod), Roxanne Hart (Brenda J. Wyatt), Clancy Brown (The Kurgan), Sean Connery (Juan Sanchez Villa-Lobos Ramírez), Beatie Edney (Heather MacLeod), Alan North (Lieutenant Frank Moran), Jon Polito (Det. Walter Bedsoe), Sheila Gish (Rachel Ellenstein), Hugh Quarshie (Sunda Kastagir), Christopher Malcolm (Kirk Matunas), Peter Diamond (Aman Fasil), Billy Hartman (Dugal MacLeod), James Cosmo (Angus MacLeod), Celia Imrie (Kate MacLeod), Alistair Findlay (Chief Murdoch), Edward Wiley (Garfield), James McKenna (Father Rainey), John Cassady (Kenny), Ian Reddington (Bassett), Sion Tudor Owen (Hotchkiss), Damie Leake (Tony the Hotdog Vendor), Gordon Sterne (Dr. Willis Kenderly), Ron Berglas (Erik Powell), Louis Guss (Newsvendor), Peter Banks (Priest), Ted Maynard (Newscaster), Anthony Mannino (Boisterous Drunk), Helena Steves (Old Woman in Car), Frank Dux (Old Man in Car), Prince Howell (Drunk in Hotel), Anthony Fusco (Barman), Ian Tyler (Lab Technician), Corinne Russell (Candy), Buckley Norris (Derelict), Richard Bonehill (uncredited), the Fabulous Freebirds (Greg Gagne, Sam Fatu, and Jim Brunzell, uncredited), Harry Fiedler (Hospital Guard, uncredited), Terry "Bam Bam" Gordy (Professional Wrestler, uncredited), Ed Montalvo (Street Tough, uncredited), Buddy Roberts (Professional Wrestler, uncredited), and Michael Seitz (Professional Wrestler, uncredited)
ALTERNATE TITLE: *Shadow Clan* (working title)

ON THE MAP

Ramírez refers to "a faraway land" where the final battle for the Prize will eventually take place. Amusingly, we find out that this is New York City circa 1985.

Connor MacLeod was born in 1518 in Glenfinnan, a village in the Highlands of Scotland. He eventually settles in another Scottish location, before that home falls as a result of the confrontation between the Kurgan and Ramírez. Other locations presented in flashbacks include 1783 France and a German-occupied region in 1943, where Connor rescues young Rachel Ellenstein.

THERE CAN BE ONLY ONE.

OUR STORY SO FAR

A supernatural event known as the Gathering draws the last of the world's Immortals together in 1985 New York City, where they battle for the legendary Prize. In the end, there can be only one. Oh, you got that part already?

ALTERNATE VERSIONS

The director's cut, which runs six minutes longer than the 110-minute theatrical cut, features a number of additions and alterations not found in previous releases, including a longer—and altogether sexier—love scene between Connor and Brenda, sound effects when Immortals sense each others' presence, a World War II flashback sequence in which Connor rescues Rachel and explains his surviving multiple gunshots as "a kind of magic," and a scene in which Connor and Brenda chat at the zoo as the Kurgan lurks in the background (which suggests that he is shadowing them and explains how he finds Brenda's apartment soon after). The final battle between Connor and the Kurgan is also longer in the director's cut.

IT'S MAGIC

It's a kind of magic for sure, but the power in this film doesn't manifest as a spell or a noxious potion; rather, it's something present in all Immortals: the power that keeps them alive forever ... or at least until they lose their heads at the hands of other Immortals. The Quickening links the Immortals to the Earth, the universe, and beyond, but the writers intentionally keep the details of the link vague. We do know that this ever-present, supernatural force, which surrounds the Immortals, lets Connor synch with the beat of a stag's heart and allows Immortals to sense one another when near. It sometimes manifests in external ways, such as when electric lights flicker, when winds mysteriously rush (even in enclosed spaces), and when showers of sparks erupt from swords during the Immortals' spectacular clashes.

Regarding the Prize: when Connor finally receives it, we see ghostly, demonic faces swirling about, biting at the air and at Connor, without explanation. Reports tell of a cut of the film in which the demons thank Connor before vanishing from sight. Has he released them to some greater reward, too?

As for Connor's reward, he loses immortality and gains the ability to father children. He also becomes at one with all living things and can read the minds of everyone in the world. Now *that's* a kind of magic!

THE QUEST FOR MEANING

This movie covers a lot of ground, from love and loss to appreciation for one's mortality. At the start, we learn that immortality is more of a curse than a blessing, with Connor banished from the lives of his friends and family on their suspicion that he is some sort of demon. He outlives the woman he loves and lives what ultimately amounts to a solitary existence. Even though desire to obtain the Prize drives the Immortals, a sense remains that the true prize might be that final stroke of the enemy's blade across the throat, releasing the Immortal from an endless and monotonous existence.

> HE FOUGHT HIS FIRST BATTLE ON THE SCOTTISH HIGHLANDS IN 1536. HE WILL FIGHT HIS GREATEST BATTLE ON THE STREETS OF NEW YORK CITY IN 1986. HIS NAME IS CONNOR MACLEOD. HE IS IMMORTAL.

WHO GOES THERE?

The first English-language film for Christopher Lambert (birth name: Christophe Guy Denis Lambert) was *Greystoke: The Legend of Tarzan, Lord of the Apes*. Apart from three *Highlander* sequels, as well as the pilot for the *Highlander* TV series, he starred in *Fortress* and its sequel, *Mortal Kombat* (as Lord Rayden), *Resurrection* (also directed by Russell Mulcahy), *Beowulf*, and *Ghost Rider: Spirit of Vengeance*.

Roxanne Hart continues to work steadily in film and television, with starring roles in TV series such as *Dream On*, *Chicago Hope*, *Oz*, *Medium*, and *Hung*.

Clancy Brown's portrayal of Rawhide in *The Adventures of Buckaroo Banzai Across the 8th Dimension* is the first exposure for many to this charismatic and talented actor. Since then, he has embraced science fiction, fantasy, and horror in films such as *The Bride*, *Starship Troopers*, *Pathfinder*, and *Cowboys & Aliens*. He has also added his voice to numerous animated television series, including *Mortal Kombat* (as Raiden, the character portrayed by Christopher Lambert in the feature-film version), *Superman* (as Lex Luthor), and *Roughnecks: The Starship Troopers Chronicles* (as Sergeant Zim, the same character he played in the feature film a few years before). Others might remember Brown as Brother Justin Crowe in HBO's *Carnivàle* [a show tragically cut off in its prime, as far as this author is concerned –SAW] or as General Eiling in *The Flash*.

After making early appearances in *Darby O'Gill and the Little People* and *Tarzan's Greatest Adventure*, Sean Connery would always be James Bond to the audience that grew up with his definitive portrayals in *Dr. No*, *From Russia with Love*, *Goldfinger*, *Thunderball*, and *You Only Live Twice*. He also had roles in *Marnie*, *Shalako*, *Zardoz*, *Murder on the Orient Express*, *The Wind and the Lion*, *The Man Who Would Be King*, *Robin and Marian*, *A Bridge Too Far*, *The Great Train Robbery*, *Meteor*, *Outland*, *Time Bandits*, *Sword of the Valiant*, *The Name of the Rose*, *The Untouchables*, *The Presidio*, *Indiana Jones and the Last Crusade*, *The Hunt for Red October*, *Medicine Man*, *First Knight*, *The Rock*, *The Avengers*, and *Entrapment*. He appeared uncredited as King Richard in *Robin Hood: Prince of Thieves* and returned to the role of Bond twice in *Diamonds Are Forever* and *Never Say Never Again*. Following an unpleasant experience on the set of *The League of Extraordinary Gentlemen*, Connery all but retired from acting, although he did play Bond once more by lending his voice to the *James Bond 007: From Russia with Love* videogame.

Alan North found himself typecast as police officers, detectives, and judges for much of his career. Most will remember him as Chief Ed Hocken in TV's *Police Squad!* alongside Leslie Nielsen. He also appeared in the films *Serpico*, *The Fourth Protocol*, *Penn & Teller Get Killed*, *Glory*, and *The Long Kiss Goodnight*. He died in 2000 at the age of 79.

Jon Polito is a veteran actor with a sour-faced look perfectly suited for playing gangsters and corrupt cops. He has more than 200 credits to his name, including in *C.H.U.D.*, *The Freshman*, *The Rocketeer*, *The Crow*, *The Big Lebowski*, and *Flags of Our Fathers*. He also appeared in a number of television series, including *Crime Story*, *The Equalizer*, *Homicide: Life on the Street*, and *Raising the Bar*.

Hugh Quarshie hails from Ghana and is a member of The Royal Shakespeare Company. He appeared in such films as *Nightbreed*, *Wing Commander*, and *Star Wars: Episode I—The Phantom Menace* (as Captain Panaka).

Apart from his portrayal as Rogue 2 in *Star Wars: The Empire Strikes Back*, Christopher Malcolm appeared in *The Dogs of War* (also featuring Huge Quarshie), *Superman III*, and *Labyrinth*. He died in 2014 at age 67.

Imposing Scottish character-actor James Cosmo appeared as another Highlander in *Braveheart*. He also appears in the films *The Four Feathers*; *Troy*; and *The Chronicles of Narnia: The Lion, the Witch and the Wardrobe*; and on TV in *Sons of Anarchy* and *Game of Thrones*.

Celia Imrie routinely bounces from the small screen to the big screen, appearing in such films as *Mary Shelley's Frankenstein*, *The Borrowers*, *Star Wars: Episode I—The Phantom Menace*, and *Nanny McPhee*.

6 DEGREES OF SORCERY

Mel Gibson might have drawn on some of this film's Scottish Highlands imagery and character designs for his film *Braveheart* a decade later. The mentor-student relationship between Ramírez and Connor is reminiscent of that of Obi-Wan Kenobi and the young and equally naïve Luke Skywalker. The existence of the aforementioned indefinable force that accompanies Immortals also rings a *Star Wars* bell. The collapse of Connor and Heather's home is similar to the destruction of the tower and lab at the end of *The Bride of Frankenstein*, and the Kurgan's modern-day "disguise" is similar to that of the monster in *Young Frankenstein*, complete with bald pate and fastened neck . . . though here, safety pins do the trick, versus a zipper. The Immortals are very much akin to the modern vampire that appears in the fiction of Anne Rice, Charlaine Harris, and any number of other contemporary takes on the creature.

In 2007, investigators revealed that a novel titled *Laura l'immortelle (Laura the Immortal)*, credited to 12-year-old Québécois author Marie-Pier Côté, was actually a *Highlander* fanfic novel penned by a different author. A lawsuit terminated publication of the novel, and the original author received compensation.

SHATTERING THE ILLUSION

As a student in UCLA's screenwriting program, writer Gregory Widen penned the first draft of Highlander—then titled *Shadow Clan*. The initial idea supposedly arose after Widen, standing before a suit of armor on display in Scotland, wondered, *What would it be like if that guy were alive today?* The original draft, much darker in tone, contained elements eventually purged from the story, such as Immortals being fertile and Connor having thirty-seven children!

Filming took place over five months, April to August 1985, in locations around Scotland, England, and New York City. For much of the shooting in the UK—especially in and around London—uniquely British environs had to undergo alterations to appear more American. For example, the Madison Square Garden parking-garage scenes were actually shot in a market in London, because the scouted garages in New York had unsuitably low ceilings.

The church scenes in which Connor meets with the Kurgan were shot after-hours, with a rabbi playing the part of the priest. Rumor has it that some of Clancy's blasphemous lines inspired a few attending priests to make the sign of the cross!

A scene introducing an Asian Immortal named Yung Dol Kim was shot but cut from the film. Unfortunately, fire eventually destroyed the footage, though some stills of the sequence still exist.

Mulcahy at first hesitated to use explosives in the alley fight between the Kurgan and the survivalist, in fear of shattering some Victorian-era glass, but production received permission upon learning that the buildings were scheduled for demolition in a few months. The final battle between Connor and the Kurgan was originally to take place atop the Statue of Liberty, but this changed first to an amusement park and then to the Silvercup Studios rooftop. The cables used to pull down the Silvercup Studios sign still show in the final cut of the film; because of the extent of damage and budgetary concerns, the crew could not reshoot any of that material. Cables for the flying harnesses also show in a few shots. Attempts at hiding them with post-production lightning effects really only served to enhance them.

The late, great Bob Anderson arranged the elaborate fight scenes and also doubled for Sean Connery. Nick Maley, who had worked on *Star Wars: The Empire Strikes Back, Clash of the Titans,* and *Krull,* designed the Kurgan's makeup.

MUSIC OF THE MINSTRELS

The late Michael Kamen presents yet another wonderful, sweeping score, but the real standout elements of this soundtrack are the contributions by rock group Queen. Rumor has it that Queen was originally approached to contribute a single track for the film, but after viewing a rough cut, the group began to write additional songs. While most people remember "Princes of the Universe," "Gimme the Prize" (Russell Mulcahy's least favorite track, incidentally), or even "Who Wants to Live Forever," Kamen's score is really worth a listen. One piece of the score accompanied the tumbling and assembling New Line Cinema logo presented before numerous films for many years.

Getting your hands on the score isn't as easy as it should be, unless you want to pay collectors' prices for promos or limited-release editions. Alternatively, more widely available collections contain selections from the film, but then you might have to listen to tracks from *Highlander II* . . . and we wouldn't want that! As for Queen's contributions, their 1986 album *A Kind of Magic* is your best bet, but some of the arrangements are slightly different from those in the film.

THE SAGA CONTINUES

There can be only one . . . and in retrospect, the people behind the many *Highlander* sequels and spinoffs should have heeded those words. The TV series that focused on Connor's cousin Duncan has its fans, but the first film ended so well, it's doubtful that anyone leaving the theaters back in 1986 were looking for the further adventures of Connor MacLeod of Clan MacLeod.

Alas, money waved before the faces of the actors and directors resulted in *Highlander 2: The Quickening*, the only film that your supernaturally tolerant author [SAW] ever had to resist the overwhelming urge to walk out of! The film series continued with *Highlander III: The Sorcerer*, *Highlander: Endgame* (bringing Duncan into the movies and killing off Connor even though he won the Prize in the first film!), and *Highlander: The Source*, which made it only as far as the Sci-Fi Channel. A remake is currently in development limbo; as of this writing, *Snow White and the Huntsman* second unit director Cedric Nicolas-Troyan was tapped to direct.

There have also been dozens of tie-in novels for both the films and the TV series, as well as comics, an anime feature, and even a Saturday morning cartoon. For collectors, a few different manufacturers and retailers have offered accurate replicas of most of the iconic swords, from Connor's katana to the Kurgan's massive two-handed sword.

For those interested in gaming in the *Highlander* universe, to date no officially licensed RPG is available, although Black Gate Publishing released *Legacy: War of Ages* in 1993—along with one supplement—that was essentially *Highlander* with all the serial numbers lovingly filed off. Fans have put unofficial home-brew versions online as well. Rumors of an official release from Margaret Weis Productions, Ltd., have flown around for years. A *Highlander* trading card game was released in 1995, with a second edition in 2007. Lastly, a couple tie-in videogames were released, including one for the British ZX Spectrum computer in 1986 and *Highlander: The Last of the MacLeods* for the short-lived Atari Jaguar CD-ROM console in 1995.

TAKE UP THY SWORD!

THE KURGAN (IMMORTAL VILLAIN)

The Kurgan (real name unknown) was born long ago to the Kurgan tribe in what is now Russia. According to Juan Sánchez Villa-Lobos Ramírez, the Kurgan's people fed children to starved dogs for amusement. As an Immortal with no concept of the value of life, he looks upon humanity as little more than playthings. He would just as easily hack a mortal woman to pieces as seduce her, and both acts would likely grant him the same amount of sadistic pleasure.

Armed with a vicious two-handed sword that can break down into multiple parts and transport easily—and that has properties akin to those of a vorpal weapon—the Kurgan is a skilled fighter who has taken many an Immortal's head over the centuries. Motivated by desire to obtain the Prize and usher in an eternity of darkness, the Kurgan will stop at nothing to achieve this, slaughtering innocents in his path.

> FROM ANOTHER TIME COMES A MAN OF GREAT POWER.
> A MAN OF INCREDIBLE STRENGTH.
> AN IMMORTAL ABOUT TO FACE HIS GREATEST CHALLENGE . . .

DON'T LOSE YOUR HEAD. Attribute-wise, the Kurgan is physically strong, dexterous, and able to endure incredible pain. He is supernaturally perceptive, like all Immortals, and unequaled in combat. Lastly, his imposing and even frightening figure can instill fear in any he wishes to threaten. He possesses worldly, experiential knowledge but likely never bothered with higher learning. The Kurgan is a brutal fighting machine—nothing more.

THE FILM'S DESTINY

Largely knocked or ignored by critics at the time, *Highlander* has since risen above that and become an adored cult film, especially among genre fans. Heck, Ricky Bobby (Will Ferrell's character in *Talladega Nights*) claimed that it won the Academy Award for Best Movie Ever Made! If you haven't seen it in a while, it is worth revisiting; it holds up well despite its distinctively '80s style, with a lot of elements that work together beautifully.

Russell Mulcahy transplants many of his music-video techniques to the big screen and does a really fine job with the assistance of cinematographer Gerry Fisher. The early sequence with the camera zooming about Madison Square Garden is way ahead of its time, utilizing computer-controlled equipment designed by Garrett Brown, the inventor of the Steadicam. It's not the last of the impressive sequences in a film that works hard to look good as well as tell an interesting story. Though a film that, at its core, is really just about a bunch of macho guys fighting it out with swords, *Highlander* exudes much more class than your average sword-and-sorcery film.

Connor MacLeod is the rich, suave, ultra-cool guy who all of us would love to be—and that many of us aspired to be back in 1986. He's not a vampire, so there's none of that blood-drinking stuff to worry about, but he has lived centuries and experienced everything the modern fan only dreams about.

Performances on the whole are excellent, but one still can't help but wonder what inspired the casting of a French actor as a Scottish Highlander or a Scottish actor as a Spanish/Egyptian. Maybe Lambert's almost otherworldly aura inspired the choice—and what better mentor could anyone have than Sean Connery?

In many ways, *Highlander* was ahead of its time and helped usher in the entire "urban fantasy" sub-genre, which still owes a hell of a lot to this movie. See the many bestselling works of Jim Butcher *(The Dresden Files)*, Simon R. Green *(Nightside)*, and Laurell K. Hamilton *(Anita Blake: Vampire Hunter)* for examples. Looks like there can be more than one, after all!

THIS YEAR IN GAMING

Speaking of Immortals, five months after the March 1986 theatrical release of *Highlander*, publisher White Wolf—a name inspired by Michael Moorcock's Elric of Melniboné—effectively began, with the launch of a gaming fanzine, *White Wolf #1*. Though it would be five more years until the company would unleash the *World of Darkness* line, with the publication of the first edition of *Vampire: The Masquerade*, this humble beginning in the hands of brothers Stewart and Steve Wieck would eventually lead to White Wolf becoming one of the top roleplaying game publishers for many years to come.

LEGEND

1986 • US/UK
EMBASSY INTERNATIONAL PICTURES / LEGEND PRODUCTION COMPANY /
TWENTIETH CENTURY FOX FILM CORPORATION / UNIVERSAL PICTURES
89M (US), 94M (EUROPE), 113M (DIRECTOR'S CUT) • COLOR • PG

WRITER: William Hjortsberg
DIRECTOR: Ridley Scott
PRODUCER: Arnon Milchan
MUSIC: Jerry Goldsmith (European version) and Tangerine Dream (US version)
CINEMATOGRAPHER: Alex Thomson
PRODUCTION DESIGNER: Assheton Gorton
SUPERVISING ART DIRECTORS: Leslie Dilley and Norman Dorme
SET DECORATOR: Ann Mollo
COSTUME DESIGNER: Charles Knode
SPECIAL MAKEUP CREATOR: Rob Bottin
SPECIAL EFFECTS SUPERVISOR: Nick Allder
STUNT COORDINATOR / UNICORN MASTER: Vic Armstrong
CAST: Tom Cruise (Jack); Mia Sara (Lili); Tim Curry (Darkness); David Bennent (Honeythorn Gump); Alice Playten (Blix); Billy Barty (Screwball); Cork Hubbert (Brown Tom); Peter O'Farrell (Pox); Kiran Shah (Blunder); Tina Martin (Nell); Robert Picardo (Meg Mucklebones); Annabelle Lanyon (Oona); Ian Longmuir and Mike Crane (Demon Cooks); Liz Gilbert (Dancing Black Dress); and Eddie Powell (Mummified Guard)
ALTERNATE TITLE: *Legend of Darkness* (working title)

ON THE MAP

Action takes place on an unnamed fantasy world in a variety of fairly typical fantasy environments, including glistening, sunlit forests (where precocious fairies dwell), expansive swamps, caves packed with treasure, and the ancient and twisted home of Darkness himself (a combination castle, fortress, and portal to hell, which real-estate agents might describe as having "old-world charm"). As the balance of the world shifts due to the savage removal of the alicorn, we also see a few of these idyllic landscapes buried in snow and shrouded in darkness.

OUR STORY SO FAR

Darkness—a being who has sat alone in shadow for untold eons—has decided that the time is right for his return. To reclaim the world, he must destroy the unicorns that walk upon the surface and that hold the powers of light and love within them, so he calls upon a gang of goblins to set things in motion. Can innocence prevail over evil?

ALTERNATE VERSIONS

No other film covered in this volume is better suited for this category than *Legend*. There is the 89-minute North American cut with a score by Tangerine Dream, the 95-minute British/European cut with Jerry Goldsmith's score, a 113-minute prerelease-tested version, and Scott's original 125-minute cut. To muddy the waters even more, a 94-minute televised cut for the syndicated Universal Debut Network package included a few variant shots and scenes, some of which actually retained the Goldsmith score. Additional sequences shot and not used in any of the commercial cuts appear as special features in the DVD and Blu-ray releases, including an alternate opening featuring *four* goblins (Blix, Blunder, Pox, and Tic) and the infamous "faerie dance": an extended sequence of the first meeting between Jack and the Gump that features several background extras, a fiddle-driven song, and a magically induced dance that explains why Jack is suddenly breathless and soaked in sweat in the final cut(s). A trimmed version of that particular sequence exists in the European cut, but the full sequence has been lost ... although the audio exists, thanks to editor Terry Rawlings.

IT'S MAGIC

Magic is inherent in many of the living creatures of this world. The unicorns are godlike beings that embody light and all that is right, just, and good. Their alicorns alone possess incredible power that can shift the balance between light and dark.

Oona is a magical being capable of weaving faerie magic, altering her appearance, and quickly transforming into a tiny flying ball of light. Honeythorn Gump can manipulate others through the use of magic and song.

Darkness is the hand of an unseen dark "father" of unimaginable power who lusts for more and makes himself vulnerable in the process. Darkness can shoot flames from his fingertips, cloud minds, distort and twist reality, and fill a glass with black wine (blech!) merely by wishing it.

As for Jack and Lili, their innocence is a form of magical power all its own, in that it makes them the greatest of enemies to Darkness. It doesn't hurt that Lili is also the object of Darkness's most carnal desires ... but who can blame him?

THE QUEST FOR MEANING

The central message of *Legend* is a fundamental one threaded through virtually this entire genre: that good and evil, light and darkness, and love and hate exist throughout nature and within each and every one of us. For the most part, these opposites maintain balance, giving us (and the universe itself) beauty and purpose. When that balance shifts, especially toward those who wish to cause harm or exert control, it can be difficult to restore. In that effort lie most of the roots of heroism and the struggle to persevere that we see in all these movies and many more besides. Even when light overcomes darkness, knowledge of the shadows remains ever present, along with the possibility that with one wrong move, the darkness will return and rise again.

Each side also finds something seductive about the other—which has a certain logic, in a system in which neither can exist without the other. Through manipulation, we shift our personal balance and occasionally stray from the path. In this film, this most basic of themes has directly personified avatars in the form of Darkness on the side of evil and the innocent Jack and Lili representing good. As Lili becomes corrupted, we see the danger of letting the balance shift and fall to the power of the dark.

WHO GOES THERE?

Tom Cruise—born Thomas Cruise Mapother IV—originally set his sights on a life in the priesthood but changed gears at the age of 18 to pursue an acting career. He made his film debut in 1981's *Endless Love*, but it wasn't until *Risky Business* two years later that his name, talent, and good looks would truly launch his long and hugely successful career, which includes a number of critically acclaimed blockbusters like *Top Gun*, *Rain Man*, *Born on the Fourth of July*, *A Few Good Men*, *The Firm*, *Interview with the Vampire*, *Mission: Impossible*, *Jerry Maguire*, *Minority Report*, and *Jack Reacher*.

Many typically remember Mia Sara for one of two roles (her very first ones): Lili in *Legend* and Sloane Peterson in *Ferris Bueller's Day Off*. Never straying far from genre productions, she also appears in the TV movie *Daughter of Darkness*, *Timecop*, the 1997 TV production of *20,000 Leagues Under the Sea*, *Dazzle*, the TV movie *Lost in Oz*, and two TV miniseries: *Nightmares & Dreamscapes: From the Stories of Stephen King* and *The Witches of Oz*. She also had a regular role on *Birds of Prey* as Dr. Harleen Quinzel / Harley Quinn.

Tim Curry is a classically trained actor who had much success on stage prior to his breakout role as Dr. Frank-N-Furter in *The Rocky Horror Show* with the Royal Court Theatre and onscreen in the feature-film adaptation *The Rocky Horror Picture Show*. His agents at the time were concerned that the role might destroy his career, but it quickly proved to be the foundation for Curry of a long and varied career in show business. Other film productions of note include *Annie*, *Clue*, *The Hunt for Red October*, *The Three Musketeers*, *The Shadow*, *Congo*, *Muppet Treasure Island*, *Scary Movie 2*, *The Secret of Moonacre*, and *Burke and Hare*. He's also racked up a wealth of TV roles both in front of the camera (*Life of Shakespeare*, *The Worst Witch*, *Wiseguy*, and *It*) and behind the microphone in animated productions, including *Peter Pan and the Pirates* (for which he won a Daytime Emmy), *Fish Police*, *Darkwing Duck*, *The Pirates of Darkwater*, *The Legend of Prince Valiant*, *Dinosaurs*, *Gargoyles*, *The Adventures of Jimmy Neutron: Boy Genius*, *Star Wars: The Clone Wars*, and *Young Justice*.

Alice Playten got her start in the 1960s via several turns on the New York stage and through a well-known commercial for Alka-Seltzer, in which she played a housewife excitedly discussing her stomach-churning recipes. Many of us, though, most fondly remember her role as Alice the babysitter in Sid and Marty Krofft's *The Lost Saucer*. Her unique voice led to a prolific career as a voice actor. You can find (or hear) her in movies like *Heavy Metal*, *Amityville II: The Possession*, *My Little Pony: The Movie*, the TV series *Doug*, and the direct-to-video *The Amazing Feats of Young Hercules*. She died in 2011 at age 63.

Legendary dwarf actor Billy Barty already had more film credits to his name than most of his *Legend* costars combined, before they were even born! His first film was a 1927 silent short at the age of 3, in which he played a baby alongside a young Mickey Rooney. He continued to appear in additional films in that long-running series (even transitioning to sound) until 1934, occasionally as a nameless infant and sometimes in the role of Rooney's younger brother. After working steadily on TV and in films, he eventually developed a relationship with producers Sid and Marty Krofft, which led to his appearances in *The Bugaloos, Sigmund and the Sea Monsters, The Lost Saucer,* and *Dr. Shrinker*. Throughout the '70s and '80s, most TV casting directors defaulted to Barty whenever they sought a diminutive comedic character: thus his appearances on *Man from Atlantis, Charlie's Angels, Supertrain, Fantasy Island,* and *ChiPs*. After *Legend,* he appeared in films like *Masters of the Universe, Willow,* and *UHF*. He founded the organization Little People of America in 1957, which continues today. He died in 2000 at age 76.

Cork "Corky" Hubbert had roles in films like *Caveman, Under the Rainbow, Sinbad of the Seven Seas,* and *The Ruby Princess Runs Away,* as well as in several TV series, such as the 1980s *Twilight Zone* revival; *The Charmings; Nowhere Man; Sabrina, the Teenage Witch;* and *Charmed*. He died in 2003 at age 51.

The bulk of Tina Martin's performances were on the British small screen in shows like *The Sweeney, Jonathan Creek,* and *The Bill,* but she's also drifted into feature films like *Leapin' Leprechauns!, Spellbreaker: Secrets of the Leprechauns,* and the TV movie *Dragonworld: The Legend Continues*.

Though audiences might now recognize character-actor Robert Picardo most often as the holographic Doctor from *Star Trek: Voyager,* he acted on the big and small screens for years, sometimes hidden under prosthetic make-up or inside costumes. You can find him in films like *The Howling, Explorers, Innerspace, 976-EVIL, Total Recall* (as the voice of Johnnycab), *Gremlins 2: The New Batch, Matinee,* and *Small Soldiers,* and in a number of television shows, like *Kojak, Alice, The Wonder Years, Stargate SG-1,* and *Stargate: Atlantis*.

Annabelle Lanyon has had a somewhat spotty film and television career, spending much of her time focused on stage productions in the UK and Los Angeles. Earlier roles as a child and teen actor had her on the small screen in *Anne of Avonlea, The Brothers, Quatermass,* and a 1980 production of *The Old Curiosity Shop*. Following *Legend,* she appeared in the films *Dream Demon, An Existential Affair, Burlesque Fairytales,* and *Brash Young Turks*.

6 DEGREES OF SORCERY

Jean Cocteau's *Beauty and the Beast* (1946) inspired several aspects of this film. Ridley Scott screened that film when he and William Hjortsberg began collaborating; Scott knew that Hjortsberg would appreciate the film's poetic quality and bring those elements into his own script.

The overall look of the film, especially the landscapes, was inspired by the work of Arthur Rackham and other storybook and traditional Christmas-card imagery from Scott's childhood, as well as classic Disney animated feature films like *Snow White and the Seven Dwarfs*. It's no surprise that Darkness and Chernabog—the colossal ghost-summoning demon featured in the "Night on Bald Mountain" sequence in Disney's *Fantasia*—bear a resemblance to one another; in turn, Darkness's design clearly went on to inspire the Destroyer of Worlds in the 1989 *Doctor Who* adventure "Battlefield." Other characters who drew much inspiration from Disney include Oona (Tinkerbell) and Meg Mucklebones (the evil queen's witch disguise in *Snow White*).

> NO GOOD WITHOUT EVIL.
> NO LOVE WITHOUT HATE.
> NO INNOCENCE WITHOUT LUST.
> I AM DARKNESS.

The riddle game between Honeythorn Gump and Jack is quite similar to that between Bilbo Baggins and Gollum in *The Hobbit: An Unexpected Journey*. A gold ring plays a notable part in this film as well.

The three goblins act a bit like a fairytale version of the Three Stooges, while the rapport between Screwball and Brown Tom is more akin to that of Laurel and Hardy or the Bowery Boys (according to Scott himself). The uninviting swamp echoes the Swamp of Sorrows from *The NeverEnding Story*, released in theaters a couple years before, and has a descendent in the Fire Swamp of *The Princess Bride*, among many others. Gump owes much to Mickey Rooney's portrayal of Puck in Max Reinhardt's 1935 version of Shakespeare's *A Midsummer Night's Dream*. The ragged mask and apron worn by the butcher are likely a nod to Leatherface from *The Texas Chainsaw Massacre*. A few of the set pieces—especially some of the large columns in Darkness's lair—also appeared in *Blade Runner*. The rescue of Blunder from the giant meat pie along with a few stray birds is a realization of the line "four and twenty blackbirds, baked in a pie" from the well-known English nursery rhyme "Sing a Song of Sixpence." Why Blunder swears upon the festering forelock of Pharisee Nicodemus when the story is set in a realm of total fantasy is anyone's guess! Many of the sets and other designs, especially those in Darkness's lair, were inspired by 18th-century Italian artist Giovanni Battista Piranesi, especially his fantastic illustrations of elaborate and altogether fictitious prisons.

The means of dispatching Darkness—thrusting the alicorn (a "stake") into him and exposing him to daylight—obviously harkens back to *Dracula* and vampire lore. Jack's retrieval of the alicorn from the bubbling and somewhat unconvincing "lava" mirrors Colwyn's retrieval of the glaive from the lava early in *Krull*. And of course, if you want to learn more about unicorns, look no further than the animated feature *The Last Unicorn* covered earlier in this book.

SHATTERING THE ILLUSION

Ridley Scott came up with the basic idea for *Legend* while shooting *The Duellists* in 1976. Believing the resulting movie would be too much of an art film with limited appeal, he moved on to other projects, including *Alien* (1979) and *Blade Runner* (1982), before putting *Legend* in front of the lens as his fourth feature film.

Scott treated the material as a classic and darker fairytale, and immersed himself in the works of the Brothers Grimm and others. He also looked at Disney animated features like *Fantasia*, *Pinocchio*, and *Snow White and the Seven Dwarfs*.

Novelist and screenwriter William "Gatz" Hjortsberg penned the script, given a relatively basic laundry list: it had to be a "classic fairytale," it had to include unicorns (with some reference to them being "the fastest steeds on Earth"), and the main villain had to be called "Darkness." Additional elements began to take form, although some of them would change as the script developed. In early drafts, Jack was a commoner—a miller's son—in love with a princess. Later, this mundane character became "Jack o' the Green," akin to the Green Man of the Forest. For a while, he was even to appear with green skin. At one point, Hjortsberg had a flash of inspiration that resulted in the princess tossing her ring, unicorns being killed, and the world going to hell while Jack sought to recover the gold band.

The initial draft, though considered good enough to present to the studios, in hindsight would have been impossible to film, because it contained armies of fairies, images of flowers springing up under every unicorn footfall, and an excessive number of effects and creatures. It also contained more sexual elements, particularly between Darkness and Lily, toned down dramatically in the final draft. Meg Mucklebones, portrayed brilliantly by Robert Picardo, was named "Jenny Greenteeth" in earlier drafts.

One early idea for Darkness had him depicted as a griffon. Ridley Scott wanted him to have an almost operatic quality. After considering Richard O'Brien for the role of Meg Mucklebones, Scott saw Tim Curry's performance as Dr. Frank-N-Furter in *The Rocky Horror Picture Show*. Thinking about how much of a challenge Curry must have had to play that sort of character—to exude charisma and achieve such an impressive performance—Scott approached him for the role. Curry agreed but admitted the whole affair seemed a bit strange. He admired the story because of its primal, psychological elements, akin to the tales of the Brothers Grimm, but resisted the development of makeup and costume, begging that his eyes be left alone. He lost even that battle: he had to wear full, often painful, scleral cat's-eye lenses. The results were impressive, however, with Curry—who normally stands about 5' 10"—elevated to almost thirteen feet from the bottom of his leg extensions to the tips of his expansive fiberglass horns. His makeup took upwards of five-and-a-half hours to apply, followed by roughly half that time to remove all the prosthetics after shooting. On one of those days, Curry grew impatient and attempted to pull some of the material off, wounding himself in the process and causing a production delay while he recovered from his injuries!

Cruise's scale-mail armor consisted of gold-painted hammered bottle caps. The serrated edges of each scale are a bit of a giveaway.

David Bennent was 19 at the time of filming, despite his youthful appearance. Although Scott loved his Swiss accent and saw no reason why Gump shouldn't sound like he was from the Black Forest—it being a fantasy story, after all—one unnamed studio executive had issues with it and even tossed out ignorant comments about Nazis. As a result, Alice Playten looped all of Bennent's lines.

Originally, Scott had considered shooting in Yosemite among the great redwoods, but due to lighting concerns, he quickly scrapped that idea in favor of constructing an artificial environment in England. The forest set occupied the entirety of the "007" soundstage at Pinewood Studios—almost 3,000,000 cubic feet—and contained a mix of fabricated and real trees.

> THERE MAY NEVER BE ANOTHER DAWN.

Tragically, on June 27, 1984, with only a

couple days of scheduled shooting left, gases that had collected in the roof of the soundstage ignited, and fire destroyed the entire forest set. Remaining scenes, such as Lili's seeing and touching the unicorns, were shot in elaborately dressed gardens on and behind the studio lot.

The search for Lili's ring consisted of high-diving shots using a 10-year-old boy to aid in scale, and Tom Cruise's own underwater diving in Silver Springs, Florida. During the shooting of those scenes, several alligators were sunning themselves nearby. Park staff assured the production that the alligators would not interfere. Cruise might still have harbored some concern, but he performed the scenes expertly.

MUSIC OF THE MINSTRELS

Jerry Goldsmith composed the original score: the one intended to accompany the film worldwide. He had previously collaborated with director Ridley Scott on *Alien*. When American test audiences reacted unfavorably to aspects of the film, one of the mandated alterations (coming mainly from Sidney Sheinberg, former president of MCA) was a complete replacement of the Goldsmith score to make the movie more appealing to younger audiences. Scott quickly went to soundtrack stalwarts Tangerine Dream, who had already proven their mettle with impressive scores for *Sorcerer, Thief, Risky Business,* and *Firestarter*. With only three weeks, Tangerine Dream produced an impressive score that mated with the slightly shorter American cut of the film and led to a very successful separate soundtrack release in its own right. The single for the track "Is Your Love Strong Enough?," featuring vocals by Bryan Ferry of Roxy Music fame and guitar work by David Gilmour of Pink Floyd, did fairly well on UK music charts and appeared frequently on MTV. The 2011 soundtrack for *The Girl with the Dragon Tattoo* featured a Trent Reznor-produced remake of that track, performed by his band How to Destroy Angels. The other vocal track on the album is "Loved by the Sun," a version of "Unicorn Theme," featuring music by Tangerine Dream and vocals by Jon Anderson of Yes.

European fans of the Jerry Goldsmith score could purchase it on vinyl in 1986. American fans (those not spending top dollar for imports) had to wait until 1992 for the CD release from Silva Screen, which featured alternate cover art and additional tracks. It was re-released in 2002 to coincide with the "Ultimate Edition" DVD. Scott prefers the original Goldsmith score and thinks it was a mistake to remove it.

Despite a long tradition of artists and bands covering the works of others, significantly fewer examples of this occur with soundtracks—especially *entire* soundtracks—but that is precisely what happened in 2012, when BSX Records released *Music from the Motion Picture Legend*, composed by Tangerine Dream and produced and arranged by Brandon K. Verrett. This seventy-four-minute, twenty-track release features all the tracks from the Tangerine Dream score, performed with more organic-sounding instruments (versus the wall-to-wall synthesizers of the original). It also features new versions of the vocal tracks "Loved by the Sun" and "Is Your Love Strong Enough?," both now performed by Katie Campbell. To be frank, I [SAW] don't find Campbell's vocals up to snuff on either of these tracks, but it's nice having options all the same.

THE SAGA CONTINUES

According to screenwriter William Hjortsberg, a novelization of the film was considered and even begun but never made it to publication. In August 2002, the now-defunct Harvest Moon Publishing released a complete script book featuring an introduction by Hjortsberg.

According to Ridley Scott, the story of *Legend* continues in a more spiritual sense, because Darkness can never be fully defeated. Thus, the villain's last words, when he splits apart at the end of the film, are that he might re-form in another time and place. Who are we to argue with the director?

TAKE UP THY SWORD!
THE ALICORN (MAGIC ARTIFACT)

While some might refer to a unicorn's spire simply as its horn, the correct term is "alicorn." Because only two unicorns are known to exist, their alicorns hold unimaginable power.

Unicorns keep darkness at bay and ensure that light and love reign. Removal of the alicorn of one of these godlike beings upsets this balance, plunging the world into chaos.

An alicorn in the possession of a magic user dramatically augments his or her abilities, increasing magical prowess significantly. In a level-based system, it doubles a spellcaster's abilities and access to spell lists. In the hands of a nonmagical character, an alicorn grants low-level magical abilities typically available to novice sorcerers. Should the wielder lose possession of the alicorn, the augmentations vanish until the wielder reacquires it.

THE FILM'S DESTINY

Legend was one of those "sweet spot" films for this author [SAW], because it appeared at precisely the right time in my life to make an impact. I might have viewed the movie with a more critical eye had I seen it even a few years later, but the glossy imagery, impressive performance of Tim Curry, superb Rob Bottin makeup creations, and Tangerine Dream score all helped turn me into an immediate fan. It remains with me to this day. For years, my friends and I routinely revisited the film, admired its gorgeous cinematography, and listened to the soundtrack. I'll never forget my jealousy when one of my best friends secured a lobby card depicting the unicorns! He tacked it to the wall of his college dorm room.

To some extent, I now agree with a few of the points that have drawn criticism over the years—although a local critic's issue with the torrent of falling goose-down still sticks in my craw, because obviously he'd never lived among cottonwoods—but I can also forgive many of those issues and still enjoy the film for what it is: a magical, living painting. As the years have passed, I've also grown to appreciate the director's cut and now believe it's the superior version, thanks to the Goldsmith score, the additional bits of character development, and the lusher appearance of the imagery. It seems that one of the studio-mandated alterations had been a desaturation of many scenes, resulting in a muddier picture. Put simply, this is yet another must-see for fans of '80s-era sword-and-sorcery films.

THIS YEAR IN GAMING

The first edition of the roleplaying game *SkyRealms of Jorune* had come out the previous year, but this year SkyRealms Publishing released the revised, thoroughly edited, and much slicker boxed second edition at GenCon 18. Designed by Andrew Leker—now a successful computer-game designer—*SkyRealms of Jorune* featured a completely alien world of floating land masses, strange races, and focusable mystical energies. Sounds a bit like James Cameron's *Avatar*, doesn't it? The printing company failed to deliver the boxes of books in time for GenCon, so SkyRealms sold the books separately, signed and promoted as a special "prerelease" edition. Much of the success of the *Jorune* line derives from the beautiful artwork by Miles Teves: a conceptual designer on a number of feature films, including *Legend, Kull the Conqueror,* and *Pirates of the Caribbean: The Curse of the Black Pearl.* Chessex published and supported a third edition starting in 1992, and the world of Jorune found its way to the PC in 1994, thanks to Strategic Simulations, Inc., and their game *Alien Logic: A SkyRealms of Jorune Adventure.* A fourth edition of the RPG is yet to appear, but third-edition contributor Joseph K. Adams has made new "official" material available online.

LABYRINTH

1986 • US/UK
Henson Associates, Inc. / Lucasfilm Ltd. / The Jim Henson Company /
Delphi V Productions / TriStar Pictures
101m • Color • PG

Story: Dennis Lee and Jim Henson
Screenplay: Terry Jones
Director: Jim Henson
Executive Producers: David Lazer And George Lucas
Producer: Eric Rattray
Score: Trevor Jones
Songs Composed And Performed By: David Bowie
Director Of Photography: Alex Thomson
Production Designer: Elliot Scott
Art Directors: Terry Ackland-Snow, Roger Cain, Peter Howitt, Frank Walsh, And Michael White
Conceptual Designer: Brian Froud
Costumes Designers: Brian Froud And Ellis Flyte
Makeup Artist: Nick Dudman
Director Of Choreography And Puppet Movement: Cheryl Mcfadden
"Chilly Down" And "Dance Magic" Choreographer: Charles Augins
Crystal Ball Manipulation Choreographed And Performed By: Michael Moschen
Cast: David Bowie (Jareth); Jennifer Connelly (Sarah Williams); Toby Froud (Toby); Shelley Thompson (Stepmother); Christopher Malcolm (Father); Natalie Finland (Fairy); Brian Henson (Voice and Performer of Hoggle); Shari Weiser (Hoggle Performer); Ron Mueck (Voice and Performer of Ludo); Rob Mills (Ludo Performer); David Shaughnessy (Voice of Didymus); Dave Goelz and David Barclay (Didymus Performers); Timothy Bateson (Voice of the Worm); Karen Prell (The Worm Performer); Michael Hordern (Voice of the Wiseman); Frank Oz (Wiseman Performer); David Shaughnessy (Voice of the Hat); Dave Goelz (The Hat Performer); Denise Bryer (Voice of the Junk Lady); Karen Prell (The Junk Lady Performer); Timothy Bateson, Douglas Blackwell, Anthony Jackson, and David Shaughnessy (Voices of the Four Guards); Anthony Asbury, Kevin Clash, Dave Goelz, and Steve Whitmire (The Four Guards Performers), David Healy (Voice of Right Door Knocker); Anthony Asbury (Performer of Right Door Knocker); Robert Beatty (Voice of Left Door Knocker); Dave Goelz (Performer of Left Door Knocker); Kevin Clash (Voice of Fiery 1); David Barclay, Kevin Clash, and Toby Philpott (Performers of Fiery 1); Charles Augins (Voice of Fiery 2); Ron Mueck, Karen Prell, and Ian Thom (Performers of Fiery 2); Danny John-Jules (Voice of Fiery 3); Sherry Amott, Dave Goelz, and Rob Mills (Performers of Fiery 3); Danny John-Jules (Voice of Ficry 4); Kevin Bradshaw, Cheryl Henson, and Steve Whitmire (Performers of Fiery 4); Richard Bodkin (Voice of Fiery 5); Anthony Asbury, Alistair Fullarton, and Rollin Krewson (Performers of Fiery 5); Michael Attwell, Sean Barrett, Timothy Bateson, Douglas Blackwell, John Bluthel, Brian Henson, Anthony Jackson, Peter Marinker, Ron Mueck, Kerry Shale, and David Shaughnessy (Goblin Voices); Donald Austen, Michael Bayliss, Fiona Beynor Brown, Simon Buckley, David Bulbeck, Martin Bridle, Sue Dacre, Geoff Felix, Trevor Freeborn, Christine Glanville, David Greenaway, Brian James, Jan King, Ronnie Le Drew, Terry Lee, Christopher Leith, Kathryn Mullen, Angie Passmore, Michael Petersen, Nigel Plaskitt, Judy Preece, Gillie Robic, Michael Quinn, David Rudman, David Showler, Robin Stevens, Ian Tregonning, Mary Turner,

Robert Tygner, Mak Wilson, and Francis Wright (Goblin Puppeteers); and Marc Antona, Kenny Baker, Michael Henbury Ballan, Danny Blackner, Peter Burroughs, Toby Clark, Tessa Crockett, Warwick Davis, Malcolm Dixon, Anthony Georghiou, Paul Grant, Andrew Herd, Richard Jones, John Key, Mark Lisle, Peter Mandell, Jack Purvis, Katie Purvis, Nicholas Read, Linda Spriggs, Penny Stead, and Albert Wilkinson (Goblin Corps)
ALTERNATE TITLES: *The Labyrinth, Magic Maze, Into the Labyrinth, Sarah's Maze, Lost in the Maze, Trapped in the Mind-Maze, Inside Outside, Inside Out, Outside Inside, Turning Inside Outside,* and *Outside In* (working titles from Jim Henson's personal notes)

ON THE MAP

Prior to Sarah entering the realm of Jareth and his mystical labyrinth—a.k.a. "the Underground"—to rescue her baby step-brother Toby, we pay a visit to the real and mundane world of Sarah and her family, featuring locations in both the UK (West Wycombe Park) and the US (North Broadway in Upper Nyack, New York). Once in the Goblin King's world, our heroes wander the labyrinth, traverse the dreaded Bog of Eternal Stench, descend into an oubliette, dance in an elaborate bubble ballroom, do battle with marauding goblin soldiers in a gated goblin city, and navigate a twisted series of chambers and stairways inspired by the work of artist M. C. Escher.

OUR STORY SO FAR

Sarah, a girl dealing with a stepmother with whom she has yet to bond and her own impending adulthood, wishes her half-brother away to the Goblin King, Jareth. She is then drawn into Jareth's world, where she has thirteen hours to traverse a labyrinth and save her baby brother from life as a resident goblin.

IT'S MAGIC

Because the adventure presented in this film is clearly—all right, *likely*—all the product of Sarah's vivid imagination, magic in the Underground and beyond (because Jareth and others can somehow breach the barrier between worlds) is limitless and unpredictable. Illusions dominate; rocks live, move of their own accord, and respond to commands; time runs backwards; and Jareth can turn the world upside down with a simple gesture or a deft juggle of a glass bauble. At the same time, the world of *Labyrinth* has also embraced technology, thus possessing mechanical sewer-cleaners, a colossal city guardian piloted by a single occupant, cannons, and even portable machine-guns!

THE QUEST FOR MEANING

It should be no shocking surprise that the events depicted are almost all allegories for aspects of the path to maturity. Sarah, a girl on the cusp of adulthood, finds solitary pleasure in her fantasies. She seems a loner, but anyone, male or female, of similar age knows how strange and seductive maturity can be. She's unhappy with her stepmother, finds life with her stepbrother difficult, distances herself from her father, and apparently has deep and confused feelings about her mother's new beau, shown as a more restrained David Bowie, sans fright wig, in photos in Sarah's bedroom. One could interpret the quest, the labyrinth itself, and the colorful characters in ways that would make Freud proud. Even the genre's common clash of magic versus technology might here further express Sarah's conflicts between the girl she is and the woman she's becoming.

WHO GOES THERE?

David Bowie was already a household name, thanks mainly to his extremely successful musical career, by the time he went before the cameras for *Labyrinth,* although he was also no stranger to the cinema, either, appearing in films like *The Man Who Fell to Earth, The Hunger,* and *Merry Christmas, Mr. Lawrence* before his casting as Jareth. Since *Labyrinth,* he also appeared in *Twin Peaks: Fire Walk with Me, Zoolander,* and *The Prestige.*

Jennifer Connelly's first big-screen role was as young Deborah (with mature Deborah played by Elizabeth McGovern) in Sergio Leone's *Once Upon a Time in America.* She played a telepath in Dario Argento's *Phenomena* before setting foot in the Underground and also appears in *The Rocketeer, Mulholland Falls, Dark City, Requiem for a Dream, A Beautiful Mind* (for which she won an Oscar, a Golden Globe, and a BAFTA), *Hulk, Dark Water, The Day the Earth Stood Still, Winter's Tale,* and *Noah.*

Brian Henson (son of Jim) started messing with Muppets onscreen in *The Great Muppet Caper* and has pretty much never stopped, manipulating and voicing characters for *The Muppets Take Manhattan, Return to Oz, The Storyteller, Dinosaurs, Muppet Treasure Island, Farscape,* and many others. He has been married to *Legend* actress Mia Sara since 2010.

Actor, producer, and director David Shaughnessy's first TV role was in *Danger UXB.* He also appeared in *Q.E.D., The Haunting of Cassie Palmer,* and *Minder,* and has more recently worked as a voice actor in videogames, such as *Mass Effect, Final Fantasy XIV, The Darkness II,* the *World of Warcraft* expansion *Mists of Pandaria,* and *Star Wars Rebels.*

British character-actor Timothy Bateson was another of those "good grief, look at all those credits" actors. With almost 200 credits to his name, stretching back to the late 1940s, you've probably seen or heard him in something over the years. You can find him alongside Sir Laurence Olivier in *Richard III* and in *Nightmare, The Avengers, Doctor Who* ("The Ribos Operation"), *Neverwhere, The Messenger: The Story of Joan of Arc,* and *Harry Potter and the Order of the Phoenix.* He died in 2009 at age 83.

Like Mr. Bateson, Michael Hordern was a British character-actor with an impressive list of credits that kept him acting all the way up to his death in 1995, also at age 83. Many genre fans know him as the voice of Gandalf in the BBC 4 radio adaptation of *The Lord of the Rings* from 1981. His first film role was in a 1939 comedy, planting the seed for the decades of film and television work that included memorable roles in *Scrooge* (with Alastair Sim), *Sink the Bismarck!, El Cid, Genghis Khan, Demons of the Mind, Theatre of Blood, Watership Down* (as the voice of Frith), *Gandhi,* and *Young Sherlock Holmes.* Rumor has it that he even once turned down the lead role in *Doctor Who* (which instead went to Patrick Troughton)!

David Healy was an American actor who had more success on the big and small screens in the UK than in the US. He appeared in TV shows like *The Saint, Mogul, The Secret Service, Land of the Lost* (for one episode), *Blake's 7, Dallas,* and *Space Precinct.* He also popped up in feature films like *Patton, Lust for a Vampire, The Ninth Configuration,* and *Supergirl.* He died in 1995 at age 66.

Robert Beatty was a versatile British character-actor who spent a lot of his time behind microphones as a voice actor. Onscreen, he appears in roles stretching back to the late 1930s, including a number of war and noir films. He also appeared in *Doctor Who, 2001: A Space Odyssey, The Pink Panther Strikes Again, Blake's 7,* and *Superman III* and *IV.* He died in 1992 at age 82.

Many of us grew up with Kevin Clash on our TVs, starting with *The Great Space Coaster, Captain Kangaroo,* and *Sesame Street,* in which he played his most famous character of all: that red, high-pitched monster named Elmo. His first work with Henson was on the feature film *Follow That Bird;* he quickly became a Muppet company regular. You can also hear his voice in *Teenage Mutant Ninja Turtles* (the first feature film) as Splinter, *Dog City, Dinosaurs, Muppet Treasure Island, Muppets Tonight, Muppets from Space,* and 10,000 TV and film projects featuring special appearances by Elmo.

Many probably know Charles Augins best as the face and voice of Queeg in a hilarious episode of *Red Dwarf.* Though he also appeared in a handful of roles in films like *Revenge of the Pink Panther* and *The Tall Guy,* he has devoted much of his career to dance choreography. He currently chairs the dance department at the Duke Ellington School of the Arts.

Yes, he's the Cat on the British science-fiction comedy show that keeps on giving, *Red Dwarf,* but Danny-John Jules has reared his head in other productions on the big and small screens, not to mention his voice in several soundtracks, in *Little Shop of Horrors; Lock, Stock and Two Smoking Barrels;* the 1995 version of *The Tomorrow People;* and *Blade II.*

Danny Blackner and Anthony Georghiou were both R.O.U.S. performers in *The Princess Bride* . . . assuming you believe they exist.

6 DEGREES OF SORCERY

Just as various toys in Kevin's room become characters that he encounters in *Time Bandits,* toys in Sarah's room (including a stuffed Sir Didymus, a Ludo doll, and a resin figure of Jareth) also join the action. When Jareth first offers a present to Sarah in the form of a glass sphere, he refers to it as "a crystal, nothing more." Is this a subtle reference to *The Dark Crystal?* The fairies seem related to Oona from *Legend.*

There's no denying similarities to *The Wizard of Oz.* The off-screen roaring from Ludo echoes the sounds heard by Dorothy and her companions prior to meeting the Cowardly Lion in the classic film adaptation.

Several links to Maurice Sendak's book *Outside Over There* include a child kidnapped by goblins. Both that book and *Where the Wild Things Are* appear in Sarah's bedroom at the start of the film, and Sendak receives a thank-you in the end credits.

One can't help but note the similarities—facial features, mannerisms, and posture—between Ludo and the longhaired hippie character Neil (Nigel Planer) from *The Young Ones.*

> JIM HENSON, GEORGE LUCAS AND DAVID BOWIE TAKE YOU INTO A DAZZLING WORLD OF FANTASY AND ADVENTURE. A 'MAZING TALE OF NEVER-ENDING FANTASY. WHERE ANYTHING IS POSSIBLE. WHERE EVERYTHING SEEMS POSSIBLE, AND NOTHING IS WHAT IT SEEMS.

Ludo's design clearly influenced the look of Sullivan in *Monsters Inc.*, as well as technical aspects of the elaborate costumes in the *Where the Wild Things Are* film adaptation directed by Spike Jonze.

Hoggle's face looks like a cross between the drunk in Will Vinton's Academy Award-winning stop-motion animated feature *Closed Mondays* (from 1974—look it up!) and actor Ernest Borgnine. On more than one occasion, Sarah refers to Hoggle as "Hogwart." Is *Harry Potter* author J. K. Rowling a fan of this film?

The Bog of Eternal Stench gets a mention in a curse featured in an episode of *Charmed*. Sir Didymus guarding the bridge harkens back to the "Old Man from Scene 24" played by Terry Gilliam in *Monty Python and the Holy Grail*. Maliciously handing the female hero a poisoned fruit first happened in *Snow White*. The attempted seduction of Sarah in an elaborate gown recalls the similar scene in *Legend* from a year before. Characters in the 2002 anime film *The Cat Returns* undertake a similar journey through an elaborate labyrinth, complete with shifting walls. No big surprise here, but the 2005 Henson-produced film *MirrorMask* includes a circus juggler manipulating his balls (stop it!) as Jareth does. The three goblin soldiers leaping out and brandishing their weapons remind us of the truncated dual between Indiana Jones and the black-clad Cairo swordsman in *Raiders of the Lost Ark*. The final confrontation with Jareth occurs in an elaborate set resembling M. C. Escher's *Relativity*.

SHATTERING THE ILLUSION

Jim Henson set out to produce a film that he believed would surpass the success of *The Dark Crystal*. To do that, he sought out people with whom he wished to collaborate, including George Lucas. Fortunately, Lucas had wanted to work with Henson for years. He admired the script because it didn't talk down to kids, and came on board to keep the script focused and to inject references to mythology that he felt were important in telling the story.

Two distinct drafts of the script—one by Terry Jones and the other by Laura Phillips, which focused more on Sarah's emotional journey into adulthood—eventually merged into a single screenplay. Jones received sole writing credit onscreen, whereas Phillips received a "special thanks" credit at the end of the film. Writer-actress Elaine May *(Heaven Can Wait, The Birdcage)* also came in to polish the script. The final draft was dated April 11, 1985.

During the development of Jareth, performers considered for the role included Mick Jagger, Sting, and even Michael Jackson, but perhaps thanks to son Brian being a Bowie fan, Henson met with the singer in the summer of 1984 to discuss the script and look at some of Froud's concept art. Bowie was more or less sold on the project, and less than a year later, the deal was set. Those working on the film recall Bowie as a great sport and a pleasure to work with.

In the autumn of 1984, Henson flew to London to start tests to determine the sizes of Ludo, Hoggle, and Sir Didymus in relation to the human actors. Before Jennifer Connelly took the role of Sarah, other strong contenders included Ally Sheedy, Jane Krakowski, and Maddie Corman.

The film took over all eight soundstages at Elstree Studios, for five months of production. For a long time, the Fieries were "Wild Things," likely changed to avoid confusion with the work of Maurice Sendak, who still received acknowledgment in the credits because his books clearly inspired certain elements of the film (as covered in "6 Degrees"). The Fieries were essentially Bunraku puppets, each of which required three operators.

Ludo proved to be one of the most complicated creatures ever built and represented the perfect blending of Froud design and Henson technique. The door-knockers came to life after Terry Jones spotted a small sketch of a face in the corner of a page in Froud's sketchbook. The prize-winning sheepdog that portrayed Ambrosius, Sir Didymus's faithful steed, had to wear specially made boots to keep the dye that colored the water in the Bog of Eternal Stench from staining its paws.

After a casting call went out for hand performers to assist with the elaborate "Shaft of Hands," several girls showed up believing they would work alongside David Bowie. Alas, most of them spent the day lying flat and in total darkness on an elaborate tower of scaffolding.

The film was a gift to Henson's daughters, on the cusp of adulthood much like Sarah. The girls' experiences inspired parts of the story and Sarah's journey.

This was the last feature film that Henson directed, mainly due to his disappointment with the movie's performance at the box office. Though it never took home any awards, it received nominations for a Visual Effects BAFTA, a couple Saturn Awards, and a Hugo for Best Dramatic Presentation, which Jim Cameron took for a little something called *Aliens*.

MUSIC OF THE MINSTRELS

Jim Henson had already collaborated with Trevor Jones on *The Dark Crystal*. Thrilled with Jones' work for that film, Henson approached him a second time. Jones was the first to suggest going for a more contemporary approach to the music, which led to the idea of casting a pop star in a lead role. The resulting score then became a total collaboration between Jones and David Bowie. In fact, Bowie delivered more or less completed tracks first, and Jones built his score around their tone.

The album, released in June 1986, performed well on the charts. The single "Underground," released as a 45, a 12" EP, and even a die-cut picture disc with Jareth's face, made it to #18 on the US Mainstream Rock chart and #21 on the UK Singles chart for that year. The track, produced by Bowie and the late Arif Mardin, featured gospel backing-vocals from a number of artists, including Chaka Khan, Luther Vandross, and Danny John-Jules (yes, the Cat from *Red Dwarf*). A CD finally came out in 1989 and has mostly remained in print ever since. One amusing side note: in 2012, Trevor Jones composed the music for a TV miniseries titled *Labyrinth* (no relation)!

THE SAGA CONTINUES

A large number of *Labyrinth* tie-in products have come out over the years, including everything from "Fiery" Halloween costumes to paper napkins, puzzles, and pencil cases. The rather high volume of stuff would require pages to discuss it all, but you can collect a few items of note to remind you of the babe!

Golden Games Incorporated published the one and only board game, *Labyrinth: The Mystical Maze Game*, in 1986, for two to four players, ages 7 and up. A spinner dictated movement. The game had a movable center section that added a bit of chaos to the proceedings. Overall it was a fairly light spin-and-move family game with a couple opportunities for strategic decisions, but the lack of art by Brian Froud—here crudely copied in a bright, rather simplistic style—makes this game a collectible only for the *Labyrinth* completist.

The lunchbox released for *The Dark Crystal* featured art and images from the film, but the bright-pink plastic monstrosity from Thermos for *Labyrinth* falls in step with the board game, opting for poorly rendered art instead of the real "Froudian" deal. Marvel Comics—continuing its early-'80s trend of adapting popular genre films—released an adaptation for this film, written by Sid Jacobson (one-time editor-in-chief for Harvey Comics) and featuring art by John Buscema, as the sixty-eight-page magazine-size *Marvel Comics Super Special* #40 and as a three-issue regular-format limited series.

A. C. H. Smith, author of the novelization for *The Dark Crystal*, returned to novelize *Labyrinth* for Henry Holt & Co. The 183-page paperback contains eight color pages of photos. Unlike the novelization of *The Dark Crystal*, this book goes for a surprisingly large amount of cash on the collectors' market, suggesting a limited print-run.

Archaia Entertainment published a deluxe hardcover reprint in 2014 featuring recently discovered Brian Froud illustrations. Henry Holt & Co. also released two elaborate tie-in books: the full-color *Labyrinth: The Photo Album* by Rebecca Grand, featuring a collection of chronological stills from the film with accompanying dialogue captions, and *The Goblins of Labyrinth* by Terry Jones and Brian Froud, a large, 138-page, glossy, full-color guide to goblins, most of which appeared in the film. Turner Publishing then condensed content from the latter book into a smaller volume titled *The Goblin Companion: A Field Guide to Goblins*. The original 138-page book was rereleased in 2006 for the film's 20th anniversary.

For the Apple IIe/IIc, Commodore 64/128, and MSX2 computers, Activision produced *Labyrinth: The Computer Game*, partially written and designed by Douglas Adams—yes, *the* Douglas Adams, of *The Hitchhiker's Guide to the Galaxy* fame. Dakin created a small line of plush toys, including Sir Didymus, Ludo, and a Fiery that featured removable limbs and head (through the miracle of Velcro).

In 2006, Tokyopop published a four-issue manga miniseries titled *Return to the Labyrinth*, written by Jake T. Forbes and illustrated by Chris Lie. The series deals with Toby, now a teenager, selected by Jareth to take over as king of the Underground.

In 2008, Toy Vault returned to the world of plushies, releasing new versions of Sir Didymus, Ludo, the Worm, and the Door-Knockers. Action-figure-producer NECA made a few collectible figures, including a couple Jareths and a nicely detailed Hoggle.

Archaia has also ventured into the realm of *Labyrinth* comics, with a short Free Comic Book Day premium released in 2012, titled *Hoggle and the Worm*, and a graphic-novel prequel released in April 2014—written by Ted Naifeh and Adrianne Ambrose, and illustrated by Cory Godbey—that tells the story of Jareth's rise to power. Because the film's story deals with timeless issues, tie-in merchandise will likely continue for years to come.

TAKE UP THY SWORD!
THE BOG (LOCATION)

Deep in the heart of the great labyrinth is a burbling expanse of foul-smelling water, muck, and mire. A few unpleasant creatures dare to call the place home, but most living beings with at least half a brain and a functional olfactory system steer clear of this horrid swamp and its perpetual pungency. According to rumors, it stretches as far as the imagination allows. Its details remain uncharted, because few visit and even fewer possess the desire to set specifics down on paper. Most goblin parents use threats of a visit to the Bog as a means to inspire their children to do household chores and keep their noses clean. Anyone accidentally setting foot in the Bog regrets it for a very long time—as do their friends, family members, and neighbors—because the foul odors supernaturally permeate anything that makes contact with the rank water. Only sorcery can purge (dispel) the stench.

THE FILM'S DESTINY

Though considered a failure at the box office, taking in roughly half of its $25 million budget, *Labyrinth* has gone on to become something much greater than Jim Henson could ever have imagined. Aside from all the merchandise discussed above, the film has also inspired things like the annual Labyrinth of Jareth masquerade ball held in Southern California, where since 1997, revelers have gathered—mostly in Venetian or fantasy-inspired costume—to dance, dine, shop, and enjoy incredible music. For many, *Labyrinth* is an adventure story on par with *The Wizard of Oz*: a tale of self-discovery and maturity, particularly for young women who see themselves in Sarah.

This film is special for this author [SAW], because thanks to this and *The Dark Crystal*, my wife and I have called the Frouds friends for some years. We attended Toby's wedding in England (coincidentally, Toby's wife is named Sarah) and have collaborated on projects, including at LAIKA Entertainment (the studio behind *ParaNorman* and *The Box Trolls*) just outside of Portland, Oregon.

Labyrinth is a magical film that, despite its flaws, continues to please audiences around the world ... and what precisely do I mean by "flaws"? Well, a few technical issues can jar the casual viewer. The sequence with the Fieries stands out in that regard: everything seems to float above the two-dimensional and slightly unfocused background, elements tossed through the air don't behave as if gravity is pulling at them, and the whole thing feels like it has tumbled out of an episode of *The Muppet Show* ("with our very special guest star, Jennifer Connelly! Yaaaaaaay!!!"). The film does require a suspension of disbelief and an appreciation for the groundbreaking techniques for its time. A final criticism perhaps unfairly levels at the soundtrack, but only because most of the tracks feel dated.

Overall, many of us happily return to the world of *Labyrinth*. It's a pleasant place to visit from time to time.

THIS YEAR IN GAMING

Finally released at Origins by Steve Jackson Games (after being publicly teased since 1983, starting as the "Great Unnamed Role-Playing System"), *GURPS (Generic Universal RolePlaying System)* made it onto gaming tables. Gamers had already tested out the game's combat system for a year, via a sixty-page book titled *Man to Man: Fantasy Combat* from *GURPS*, but the entire system—contained in a boxed set—first appeared in game shops in 1986. *Man to Man* borrowed from designer Steve Jackson's *The Fantasy Trip* (published by Metagaming), but *GURPS* strayed from those ideas and introduced a number of unique gaming concepts that would ensure the game's enduring success. A couple supplements supported the initial release, including *GURPS Fantasy* and *GURPS Autoduel*, which tied *GURPS* in with Steve Jackson's hugely popular *Car Wars* universe. *GURPS* continued to be one of the most supported generic RPG systems available, with tie-ins for licensed properties like Conan, Discworld, Horseclans, The Prisoner, and Witch World, and rules conversions for other roleplaying games, like *Deadlands*, *Traveller*, and *Vampire: The Masquerade*. Perhaps the most famous real-life tale connected to *GURPS* involved a 1990 raid on Steve Jackson Games, during which the Secret Service seized the manuscript for *GURPS Cyberpunk* and declared it a "handbook for computer crime"! The fourth edition of *GURPS* came out in 2004.

BIG TROUBLE IN LITTLE CHINA

1986 • US • 20TH CENTURY FOX • 99M; COLOR; PG-13

WRITERS: Gary Goldman and David Z. Weinstein
ADAPTATION BY: W. D. Richter
DIRECTOR: John Carpenter
PRODUCER: Larry J. Franco
MUSIC: John Carpenter and Alan Howarth
DIRECTOR OF PHOTOGRAPHY: Dean Cundey
VISUAL EFFECTS PRODUCED BY: Richard Edlund
VISUAL EFFECTS CREW: Boss Film Corporation
VISUAL EFFECTS ART DIRECTOR: George Jensen
CREATURES CREATED BY: Steve Johnson
SPECIAL EFFECTS COORDINATOR: Joseph Unsinn
PRODUCTION DESIGNER: John J. Lloyd
ART DIRECTOR: Les Gobruegge
COSTUME DESIGNER: April Ferry
STUNT COORDINATOR: Kenny Endoso
MARTIAL ARTS CHOREOGRAPHER: James Lew
MARTIAL ARTS CONSULTANT: Jim Lau
CONTACT LENSES BY: Dr. Morton Greenspoon
CAST: Kurt Russell (Jack Burton); Kim Cattrall (Gracie Law); Dennis Dun (Wang Chi); James Hong (Lo Pan); Victor Wong (Egg Shen); Kate Burton (Margo); Donald Li (Eddie Lee); Carter Wong (Thunder); Peter Kwong (Rain); James Pax (Lightning); Suzee Pai (Miao Yin); Chao Li Chi (Uncle Chu); Jeff Imada (Needles); Rummel Mor (Joe Lucky); Craig Ng (One Ear); June Kim (White Tiger); Noel Toy (Mrs. O'Toole); Jade Go (Chinese Girl in White Tiger); Jerry Hardin (Pinstripe Lawyer); James Lew, Jim Lau, Ken Endoso, Stuart Quan, Gary Toy, and George Cheung (Chang Sing Members); Jimmy Jue (Wounded Chang Sing); Noble Craig (Sewer Monster); Danny Kwan (Chinese Guard); Min Luong (Tara); Paul Lee (Chinese Gambler); Al Leong, Gerald Okamura, Willie Wong, Eric Lee, Yukio G. Collins, Bill M. Ryusaki, Brian Imada, Nathan Jung, Daniel Inosanto, and Vernon Rieta (Wing Kong Hatchet Men); Daniel Wong and Daniel Eric Lee (Wing Kong Security Guards); Lia Chang, Dian Tanaka, Donna L. Noguschi, and Shinko Isobe (Female Wing Kong Guards); John Carpenter (Chinatown Worker, uncredited); Dawna Lee Heising (Chinese Guard, uncredited); and Leo Lee (Fighter, uncredited)
ALTERNATE TITLES: *John Carpenter's Big Trouble in Little China* and *Ghost Hunters* (Japanese title)

ON THE MAP

The action takes place in Chinatown of San Francisco, California, mostly beneath the streets in Lo Pan's Evil Underground Lair™.

OUR STORY SO FAR

Often clueless truck-driver Jack Burton accompanies his friend Wang Chi to the airport to pick up Wang Chi's green-eyed mail-order bride Miao Yin, only to become embroiled in an evil plot that stretches back millennia. Ancient cursed wizard Lo Pan needs the girl to

> SOME PEOPLE PICK THE DARNEDEST PLACES TO START A FIGHT! (US)

regain his flesh and former glory, so now Jack, Wang Chi, a local maitre d', and a bus-driver-cum-sorcerer must venture deep under Chinatown to rescue Miao Yin and another victim of Lo Pan's scheme, the coincidentally also green-eyed reporter Gracie Law. Let's hope they feel kind of invincible.

ALTERNATE VERSIONS

In an alternate ending, Jack Burton rams his newly recovered truck into a sports car containing Miao Yin's three original kidnappers, the Lords of Death, sending them off the dock and into the water. This ending didn't sit well with test audiences, who thought it was too mean-spirited. It appears on DVD along with other deleted material. The UK DVD release restored very minor trims—only seconds—in 2002.

IT'S MAGIC

The movie dumps a great deal of slightly underdeveloped but detailed magical mythology on viewers in bits and pieces. We get some insight into the underlying cosmology of the universe, the ongoing tension between good and evil furies, the offensive environmental upheaval of the planet to feed humanity's desire for its "black blood," the presence of nether-realms with names like "The Hell of Being Cut to Pieces" and "The Hell of Upside-Down Sinners," and the existence of inexplicable monstrous creatures, like hairy, jaw-heavy apes and creepy giant insects.

Eldritch green fire, apparently a manifestation of "Chinese black magic," destroys a good bit of Chinatown. This form of energy seems to play on elemental forces, with human-shaped avatars that embody the powers of thunder, rain, and lightning: the Three Storms. Complicated rituals and blood magic are also part of the mix, even involving vaguely vampiric behavior. As with many of our other movies, green and blue are the dominant colors of magic.

At the center of it all is the ghostly warrior-wizard Lo Pan, cursed 2,258 years ago to walk the Earth as an immortal demon after he unsuccessfully challenged the first sovereign emperor of China, Qin Shi Huang. He can break the Curse of No Flesh—which seems to have its good side, because although it robs him of flesh and the delights thereof, it gives him spiritual indestructibility and the power to pass through solid matter—only if he marries and sacrifices a girl with green eyes. Marrying her is enough to appease Ching Dai, the demon-god of the East; the emperor added the sacrifice component. He was a harsh guy.

Egg Shen's confidence and senses-boosting potion are a "dream" to counter another dream. We wonder: is this all real? He also has a six-demon bag with exploding jewels that *World of Warcraft* players might recognize. Speaking of which....

THE QUEST FOR MEANING

Gaming plays a pretty high-profile role in this film, from the opening scene's rousing game of Fan-Tan to the epic wedding-battle sequence in which Egg Shen and Lo Pan square off in a contest of magical Rock 'Em Sock 'Em Robots reminiscent of a videogame, complete with Lo Pan appearing to operate an invisible controller! But the film plays the real game on the audience, by turning nearly every major Asian film stereotype and the familiar hero-sidekick paradigm upside down, sideways, and every which way but loose (wrong movie). In another movie, Wang Chi would be the sidekick, and Jack the lantern-jawed all-American hero—not the clumsy, arrogant, but occasionally lovable fool that he is. A bit like Indiana Jones, he's a hero in spite of himself: rarely effective, and unconscious through a lot of the action. Yet he kills Lo Pan in the end.

David Lo Pan embodies the Fu Manchu–like concept of the predatory "Yellow Peril," not only as an evil wizard but also as a human trafficker. He preys on innocent girls "fresh off the boat," selling them into brothel work as a lucrative sideline.

Egg Shen is our Charlie Chan, a mysterious man inexplicably in possession of all the facts, dispensing them, along with snippets of ancient Chinese wisdom, like fortune cookies. The two female stereotypes, the Dragon Lady and the Lotus Blossom, are also present but not as evident. The brothel's madam only fleetingly suggests the Dragon Lady. As the Lotus Blossom or China Doll, Miao Yin plays it totally straight. That's probably because she spends most of the film either out cold or in a trance, and never gets a chance to be anything other than cowed or comatose.

But appearances can be deceiving: the Great White Hope is an arrogant, incompetent bumbler, the Girl Friday doesn't get the guy, the Asian leads for the most part don't even have stereotypically Asian accents and in fact are not portrayed as "other"; that's Jack's job. Everyone storms the castle and saves the damsels in distress, but Wang Chi and Eddie get the girls. You know what Jack Burton says, though . . . oh, you do?

WHO GOES THERE?

Not many actors can be iconic heroes three or four times over, but Kurt Russell has done it more than that, in an impressive career that began when he was just a kid: he appeared with Elvis in *It Happened at the World's Fair*. He spent years appearing in classic Disney fare like *Follow Me, Boys!; The One and Only; Genuine; Original Family Band; The Horse in the Gray Flannel Suit; Guns in the Heather; The Computer Wore Tennis Shoes; The Barefoot Executive; Now You See Him, Now You Don't; Superdad;* and *The Strongest Man in the World;* as well as TV shows such as *Dennis the Menace, The Man from U.N.C.L.E., Gilligan's Island, Lost in Space,* and *Daniel Boone*. Successfully crossing over into adult roles after briefly switching over to minor-league baseball, Russell played Elvis in a TV movie by John Carpenter, which established a productive partnership that led to projects like *Escape from New York, The Thing,* this film, and *Escape from L.A.* Russell became one of cinema's most likable rogues in movies like *Used Cars, Overboard, Tango & Cash, Backdraft, Captain Ron, Tombstone, Stargate, Soldier, 3000 Miles to Graceland, Sky High* (in which he revisited his Disney roots, this time as a father figure), *Grindhouse (Death Proof), Furious Seven,* and *The Hateful Eight*.

Now permanently associated with her role as sexually ravenous Samantha Jones from the *Sex and the City* cable-television series and films, Kim Cattrall began her career with appearances in TV shows like *Logan's Run, Columbo, The Incredible Hulk, Vega$,* and *Charlie's Angels,* before her memorable role as the very vocal Honeywell in the raunchy comedy film, *Porky's.* She also appeared in *Police Academy, City Limits, Turk 182!, Mannequin, Star Trek VI: The Undiscovered Country, Above Suspicion,* and *Baby Geniuses.*

Dennis Dun appeared in *Year of the Dragon, The Last Emperor,* and *Prince of Darkness.*

You have seen James Hong more times in your life than you can possibly count. With more than 350 film and television roles to his credit, he is one of the most recognizable Asian character-actors in pop-culture history, with memorable genre appearances in TV shows like *The Outer Limits, I Spy, Kung Fu, The Bionic Woman, The New Adventures of Wonder Woman, Fantasy Island, The Dukes of Hazzard, Tales from the Darkside, The A-Team, Airwolf, Beauty and the Beast, War of the Worlds, Seinfeld* ("Seinfeld, four!"), *MacGyver, The Adventures of Brisco County Jr., Lois & Clark: The New Adventures of Superman, The X-Files, Ellen, Friends, Millennium, Charmed,* and *The Big Bang Theory.* He has also appeared in the films *Colossus: The Forbin Project, Blade Runner, Missing in Action, The Golden Child, Revenge of the Nerds II: Nerds in Paradise, The Two Jakes, Wayne's World 2, The Shadow, Tank Girl, Balls of Fury,* and the remake of *The Day the Earth Stood Still,* and has lent his voice to *Godzilla, King of the Monsters!; Mulan;* and the *Kung Fu Panda* franchise.

Victor Wong's career as a distinctive character-actor began later in life, after his stint as a San Francisco public-television news reporter. He appeared in *Year of the Dragon, The Golden Child, The Last Emperor, Prince of Darkness, Tremors, The Joy Luck Club,* and the *3 Ninjas* film series. He died in 2001 at age 74.

Kate Burton is one of the most prolific and popular readers for bestselling audio books.

Genre fans know Jerry Hardin well, as Deep Throat in *The X-Files* and Mark Twain in the two-part "Time's Arrow" story from *Star Trek: The Next Generation.* His career also includes roles in numerous other TV shows from the '70s to the present, as well as films like *Thunder Road, Mitchell, 1941, Cujo, The Falcon and the Snowman, Warning Sign, The Milagro Beanfield War, Little Nikita, The Firm, Ghosts of Mississippi,* and *Hidalgo.*

George Cheung played Genghis Khan in the "Back in the Bottle" episode of *Xena: Warrior Princess.*

Al Leong's first film role was in the Vietnam sequence of *Twilight Zone: The Movie,* which was marred by real-life tragedy. He has been a ubiquitous presence in action movies since the mid-'80s, and he played Genghis Khan in *Bill & Ted's Excellent Adventure.*

Nathan Jung played Genghis Khan, too, in "The Savage Curtain" episode of *Star Trek.* If you were following along, you'd have counted three Genghis Khans in one film, which might be a record.

Vernon Rieta appeared in *Highlander: Endgame.*

6 DEGREES OF SORCERY

This film has a huge number of visual references, especially because Carpenter intended it as an homage to "Chopsocky" films, spaghetti westerns, *wuxia* films, and about a half-dozen other genres. The old lady at the beginning of the film who closes her door and refuses to talk to Jack is a familiar visual from westerns. Lightning might remind you of a character from the *Mortal Kombat* franchise. Jack's incognito outfit and behavior in the brothel is reminiscent of Clark Kent. Jack's attempt to punch out Rain is a humorous mirror of James Bond's continual failed

> JACK BURTON'S IN FOR SOME SERIOUS TROUBLE AND YOU'RE IN FOR SOME SERIOUS FUN.

attempts to damage the steel-toothed Jaws with a well-placed haymaker in two Bond films, and Indy's attempts to punch out the Nazi who Marion neatly minces with a plane propeller in *Raiders of the Lost Ark*.

Lo Pan's lair looks like a cross between the bases in *You Only Live Twice* and *Enter the Dragon*. Lo Pan is initially very polite, much like a classic Bond villain—he's even in a wheelchair with a slight Blofeld air about him—and his wizard get-up is similar to Ming the Merciless's robes from *Flash Gordon*. His ultra-long fingernails might suggest those of Lady Deathstrike in *X2*.

Egg Shen appears to have a kind of Batpole to Chinatown's underworld, like Bruce Wayne's into the Batcave in the '60s *Batman* TV series. The aerial battle between Wang Chi and Rain is very similar to the wire-fu used by everyone from the Wachowskis in the *Matrix* trilogy to Uwe Boll in the *BloodRayne* films; now there's a range. Egg Shen's use of his mirror fan to reflect back Lightning's bolt is similar to Superman returning General Zod's heat vision in *Superman II* and Perseus's use of his shield in *Clash of the Titans*. Lo Pan and Egg Shen's beam duel is reminiscent of magical duels in many films, such as the one in Roger Corman's *The Raven*, the climactic final battle in *Howard the Duck* (yeah, we went there!), the fight between Iron Man and Rhodey in *Iron Man 2*, and various *Harry Potter* duels up to and including the final battle between Harry and Voldemort. The moment when Lo Pan throws the knife and Burton catches and returns it is echoed in an exchange between the Bride and one of the members of the Crazy 88 in *Kill Bill*. Finally, a major influence on Carpenter's creative decisions for this film (apart from *The Wizard of Oz* and a film he refers to as *Swords of Fame*, for which we can't locate any details) is a movie listed in our index: *Zu: Warriors from the Magic Mountain*, which itself drew inspiration from *Star Wars* and therefore *The Hidden Fortress*. And of course, a similar curse that has its ups and downs also afflicts the crew of the Black Pearl in *Pirates of the Caribbean: The Curse of the Black Pearl*.

SHATTERING THE ILLUSION

The first version of what became *Big Trouble in Little China* was a period western, set in the 1880s, written by Gary Goldman and David Weinstein in the early 1980s. In it, Jack Burton loses his horse and not his truck. Then 20th Century Fox acquired the script, removed the writers from the project, and commissioned W. D. Richter—creator of *The Adventures of Buckaroo Banzai*—to overhaul the script, which he did by moving the setting to the present day and eliminating almost everything else, apart from the basic thread of Lo Pan and his quest. Richter credited the balance between the real world and a darker underworld in *Rosemary's Baby* for his approach to the new script. When John Carpenter came on as director, he, too, contributed to the writing, but a Writers Guild of America decision resulted in Goldman and Weinstein retaining credit for the script and Richter and Carpenter receiving none.

The studio put a great deal of pressure on production, because it wanted to release the movie before Paramount's *The Golden Child* (with Eddie Murphy). *Big Trouble* had only ten weeks for preproduction and rehearsals and fifteen weeks of principal photography and post-production effects work. It made it to theaters just five months before its rival, which Carpenter had originally been asked to direct. To equal Murphy's star power, Carpenter first considered casting big names like Jack Nicholson or Clint Eastwood before turning to frequent collaborator Kurt Russell. Initially uncertain about the role, Russell warmed to it when he and Carpenter figured out that Burton was a guy who thought he was the hero but wasn't.

Russell based his swaggering performance on screen-legend John Wayne. Russell and Carpenter also spontaneously worked up the business involving Burton kissing Gracie and getting smeared with lipstick, as an extra comedy layer for the sequence. Carpenter was impressed with how willing Russell was to poke fun at himself. Dennis Dunn was also dedicated to his part, keeping a wooden practice sword with him on set so he could constantly prepare for his final battle when not shooting another scene.

During the making of the scene after Burton leaves the bordello, Russell suffered from a 104-degree fever and had to sit and rest as much as possible while still doing his best to keep production going. He wasn't the only one to risk his health; during underwater shooting, Carpenter, also submerged, wound up getting an ear infection.

Carpenter regularly worried about special-effects mishaps, such as the risk of James Pax's straw hat catching fire. He got very mad when an explosive squib set into the wall behind Russell went off early, potentially injuring the actor. An air ram hurled a stuntwoman at what was supposed to be a breakaway door, but the door was solid. Fortunately, the stuntwoman did not suffer injuries from the surprising impact.

Carpenter found Boss Film's effects lacking in quality, but Boss boss (heh) Richard Edlund blamed the limited $2 million budget. That team still created a new matte method specifically for the eyeball-festooned guardian and achieved other visuals using extremely low-tech methods, like rolling James Hong on a dolly when Lo Pan "floats" and using all sorts of trick sets and trampolines to create the illusion of complex, choreographed fight sequences. Sets served as the exteriors of Chinatown, so the production could maintain controlled locations.

Following completion of the film, producer Barry Diller asked Carpenter to make adjustments, including the addition of the somewhat inconsistent opening scene in the lawyer's office, to give the audience more setup and enhance Russell's heroic stature. This clashed a bit with the intention of flipping the traditional roles between the hero and sidekick.

The making of the movie was fun for the entire team, but a lack of advertising and poor support from the studio sank the film at the box office—all the more aggravating because the movie consistently impressed critics, who even told the filmmakers they had a surefire hit on their hands. It made less than half of its $20–25 million budget back when first released in theaters. It eventually found its audience via home video and grew into a beloved cult classic. Nevertheless, its failure convinced Carpenter to eschew the studio system from then on and go back to his roots as an independent filmmaker.

> Some people pick the damnedest places to start a fight! (UK)

MUSIC OF THE MINSTRELS

Joe Regis assembled the distinctive soundtrack album by Carpenter and Alan Howarth, which includes Carpenter's group, the Coupe de Villes, performing the title song. Besides Carpenter, you can also hear the voices of Nick Castle and Tommy Lee Wallace. Enigma / Demon Records put out the vinyl LP in 1986 and a CD version in 1992. A UK single of the Coupe de Villes song came out in 1986, with the main orchestral theme from the movie, "The Pork Chop Express," on the flipside. In 1999, Supercollector picked up the gauntlet and added material not included in the original release. That version is hard to find. In 2009, La La Land stepped up to the plate and offered fans a definitive, remastered edition with the complete score and extensive liner notes, limited to only 3,000 copies. It became available on iTunes as a digital download in 2011 but without the Coupe de Villes' title song.

THE SAGA CONTINUES

Owners of a Commodore 64 [oh, those were the days —ATB], Amstrad CPC, or ZX Spectrum could play Electric Dreams Software's side-scrolling videogame, released in conjunction with the film. N2 / Mirage Toys released a series of six-inch action figures in the early 2000s and teased the production of a twelve-inch Jack Burton figure that never made it to market. The line saw limited distribution and is now very rare. In 2014, BOOM! Studios began a sequel comic-book series.

As we concluded work on this book, the announcement came that Dwayne Johnson would play Jack Burton in a *Big Trouble* remake. Do you think he gets the part about how Jack isn't really the hero of the movie?

TAKE UP THY SWORD!

EYEBALL-GUARDIAN (MONSTER)

DEFENSE: Eyeball-guardians possess no offensive abilities and thus turn and flee when in danger.

POWERS/VULNERABILITIES: Because they psychically bond with their masters, eyeball-guardians can transmit images directly into their masters' minds. A master can, in turn, speak through an eyeball-guardian to address anyone in its vicinity. Eyeball-guardians lack limbs, so they cannot perambulate. Instead, they move via magical levitation. Because eyes cover their spherical bodies, nothing can get past them without detection.

DETAILS: A summoner can call an eyeball-guardian to protect a lair or treasure. It serves only one master. Whatever an eyeball-guardian observes, its master also sees. An enemy can slay it in standard combat; however, this timid and swift-moving creature does everything in its power to escape from harm. If ever anything blinds all of its eyes, it vanishes from this plane to recover and returns soon after to continue to fulfill its mandate.

THE FILM'S DESTINY

How many movies could manage to throw in everything *and* the kitchen sink and still come out on top with a quotable cult hit that lives on long after a relatively shaky original release?

True, *Big Trouble in Little China* isn't everyone's cup of tea. It's one of the stranger films in this book, as far as the sword-and-sorcery genre goes, but it qualifies by our criteria just as much as it trades on tropes from the schools of action, science-fiction, horror, western, and "Chopsocky" cinema. In fact, it straddles all these genres with such brazen arrogance that it dares you to dislike it. If you're not happy, it tells you, wait five minutes: I'll be another movie by then.

Perhaps the movie's slyest gambit is to take '80s hero Kurt Russell—none other than Snake Plissken and R. J. MacReady—and make him a clueless sidekick who constantly asks what's going on, spouts macho aphorisms, and succeeds (partially) by little more than sheer bravado and a mystical boost. His abrasive relationship with Gracie also recalls the Howard Hawks school of fast-talking screwball romantic-comedy pairings, giving the movie an old-style Hollywood energy at its emotional core.

Glaringly embarrassing '80s style surrounds the film's retro characterizations, especially the chamber in which the climactic battle takes place, which has an escalator, neon tubing everywhere you look, and a skull that might be stage dressing for Spinal Tap. Are they in an evil underground lair, or a mall? Maybe both.

With tongue firmly in cheek, the movie still takes itself seriously when it counts. Hong's Lo Pan in particular is a delightful villain, somehow endearing and terrifying in his different guises, and ultimately tragic, like so many of his cinematic comrades. As for the final scene, it almost makes you wish that Jack Burton's confounding adventures would continue, so he'd have more chances to shake the pillars of heaven.

THIS YEAR IN GAMING

West End Games (in cooperation with Chaosium) released the first edition of *Ghostbusters*, an officially licensed roleplaying game based on the hugely popular motion picture released two years prior. The core dice-pool mechanics of the system represented the first version of the d6 system that West End would eventually feature in its long-running *Star Wars: The Roleplaying Game* (1987 to 1998) and in its in-house generic rules known as *The D6 System* (1996). *Ghostbusters* would do well enough for West End to merit a revised "second" edition, *Ghostbusters International*, released in 1989 to tie in with the release of *Ghostbusters II*. The company supported both editions with adventures and supplemental materials.

THE BARBARIANS

1987 • US/Italy • Cannon Films / Cannon Italia Srl • 87m • Color • R

Screenplay/Story: James R. Silke
Dubbing Dialogue: Aberto Piferi
Director: Ruggero Deodato
Producers: Yoram Globus and Menahem Golan
Music: Pino Donaggio
Director of Photography: Lorenzo Battaglia
Make-Up & Visual Effects: Francesco and Gaetano Paolocci
Production Designer: Giuseppe Mangano
Costumes: Francesca Panicali
Costumes For The Barbarian Brothers: Michela Gisotti
Master Of Arms: Benito Stefanelli
Weapons: Umberto D'Aniello
Cast: Peter Paul (Kutchek); David Paul (Gore); Richard Lynch (Kadar); Eva La Rue (Ismene/Kara); Virginia Bryant (Canary); Sheeba Alahani (China); Michael Berryman (Dirtmaster); Franco Pistoni (Ibar); Raffaella Baracchi (Allura); Pasquale Bellazecca (Kutchek as a Young Boy); Luigi Bellazecca (Gore as a Young Boy); Wilma Marzilli (Fat Woman); Pailo Risi (Clown); Giovanni Cianfriglia (Strongman); Angelo Ragusa, Nanni Bernini, and Lucio Rosato (Kadar's Men); George Eastman (Jacko); Franco Dadi (Bluto); L. Caroli (Nose, uncredited); Tiziana Di Gennaro (Kara as a Young Girl, uncredited); Marilda Donà (Kadar's Woman, uncredited); Paolo Merosi (Kadar's Man, uncredited); Nello Pazzafini (Jacko's Man, uncredited); Renzo Pevarello (Bones, uncredited); and Benito Stefanelli (Greyshaft, uncredited)
Alternate Title: *The Barbarian Brothers*

ON THE MAP

We're in an ancient, medieval world of "savage splendor." Kadar rules the kingdom of Talchet, a decadent, class-based society in which the wealthy ride on the backs of the poor and the enslaved ... figuratively and literally. Other environments include war-scarred fields, mountain ranges, and the Forbidden Lands (accessible through a tunnel hidden behind a waterfall). In the last, the Gravemaker, an ancient dragon, dwells.

OUR STORY SO FAR

Vicious King Kadar somewhat justifiably enslaves twin brothers Kutchek and Gore as youths after one of them gnaws his fingers off; you can't just do that kind of thing and expect to get away with it. Upon reaching manhood, they escape their bondage and head out to save their people, rescue their queen, and defeat Kadar.

ALTERNATE VERSIONS

Comparisons between the very few releases of the film have revealed running-time variations of 84 to 87 minutes, but no details as to those missing three minutes. As of this writing, a

US DVD or Blu-ray has not been released. Until that time—when we will likely see an uncut version of the film—the mystery, if there is one, remains.

IT'S MAGIC

We witness a few spells cast in stereotypical fashion—China even casts an old-school web spell onto the young versions of the barbarians—but magic manifests in unusual ways as well. Canary can somehow charm Kadar in the swamp, and her cries for Kutchek and Gore carry for miles. Canary also shares a link with the Belly Stone, so that when she dies, the stone temporarily becomes a normal stone, perhaps to hide from malevolent eyes. The fact that Kadar's severed fingers must be destroyed so they are not used against him acknowledges the existence of sympathetic magic. The Belly Stone itself—the object of Kadar's greed—is not only a valuable stone; it also contains the secrets of music, art, and story, granting such blessings upon those who possess it. That's some stone.

THE QUEST FOR MEANING

This film presents the bonds of love—oh, stop gagging—in a variety of ways. The Ragnicks, with Kutchek and Gore as precocious twins, epitomize the close-knit, bonded family. They in turn express their love for those around them to such an extent that they risk their lives to prevent Canary's capture. Although they become separated from one another, their love for each other remains even after the twins become savage gladiators.

It does not become clear, however, whether Kadar's infatuation with Canary is the product of her sorcery or a genuine feeling. As king of Talchet, he can have anything—and anyone—he wants, yet he practically bows and scrapes at Canary's feet, even agreeing to spare the twins provided she gives herself to him. Yet for at least a decade, though he dresses Canary in the finest clothes and drowns her in precious jewels and pearls, he keeps her locked away in his harem. He kowtows to her there in the hopes that his caged Canary will "sing" (see where we went there?) and reveal the whereabouts of the precious Belly Stone. By the end of the film, the Ragnick "family" is reborn, despite the tragic loss of Canary, and happiness of a kind prevails.

WHO GOES THERE?

Professional bodybuilders Peter and David Paul got their big break in show business thanks to Joel Schumacher, in the 1983 comedy *D.C. Cab*. They continued to do the double-act in a few other films, like *Think Big*, *Double Trouble*, and *Twin Sitters*, as well as in television series, including *Knight Rider*. They shot a segment for *Natural Born Killers* that was cut from the final film but appears on the DVD/Blu-ray as a special feature.

This was the debut role for the always adorable Eva La Rue. With an unwavering career in both television and movies, La Rue has had healthy runs in a few soap operas and other series over the years, such as *Third Watch* and *CSI: Miami*. In film, she appears in *Crash and Burn*, *Ghoulies III: Ghoulies Go to College*, and *RoboCop 3*.

Despite bearing a slight resemblance to Sybil Danning, Virginia Bryant appeared in only a few other films of interest, including *Demons 2* and *The Ogre: Demons 3*.

> **WARRIORS.
> CONQUERORS.
> HEROES.**

Originally discovered by producer-director George Pal, Michael Berryman perhaps best sparks memories for his role as one of the modern-day savages in Wes Craven's *The Hills Have Eyes* and its sequel, but he has graced our screens with his unusual countenance (the effects of hypohidrotic ectodermal dysplasia) in many other films, such as *Doc Savage: The Man of Bronze*, *One Flew Over the Cuckoo's Nest*, *Weird Science*, *Star Trek IV: The Voyage Home*, *Beastmaster 2: Through the Portal of Time*, *Double Dragon*, *The Devil's Rejects*, and *The Lords of Salem*. He has also played roles in TV shows like *The Fall Guy*, *ALF*, *Star Trek: The Next Generation*, *Tales from the Crypt*, and *Scooby-Doo! Curse of the Lake Monster*.

Raffaella Baracchi was Miss Italy 1983.

Paolo Risi played a "pantomime dwarf" in the 1999 production of *A Midsummer Night's Dream* starring Kevin Kline and Michelle Pfeiffer. He also appeared in a couple episodes of the HBO series *Rome*, in which he played Cato the dwarf.

Giovanni Cianfriglia has worked as an actor and stuntman in more than a hundred movies since his start in 1958, when he doubled for Steve Reeves in *Hercules*. That relationship with Reeves continued for a total of six films, including *Morgan, the Pirate* and *Duel of the Titans*. Though the vast majority of his pictures were Italian *peplum* or westerns, he crossed over for a few films but often in uncredited roles, including the 1983 *Hercules*, *Ladyhawke*, and *The Last Temptation of Christ*.

Apart from playing a zombie in *Zombie Holocaust* (a.k.a. *Dr. Butcher M.D.*) as well as a few soldiers and goons in Italian pictures, Angelo Ragusa has a long and impressive career as a stuntman in such productions as *1990: The Bronx Warriors*, *Ladyhawke*, *King David*, *The Name of the Rose*, *The Adventures of Baron Munchhausen*, *The Mummy*, *Quantum of Solace*, and *The Twilight Saga: New Moon* ... although we're not sure if he sparkled in that one or not.

Writer-actor George Eastman (born Luigi Montefiori) has both penned and appeared in a number of films, often under one of fifteen different pseudonyms. Though known for his good looks, he buried himself under makeup for the lead role in the cannibal film *Anthropophagus*, a movie he both wrote and starred in. Over the many years of his career, he has also been a gunslinger (sporting both color hats) in a number of spaghetti westerns, including *Django Kills Softly* (in which he played the title role) and *Django, Prepare a Coffin*. He also appeared in *Fellini Satyricon*, played opposite Charlton Heston in *Call of the Wild*, and worked on several unsavory pictures with Joe D'Amato, including *Sexy* (or *Erotic*) *Nights of the Living Dead* and *Porno Holocaust*.

Franco Dadi is an actor, a stuntman, and "master of the sword," a credit he received for his work on *Iron Warrior*, the third film in the *Ator* series. He also earned credit as the stunt coordinator for *The Curse* and *Bill & Ted's Excellent Adventure*.

Nello Pazzafini also had roles in *Ator, the Fighting Eagle*; *Yor, the Hunter from the Future*; *The Blade Master*; and tons of other adventure epics. He died in 1997 at age 63.

Benito Stefanelli was also in *Ladyhawke* and provided vital translation services between director Sergio Leone and actor Clint Eastwood on the set of *A Fistful of Dollars*. He died in 1999 at age 71.

6 DEGREES OF SORCERY

Fellini's *La Strada* likely inspired the Ragnick caravans. The chase sequence at the top of the film plays like a medieval version of *The Road Warrior* (a.k.a. *Mad Max 2*). The striking sorceress China resembles the witch Ban Urlu of *The Sword and the Sorcerer* (which also featured Richard Lynch). Her role and appearance are somewhat similar to those of General Kala from *Flash Gordon*. There's also no denying her similarity, at least in appearance, to Zula of *Conan the Destroyer*, released three years before.

The treatment of the brothers and the various depictions thereof come from *Conan the Barbarian*, right down to the slowly marching feet in the sand, like Conan's feet around the Wheel of Pain. Kadar's harem and Canary's imprisonment are similar to Ming's harem and Dale's imprisonment in *Flash Gordon*. The helmeted monstrosities scream Master Blaster from 1985's *Mad Max Beyond Thunderdome*, further copied when Kutchek and Gore battle one another while the townspeople look on and cheer through the lattice surrounding the arena. The Ragnicks capture Kutchek and Gore beneath a large net not unlike the way the Amazons capture Ator in *Ator, the Fighting Eagle*. Gore's bizarre laugh makes him sound a bit like an inebriated Tauntaun from *Star Wars: The Empire Strikes Back*. The acquisition of special gold weapons and armor from a secret location—the Tomb of the Ancient King—happens much the same way as in *Legend*. The dragon bears a striking resemblance to a Drashig from the 1973 *Doctor Who* story "Carnival of Monsters." When Kadar has his final showdown with Kutchek and Gore, he wields a facsimile (in both appearance and function) of Ator's Shield of Mordor, even using its mirrored surface to blind his opponents.

SHATTERING THE ILLUSION

With a story and screenplay by screenwriter *(American Ninja, King Solomon's Mines)* and author *(Frank Frazetta's Death Dealer* series) James R. Silke, *The Barbarians* went before the cameras from August 4th to October 9th, 1986. Several shoots took place in the Tor Caldara Nature Reserve, south of Anzio. Additional scenes were shot around Campo Imperatore, L'Aquila, Abruzzo, Italy—a location used by a number of other films of note, including *Krull*, *Ladyhawke*, and *The Name of the Rose*.

Ottaviano Dell'Acqua perhaps gained the most fame for being the iconic worm-eyed zombie in Lucio Fulci's *Zombi 2*. His image on that movie's posters now appears on t-shirts and other merchandise around the world. During this production, he was a stuntman, a role he has fulfilled in more than 180 other films.

By 1987, big-budget Hollywood entries were replacing the low-budget sword-and-sorcery genre of the early '80s, with films like *The Princess Bride, Highlander, Labyrinth,* and *Big Trouble in Little China*. (Boy, those titles sure do sound familiar. . . .) Sure, a few outfits still produced things like *Gor, Iron Warrior,* and *Amazons*, but the tone had shifted. Whereas those older films had made their money via 99-cent theaters and local drive-ins, the new market for low-budget films was now in the direct-to-video industry via local video-store shelves. That was where *The Barbarians* was headed.

FEEL THE POWER!

MUSIC OF THE MINSTRELS

Pino Donaggio was already a familiar name in genre films by the time he came to compose the score for *The Barbarians*. Because he had already composed the memorable scores for *Don't Look Now* (his first feature film), *Carrie, Piranha, The Howling, Hercules* (discussed elsewhere in this volume), and *Body Double,* securing his services for *The Barbarians* was a good and marketable move. This was his first collaboration with Deodato. They would go on to work together on a couple additional projects over the next two years.

The score is a good mix of contemporary synth-pop and dynamic orchestral pieces conducted by Natale Massara, who had worked with Donaggio on dozens of other film and television projects. Intrada released the complete soundtrack on CD in 1990, limiting it to only 1,200 copies. It features sixteen tracks, including the song that plays over the credits, "Ruby Dawn," performed by singer-songwriter Ronnie Jackson, with lyrics by Paolo Steffan.

THE SAGA CONTINUES

With an estimated budget of $4 million—pretty significant for an '80s Italian *Conan* knock-off—and a domestic total gross of only $800,000, *The Barbarians* did not fare well enough to merit the sequel that at least a few of us would have liked to see. (Oh, come on, there have to be a couple of you out there.)

This film's failure didn't put an end to the careers of Peter and David Paul, however. They appeared together in a few more films. They would typically play other bumbling, muscle-bound twins, so they weren't looking for much in the way of acting challenges.

An odd selection of tie-in apparel came out at the time of the video release, promoted on the tape itself. Items offered included white, puff-printed tank tops, t-shirts, sweatshirts, and gym shorts. Sexy!

TAKE UP THY SWORD!

THE BOG DRAGON (MONSTER)

ATTACKS: The bog dragon attacks with either two large sets of claws or one aggressive bite.

POWER/VULNERABILITY:

WATER-BREATHING: The bog dragon can breathe freely under even the murkiest swamp water.

SACRED-WEAPON WEAKNESS: Mundane weapons can harm the bog dragon, but it takes double damage from successful attacks with sacred weapons plundered from tombs of ancient kings. Normal weapon damage incapacitates the bog dragon for a time but does not destroy it.

DETAILS: The bog dragon is an ancient beast that has lived in the Forbidden Lands from time immemorial. Some legends tell of the creature possessing a breath weapon, but no one has ever witnessed its use. Perhaps the dragon has lost the ability due to age.

THE FILM'S DESTINY

Most of us didn't have the opportunity to see something like *The Barbarians* on the big screen, but that's what access to a VHS or Betamax machine was all about. In some ways, however, it's a shame that more people didn't get to see this film on the big screen. Yes, that's right: despite clichés, unrefined performances, and a pretty sad-looking bestiary, the worthwhile elements win out, including the chemistry between the Paul brothers (unfairly nominated for the Razzie for Worst New Star that year), the costuming, some of the cinematography, and Donaggio's score. It's like watching a stormy sea, in that, at one moment, things dip and you cringe, but then Richard Lynch lights up the screen with a sinister aside or Eva La Rue flashes one of her irresistible smiles, and you're back on the crest of the wave.

That's not to say there aren't plenty of things to legitimately criticize about this film. One huge issue is that the boys must have been imprisoned for at least ten or twelve years and yet no one—not Kadar, not Canary, and not any of the Ragnicks (apart from Kara)—appears to have aged a day. Even the costumes, hairstyles, and makeup are unaltered by the passage of time. Sorcery, perhaps? Also, it makes absolutely no sense at all why Ismene doesn't reveal herself as Kara right away, once she knows the barbarians' identity. Those issues aside, if you're looking for a lighthearted example of the sword-and-sorcery genre that still presents some pretty nifty story ideas—at the very least, fodder for your next RPG campaign—you really can't go wrong with *The Barbarians*.

THIS YEAR IN GAMING

After his departure from TSR in 1985, Gary Gygax cofounded New Infinities Productions, Inc., with the intention of releasing new fiction and roleplaying-game materials. He started with the *Cyborg Commando* RPG, written primarily by TSR alumnus Frank Mentzer and based on detailed notes from Gygax. The concept behind the game seemed sound, but it would prove a disaster, even with the support of three supplements. The mechanics were faulty, generated characters weak, and the system sloppy and confusing. As a result, many consider it one of the worst and least-successful roleplaying games ever released, especially in light of its pedigree.

THE PRINCESS BRIDE

❋

1987 • US • 20TH CENTURY FOX • 98M • COLOR • PG

SCREENPLAY: William Goldman (based on his book)
DIRECTOR: Rob Reiner
PRODUCERS: Andrew Scheinman And Rob Reiner
MAKE-UP SUPERVISOR: Lois Burwell
BILLY CRYSTAL'S AND CAROL KANE'S MAKE-UP CREATED BY: Peter Montagna
SPECIAL EFFECTS SUPERVISOR: Nick Allder
MUSIC: Mark Knopfler, Guy Fletcher, and Willy De Ville (vocalist)
DIRECTOR OF PHOTOGRAPHY: Adrian Biddle
PRODUCTION DESIGNER: Norman Garwood
ART DIRECTOR: Richard Holland
COSTUME DESIGNER: Phyllis Dalton
STUNT COORDINATOR: Peter Diamond
SWORDMASTER: Bob Anderson
ADDITIONAL SWORDFIGHTING CHOREOGRAPHY: Bill Tomlinson (uncredited)
CAST: Cary Elwes (Westley), Mandy Patinkin (Inigo Montoya), Chris Sarandon (Prince Humperdinck), Christopher Guest (Count Rugen), Wallace Shawn (Vizzini), Andre the Giant (Fezzik), Fred Savage (The Grandson), Robin Wright (Buttercup, the Princess Bride), Peter Falk (The Grandfather), Peter Cook (The Impressive Clergyman), Mel Smith (The Albino), Carol Kane (Valerie), Billy Crystal (Miracle Max), Anne Dyson (The Queen), Margery Mason (The Ancient Booer), Malcolm Storry (Yellin), Willoughby Gray (The King), Betsy Brantley (The Mother), Paul Badger (The Assistant Brute), Anthony Georghiou and Danny Blackner (R.O.U.S. Performers), and Derek Pykett (Villager, uncredited)

ON THE MAP

The grandson lives in Evanston, Illinois (note all the Chicago sports paraphernalia in his room), but the tale of Westley and Buttercup takes place a long time ago in a land called Florin (celebrating its 500th anniversary), which is teetering on the verge of war with its rival across the sea, Guilder. When, exactly? Impossible to tell, because the story deliberately includes a number of anachronisms, including references to the settlement of an Australian penal colony in 1788 and a quip about Asian warfare paraphrased from a speech by field marshal Bernard Law Montgomery in 1962. After all, it's a storybook story.

OUR STORY SO FAR

Westley and Buttercup are two young lovers destined for happiness if they can just overcome a few obstacles: Evil Prince Humperdinck intends to marry and then murder Buttercup in a plot to instigate war. A pair of good-hearted outlaws get swept up in the plan, with one also pursuing vengeance for the murder of his father. And when Humperdinck's men capture Westley and kill him with a nightmarish machine that drains the human soul, there might be no way to bring him back. Can true love see them through?

IT'S MAGIC

You could argue that this is one of the weaker choices for us in this book, because magic does not play a huge role. On the other hand, is not true love the most magical thing of all? Okay, okay, don't get the dry heaves; we figured it was worth a try.

At the very least, magic is likely at work in the humble home of Miracle Max, because the evidence suggests that Count Rugen's machine does indeed kill Westley, in which case Max's chocolate-coated pill is a form of mystical cure-all that resurrects the dead. On the other hand, the machine might merely have rendered Westley comatose or extremely injured, in which case Max is just a flimflam man with a sweet tooth. Either way, Max's lack of employment fits neatly with our usual theme of magic passing out of the world, although that's more of a "Quest for Meaning" topic.

But come on now: how could we leave this movie out? Inconceivable!

THE QUEST FOR MEANING

Are you kidding? True love!

... Not enough? One of the things that makes this the perfect fairytale film for all ages is that it contains pure, well-illustrated messages about the best that humans can be. In addition to the main theme—the old reliable saw that love conquers all—magic overcomes death-by-machine: another expression of the familiar nature-versus-technology struggle seen often in this genre. There is also a consistent thread about loyalty and honor, and even commentary on basic politeness. During the quick montage in which Buttercup realizes Westley's true feelings on the farm, she exchanges her brusque tone for one of humility and kindness. In doing so, she opens the door to love, and decency wins the day.

When Inigo finally gets his revenge, he wounds Rugen only as many times and in the same way as Rugen wounded him: two cuts to the face, two stabs in the shoulders, and the killing blow in the stomach (from when Rugen hurled his knife at Inigo). Though enraged and motivated by vengeance, Inigo nonetheless shows admirable nobility.

Even Humperdinck and Rugen, loathsome people by any stretch of the imagination, demonstrate unswerving devotion to one another, especially in an affectionate scene by the tree that leads to Rugen's devilish dungeon. Because Humperdinck isn't really interested in Buttercup romantically, you might almost wonder . . . ? He and Rugen do make a nice couple.

Ultimately, not only love conquers, but so do friendship and honor. These things surely shouldn't be limited to storybooks.

This movie is also steeped in gaming ideas, from the kid playing his baseball videogame at the film's start to Westley's systematic dispatching of various "bosses" in

> SCALING THE CLIFFS OF INSANITY.
> BATTLING RODENTS OF UNUSUAL SIZE.
> FACING TORTURE IN THE PIT OF DESPAIR.
> TRUE LOVE HAS NEVER BEEN A SNAP.

his journey to retrieve Buttercup from Vizzini's clutches. Each match draws upon a different set of skills and requires a unique solution.

For gamers devoted to roleplaying systems: the creators as well as fans of *The Princess Bride* often credit it as a celebration of storytelling. Anyone who appreciates the value of a tale well told, of instilling the joy of reading and imagination in young people, and of finding happiness in sharing those things with friends gathered to venture into worlds of adventure should find something to love in this sweet fairytale.

WHO GOES THERE?

Dashing Cary Elwes also appeared in movies like *Oxford Blues, The Bride, Lady Jane, Glory, Days of Thunder, Hot Shots!* (what is a chafing dish?), *Dracula, The Crush, Robin Hood: Men in Tights, The Jungle Book, Twister, Liar Liar, Cradle Will Rock, Shadow of the Vampire, Saw, Ella Enchanted, Saw 3D: The Final Chapter*, and *The Adventures of Tintin*, and on TV shows such as *Seinfeld, From the Earth to the Moon, The Outer Limits, Batman Beyond*, and *The X-Files*. Oh, and if you've ever been as confused as we were, given Elwes's there/not-there accent: he was born and raised in the UK.

Mandy Patinkin's first true love is the musical-theater stage, where he is a tenor vocalist, but he has also appeared in films like *Ragtime, Yentl, Alien Nation*, and *Dick Tracy*, and on television in *Picket Fences, The Simpsons, Homicide: Life on the Street, Chicago Hope, Touched by an Angel* (as Satan!), *Boston Public, Law & Order, Dead Like Me, Criminal Minds*, and *Homeland*.

Chris Sarandon was the only Jerry Dandridge, and don't let anyone tell you differently. As the suave vampire in the original *Fright Night*, he made a generation reconsider joining the creatures of the night, but he started his career on television in *Guiding Light* and moved on to appearances in films such as *The Sentinel, Nausicaä of the Valley of the Winds* (the English-dubbed version), *Child's Play, Shatterbrain, The Nightmare Before Christmas* (as the voice of Jack), *Bordello of Blood*, and (sadly) the remake of *Fright Night*. He's also turned up on TV in *A Tale of Two Cities, Sisters, Picket Fences, Star Trek: Deep Space Nine, The Practice, Chicago Hope, Felicity, ER, Judging Amy, Charmed, Cold Case, Law & Order*, and *Psych*. He was Jesus in the TV movie *The Day Christ Died* and the Frankenstein monster in a 1987 TV-adaptation of *Frankenstein*.

Christopher Guest turned his participation in Rob Reiner's *This Is Spinal Tap* into a cottage industry, directing and starring in a successful series of mockumentary films like *Waiting for Guffman, Best in Show, A Mighty Wind*, and *For Your Consideration*. He was part of the cast of *Saturday Night Live* for one memorable year in the 1980s and has also appeared in movies like *Death Wish, Shame of the Jungle* (the English-dubbed version), *Heartbeeps, Little Shop of Horrors*, and *A Few Good Men*, and television series like *All in the Family, Laverne & Shirley*, and *St. Elsewhere*.

Wallace Shawn is a complex, creative fellow with credits that stretch across nearly all media. Although he's an award-winning playwright, he tends to be intellectual comic relief in films and television due to his unique appearance and lisp, with roles in movies such as *Manhattan, All That Jazz, Simon, My Dinner with Andre* (as himself), *Strange Invaders, Mom and Dad Save the World, The Meteor Man, Clueless*, and *Vegas Vacation*, and in TV shows like *Clueless* (yup, again), *Murphy Brown, Crossing Jordan, The L Word, Eureka*, and *Gossip Girl*. He was also the voice of Rex in the *Toy Story* series and the Grand Nagus on *Star Trek: Deep Space Nine*.

Born André René Roussimoff, Andre the Giant suffered from acromegaly but turned his disorder into an asset as one of the most popular and distinctive wrestlers of the WWF. He was the first Bigfoot in two hugely popular episodes of *The Six Million Dollar Man* and also appeared uncredited as Dagoth in *Conan the Destroyer*. He died in 1993 at age 46. After his death, *The Princess Bride* costar Billy Crystal made the movie *My Giant* as a tribute to him.

Fred Savage was contemplative Kevin Arnold on *The Wonder Years* and also appeared in films like *The Boy Who Could Fly*, *Vice Versa*, *Little Monsters*, *The Wizard*, and *Austin Powers in Goldmember*. He was also the voice of Hawk in the animated *Justice League* TV series, but in recent years he's moved behind the camera to direct episodes of television shows like *Boy Meets World* (starring younger brother Ben), *Zoey 101*, *Hannah Montana*, *Wizards of Waverly Place*, and *It's Always Sunny in Philadelphia*.

Robin Wright became part of a Hollywood power-couple when she married outspoken actor and activist Sean Penn in 1996 (they divorced in 2010), but she started out with appearances in *Hollywood Vice Squad* and in this film. She also had a regular role in *Santa Barbara* and roles in *Forrest Gump*, *Unbreakable*, *Beowulf*, and *The Girl with the Dragon Tattoo*, as well as in the Netflix TV series *House of Cards*.

Audiences will always remember Peter Falk as rumpled detective Columbo, a role he played in two television movies, in an ongoing series in the 1960s and '70s, and in specials from 1989 to 2003. After early roles in the golden age of television, including a memorable episode of *The Twilight Zone* in which he played a thinly-veiled version of Fidel Castro, Falk appeared in movies like *It's a Mad Mad Mad Mad World*, *Robin and the 7 Hoods*, *Murder by Death*, *The Cheap Detective*, *The In-Laws* (Serpentine!), *The Great Muppet Caper*, . . . *All the Marbles*, and *Vibes*. He died in 2011 at age 83.

Peter Cook teamed with Dudley Moore, and together they became one of the most influential comedy teams of their time. Cook's film roles include *Bedazzled*, *Those Daring Young Men in Their Jaunty Jalopies*, *The Rise and Rise of Michael Rimmer*, *The Hound of the Baskervilles*, *Yellowbeard*, *Supergirl*, *Without a Clue*, and *Black Beauty*. He died in 1995 at age 57.

Mel Smith is half of the British comedy team Smith & Jones and also turned up in the movies *Morons from Outer Space*, *European Vacation*, and *Brain Donors*. He died in 2013 at age 60.

Television viewers of the '80s remember Carol Kane as Latka's girlfriend/wife Simka on *Taxi*. She's also appeared in films like *Carnal Knowledge*, *Annie Hall*, *The Muppet Movie*, *When a Stranger Calls*, *Transylvania 6-5000*, *Jumpin' Jack Flash*, *Ishtar*, *Scrooged*, and *Addams Family Values*, and on TV series such as *Faerie Tale Theatre*, *Cheers*, *Tales from the Darkside*, *The Ray Bradbury Theater*, *Seinfeld*, *Aladdin*, *Ellen*, *Pearl*, *Family Guy*, *Monk*, and *Gotham*. Horror fans might be mad if we didn't mention that she also reprised her role as Jill for the TV-movie sequel, *When a Stranger Calls Back*.

Early in his career, Billy Crystal performed stand-up comedy and made history as the first openly gay regular character on television in *Soap*. He joined Christopher Guest for that season of *Saturday Night Live* and appeared in the films *This Is Spinal Tap*, *Running Scared*, *Throw Momma from the Train*, *When Harry Met Sally . . .* , *City Slickers*, *Mr. Saturday Night* (which he also cowrote and directed), *City Slickers II: The Legend of Curly's Gold*, *Hamlet*, *My Giant*, *Analyze This*, *Monsters Inc.*, its 2013 sequel *Monsters University*, *Analyze That*, *Howl's Moving Castle* (the English-dubbed version), and *Cars*.

Anne Dyson worked largely on UK TV, with roles in *Dixon of Dock Green, Coronation Street, Z Cars*, the landmark *I, Claudius* miniseries, *The Sweeney, Hammer House of Horror, Juliet Bravo, The Box of Delights*, and *Tales of Sherwood Forest*. She died in 1996 at age 88.

Margery Mason also had a prolific career on British television, beginning with multiple appearances in *Quatermass and the Pit*. Much later in her career, she had roles in films like *Howards End, 101 Dalmatians, Love Actually*, and *Harry Potter and the Goblet of Fire*. She died in 2014 at age 100 (!).

Malcolm Storry played the knight (the green one, that is) in a TV-movie version of *Gawain and the Green Knight*.

Willoughby Gray was Dr. Hans Glaub in *A View to a Kill* and Canis in *Solarbabies*. He died in 1993 at age 76.

Betsy Brantley first appeared in *Shock Treatment* and was the performance model for Jessica Rabbit in *Who Framed Roger Rabbit*. She also appeared on TV shows like *Beauty and the Beast, Tour of Duty, Second Noah*, and the *From the Earth to the Moon* miniseries.

Paul Badger was the mummy in *Waxwork*.

6 DEGREES OF SORCERY

Monty Python and the Holy Grail also presents as a story told from a book. Piracy coming between a couple's romance turns up as a theme in *Pirates of the Caribbean: The Curse of the Black Pearl*. It might surprise you to know that many references in the film to historic figures are *not* fiction: the sword experts that Inigo and Westley cite during their duel and the Dread Pirate Roberts were real people.

The look of Westley's pirate alter-ego was based on legendary swashbuckler Zorro, while cinema Robin Hoods Douglas Fairbanks and Errol Flynn influenced much of his bearing and characterization. Elwes would go on to play Robin in the Mel Brooks parody *Robin Hood: Men in Tights;* his fencing training from this film would come in handy. The swordplay draws on cinema sources too numerous to list here. Reiner has suggested that Buttercup's failure to recognize Westley in his pirate guise is the same as Lois Lane's failure to notice Clark Kent's obvious resemblance to Superman.

The Thieves' Forest probably parallels Robin Hood's Sherwood. Other wooded areas that pose life-threatening challenges, like the Fire Swamp, appear in *The Lord of the Rings* films. The quicksand sequence recalls one in *The Beastmaster*.

Our heroic group of a blonde farm boy, a rogue with a heart of gold, and a large, hairy oaf storming the castle for a princess in distress mirrors their counterparts in *Star Wars*. (Miracle Max might be an Obi Wan who wisely stays at home.) By extension, this means we can link this movie to Akira Kurosawa works like *The Hidden Fortress* and *Yojimbo*, as well as the inspiration for *Yojimbo*—Dashiell Hammett's novel *Red Harvest*—and its cinematic successors, Sergio Leone's *A Fistful of Dollars* and John C. Broderick's *The Warrior and the Sorceress*. Also, obvious parallels shared with *Star Wars* link this film to Tolkien's *The Lord of the Rings* and to *The Wizard of Oz*. That's quite a lineage! Although we noted at least one link to *Monty Python and the Holy Grail* at the start of this section, we feel compelled to point out that—despite overzealous reporting on various Internet sites—that is *not* Eric Idle in an uncredited cameo in the background of one crowd scene.

SHATTERING THE ILLUSION

William Goldman's 1973 fantasy novel featured a similar narrative conceit of a framing sequence referring to an older story, although in the book the framing was from the point of view of Goldman as he edited and annotated the work of "S. Morgenstern." Early attempts to adapt the book into film went nowhere until Goldman's friend Carl Reiner shared the book with his son, actor and director Rob Reiner of *This Is Spinal Tap* and *Stand by Me*, while the younger Reiner was still a regular cast member of the TV series *All in the Family*.

As with most book-to-film adaptations, some of the subplots and backstory in the novel fell away for the screenplay, including details about Inigo and Fezzik as well as a sequence in which Miracle Max sends the heroes to fetch the materials needed to make his magic pill for Westley. The shrieking eels replaced a slightly more disturbing sequence, in which Vizzini pours blood into the water to attract sharks after Buttercup attempts to escape the boat. The Pit of Despair replaced a setting called the Zoo of Death, to save money and contain the action. In the book, Inigo's father withholds the sword that he designed for the six-fingered man after the villain denigrates its workmanship, but in the film, the father refuses to accept payment that isn't equal to the sword's quality.

Arguably the biggest change is in Buttercup's character. The book paints her as a far more self-interested and unsympathetic person, willing to give up Westley and marry Humperdinck in order to stay alive and have money instead of love.

Goldman had always wanted Andre the Giant to play Fezzik and wrote the character with the wrestler in mind, but when Goldman had tried to get a film deal for the book years earlier, Arnold Schwarzenegger wanted the part. By the time the movie went into production, Schwarzenegger was much too successful to participate, and Goldman's first choice became a reality.

Andre was, according to everyone who knew him, every bit the gentle giant that Fezzik wanted to be. Robin Wright has commented that when it grew cold on location, Andre would place his enormous hand on top of her head to keep her warm. He suffered from back trouble and other ailments related to his size, and could not handle arduous physical tasks. Shots of Westley wrestling Fezzik and Fezzik catching Buttercup at the end of the film required clever editing and camera trickery to avoid potentially injuring Andre. His thick accent made dialogue delivery difficult, but Mandy Patinkin helped by smacking the towering actor in the face to encourage him to speed up.

While everyone was protecting Andre, they should have been watching Elwes during the scene in which Christopher Guest's Count Rugen hits him on the head. Elwes told Guest to make it as real as possible; the resultant blow sent Elwes to the hospital and suspended shooting for an entire day. Elwes also suffered an injury to his foot that required costume designer Phyllis Dalton to customize his footwear so he could continue shooting. It was clearly not a very lucky set for the star.

He wasn't the only one. Reiner nearly drowned in hip waders while looking for a good angle inside the water tank during shooting of the shrieking-eels sequence. Less dangerous but no less aggravating, Reiner's turn as the voice of the R.O.U.S.es took longer than planned because his first sessions of grunts and growls went accidentally unrecorded.

> HEROES. GIANTS. VILLAINS. WIZARDS. TRUE LOVE. NOT JUST YOUR BASIC, AVERAGE, EVERYDAY, ORDINARY, RUN-OF-THE-MILL, HO-HUM FAIRY TALE.

One of the most impressive aspects of the film (no, not the clergyman) is the extensive swordfight between Westley and Inigo. It owes part of its success to the two actors' visibility and their performance of their own stunts, aided by expert choreography from legendary swordmaster Bob Anderson. They had trained to handle their swords with each of their hands. Stunt doubles came in only for the somersaulting leaps.

Patinkin is a contentious figure in Hollywood, more focused on his musical career than his acting and often a source of friction among casts that work with him. Nevertheless, he cites this role as his favorite, especially because it was an emotional experience for him. Having lost his father in 1972 from cancer, he played the final scene of Inigo confronting Count Rugen as though he were vanquishing the disease that had claimed his father's life. Christopher Guest picked up on Patinkin's passion in that confrontation, suffering a stab wound to his thigh. He commented to the on-set swordmaster that he thought Patinkin was really trying to kill him. Subsequently, he ignored the choreography he had learned and concentrated on defending himself.

When 20th Century Fox released the film with little marketing or fanfare, Reiner complained that he didn't want it to become "another *Wizard of Oz*," referring to that film's disappointing initial release. Considering how *The Princess Bride* has grown in reputation to become a timeless modern classic, that comparison was more astute than perhaps Reiner realized, and not at all something to complain about. Reiner has said that the best evidence of the film's timeless quotability was when one of John Gotti's men met him outside a New York restaurant while guarding the mob boss's limo, eyed the director, and said, "You killed my father. Prepare to die." Fortunately, he was just a big fan.

. . . And for the record, the grandson is playing a Commodore 64 baseball game from Accolade called *Hardball*, although the sound effects in the film don't match the actual sound in the game.

MUSIC OF THE MINSTRELS

As with many of our films, a good portion of this one's success comes from the musical score. In this case, however, it's not bombastic battle themes and sweeping orchestral arrangements that make the mood, but a soft, sweet, guitar-driven soundtrack composed and performed by Dire Straits' Mark Knopfler. It infuses the movie with just the right romantic atmosphere. The melodic work evokes a subtle sense of nostalgic longing, too, as if everyone in the story is aware that this quest for true love is something left behind in a long-lost past, but still just reachable if your heart is up to the task.

Knopfler was apparently an immediate choice for Reiner. He responded that he'd score the film only if Reiner included, in the movie, the distinctive baseball cap he had worn in his role as Marty Di Bergi in *Spinal Tap*. Reiner did work in a replica cap for scenes set in the grandson's room, only to find out that Knopfler had been kidding.

Although Knopfler's score did not garner an Academy Award nomination, the original song "Storybook Love," sung by Willy De Ville, did. De Ville performed the song live on the 60th Oscar telecast [when's the last time you read or heard *that* word? —ATB], but "(I've Had) The Time of My Life" from *Dirty Dancing* got the statuette.

Warner Bros. Records and Vertigo Records released the soundtrack. It is not hard to track down, which is unusual in this genre.

THE SAGA CONTINUES

Obviously William Goldman's novel was the basis for the film. There was no other novelization.

At one point, Goldman teamed with Tony Award–winning composer Adam Guettel to craft a musical stage-version of *The Princess Bride*, but they scrapped the plans in 2007 during a dispute over the division of potential proceeds. Guettel did complete some of the music, though, and it has seen performances on a limited basis at workshop and concert venues. At the end of 2013, Disney announced development of a stage adaptation of its own but did not disclose what form that would take.

Vestron Video offered a promotional board game in conjunction with the home-video release of the movie in 1988. It was a bare-bones effort, with rules printed on the board. It required gamers to provide the other components themselves. Warp Spawn Games offered a *Quest for the Princess Bride* card game in 2005. Playroom Entertainment and Toy Vault Inc. published *Princess Bride: Storming the Castle* in 2008. It was a redesign of *Temple of the Monkey*, a Playroom release from the previous year. Using cardboard character tokens and cards arranged in a cross layout, players attempted to save Buttercup from Humperdinck's castle. *The Princess Bride* game released by Worldwide Biggies for Mac and PC in 2008 featured five minigames but suffered from simplistic play, generic graphics, and a bland soundtrack, despite use of the "Storybook Love" song and dialogue by some of the original actors.

Although Goldman has not yet succumbed to pressure for a follow-up book, he wrote and released a "sample chapter" from an otherwise nonexistent novel called *Buttercup's Baby*. In this mini-sequel, Westley and Buttercup's daughter Waverly is kidnapped, prompting Fezzik to attempt a rescue. It also explores Inigo's romantic past.

No further plans for a sequel have come to fruition. In the meantime, you can read Cary Elwes's memoir of the making of the film: *As You Wish: Tales from The Princess Bride* (Simon & Schuster, 2014).

TAKE UP THY SWORD!

UNUSUALLY LARGE RODENTS (MONSTROUS ANIMALS)

ATTACK: An unusually large rodents attacks with a bite that inflicts fairly low damage, but each successful bite has a ten percent chance of spreading disease.

DETAILS: These creatures shy away from light and prefer find dark swamplands as their habitat. For the most part, these timid creatures avoid combat, particularly with larger opponents, but when threatened—or perhaps when riddled with disease—they boldly attack. They are omnivorous, typically feeding on carrion, seeds, and nuts, but wounded prey unable to defend itself is also an attractive target.

THE FILM'S DESTINY

One of the (arguably) three most quotable movies of the 20th century, *The Princess Bride* is less a movie than a watershed collective pop-culture experience. In the years that followed its only moderately successful release, its reputation as a cult film grew and grew, until today most people can associate with the "inconceivable" and "I am Inigo Montoya . . . ." Well, you know the rest.

Part of the film's charm is that it is a sincere and simple fairytale incorporating familiar clichés while also satirizing the genre: poking fun at everyone and everything, but with an affection that takes off any mean-spiritedness. The script, though sharp and witty, never talks down to the audience or denigrates its subject matter. Perhaps its self-awareness sells the theme of true love more effectively than would a story without all those delightful winks and nods peppering its plot.

The cast is as perfectly chosen as anyone could hope for, the music is touching and complements the sun-dappled scenery . . . and that dialogue! Rarely has there been a film in which every single line was poetry waiting to be repurposed into daily life, making *The Princess Bride* a sort of pop-culture *I Ching* that provides endless opportunities to connect with fellow fans. As a story that revels in love and honor and what makes us human, and with so much twinkling heart and humor threaded expertly throughout, viewers of any age can find something that appeals to them. It's a movie you can wrap around yourself like a warm blanket on a calm, comfortable night. Find it running on some cable station, and you're set for the next ninety-eight minutes.

Now if only *Office Space* had an enchanted sword instead of a Swingline stapler, we could have had the hat trick in this book.

THIS YEAR IN GAMING

Lion Rampant, founded by Jonathan Tweet and Mark Rein-Hagen, released the first edition of the groundbreaking medieval fantasy roleplaying game *Ars Magica*. Its innovative new system presented unique concepts not seen in previously published RPGs, including a freeform spellcasting system, a setting akin to that of medieval Earth (but one in which magic and myth truly existed), and a significant portion of the game devoted to improving one's home or covenant. The game also introduced a new style of play referred to as the "troupe system," whereby each player would control more than one character in the campaign. No less than four publishers have handled the line since its inception, including White Wolf, Wizards of the Coast, and currently Atlas Games, who released its fourth and fifth editions in 1996 and 2004, respectively.

> IT'S AS REAL AS THE FEELINGS YOU FEEL.

DEATHSTALKER II

1987 • Argentina/US • Aries Films International / New Horizon Picture Corp
85m • Color • R

Screenplay: Neil Ruttenberg
Story: Jim Wynorski
Additional Dialogue: R. J. Robertson
Director: Jim Wynorski
Producers: Roger Corman, Frank Isaac, Jr., and Hector Olivera
Music: Chuck Cirino, Oscar Camp, and Chris Young
Director of Photography: Leonard Solis
Stunt Coordinator: Arthur Noal
Costume Special Effects: Marisa Urruti
Special Effects: Nicky Morgan
Make-Up: George Barry and Maria Laura
Art Director: Marta Albert
Costume Designer: Marta Albertinazzi
Cast: John Terlesky (Deathstalker), Monique Gabrielle (Reena the Seer / Princess Evie), John La Zar (Jerak the Sorcerer), Toni Naples (Sultana), Maria Socas (Amazon Queen), Marcos Wolinsky (Pirate), Queen Kong (Gorgo, Amazon Champion Wrestler), Jake Arnt (High Priest), Carina Davi (Young Amazon), Arch Stanton (Dying Soldier), Douglas Mortimer (Man in Black), Maria Luisa Carnivani (Woman Guard), Leo Nichols (Pirate's Hitman One), Frank Sisty (Pirate's Hitman Two), Red Sands (Pirate's Hitman Three), Dan Savio (Pirate's Hitman Four), William Feldman (Pirate's Hitman Five), Nick Sardansky (Evie's Victim), and Victor Bo (Kang, uncredited, from archive footage)
Alternate Title: *Deathstalker II: Duel of the Titans*

ON THE MAP

We go from one unnamed kingdom—home to the castle from which Deathstalker first steals the gem and to Abūd's tavern—to the Kingdom of Jafir, ruled by Princess Evie, as well as a variety of places in between, including a disused quarry, a graveyard populated by the walking dead, and a village of Amazon women.

OUR STORY SO FAR

After evil sword-wielding sorcerer Jerak magically clones Princess Evie in order to usurp the throne, the real princess—in the guise of Reena the Seer—enlists the aid of noted rogue and rapscallion Deathstalker to help her defeat the vampiric doppelganger and reclaim her kingdom. Along the way, they battle Amazon women, walking dead, and a ragtag gang of inept thugs armed with explosive arrows and light beer.

Twice the action.
Twice the passion.
Twice the adventure.

ALTERNATE VERSIONS

The version of the film available as part of the four-film *Sword and Sorcery Collection* from Shout Factory is actually a shorter "director's cut" that runs 77 minutes, despite the disc label's claim that it's 85. If you want a cut that runs 85 minutes, believe it or not that doesn't exist. The previously released DVD from New Concorde clocks in closer to 88! Confused? So are we.

The earlier release contained footage never before seen in a US version, but Wynorski decided there were reasons for its absence and excised it all from the more recent cut. The Shout Factory release looks and sounds better than the New Concorde version, despite the edits, but the commentary is also trimmed accordingly. The UK release suffered from a few censor adjustments, including most shots of throwing-star use and a few of the more graphic seconds of Reena's rape.

IT'S MAGIC

Jerak is the only character capable of using magic. Reena/Evie *claims* to be a prophetess, but her abilities are somewhat suspect . . . and you can't really trust the fortunetelling capabilities of a crystal doorknob. (You can blame the mysterious lightning strikes during the film's final battle on a sorcerer from another film, because they are borrowed footage randomly inserted into this movie.)

Jerak uses alchemy to spawn the clone of Evie. He can also communicate through burbling ponds, slay people through these portals, project transparent images of himself over great distances, telekinetically manipulate mechanisms from afar, and resurrect the dead. Inserting him into a traditional tabletop fantasy-RPG would be tricky, because he is a multi-classed fighter/wizard/illusionist/necromancer!

THE QUEST FOR MEANING

This straightforward fantasy romp has kicked aside most meaningful themes, but one that remains is trust. From the opening scene, in which Stalker procures the gem from the treasure chamber, we see that he trusts a woman (with teased '80s hair, of course) to deliver him to the treasure (sending her off to safety with a kiss before advancing into the chamber to face unknown dangers). For the most part, he is the archetypal rogue, like Han Solo, Indiana Jones, or Ash Williams—but also like those characters, when the going gets tough, he puts his trust in those around him and likewise earns their trust. Sure, he cracks wise and is almost always in it for himself—robbing from the rich and pretty much keeping whatever he steals—but at the end of the day, he is a decent guy.

On the other hand, those who put their trust in villains like Jerak and Sultana always end up dead at the hands of Deathstalker or their so-called allies. The pirate employed by Sultana to kill Stalker and capture Evie brings along a band of incompetent bounty hunters to do the job, but when Stalker and Reena escape and slaughter the gang of assassins as well, they reward the pirate for his efforts with a sword to the gut. The bloodthirsty clone of Evie cannot even trust Jerak, her very creator, though he is the only one who can keep her alive.

WHO GOES THERE?

John Terlesky hasn't acted since 2005. His career has taken him to the other side of the camera, where he has enjoyed a successful career as a film and television director for shows like *Boston Legal, Ugly Betty,* and *Castle*. Before shifting his focus, he appeared in the films *Chopping Mall* (also directed by Jim Wynorski), *Appointment with Death, Crazy People,* and *Vampirella,* as well as on the small screen in *Guns of Paradise, Walker Texas Ranger, The Last Frontier,* and *CSI: Miami*.

Monique Gabrielle bared all in *Penthouse* in 1982. She transitioned into an acting career shortly after, appearing in films like *Young Doctors in Love, Night Shift, Airplane II: The Sequel, Chained Heat, Bachelor Party, Amazon Women on the Moon, Not of This Earth, The Return of Swamp Thing,* and *Evil Toons*. Alongside her mainstream film career, she also continued to appear in softcore fare and even dipped into a bit of the harder stuff in the '90s.

With the most impressive pedigree of all the cast, John LaZar is a veteran actor of both stage and screen. Some of his most famous films include the Russ Meyer–directed *Beyond the Valley of the Dolls*—which he believes might have permanently damaged his career—*Supervixens, Scorpion, Night of the Scarecrow,* and *Maximum Revenge*. Recently he costarred with Adrienne Barbeau in award-winning zombie short film *Alice Jacobs Is Dead*. He is also an accomplished martial artist and fencer.

Southern California native Toni Naples (born Karen Rosemary Chorak) rode high on a B-movie wave through the '80s and '90s. Her first role was alongside Lana Clarkson *(Barbarian Queen)* in 1983's *Female Mercenaries*. She also appeared in *Doctor Detroit, Chopping Mall, Transylvania Twist, Sorority House Massacre II, Munchie,* its sequel *Munchie Strikes Back, Dinosaur Island,* and *Sorceress* (for which she also served as executive producer).

Born Deanna Booher, Queen Kong often uses her roller-derby name. She was also a member of G.L.O.W. (Gorgeous Ladies Of Wrestling), in which she went by Matilda the Hun, a name lifted from the 1975 Roger Corman–produced film *Death Race 2000*. On the big screen, she appeared in *Spaceballs, Slash Dance, Cage,* and *Theodore Rex*. She also had a few comedic roles on TV, for *Night Court, Dream On,* and *Married with Children*.

Jake Arnt (Jacques Arndt) appeared in *Amazons* and *Highlander II: The Quickening*.

6 DEGREES OF SORCERY

More than most films covered in this volume, *Deathstalker II* features a significant number of unashamed (freely admitted) nods and homages to other films and television shows. The alternate title *Duel of the Titans*—not so much an alternate as disused, despite its appearance in the title sequence—is a slightly adjusted variant of the well-known Harryhausen film covered elsewhere in this volume.

Our wisecracking protagonist shares plenty of mannerisms with medieval Ash from *Army of Darkness*... although *Deathstalker II* predates that film by a few years, so who stole from whom, eh? The initial shot of the castle's illumination by flashes of lightning is lifted wholesale from the 1963 Roger Corman production *The Raven*. The scene following that one mirrors *Raiders of the Lost Ark*, with Deathstalker liberating a valuable gem instead of a Cachapoyan fertility idol. Many of the props and sets appeared in other films of that time, including the first *Deathstalker*, although this would be their last use; note the decrepit state of some of the styrofoam walls. One of the guards refers to "Merlin the magician," thus linking to Arthurian legend. Several shots from the first *Deathstalker* are reused. The armor worn by various guards is clearly the armor from *The Warrior and the Sorceress*, here spray-painted black. Elements of the fight between Stalker and the bald thug in the tavern, even down to his request for a bottle on the bar, are once again from *Raiders of the Lost Ark*. The dialogue between Reena and Stalker as she tells his future using a doorknob (seriously, it really was) includes a few adapted lines from *Star Wars* and name-drops Conan. The buccaneer is called Chin (from *Hawaii Five-O*), solely to allow for the line "Give it to me, Chin. Whaddya got?" The exploding arrows are straight from *Rambo: First Blood Part II*. "Crazy" Otto Reingold, the Mad Prussian, looks shockingly like Curly Howard of *The Three Stooges;* check out the look he gives when Stalker snaps his neck in the quarry. The cemetery, though a lot smaller, has a similar layout to the one in the finale of *The Good, The Bad and the Ugly*.

The walking dead behave like those in *Night of the Living Dead*. Driving them back with torches also echoes scenes from that seminal horror film—and there's no denying the nod to Michael Jackson's *Thriller*.

Stalker's "son-of-a-bitch" line inside the tomb is lifted from *Raiders of the Lost Ark*. There are a number of homages to Warner Bros. cartoons, Bugs Bunny in particular, including shots and even lines ("Yipe!" and "Mother!"). The signpost features several amusing references, including Altair IV *(Forbidden Planet)*, Cimmeria *(Conan)*, and El Kabong (Quick Draw McGraw's Zorro-like alter-ego). Stalker's wrestling match with Gorgo brims with nods to *Rocky*.

Stalker and Reena peeking through the reeds is an homage to a recurring gag on the television series *Laugh-In* featuring Arte Johnson . . . and yes, Deathstalker does actually say "Very interestink!" The line "I thought you was dead" also comes up repeatedly in *Big Jake* and *Escape from New York*.

Stalker's imminent demise beneath the swinging pendulum is an acknowledged (by Jim Wynorski) nod to the 1961 film version of *The Pit and the Pendulum*, directed by *Deathstalker II* producer Roger Corman. The exchange at the pendulum between Sultana and Deathstalker is a mirror of the dialogue between James Bond and Auric Goldfinger in, of course, *Goldfinger*.

Shots of lightning strikes and at least one shot of a man running on fire were lifted from the movie *Amazons*. Reena skulking around the dungeons is straight out of an episode (or maybe *most* episodes) of *Scooby Doo*. The fake princess Evie melts away like the Wicked Witch of the West in *The Wizard of Oz*. Deathstalker grabbing the sword blade between his hands comes from the Hong Kong classic *5 Fingers of Death*. The talk of future players enacting their adventures, both at the end as well as earlier in the film as part of Reena's prophecy, is similar to an exchange between Samwise and Frodo Baggins in *The Lord of the Rings: The Two Towers*. As if the film weren't already replete with homages and inside gags, the end credits feature a list of eighty-seven fake names, like Lotta Bush and April May, as well as characters and actors from other films, TV shows, and even comics, including Carl Denham *(King Kong)*, Napoleon Solo *(The Man from U.N.C.L.E.)*, Norman Bates *(Psycho)*, Julius Kelp *(The Nutty Professor)*, Billy

Batson (Captain Marvel's alter-ego), Paul Kersey *(Death Wish)*, Harry Callahan *(Dirty Harry)*, Martin Brody *(Jaws)*, and Damien Thorn *(The Omen)*.

SHATTERING THE ILLUSION

The original script for this first sequel to *Deathstalker* was a more serious attempt at a *Conan* knockoff and in keeping with the tone of the first film in the "series." Wynorski and Terlesky abandoned that, however, and instead came up with something more fun, in answer to the question, "What would happen if Bugs Bunny played *Deathstalker II*?" Terlesky preferred having people laughing *with* them rather than *at* them: a wise choice.

They shot the film in just nineteen days. Interiors were shot at the Baires Studios (Estudios Baires), a facility located about a hundred miles outside of Buenos Aires. Other Roger Corman sword-and-sorcery productions, including *Amazons*, also used that facility.

Much of the armor appears the same as that used in *The Warrior and the Sorceress*, filmed a few years before. For this film, it was painted black. To help disguise the fact that there was only a tiny crew of stuntmen on the film, they often wear masks or hoods.

Roger Corman insisted on a few odd additions of nudity, most of which came from other films in the studio's catalog. Shots of the bargain-basement Gamorrean guard in Abūd's tavern were also borrowed, from the first *Deathstalker*.

Many of the exterior shots took place at night to help hide modern elements: a nearby freeway, houses, chainlink fences, and so on. In a notorious shot, pointed out in the audio commentary, a tire is visible as Stalker and Reena ride along the edge of a pond.

The first soldier shown dueling Jerak—again, hidden under a mask—is none other than John Terlesky, and "Arch Stanton" is really director Wynorski under a pseudonym. If you recognize the name, that's because it appears on a grave in the finale of *The Good, The Bad and the Ugly*.

Some have criticized Monique Gabrielle's performance, but Wynorski takes partial responsibility for her often larger-than-life delivery. He frequently pushed her to go "bigger."

Often scenes were hastily rewritten the night before shooting, taking inspiration from Warner Bros. cartoons and Spanish-language game shows. The final, genuinely exciting showdown between Jerak and Deathstalker was carefully choreographed by the two actors involved. Terlesky stepped in to direct the sequence as well.

MUSIC OF THE MINSTRELS

Part of the original production deal was that an Argentine composer—likely Oscar Cardozo Ocampo, who had scored the first *Deathstalker*—would provide the score, but that decision had been based on the original, straightforward sword-and-sorcery script. Once Wynorski and Terlesky turned the film into a comedy, they required a more suitable score. Having worked with and befriended Chuck Cirino for the movie *Chopping Mall*, Wynorski wanted him to provide the music.

By the time Cirino came along, the work print was no longer available, so Wynorski's description and a copy of the screenplay had to provide details about the film. The results are a synth-heavy, adventurous score with a number of comedic nods to the work of Ennio Morricone, along with elements lifted directly from the *Chopping Mall* soundtrack. To link the film to the previous

Deathstalker, a tiny bit of Ocampo music occurs at the very beginning (credited to "Oscar Camp"), but it quickly segues into iconic Cirino '80s synthpop beats. Chris Young also receives credit, because a few bits of his previous Corman scores slip into the soundtrack on occasion, especially during the final battle between Stalker and Jerak. Fan demand led to BSX Records releasing the score in the form of a 2008 limited-edition CD alongside the score for *Chopping Mall*, featuring liner notes by Steve Mitchell (writer of *Chopping Mall*) and Wynorski.

> HIS BATTLE ISN'T OVER YET . . .

THE SAGA CONTINUES

You can check out the index in the back to learn more about the other installments in this series. Not only was there a *Deathstalker* film that preceded this one; there were also two additional sequels. Three actors played the title role—Rick Hill in I and IV, John Terlesky here, and John Allen Nelson in III—with little or no regard for the other installments. Also, four years separated the first film (in 1983) from the second, one year passed between the second and third (1988's *Deathstalker and the Warriors from Hell*), and three more years separated that from the fourth and final film, 1991's *Deathstalker IV: Match of Titans*.

A couple other links of note exist among the four films, including executive producer Roger Corman and poster-artist Boris Vallejo. Howard R. Cohen wrote the screenplays for I, III, and IV. Amusingly, he was also a series writer on *Rainbow Brite* and *The Care Bears*! Note that though they share the name, the *Deathstalker* series of novels by Simon R. Green have absolutely nothing to do with the films . . . although they are great reads all the same.

TAKE UP THY SWORD!

DRAUGHT OF DUPLICATION (MAGIC POTION)

Once imbibed, this elixir invades the target's body, exploring every aspect of it, physical and mental. Then, through sorcery, it uses that information to replicate the person, causing the copy to materialize outside the person.

For all intents and purposes, the clone is a perfect mirror-image, but with a few shortcomings. First, it is soulless and can stay alive only through vampirism: draining others' souls. Second, it links to its "host" (the original) on the astral plane, so if the host perishes, it does as well, regardless of its location on this or any other plane of existence.

The sword-wielding wizard behind this concoction took its secrets with him to his grave. He had been close to improving it to allow the copy to have a more permanent and independent existence.

THE FILM'S DESTINY

With four possible representatives of this series to choose from, we decided on this one because it's friggin' hilarious—and for once, the laughs are intentional! Stay through the end credits for some funny outtakes.

Despite some clunky acting on the part of Monique Gabrielle—partly Wynorski's responsibility, as noted earlier—she still does a great job performing two completely distinct roles. Though creative hair and costume design get credit for some of that, the rest relies on Gabrielle really giving it her all, with different mannerisms and vocalizations for Reena and Evie.

Unlike a few of the joyless films covered in this volume (representing the worst this genre has to offer), *Deathstalker II* is a fun romp worthy of a screening or two with friends. You'll laugh at the wacky, over-the-top comedy—and if frequent displays of naked flesh are your cup of tea, you'll also be happy with that. To be fair, however, it doesn't go as far as the nudity in *The Warrior and the Sorceress*.

THIS YEAR IN GAMING

Magazine ads proclaimed "no elves" in a new setting and roleplaying game from Bard Games (of Greenwich, Connecticut): the *Talislanta* line. The promotion probably enticed gamers tired of the same old Tolkien-esque tropes.

Bard had already released a series of generic fantasy RPG *Compleat* books *(The Compleat Alchemist, The Compleat Adventurer,* and *The Compleat Spell Caster),* as well as *The Atlantis Trilogy,* an antediluvian alternative to *Dungeons & Dragons* that consisted of *The Arcanum* (core rulebook), *The Lexicon* (gazetteer and atlas), and *The Bestiary,* all co-designed by Stephan Michael Sechi.

Creators of *Talislanta* drew much of their inspiration from the *Dying Earth* stories of Jack Vance, versus the straightforward sword-and-sorcery of Howard, Leiber, or Tolkien. Three core books mirrored the format of *The Atlantis Trilogy*: *The Talislantan Handbook* (core rulebook), *The Chronicles of Talislanta* (gazetteer and atlas), and *A Naturalist's Guide to Talislanta* (bestiary). All three volumes featured cover art and interior illustrations by P. D. Breeding (now P. D. Breeding-Black). Sales merited additional volumes and even a second edition, but Bard Games folded following the release of *The Cyclopedia Talislanta Volume VI: The Desert Kingdom* in 1990.

That would not mean the end of Talislanta, however. Wizards of the Coast released a third edition, Shooting Iron a fourth, and Morrigan Press a fifth—as well as a d20 conversion. Most recently, Sechi, who now works mainly as a musician, set up a website to offer scans of previously released Talislanta books free of charge . . . and there are still no elves.

WILLOW

1988 • US • IMAGINE FILMS ENTERTAINMENT / METRO-GOLDWYN-MAYER (MGM) / LUCASFILM
126M • COLOR • PG

STORY: George Lucas
SCREENPLAY: Bob Dolman
DIRECTOR: Ron Howard
PRODUCERS: George Lucas, Joe Johnston, and Nigel Wooll
MUSIC: James Horner
DIRECTOR OF PHOTOGRAPHY: Adrian Biddle
PRODUCTION DESIGNER: Allan Cameron
ART DIRECTORS: Tim Hutchinson, Jim Pol, Tony Reading, Kim Sinclair, And Malcolm Stone
COSTUME DESIGNER: Barbara Lane
MAKEUP DESIGNER: Nick Dudman
PROSTHETIC MAKEUP SUPERVISOR: Suzanne Reynolds
SPECIAL EFFECTS SUPERVISOR: John Richardson
CHIEF PUPPETEER: David Allen
VISUAL EFFECTS: Phil Tippett (ILM)
CREATURE SUPERVISOR: Nick Dudman
FIGHT ARRANGER: William Hobbs
CAST: Val Kilmer (Madmartigan); Joanne Whalley (Sorsha); Warwick Davis (Willow Ufgood); Jean Marsh (Queen Bavmorda); Patricia Hayes (Fin Raziel); Billy Barty (High Aldwin); Pat Roach (General Kael); Gavan O'Herlihy (Airk Thaughbaer); David Steinberg (Meegosh); Phil Fondacaro (Vohnkar); Tony Cox and Robert Gillibrand (Vohnkar Warriors); Mark Northover (Burglekutt); Kevin Pollak (Rool); Rick Overton (Franjean); Maria Holvöe (Cherlindrea); Julie Peters (Kiaya Ufgood); Mark Vande Brake (Ranon Ufgood); Dawn Downing (Mims Ufgood); Michael Cotterill (Druid); Zulema Dene (Ethna); Joanna Dickens (Barmaid); Jennifer Guy (The Wench); Ron Tarr (Llug); Sallyanne Law (Mother); Ruth Greenfield and Kate Greenfield (Elora Danan); Edwin Alofs (Villager); Kenny Baker, Jack Purvis, and Malcolm Dixon (Nelwyn Band Members, uncredited); Peter Burroughs, Sadie Corre, Kim Davis, Samantha Davis, Valerie Gale, Rusty Goffe, Cheryl Howard, Nosher Powell, and Ashley C. Williams (Nelwyn Villagers, uncredited); Gerry Crampton and Greg Powell (Nockmaar Lieutenant, uncredited); Craig Salisbury (Nelwyn Jester, uncredited); and David Sibley (Galladorn Warrior, uncredited)
ALTERNATE TITLE: *Munchkins* (original title)

OUR STORY SO FAR

An evil queen seeks a baby foretold by prophecy to one day defeat her. The child falls into the hands of reluctant guardian and farmer Willow Ufgood. When the queen's forces capture the baby, Willow allies with a sword-wielding rogue, an aged sorceress, and a couple of precocious brownies to rescue the child before the queen sacrifices her and averts the prophecy.

IT'S MAGIC

Magic in this universe is fairly stereotypical, with a spellcasting system that relies on elaborate hand-gestures, intense focus, and ancient words of power. Spell effects are also traditional:

> ADVENTURE DOESN'T COME ANY BIGGER THAN THIS.

flashing lights, explosions, transformations, and bolts of lightning. Magic wands make an appearance, along with enchanted items like the flesh-to-stone transforming acorns. Bavmorda comes across as an unbelievably powerful sorcerer—greater than all the other characters—capable of transforming an entire army into pigs with a single spell.

THE QUEST FOR MEANING

Maybe it stems from childhood bullying, but George Lucas has spent a lot of energy telling stories about small (in both stature and ability), usually underestimated characters who wind up becoming heroes. There's Luke Skywalker, the naïve farm boy who becomes a great Jedi; his master, Yoda, the comical, big-eared clown who hides an ancient secret; Willow Ufgood, the Nelwyn farmer who realizes his potential as a sorcerer; and of course baby Elora, who will eventually grow to become a formidable opponent to the forces of darkness. In *Star Wars: The Empire Strikes Back*, Yoda—in his usual anastrophic way—tells Luke that "size matters not." This doesn't end with Lucas's major characters, either: Ewoks, Jawas, droids, and the brownies of *Willow* are all initially misjudged or ignored for being diminutive and cute, but they surprise the characters they interact with as well as the audience. For those wondering where Howard the Duck fits into all this . . . do we really need to go there? After all, every duck has his limit. . . .

WHO GOES THERE?

For several years, it seemed you couldn't see a big-budget action film without Val Kilmer's mug showing up onscreen. His first big-screen role was in the 1984 spy parody *Top Secret!* Not long after, he appeared in two films that helped him become a household name: *Real Genius* and *Top Gun*. Other movies of note include *The Doors, Tombstone, Batman Forever, Heat, The Island of Dr. Moreau, The Saint, Kiss Kiss Bang Bang,* and *MacGruber*. He was also the uncredited voice of K.I.T.T. in the 2008 reboot of *Knight Rider* and the voice of Bravo in *Planes*.

Joanne Whalley—for a time, Whalley-Kilmer—got her start on British television in a number of well-known soaps and series. She appeared in *Pink Floyd—The Wall*, played the title character in the 1994 TV-miniseries *Scarlett,* and recently had roles on *Gossip Girl* and *The Borgias*. *Willow* is her only foray into the sword-and-sorcery genre to date.

Warwick Davis's first big film role came when he was only 11 years of age. Unfortunately, he was unrecognizable in that part—hidden under layers of latex and fur—but fortunately, the costume he was wearing was that of Wicket the Ewok in *Star Wars: Return of the Jedi*. He reprised the role in two relatively infamous TV-movie spinoffs and wore a goblin costume for a few scenes in *Labyrinth*. Then came *Willow*. No stranger to genre films, Davis has appeared in a slew of productions likely found in most of our movie collections, including the *Leprechaun* series (yes, even the ones set in outer space and the ghetto), *Star Wars: Episode I—The Phantom Menace,* the *Harry Potter* films, *The Hitchhiker's Guide to the Galaxy, The Chronicles of Narnia: Prince Caspian, Jack the Giant Slayer,* and even a 2013 episode of *Doctor Who*.

Some remember Jean Marsh for her three memorable appearances in *Doctor Who*: two in the '60s and one in the late '80s. She was even married to Third Doctor Jon Pertwee for a few years in the late '50s. Beyond her adventures in time and space, she has worked on the small screen in a number of productions, including *The Twilight Zone; The Saint; UFO; Upstairs, Downstairs; Hawaii Five-O;* and *The Tomorrow People;* as well as in films, like *Frenzy* (by Alfred Hitchcock), *Dark Places, The Changeling,* and *Return to Oz.*

Patricia Hayes had a long and illustrious acting career that began in the 1930s. She appeared in a number of films and TV shows of note, including *The Terrornauts, Fragment of Fear, The NeverEnding Story,* and *A Fish Called Wanda.* She died in 1998 at age 88.

Gavan O'Herlihy is often remembered for a role he is often not remembered for (if you can follow that): forgotten son Chuck Cunningham from the first season of TV's *Happy Days.* During his career, he usually played heavies and villains. He appeared on television in *The Six Million Dollar Man,* the *Lonesome Dove* miniseries, *Twin Peaks,* and *Star Trek: Voyager,* and in movies like *Superman III, Never Say Never Again, Death Wish 3, Prince Valiant,* and *The Descent: Part 2.*

David Steinberg (no relation to the comedian of the same name) stood only 3' 11" tall. This, along with his acting prowess, led to roles in TV shows like *The Equalizer, Charmed, Ugly Betty,* and *Zoey 101,* as well as films like *Epic Movie* and *Transylmania.* He died in 2010 at age 45.

With more than seventy-five film, television, and music-video roles on his resume, Tony Cox has kept busy since starting his career in the early '80s. He turned up on the small screen in *Buck Rogers in the 25th Century, The Greatest American Hero, The Ewok Adventure* and *Ewoks: The Battle for Endor* TV movies, *Faerie Tale Theatre,* and *Frasier,* and on the big screen in *Under the Rainbow, Jekyll and Hyde... Together Again, Star Wars: Return of the Jedi, Invaders from Mars, Spaceballs, Beetlejuice, Spaced Invaders, Mom and Dad Save the World, Leprechaun 2, Bad Santa,* and *Oz the Great and Powerful.*

Kevin Pollak still does one of the best Captain Kirk / William Shatner impersonations in the world, but audiences also know him for his many comic and impressive dramatic roles, in movies like *Avalon, L.A. Story, A Few Good Men, Wayne's World 2, Grumpy Old Men, The Usual Suspects, Casino, That Thing You Do!, End of Days, The Whole Nine Yards* and its sequel *The Whole Ten Yards,* and *The Santa Clause 2* and its sequel *The Santa Clause 3: The Escape Clause.*

Rick Overton began his career in comedy's stand-up circuit. He appeared on TV in *Amazing Stories, Bill & Ted's Excellent Adventures* (as the uncredited voice of Rufus), *Seinfeld* (hate the Drake!), *Lois & Clark: The New Adventures of Superman, Married with Children, Mad About You, The Secret Adventures of Jules Verne, Alias,* and *Lost,* and in films like *Young Doctors in Love, Airplane II: The Sequel, Beverly Hills Cop, Gung Ho, Earth Girls Are Easy, The Rocketeer, Groundhog Day, Eight Legged Freaks, The Astronaut Farmer,* and *Cloverfield.*

Ron Tarr was a bit of a British TV fixture for several years, appearing in such series as *Space: 1999, Doctor Who, Blake's 7, Lovejoy, The Comic Strip Presents...,* and *EastEnders*—as Big Ron. In 1997, he appeared as that character in the infamous *Doctor Who* 30th-anniversary two-part short feature for charity, *Dimensions in Time.* He died that same year at age 60.

Sadie Corre was one of the Transylvanians in *The Rocky Horror Picture Show* and an Ewok in *Star Wars: Return of the Jedi.* She died in 2009 at age 91.

Rusty Goffe is another dwarf actor who has been gracing screens for decades, beginning with an uncredited but recognizable role as an Oompa Loompa in *Willy Wonka & The Chocolate Factory*. Another memorable but uncredited role was that of the "GONK" droid in *Star Wars*. He also appears in *Flash Gordon, History of the World: Part I, MirrorMask, Harry Potter and the Order of the Phoenix, Fred Claus*, and *Harry Potter and the Deathly Hallows: Part 2*, as well as an episode of *Doctor Who* as Little John.

Ashley C. Williams was in kindergarten when cast as a Nelwyn child in this movie. More recently, she appeared as the middle segment in *The Human Centipede*.

Craig Salisbury was Panto Erik the Great in *Jack the Giant Slayer*.

6 DEGREES OF SORCERY

Like Herod the Great and the high priest of the spider cult in *Ator, The Fighting Eagle*, Bavmorda orders the deaths of children to avert prophecy. The motif of a baby set adrift and eventually falling into a caregiver's hands has appeared in legends throughout history, including those of Moses, Romulus and Remus, Karna, and Sargon I, not to mention films in this book, like *Clash of the Titans*.

The interior of Willow Ufgood's home bears more than a slight resemblance to that of Bilbo and Frodo's hobbit hole in the Peter Jackson *Lord of the Rings* films . . . and that's hardly where the comparisons to those films end: a "fellowship" of seven Nelwyns sets off on the initial adventure, Willow and Meegosh have a number of Sam-and-Frodo moments, Cherlindrea flutters about and glows like Galadriel in *The Fellowship of the Ring* (although with significantly less menace), Airk Thaughbaer's appearance mirrors that of a Rohan rider, the human tavern is like the Prancing Pony, Bavmorda's castle resembles the Black Gate, and during the climatic magic duel, Fin Raziel tosses Bavmorda around much as Saruman does to Gandalf.

The scene in which the group hides under the floor is right out of *Chitty Chitty Bang Bang*, although Benny Hill as a toymaker is nowhere to be seen.

The throne of the High Aldwin would reappear as the throne of another diminutive actor in the opening sequence of *Your Highness* (covered elsewhere in this volume).

The line "your reign of terror is at an end" has appeared in a variety of forms in numerous films (*Legend*, for example), TV shows, and professional-wrestling events, to the point of parody.

Considering Lucas's earlier work on *Star Wars*, it's no surprise to find similarities there, too: for one thing, Madmartigan is a sword-wielding fantasy version of Han Solo. The brownies tie down Willow and Meegosh in the same way that the Lilliputians secure Gulliver in *Gulliver's Travels*.

The carriage and sled chases feel as though they came right out of an *Indiana Jones* film (another Lucas connection); the music nods to those movies a few times as well.

The love potion is effectively Oberon's potion in *A Midsummer Night's Dream*.

You can hear the notorious "Wilhelm scream" a few times; we counted three.

The structure of the magic words is similar to the Charm of Making from *Excalibur*.

The creature in *The Magic Sword* might have inspired the two-headed dragon.

When the dragon picks up and eats a soldier, comparisons to *The Beast from 20,000 Fathoms* are inevitable.

Bavmorda wears a bandage wrap similar to the one worn by the Bride in *The Bride of Frankenstein*.

Speaking of *Star Wars*, when pinned, Raziel attempts to "use the Force" to draw her wand back into her hand.

SHATTERING THE ILLUSION

George Lucas had been kicking around the idea for *Willow* for fifteen years prior to production. Finally he set out to make an adventure film that would appeal to kids. (Wasn't *Star Wars* . . . ? Never mind.) Amusingly, in the behind-the-scenes featurette released in 1988, Lucas stated that he didn't make "effects movies"; take that as you will.

Legendary French artist Jean "Moebius" Giraud did some of the preliminary (and sadly unused) concept art. He died in 2012 at age 73.

Before *Willow*, Ron Howard had directed *Splash* and *Cocoon*, both highly successful films, proving he could tackle a big-budget sword-and-sorcery epic. For the first time in his directing career, he took advantage of video assist, whereby a feed from the camera recorded to video, allowing him to review shots immediately on set. These days, with most films shot digitally, timely review of shots is no longer an issue.

Warwick Davis was 17 when principal photography began, in April 1987. He had been interested in stage magic as a boy, so he was thrilled not only to portray a wizard but also to perform a few of his favorite illusions on the big screen.

Before Val Kilmer got the part of Madmartigan, both John Cusack and Matt Frewer were in the running. The casting of the Nelwyn villagers proved quite a challenge. In the end, very few working actors were chosen. The two-headed dragon (a.k.a. the Eborsisk) was a "go-motion" computer-controlled mechanical puppet.

In a long-running tradition with films directed by Ron Howard, he has included his brother Clint. Unable to find a suitable role for Clint in this film, though, Howard opted instead to have the Eborsisk partially modeled after aspects of his brother. If you look at the rather repulsive creature sideways, you might catch a few hints of Clint Howard in the beady eyes and leathery skin. "Eborsisk" is a combination of the names of late movie-critics Roger Ebert and Gene Siskel, although the name never comes up in the film. Another nod to critics was the name General Kael, after the late *New Yorker* film critic Pauline Kael.

The first major use of the digital technique known as morphing appeared in this film, pushed by Dennis Muren to Ron Howard and George Lucas. This was also likely the first time artists digitally "blended" real-world objects for a feature film. Muren believes the production was right on the edge of full digitalization, several years before that became the Hollywood standard. All these techniques helped prepare visual-effects company Industrial Light & Magic (ILM) for the computer-generated creations that appeared in *The Abyss* and *Terminator 2*.

In the sequence involving release from the cage during the crossroads scene, the rope holding the cage snapped, dropping the unit on Kilmer's foot and nearly breaking it. At a later point in the film, Kilmer thus exhibits a limp.

Kilmer often twirls objects in his films—pens, cups, guns, and so on. In *Willow*, he twirls his sword during the fight in the snow camp.

THE NEXT GREAT ADVENTURE

Kilmer and costar Joanne Whalley married in February 1988. They divorced eight years later: a rather impressive duration for a Hollywood marriage.

In an interview, Warwick Davis has recently explained a somewhat notorious issue: that of the missing third magic acorn. Apparently a scene was shot in which Bavmorda raises a terrible storm in an attempt to drown Willow and Raziel (in her recently rescued possum form). As their boat tosses about on the water, Willow accidentally drops one of the acorns, turning the boat to stone and sending it to the bottom of the lake. If you watch the following scene in the hut, you can see that Willow is still wet from swimming to shore. Diehard *Willow* fans: you can now rest easy, knowing the reason for this egregious continuity mystery.

MUSIC OF THE MINSTRELS

James Horner's sweeping score for *Willow* is effectively the sister score to the Don Bluth animated feature *The Land Before Time,* released the same year. Both feature many of the same production crew-members and musicians.

Though some have criticized Horner for copying his own scores, he drew much of the inspiration for this soundtrack from classical music and folk songs of old. "Mari Stanke Le," a Bulgarian harvest song, clearly inspired Elora Danan's theme. Willow's theme derives from Robert Schumann's third symphony, *Rhenish*. Bits of the softer, choir-driven material come from Bartok's "Cantata Profana," and Bavmorda's spellcasting horn-blasts seem linked to Prokofiev's "October Revolution Cantata." Some have compared the main theme to the "Redemption" motif from Wagner's operatic tetralogy *Der Ring des Nibelungen* (and you sure can read a *lot* about that story in our index!). A Lucas-inspired (or Lucas-insisted) track at the end of the film sounds like a carryover from the Ewok celebration (a.k.a. "Yub Nub") in *Star Wars: Return of the Jedi.*

Although the soundtrack originally suffered from a fairly limited release on vinyl, it was eventually fully released in the '90s. Sadly, as of this writing, it appears to be out of print.

THE SAGA CONTINUES

Del Rey published the official novelization in January 1988. Written by Wayland Drew, author of *The Erthring Cycle* and the novelizations of *Dragonslayer* and **batteries not included,* the book included a few elements not in the film, such as appearances by Sorsha's father.

A trilogy of novels called *Chronicles of the Shadow War* followed the release of the film, all cowritten by comic-book writer Chris Claremont and George Lucas. Set fifteen years after the film and focusing on Elora Danan, now a teenager, the books often come across as dark and plodding. Harsh criticism of them centers on their killing off of characters from the film. If you still want to read more about Elora and Willow: the individual *Chronicles* titles are *Shadow Moon* (1995), *Shadow Dawn* (1996), and *Shadow Star* (2000).

Marvel Comics released the official comic-book adaptation, written by Jo Duffy and spread over three issues later compiled into a graphic novel (as well as a mass-market paperback "illustrated version"). Bob Hall, Romeo Tanghal, and Joe Rosen illustrated.

The adventures of Willow Ufgood could continue on your dining room table with a children's roll-and-move board game from Parker Brothers, or with a more adult strategy game called *The*

Willow Game, designed by Greg Costikyan and published by Tor Books. Costikyan already had a relationship with Lucas, having worked as a designer on *Star Wars: The Role-Playing Game*

> FORGET ALL YOU KNOW, OR THINK YOU KNOW.

for West End Games, and was thrilled to take on the gaming project for *Willow.* His board game sold roughly 25,000 units, making it a success by hobby-gaming standards, but Tor got a little overenthusiastic and published 75,000 copies, which made it a commercial failure. For roleplaying gamers, Tor published *The Willow Sourcebook,* written by Allen Varney, with additional material by Costikyan, in August 1988. Though the ninety-page tome (including eight pages of color photos) functioned primarily as a general encyclopedia of information about the world (including its people, monsters, and magic), some sections also contained generic stats for use in tabletop fantasy-RPGs; however, the stats clearly derived from *Advanced Dungeons & Dragons,* with Bavmorda presented as a (gasp!) 36th-level magic-user! A brief recommendation by the one and only Gary Gygax appears on the back of the book. There were also three videogame adaptations: Mindscape released the first in 1988 for Amiga, Atari ST, and PC, and Capcom released two more (both different) in 1989 for arcades and NES consoles.

Finally, an animated series was proposed in 1988. Had it moved forward, Canadian animation studio Nelvana *(Heavy Metal, Rock & Rule)* might have handled it. Artists completed a number of concept drawings and character designs; a portfolio of those, now in the hands of a private collector, appeared online in early 2012. The illustrations feature Willow, Madmartigan, Sorsha, the brownies, and a slightly older version of Elora Danan.

Rumors of a proper, live-action sequel have circulated for ages. In a 2013 interview in honor of the film's 25th anniversary and Blu-ray release, Davis expressed interest in returning to the role as an older and much wiser Willow. Now *that's* something we would pay to see! He even lampooned the idea, joined by former costar Kilmer, supposedly to seek financing for the sequel, in the series finale of Davis's *Life's Too Short* comedy series. That's probably as close as we'll ever get.

TAKE UP THY SWORD!

ACORNS OF PETRIFICATION (MAGIC ITEM)

Such an enchanted oak nut appears as a mundane acorn, but when thrown at a target, it works as a successful petrifaction or flesh-to-stone spell. It affects a single target as well as any clothing, armor, gear, and weapons held or carried. The target can resist as with the equivalent spell.

The acorns petrify *any* object or even surface they strike. In other words, an acorn tossed at a tree—or a door, or a table, and so on—with a bit of force turns the target to stone without resistance. Because the acorns are enchanted, the user need not be a spellcaster to use them: an acorn tossed by a monkey has the same effect.

THE FILM'S DESTINY

Despite the enormous budget, experienced crew, and competent cast, *Willow* is little more than an overblown American remake of Joe D'Amato's *Ator, the Fighting Eagle.* Yes, you read that right! Both feature a child of prophecy with an arm birthmark, destined to someday defeat

> A WORLD WHERE HEROES COME IN ALL SIZES AND ADVENTURE IS THE GREATEST MAGIC OF ALL.

an evil ruler. In both, soldiers scour the lands and terrorize villages in search of the child, and a good guy becomes bad . . . but because *Willow* is a remake, the bad guy becomes good. (See, it's a twist.)

To be fair, a villainous ruler threatened by a child of prophecy is right out of legend, with Herod the Great's massacre of the innocents in the New Testament. And many know that Lucas worships at the feet of Joseph Campbell, author of *The Hero with a Thousand Faces*, frequently citing his influence. So even if D'Amato treaded this ground earlier, Lucas drawing on existing myths is no surprise.

This is an uneven, two-dimensional film that never achieves its potential. On the one hand, it has some nice visuals, a few likeable characters, a great villain in Jean Marsh, and some groundbreaking effects, but on the other hand, a number of scenes are campy or just downright stupid. The snow-sled escape is exciting and nicely shot, but just when it should end, Madmartigan—at the core of a giant snowball—rolls into town in a scene right out of a Warner Bros. cartoon. The brownies are cute, but their double act becomes tiresome after about three minutes. Far too many of the gags are pushed way too hard. Subtlety has never been Lucas's strong point. Lastly, the target audience for the film is unclear. Seventy-five percent of the film has the potential to be a great sword-and-sorcery adventure for adults, with well-choreographed and downright brutal swordfights and some seriously dark characters and themes. The remaining twenty-five percent has Nelwyns being pooped on, wisecracking, pratfalling brownies, cooing babies, and that aforementioned snowball bit. In fact, this is the same problem many had with the *Star Wars* prequels a decade later!

All that aside, you won't feel like you've completely wasted 126 minutes of your life watching *Willow*. It has its moments, but it could have been—and *should* have been—so much more.

THIS YEAR IN GAMING

Released by R. Talsorian Games, Cyberpunk—also known as *Cyberpunk 2013*—came from the mind of game designer Mike Pondsmith *(Mekton, Teenagers from Outer Space, Fuzion)*. Drawing from cyberpunk literature, such as the works of William Gibson, Bruce Sterling, and Walter Jon Williams, as well as films like *Blade Runner* (cited as Pondsmith's favorite movie), the game introduced players to a dystopian near future in which they took on the roles of cybernetically enhanced fixers, netrunners, nomads, rockerboys, and techies in a world dominated by sprawling megacorporations. In its gritty and potentially lethal combat system called "Friday Night Firefight," one lucky shot could spell death, distinguishing the game from a lot of the "grindy" and drawn-out hit-point systems of the day. The boxed set contained three booklets: *View from the Edge: The Cyberpunk Handbook, Welcome to Night City: A Sourcebook for 2013*, and *Friday Night Firefight*, as well as a collection of player aids. Supporting this first edition of the game, a handful of supplements came out the following year. The far more successful *Cyberpunk 2020* supplanted it in 1990.

Another event worthy of note this year was the 30th-anniversary celebration of GenCon.

BARBARIAN QUEEN II: THE EMPRESS STRIKES BACK

1992 • US/MEXICO • TRIANA FILMS / CONCORDE PRODUCTIONS • 80M • COLOR • R

SCREENPLAY: Howard Cohen and Lance Smith
STORY: Lance Smith
DIRECTOR: Joe Finley
PRODUCERS: Alan Krone, Anthony Norway, and Roger Corman (uncredited)
MUSIC: Chris Young
DIRECTOR OF PHOTOGRAPHY: Francisco Bojorquez
ART DIRECTOR: Francisco Magallón
SPECIAL EFFECTS: Federico Farfán
MAKE-UP: Lucrecia Muñoz
WARDROBE: Ignacia Aguilar
CAST: Lana Clarkson (Athalia / Barbarian Queen), Greg Wrangler (Aurion), Rebecca Wood (Zarla), Elizabeth Jaeger (Noki), Roger Cudney (Hofrax), Alejandro Bracho (Ankaris), Cecilia Tijerina (Tamis), Orietta Aguilar (Erigena), Carolina Valero (Nabis), Monica Steuer (Ethbek), Carlos Romano (Peasant), Manuel Benítez (Captain), Antonio Zubiaga (King's Soldier), George Belanger (Noble 1), John Sterlini (Noble 2), Patrick Welch (Noki's Father), Arturo Ostos (Soldier 1), Alejandro Landero (Soldier 2), Francisco Tostado (Soldier 3), Hector De Rubin (Soldier 4), and Memo Ayala (Iron Man)

ON THE MAP

Set in an unknown time and place "long ago," with nods to the Crusades and deliberate parallels to the legend of Robin Hood, the action moves from the castle of Athalia's father to the lands beyond the kingdom's borders, where roguish, Amazon-like warrior-women dwell . . . and then the story takes us back and forth between the two places a few more times.

OUR STORY SO FAR

Believing the king dead upon the field of battle, Ankaris usurps the throne and orders his sister, Athalia, to release a magical scepter to him. She refuses to speak the magic words that would grant him the scepter's full powers, so he sends her to the gallows for execution. En route, she frees herself and flees the castle, eventually joining forces with a band of rogues. Together they rise up against Ankaris and his forces to reclaim the kingdom for the people.

ALTERNATE VERSIONS

The BBFC cut down the UK (18-rated) version of the film by almost three minutes. Most of the edits affected scenes of rape and torture.

IT'S MAGIC

The magical scepter secures the king's authority, as well as his life, because it has a magical bond with his mortality. He has entrusted its secret to Athalia in the event of his death, so she can speak words that release the scepter from its protected vault: something only a female can do. Two unique phrases transfer the scepter's power: one releases it from its vault, and the other severs the tie with the current king—which can prove fatal—and links it to a new king, granting him immortality.

The young Tamis's dead mother had been a user of magic. Before she died, she promised to pass her power to her daughter when Tamis was old enough. Believing herself mature enough, Tamis dons a medallion, speaks the magical phrase Athalia used to free the scepter from its vault, and then begs the deceased spirit of her mother to influence her destiny. As a result, Tamis ages, so that she might seduce Aurion as a grown woman.

Ultimately, this fantasy world revolves around a maternal order of mages, wherein even when the scepter's power influences a man, a woman must first grant it to him. Considering how often this genre is steeped in patriarchal themes, this is worth highlighting.

THE QUEST FOR MEANING

We are told in a not-so-rousing speech delivered by Athalia from the castle battlements that the magical powers of the scepter have enabled the rule of the kingdom, but ultimately the people's respect for the one on the throne—regardless of the artifact's influence—makes for a true and honorable ruler. Ankaris seeks control of the scepter early on, desiring nothing but power and immortality, but words and some sort of bond to womankind protect it. In the end, Athalia takes control of the kingdom, presumably along with Aurion, and tosses the scepter into the hands of the people, claiming that their belief in the kingdom's ruler is magic enough to ensure competent rule from that day forth. That is, of course, until the people figure out how to use the scepter's powers and rise up against Athalia in *Barbarian Queen III* (not!).

WHO GOES THERE?

Lana Clarkson got her big break with just a couple lines in *Fast Times at Ridgemont High*. From there, she enjoyed a steady stream of roles both big and small in films like *Deathstalker, Brainstorm, Scarface, Amazon Women on the Moon,* and *The Haunting of Morella*. She also frequently played TV roles throughout the '80s and '90s. Though never quite the star she had always dreamed of becoming, she became a household name in a tragic final role in 2003: she was found shot dead at the age of 40 in the home of record producer Phil Spector.

Those of us who grew up in the '80s and even '90s might remember Greg Wrangler in the role of Peter in a long-running Christmas-themed Folger's coffee commercial. Go look it up for a bit of holiday nostalgia. Wrangler continued to act, appearing in a few soap operas as well as guest roles in *Freddy's Nightmares, Babylon 5, Arrested Development, Heroes,* and *The Event*. Other films of note include *The Runestone, The Mummy Lives,* and *Sorceress II: The Temptress*.

Rebecca Wood (sometimes credited as Rebecca Sharkey) started her film career in *Mask* alongside Cher and Eric Stoltz. She flashed her breasts and took an axe to the stomach in *Fri-

day the 13th: A New Beginning and had a small role in the 1989 ghost story *The Forgotten One*. *Barbarian Queen II* was her final film; she gave up acting soon after.

> SHE'S WILD. SHE'S SEXY. SHE'S THE BARBARIAN QUEEN.

Ohio-born Roger Cudney visited Mexico in the 1960s to perform with a traveling musical-theater group but wound up staying and enjoying a long career in Mexican cinema and television, where he often plays a villainous gringo. The majority of his roles are in little-known Mexican productions, but he has popped up in Hollywood films from time to time, including *The Bees, Deathstalker and the Warriors from Hell* (a.k.a. *Deathstalker III*), *License to Kill, Total Recall,* and *Species: The Awakening.*

Puerto Rican actor Alejandro Bracho also appeared in *Deathstalker III, License to Kill,* and *Clear and Present Danger.*

Former child star Cecilia Tijerina appears in a number of Spanish-language productions as well as in *The Taking of Beverly Hills, Picking Up the Pieces,* and *Once Upon a Time in Mexico.*

Trilingual actor Monica Steuer has an impressive resume, with award-winning roles on stage, television, and film. She appears in *Total Recall* (in which she played the "mutant mother" under makeup created by Rob Bottin), *Empire, The Ministers,* and the videogame *Max Payne 3* (as the voice of Rodrigo's secretary).

Carlos Romano's first role was back in 1966. As with most of his roles, it was in a Mexican production. He has, however, also appeared in a number of well-known Hollywood films, including *The Octagon, Yellowbeard, Amityville 3-D, The Falcon and the Snowman,* and *Deathstalker III.*

Would it surprise you to know that Manuel Benítez appeared in *Deathstalker III* as well? He also appears in *Fist Fighter* (along with George Rivero of *Conquest*), *The Assassin,* and an episode of *Acapulco H.E.A.T.*

Surprisingly, actor George Belanger did *not* appear in *Deathstalker III* with so many of his *Barbarian Queen II* costars, but he has played roles for a few other familiar titles, including *The Bees, The Falcon and the Snowman,* and *License to Kill,* as well as *Beyond the Limit, Original Sin,* and *The Air I Breathe.*

6 DEGREES OF SORCERY

The title is a rather lame parody of a certain sequel to *Star Wars,* but you probably got that one already. The order to kneel is like that from Zod in *Superman II.* Clarkson's performance surely inspired *Xena: Warrior Princess;* not to leave any ambiguity, Roger Corman has referred to Clarkson's character in this and its predecessor as "the original Xena." Ankaris is a bit like the old *Saturday Night Live* character Father Guido Sarducci.

The gallows rescue is modeled on a similar rescue in *The Adventures of Robin Hood* starring Errol Flynn. The film overall is very much a female-centric version of the Robin Hood legend, with Ankaris standing in for Prince John.

The topless rack-torture mirrors the same type of thing, also featuring Lana Clarkson, depicted in *Barbarian Queen* ... although director Joe Finley steps it up a notch and presents *two* scenes of topless torture in this sequel! The gem pictured in the movie poster bears a similarity to a d20. Tying some of the magical power only to females also turns up in *Red Sonja.*

SHATTERING THE ILLUSION

The movie was shot in 1989 at Estudios America—the site of the castle sets' construction—and Bosque del Ajusco, Mexico City, Mexico. Unlike the first *Barbarian Queen*, which enjoyed a brief but limited theatrical release, at least in part thanks to all the post-*Conan* enthusiasm for the genre, this one went direct to video. This was writer Howard R. Cohen's last produced screenplay.

Lana Clarkson's sword-and-sorcery legacy began when she worked on Roger Corman's 1983 release, *Deathstalker*. Though her role was small, Corman—and even a few critics, many of whom weren't particularly kind to that film—took note of Clarkson, which led to her playing the title role in 1985's *Barbarian Queen* and, seven years later, this "sequel."

Maybe stardom went to her head. Her demanding nature on set might be the main reason we never saw a *Barbarian Queen III*—or a timely sequel to the first film, for that matter. That said, she was well liked in some circles. There are even tales of her enjoying a day off, during production of this film, aboard an Acapulco-moored yacht belonging to Kirk Douglas.

Recently, completely original scenes designed to look as though they were lifted from one of the *Barbarian Queen* films appeared in the 2013 HBO original movie *Phil Spector*. For those, actress Meghan Marx appeared as Lana Clarkson, complete with skimpy leather outfit and teased, '80s blonde hair.

MUSIC OF THE MINSTRELS

Chris Young—or Christopher Young, as he's more widely known—has been scoring films since the early '80s. His work on movies such as *Wizards of the Lost Kingdom, A Nightmare on Elm Street Part 2: Freddy's Revenge, Hellraiser, The Fly II, The Dark Half, Species, The Core, The Grudge, Ghost Rider, Spider-Man 3*, and *Drag Me to Hell* has garnered him numerous award nominations and wins, including a Saturn Award for his score for *Hellbound: Hellraiser II*; BMI Film Music Awards for *Entrapment, Swordfish*, and *The Grudge;* and a Golden Globe nomination for *Last Flight Out*. The master Bernard Herrmann inspired his earlier work, having motivated Young to pursue a career in scoring movies.

That said, this might not be the pinnacle of Young's career . . . but it is surprisingly decent, with a nicely constructed, triumphant theme. Alas, all the music that played in this film came from previous films. Unfortunately, as of writing, the score remains unreleased, despite ongoing efforts of fans. Yes, there are fans.

THE SAGA CONTINUES

Let us dissuade you from any misconceptions: despite this movie's attempt, in both title and promotion, to seem like a follow-up to Clarkson's first *Barbarian Queen* romp, little connects the two films other than the late Clarkson in the lead role and perhaps a couple similar scenes of topless torture. Likely the original intent was to launch a female-driven series similar to the *Deathstalker* films, but alas, such was not to be.

If, however, you are looking for an evening of films in a similar vein to satisfy your longing for an ongoing saga, a compatible set of four movies includes (in chronological order) *Sor-

ceress, Barbarian Queen, Amazons, and *Barbarian Queen II.* Three of those have poster art by none other than fantasy artist extraordinaire Boris Vallejo. It is a brave soul who attempts this lineup in one sitting!

TAKE UP THY SWORD!

THE KING'S SCEPTER (MAGICAL ARTIFACT)

Royals pass this relic from one generation to another. It possesses powers entrusted only to one member of the royal family at a time, usually the king or queen. In the hands of such a guardian, it can control the minds of others and also grants its possessor extended life—if not immortality. While magically suspended in its vault, it protects itself from any attempt to retrieve it by unauthorized hands: powerful flames can immediately reduce a thief to ash.

Perhaps the scepter's greatest power, however, is not mystical; rather, it is in its symbolism to those ruled by whoever controls it. Merely revealing it to the citizenry can encourage them and unify them in loyalty.

THE FILM'S DESTINY

This is predictably a Z-grade fantasy adventure with Roger Corman's stamp of approval on every cheesy frame: low-budget, clunky, poorly acted fare that really only appeals to a certain type of viewer—which is, actually, probably you, our reader! If you want a mindless—or mind-numbing—eighty minutes of movie that doesn't take itself too seriously and offers a nice mix of silliness with swordplay (unlike, say, the grim, humorless films *Conquest* and *The Warrior and the Sorceress*), along with a few gratuitous topless scenes to spice things up, and a bit of mud wrestling thrown in for good measure, then *Barbarian Queen II* is the cinematic experience for you. Only 14 years old at the time of production, Cecilia Tijerina in particular delivers a pretty impressive performance as the bratty—and kind of creepy—Tamis. This is one of those laughably chintzy entries in the genre that will have you smiling throughout—that is, of course, if you approach it with low expectations and the right attitude. If you saw the first *Barbarian Queen* and felt somehow empty afterward, as though the world wouldn't be complete without a second film featuring Lana Clarkson being tortured topless on a rack (a rack on a rack . . . sorry, yes we went there), your prayers have been answered.

THIS YEAR IN GAMING

TSR released the first product for their *Al-Qadim—Arabian Adventures* setting. Designed by Jeff Grubb, this beautifully produced and illustrated 160-page trade paperback introduced Dungeon Masters and players alike to a place known as Zakhara, located in the Forgotten Realms. The core book offered new rules for character classes, kits, proficiencies, and spells, as well as new and exotic equipment. TSR supported the setting with additional products, such as sourcebooks, boxed sets, and adventures. The effort even inspired a successful 1994 PC game from Strategic Simulations titled *The Genie's Curse.*

ARMY OF DARKNESS

1993 • US • UNIVERSAL PICTURES • 81M • COLOR • R

WRITERS: Sam Raimi and Ivan Raimi
DIRECTOR: Sam Raimi
PRODUCERS: Robert Tapert and Bruce Campbell
MUSIC: Joseph LoDuca and Danny Elfman ("March of the Dead" theme)
DIRECTOR OF PHOTOGRAPHY: Bill Pope
DIRECTOR OF VISUAL EFFECTS: William Mesa
SPECIAL MAKE-UP EFFECTS: Robert Kurtzman, Greg Nicotero, And Howard Berger (KNB Efx Group)
ASH & SHEILA MAKEUP EFFECTS: Tony Gardner and Alterian Studios, Inc.
PRODUCTION DESIGNER: Tony Tremblay
COSTUME DESIGNER: Ida Gearon
ART DIRECTOR: Aram Allan
STUNT COORDINATOR: Chris Doyle
SWORDMASTER: Dan Speaker
SPECIAL ARMOUR AND WEAPONS DESIGNED AND CONSTRUCTED BY: Jeff Hedgecock and Vorhut Fahnlein Arms
CAST: Bruce Campbell (Ash); Embeth Davidtz (Sheila); Marcus Gilbert (Arthur); Ian Abercrombie (Wiseman); Richard Grove (Duke Henry); Michael Earl Reid (Gold Tooth); Timothy Patrick Quill (Blacksmith); Bridget Fonda (Linda); Patricia Tallman (Possessed Witch); Theodore Raimi (Cowardly Warrior / Supportive Villager / Eye-Patch / S-Mart Clerk); Deke Anderson (Tiny Ash #1); Bruce Thomas (Tiny Ash #2); Sara Shearer (Old Woman); Shiva Gordon (Pit Deadite #1); Billy Bryan (Pit Deadite #2); Nadine Grycan (Winged Deadite); Bill Moseley (Deadite Captain); Michael Kenney (Henry's Man); Andy Bale (Lieutenant #1); Robert Brent Lappin (Lieutenant #2); Rad Milo (Tower Guard); Brad Bradbury (Chief Archer); Sol Abrams, William Lustig, Lorraine Axeman, David O'Malley, Josh Becker, David Pollison, Sheri Burke, Ivan Raimi, Don Campbell, Bernard Rose, Charlie Campbell, Bill Vincent, Harley Cokeliss, Chris Webster, Ken Jepson, and Ron Zwang (Fake Shemps); Angela Featherstone (S-mart Girl, uncredited); Patricia Anne Isgate (Peasant Woman, uncredited); Kevin O'Hara and Courtney Pakiz (Deadites, uncredited); and Sam Raimi (Knight in Sneakers, uncredited)
ALTERNATE TITLES: *Evil Dead II: The Medievil Dead* (working title), *Bruce Campbell vs. Army of Darkness* (opening credits), *Army of Darkness: The Ultimate Experience in Medieval Horror* (closing credits), and *Evil Dead 3: Army of Darkness*

ON THE MAP

Ash's journey begins at that creepy cabin in the woods before he's flung back to 14th-century England, presumably near London, if the presence of Big Ben in the post-apocalyptic alternate ending is any indication.

OUR STORY SO FAR

Reluctant Deadite fighter Ash is caught up in a temporal whirlpool that sends him back through time to medieval England. There our hero must overcome an army of skeletal marauders led by his demonic doppelganger, unite a downtrodden rabble against impossible odds, and save an innocent girl from the clutches of his decayed twin while trying to overcome his tendency to behave like a complete and utter prick.

ALTERNATE VERSIONS

This film has at least three distinct cuts, and it doesn't help that it's one of the most re-released films in the history of the DVD format. (*Halloween* probably edges it out. Thank you, Anchor Bay.) The 81-minute version listed above is the US theatrical cut and the most familiar version to most viewers. The director's cut runs 96 minutes, not only adding a lot of footage, but also replacing dialogue. Most significantly, the line "Good, bad—I'm the guy with the gun" turns up in the theatrical version but *not* the director's cut. The latter features the alternate, apocalyptic ending, in contrast with the shorter cut's more familiar [and in one author's opinion, more satisfying –ATB] "S-Mart" ending. If you want to see the longest cut of the film, grab the Region 3 edition of the director's cut from Hong Kong, which runs 97 minutes and includes a slightly longer scene (by seconds) of Evil Ash ravishing Sheila.

IT'S MAGIC

Good and evil exists in this universe, with both forces capable of manifesting through magic. The bad side of the equation can call forth armies of undead and cause havoc via that mischievous little *Necronomicon Ex-Mortis*, but the positive side has it a bit harder. These forces might be sentient, because one thing is certain: if you're fighting on the side of good, you'd better get those words *exactly* right. The benevolent powers do *not* take intentions into consideration.

THE QUEST FOR MEANING

Dropping a man from the present into the past and demanding that he take the heroic lead in a battle against evil nicely mirrors almost any modern gaming experience, especially if you like a little genre-bending sci-fi and steampunk, courtesy of the retrofitted Oldsmobile "Deathcoaster" and Ash's cyborg-like modifications to his body via the chainsaw and super-strong robotic armored hand. True, Ash isn't exactly a willing participant initially, but he comes around and lets the better part of himself out to play by adventure's end . . . though his sudden advanced skills in engineering, chemistry, and combat mechanics are a bit hard to swallow. He's even a genre fan himself: his trunk contains issues of *Dark Horse Presents* and *Fangoria*!

A big question some might ask, especially given the obvious parallels with a certain Connecticut Yankee's experience, is whether we're supposed to believe this is *the* Arthur of legend who allies with Ash. Could this ramshackle castle and its dirt-covered denizens be the remnants of a once-great Camelot worn down by battle on two fronts against Henry's army and the Deadite attacks? Or will the Ash-inspired victory and unification of Arthur's and Henry's men lead to the glory days we know so well from all those classic tales of chivalry and romance? Could that "wiseman" even be Merlin? Food for thought.

> TRAPPED IN TIME.
> SURROUNDED BY EVIL.
> LOW ON GAS.

WHO GOES THERE?

Bruce Campbell is one of genre entertainment's most enduring lead/character-actor through his work with friend Sam Raimi on the *Evil Dead* series, cameo appearances in the first three *Spider-Man* films (all helmed by Sam Raimi), and roles in *Maniac Cop, Moontrap, Darkman, Waxwork II: Lost in Time, Mindwarp, The Hudsucker Proxy, Congo, Escape from L.A., McHale's Navy, Bubba Ho-Tep, Man with the Screaming Brain* (which he also wrote and directed), and *My Name Is Bruce* (which he directed—and appeared in, as a heightened version of himself). On television, he starred in the popular cult series *The Adventures of Brisco County Jr.*, had recurring guest roles on *Ellen, Xena: Warrior Princess,* and *Hercules: The Legendary Journeys,* starred in the short-lived series *Jack of All Trades,* appeared as Sam Axe in *Burn Notice* and a prequel TV movie, and returned as Ash in the Starz TV series *Ash vs. Evil Dead!* He's also written two books: *If Chins Could Kill: Confessions of B Movie Actor* and *Make Love! The Bruce Campbell Way.* "Groovy."

The same year she appeared in this movie, Embeth Davidtz was in *Schindler's List* and went on to star in the films *Mansfield Park, Bicentennial Man, Bridget Jones's Diary, Thir13en Ghosts, The Girl with the Dragon Tattoo,* and two *Amazing Spider-Man* films (ones *not* directed by Sam Raimi). She has also appeared on the television shows *Citizen Baines, Grey's Anatomy, Californication,* and *Mad Men.*

This wasn't Marcus Gilbert's first brush with Arthurian legend. He also played a version of Lancelot—Ancelyn—in the 1989 *Doctor Who* adventure "Battlefield."

Ian Abercrombie played nearly 200 roles in film and television productions alone, with an extensive career that included stage and voiceover work. For one generation of television viewers, he was Mr. Pitt on *Seinfeld.* Younger viewers know him best as Professor Crumbs on *Wizards of Waverly Place.* *Star Wars* fans might recognize his voice as that of Darth Sidious in the *Clone Wars* animated series and related videogames. He died in 2012 at age 77.

Blink and you miss her, but that's Bridget Fonda as Linda. She comes from an acting dynasty, including Peter (her father), Jane (her aunt), and Henry (her grandfather). Appearing first as a child in *Easy Rider,* she also turned up in *Aria, Shag, Frankenstein Unbound, The Godfather: Part III, Doc Hollywood, Single White Female, Jackie Brown, A Simple Plan, Lake Placid, Monkeybone,* and *Kiss of the Dragon.* Following a car crash and marriage to composer Danny Elfman (in that order), she retired from acting.

Patricia Tallman is a genre icon as an actress and stuntwoman in a number of sci-fi, horror, and fantasy films and television series. Her more prominent roles include Barbara in the 1990 remake of *Night of the Living Dead,* multiple appearances on the *Star Trek* TV-shows, and in the role of Lyta on *Babylon 5.*

Ted Raimi might always have work in the business with his brother Sam, but he really doesn't need that help. He's a reliable, often comedic character-actor in the films *Patriot Games, Candyman, Clear and Present Danger, Wishmaster,* his brother's three *Spider-Man* films, and *The Midnight Meat Train.* He also appeared in recurring roles on *SeaQuest 2032, Xena: Warrior Princess,* and *Hercules: The Legendary Journeys,* and did a variety of celebrity voice impersonations on *Code Monkeys.*

> 1 Man, 1 Million dead,
> The odds are just about even.

Bill Moseley is a horror icon, thanks to roles in movies like *The Texas Chainsaw Mas-*

sacre 2, the 1990 remake of *Night of the Living Dead*, *House of 1000 Corpses*, *The Devil's Rejects*, *Grindhouse*, Rob Zombie's *Halloween*, *Repo! The Genetic Opera*, and *2001 Maniacs: Field of Screams*. He also had a regular part on the cable television series *Carnivale*. Among many other credits, he did a memorable guest turn on *Z Nation*.

> SOUND THE TRUMPETS, RAISE THE DRAWBRIDGE, AND DROP THE OLDSMOBILE.

6 DEGREES OF SORCERY

The most obvious overall thematic parallels are with classic literary flights of fantasy like *A Connecticut Yankee in King Arthur's Court*, *Gulliver's Travels*, and *Don Quixote* (tilting at windmills?), as well as numerous allusions to cinematic classics like Errol Flynn's swashbuckling escapades and the Ray Harryhausen films covered in this book, especially the skeleton battle in *Jason and the Argonauts*. Shakespeare's *Julius Caesar* and *King John* are quoted. There are also a fair few connections to *The Lord of the Rings* books and movies, such as in the fog-enshrouded path to the cemetery where the books wait, as well as the castle siege that echoes battles at Helm's Deep and Minas Tirith, and Henry's nick-of-time arrival, resembling that of Théoden and the Rohirrim. Many members of the production team were Three Stooges devotees, so there are also nods and debts owed to *Restless Knights* and *Squareheads of the Round Table*.

In case you didn't know, those words Ash can't quite get right are a reference to the command that could make the formidable robot Gort stand down in the original sci-fi masterpiece *The Day the Earth Stood Still*. For the record, the actual words (not quite said or captioned correctly in any version of *Army of Darkness*) are "klaatu barada nikto."

In addition to the Harryhausen connections, the sequence with the undead army rising from their graves and marching into combat also echoes *The Legend of the Seven Golden Vampires*. Ash somersaults over a standing Evil Ash and stabs him from behind in a move like Dar's in *The Beastmaster*. Anyone get an *Animal House* Deathmobile vibe from the arrival of the Deathcoaster? The progression of Evil Ash from fleshy duplicate to skeletal warrior might have inspired the Black Knight, Bony Black Knight, and Ghost Black Knight triad in *World of Warcraft*. The passing of time in the apocalyptic alternate ending recalls the look of the time traveler's journeys in George Pal's *The Time Machine*.

You want something *really* obscure? Some of this film's battle scenes supposedly came from storyboards dating back to the 1948 Ingrid Bergman film *Joan of Arc*!

SHATTERING THE ILLUSION

To make the first *Evil Dead* film—independently and on a shoestring—Sam Raimi and his partners gathered a like-minded team eager to make its mark on horror with a fun romp. The successful result led to a marginally more elaborate remake/sequel. After the two films—and their hapless hero, Ash—gathered a growing fan base, Universal Pictures expressed interest in backing a third *Evil Dead* through producer Dino De Laurentiis. The studio demanded, however, that the film stand alone as much as possible, and did not want even the title to reflect that the movie was the third installment in a series.

> HOW CAN YOU DESTROY AN
> ARMY THAT'S ALREADY DEAD?

Plans for what would become *Army of Darkness* were already in the works during production of Raimi's *Darkman*, which became a success. Now given a budget of $12 million, Raimi assembled a non-union crew and went back to his roots as a fan of EC Comics to storyboard the entire film in the style of those classic horror comic books before shooting began. Despite the huge increase in financial support, the crew still approached the shoot economically, with principal photography taking place over fifty-five days. Most of the exterior work was done in familiar scenic locations outside Los Angeles, including the Vasquez Rocks formations recognizable in countless cult films and TV appearances (most famously as the backdrop for Captain Kirk's battle with the Gorn in the *Star Trek* episode "Arena") and Bronson Canyon, where the entrance to the Batcave was filmed for the '60s *Batman* TV show.

Continuity was often a nightmare, due to sand and dust blowing on the actors as well as the crew. Another challenge was keeping Ash's facial cuts consistent via a plastic stencil for applying makeup. This led to a minor complication when Campbell had to go to the hospital for an actual facial injury during filming. Initially the doctor couldn't figure out which of the cuts was the real one but later claimed the other cuts weren't very convincing. Campbell happily reminded him that he couldn't tell the difference earlier.

The army of the dead consisted of a complex mix of stunt actors in makeup, puppets, and stop-motion models, often combined in a single shot to create a sense of scope and depth. Some of the battle sequences had more than a hundred soldiers and nearly fifty horses.

The KNB effects team comprised artists Bob Kurtzman, Greg Nicotero, and Howard Berger. They had met while working on *Evil Dead II* and returned under their new firm name, with additional special-effects support provided by Tony Gardner and Alterian Studios, the latter of which handled the detailed work on Campbell and Davidtz in their Deadite guises. To keep the gore quotient low, the production used no fake blood—only black Deadite "bile," and plenty of it.

A month after production wrapped, the team reassembled to create a more upbeat ending at the behest of the studio. The "S-Mart" finale was more elaborate than the original apocalyptic ending. Additional reshoots expanded the windmill sequence.

Some real-life drama accompanied the release of the movie, when Universal and De Laurentiis entered a tug-of-war over the rights to a Hannibal Lecter film following the success of *Silence of the Lambs*. This put the release of *Army of Darkness* in jeopardy, but the factions resolved the conflict in time for the movie to reach theaters in February 1993.

MUSIC OF THE MINSTRELS

The score for this film benefits from a central theme titled "March of the Dead," contributed by Oingo Boingo's Danny Elfman. His percussive, driving compositions had graced the soundtracks of *Beetlejuice* and *Batman* as well as Raimi's previous film, *Darkman*, but that was his sole piece for this movie.

Following reshoots, *The Evil Dead* series composer Joseph LoDuca took on the rest of the score, with Raimi's participation. Varese Sarabande released the entire score on CD. It is now out of print but not difficult to find. In Japan, a compilation CD of all three LoDuca *Evil Dead* scores was released. It poses a bit more of a challenge to locate.

THE SAGA CONTINUES

For further adventures, you can read a long and labyrinthine collection of *Army of Darkness* licensed comic books, published by Dark Horse Comics and later Dynamite Publications, starting with a three-issue adaptation of the film. Ash has also chainsawed his way through Deadites in videogames like *The Evil Dead, Evil Dead: Hail to the King, Evil Dead: A Fistful of Boomstick*, and *Evil Dead Regeneration*, including two adventures for mobile devices titled *Army of Darkness Defense* and *Evil Dead: The Game*.

The year of the film's release, Leading Edge Games released a board game focusing on the climactic castle siege. It employed cooperative play and featured extensive photography from the film. A line of associated 25mm lead miniatures was also available in twelve different packs that included Deadites, knights, and even Ash's retrofitted, siege-ready Ashmobile!

In 2004, Eden Studios got into the Deadite-fighting business with a card game that featured lots of photos from the film, and then with an RPG penned by *Deadlands* creator Shane Hensley in 2005. The core rulebook, available both in print and as a PDF, taught players how to use the "Army of Darkness Unisystem."

Would you believe *Evil Dead: The Musical?* The off-Broadway play continues to run in regional productions and has prompted *The New York Times* to anoint it "the next *Rocky Horror*." Well, we'll see about that.

If you're interested in seeing how Ash's ordeal began, you'll have to step out of the sword-and-sorcery genre and back into the first two (horror-comedy) installments in the *Evil Dead* series: the ultra-low-budget *Evil Dead* (of course) and its semi-remake sequel *Evil Dead II: Dead by Dawn*. As for a continuation of the saga, therein lies a tale.

Fans have clamored for *Evil Dead 4* (or *Army of Darkness 2*) since long before Bruce Campbell went gray and paunchy. In one missed opportunity, theatrical success of the horror crossover *Freddy vs. Jason* prompted the development of a possible follow-up, *Freddy vs. Jason vs. Ash*, but Raimi nixed that because *Evil Dead* remake/sequel talk was having one of its surges. The concept did see the light of day as one of the many *Army of Darkness* comic books.

Then there was the sly not-quite-remake/somewhat-sequel *Evil Dead* in 2013 (which both authors highly recommend). It features a split-second appearance by Campbell/Ash after the end credits.

As we concluded work on this book, the news broke that at long last we would soon enjoy a full-fledged multi-episode sequel series on the Starz channel, *Ash vs. Evil Dead!* That's right, *Evil Dead* fans . . . come get some.

TAKE UP THY SWORD!

THE BIG GUN (MAGIC WEAPON)

Manufactured in Grand Rapids, Michigan, and originally sold in a well-known department store's sporting-goods department, this double-barreled, twelve-gauge firearm is more than just your typical gun. Inside its finely polished walnut stock and cobalt-blue steel exterior, this weap-

> They move.
> They breathe.
> They suck.

on, upon being tossed through a dimensional vortex (throwing it back in time 700 years), has been "altered" by the influence of *the Dark Ones*.

It has *double* the range of a similar, ordinary weapon and double the damage of all successful shots versus standard living targets. Shells fired from it can strike (with normal damage) undead normally resistant to mundane weapons. Lastly, its wielder can load both barrels in the same round.

THE FILM'S DESTINY

Sure, Ash is a bastard most of the time, but it's hard not to root for the poor guy as he finds himself in one horrifying situation after another, with everyone looking to him as the "Chosen One" who will lead humanity to victory against hordes of living-dead demons. Who wouldn't have some personality issues under all that pressure? Continuing the frenetic, cartoonish approach that made the first two *Evil Dead* films so much fun, *Army of Darkness* ramps up the humor and the horror with slapstick and splatter, and even offers genuinely touching moments of romance in Ash's relationship with Sheila. It's rare to have a hero in this genre whose primary motivation is personal—the sorry sap just wants to get home—and who directly causes nearly every bad thing that happens to anyone in this movie. Yet when the going... et cetera, Ash surprises everyone, including viewers, by taking the reins and becoming the hero he is apparently destined to be. It's a rousing subversion of the series' tongue-in-cheek inanity that Ash becomes a responsible leader, excusing the dodgier aspects of the film by making us care about this idiot and hope he makes it out alive.

To be fair, there's also a bit of glee in seeing Ash put through his paces too, which makes it all the more shocking that this tour-de-force performance didn't get Campbell more mainstream attention. A quotable, infinitely re-watchable cult classic from first frame to last, *Army of Darkness* might be the final exciting adventure for Ash (and depending on the version you watch, leaves him either as the king of his own little world or trapped in a nightmare from which there might be no escape). Regardless of the choice of ending, Ash ends up exactly where he should be: trapped by fate, plagued by horrors no one should face, and more than capable of snatching victory from the jaws of Deadite harpies.

THIS YEAR IN GAMING

The future of Wizards of the Coast—reeling from a devastating lawsuit by RPG publisher Palladium Books and still four years from acquiring *Dungeons & Dragons*—was dangling by a thread when Peter Adkison, desperate to find a new low-cost and portable product, spoke with game designer Richard Garfield about combining the collectability of baseball cards with some sort of game. The initial concept dated back to 1982, when the prototype game was called "Manaclash." The *Magic: The Gathering* "Alpha" set premiered at the Origins gaming convention in mid-July, and Wizards officially released it to the public on Thursday, August 5. It was an overnight success, quickly selling out its initial run of 2.6 million cards. A "Beta" printing consisted of a further 7.3 million cards, and December saw the release of the *Unlimited Edition*. Several dozen expansions later, the rest is history!

DRAGONHEART

1996 • Slovakia/UK/US • Universal Pictures • 103m • Color • PG-13

Screenplay: Charles Edward Pogue
Story: Patrick Read Johnson and Charles Edward Pogue
Director: Rob Cohen
Producer: Raffaella De Laurentiis
Music: Randy Edelman
Director of Photography: David Eggby
Production Designer: Benjamin Fernandez
Art Directors: Maria Teresa Barbasso and Jan Svoboda
Costume Designers: Thomas Casterline and Anna Sheppard
Make-Up Supervisor: Giannetto De Rossi
Special Visual Effects and Animation By: Industrial Light & Magic
Visual Effects Supervisor: Scott Squires
Dragon Designs By: Phil Tippett
Character Animation Supervisor: James Straus
Special Effects Supervisor: Kit West
Stunt Coordinator: Paul Weston
Armourer: Scot Ellis
Horse Master: Ivo Kristof
Sword Trainer / Choreographer: Kiyoshi Yamazaki
Cast: Dennis Quaid (Bowen), David Thewlis (Einon), Pete Postlethwaite (Gilbert), Dina Meyer (Kara), Jason Isaacs (Felton), Brian Thompson (Brok), Lee Oakes (Young Einon), Wolf Christian (Hewe), Terry O'Neill (Redbeard), Peter Hric (King Freyne), Eva Vejmelkova (Felton's Minx), Milan Bahul (Swamp Village Chief), Sandra Kovacicova (Young Kara), Kyle Cohen (Boy in Field), Thom Baker (Aislinn's Chess Partner), Julie Christie (Aislinn), Sean Connery (Voice of Draco), John Gielgud (Voice of King Arthur, uncredited), and Buddy Quaid (Cook/Servant, uncredited)

ON THE MAP

It's a version of 10th-century England in which the Arthurian legend was real.

OUR STORY SO FAR

A bitter, aging knight and the last living dragon form an unlikely partnership, but one of them might have to make the ultimate sacrifice in an attempt to end the reign of a vicious despot who was once the knight's student.

ALTERNATE VERSIONS

In the UK, a single sound effect of a neck snapping changed, to lower the film's rating. No need to rush out and get that Region 2 DVD.

IT'S MAGIC

Although this is one of those movies that has no overt magic apart from the existence of dragons, the dragons possess mystical powers and a spiritual affinity with the universe that marks them as more than just fanciful but natural animals. They have unpronounceable names (or so Draco says), can camouflage as rock, and can heal humans, either via an elixir (secreted by them or distilled from their bodies?) or by sharing their vitality. Once linked to a dragon in such a way, a person becomes impervious to normal damage and can die only when that dragon also dies.

Technically speaking, though, there is a bit of magic beyond Draco's. If Arthur and his legendary Knights of the Round Table are real, perhaps Merlin, too, exists? And Arthur's resting place at Avalon still resonates with his spirit. There, the lasting lessons of valor, virtue, and truth still remind a warrior of his calling from beyond the grave.

THE QUEST FOR MEANING

There's a lot of discussion about honor, virtue, and chivalry, as well as adherence to "the old code"—all of which apply to both humans and dragons. But when corruption rears its head, it comes entirely from the race of Man. Dragons serve as guardians of Man in his folly and can thus earn their place in dragons' heaven, in the stars, with the immortal spirits of their brethren. Draco attempts to unite humans and dragons through curing Einon, but we know how that one goes.

Draco, as the last dragon, represents a theme of many other movies in this book: the world of magic and myth fading away, supplanted by the industrial civilization of modern Man. In the midst of that shift, Bowen and Draco bond; they're both relics of the passing age and need each other to survive.

This movie inverts a common sword-and-sorcery trope: that of a burned-down village inspiring heroism in an observer or survivor. In this case, destruction of a village leads to the vengeful murder of the king responsible while his impressionable son observes, thus embittering the son, who turns to evil. The movie follows the usual gaming rhythm of stacking up "boss" fights at the end, with Felton and Brok providing two levels of challenge before the final showdown between Bowen and Einon.

WHO GOES THERE?

Dennis Quaid's good-natured grin and roguish personality have stood him in good stead in films such as *Breaking Away, Caveman, Jaws 3, The Right Stuff, Dreamscape, Enemy Mine, The Big Easy, Innerspace, D.O.A., Great Balls of Fire!, Wyatt Earp, Frequency, The Alamo, The Day After Tomorrow*, the 2004 remake of *Flight of the Phoenix, Legion, G.I. Joe: The Rise of Cobra, Pandorum, Soul Surfer*, and the 2011 remake of *Footloose*.

David Thewlis is the occasionally hairy Professor Remus Lupin in the *Harry Potter* films and has also played roles in *Naked, Black Beauty, James and the Giant Peach, The Island of Dr. Moreau, Seven Years in Tibet, The Big Lebowski, Timeline, Kingdom of Heaven*, the 2006 remake of *The*

Omen, War Horse, and *The Zero Theorem*. He also lent his voice, uncredited, to the *World of Warcraft* online game as Lord Darius Crowley.

> HONOUR BEFORE FEAR

The distinctive cheekbones of Pete Postlethwaite have appeared in *A Private Function*, Mel Gibson's *Hamlet*, *Alien³*, *The Usual Suspects*, *James and the Giant Peach* (okay, it was just his voice in this one), *Romeo + Juliet*, *The Serpent's Kiss*, *The Lost World: Jurassic Park*, *Amistad*, *Æon Flux*, the 2006 remake of *The Omen*, *Solomon Kane*, and the 2010 remake of *Clash of the Titans*. He died in 2011 at age 64.

Dina Meyer appeared in TV shows like *Beverly Hills 90210*, *Friends*, *Birds of Prey*, *Point Pleasant*, and *CSI: Crime Scene Investigation*, and films such as *Johnny Mnemonic*, *Starship Troopers*, *Stranger Than Fiction*, *Star Trek: Nemesis*, *Saw*, *The Storyteller*, *Saw II*, *Saw III*, *Saw IV* (seeing a pattern here?), and *Piranha 3D*.

A generation of moviegoers knows Jason Isaacs as Death Eater Lucius Malfoy in the *Harry Potter* films. He also appeared in *Event Horizon*, *Armageddon*, *Soldier*, *Peter Pan*, *Elektra*, and *Grindhouse*, and had roles in TV series like *Highlander*, *Avatar: The Last Airbender*, *Awake*, *Star Wars Rebels*, and *Dig*. In videogames, he was the voices of Ra's al Ghul in *Batman* and Satan in *Castlevania*.

Brian Thompson is a ubiquitous and instantly recognizable presence in genre film and television, appearing in movies like *The Terminator*, *Cobra*, *Three Amigos*, *Alien Nation*, *Fright Night Part 2*, *Moon 44*, *Lionheart*, *Doctor Mordrid*, *Star Trek: Generations*, *Mortal Kombat: Annihilation*, *Fist of the Warrior*, *Flight of the Living Dead*, and *Dragonquest*, and in TV shows like *Otherworld*, *Knight Rider*, *Werewolf*, *Star Trek: The Next Generation*, *Alien Nation*, *The Adventures of Superboy*, *Kindred: The Embraced*, *Star Trek: Deep Space Nine*, *Buffy the Vampire Slayer*, *Seven Days*, *The X-Files*, *Birds of Prey*, *Charmed*, *Star Trek: Enterprise*, and *Chuck*. He also played Hercules in the TV movie *Jason and the Argonauts*.

Wolf Christian had a bit part in *First Knight*.

Terry O'Neill turned up in *Conan the Destroyer* and *Kull the Conqueror*, and you can call him Ishmael ... in *The League of Extraordinary Gentlemen*.

Peter Hric returned in a different role for *Dragonheart: A New Beginning*.

Julie Christie is an acting legend with a career that includes films such as *Doctor Zhivago*, *Fahrenheit 451*, *Far from the Madding Crowd*, *McCabe & Mrs. Miller*, *Shampoo*, *Demon Seed*, *Heaven Can Wait*, Kenneth Branagh's *Hamlet*, *Troy*, *Harry Potter and the Prisoner of Azkaban*, *Finding Neverland*, and *Red Riding Hood*.

John Gielgud's reputation as perhaps the greatest Shakespearean actor of the last century started forming when, at 26 years old, he first played Hamlet. Although much of the work that defined him occurred on stage, he also crafted a prolific film and television career that included cinematic adaptations of *Julius Caesar* (two film versions, once as Caesar), *Richard III*, and multiple productions of *Romeo and Juliet* and *Hamlet*, as well as *Around the World in Eighty Days*, *Becket*, *Murder on the Orient Express*, *Murder by Decree*, and the infamous *Caligula*. Later in life, he experienced a renewed appreciation for his work through appearances in films like *The Elephant Man*, *Arthur*, *Gandhi*, and *First Knight*, and in TV productions such as *Frankenstein: The True Story*, *Brideshead Revisited*, *Marco Polo*, *The Far Pavilions*, *The Canterville Ghost*, *War and Re-*

YOU WILL BELIEVE

membrance, and *Merlin* (but not as the wizard). Two of his last roles were as Merlin in the animated film *Quest for Camelot* and as the Pope in *Elizabeth*. He died in 2000 at age 96.

Though we usually don't focus on non-actors in this section, we'll make an exception for makeup supervisor Giannetto De Rossi. He designed the iconic "worm-eye zombie" seen on countless posters and t-shirts, originally from the film *Zombie* (also known as *Zombi 2* and *Zombie Flesh-Eaters*). He also toiled on zombie films *The Beyond*, *The House by the Cemetery*, and *Let Sleeping Corpses Lie* (also known as *The Living Dead at the Manchester Morgue*), and sword-and-sorcery movies like *Conan the Destroyer* and *Kull the Conqueror*.

6 DEGREES OF SORCERY

A joke about the peasants revolting recalls a similar gag in Mel Brooks' *History of the World: Part I*. *Dragonheart* has many visual and thematic connections to its spiritual predecessor, *Dragonslayer*, including the lava-filled lair of Draco. Can we link Draco, the last dragon, to Amalthea in *The Last Unicorn*? Okay, maybe that's a stretch.

Bowen rides down the ranks of assembled warriors like Aragorn and Theoden in *The Lord of the Rings* films. A spear-firing weapon resembles one used in *The 7th Voyage of Sinbad*. Draco is chained to the ground like Ash in *Army of Darkness* (both of which mimic the treatment of Gulliver in *Gulliver's Travels*). The slowing of Draco's beating heart echoes a similar scene at the end of the 1976 *King Kong*. The golden mist that carries Draco's spirit to the stars is a lot like the Time Lord energy that accompanies many of the Doctor's regenerations in the BBC science-fiction television series *Doctor Who*. Draco's final words once again put Connery in the role of off-camera mentor and voice of wisdom, as he was in *Highlander*. Stellar constellations forming because of actions in the film also appear in *Clash of the Titans*.

SHATTERING THE ILLUSION

Writer Patrick Read Johnson pitched the story idea for the film as *Butch Cassidy and the Sundance Dragon*, citing the partnership between a knight and a dragon as both amusing and endearing at the same time. Producer Raffaella De Laurentiis first offered the directorial role to John Badham, but he passed on the project.

Johnson took the reins. After obtaining a puppet dragon designed by Jim Henson's Creature Shop in just two months, he began shooting in England. The production immediately encountered problems staying within budget, so once again, De Laurentiis shopped for a director who could save the film.

Rob Cohen accepted the challenge. One of his strategies for making the movie work was to replace the puppet dragon with a CGI version like the dinosaurs that had recently appeared in the blockbuster extravaganza *Jurassic Park*.

In casting the film, Cohen began with a lead actor who embodied the traits that Bowen possessed. Dennis Quaid trained in swordfighting under master Kiyoshi Yamasaki *(Conan the Barbarian, Conan the Destroyer, Red Sonja)* so his character could exhibit an Eastern style of combat. As for the voice of Draco, Cohen considered the distinctive and dignified tones of Sean Connery to be the only option.

Cohen shot Quaid's live-action footage using the tried-and-true method of a stick to indicate Draco's eye line and Cohen reading Connery's dialogue for each take. A small aircraft stood in for some of the material filmed for later insertion of the CGI Draco. The only real Draco props were a foot and jaw, for close-contact sequences with Quaid.

Despite a grueling shoot, Quaid suffered only one injury: a broken finger sustained during a fight sequence with Thewlis. He completed the film wearing a plaster cast kept out of sight.

ILM's Phil Tippett, in conjunction with sculptor Pete Konig, oversaw Draco's design. Cohen briefed them to steer the look of the dragon toward that of the traditional Chinese guardian-lion figures that stand in front of many of that country's government buildings. Those, combined with elements of horses and snakes, led to the final look. Physical models saw use only as references in lighting the character. Early computer tests employed the *Jurassic Park* T-rex CGI model, warped to fit the requirements of Draco's performance.

Motion-capture was not an option yet. To make Draco resemble Connery, Cohen filmed Connery's three voice-recording sessions. Crew members assembled hundreds of still shots from Connery's previous work to provide animators with material from which to create Draco's expressions.

Cohen worked on the film for more than a year after the half-year of principal photography wrapped, because the lengthy process of finalizing all the computer-generated effects required frequent feedback and approval. The film received nominations for two effects Oscars but won neither award.

MUSIC OF THE MINSTRELS

If the movie's main theme sounds familiar, it should. Very often a studio recycles a score again and again, usually for upcoming-movie trailers. This phenomenon occurs frequently with Edelman's compositions. His "To the Stars" turned up for other films, trailers, television ads, the Olympics, and an Academy Awards montage. MCA Records released the *Dragonheart* soundtrack.

THE SAGA CONTINUES

Despite its less-than-spectacular performance, *Dragonheart* spawned quite a bit of merchandise in its marketing to a youthful audience. Cowriter Charles Edward Pogue novelized his own script. Boulevard Books published the novel, which named the dragonslayers who go unnamed in the film. Topps Comics released a two-issue adaptation of the movie. A plethora of other books came out, including a movie storybook by Dina Anastasio and Leslie McGuire, a junior novelization by Adriana Gabriel, and a variety of activity books for children.

Acclaim Entertainment produced a much-maligned videogame tie-in for Sony PlayStation, Sega Saturn, and PCs. Reviewers criticized the game mechanics and design. Acclaim also released a separate tie-in game for the Game Boy. It didn't draw as much vitriol, but it, too, was not a huge success.

In 2000, a direct-to-DVD sequel titled *Dragonheart: A New Beginning,* aimed at younger viewers, recycled some of the fiery destruction footage of the first film. In 2015, a prequel titled *Dragonheart 3: The Sorcerer's Curse* came out. A fourth installment is reportedly in the works.

TAKE UP THY SWORD!
DRAGONSLAYER'S BOLA CASTER (WEAPON)

Mounted inside two specialized, linked saddlebags, the bola caster is an impressive feat of medieval engineering and an essential tool in the professional dragonslayer's arsenal. The operator must open both bags simultaneously and then hook a trio of bolas from one bag to a line on a ratcheting spool in the other bag. With the unit thus assembled, the operator launches it at an airborne target, whereupon, with a successful attack roll, the device wraps itself around leg, tail, neck, or any other part of the dragon that it can ensnare. In comparison to standard bolas, which have an accuracy range of fifty feet, the bola caster hurls the bolas up to six times that range, thanks to a launching mechanism that assists the user's throw! Once the bolas have locked onto their target, the knight errant typically wraps the line around the saddle-horn and uses the mount to help draw the captured dragon down. The bola caster works best versus small or adolescent dragons, but it can also entangle greater dragons and slow their escape.

THE FILM'S DESTINY

With so much *Dragonslayer* DNA in the mix, *Dragonheart* should have been a much better movie. Although the results aren't entirely bad, the proceedings have a disappointing flatness.

Part of it has to do with the two lead performances. Dennis Quaid was always a poor man's Harrison Ford: a scrawnier version with the same lopsided smile and cocksure swagger. In the opening moments of the film, when he should capture our hearts, he comes across as an annoying bully. He predictably reaps what he sows when facing his protégé again years later, but he's not quite old enough to pull off the burnt-out knight portrayal. He shares zero chemistry with Dina Meyer, making the supposed pairing of Bowen and Kara at film's end questionable at best, if not flat-out laughable.

There couldn't be a better choice than Connery for the voice of Draco, but his performance never quite convinces us that he's there, living and breathing as the dragon. He sounds exactly like an actor sitting in a sound booth reading from script pages. In terms of pure design, Draco is one of cinema's better dragons, but the combination of visuals and voice never quite meshes.

> FROM THE DIRECTOR WHO BROUGHT YOU DRAGON AND THE SPECIAL EFFECTS WIZARDS WHO BROUGHT DINOSAURS TO LIFE.

The usually gruff Pete Postlethwaite seems slightly miscast as the comic-relief scribe. David Thewlis's Einon is discordant: buffoonish one moment, cruel and lethal the next. The tone is extremely uneven, failing at balancing light, comedic moments, outright slapstick, and juvenile body humor with much darker drama and pathos. There are some nice shots, especially those that hide Draco from view before his first big reveal, and one in which he rises behind Bowen, lit by the sun. Like several other movies in this book, this one sits uncomfortably between success and failure: never achieving its potential, and aggravating viewers with the promise of what could have been.

THIS YEAR IN GAMING

In 1994, while attending GenCon 27, RPG designer Shane Lacy Hensley saw the cover art for an upcoming sourcebook from White Wolf Studios: *Necropolis: Atlanta* for their *Wraith: The Oblivion* line. The striking image of an undead Confederate soldier by artist Brom inspired Hensley to develop a unique new roleplaying game. Drawing on his affection for spaghetti westerns and gothic horror, he released the first edition of *Deadlands: The Weird West*—Pinnacle Entertainment Group's first roleplaying game—at GenCon in 1996, to critical acclaim . . . and a few Origins awards the following year. Sporting a cover by Brom (of course) and an exotic combination of Old West adventure and mad steampunk science with ancient evils, sorcery, and things that go bump in the night, the game was an immediate, huge success. It quickly proved the favorite roleplaying game setting for this author [SAW]! Supplemental material followed for seven more years, including a post-apocalyptic sequel, a version set on a faraway planet, a miniatures game, a collectible card game, a board game, and RPG conversions for use with d20 and GURPS. To celebrate the game's 10th anniversary in 2006, Pinnacle released *Deadlands: Reloaded!* for use with *Savage Worlds*.

DUNGEONS & DRAGONS

2000 • US / Czech Republic
New Line Cinema / Sweetpea Entertainment / Behaviour Worldwide / MDP Worldwide / Silver Pictures / Station X Studios / Stillking Films
107m • Color • PG-13

Writers: Topper Lilien and Carroll Cartwright
Based on: the *Dungeons & Dragons* Property owned by Wizards Of The Coast, Inc.
Director: Courtney Solomon
Producers: Courtney Solomon, Kia Jam, and Tom Hammel
Music: Justin Caine Burnett
Director of Photography: Doug Milsome
Production Designer: Bryce Perrin
Art Directors: Jindrich Kocí and Ricardo Spinace
Costume Designer: Barbara Lane
Special Effects: John Frederick Bryant, George Gibbs, and Peter Hawkins
Special Mechanical Effects Supervisor: George Gibbs
Creatures, Weapons, And Armor Designed By: Tully Summers
Armorer: Petr Bousek
Stunt Coordinators: Graeme Crowther and Petr Drozda
Cast: Justin Whalin (Ridley Freeborn), Marlon Wayans (Snails), Zoe McLellan (Marina Pretensa), Thora Birch (Empress Savina), Kristen Wilson (Norda), Richard O'Brien (Xilus), Tom Baker (Halvarth), Lee Arenberg (Elwood Gutworthy), Edward Jewesbury (Vildan Vildir), Robert Miano (Azmath), Bruce Payne (Damodar), Jeremy Irons (Profion), Tomas Havrlik (Mage), Martin Astles (Orc #1), Matthew O'Toole (Orc #2), David O'Kelly (Three Eyes), Kia Jam (Thief #1), Nicolas Rochette (Thief #2), David Mandis (Thief #3), Robert Henny (Crimson Brigade), Stanislaw Ondricek (Another Mage), Roman Hemala (Council Mage), Andrew Blau (Elf #1), Marta Urbanova (Elf #2), and Jiri Machacek (Loyalist General)
Alternate Titles: *Dungeons & Dragons: The Movie* and *Dungeons & Dragons I*

ON THE MAP

We're in the empire of Izmer, a divided land ruled by a council of mages and a benevolent empress at its heart, the capital city of Sumdall.

OUR STORY SO FAR

Dark mage Profion wishes to depose Empress Savina and assume control of Izmer. Savina controls gold dragons, so to wage war, Profion must secure the Rod of Savrille, a magical scepter that can control red dragons. He sends the evil Damodar to find it, but Ridley Freeborn and his companions reluctantly quest for the rod to find it first.

> Adventure hinges on more than just a throw of the dice.

ALTERNATE VERSIONS

Several scenes cut primarily for budgetary reasons all appear in the DVD and Blu-ray releases. A few audio modifications to the original theatrical UK release reduce the impact of violent scenes to drop the rating from a "15" to a "12." These changes are reversed in the UK DVD and Blu-ray releases.

IT'S MAGIC

Because director Courtney Solomon intended the movie to faithfully represent the *Dungeons & Dragons* roleplaying-game universe, magic tends—for the most part—to obey laws and depict spells as described in the various rulebooks spanning multiple editions. We see references to the "Feeblemind" spell, some version of "Teleport" used multiple times, "Magic Missile," "Hold Person," and even a form of "Repulsion." The fact that Marina can cast some of these spells suggests that within the framework of the *Dungeons & Dragons* universe—despite Ridley commenting on her status as a "low-level" mage—she is at least a fifth-level wizard (though her pre-generated character in the free tie-in promotional materials from Wizards of the Coast is third level). Profion and his fellow mages are clearly all very high-level magic-users capable of wielding powerful spells.

THE QUEST FOR MEANING

The film explores the value of friendship throughout, which only makes sense, considering the concept of the allied adventuring party in most roleplaying games. There's strength in numbers against often incredible odds presented by a games master; splitting the party can lead to pain, suffering, and character death . . . as we see depicted so brutally in the film with the death of Snails at the savage hands of Damodar.

The almost brotherly bond between Ridley and Snails from the outset suggests a long history. Snails' murder could effectively have ended the adventure, because Ridley on his own, motivated solely by revenge, would probably have rushed straight to his own destruction. Thanks to the presence of Marina, Norda, and Elwood, he shakes off the tragedy and pushes on, motivated by the loftier and morally correct goals that inspired the quest in the first place. The death of Snails also matures Ridley as he says farewell to his childhood companion and focuses his attention on Marina and their growing love. Of course, once Ridley explores this aspect of his journey into adulthood, Snails somehow reaches out from beyond the grave, reconnects with his best friend, and draws them all into a new adventure—one we will never see (for better or for worse).

WHO GOES THERE?

Justin Whalin won a Daytime Emmy Award for his role as the son of a lesbian couple in a 1994 CBS after-school special. His first big-screen appearance was in 1988's *The Dead Pool*. You can also find him in the films *Child's Play 3*, *Serial Mom*, *Blood of Beasts*, and *Super Capers*. Audiences might remember him best as Jimmy Olsen (a role he took over from Michael Landes) on TV's *Lois & Clark: The New Adventures of Superman*, but he also had TV roles in *Charles in Charge*, *The Wonder Years*, *Blossom*, and *It Had to Be You*.

THIS IS NO GAME. One of the seemingly infinite Wayans family of entertainers, Marlon is an accomplished comedic and dramatic actor, as well as a writer and producer. He got his start in *I'm Gonna Git You Sucka* (written and directed by older brother Keenan Ivory Wayans). Other notable films include *Mo' Money*, *Above the Rim*, *Requiem for a Dream*, *Scary Movie*, *Scary Movie 2*, *The Ladykillers*, *G.I. Joe: The Rise of Cobra* (in the role of Ripcord), and *A Haunted House* and its sequel. He was also a series regular on the sketch comedy show *In Living Color* and in the sitcom *The Wayans Bros.* (with brother Shawn).

Zoe McLellan has worked primarily in television, appearing in *Nowhere Man*, *Sliders*, *Star Trek: Voyager*, *The Invisible Man*, *JAG*, *Dirty Sexy Money*, *House M.D.*, *NCIS*, and *NCIS: New Orleans*.

Thora Birch is the type of actor who seems to reinvent herself in every role. She debuted in the family-friendly comedy *Purple People Eater* and also had recurring parts in a few TV series, including *Day by Day* and *Parenthood*. She played the president's daughter in *Patriot Games* and *Clear and Present Danger*, and also appeared (often in quirky roles) in *Hocus Pocus*, *Monkey Trouble*, *Alaska*, *American Beauty*, *Ghost World*, *Silver City*, *Deadline*, and *Winter of Frozen Dreams*.

Kristen Wilson played Dr. John Dolittle's wife in three of the *Dr. Dolittle* films. She also appeared in *Bulletproof*, *Confessions of a Dangerous Mind*, *Walking Tall*, and *Mega Python vs. Gatoroid*.

The world knows Richard O'Brien as Riff Raff of *The Rocky Horror Picture Show*. Not only did he write the stage musical upon which the film was based; he also created the catchy tunes that haunt us to this day. He wrote and costarred in the pseudo-sequel, *Shock Treatment*, released a few years later, and has also appeared in the films *The Odd Job*, *Flash Gordon*, *Dark City*, *Ever After: A Cinderella Story*, and *Elvira's Haunted Hills*. On television, he hosted the British children's game show *The Crystal Maze* and portrayed the villainous Gulnar in *Robin of Sherwood*. More recently, he lent his distinctive voice to the cartoon series *Phineas and Ferb*.

One of the founding members (alongside Tim Robbins) of The Actors' Gang (one of Los Angeles's oldest theater companies), Lee Arenberg has been acting since 1987, starting with small film roles in the comedies *The Underachievers* and *Cross My Heart*. He has appeared in a number of notable genre films since then, including *Martians Go Home*, *Brain Dead*, *Class of 1999*, *RoboCop 3*, *Freaked*, *Waterworld*, and *Warriors of Virtue*, but viewers probably know him best for his role as Pintel in the first three *Pirates of the Caribbean* films. He's also racked up numerous TV appearances in *Tales from the Crypt*, *Seinfeld*, *Lois & Clark: The New Adventures of Superman*, *Charmed*, *Scrubs*, *Once Upon a Time*, and every *Star Trek* series from *The Next Generation* through *Enterprise*.

A member of Kenneth Branagh's Renaissance Players, Edward Jewesbury had a very long and respectable acting career going back to the 1930s. Though the majority of his roles were on the small screen, he made an impression in films such as *Henry V*, *Much Ado About Nothing*, *Frankenstein*, and *Richard III*. He died in 2001 at age 83.

Since his first role as a mugger in the original *Death Wish*, now-veteran actor Robert Miano has worked nonstop. You can find him in films like *Chained Heat*, *Firestarter*, *Fear City*, *The Rain Killer*, *Donnie Brasco*, and *Fast & Furious*, as well as in TV shows like *The Amazing Spider-Man*, *CHiPs*, *Fantasy Island*, *T.J. Hooker*, *The A-Team*, and many more.

Classically trained actor Bruce Payne's first feature-film role was alongside Monty Python alumnus John Cleese in *Privates on Parade*. He also appeared in *The Keep*, *Solarbabies*, *Howling*

VI: The Freaks, Passenger 57, Warlock III: The End of Innocence, Highlander: Endgame, and the sequel to this film, *Dungeons & Dragons: Wrath of the Dragon God* (in which Damodar has lost his strange blue lips).

Jeremy Irons won an Oscar for *Reversal of Fortune*, as well as a few Emmys, some Golden Globes, a SAG Award, and even an Annie for his portrayal of Scar in *The Lion King*. Other feature films of interest include *The Mission, Dead Ringers*, the surreal *Kafka, Die Hard: With a Vengeance, The Man in the Iron Mask, The Time Machine, Kingdom of Heaven*, and *Eragon*. On television, he's had roles in the miniseries *Brideshead Revisited, Law & Order: Special Victims Unit*, and *The Borgias*.

David O'Kelly appeared in different roles in the TV adaptations of *Dune* and its sequel *Children of Dune*, as well as in a handful of C-grade science-fiction "Czechploitation" flicks, including *Chained Rage: Slave to Love, Rage of the Innocents*, and *Dakota Bound*. He also appears in *The Prince and Me* and *The Illusionist*.

6 DEGREES OF SORCERY

The opening of *Eragon* reproduces this movie's opening sequence of moving through clouds—and it also features Jeremy Irons and some dragons. The dragon in the lab is dispatched in a similar fashion to the Rancor in *Star Wars: Return of the Jedi*. Ridley says "trust me" in typical Indiana Jones style: not the last Indy nod in the film, as you will see. The twin moons are a nod to *Krull* as well as a nocturnal nod to Tattooine and its twin suns in *Star Wars*. The political nonsense against the empress is just as convoluted as when Palpatine plots against Amidala in the *Star Wars* prequels, down to the vote—although all this is purely coincidental, because these scenes were written years before the release of *Episode I* (just lucky, we guess). The magic school resembles Hogwarts. Snails screams like Chris Tucker's Ruby Rhod from *The Fifth Element*.

As noted in **It's Magic**, some of the spell names and other references come directly from the *Dungeons & Dragons* core rules. The tavern's design represents the stereotypical *D&D* tavern, and the beholders also come from the *Dungeons & Dragons* universe, being unique to the game.

A crossbow bolt strikes Elwood in the helmet in the same way that an arrow hits Brown Tom in the "brain pan" in *Legend*. To escape from Damodar, the group uses a trash chute just like the group in *Star Wars*. The creature is placed in Damodar's body in a similar way to the insertion of the Ceti Alpha V creatures into Commander Chekov's and Captain Terrell's ears in *Star Trek II: The Wrath of Khan*. Profion's assurance that the creature will be removed once Damodar succeeds in his quest harkens back to a similar promise made to Snake Plissken in *Escape from New York*.

The musical sting that announces Damodar's entrance in the tavern is similar to the imperial march in the *Star Wars* films. The orcs look a bit like the Garthim from *The Dark Crystal*, at least from the back. The work of legendary fantasy artist Chris Achilleos inspired Norda's chest plate. Xilus allows people into his elaborate maze to face a number of challenges in the same way that O'Brien, as himself, allowed contestants into his maze in the early '90s *Dungeons & Dragons*–inspired British game show, *The Crystal Maze*. Breaking a light beam in the maze releases a trap much like one in the temple at the start of *Raiders of the Lost Ark*,

THE GAME HAS JUST BEGUN.

and the Eye of the Dragon—the gem at the maze's heart—resembles the Chachapoyan fertility idol from the same film and sequence.

The rotating tiles in the flame-filled corridor of eyes are a deliberate deception that might be a nod to the reorientation of similar stone slabs to confuse Sarah in *Labyrinth*. A bit of a retroactive in-joke about this entire fiery sequence of the film appears in a two-page painting in the "Skills" chapter of the fourth edition of the *Player's Handbook*.

The long-distance conversation between Savina and Norda reflects—pun intended—the evil queen's consultation with the magic mirror in *Snow White and the Seven Dwarfs*. The elves' healing of Ridley's life-threatening stab wound, and his subsequent recovery in their village, is similar to Frodo's experiences in Rivendell in *The Lord of the Rings: The Fellowship of the Ring*. The Rod of Savrille possesses a corrupting influence akin to that of the One Ring in those films. Ridley sliding through the tunnel in the caves harkens back to *The Goonies*. The swordfight between Ridley and Damodar is very much a *Star Wars* lightsaber duel, even down to the "electrified" coloration of the swords—"heroic" blue for Ridley and "evil" red for Damodar.

SHATTERING THE ILLUSION

In the mid-1980s, a young director named James Cameron (perhaps you've heard of him) and practical-special-effects wizard Stan Winston approached TSR's manager, Lorraine Williams, with the intent of securing the *Dungeons & Dragons* license for a feature film. Cameron wished to produce, with Winston in the director's chair. Rumors abound as to exactly what transpired in that meeting—including one in which Williams physically chased the two movie heavyweights out of TSR—but they never reached an agreement, and the world never saw a Cameron-produced *Dungeons & Dragons* feature. According to Dave Arneson, this was not the only time a big-name director had approached TSR. He recalls that both George Lucas and Steven Spielberg expressed interest as well!

When it finally happened with Courtney Solomon at the helm, the estimated budget for Solomon's first draft of the script was $125 million: too much. The resulting adjustments included the removal, sadly, of numerous sequences, including an elaborate dungeon crawl featuring iconic *D&D* monsters, such as carrion crawlers and giant spiders.

During script read-throughs in Prague, word came that Jeremy Irons had been cast as Profion. Irons had recently purchased Kilcoe Castle in Count Cork, Ireland. He has since stated that he accepted the role because of that; he had to pay for it somehow.

Actor Bruce Payne performed the film's opening narration using a slightly different voice than the one he used for Damodar. Principal photography began with the scenes of the Antius market in a castle and featured 300 extras. The first dialogue scenes shot were those involving Richard O'Brien.

Irons' first day of shooting—a jam-packed, twenty-one-hour workday—was in the Sedlec Ossuary of the incredible Cemetery Church of All Saints, also known as the Bone Church, located about an hour from Prague in the city of Kutná Hora. *Dungeons & Dragons* was the first production allowed to shoot in

ADVENTURE WILL NEVER BE THE SAME.

that historic location, although it would not be the last.

This was Irons' first experience performing for CG and in front of a blue screen. It took him a little while to get used to working with things like forty-foot sticks with googly eyes mounted on them to ensure accurate eye-lines for the post-production insertion of computer-generated dragon models.

> THIS IS MORE THAN A GAME . . .

The dragons were accomplished via motion-capture, with actors performing their movements ahead of time, although the massive dragon skeleton was a beautifully executed fifty-foot prop. The winged imp replaced a "pocket dragon" cut from the script prior to production.

Because production had access to Marlon Wayans only for a few short days—he was simultaneously shooting *Requiem for a Dream* back in New York—all his scenes had to be shot out of sequence and with great haste. A number of alternate, often foul-mouthed, takes with Wayans exist that would have dramatically shifted the final MPAA rating of the film! His constant improvisation kept his costars, particularly Justin Whalin, on their toes. The most unpleasant sequence for Wayans involved the rug trap, with its submerged mechanical lift and hundreds of gallons of rancid oatmeal, all done in one take. Some of the oatmeal had to remain on Wayans' costume for certain scenes, and the stench accompanied him everywhere he went.

The Crimson Brigade soldiers who accompany Damodar were meant to have a slight Nazi vibe to them, but Solomon strongly disliked the results. One costume choice that Solomon *did* approve was the deliberate use of black for the "real" Profion and bright white for his friendlier persona in the council chambers.

Academy Award–winning special-effects supervisor George Gibbs designed the maze, one of Whalin's favorite sequences—although Whalin almost didn't leave the set unscathed, because the falling-pendulum trap came dangerously close to him when released. That part appears in the film.

Overall, the movie featured 517 digital shots, a shocking 284 of which appeared in the seven-minute climactic battle sequence. This alone explains the year and a half it took to complete post-production.

Besides Whalin's close call, a few notable injuries—some of which made the final cut—include Wayans getting smacked by a scroll case during the leap down the trash chute, Whalin getting knocked around and bruised during the duel with the giant warrior, a stuntman breaking his nose in the struggle against Damodar for the rod, and Whalin breaking a finger during his final fight. Fortunately, all involved had more than enough hit points to handle the damage!

The film's final scenes underwent a few changes. The first was Profion being eaten by the gold dragon, which replaced a scene much greater in scope. Another involved a final scene, apparently filmed and scrapped, that involved a *Star* Wars–like celebration in honor of the heroes. An alteration reintroduced among the DVD's special features involved Ridley at Snails' grave. The original version had a more melancholy, final quality to it.

MUSIC OF THE MINSTRELS

This was Justin Caine Burnett's first big solo score. Prior to this, he had worked as a composer's assistant on such films as *The Rock*, *Armageddon*, and *The Peacemaker*. He clearly draws

IT'S NO GAME!

inspiration from the likes of Howard Shore, John Williams, and Hans Zimmer (under whom he trained), but in no way is this a negative. Some consider this one of the best scores of 2000.

Featuring the West Australian Symphony Orchestra, the soundtrack is a must-have for any gaming table. The piece Burnett composed for the maze is one of the strongest. Watertower Music, a division of Warner Bros., handled the official soundtrack's release, which featured fourteen tracks directly from the score and one high-energy bonus track titled "This Is Not a Game," credited to Fountains of Wayne bassist Adam Schlesinger and advertising jingle composer Steven M. Gold, under the name Buck 250.

THE SAGA CONTINUES

Neil Barrett, Jr. novelized the film in paperback form, and John Baxter authored a glossy 128-page book on the making of the movie, both published by Wizards of the Coast. The original DVD release contained additional DVD-ROM content, including "Fastplay" printable gaming materials so you could roleplay as Ridley, Marina, Elwood, or Snails in an adventure titled *The Sewers of Sumdall*.

This film has two sequels. *Dungeons & Dragons: Wrath of the Dragon God* (2006) is a superior film in some ways despite a much smaller budget. *Dungeons & Dragons: The Book of Vile Darkness* was a 2012 tie-in TV-movie originally meant to synchronize with the release of a 2011 *Dungeons & Dragons* fourth-edition game product bearing the same name. Both sequels credit Courtney Solomon as executive producer, with producer Steve Richards also along for the long game.

In May 2012, Warner Bros. announced that it had acquired the rights to produce a big-budget *Dungeons & Dragons* film, scripted by *Wrath of the Titans* writer David Leslie Johnson. Oddly, his original script, titled *Chainmail*, drew inspiration from the pre-*D&D* miniature-battle rules of the same name cowritten by Gary Gygax and Jeff Perren and released in 1971. Other names linked to the production included executive producer Alan Zeman, producer Roy Lee and, yes, producer Courtney Solomon. Alas, only days after that announcement, Hasbro—owners of Wizards of the Coast—claimed that it had a feature film in development with Universal, not Warner Bros., in the hands of Chris Morgan (writer of several of *The Fast and the Furious* films). This launched a long-running and messy legal battle between the studios.

The Monday after GenCon 2015, the announcement came that Warner Bros., Hasbro's Allspark Pictures, and Sweetpea Entertainment had come to an "undisclosed arrangement," ending the lawsuit and ensuring production of a David Leslie Johnson–scripted big-budget feature. Regardless of the budget and scope, we assume Jeremy Irons will sit this one out.

TAKE UP THY SWORD!

DRAGON-EYE RUBY (MAGICAL ITEM)

This mysterious egg-sized ruby possesses properties both mechanical and magical. On the one hand, it acts as a key when inserted into the eye socket of a dragon statue. By balancing a locking mechanism, it allows entry into a vast treasure trove.

On the other, far more secretive hand, the ruby can resurrect the dead (per the spell) and function as a focusing device for a long-distance, intraplanar spell of teleportation. In ancient times, the owner of the stone utilized its teleportation ability to shift people and items across great distances. This stone is the means by which the contents of the aforementioned treasure trove arrived.

THE FILM'S DESTINY

Okay, so it was never going to win any awards or inspire millions of people to rush out to their game shops and purchase *Dungeons & Dragons*. But despite a massive pile of insanely negative reviews, this movie really isn't all that bad. Please put the torches down and listen: This author [SAW] admits to having a strong adverse reaction the first time, but my feelings have mellowed with age and I now find myself amused—or is that bemused?—by it. Aware of the numerous problems that plagued production, the biggest of which was lack of funds, an open-minded sort might nonetheless find that the film is still a fun adventure worthy of at least one viewing. It dares to stray from the fun-adventure path and bravely presents us with a pretty brutal and tragic death scene that significantly shifts the tone, even elevating it slightly.

The movie's fair share of problems includes the cringeworthy, over-the-top performance of Jeremy Irons, which some have said should have made him surrender his Oscar. There are plenty of reasons for annoyance with Marlon Wayans' half-assed performance as well. Despite the efforts of what for the time was a competent crew of CG artists, a lot of the rendered environments and monsters come across as crude, especially considering that the shockingly convincing dinos of *Jurassic Park* had graced screens seven years before.

Keep your eyes peeled during the end credits for this amusing disclaimer: "No dragons or other animals were hurt or injured during the filming of this motion picture." Cute.

THIS YEAR IN GAMING

The year 2000 was an incredibly significant one for *Dungeons & Dragons* and parent company Wizards of the Coast. Though this movie was almost universally panned, it pushed the brand back into the public consciousness in time to celebrate the release of the roleplaying game's third edition, released at GenCon 33 (in August) after almost three years of development and a year and a half of closed playtesting. Wizards released the three core books—*The Player's Handbook, The Dungeon Master's Guide,* and *The Monster Manual*—simultaneously to allow players to dive right into that radically reworked update to the first and second editions. It drew concepts from previously published RPG lines, including *Alternity,* one of TSR's final RPGs, released a couple years prior to the company's acquisition by Wizards of the Coast.

The launch of Third Edition also marked the release of both the official d20 license and the Open Gaming License that allowed publishers around the globe to produce and sell materials compatible with the Third Edition core rules. If a publisher wanted to produce *Dungeons & Dragons*–compatible products, it would have to abide by the d20 license. Publishers wanting to produce RPGs using the core rules of the d20 system could adopt the Open Gaming License. Both of these programs ultimately resulted in a glut of products of varying quality. A number of publishers rose and fell during this time.

THE LORD OF THE RINGS: THE FELLOWSHIP OF THE RING

2001 • NZ/US • NEW LINE CINEMA / WINGNUT FILMS • 178M/228M • COLOR • PG-13

SCREENPLAY: Fran Walsh, Philippa Boyens, and Peter Jackson
BASED ON THE BOOK BY: J. R. R. Tolkien
DIRECTOR: Peter Jackson
PRODUCERS: Barrie M. Osborne, Peter Jackson, Fran Walsh, and Tim Sanders
MUSIC: Howard Shore. ("May It Be" and "Aníron" composed and performed by Enya.)
DIRECTOR OF PHOTOGRAPHY: Andrew Lesnie
MAKEUP & HAIR DESIGN: Peter Owen and Peter King
SPECIAL MAKE-UP, CREATURES, ARMOUR, WEAPONS, AND MINIATURES: Richard Taylor & WETA Workshop
DIGITAL VISUAL EFFECTS DESIGNED AND CREATED BY: WETA Digital
FORD BF BRUINEN SEQUENCE BY: Digital Domain
VISUAL EFFECTS SUPERVISOR: Jim Rygiel
PRODUCTION DESIGNER: Grant Major
SUPERVISING ART DIRECTOR: Dan Hennah
COSTUME DESIGNERS: Ngila Dickson and Richard Taylor
CONCEPTUAL DESIGNERS: Alan Lee and John Howe
CULTURAL FIGHTING STYLES: Tony Woolf
TOLKIEN LANGUAGE TRANSLATION: David Salo
STUNT COORDINATOR: George Marshall Ruge
SWORDMASTER: Bob Anderson
HEAD ANIMAL WRANGLER: Dave Johnson
HORSE COORDINATOR: Stephen Old
HORSE TRAINER: Don Reynolds
CAST: Elijah Wood (Frodo Baggins); Ian McKellen (Gandalf the Grey); Liv Tyler (Arwen); Viggo Mortensen (Aragorn); Sean Astin (Samwise Gamgee); Cate Blanchett (Galadriel); John Rhys-Davies (Gimli); Billy Boyd (Peregrin "Pippin" Took); Dominic Monaghan (Meriadoc "Merry" Brandybuck); Orlando Bloom (Legolas); Christopher Lee (Saruman); Hugo Weaving (Elrond); Sean Bean (Boromir); Ian Holm (Bilbo Baggins); Andy Serkis (Gollum / Voice of the Witch-King); Marton Csokas (Celeborn); Craig Parker (Haldir); Lawrence Makoare (Lurtz); Alan Howard (Voice of the Ring); Noel Appleby (Everard Proudfoot); Sala Baker (Sauron); Peter Corrigan (Otho); Lori Dungey (Mrs. Bracegirdle); Megan Edwards (Mrs. Proudfoot); Michael Elsworth (Gondorian Archivist); Mark Ferguson (Gil-Galad); Norman Forsey (Gaffer Gamgee); William Johnson (Old Noakes); Brent McIntyre (Witch-King); Peter McKenzie (Elendil); Sarah McLeod (Rosie Cotton); Elizabeth Moody (Lobelia); Ian Mune (Bounder); Cameron Rhodes (Farmer Maggot); Martyn Sanderson (Gate Keeper); Brian Sergent (Ted Sandyman); Harry Sinclair (Isildur); David Weatherley (Barliman Butterbur); Victoria Beynon-Cole, Lee Hartley, Sam La Hood, Chris Streeter, Philip Grieve, Jonathan Jordan, Semi Kuresa, Clinton Ulyatt, Paul Bryson, Lance Fabian Kemp, Jono Manks, Ben Price, Kate O'Rourke, and Thomas McGinty (Hero Orcs, Goblins, Uruks, and Ringwraiths); Billy and Katie Jackson (Cute Hobbit Children); Timothy Bartlett (Hobbit, uncredited); Jarl Benzon (Elf, uncredited); Jorn Benzon (Rumil, uncredited); Rachel Clentworth (Goblin, uncredited); Sabine Crossen (Rivendell Elf, uncredited); Taea Hartwell (Cute Hobbit Child, uncredited); Peter Jackson (Albert Dreary, uncredited); Alan Lee (King of Men, uncredited); Bret McKenzie (Elf at Council of Elrond, uncredited); and Shane Rangi (Witch-King of Angmar, uncredited)

ON THE MAP

The journey to deliver the One Ring to the fires of Mount Doom begins in Hobbiton. Frodo and Sam head to Bree, and then attend the Council of Elrond in Rivendell, where they meet up with Gandalf, who took an ill-fated side-trip to Isengard. Together the Fellowship passes through the Mines of Moria and passes the Argonath before splitting into two smaller parties.

OUR STORY SO FAR

Middle-earth faces great danger from the growing power of the evil Sauron. Hobbit Frodo Baggins volunteers to take the One Ring of Power—a magical artifact with the potential to facilitate Sauron's victory over all the forces of good in the world—to destroy it in the fires of Mount Doom. A fellowship gathers to aid Frodo in his quest, and the journey begins ... but will the oppressive will of the Ring divide and destroy this band of heroes before they complete their mission?

ALTERNATE VERSIONS

As with the next two films in the trilogy, this one has two versions for home viewing. In our credits above and for the following two movies in the series, we defer to the extended editions.

The theatrical cut largely keeps the film as shown in theaters (with a minor difference or two that technically mean the film has three versions). An extended edition includes material that fleshes out the story and adds a number of welcome touches. One annoying quirk, however, is that it lacks one of Gandalf's first lines in the theatrical version, about being thankful that the hobbits have gone unnoticed by Sauron and the world at large. Perhaps more egregiously, for the Blu-ray release, Peter Jackson tweaked the color palette to make the entire movie greener, giving it a sickening cast that sometimes makes it seem as if you're watching through a haze of green goo.

IT'S MAGIC

This film introduces us to Middle-earth and therefore the way its magical forces operate. Magic-users can forge magic into artifacts, manipulate it at will, and draw it from nature. The methods used and manifestations enacted in different cultures say everything about the peoples who populate this fantasy world.

Magical objects have huge importance, if only because the entire plot hinges on One of them: the One Ring. Its powers are many, and it seems to have sentience, seeking out those who might suit its purposes and weighing heavily upon them (literally) as it corrupts their spirits. It physically sizes itself to fit its wearer's finger, manifests a runic inscription only when exposed to flame, and offers its bearers unnaturally long (and tortured) life.

> ONE RING TO RULE THEM ALL, ONE RING TO FIND THEM, ONE RING TO BRING THEM ALL, AND IN THE DARKNESS BIND THEM.

THE LEGEND COMES TO LIFE

One of the most intriguing visual depictions of magic in this series—and one that carries all the way through to *The Hobbit* films—is the "shadow realm," into which the Ring's wearer shifts while becoming invisible in the ordinary world. Therein, a storm and the windswept, desaturated reality of the Ringwraiths make it a frightening, inhospitable place, perhaps demonstrating the ravaging forces that act upon anyone who dabbles in that power and takes on the weight of the Ring.

Enchanted objects behave in other ways, too. For example, runes etched on a door can prevent entry except by the proper spoken incantation. Exactly how power binds to these physical artifacts is unclear. When Gandalf and Saruman wield their staves, they seem to use them actively to direct or manipulate magical energy, like giant wands. Bilbo's sword Sting glows blue when orcs (or goblins) are nearby . . . except when the producers lost track of when it should do that. In one of the less-physical manifestations of magic, Gandalf has a rapport with winged creatures like butterflies and eagles: a profound connection to nature and life that later comes up as one of the most significant traits of his wizard colleague, Radagast, in *The Hobbit* prequels.

Sting is one of many elven weapons; the race of elves has a particular affinity for magic. Galadriel's mirror serves as a crystal ball, showing its viewer a possible future. The elves' silvery mithril mail rests lightly on its wearers but provides protection equivalent to that of dragon scales. Elven medicine is the only thing that can combat the evil magic of a Morgul blade . . . but even then, a wound sustained from such an evil weapon never truly heals.

THE QUEST FOR MEANING

This is a campaign setting brought to life in a way that few other films or movie series have managed, which is really no surprise, because Tolkien, among others, helped fuel the imaginations that led to RPGs like *Dungeons & Dragons* and its imitators. The themes underlying this complex saga can overwhelm—after all, entire books discuss them already. This first film starts off small for a reason, though, so let's follow the same path.

Recurring elements pervade the series and many other films in this book, such as the idea of nature versus mechanized industry (to say nothing of the emergence of connective technology—that One Ring does link with all the others, just as the Palantírs provide a global communications network). We also see the passage of time and knowledge as an old era gives way to a new. Disturbingly, the heroes are all white-skinned humans (or at least familiar-looking humanoids), and the villains are dark-skinned monsters.

Here at the beginning of all things (see what we did there?), one of the strongest messages is about what it means to leave home. It's a childlike feeling: that first day off to school, or that first time you venture past the boundaries of your own neighborhood. Suddenly a larger world comes into focus. For Frodo, even more than for Bilbo years earlier, the beginning of this journey is the beginning of maturation and wisdom. Sadly, in gaining a world, Frodo loses not only his innocence but eventually his future. Fortunately, his sacrifice ensures that the world *does* have a future. His powerful legacy will surely resonate into the Fourth Age.

WHO GOES THERE?

Gwaihir-eyed moviegoers might remember a tiny Elijah Wood making a brief first film appearance in *Back to the Future Part II*, although he had a much larger role in *Avalon*. He went on to roles in the movies *Radio Flyer*, *Flipper*, *Spy Kids 3-D: Game Over*, *Eternal Sunshine of the Spotless Mind*, *Sin City* (as a seriously depraved murderer), *Happy Feet* and *Happy Feet Two* (as the voice of Mumble), and the remake of the slasher film *Maniac* (as another seriously depraved murderer ... did the Ring have that much of an effect?). He returned to play Frodo in *The Hobbit: An Unexpected Journey*, played Ryan on the very odd television show *Wilfred*, and provided his voice for the animated film *9*, various episodes of *Robot Chicken* and the *TRON: Uprising* TV series, *The Legend of Spyro* videogames, and *The Lord of the Rings* tie-in games.

Sir Ian McKellen's extensive Shakespearean and other theater work honed the skills he would bring to an eclectic film career. He had an uncredited role in *Corvette Summer* and played D. H. Lawrence in *Priest of Love*. He also appeared in *The Keep*, *Last Action Hero* (as a Bergman-esque Death), *Six Degrees of Separation*, *The Shadow*, *Gods and Monsters* (as director James Whale), *Apt Pupil*, *The Da Vinci Code*, *Stardust*, and *The Golden Compass*. He played Number 2 in the 2009 TV miniseries version of *The Prisoner*, was the voice of the Great Intelligence in the 2012 *Doctor Who* Christmas special "The Snowmen," and played Magneto in *X-Men* and its four follow-up films. He also returned as Gandalf in *The Hobbit* trilogy.

The daughter of Aerosmith's Steven Tyler, Liv Tyler got her first big pop-culture exposure—somewhat creepily—as a model alongside a young Alicia Silverstone in Aerosmith's music video for the song "Crazy." She had roles in the films *Empire Records*, *That Thing You Do!*, *Armageddon*, *Jersey Girl*, *The Strangers*, and *The Incredible Hulk*.

Viggo Mortensen's first film role was a small appearance in *Witness*. He went on to appear in *Leatherface: Texas Chainsaw Massacre III*, *Young Guns II*, *Crimson Tide*, the ill-advised remake of *Psycho*, *Hidalgo*, *A History of Violence*, and *The Road*.

Sean Astin came from an acting dynasty. He made his feature-film debut in *The Goonies* and followed that up with roles in *Toy Soldiers*, *Encino Man*, *50 First Dates*, and *Slipstream*. He also appeared in the TV series *Jeremiah*, *24*, *Alphas*, and *The Strain*, was the voice of *Special Agent Oso*, and played Raphael in the revival of *Teenage Mutant Ninja Turtles*. Like some of his *Lord of the Rings* costars, he voiced his character for a variety of tie-in videogames.

Cate Blanchett has a number of theater credits. She also appeared as the titular queen in *Elizabeth* and *Elizabeth: The Golden Age*, as well as in films like *The Life Aquatic with Steve Zissou*, *The Aviator* (as Hollywood legend Katharine Hepburn), *Hot Fuzz* (uncredited and under a mask), *Indiana Jones and the Kingdom of the Crystal Skull* (it hurt just to type that), *The Curious Case of Benjamin Button*, the 2010 *Robin Hood*, and *How to Train Your Dragon 2* as the voice of Valka. She returned as Galadriel for *The Hobbit* trilogy.

John Rhys-Davies had already achieved lasting pop-culture fame as Indiana Jones' friend Sallah in *Raiders of the Lost Ark* and *Indiana Jones and the Last Crusade*, as well as from his appearances in early (better) episodes of the time- and dimension-hopping television series *Sliders*. With more than 200 acting credits to his name, he has been a ubiquitous presence. He played roles in the *I, Claudius* television miniseries, more TV shows and TV movies than we can list here (including voices for numerous animated series and videogames), and films like *Sphinx, Sword of the Valiant: The Legend of Sir Gawain and the Green Knight, King Solomon's Mines, The Living Daylights, Waxwork, The Lost World, Return to the Lost World, Sinbad: Beyond the Veil of Mists, The Princess Diaries 2: Royal Engagement*, and *In the Name of the King: A Dungeon Siege Tale.*

Billy Boyd went on to play the voice of Glen (or Glenda) in *Seed of Chucky* and also provided his voice for several *Lord of the Rings* videogames.

Besides joining costar Boyd in voicing his character for tie-in videogames, Dominic Monaghan appeared in *X-Men Origins: Wolverine* and had regular roles in the TV series *Lost* and *FlashForward.*

Orlando Bloom scored two major franchises one after the other, following up his elven role in *The Lord of the Rings* films (to which he returned in the last two *Hobbit* films) with the role of Will Turner in the first three *Pirates of the Caribbean* movies. He also appeared in *Black Hawk Down, Troy, Kingdom of Heaven*, and the 2011 version of *The Three Musketeers.*

Hugo Weaving has probably heard "Welcome to Rivendell, Mr. Baggins" (which Elrond never says, but you know that) more than once, because a similar greeting is one of his quotable lines as Agent Smith in *The Matrix* film trilogy. He has also appeared in *The Adventures of Priscilla, Queen of the Desert; Babe* and *Babe: Pig in the City* (as the voice of Rex); *V for Vendetta* (playing the entire lead role under a mask); *The Wolfman; Legend of the Guardians: The Owls of Ga'Hoole* (playing the voices of two characters); and *Captain America: The First Avenger* (as the Red Skull). He returned to play Elrond in a number of *The Lord of the Rings* videogames and the first and last *Hobbit* films. He has made dismissive statements about his voice work as Megatron in the *Transformers* movies.

Sean Bean often plays characters who don't have much luck, in films such as *Patriot Games, Black Beauty, GoldenEye, Ronin, Troy, National Treasure, The Island, Silent Hill*, the remake of *The Hitcher, Percy Jackson & the Olympians: The Lightning Thief* (as Zeus!), and *Silent Hill: Revelation 3D*. On television, he has appeared in a series of TV movies based on the Richard Sharpe books by Bernard Cornwell, a role to which he returned as recently as 2008, but HBO viewers now know him best as Ned Stark from the first season of *Game of Thrones*. (Spoiler: we told you he never has much luck.)

Sir Ian Holm had an extensive and occasionally dangerous theater background in the Royal Shakespeare Company. Laurence Olivier nicked Holm's finger in a swordfight while performing *Coriolanus*. After appearing in TV miniseries like *Jesus of Nazareth* and *Holocaust*, as well as a TV-movie adaptation of *The Thief of Baghdad*, Holm caught genre fans' attention as Ash in *Alien*. Other film roles include *Chariots of Fire, Time Bandits, Greystoke: The Legend of Tarzan, Lord of the Apes, Brazil,* Mel Gibson's *Hamlet, Naked Lunch*, Kenneth Branagh's *Frankenstein, The Fifth Element, eXistenZ, From Hell, The Day After Tomorrow*, and *Ratatouille* (as the voice of Skinner). In a fun bit of pop-culture synergy, he played Frodo in a 1981 BBC Radio production of *The Lord of the Rings*, only to return to play his own uncle Bilbo, a role to which he returned in the first and last *Hobbit* movies.

> EVEN THE SMALLEST PERSON CAN CHANGE THE COURSE OF THE FUTURE. FELLOWSHIP WILL PROTECT HIM. EVIL WILL HUNT THEM.

Andy Serkis had a variety of television and film roles—including playing Bill Sikes in a TV miniseries version of *Oliver Twist*—before Gollum catapulted him to worldwide fame and made him the go-to performer for motion-capture creations with personality. He went on to "play" King Kong in Peter Jackson's 2005 remake and appeared in human form as Lumpy. He was Capricorn in *Inkheart*, Hare alongside Simon Pegg's Burke in *Burke and Hare*, and Caesar in *Rise of the Planet of the Apes* and *Dawn of the Planet of the Apes*. He also played roles in *The Adventures of Tintin*, *Avengers: Age of Ultron*, and *Star Wars: Episode VII—The Force Awakens*. In addition to returning as Gollum in *The Hobbit: An Unexpected Journey*, Serkis shouldered extra responsibility as second unit director for the entire *Hobbit* trilogy.

Marton Csokas is often a reliably menacing presence, appearing on television in *The Ray Bradbury Theater*, *Hercules: The Legendary Journeys*, *Farscape*, *BeastMaster*, *Cleopatra 2525*, *Xena: Warrior Princess*, and *Rogue*, and in films such as *Star Wars: Episode II—Attack of the Clones* (in voice only), *xXx*, *The Bourne Supremacy*, *Kingdom of Heaven*, *Æon Flux*, *Alice in Wonderland*, *Abraham Lincoln: Vampire Hunter*, *The Amazing Spider-Man 2*, and *Sin City: A Dame to Kill For*.

Craig Parker had roles in TV shows like *Xena: Warrior Princess*, two *Power Rangers* shows, *Spartacus: War of the Damned*, and *Reign*, as well as in movies, such as *The Lord of the Rings: The Two Towers* (returning as Haldir), and *Underworld: Rise of the Lycans*.

Lawrence Makoare appeared on *Xena: Warrior Princess* and *Young Hercules*, played Mr. Kil in *Die Another Day*, and returned to Middle-earth in *The Lord of the Rings: The Return of the King* and *The Hobbit: The Desolation of Smaug*.

Sala Baker returned for the next two *Lord of the Rings* films and had an uncredited appearance in the 2009 *Star Trek*.

Peter Corrigan is not the character that this author [ATB] always wrote about in childhood fiction (not sure why that name always came up), but he did have a role in *King Kong*.

Lori Dungey is one of many in this list who appeared in the television series *Xena: Warrior Princess* and *Hercules: The Legendary Journeys*. She also appeared in *Young Hercules* and a plethora of *Power Rangers* shows.

Mark Ferguson was Prometheus in *Hercules: The Legendary Journeys—Hercules and the Circle of Fire* and was Hades in *Hercules in the Underworld*. He then appeared in the *Hercules* series, *Xena: Warrior Princess* (in multiple roles), *Cleopatra 2525*, two *Power Rangers* shows, and *Spartacus: War of the Damned*.

Norman Forsey played multiple roles in *Hercules: The Legendary Journeys* and *Xena: Warrior Princess*.

William Johnson also did his duty on *Xena: Warrior Princess* and *Hercules: The Legendary Journeys*, and appeared in the films *Ocean's Eleven* and *King Kong*.

Peter McKenzie appeared in *King Kong*. He also happens to be Bret (Figwit/Lindir) McKenzie's father.

Sarah McLeod's Rosie turns up again in *The Lord of the Rings: The Return of the King* to marry dear Sam.

Elizabeth Moody was Mum in *Dead Alive*. She died in 2010 at age 70.

Ian Mune appeared in the TV shows *The Ray Bradbury Theater* and *Hercules: The Legendary Journeys*.

Cameron Rhodes was in *Xena: Warrior Princess* and numerous *Power Rangers* series, and lent his voice to the Gryphon in *The Chronicles of Narnia: The Lion, the Witch and the Wardrobe*.

Martyn Sanderson played a variety of roles in *Hercules: The Legendary Journeys* and two of its TV-movie predecessors. He died in 2009 at age 71.

Brian Sergent did voices for *Meet the Feebles* and *The Hobbit: The Desolation of Smaug*, and appeared in two episodes of *The Ray Bradbury Theater*.

Harry Sinclair also appeared in *Dead Alive*.

David Weatherley did the TV rounds in *Xena: Warrior Princess, Hercules: The Legendary Journeys* (haven't they all?), and *Power Rangers Operation Overdrive*. He also provided a voice for the videogame *Star Wars: Knights of the Old Republic II—The Sith Lords*.

Sam La Hood was a satyr in *The Chronicles of Narnia: The Lion, the Witch and the Wardrobe* and Strigol in *30 Days of Night*.

Philip Grieve also turns up in *King Kong, Bridge to Terabithia*, and the *Spartacus: War of the Damned* television series.

Kate O'Rourke was a hag in *The Chronicles of Narnia: The Lion, the Witch and the Wardrobe* and Inika in *30 Days of Night*.

It's amazing how many kids of various races look identical in Middle-earth, because Billy and Katie Jackson turn up in both sequels as completely different children. They also wind up in New York in *King Kong*, and Katie returns for three more roles in *The Hobbit* films.

Timothy Bartlett was in *The Tommyknockers* TV-miniseries and played Master Worrywort in the first and last *Hobbit* films.

Taea Hartwell was just a baby in *The Frighteners*.

Bret McKenzie's unnamed elf became such a fan favorite, he even received the unofficial character name "Figwit." He appeared again in *The Lord of the Rings: The Return of the King* ... but *The Hobbit: An Unexpected Journey* solved (probably) the mystery of his identity: it credited him as Lindir (assuming he plays the same elf). In other circles, he is half of the musical comedy team Flight of the Conchords.

Shane Rangi also had roles in *The Lord of the Rings: The Return of the King*, the *Chronicles of Narnia* films, the *Spartacus: Gods of the Arena* STARZ TV series, and *The Hobbit: The Battle of the Five Armies*.

6 DEGREES OF SORCERY

The early incarnation of Sauron as masked, armored evil energy is similar to that of Omega in the 10th-anniversary *Doctor Who* story "The Three Doctors." Much of the portrayal of the Black Riders has direct visual links to one of Peter Jackson's favorite horror movies, *Tombs of the Blind Dead*—in particular, the way they encircle their prey at Amon Sul and their V-formation pursuit of Arwen. The water at the Ford of Bruinen takes the shapes of galloping horses just as the ocean waves take the shapes of unicorns in *The Last Unicorn*. Gandalf jumps off the edge of the tower and flies to safety on the back of an eagle, similar to the way Marty McFly dropped off the side of a tall building to catch a ride on a flying Delorean in *Back to the Future Part II*. What—too much of a stretch?

The cave-troll might have cousins who appear as the Rancor in *Star Wars: Return of the Jedi* and the mountain troll in *Harry Potter and the Sorcerer's Stone*. Bridge crossings figure in many other fantasy epics, including *The 7th Voyage of Sinbad* and *Star Wars*, to say nothing of *The Lord of the Rings* and *Hobbit* films. The towering Argonath statues are Harryhausen-esque, recalling the Colossus-like Talos and similar creations in *Jason and the Argonauts* and *Clash of the Titans*. Lurtz the Uruk-hai has a limb severed like the Black Knight of *Monty Python and the Holy Grail*. Shinzon in *Star Trek: Nemesis* steals Lurtz's bold move of pulling Aragorn's blade deeper into his own body. Sauron's link to the Ring is that of a lich to its phylactery, something that becomes an even more elaborate plot point with the Dark Lord Voldemort in the *Harry Potter* series. The sky cells seen in the TV series *Game of Thrones* echo Gandalf's place of imprisonment at the top of Isengard.

SHATTERING THE ILLUSION

The road to the making of this monumental movie achievement was as long and torturous as the ones that a few well-known hobbits trod in their own adventures. It would take an entire book—or two, or twelve—to chronicle this history in depth. Others have done just that, so we'll give you the short version.

The popularity of J. R. R. Tolkien's fantasy novel series guaranteed that one day someone would adapt it for the small or large screen. A few abortive attempts happened along the way. In one bizarre attempt to produce a *Lord of the Rings* feature film, the Beatles tried to develop a version that would feature John Lennon as Gollum, Paul McCartney as Frodo, George Harrison as Gandalf, and Ringo Starr as Samwise. *Yellow Submarine* art director and designer Heinz Edelmann was also interested in making an opera-like musically driven animated version. Director John Boorman nearly traveled to Middle-earth, too. That story appears in our chapter on *Excalibur*.

When Tolkien's world *did* make it to feature-length animation, the results were piecemeal, such as with the 1978 Ralph Bakshi film or the 1980 Rankin/Bass special that served as an unofficial sequel/conclusion to that film. (You can find both of these in our index.) Now, after the success of this recent series, the first fully produced adaptation of *The Lord of the Rings* has received more attention and appears in its entirety on YouTube.

In 1997, Peter Jackson and Fran Walsh took the Tolkien books and turned them into a ninety-page film treatment. When the project was still under the auspices of Miramax, that company insisted on making the trilogy into one film, which sent Jackson searching for another studio. At New Line, he pitched a two-movie structure. New Line replied that the saga simply had to be three films . . . and a proper trilogy was born. With the addition of third writer Philippa Boyens, the scriptwriters went to work.

Jackson relied on extensive storyboarding by illustrator Christian Rivers, as well as pre-visualization and animatics for almost everything throughout the trilogy. The goal of the

> FATE HAS CHOSEN HIM.
> A FELLOWSHIP WILL PROTECT HIM.
> EVIL WILL HUNT THEM.

Power Can Be Held In the Smallest of Things

team was to make a fairytale world seem like a realistic vision of history.

Jackson naturally recruited Tolkien artists Alan Lee and John Howe as designers, because the two men had become synonymous with Middle-earth. Not only could the production use everything the two men had drawn before, but in some cases Jackson prevailed upon them to revisit earlier artwork and expand upon it to provide additional details needed to bring those images to life. The men gave the cultures of the world distinctive styles that carried throughout architecture and wardrobe and instantly cued the audience as to which race created any given design.

Weta did often-groundbreaking digital work across all three films. In this first, it used a number of techniques to achieve the imagery of everything from the fiery Balrog to the Lovecraftian Watcher in the Water. Jackson always returned to the work of Ray Harryhausen when conceptualizing monsters for the trilogy.

Steve Regelous wrote the AI computer program Massive, which would also drive the enormous battles in the next two movies. He first used it for the army in the *Fellowship* prologue. Cast members underwent scans to create digital doubles for a variety of uses, ranging from the staircase-running sequence in Moria to Legolas's many audience-pleasing feats. When shooting the cave-troll scene, Jackson used a then-innovative technological approach, in which he viewed a virtual recreation of the set and all the characters via a monitor live on set.

It wasn't all ones and zeroes in computers or paint on canvas. A thirty-person core stunt team led by George Ruge handled many of the physical fights and gags. Some of these stuntpeople had previously worked on the New Zealand–based fantasy television series *Hercules: The Legendary Journeys* and *Xena: Warrior Princess*. As the design team devised ways to make the cultures of Middle-earth look distinctive, this team labored to create different approaches to fighting that would define the body language and movement of the various races.

Legendary swordmaster Bob Anderson trained actors and designed battles. Despite Viggo Mortensen's late casting, he not only proved up to the challenge but quickly became a favorite member of the ensemble and impressed Anderson, who called the actor the best swordsman he had ever trained.

For all those battles, Weta swordsmith Peter Lyon forged *real* weapons, and workers sat for three years linking 12.5 million plastic ringlets together for the faux chain mail in many of the costumes. They supposedly worked so hard, their fingerprints partially wore off!

Amid all the other fabrication work that created an entire universe of fantasy through 45,000 distinct props and objects—including nearly sixty "bigatures" for various architectural features, 10,000 prosthetic appliances, 1,800 pairs of hobbit feet (cooking the foam latex ran around the clock for three and a half years), and almost 20,000 costumes (forty for every lead actor and for each of their requisite body, scale, and stunt doubles)—surely the most important prop was the One Ring. Jens Hansen designed fifteen versions before basing it on co-producer Rick Porras's wedding band.

As noted earlier, Mortensen won over Bob Anderson, but Anderson wasn't the only one. The entire cast and crew had great respect for their Aragorn, especially because of his late arrival to replace original choice Stuart Townsend, whom Jackson let go one day before the start of principal photography when the director realized he just wasn't right for the part.

Cameras began rolling on the entire saga, starting with the scene of the hobbits hiding from the Ringwraiths. From there, the team was off and running, filming three movies in fifteen months, with real-world adventures at least as exciting as the story they were telling.

As with many of these films, actors suffered for their art. John Rhys-Davies had the most difficult time with his makeup. He had to deal with major skin irritation and other problems. He would eventually throw one of his dwarf "foreheads" into a fire to celebrate the conclusion of shooting when *The Return of the King* wrapped. In a river scene, Orlando Bloom had to rescue Rhys-Davies' Gimli scale double Brett Beattie when he fell out of their boat and sank in his heavy armor. During shooting of one of the last scenes, in which Sam runs into the water from the shore to catch Frodo, Sean Astin stepped on a shard of glass, which sliced into his foot and filled his prosthetic hobbit-foot with blood. None other than famous explorer Jacques Cousteau's pilot airlifted him out for medical attention.

The post-production process proved more and more difficult with each successive installment. Sound technicians had to "loop" or rerecord almost all the dialogue here for various reasons. The digital team had plenty of effects to handle, including the completion of some of them during filming, thanks to Jackson's reliance on in-camera tricks like cleverly designed sets and cagey camera angles for the scale issues between the various characters, or Christmas lights rigged to reflect in Cate Blanchett's eyes to give her that otherworldly elven look.

The film premiered in London on December 10, 2001; in LA on December 16; and then back in New Zealand on December 18. As the series went on, the Wellington premieres would take on more and more pageantry....

MUSIC OF THE MINSTRELS

Canadian composer Howard Shore had a varied early career, including a run as musical director of *Saturday Night Live* (he reportedly named the Blues Brothers during that time) and an earlier stint writing accompaniment for magician Doug Henning's *Spellbound*, but the musical magic he added to this trilogy and its successive *Hobbit* prequels will likely stand as his principal professional legacy. Employing the New Zealand Symphony Orchestra, London Philharmonic Orchestra, and numerous vocal and choral performers, Shore crafted more than ninety themes tied to the many characters and settings of Middle-earth. He worked on the project from the end of 2000 to March 2004.

To ensure that he keyed into the emotional core of the saga, Shore visited the set many times. The many leitmotifs introduced in *Fellowship* would define melodic Middle-earth for the remainder of the saga. From the melancholy strains of "The History of the Ring" and the pastoral music for the Shire and its hobbit inhabitants to the rousing heroic theme for the Fellowship, the score created a complex aural accompaniment to a world of adventure, enhanced by several vocal performances, including two songs—"May It Be" and "Aníron"—composed and sung by the world-renowned Enya.

Viggo Mortensen provided the melody for the "Song of Beren and Luthien" that Aragorn briefly sings, with Roisin Carty serving as his dialect coach. Fran Walsh wrote the lyrics for "In

Dreams," performed by soprano Edward Ross. Philippa Boyens wrote some of the choral pieces, and Tolkien scholar David Salo translated one poem.

Shore composed an additional thirty minutes of music for the extended edition of the film. In November 2001, Reprise Records released the first soundtrack for *The Fellowship of the Ring* in a regular CD edition with multiple cover designs, and in a limited version with a red leather-like box. In December 2005, Reprise brought out this film's installment in *The Complete Recordings* series on CD, with an accompanying DVD-audio featuring two stereo mixes. An "Annotated Score" was distributed for free online. As with the other two films, *Complete Recordings* liner-notes author Doug Adams chronicled the story of Shore's work on the saga in his book, *The Music of the Lord of the Rings Films*. The book included another CD, *The Rarities Archive*, which provided still more material for eager fans to hear, plus insights from Shore.

The score garnered an Oscar for Best Original Score, a Grammy for Best Score Soundtrack Album, and the World Soundtrack Award for Best Original Soundtrack: not a bad start. At least one author [ATB] can testify that Shore's pastoral "Concerning Hobbits" makes a beautiful piece of music to accompany the bride down the aisle for a wedding ceremony.

THE SAGA CONTINUES

A novelization of the film was conveniently already available, having been written by J. R. R. Tolkien decades before the film was even shot. (Yes, we're kidding.) The film trilogy continues with *The Lord of the Rings: The Two Towers* and concludes with *The Lord of the Rings: The Return of the King*, but those are for other chapters. . . .

Although we do our best in this book to chronicle the tie-ins and related items that accompany the films, some movies or properties are just too monumental. In the case of this, one of the most merchandised series of recent years, we're not going to provide anything more than a cursory sampling.

As with the following two installments, there were books, magazines, toys of all kinds (including action and plush figures), statues, sculpted environments, sword and jewelry replicas, costumes, cloaks, wedding One Rings, and so on. WETA and Sideshow Collectibles, among other licensees, made lots of collectibles.

Even when it comes to the world of gaming, a great many *Lord of the Rings* games—tabletop, RPG, video, and online—cover the entire saga . . . but only certain releases directly tied to the films (rather than to Tolkien's tale in general). In 2001, Decipher launched *The Lord of the Rings Trading Card Game*, with releases that extended well beyond the years during which the movies ran in theaters. By 2007, Decipher lost the license and ended the game with its nineteenth expansion, *Ages' End*. In 2013, Cryptozoic Entertainment released *The Lord of the Rings: The Fellowship of the Ring Deck-Building Game*. It made two Arwen promo cards available through participating stores. In 2001, Games Workshop started a *Warhammer*-like tabletop battle-and-strategy system with a boxed *Fellowship of the Ring* tie-in game supported by a variety of miniature figures. In 2005, the company released a *Fellowship* tie-in titled *The Mines of Moria*. The 2000 Reiner Knizia–designed

MIDDLE EARTH COMES ALIVE · · ·

Lord of the Rings game from Rio Grande Games preceded this film by a year, but it and its expansions became a recognizable part of the film-era gaming experience. A limited edition arrived in the fall of 2001, with pewter pieces, a gold-plated ring, numbered prints signed by John Howe, and the box itself signed by Knizia. A *Friends & Foes* expansion also came out in 2001. That same year, Rio Grande released a two-player game titled *Lord of the Rings: The Search*. In 2002, Impact Games and RoseArt both put out board games based on the film. As for role-playing in Middle-earth, Decipher released the only film-based game in 2002, calling it—un-originally—*The Lord of the Rings Roleplaying Game*. For details on that, look no further than our "This Year in Gaming" section of the *The Lord of the Rings: The Two Towers* chapter.

TAKE UP THY SWORD!

MAGICAL FIREWORKS (MAGICALLY AUGMENTED OBJECTS)

TARGET: A single skyrocket

RANGE: 500 yards (once launched)

DURATION OF EFFECT: 1 round per caster's experience level

RESULT: Enchants a mundane firework to expand it into an augmented display of the caster's design (a swooping dragon, a rush of water, and so on).

The basic components required to manufacture these glorious pyrotechnic displays—sweeping, dancing, and roaring productions—are fairly mundane until manipulated magically. Each enwrapped cylinder contains elements tweaked by sorcerous hands, so that, when launched into the night sky, it activates in impressive or even frightening ways.

The initial display is often a flash and boom of sparks, enough to impress even the most apathetic witness. Shortly after that, the magical elements rally to create a pre-programmed extravaganza that can distract or intimidate any who fail saving throws versus magic.

The caster, often a halfling (because many halflings are experts at manufacturing such things), begins with a standard firework. Through design and concentration (1d4 x 10 minutes per firework) the caster enchants the skyrocket, impressing the desired display upon its explosive components.

THE FILM'S DESTINY

One of the biggest challenges facing this first film was to economically introduce the vastness of Middle-earth to mainstream moviegoers while satisfying as many Tolkien fans as possible (and that, let's be fair, was *never* going to be easy). That it did that and instantly invested us completely in a simultaneously fantastical and very real place is one of this movie's greatest strengths.

The opening montage to the idyllic initial view of the Shire immediately enthralls us, and then we begin to get a sense of what's at stake as the looming evil of Sauron grows. The most carefree culture of Middle-earth is the most vulnerable to the darkness, and yet from its ranks will come his undoing.

> ALL WE HAVE TO DECIDE IS WHAT TO DO WITH THE TIME THAT WE ARE GIVEN.

In a sense, one can view the trilogy as a single film released in three chapters, but the individual movies have distinct tones. As huge as the overall tale is, *Fellowship* is the warmest and most intimate of the three installments, and with good reason. The hobbits are the spiritual and emotional core of the story, and so, because the scope of the saga grows to encompass many peoples and lands, these small folk provide grounding for all that will follow, with their simple, bucolic life and placid community. Once the road trip starts, we're off on an amazing journey, aided by Howard Shore's memorable musical motifs and by remarkably complete designs that distinguish the cultures of the various races—hobbits, humans, dwarves, and elves—while uniting them in a convincing reality.

Setting a new benchmark for fantasy film, *Fellowship* gives the next two movies a lot to live up to. In some ways, they don't quite match the sense of wonder we see here . . . but beginnings are like that. What we'll lose in newness we'll more than make up for with a deeper, richer exploration of this world, truly brought to life onscreen for the first time.

THIS YEAR IN GAMING

Desiring to explore new career paths, long-time friends Matthew Sprange and Alex Fennell came together to form a new gaming company based in Swindon, England. Taking the name Mongoose Publishing—after rejecting "Bitter Tart" and "Cosmic Mongoose," among other names—they began by publishing supplemental d20 materials, primarily for the third edition of *Dungeons & Dragons*, thanks to the Open Gaming License from Wizards of the Coast. Their first release was *The Slayer's Guide to Hobgoblins*, a thirty-two-page monster book inspired by the "Ecology of . . ." articles that appeared in *Dragon* magazine. The book sold thousands of copies worldwide, giving birth to a series that would total twenty-nine volumes by 2004. Other releases in 2001 included the first of their *Encyclopaedia Arcane* series, *Demonology—The Dark Road* (a sixty-four-page book containing information on the Demonologist character class), *Gladiator: Sands of Death* (an eighty-page campaign guide), and *Seas of Blood: Fantasy on the High Seas* (a 128-page guide to ocean adventures).

VERSUS

2002 • JAPAN
KSS Inc. / Suplex Inc. / WEVCO Produce Company / napalm FiLMS/ Miramax Films
119M • Color • R

Writers: Ryuhei Kitamura and Yudai Yamaguchi
Director: Ryuhei Kitamura
Action Director: Yuji Shimomura
Producer: Hideo Nishimura
Producer: Keishiro Shin
Music: Nobuhiko Morino
Cinematographer: Takumi Furuya
Special Make-Up Effects: Susumu Nakatani
Costume Designer: Mamo And Chaico
Creative Director: Takehito Iizuka
Cast: Tak Sakaguchi (Prisoner KSC2-303), Hideo Sakaki (The Prisoner's Foe), Chieko Misaka (The Girl), Kenji Matsuda (Yakuza Leader), Yuichiro Arai (Motorcycle-Riding Yakuza), Minoru Matsumoto (Crazy Yakuza with Amulet), Kazuhito Ohba (Yakuza with Glasses), Takehiro Katayama (Red-Haired Assassin), Ayumi Yoshihara (Long-Haired Female Assassin), Shoichiro Masumoto (One-Handed Cop), Toshiro Kamiaka (Samurai Warrior), Yukihito Tanikado (Cop with Barrett), Hoshimi Asai (Short-Haired Female Assassin), Ryosuke Watabe (Yakuza Zombie in Alligator Skin Coat), and Motonari Komiya (Prisoner POCH-1835)
Alternate Titles: *The Return: Down to Hell 2* (working title) and *The Ultimate Versus* (director's cut)

ON THE MAP

The Forest of Resurrection is a dark, enchanted wood somewhere in Japan.

OUR STORY SO FAR

A bizarre collection of Yakuza gang members, escaped convicts with memories of former lives, and assorted bystanders are caught up in an eternal struggle between good and evil centered around a portal in a mysterious forest that links Earth to . . . somewhere else.

ALTERNATE VERSIONS

Two versions of the film were released on DVD in the US, one with the R-rated cut and another with an uncut, unrated version. German releases also cut some of the more violent scenes. *The Ultimate Versus,* released as a three-disc DVD set from Media Blasters, is an enhanced and extended cut of the original movie, with new effects, additional action sequences, and more explanatory material to flesh out the story. It runs 153 minutes, so it really is the ultimate *Versus* experience if you want the most of this movie that you can get. (See **Shattering the Illusion** for more.)

IT'S MAGIC

The zombie genre has a set of constantly shifting, evolving rules for the behavior of these sometimes dead, sometimes living creatures. In this movie, the zombies in the Forest of Resurrection are manifestations of an extradimensional power that permeates the geographic area surrounding the 444th portal connecting Earth to another reality. What reality? We're told there are 666 such portals around the globe, which might suggest one possible destination. Better dress lightly.

Anyone who dies in the Forest reanimates as an aggressive, flesh-eating monster. Some of these creatures shamble around as they do in most of George Romero's classic "modern zombie" movies, but some retain their personalities and physical abilities. These "hyper zombies," in the thrall of the Prisoner's Foe, are an intriguing hybrid of modern zombies, possessed voodoo-slaves, and Asian "hopping corpse" creatures. Frighteningly resilient, a hyper zombie can survive the usual head shot but not necessarily a large hail of bullets. You can also dismember one if you're brave enough to try the messy, close-quarters approach.

Blood magic also exists in this world. The sacrifice of a girl with the "power of resurrection" blood type (we don't remember that from among A, B, AB, and O) can tear open a doorway between realities ... but only once every 500 years. If anything disrupts the process, the ritual's completion might then require blood from a second subject. No one ever said bridging boundaries between dimensions was easy.

THE QUEST FOR MEANING

Much of this movie depends on at least a basic knowledge of Japanese mythology and narrative themes. With a blend of religious traditions, symbolism from decades of martial-arts movies, and the latest gaming clichés, *Versus* is an amalgam of metaphors from the history of Japanese pop culture. It also goes beyond that one heritage, however, touching on universal notions of heroism, self-sacrifice, and the power of love (true love?).

At its core, though, it's basically a take on the eternal struggle between good and evil, embodied by two individuals who battle throughout time for control of a third—a symbol of purity, love, and selflessness—and who even switch roles from time to time. The individuals seem less important than the fight itself, by which they contribute to the preservation of some unknown cosmic balance. It's human nature to fight for survival. Here that fight reaches epic proportions, in a place that supposedly exists on Earth, but in a timeless loop that connects past, present, and future.

WHO GOES THERE?

Hideo Sakaki appeared in *Ju-on (The Grudge)*, *Battlefield Baseball*, and *Godzilla: Final Wars* (also written and directed by Ryuhei Kitamura).

Tak Sakaguchi turned up in *Alive*, *Azumi*, *Battlefield Baseball*, *Godzilla: Final Wars*, *Azumi 2: Death or Love*, *Death Trance*, *Tokyo Gore Police*, *Samurai Zombie*, *Mutant Girls Squad*, and *A Yakuza's Daughter Never Cries*.

6 DEGREES OF SORCERY

This film draws on a multitude of pop-culture sources from around the globe, especially films, anime, and videogames, starting with the *Highlander* premise of eternal warriors meeting each other throughout time and battling with coats and swords, and including the *Mortal Kombat* motif of a contest at a remote location. Other films, including *The Crow, Predator, The Matrix,* and the *Terminator* films, contribute a variety of visual and narrative effects. Sergio Leone's penchant for tight close-ups influences the film as well.

The zombies don't stand up well to dismemberment: the method used for dispatching undead schoolgirls in the truly warped *Stacy* and for the demon-possessed corpses in *The Evil Dead* movies (which of course include *Army of Darkness*). Quite a few of the camera moves in this movie replicate similar signature shots used by *The Evil Dead* director, Sam Raimi, which is understandable because both films take place in cursed woods with disembodied, malevolent, magical forces. Kitamura even began this project with a shorter version before expanding it to feature length.

Cultural influences run both ways, because *Metal Gear* videogame producer-director Hideo Kojima served as an extra in this movie. In return, Kitamura directed the cut scenes in *Metal Gear Solid: The Twin Snakes*, bringing the distinctive style of *Versus* to sword combat in that game.

SHATTERING THE ILLUSION

Inspired by the likes of Italian horror directors Dario Argento and Lucio Fulci, American counterparts such as Sam Raimi and George Romero, and a plethora of other genres, from the post-apocalyptic milieu of the *Mad Max* movies to '80s American action fare like *Commando*, director Ryuhei Kitamura attended an Australian film school. He made one short zombie film with a forest setting before returning to Japan, where he shot *Down to Hell* in less than two weeks for just $3,000. The Hi8 video, completed in 1997, ran forty-seven minutes and was the core of what would evolve into *Versus*.

Kitamura completed his first full-length feature before returning to the world of *Down to Hell* for a follow-up. Rallying support from friends and family, he gathered the funds to produce the movie on his own, starting with just $10,000. For a few months he shot footage in the daytime and spent nights raising more money. Although he planned to use every set piece and idea he ever had, just in case he never had another chance, he could not afford a planned car-based homage to *Mad Max*.

Actor Tak Sakaguchi was a street fighter when Kitamura found him and invited him to a party. There, Sakaguchi witnessed Kitamura fighting somebody, while his future costar, Hideo Sakaki, focused on hooking up with a girl.

Fighting on film was new to many cast members, whose only experience was during controlled, choreographed indoor rehearsals that did not take into account the wet, tangled

> BEWARE THE PAST. FIGHT THE PRESENT. FEAR THE FUTURE.

> WITNESS A BATTLE NO ONE HAS EVER SEEN.

terrain of a forest location. Sakaguchi alone broke several ribs and a tooth during filming.

Near the end of shooting, Kitamura expressed displeasure with the title of the film: *Return to Hell: Down to Hell 2*. While covering the production for a documentary, Kitamura's friend, former film-school classmate, and crew member for this film, Ryuichi Takatsu, suggested an alternative: he thought that *Versus* best summed up Kitamura's passion for the movie and his life of fighting for what he wanted. Obviously, Kitamura liked the idea.

The film's twist ending came about as a last-minute change. Just half an hour before the scheduled shooting of the epilogue, Kitamura swapped the roles of the two leads, placing the hero and villain in opposing positions, purely to throw the audience for a loop in the closing moments.

In 2004, Kitamura reunited the majority of his team from the original production back at the same location for five days. Because time and budgetary constraints, as well as technical limitations, had hampered the making of the movie, Kitamura took this opportunity to enhance the film and bring it more in line with his vision. Sakaguchi replaced Yuji Shimomura as the director of action sequences for the new shoot. (See "**Alternate Versions**.")

MUSIC OF THE MINSTRELS

Ryuhei Kitamura's high-school classmate, Nobuhiko Morino, composed the *Versus* music: another elusive fantasy-film soundtrack that seems only to exist as a bootleg through occasionally available Internet downloads. Morino's first film score was for the *Versus* precursor *Down to Hell*, for which he bought a keyboard. He presumably used more equipment for the scoring of *Versus*.

THE SAGA CONTINUES

Original plans to follow the film with a sequel, slated to shoot in 2005, never came to pass. In the last few years, Kitamura began discussing *Versus 2* again, not as a direct continuation of the first movie with any returning characters but as a story taking place in the United States simultaneously with the original one, at one of the other 665 portals. This combination reboot/sequel also has not yet materialized.

TAKE UP THY SWORD!

FORESTS OF RESURRECTION (MYSTICAL GATEWAY)

Hidden among the world's naturally occurring forests are non-navigable gateways from evil-aligned planes of existence, through which energies can leak. Here in the primary realm, these dark powers can manifest as frightening and dangerous constructs, including various forms of undead. Such twisted woodlands often draw necromancers, who can easily raise the dead there and, through the use of elaborate blood magic, tear rents in the fabric of existence to allow direct access from the outer planes (but only once every few centuries).

Because forces prowling for hosts in these forests vary in power and temperament, a traveler to the realm should prepare for anything from slow-moving, mindless walking dead to extremely powerful liches. In fact, one should not travel through these forests at all unless expertly skilled in tracking or outdoor survival, or in possession of applicable magical items or sorcerous abilities. Unaware wanderers can find themselves trapped in these zones for the rest of their lives ... and even beyond! Villages neighboring such forests are replete with tales of lost children or missing shepherds or hunters. One should consider any maps of the area suspect, because the dimensions and configurations of the forests change without warning.

THE FILM'S DESTINY

Though not a traditional sword-and-sorcery movie—sitting on the periphery of that genre as well as half a dozen others—this film takes an enthralling, rollercoaster-ride approach to entertainment. From the moment it begins, *Versus* straps you in and hurtles you through a frenetic world of insane mythic fantasy, over-the-top action, and compelling if incompletely drawn characters. Archetypes abound, as does copious gore. Though the second half flags in intensity, the movie more than makes up for it with a one-two punch of a finale.

Handsome lead Tak Sakaguchi and saturnine Hideo Sakaki command attention—unlike Chieko Misaka's damsel-in-distress cipher—but Kenji Matsuda's gleefully deranged, almost Joker-like Yakuza leader steals the movie out from under them in the first half. His body language, cartoonish facial expressions, and bemused reaction to the lunacy of the situation are so endearing that it's a shame when he becomes a far less interesting zombie only an hour into the proceedings.

A masterpiece of rapid-fire editing and time-spanning storytelling that serves up a few surprises despite its clichéd components, this film might nevertheless become tedious viewing for those with knowledge of gaming and anime. So much of this movie trades in motifs and elements made popular in other media that, rather than a cohesive film experience or even a casual action romp through the woods, *Versus* can feel more like a catalogue of "greatest hits" references to superior source material. But if that doesn't stop you, and if you're willing to let the obvious enthusiasm of everyone involved sweep you up, this adrenaline-fueled comic-book of an adventure movie will win you over with its delightful blend of the familiar and the unexpected.

THIS YEAR IN GAMING

After publicly announcing the officially licensed *Buffy the Vampire Slayer Roleplaying Game Core Rulebook* in December 2001, Eden Studios—publishers of roleplaying games like *All Flesh Must Be Eaten*, *Conspiracy X*, and *Witchcraft*—released the game in August 2002. Using a modified version of the in-house *Unisystem* rules (referred to by system designer C. J. Carella as "the cinematic variant"), designers based the game on the popular TV series created by Joss Whedon. The show entered its seventh season on the United Paramount Network (UPN) one month after the game's publication. The release was Eden's most successful to date. A number of supplemental products soon followed it, as well as another RPG, based on the *Buffy* spinoff series *Angel*, in 2003. With *Buffy* and *Angel* off the airwaves by 2004, Eden dropped both licenses in 2006.

> NON-STOP FREE-FALL ULTRAVIOLENCE ACTION ENTERTAINMENT.

THE LORD OF THE RINGS: THE TWO TOWERS

2002 • NZ/US • NEW LINE CINEMA / WINGNUT FILMS • 179M/235M • COLOR • PG-13

SCREENPLAY: Fran Walsh, Philippa Boyens, Stephen Sinclair, and Peter Jackson
BASED ON THE BOOK BY: J. R. R. Tolkien
DIRECTOR: Peter Jackson
PRODUCERS: Barrie M. Osborne, Fran Walsh, and Peter Jackson
MUSIC: Howard Shore. ("Gollum's Song" music by Howard Shore, lyrics by Fran Walsh, and performed by Emiliana Torrini.)
DIRECTOR OF PHOTOGRAPHY: Andrew Lesnie
MAKEUP & HAIR DESIGN: Peter Owen and Peter King
SPECIAL MAKE-UP, CREATURES, ARMOUR, WEAPONS AND MINIATURES: Richard Taylor And Weta Workshop
DIGITAL VISUAL EFFECTS DESIGNED AND CREATED BY: Weta Digital
VISUAL EFFECTS SUPERVISOR: Jim Rygiel
PRODUCTION DESIGNER: Grant Major
SUPERVISING ART DIRECTOR: Dan Hennah
COSTUME DESIGNERS: Ngila Dickson And Richard Taylor
CONCEPTUAL DESIGNERS: Alan Lee And John Howe
CULTURAL FIGHTING STYLES: Tony Woolf
TOLKIEN LANGUAGE TRANSLATION: David Salo
STUNT COORDINATOR: George Marshall Ruge
SWORDMASTER: Bob Anderson
HEAD ANIMAL WRANGLER: Dave Johnson
HORSE COORDINATOR: Steve Old
HORSE TRAINER: Don Reynolds
CAST: Elijah Wood (Frodo Baggins); Ian McKellen (Gandalf the Grey / Gandalf the White); Liv Tyler (Arwen); Viggo Mortensen (Aragorn); Sean Astin (Samwise Gamgee); Cate Blanchett (Galadriel); John Rhys-Davies (Gimli / Voice of Treebeard); Bernard Hill (King Theoden); Christopher Lee (Saruman); Billy Boyd (Peregrin "Pippin" Took); Dominic Monaghan (Meriadoc "Merry" Brandybuck); Orlando Bloom (Legolas); Hugo Weaving (Elrond); Miranda Otto (Eowyn); David Wenham (Faramir); Brad Dourif (Grima Wormtongue); Andy Serkis (Gollum); Sean Bean (Boromir); Karl Urban (Eomer); Craig Parker (Haldir); John Noble (Denethor); Bruce Allpress (Aldor); John Bach (Madril); Sala Baker (Man Flesh Uruk); Jed Brophy (Sharku/Snaga); Sam Comery (Éothain); Calum Gittins (Haleth); Victoria Beynon-Cole, Lee Hartley, and Philip Grieve (Hero Orcs); Bruce Hopkins (Gamling); Paris Howe Strewe (Theodred); Timothy Lee (Wildman); Nathaniel Lees (Ugluk); John Leigh (Hama); Robbie Magasiva (Mauhur); Robyn Malcolm (Morwen); Bruce Phillips (Rohan Soldier); Robert Pollock (Mordor Orc); Phillip Spencer-Harris (Ranger I); Olivia Tennet (Freda); Ray Trickett (Bereg); Stephen Ure (Grishnakh); Billy and Katie Jackson (Cute Rohan Refugee Children); Josh Wood (Warrior); Jarl Benzon and Sandro Kopp (Elves, uncredited); Jorn Benzon (Elf Archer, uncredited); Karlos Drinkwater and Paul Norell (Easterlings, uncredited); Daniel Falconer (Elven Warrior, uncredited); Dan Hennah and Alan Lee (Men of Rohan, uncredited); Paul Holmes and Marcus Thorne (Orcs, uncredited); Peter Jackson and Barrie M. Osborne (Rohirrim Warriors, uncredited); Joseph Mika-Hunt and Piripi Waretini (Uruk-Hai, uncredited); Henry Mortensen (Reluctant Rohan Child Warrior, uncredited); and Hannah Wood (Woman in Cave, uncredited).

ON THE MAP

As Frodo, Sam, and Gollum slowly make their way from Emyn Muil to the Black Gate of Mordor and briefly to Osgiliath—just a skip over the river from Minas Tirith—the rest of the Fellowship finds itself in Fangorn Forest and Rohan, King Theoden's land.

OUR STORY SO FAR

The Fellowship is divided. As Frodo and Sam tentatively team up with the withered former custodian of the ring—the treacherous Gollum—to make their way to Mordor, the others must contend with an army of orcs sent by Sauron's ally Saruman, as the monstrous creatures lay siege to Helm's Deep, which could be the last stronghold of Men. As the cliché goes, it's always darkest just before the dawn....

ALTERNATE VERSIONS

The extended edition of this film most notably brings us John Noble's Denethor one film early. We learn a bit more about the family dynamics of the steward of Gondor and his two sons, Sean Bean's Boromir and David Wenham's Faramir. Alterations, additions, and other tweaks run throughout this version as compared with the theatrical release, including intriguing tidbits about female dwarves and Aragorn's true age, both shared with Eowyn on the long march to Helm's Deep.

Of all the restored material, however, one key sequence would have shown a possible future for Frodo should he claim the Ring—with Elijah Wood in truly unnerving makeup, transitioning from our lovable hobbit into a Gollum-like creature—but it does *not* appear in the extended cut of the film and remains one of the more intriguing "lost" bits of footage that has yet to return to the saga.

IT'S MAGIC

The first film already established a lot of the magic now in play in this middle chapter. One of the most significant enchantments in this installment is Saruman's enslavement of King Theoden via the slimy machinations of Grima Wormtongue. Only the intervention of a more powerful wizard can save this Theoden addled, twisted, and aged beyond his years ... but didn't Gandalf die last time?

When Gandalf returns as "the White," he has increased his command of magical forces, especially notable in his ability to turn back Saruman's power over Theoden and shatter the other wizard's staff—at long distance, no less! Fascinatingly, in Gandalf's first appearance in this incarnation, he seems not to remember his earlier life until reminded, and his voice fluctuates between Ian McKellen's and Christopher Lee's. Could it be that in assuming the role of the White Wizard, Gandalf has taken on a bit of Saruman's formerly good spirit?

The Palantírs are a magical manifestation of a sort of networking communications device that Tolkien could only dream of, but they also resemble the clichéd seeing-stones or crystal balls favored by witches and other supernatural beings in countless classic tales. Elven cloaks seem to live up to their name: they mimic rock and perhaps other terrain when their wearers wish to hide. Elven rope also has a mind of its own, unknotting itself when necessary, and the elves' lembas bread can fill the average stomach with just a few bites. Best not to overdo it, then.

THE QUEST FOR MEANING

With the entire *Lord of the Rings* series thematically rich in story threads and characters, reflecting a variety of interlinking ideas, perhaps it befits a film with *Two* in the title—and perhaps we can save ourselves from writing what could be an entire book in and of itself—to boil down a lot of what this installment has to offer by looking at two characters: Theoden and Gollum. Theoden embodies everything the series is about: one age passing the world to the next, with reluctance but resignation and understanding; honor and loyalty and the legacy of one's time on Middle-earth; and weariness giving way to resolute determination and heroism in tragic times. Once this man, unaccustomed to being out of control, regains his true self, he still encounters a situation in which power has shifted and he can no longer determine the future. His love for Eowyn shows the softer side of a stern leader who doubts the strength of his heart. When he physically and mentally emerges from bewitched lethargy, his turning to her with a wistful "I know that face" sets up one of the following film's most moving moments. Can you guess that the king of Rohan ranks as one of the best characters in this entire volume, at least according to one of your authors [ATB]?

Gollum is also an embodiment—but in his case, of greed and desire. He conveys the power and tragedy of the Ring's effect on its bearers. He elicits sympathy, even while chilling the blood because of his genuine menace to our hobbit duo. Not just at once threatening and pitiable, Gollum is also a frightening warning of what Frodo might become if he, too, were to succumb to the Ring (a potential future creepily glimpsed in that unused scene described in **Alternate Versions**).

That duality is another handy connection to our "two" theme, but if we follow that through, we'll be here all day. After all, the returned Gandalf the White now contrasts the sullied Saruman the White, Eowyn futilely fights the absent spirit of Arwen in her attraction to Aragorn, and Faramir dwells in the shadow of his dead brother (and thus cannot prove himself to his father).

And did we bring up the recurring theme of technological advancement crushing the natural world? All right, then.

WHO GOES THERE?

Bernard Hill had early television roles in the *I, Claudius* miniseries and a number of Shakespearean TV-movies. He also played John Lennon in *John Lennon: A Journey in the Life* and appeared in feature films like *Gandhi*, *The Bounty*, *First Knight*, *Mr. Toad's Wild Ride*, *Titanic* (as Captain Smith), *The Scorpion King*, and *The Lord of the Rings: The Return of the King*. He also provided his voice for the judge in *ParaNorman*.

Miranda Otto also appeared in *The 13th Floor*, *The Thin Red Line*, *What Lies Beneath*, *The Lord of the Rings: The Return of the King*, the 2004 *Flight of the Phoenix*, the 2004 *War of the Worlds*, and HBO's *Westworld* series.

David Wenham started in television, including roles in *A Country Practice, Twisted Tales,* and *SeaChange*, and appeared in movies like *Dark City, Moulin Rouge!, The Lord of the Rings: The Return of the King, Van Helsing, 300, 300: Rise of an Empire,* and *Pirates of the Caribbean: Dead Men Tell No Tales*. He also lent his voice to the animated film *Legend of the Guardians: The Owls of Ga'Hoole*.

> THE JOURNEY CONTINUES
> DECEMBER 18TH.

Brad Dourif is a genre-entertainment institution, probably known best for the voice coming out of a murderous little doll named Chucky in the *Child's Play* movie franchise. He often plays twisted, wild-eyed characters you wouldn't want to meet in an elevator or dark alley. He made his mark early, in the movie *One Flew Over the Cuckoo's Nest*, and moved on to roles in *Eyes of Laura Mars, Heaven's Gate, Dune, Blue Velvet, The Exorcist III, Graveyard Shift, Critters 4, Trauma, Alien: Resurrection, Urban Legend, The Lord of the Rings: The Return of the King,* and Rob Zombie's *Halloween* and *Halloween II*, as well as TV series like *Wild Palms, Tales from the Crypt, The X-Files, Babylon 5, Star Trek: Voyager, Millennium, Deadwood, Fringe,* and *Once Upon a Time*.

Like so many actors in this series, Karl Urban drew attention early on with appearances in *Hercules: The Legendary Journeys* and *Xena: Warrior Princess*, but nearly always as the same character: none other than Julius Caesar. Other film appearances include *Ghost Ship, The Lord of the Rings: The Return of the King, The Chronicles of Riddick, The Bourne Supremacy, Doom, Pathfinder, Red, Dredd* (as the title character), and *Riddick*. In 2009 he joined another monumental pop-culture franchise by taking over the role of Dr. Leonard "Bones" McCoy in *Star Trek* and its sequels.

John Noble (credited as "John Nogle" by mistake) followed up the troubled-parent character in this and *The Lord of the Rings: The Return of the King* with a regular role as Dr. Walter Bishop in the television series *Fringe*. He also appeared in the TV shows *Time Trax, Stargate SG-1, 24,* and *Sleepy Hollow*, was the dragon spirit in *The Last Airbender*, and voiced Unicron in *Transformers Prime*, Brainiac in *Superman: Unbound*, and the Scarecrow in *Batman: Arkham Knight*.

John Bach had roles in TV shows like *The Ray Bradbury Theater, Time Trax, Mysterious Island, Farscape,* and *Spartacus: War of the Damned*, and in films such as *The Lord of the Rings: The Return of the King* (returning as Madril) and *The Chronicles of Narnia: Prince Caspian*.

Jed Brophy had roles in films like *Dead Alive, The Lord of the Rings: The Return of the King, King Kong,* and *District 9*, and returned for all three *Hobbit* films as Nori.

Calum Gittins also appeared in *The King's Speech*.

Bruce Hopkins played lots of different characters in (you know where this is going) *Young Hercules, Hercules: The Legendary Journeys,* and *Xena: Warrior Princess* and returns in the final film of this trilogy.

Nathaniel Lees had multiple roles in *Xena: Warrior Princess, Hercules: The Legendary Journeys* (and one of its TV-movie predecessors), and *Young Hercules*. He also played Mifune in *The Matrix Reloaded* and *The Matrix Revolutions* and appeared in *30 Days of Night*.

John Leigh appeared in the movie *The Frighteners* and the TV shows *Jack of All Trades* and *Xena: Warrior Princess*, as well as a half-dozen *Power Rangers* series.

Bruce Phillips was in multiple episodes of *Hercules: The Legendary Journeys* and played Grimbold in *The Lord of the Rings: The Return of the King*.

Stephen Ure did the usual turns on *Hercules: The Legendary Journeys* and *Xena: Warrior Princess* and also appeared in *Spartacus: Gods of the Arena* and *Spartacus: War of the Damned*. He played Gorbag in *The Lord of the Rings: The Return of the King*; Satyr in *The Chronicles of Narnia: The Lion, the Witch and the Wardrobe*; and two roles in the first two *Hobbit* films.

Paul Norell appeared in *Young Hercules, Hercules: The Legendary Journeys, Jack of All Trades,* and *Xena: Warrior Princess,* and returned as the king of the dead in *The Lord of the Rings: The Return of the King*.

Joseph Mika-Hunt also made uncredited appearances in *Avatar* and all three *Hobbit* movies.

Hannah Wood's only other credited film appearance was in *Radio Flyer,* starring Elijah Wood. (Think they're related? Hint: siblings.)

6 DEGREES OF SORCERY

Some might draw a visual connection between Gollum and Dobby from the *Harry Potter* films. The "zombie ghosts" under the waters of the Dead Marshes resemble creatures from movies like *Zombie Lake, Zombies of Mora Tau,* and *The Fog*. Gandalf's journey out of himself following the battle with the Balrog has a vague, trippy *2001: A Space Odyssey* vibe ... man. His reunion with Shadowfax underscores the image of the white horse in various guises as a symbol of strength or purity, echoed in countless other films in the genre, such as *Clash of the Titans, Krull,* and *The Last Unicorn*. The trolls working on the Black Gate are like Conan on the Wheel of Pain in *Conan the Barbarian*. Theoden's cursed, aged form seems very like a Rankin/Bass character brought into the live-action realm, especially when cackling madly. Moving under hooded cover, Faramir and his men look like Robin Hood and his merry band. Saruman prevents Grima from accidentally igniting gunpowder just as Ash prevents a similar mistake in *Army of Darkness*. Treebeard's comment about "a fine hit" is similar to Osric's line about "a very palpable hit" in Shakespeare's *Hamlet*.

SHATTERING THE ILLUSION

Knowing that this volume would probably be the most trouble to adapt to film, due to it being a "middle child," the team budgeted time early in the schedule to crack the complexity of its narrative and to determine how to take the linear approach of *Fellowship* to a different level. One of the biggest decisions made by Peter Jackson and company when shaping this middle chapter involved weaving (not Hugo) together the two halves of the *Two Towers* novel. Following the broken Fellowship to Rohan in its first half and rejoining Frodo's team on the way to Mordor in the second, the divided book meshed into a script that moved among three groups to maintain audience investment in all sides of the story.

The film built on associations either that Tolkien intended or that the team inferred from the material, whether it was the WWI parallel of the Dead Marshes and the relationship between Frodo and Sam that echoed that of an English officer and his batman, or Treebeard as an avatar of Tolkien's friend C. S. Lewis, or the Hitlerian posturing of Saruman.

Another question that came to mind was: which *are* the two towers of the title? Even Tolkien wasn't entirely clear on that point, offering differing answers on several occasions. For the film, however, the two towers became—as one of Tolkien's answers had it—Saruman's Orthanc and Sauron's Barad-Dur.

As with the rest of the series, the production had to cut and alter some of Tolkien's material, leaving out Old Man Willow, for example—although Merry and Pippin's experience in the woods with entwining roots allowed for a "cameo" of sorts. One character *had* to remain—one of the trilogy's most glorious accomplishments: the marriage of CGI and performance that was Andy Serkis's Gollum. Many new cast members joined the story, including everyone at Rohan, but Gollum was the tour de force of the film, with artists John Howe and Alan Lee devising an Iggy Pop–inspired look to adapt into a crude computer simulation. When Serkis proved valuable not just as the voice of Gollum but as the driver of his physical performance, creators devised a complex approach using Serkis in a "gimp suit" for takes with the other actors, adding takes without him for use in post-production. Serkis encountered difficulties with his fellow actors, because they didn't know whether to treat him as an equal or as an effect. His frequent imbibing of honey lemon and ginger to soothe his ravaged throat after hours of the Gollum voice led to some juicy dialogue; his spit even appears onscreen. Airbrushing techniques, adapted into digital form, created Gollum's realistic thin skin. In collaboration with Fran Walsh, Serkis also enhanced the dual nature of Gollum, with the evil side holding dominance over the sweeter but more gullible Smeagol of old, leading to the scene in which Serkis acted a conversation between both personalities in real time.

Of the extensive design work undertaken by John Howe and Alan Lee, Edoras drew at least partly from the feast hall of Danish King Hrothgar in the epic *Beowulf*, and Osgiliath came from the bombed-out environs of London and Berlin during World War II. Multiple sizes of "bigatures" became Helm's Deep and other locations, with digital post-production involving nearly 800 special-effects shots. The team had to double its workforce, triple its storage, and quadruple its processors to make it all happen. Even then, it completed some work, like the flooding of Isengard, only months before the film's December release.

The program Massive, used to generate the huge armies that battle here and in the third film, utilized AI that allowed individual figures to make decisions on their own. In early testing, some of the soldiers actually fled rather than fight—not because of cowardice, but because they didn't trigger to engage an enemy in close proximity!

Some of the evil "black speech" in the film came from a recording session involving the intonations of an entire cricket stadium-crowd. As for Brad Dourif, he maintained a convincing English accent even when the cameras weren't rolling, and talked in his normal accent only when finished with his role. Fellow cast member Bernard Hill couldn't believe his natural accent, thinking he sounded unconvincing as an American.

As the story grew more complex, so, too, did the production. Deep into its fourteen-month main schedule, multiple units had split off to shoot material. Jackson employed a satellite system to keep tabs on activity.

Injuries mounted, too, from Orlando Bloom breaking a rib to Viggo Mortensen breaking two toes on a helmet—an incident shown in the final cut of the film. Also, a sword chipped

> THE BATTLE FOR MIDDLE-EARTH BEGINS!

one of Mortensen's teeth, and Bernard Hill needed stitches for a head wound. Psychological tensions also rose, such as when Andy Serkis accidentally pulled off Sean Astin's wig during a take, and the annoyed actor stormed off the set.

The Helm's Deep sequence, which took more than four months to complete, naturally suggested itself as the perfect climax for this chapter, though it moved the confrontation with Shelob to the next film. Even the physical construction of the sequence had its share of problems, including a door built so well by the art department that it withstood a battering instead of falling as planned! Night shooting on the Helm's Deep sequence made an arduous shoot even harder, especially for the horde of orc actors clothed in heavy prosthetics, armor, and gear.

Basing some of the action on the historic clash between British and Zulu forces, Jackson and his team made a number of changes to the source material that would make Tolkien purists uncomfortable if not outright enraged. Liv Tyler had trained for a plan to include Arwen in the battle, nixed in the editing—but battle scenes with her were shot. A few still photos and one or two very quick screen grabs even from the finished film betray the original intent to have Aragorn's love ride to the rescue alongside the other elves during the siege. With her removed from that sequence, the filmmakers faced the issue of keeping her romance with Aragorn alive throughout a movie in which she played no active role. They found the solution in Tolkien's appendices: the psychic bond between the two lovers. They also used flashbacks to incorporate Arwen wherever they could.

Perhaps more contentious for Tolkien aficionados than the possibility of Arwen's inclusion in Helm's Deep and the elves' involvement in the final version of the battle, or even the Warg attack (not included in the original text), was the tweaking done to Faramir's story. The book portrays the character as predominantly unaffected by the wooing of the Ring, but the film Faramir is not as nice and also decides to take the hobbits to Osgiliath. This leads to one of the most criticized aspects of the film: Frodo actually revealing the Ring to a Nazgul.

Later pickup shooting expanded on scenes with Gollum and Faramir. Jackson held off on including the final confrontation with Saruman, to use it as the opening of the next movie—a choice that would lead to serious contention between him and Lee. (More on that in *The Return of the King* chapter.) Just about everyone involved, Jackson included, remembers the post-production process of this middle chapter as the most psychologically draining part of the long years spent on the trilogy. The film premiered in Wellington on December 18, 2002, about two weeks after its debuts in the US and UK, with an enormous Gollum and One Ring adorning the marquee of the Embassy Theater.

MUSIC OF THE MINSTRELS

Howard Shore found that composing music for this installment presented problems in the sense that it joined a story in progress and left it the same way, providing no true beginning or end. He carried some of the motifs from *Fellowship* into the second film and connected the two (yes, we can't help it) most significant new melodies in this film to characters we highlighted in **The Quest for Meaning** section.

A NEW POWER IS RISING.

First, a Norwegian Hardanger fiddle created a distinctive rustic sound for the string-heavy Rohan theme presenting Theoden and his people. A plaintive theme accompanies the real star of this film: the combination of actor Andy Serkis and CGI wizardry that is Gollum. It mixes equal parts calculating menace and mournful regret, along with the familiar "History of the Ring." The film's end-credits song this time around is an extension of the musical exploration of Gollum, in "Gollum's Song," with lyrics by Fran Walsh and a vocal performance by Emiliana Torrini, who came in when international singing star Björk could not perform the song due to her pregnancy.

Shore employed additional vocal and choral work for Arwen's spiritual restoration of Aragorn by the riverside, Haldir's death, and the march of the Ents. Even Peter Jackson got in on the act, banging a gong (all day?) for the ride into Edoras! Shore also composed an extra forty minutes of music for the extended edition of the film.

In December 2002, Reprise Records released the first soundtrack for *The Two Towers* in a regular CD edition, with poster cover art and two limited versions that featured either a blue or brown (Internet exclusive) leather-like box. The limited editions added one bonus track but cut two others. In November 2006, Reprise brought out this film's installment in *The Complete Recordings* series on CD, with an accompanying DVD-audio featuring two stereo mixes. An annotated score was distributed for free online.

As with the other two films, *Complete Recordings* liner-notes author Doug Adams chronicled the story of Shore's work for the saga in his book, *The Music of the Lord of the Rings Films*. The book included another CD, *The Rarities Archive*, which provided still more material for eager fans to hear, plus insights from Shore. This was the only film in the trilogy *not* to win an Oscar for its score, but it did join the others in grabbing a Grammy for Best Score Soundtrack Album.

THE SAGA CONTINUES

As we noted in **The Saga Continues** for the first film, there's no way to do all the related merchandise justice here, but in terms of gaming, we can at least highlight the tie-ins to the film. In this case, Hasbro / Parker Brothers released *Risk: The Lord of the Rings* in 2002. In 2013, Cryptozoic Entertainment released *The Lord of the Rings: The Two Towers Deck-Building Game*, which players could combine with the previous *Fellowship* release or play by itself. Participating stores also offered two Eowyn promo cards.

In 2002, Games Workshop continued their *Warhammer*-like tabletop battle-and-strategy system with a boxed *Two Towers* tie-in game. That same year, the Reiner Knizia–designed *Lord of the Rings* game from Rio Grande Games added a *Sauron* expansion, and Rio Grande also released a two-player game titled *Lord of the Rings: The Duel*. Another Reiner Knizia game, titled *Lord of the Rings: The Confrontation*, came out as well, this time from Fantasy Flight Games; a deluxe edition followed in 2005. Impact Games and RoseArt both put out board games based on the film in 2003.

In 2002, Electronic Arts released a console videogame for the Xbox, PlayStation 2, Nintendo GameCube, and Game Boy Advance that used footage from *The Lord of the Rings: The*

> THE FELLOWSHIP IS BROKEN.
> THE POWER OF DARKNESS GROWS...

Fellowship of the Ring and this movie, garnering positive reviews for its design and play. Many of the film's cast provided specially recorded vocals as well.

In 2013, Lego released a buildable game with microfigures based around *The Battle of Helm's Deep* as part of its Lego Games line.

Of course, this trilogy has one more installment: *The Lord of the Rings: The Return of the King*. Check out our chapter on that film for more....

TAKE UP THY SWORD!

MIND PARASITE (MAGIC SPELL)

In the hands of a mighty wizard, this powerful spell can affect the mind of a chosen target many leagues away. Featuring a sorcerous combination of effects, including enfeeblement (physical exhaustion and weakness), bewitchment (vulnerability to illness and the premature effects of aging), mind control, and mesmerization, the mind-parasite spell can force a single target to do the bidding of the caster—even things that could potentially cause the victim bodily harm. The controller can also perceive the world through the victim's senses, even smelling the sweet fragrance of barrow flowers or tasting the seasonings in a fine stew. The effects of the spell last as long as the magic user maintains them or until the target successfully resists the spell in a duel of wills or a wizard of equal or greater ability dispels it. Only those in league with the darkest forces employ this charm, because its purpose is solely sinister.

THE FILM'S DESTINY

Though it befits a film with *Two* in the title to split storylines and follow multiple tracks, oddly, we're dealing with not two but *three* threads. Frodo, Sam, and Gollum head to Mordor; Aragorn and the others face the orc hordes of Saruman at Helm's Deep alongside Theoden and his Rohirrim; and Merry and Pippin team up with Treebeard to take on Saruman's threat at its source! That the movie doesn't feel anthological or divisive is a feat. It juggles all the characters and shifts to a new location every time you wonder what's going on elsewhere.

For this reviewer [ATB], the movie might have a great deal going for it, but it primarily comes down to the two powerful and moving characters mentioned previously. Andy Serkis's Gollum is a technological tour de force, one of the few instances in cinema history to date in which a fully CGI character (relying of course on the actor's voice and motion-capture performance in addition to the efforts of talented animators) can engage the audience emotionally and hold his own alongside living actors. As for my other favorite newcomer to the saga, Theoden is a far richer character than perhaps he even needs to be, owing to a great combination of writing and Bernard Hill's nuanced performance.

The movie expertly fulfills the by-now expected pop-culture role of the middle chapter in a trilogy by serving as this series' *Empire Strikes Back*, placing its heroes in dark danger and contrasting that successfully with one of the saga's most moving speeches. Samwise's climactic summation of the stakes when all seems at its worst not only propels the story into its final installment but provides one of the series' lynchpin thematic moments. Despite the ending on another cliffhanger, there's a sense not as much of foreboding as of victory moving closer. Sam's speech and Gandalf's arrival at Helm's Deep provide a dual (there it is again) note of hope. And there's just one more to go....

THIS YEAR IN GAMING

From 1984 to 1999, if you wanted to adventure in Middle-earth, you turned to Iron Crown Enterprises (I.C.E.) for the officially licensed *Middle-earth Role Playing (MERP)* line. It wasn't until 2002 and the release of *this film* that a new licensed option appeared, in the form of the aptly named *The Lord of the Rings Roleplaying Game* published by Decipher, Inc. Using that company's in-house d6-based CODA system, the line launched with five products: the *Core Book*; the introductory *Adventure Game* boxed set; a second introductory boxed set for *The Two Towers*; a booklet of character forms for players, called *The Hero's Journal*; and *Maps of Middle-earth*, a boxed set containing a series of large, beautifully rendered foldout maps. Additional boxed sets and books followed, but the well eventually dried up in 2005 with the publication of the final supplement, the *Helm's Deep Sourcebook*. Promoted products that sadly never saw the light of day include *Paths of the Wise: The Guide to Magicians & Loremasters, Fields of Battle: The Guide to Barbarians & Warriors, Isengard Sourcebook,* and *Rohan: Among the Horse-Lords*.

The game, designed by Matt Forbeck, Steven S. Long, Christian Moore, and John Rateliffe, among others, won the Origins Award for Best Role-Playing Game of 2002. After Decipher abandoned the line, the license lived on with a successful trading card game through 2007.

PIRATES OF THE CARIBBEAN: THE CURSE OF THE BLACK PEARL

2003 • US • WALT DISNEY PICTURES / JERRY BRUCKHEIMER FILMS • 143M • COLOR • PG-13

SCREENPLAY: Ted Elliott and Terry Rossio
STORY: Ted Elliott, Terry Rossio, Stuart Beattie, and Jay Wolpert
DIRECTOR: Gore Verbinski
PRODUCER: Jerry Bruckheimer
MUSIC: Klaus Badelt
ADDITIONAL MUSIC: Bob Badami, Hans Zimmer, Ramin Diawadi, James Dooley, Nick Glennie-Smith, Steve Jablonsky, Blake Neely, James McKee Smith, Geoff Zanelli, Craig Eastman, and Trevor Morris (uncredited)
DIRECTOR OF PHOTOGRAPHY: Dariusz Wolski
VISUAL EFFECTS: John Knoll and Jill Brooks
MAKE-UP EFFECTS: Keith Vanderlaan, Ve Neill, and Greg Cannom
COSTUME DESIGNER: Penny Rose
PRODUCTION DESIGNER: Brian Morris
ART DIRECTORS: Derek R. Hill, Donald B. Woodruff, and James E. Tocci
STUNT COORDINATOR: George Marshall Ruge
MASTER SHIP TECHNICIAN: Courtney J. Andersen
LEAD ANIMAL TRAINER: Ursula Brauner
ARMORER: Harry Lu
SWORD MASTER: Mark Ivie
ADDITIONAL SWORD TRAINER: Bob Anderson
SWORD MAKER: Tony Swatton
CAST: Johnny Depp (Captain Jack Sparrow); Geoffrey Rush (Captain Hector Barbossa); Orlando Bloom (Will Turner); Keira Knightley (Elizabeth Swann); Jack Davenport (Commander James Norrington); Jonathan Pryce (Governor Weatherby Swann); Lee Arenberg (Pintel); Mackenzie Crook (Ragetti); Damian O'Hare (Lt. Gillette); Giles New (Murtogg); Angus Barnett (Mullroy); David Bailie (Cotton); Michael Berry, Jr. (Twigg); Isaac C. Singleton, Jr. (Bo'sun); Kevin R. McNally (Joshamee Gibbs); Treva Etienne (Koehler); Zoe Saldana (Anamaria); Guy Siner (Harbormaster); Ralph P. Martin (Mr. Brown); Paula Jane Newman (Estrella); Paul Keith (Butler); Dylan Smith (Young Will); Lucinda Dryzek (Young Elizabeth); Luke de Woolfson (Frightened Sailor); Michael Sean Tighe (Seedy-Looking Prisoner); Greg Ellis (Officer); Dustin Seavey (Sentry); Israel Aduramo (Crippled Man); Christian Martin (Steersman); Trevor Goddard (Grapple); Vince Lozano (Jacoby); Ben Wilson (Seedy Prisoner #2); Antonio Valentino (Seedy Prisoner #3); Lauren Maher (Scarlett); Matthew Bowyer (Sailor/Edinburgh); Brye Cooper (Mallot); Mike Babcock (Seedy Prisoner #4); Owen Finnegan (Town Clerk); Ian McIntyre (Sailor); Vanessa Branch (Giselle); Sam and Ben Roberts (Crying Boy); Martin Klebba (Marty); Felix Castro (Moises); Mike Haberecht (Kursar); Rudolph McCollum (Matelot); Gerard Reyes (Tearlach); M. Scott Shields (Duncan); Chris "Sully" Sullivan (Ladbroc); Craig Thomson (Crimp); Fred Toft (Quartetto); D. P. Fitzgerald (Weatherby); Jerry Gauny (Ketchum); Maxie J. Santillan, Jr. (Maximo); Michael Lane (Monk); Tobias McKinney (Dog Ear); David Patykewich (Clubba); Tommy Schooler (Scarus); Michael A. Thompson (Simbakka); Michael W. Williams (Hawksmoor); Jose Zelaya (Katracho); Finneus Egan (Scratch); Don LaDaga (Nipperkin); LeJon Stewart (Lejon); Christopher S. Capp (Voice of Parrot); Gregory R. Alosio, Jordi Caballero, and James McAuley (Pirates, uncredited); Paul Gagne (Sailor, uncredited); and Joe Grisaffi (Marine, uncredited)
ALTERNATE TITLE: *Pirates of the Caribbean* (working title)

ON THE MAP

Jack drifts into Port Royal before heading to Tortuga and the Isla de Muerta. Naturally, everyone spends plenty of time on the open sea as well.

OUR STORY SO FAR

Captain Jack Sparrow, irrepressible adventurer and former commander of the pirate ship called the *Black Pearl*, teams up with a lovestruck blacksmith named Will Turner to save Turner's would-be bride, the headstrong daughter of Port Royal's governor, after a vicious band of cursed cutthroats now in possession of the *Black Pearl* (Sparrow's old crew, including the treacherous and desperate Captain Hector Barbossa) kidnap her.

ALTERNATE VERSIONS

Home-video releases offer plenty of deleted and additional scenes, but only as separate, selectable clips and not cut into an extended version.

IT'S MAGIC

This is a world filled with magic, but we learn the full extent of that only in the sequels. If we focus just on this one film, the power emanates entirely from a curse placed upon a store of 882 pieces of Aztec gold that must remain undisturbed. Having disturbed them, the tormented crew of the *Black Pearl* are now a strange amalgam of undead skeletons and immortal ghosts, neither alive nor truly dead, existing in a timeless limbo. They also cannot feel any sensations or derive pleasure from simple human activities like eating, a part of the curse that intensified as they traveled and spent their cursed gold. Strangely, though, the curse enables them to live virtually forever and survive what would otherwise be life-threatening injuries, presumably only so their emotional torture can continue indefinitely. Although they still look like their human selves, direct moonlight reveals their true, undead forms. Through unknown means, the stricken pirates discovered that returning the gold and performing an accompanying blood ritual could break the curse. But a certain monkey might decide the pros outweigh the cons. . . .

THE QUEST FOR MEANING

Surely one of the most powerful messages of this otherwise freewheeling, fun action adventure is that despite what Gordon Gecko once told Mr. "Winning," greed is bad. Anyone who has paid attention to global financial news of the last few years shouldn't find that too surprising.

But there's an odd imbalance in the ethical center of the film, in that we grow to respect Jack despite his eccentricities, and we celebrate Will's transformation from humble apprentice to full-fledged pirate in the footsteps of his father. Then there's that pirate code, which shows that though they are criminals in the eyes of some, they try to abide by a system of honor that guides their actions. By the end of the film, we even feel for Barbossa and appreciate that he at least finds peace and feeling in death . . . well, for another movie or so.

> PREPARE TO BE BLOWN
> OUT OF THE WATER.

Pirates symbolize the pure spirit of adventure that flows through many of these fantasy films, not least the desire to throw away the trappings of ordinary life, get rid of our jobs and our other responsibilities—anything else tying us to land—and set sail on the high seas to a far horizon and a swift sunrise. (Hmm, that sounds like something else.) So although some of the pirates in this film are monsters through much of the movie, what are we to think: are pirates bad or good? Is the curse a just one, a reflection of the wrongness of their choice of occupation, or was it merely one poor choice on a lousy day? Food (heh) for thought. If nothing else, perhaps we should simply reduce it to this: money can never buy happiness . . . but it can buy the pain of eternal, unfeeling limbo, and that's a choice you'll have to make yourselves.

WHO GOES THERE?

Before he became a global icon, Johnny Depp started with memorable roles in the Wes Craven horror movie *A Nightmare on Elm Street* and the TV show *21 Jump Street*. Soon he was a unique combination of character-actor and intellectual or quirky lead in films like *Cry-Baby, Benny & Joon, What's Eating Gilbert Grape, Don Juan DeMarco, Donnie Brasco, Fear and Loathing in Las Vegas, The Ninth Gate, Chocolat, From Hell, Once Upon a Time in Mexico, Finding Neverland, Public Enemies*, and *Mortdecai*, but his ongoing collaboration with director Tim Burton catapulted him into the mainstream, via films like *Edward Scissorhands, Ed Wood, Sleepy Hollow, Charlie and the Chocolate Factory, Corpse Bride, Sweeney Todd: The Demon Barber of Fleet Street, Alice in Wonderland*, and the remake of *Dark Shadows*. He has also returned as Captain Jack in all the *Pirates* sequels to date, turned up in the film version of *21 Jump Street*, and appeared as Tonto in the 2013 train-wreck *The Lone Ranger*.

Geoffrey Rush started his career with an unlikely turn as Snoopy in a production of the musical *You're a Good Man, Charlie Brown!*, but audiences know him better as a chameleonic character-actor in such films as *Twelfth Night, Les Misérables, Elizabeth, Shakespeare in Love, Mystery Men, House on Haunted Hill, Quills, The Life and Death of Peter Sellers* (in an uncanny incarnation of the comedian), *Elizabeth: The Golden Age, The King's Speech, The Book Thief*, and every *Pirates* sequel. He also lent his voice to *Finding Nemo, Legend of the Guardians: The Owls of Ga-Hoole*, and *Green Lantern*.

After a brief appearance in *Star Wars: Episode I—The Phantom Menace*, Keira Knightley kicked open Hollywood doors with her role in *Bend It Like Beckham*. She also appeared in *Love Actually, King Arthur, Pride & Prejudice, Seeking a Friend for the End of the World*, and the next two *Pirates* films.

Jack Davenport appeared in movies such as *Tale of the Mummy, Pirate Radio, Kingsman: The Secret Service*, and the next two *Pirates* films, as well as television series like *Ultraviolet, Coupling, FlashForward*, and *Smash*.

Although Jonathan Pryce's cultured British tones make him a perfect choice for classical stage productions, he has shown equal flair for everything from camp comedy to dark drama, with appearances in films like *Something Wicked This Way Comes, Brazil, Jumpin' Jack Flash, The Adventures of Baron Munchausen, Evita, Tomorrow Never Dies, What a Girl Wants, The Brothers*

Grimm, G.I. Joe: The Rise of Cobra, G.I. Joe: Retaliation, and the next two *Pirates* movies. He also put in memorable turns as the Master in the *Doctor Who* sketch "The Curse of Fatal Death" for Comic Relief in 1999 and as the High Sparrow in *Game of Thrones.*

Mackenzie Crook shot to fame in the original UK incarnation of *The Office* and has also appeared in TV shows like *Merlin* and *Game of Thrones,* and films like *The Life and Death of Peter Sellers, The Merchant of Venice, Finding Neverland, The Brothers Grimm, City of Ember, Solomon Kane,* and *Ironclad,* as well as the next two *Pirates* movies.

Damian O'Hare returned in *Pirates of the Caribbean: On Stranger Tides* and provided voice work for videogames like *Risen, Killzone 3,* and the *Assassin's Creed* series.

Angus Barnett appeared in *Finding Neverland, Pirates of the Caribbean: At World's End, Hugo,* and the remake of *Jack the Giant Killer.*

David Bailie turned up in the next two *Pirates* films, *The Creeping Flesh,* the very strange *Son of Dracula* (also featuring Ringo Starr as Merlin!), *Legend of the Werewolf, Cutthroat Island,* and *Gladiator,* and also played Dask in the *Doctor Who* story "Robots of Death."

Michael Berry, Jr. also appeared in *Mission: Impossible III, Star Trek,* and *The Hangover Part II.*

Isaac C. Singleton, Jr. had roles in films like *Galaxy Quest* and *Charlie's Angels,* and did voice work for videogames based on *The Lord of the Rings, Spider-Man, Transformers, Street Fighter,* and *StarCraft II.*

Kevin R. McNally began his career with television appearances in *Survivors; I, Claudius;* and the *Doctor Who* story "The Twin Dilemma." He also had roles in films like *The Spy Who Loved Me, Spice World, Sliding Doors, Entrapment, Johnny English, The Phantom of the Opera, Valkyrie,* and all the *Pirates* sequels. He played roles on TV shows like *Downton Abbey, Supernatural,* and *TURN: Washington's Spies* as well.

Treva Etienne appeared in *Falling Skies.*

Zoe Saldana warped to stardom as Uhura in the J. J. Abrams feature-film reboot of *Star Trek* and its sequels, and as Neytiri in *Avatar.* She then turned green as Gamora in *Guardians of the Galaxy.*

Guy Siner appeared in the classic "Genesis of the Daleks" episodes of *Doctor Who,* as well as *I, Claudius; 'Allo 'Allo!; Babylon 5;* and *Star Trek: Enterprise.*

Lucinda Dryzek appeared in *City of Ember* and the "School Reunion" episode of *Doctor Who.*

Greg Ellis is a prolific cartoon and videogame voice artist for titles like *Dragon Age: Origins, Batman: The Brave and the Bold,* and various *Star Wars* projects. He was also the net mender in *The Hobbit: The Desolation of Smaug.*

Trevor Goddard was Kano in *Mortal Kombat* and also appeared in the TV shows *Babylon 5* and *The X-Files.* He died in 2003 at age 40.

Martin Klebba appeared in movies such as *Run Ronnie Run, Death to Smoochy, Men in Black II, Austin Powers in Goldmember, Ted 2,* and three more *Pirates* films. He also had a recurring role as Randall in the TV series *Scrubs.*

6 DEGREES OF SORCERY

Because the movie was based on the famous Disney theme-park ride, a number of visuals directly reference the ride throughout the film, mostly during the sequence set on the island of

Tortuga. Prisoners trying to get their cell key from a reluctant dog, wine draining out through Barbossa's exposed ribcage, and numerous scenes of pirates carousing are replications from familiar ride tableaux.

The fog that enshrouds the characters recalls another movie featuring pirate zombies, John Carpenter's *The Fog*. Some of Captain Jack's dialogue references one of Depp's favorite British comedy television shows, once in the theatrical cut and once in a deleted scene available on DVD. Disney might be coyly referring to its own legendary animated adaptation of the fairytale *Snow White* when Barbossa offers an apple to Elizabeth, prompting her to suspect that it might be poisoned.

Countless zombie movies have featured grasping, skeletal hands reaching through shattered windows for living victims, perhaps best epitomized by corpses laying siege to a farmhouse in *Night of the Living Dead*, itself referenced again in *The Fog*. Waterlogged, seaweed-enshrouded zombies also take to the ocean floor in *Zombies of Mora Tau*, but it isn't just the undead that creep underwater. Jack and Will use a rowboat to form a pocket of oxygen, in a strategy lifted from the Burt Lancaster vehicle *The Crimson Pirate* and also employed by none other than Indiana Jones in *Indiana Jones and the Last Crusade*.

SHATTERING THE ILLUSION

Who would have thought that adapting a Disney theme-park ride into a feature film would not only work but also spawn a long-lasting franchise? When writers Ted Elliott and Terry Rossio first pursued the idea in the 1990s, it did not necessarily draw favorable attention.

Perhaps more was on Elliott's mind than Disney's famous ride. Ron Gilbert's series of *Monkey Island* computer games contain an astonishing number of similarities to the visuals, characters, and plot elements of not just this but subsequent *Pirates* films. Gilbert credited the ride as inspiration for his games, as well as a 1987 novel by Tim Powers titled *On Stranger Tides*. (If that sounds familiar, check **The Saga Continues** for more.) For a brief time, just a few years before this first *Pirates* film got underway, plans to adapt *Monkey Island* into a film went as far as Elliott writing the screenplay. Could *Pirates* owe a lot of its conceptual design and script to the failed *Monkey Island* adaptation?

Two failed attempts to craft a *Pirates* script with a more straightforward story led to Elliott and Rossio's version, which blends piracy and fantasy. The budget ballooned, but the chance to reinvigorate a classic cinematic genre kept Disney committed, and attracted director Gore Verbinski as well as a cast led by the incomparable Johnny Depp. The mercurial actor accepted the part so that his daughter could see him in a movie, for a change.

Crossing the personas of hard-rocking, hard-living Keith Richards of the Rolling Stones with the endlessly optimistic but annoying Pepe Le Pew from Warner Bros. cartoons, Depp created an eccentric take on the character of Captain Jack that caused some studio execs to worry. Their concern proved completely unwarranted, because Depp's choices created a modern film icon and won him a Screen Actors Guild Award for Outstanding Performance by a Male Actor, an MTV Movie Award for Best Male Performance, and an Academy Award nomination for Best Actor (taken by Sean Penn for *Mystic River*).

Keira Knightley was disappointed that she had no swashbuckling swordplay in the film but dutifully went to see the Disneyland ride. Apparently she had to wait in line with other park visitors.

Depp wasn't the only thing about the movie that had people skeptical. Besides the studio, plenty of people in the press thought that a big-budget would-be blockbuster based on a ride would never be a success. Of course, they were all wrong, too. The movie was the first to break Disney's PG-rating barrier and also the first film to premiere at Disneyland in California, where the ride had debuted decades earlier.

MUSIC OF THE MINSTRELS

Some have leveled criticism at the soundtrack for being too generic or repetitive, but for at least one of your authors [ATB], the main theme is a rousing tribute to the swashbuckling adventures of the past and a stirring melody that works every time it punctuates another death-defying escape or heroic escapade. The story behind the music has some intrigue of its own. Alan Silvestri was the first choice to provide the score, but his approach apparently clashed with producer Jerry Bruckheimer's sensibilities. After Silvestri's departure, director Gore Verbinski turned to a colleague from *The Ring*, Hans Zimmer, but Zimmer was working on another project at the time and recommended Klaus Badelt. Still, Zimmer knocked out a range of tunes for the score in one night. With three weeks left to complete all the music for the film, Badelt pressed a veritable crew of composers into work to provide support and more material, recording at a variety of studios in just four days.

Walt Disney Records released a soundtrack album in the summer of 2003 with less than forty-five minutes of music that didn't quite match the cues as heard in the film and had some oddly vague track names. Listeners have also noted that the album painfully distorts the sound of the recording on some tracks.

The most recognizable melody from the film, "He's a Pirate," has lived well beyond the initial score, turning up in a synthesized adaptation by Yoko Shimomura in the *Kingdom Hearts II* videogame and in several versions on the *Pirates Remixed* EP available only through iTunes. DJ Tiësto, who contributed to the EP, also features a remix of "He's a Pirate" on his album *Elements of Life*. . . . And no, this isn't official, but there can be no better musical homage than Michael Bolton's impassioned ode "Jack Sparrow" from *The Lonely Island* ("the jester of Tortuga!").

THE SAGA CONTINUES

Two sequels shot back to back followed this film: *Pirates of the Caribbean: Dead Man's Chest* and *Pirates of the Caribbean: At World's End*, released in 2006 and 2007 and concluding the story of Will and Elizabeth as well as apparently ending the series. In 2011, however, a fourth film eventually arrived to revitalize the saga, with Depp's Jack returning sans most of his previous supporting cast—apart from the welcome presence of Geoffrey Rush as Barbossa—in *Pirates of the Caribbean: On Stranger Tides* (yup, loosely based on the aforementioned Powers novel that also inspired the *Monkey's Island* games). A fifth installment is on the way for 2017.

As for home release, this movie actually turned up on VHS but also had three DVD releases: a single disc, a two-disc special edition, and a three-disc edition, the last featuring a "Lost Disc"

328 • CINEMA AND SORCERY

of still more extra features than on the previous releases. And yes, there's also a Blu-ray version.

The original film had a host of publishing tie-ins, from a graphic novel by Michael Stewart to story and sticker books and a junior novelization by Irene Trimble. A videogame released in 2003 for PC and Xbox featured a character called Captain Nathaniel Hawk. There was also a separate game for mobile devices, and a Game Boy Advance prequel set ten years before the film, with a young Jack Sparrow. Consensus had it that the Game Boy effort was less than satisfying. Hasbro / Milton Bradley put out a *Pirates*-branded adaptation of their classic *Game of Life* board game in a special collector's-tin, mainly focusing on the ride. Only Disney parks carried it.

Most of the franchise's merchandising, including tons of games in traditional and digital formats, kicked in with the sequels, although if you want to reach further back than this film, Parker Brothers based a 1967 board game on the Disneyland park, and a 1975 "Action Game" based on the ride allowed players to down cardboard ships with plastic cannonballs. Yo ho!

TAKE UP THY SWORD!
CURSED MONKEY (ANIMAL)

ATTACKS: The cursed monkey can make a natural (unarmed) attack with a nasty bite and can also wield small melee weapons like daggers or clubs, as well as firearms like pocket pistols.

POWERS/VULNERABILITIES: In his cursed state, this animal is essentially an undead immortal. He is invulnerable to any sort of magical influence that would normally affect living beings, and he cannot be poisoned or diseased. Should the curse lift, however, he becomes just another capuchin monkey.

DETAILS: Victim of an ancient curse that enchanted a treasure of gold pieces (which transforms anyone who steals even one coin into an unliving creature), this monkey is nevertheless a clever and loyal companion.

THE FILM'S DESTINY

Raise your rum and drink up, me hearties, because this stirring, seafaring action-adventure seamlessly blends pirate movies of old with basic elements of the sword-and-sorcery genre to create a fun ride of a film with more than a few knowing winks to a 21st-century audience, while never losing respect for its source material. That it began with the idea of bringing an amusement-park experience to the theater—something that didn't sound very promising—and resulted in an insanely popular blockbuster that spawned a franchise and gave the world Johnny Depp's Captain Jack Sparrow is some kind of minor magic in itself.

> OVER 3000 ISLANDS OF PARADISE—FOR SOME IT'S A BLESSING—FOR OTHERS . . . IT'S A CURSE.

The movie also comfortably straddles a line by evoking a lot of the horror genre's motifs while never tipping over into the purely grotesque. The skeletal cursed pirates are merely a more realistic version of the animated types that chased Disney's classic characters in Halloween short cartoons in days of yore.

Often bathed in moonlight, the film's atmosphere is palpable and invigorating, leading to a wonderful climactic battle in partially lit caverns, with brilliant effects shifting the two combatants—Sparrow and Barbossa—between their human and skeletal appearances. True, this movie doesn't share the aesthetic of the more obvious sword-and-sorcery selections in this book, but it qualifies where it counts, with romantic heroes, thrilling blade-filled battles, magical forces, a quest for treasure (or, rather cleverly, to *return* it) and for salvation, and a spirited score that carries you through the experience like a ship sailing in a brisk breeze. The sequels might overcomplicate matters with excess mythology and morose meandering, but this single movie is a tribute to adventure and well worth the journey.

THIS YEAR IN GAMING

To support the release of the first printing of the *Savage Worlds* core rules published this year, Pinnacle Entertainment Group / Great White Games released the first edition of *50 Fathoms*, a Plot Point setting book that takes players to Caribdus, a drowned world cursed by a trio of ancient sea hags. New races dwell on this fantastic planet, but mysterious portals link it to Earth, allowing pirates and privateers from the 16th through the 19th centuries occasionally to find their way to it. Designer Shane Lacy Hensley has said (in the foreword to the second printing of *50 Fathoms*, released in 2011) that the setting was inspired by elements from the 1995 Kevin Costner movie *Waterworld*, the animated series *The Pirates of Dark Water*, and ... wait for it ... *Pirates of the Caribbean: The Curse of the Black Pearl*.

THE LORD OF THE RINGS: THE RETURN OF THE KING

2003 • NZ/US • NEW LINE CINEMA / WINGNUT FILMS • 201M/251M • COLOR • PG-13

SCREENPLAY: Fran Walsh, Philippa Boyens, and Peter Jackson
BASED ON THE BOOK BY: J. R. R. Tolkien
DIRECTOR: Peter Jackson
PRODUCERS: Barrie M. Osborne, Peter Jackson, and Fran Walsh
MUSIC: Howard Shore. (Featuring "Into the West," with words and music by Howard Shore, Fran Walsh, and Annie Lennox, and performance by Annie Lennox; "The Edge of Night," with music by Billy Boyd, lyrics by J. R. R. Tolkien, and adaptation by Philippa Boyens; and "Aragorn's Coronation," with music by Viggo Mortensen annd lyrics by J. R. R. Tolkien.)
DIRECTOR OF PHOTOGRAPHY: Andrew Lesnie
MAKEUP & HAIR DESIGN: Peter Owen And Peter King
SPECIAL MAKE-UP, CREATURES, ARMOUR, WEAPONS AND MINIATURES: Richard Taylor And Weta Workshop
DIGITAL VISUAL EFFECTS DESIGNED AND CREATED BY: Weta Digital
VISUAL EFFECTS SUPERVISOR: Jim Rygiel
PRODUCTION DESIGNER: Grant Major
SUPERVISING ART DIRECTOR: Dan Hennah
COSTUME DESIGNERS: Ngila Dickson And Richard Taylor
CONCEPTUAL DESIGNERS: Alan Lee And John Howe
CULTURAL FIGHTING STYLES: Tony Woolf
TOLKIEN LANGUAGE TRANSLATION: David Salo
STUNT COORDINATOR: George Marshall Ruge
SWORDMASTER: Bob Anderson
HEAD ANIMAL WRANGLER: Dave Johnson
HORSE COORDINATOR: Steve Old
HORSE TRAINERS: Don Reynolds and Grahame Ware, Jr.
CAST: Elijah Wood (Frodo Baggins); Ian McKellen (Gandalf the White); Liv Tyler (Arwen); Viggo Mortensen (Aragorn); Sean Astin (Samwise Gamgee); Cate Blanchett (Galadriel); John Rhys-Davies (Gimli / Voice of Treebeard); Bernard Hill (King Theoden); Christopher Lee (Saruman); Billy Boyd (Peregrin "Pippin"Took); Dominic Monaghan (Meriadoc "Merry" Brandybuck); Orlando Bloom (Legolas); Hugo Weaving (Elrond); Miranda Otto (Eowyn); David Wenham (Faramir); Brad Dourif (Grima Wormtongue); Karl Urban (Eomer); John Noble (Denethor); Andy Serkis (Gollum); Ian Holm (Bilbo Baggins); Sean Bean (Boromir); Lawrence Makoare (Witchking/Gothmog); Paul Norell (King of the Dead); Marton Csokas (Celeborn); Alan Howard (Voice of the Ring); Noel Appleby (Everard Proudfoot); Alexandra Astin (Elanor Gamgee); David Aston (Gondorian Soldier 3); John Bach (Madril); Sadwyn Brophy (Eldarion); Alistair Browning (Damrod); Richard Edge (Gondorian Solider 1); Jason Fitch (Uruk 1); Phillip Grieve (Orc Commander); Bruce Hopkins (Gamling); Ian Hughes (Irolas); Bret McKenzie (Elf Escort); Sarah McLeod (Rosie Cotton); Maisie McLeod-Riera (Baby Gamgee); Bruce Phillips (Grimbold); Robert Pollock (Orc Sergeant); Shane Rangi (Harad Leader 2); Todd Rippon (Harad Leader 1); Thomas Robins (Deagol); Harry Sinclair (Isildur); Bruce Spence (The Mouth of Sauron); Peter Tait (Shagrat / Corsair Captain); Joel Tolbeck (Orc Lieutenant 1); Stephen Ure (Gorbag); Tom George, Anthony May, Andy Serkis, Craig Parker, Joel Tolbeck, Kevin Howarth, Mark Bowden, Con O'Neil, Brian Sergent, Martin Kwok, and Chris Ward (Additional Character Voices); Sala Baker, Ross Duncan, Pete Smith, Jed Brophy, and Lee Hartley (Featured Orcs); Billy and Katie Jackson (Featured Children); Jorn Benzon (Traveling Elf, uncredited); Peter Jackson (Mercenary on Boat, uncredited); and Royd Tolkien (Ranger, uncredited)

ON THE MAP

The war is reaching its climax, so we spend a good amount of time at the once-great city of Minas Tirith, although various characters visit the Paths of the Dead, Minas Morgul, a disgustingly sticky cave inhabited by Shelob the spider, and the Black Gate. At that last, the final battle takes place, while the Ring sinks into oblivion at the Crack of Doom. Then there's a melancholy return to the Shire before setting off on that last boat ride west. . . .

OUR STORY SO FAR

As Aragorn moves closer to embracing his destiny and facing the full might of Sauron in the final battle for Middle-earth at Minas Tirith and the Black Gate, Frodo and Sam edge nearer to destroying the One Ring and vanquishing evil from the world once and for all. But will Gollum become their greatest obstacle or their most unwitting ally . . . and who will survive to witness the return of the king?

ALTERNATE VERSIONS

As with the previous two installments in the trilogy, an extended edition followed the theatrical cut on home-video release and added a great deal to the film . . . but in this case, in our humble opinion, it is a rare occasion in which much of the additional material unnecessarily slows the pacing at crucial points, adds humor that falls flat and seems tonally wrong with certain characters, and ruins a vital surprise late in the movie that everyone thought would turn out well for our heroes but still depends on a sense of suspense to feel triumphant. Therefore, unlike with the previous two movies, we argue that this movie's extended version is inferior to the cut seen in theaters.

. . . So after all this, you might wonder: what is our recommendation for the best way to experience the trilogy, given the different editions of each film? It's simple: Watch the extended editions of *The Fellowship* and *The Two Towers*, and then watch the opening sequence with Saruman from the extended edition of *The Return of the King*. Stop it immediately after that and switch to the theatrical edition of *Return*. You're welcome.

IT'S MAGIC

Wrapping up our look at magic in this trilogy, one of the most significant bits of necromancy here is on the side of good and not evil: the oath that binds the army of the dead to Aragorn by his lineage and guarantees him a uniquely half-ghost, half-corporeal green-zombie legion just when he needs it! We see Galadriel's gift of the Light of Earendil employed in the dark depths of Shelob's lair. Another kind of magical light strikes a blow when Gandalf holds off the Nazgul with a beam from his staff. He's clearly still got it, even if he seems a bit less tolerant of smoking than he was in his Grey incarnation.

Speaking of the Nazgul, while Sauron and his power drive the narrative from beginning to end, the witch king of Angmar—a sorcerer so powerful he can even break Gandalf the White's staff—is a devastating foe with one significant weakness. It is said that no man can hinder him;

> THE EYE OF THE ENEMY IS MOVING.

a woman like Eowyn, on the other hand.... (Maybe she *is* a good match for Faramir, after all.) And does he crumble at the assault!

Though sailing off into the West is of course a death metaphor, in Tolkien's universe the notion exists that many of the beings populating Middle-earth, like the wizards (Istari or Maiar), come from somewhere else and dwell in more than one dimension or on more than one level of reality at once. The voyage we see at the end of this film is perhaps their withdrawing from our world and going back home . . . if you want to believe that.

Finally, one of the more powerful threads running through this narrative is that the forces of magic as represented by the good beings of Middle-earth all derive from an affinity with the natural world, whereas those that trade in the trappings of technology—steam-belching factories in the fiery pits of Isengard, siege machines crushing the landscape, and suicide bombers delivering explosives—are evil. The encroaching of the modern, nonmagical world on an ecologically balanced one of magic and nature is at the core of the struggle in Tolkien's saga. Although we side with those who find harmony with nature—itself just one planar projection of a multidimensional reality—we also accept by the story's end that the modern world of Men is inevitable. The real message then is one of caution: can we preserve that harmony with nature and still progress industrially? If Peter Jackson hadn't omitted the crucial epilogue featuring a still-living Saruman enslaving Hobbiton and turning it into another factory that must be shut down, we might have a definitive answer: no.

THE QUEST FOR MEANING

As we come to the end of the trilogy, one of the most pervasive themes is not just the old reliable triumph of good over evil but the more melancholy notion that even in victory one must accept that nothing can stop the passage of time and that some wounds never heal. Aragorn will become king, but he will also one day die. Our heroes will soon take that trip across the sea and leave the world to others (like Sam's children) to inherit. There is something of immortality in that idea. Individuals pass on, but life continues. A bittersweet, almost elegiac quality pervades this otherwise bombastic conclusion to an epic saga. After all the battles are fought and the world is saved from darkness and oblivion, the larger challenge of simply facing life lies ahead. All things end, but endings can be beginnings, too . . . and oh, yes, there's a prequel trilogy, isn't there . . . ?

WHO GOES THERE?

We don't have many people left to cover in this section, because so many of the cast members recur from the previous two films, but on we go.

Alexandra Astin and Maisie McLeod-Riera do a great job of playing the roles of Sam and Rosie's children, and why not? After all, they're the actual daughters of Sean Astin and Sarah McLeod, respectively (who are not together in real life).

David Aston quickly popped in on *Hercules: The Legendary Journeys* and *Xena: Warrior Princess*, and then had roles in *The Matrix* and *Underworld: Rise of the Lycans*.

Yes, Alistair Browning was on *Hercules: The Legendary Journeys* and *Xena: Warrior Princess*, as well as *Jack of All Trades* and three *Power Rangers* shows.

Of course Ian Hughes also appeared in *Hercules: The Legendary Journeys* and *Xena: Warrior Princess*, as well as *Robin Hood* and *Torchwood*.

Todd Rippon turned up in *Hercules: The Legendary Journeys*, one of its TV-movie predecessors, *Xena: Warrior Princess*, and Peter Jackson's film *The Frighteners*.

Thomas Robins returned as Young Thrain in *The Hobbit: An Unexpected Journey*.

Bruce Spence had roles in *The Cars That Eat People*, both *Mad Max 2: The Road Warrior* and *Mad Max Beyond Thunderdome* (possibly his most memorable appearances), *Hercules Returns*, *Ace Ventura: When Nature Calls*, *Dark City*, *Queen of the Damned*, *Finding Nemo* (as the voice of Chum), *The Matrix Revolutions*, *Peter Pan*, *Star Wars: Episode III—Revenge of the Sith*, and *The Chronicles of Narnia: The Voyage of the Dawn Treader*. He also appeared on the *BeastMaster* TV series.

Peter Tait was Gyorg in *Underworld: Rise of the Lycans* . . . and guess which TV shows he's appeared on?

Joel Tobeck (miscredited as "Tolbeck" in the film) works extensively on stage but made the usual other appearances: *Young Hercules*, *Hercules: The Legendary Journeys*, and *Xena: Warrior Princess*. He also appeared in *Cleopatra 2525* and a number of *Power Rangers* series. In film he's had roles in *Ghost Rider* and *30 Days of Night*.

Royd Tolkien is part of the family: he's J. R. R.'s great-grandson.

6 DEGREES OF SORCERY

Saruman's death by impalement on the wooden wheel echoes many of Christopher Lee's final moments in his Hammer *Dracula* films, especially in the pre-credits sequence of *Dracula A.D. 1972*. Gandalf's suggestion that Minas Tirith might fall at "the whim of a madman" recalls one of Dennis Hopper's lines in the action movie *Speed*. We're sure it's not intentional. When the orcs arrive to attack Osgiliath, their ramped boats bring to mind the beach landings during the invasion of Normandy in World War II. Keep your eyes peeled, but what is young Boba Fett from *Star Wars: Episode I—The Phantom Menace* doing in the crowd at Minas Tirith? (We know: it's only actor Daniel Logan in a blink-and-you-miss-him appearance.)

The Paths of the Dead sure look familiar, almost like they might be the home turf for the Sumatran rat-monkey in Peter Jackson's earlier film, *Braindead* (but that's just because he used the same location, the Putangirua Pinnacles, both times). The army of the dead and their king have an old-school Disney's Haunted Mansion look to them, with their greenish, funhouse glow. Some of them also slightly resemble the Blind Dead from the series of horror movies by that name.

The wild-man oliphaunt rider sports a little bit of a *Mad Max* post-apocalyptic style. The witch king collapses like a more frenetic version of the Wicked Witch of the West, when she melted away in *The Wizard of Oz*. Our heroes taking out the oliphaunts resembles the Rebels bringing down the AT-AT walkers in *Star Wars: The Empire Strikes Back*. The lineage of Aragorn's rallying speech at the Black Gate stretches back to the St. Crispen's Day speech in

Shakespeare's *Henry V.* The image of Frodo with the red book at the desk in Bag End echoes Bilbo's similar scene at the start of the trilogy; see, these movies even come full circle and reference themselves!

SHATTERING THE ILLUSION

While this production didn't face the "middle chapter" struggles that *The Two Towers* had to overcome, crafting an epic ending to the trilogy was surely no easy task. As with the other films, changes from the source material rankled some fans, such as Sam being sent home prior to the confrontation with Shelob, to increase the threat and power of Gollum.

Arwen turning up at Helm's Deep might have given dedicated fans cause to wail in *The Two Towers*, but even more shocking might have been a physical final duel between Aragorn and Sauron, the latter reassuming the huge humanoid form of the first film's flashback to the previous war. Serious thought was given to the idea that audiences would want to see their hero defeat Sauron face to face, but after three days of shooting that fight, Jackson and his team decided it was the wrong way to go and that Sauron should remain a distant, incorporeal force. They made use of that battle footage by replacing Sauron with the troll that faces Aragorn at the Black Gates.

Once again the script omits part of Tolkien's story, but here it is a truly profound change: the entire "Scouring of the Shire" epilogue is missing, and the return to Hobbiton has none of the terror of finding home turned into a factory, nor a last meeting with Saruman. (Galadriel's mirror prediction at least gave the Scouring a nod.)

Crew members built the enormous Minas Tirith set—the trilogy's most extensive construction, inspired by architecture from Italy, France, and Cornwall, England—on the remains of the Helm's Deep set from the previous film. The City of the Dead was based on Petra in Jordan. (Remember that place?)

As for the army of the dead—something the entire team was thrilled about, because it meant creating *zombies*—a brief period of trepidation transpired when the trailer for Disney's *Pirates of the Caribbean: The Curse of the Black Pearl* came out, showcasing a face (Barbossa's) that looked shockingly similar to the design of this movie's zombie king. Still the team forged ahead.

The truly disturbing Shelob was designed to scare Jackson himself, with a lot of her look based on local New Zealand tunnel-web spiders. Artists rendered the elephantine Mumakils in CGI most of the time, but others also created a life-size mockup of a dead one, which later gave the Weta team the perfect backdrop for their crew photo.

Most of the shooting for this installment was scheduled toward the end of the fourteen-to-fifteen-month filming of the trilogy. A Queenstown flood required a few changes to the original plan. Part of the sequence with Sam being sent home by Frodo was shot before Serkis was even cast, and wouldn't be completed with Serkis until a year later.

When directing Christopher Lee for his final scenes as Saruman, Jackson tried to coach him on how to react to being stabbed, only to have the elderly actor explain the *real* way someone sounds when being stabbed to death. His war experience apparently gave him firsthand knowledge. Jackson deferred to his expertise. On a less grisly note, Sean Astin appreciated that the Cirith Ungol setting gave him a chance to feel like Errol Flynn.

The film—and the entire trilogy—finished principal photography on December 21, 2000. Three years after that, pickups were shot.

> "THIS DAY DOES NOT BELONG TO ONE MAN BUT TO ALL. LET US TOGETHER REBUILD THIS WORLD THAT WE MAY SHARE IN THE DAYS OF PEACE."

During that time, the final wrestling for the Ring between Frodo and Gollum was finessed to make it more of a back-and-forth struggle between addicts, in an echo of the earlier confrontation between Smeagol and Deagol. The battle on Mount Doom was also enhanced, making movie history by using 35mm full-motion capture on Serkis for those shots. The coronation scene benefited from the pickup schedule, particularly the wildly passionate kiss between Aragorn and Arwen that had never quite reached that level in the original shoot.

Jackson was visibly shaken and in tears while shooting the last-ever live-action scene of Elijah Wood as Frodo in Bag End. And then it was over.

While the post-production process for *The Two Towers* was arduous, this one was a desperate, chaotic race to the finish line, with Jackson pushing the crew to the limits. He dumped 2 million feet of film on them for editing and added special-effects shots (more in the final two months than in the previous two films) to the nearly 1,500 required, creating new footage, jeopardizing the release date, and editing right to the last minute. One shot of a Mumakil that originally took six months to complete had to be scrapped and redone in just two days.

The somewhat odd Smeagol/Deagol scene feels unfinished in comparison to much of the rest of the movie. Originally intended as a flashback for *The Two Towers*, it became the prologue here. The vital confrontation that concludes Saruman's story, removed from the second movie with the intent for it to open *The Return of the King*, was cut *again* for this film's theatrical release. Christopher Lee was none too pleased to see his character given no closure except on home video releases, but fortunately he and Jackson would resolve the bad blood by the time he returned for the *Hobbit* films.

The film opened in Wellington—its world premiere—on December 1, 2003. Not only did a fell beast now loom over the Embassy Theater; the entire city celebrated the trilogy's final film. An Oslo acting troupe followed the film around the world and performed live recaps of the first two movies, having spent six months preparing for the tour with no compensation.

For fans of the trilogy and of fantasy in general, one of the most moving moments in this monumental achievement came with its phenomenal sweep at the 76th Academy Awards. The film took all eleven awards for which it was nominated, tying with *Ben Hur* and *Titanic* for most wins to date. Steven Spielberg presented the final award, for Best Picture, announcing a "clean sweep" that for many watching that night served as a vindication and validation not only of the extraordinary production effort that shaped the trilogy but for genre filmmaking, including movies like *King Kong* and *The 7th Voyage of Sinbad* that inspired Jackson in the first place and led him to create a saga that he hoped would continue that legacy for generations to come. Accepting the award, Jackson quipped, "Fantasy is an f-word that hopefully the five-second delay won't do anything with."

... And *still* it wasn't over, because less than a month after Oscar night, the team was shooting one last insert of model skulls for the extended-edition DVD release. Alan Lee completed his drawing for the DVD release a week before it hit shelves.

Perfectionists.

MUSIC OF THE MINSTRELS

Although many themes from the trilogy return (appropriately enough) for the final installment, in some cases providing just the right sense of accompanying aural closure for the cast of characters and their various roles in the saga, that doesn't mean composer Howard Shore didn't find places to introduce new material this late in the game. Themes for Gondor and Minas Tirtih debuted in full here, drawing from elements as far back as those in *Fellowship*. Shore also weaved the melody that would accompany Annie Lennox's vocals for "Into the West" (more on that in a minute) into the score, especially during the contemplative scene in which Gandalf comforts Pippin on the eve of battle. To be sure, some of the most emotional, rousing moments come when the strains of the Shire or Fellowship themes bring the saga full circle.

As with past installments, a number of vocal performances added depth, including Billy Boyd's dark rendition of "The Edge of Night" and Viggo Mortensen's short but sublime vocals during the coronation of Aragorn. Anyone with a heart can't help but be moved by the extraordinary end-credits song "Into the West," sung by Lennox (full composition credits detailed above). Shore also rescued an unused song sung by Arwen, featuring Liv Tyler's vocals from *The Two Towers*, for the extended-edition cut of this film: specifically, the scene set in the Houses of Healing. He saved another piece planned for that scene by moving it to accompany the long scroll of fan names featured in the end credits.

In November 2003, Reprise Records released the first soundtrack for *The Return of the King* in a regular CD edition with poster cover-art. A limited edition added an extra DVD with a variety of bonus features, including an Annie Lennox track, "Use Well the Days," originally planned for the end credits but rejected in favor of "Into the West." In November 2007, Reprise brought out this film's installment in *The Complete Recordings* series on CD, with an accompanying double-sided DVD-audio. An annotated score was, as before, distributed for free online. This was the only one of the three *Complete Recordings* releases also made available digitally.

As with the other two films, *Complete Recordings* liner-notes author Doug Adams chronicled the story of Shore's work on the saga in his book, *The Music of the Lord of the Rings Films*. The book included another CD, *The Rarities Archive*, which provided still more material for eager fans to hear, plus insights from Shore.

During this film's historic Academy Awards sweep in 2004, "Into the West" won the Best Song Oscar. The score in its entirety won Best Original Score as well as a Grammy for Best Score Soundtrack Album. Shore later created a *Lord of the Rings Symphony* for performances in various venues, with an accompany-

> THERE CAN BE NO TRIUMPH WITHOUT LOSS.
> NO VICTORY WITHOUT SUFFERING.
> NO FREEDOM WITHOUT SACRIFICE.

ing visual-art and light show, as well as a DVD release on the making of the six-movement *Symphony* experience. In September 2011, a double album of the symphony became available digitally and on CD.

THE SAGA CONTINUES

One last time we'll take as read the plethora of items released in conjunction with this and the previous two films, and take a look at a few gaming-related highlights. Hasbro / Parker Brothers released versions of classic board games *Risk, Monopoly,* and *Trivial Pursuit* in *The Lord of the Rings Trilogy Edition*s in 2003 (with *Risk* getting a *Siege of Minas Tirith* expansion). A DVD *Trivial Pursuit* edition followed in 2004, and a *Collectors Edition* of the *Monopoly* tie-in, with different art and playing-pieces, came out in conjunction with USAopoly. In 2004, Hasbro / Milton Bradley offered a *Stratego* tie-in as well.

A puzzle-based game from WizKids called *Connect with Pieces: The Lord of the Rings* came out in 2013, as did a *Dice Building Game*. A year earlier, WizKids released *The Lord of the Rings: Nazgûl* game, and in 2011 the company added *The Lord of the Rings* characters to their pantheon of Heroclix game figures.

In 2011, Fantasy Flight Games launched *The Lord of the Rings: The Card Game*. Then the company ensured that fans would never again be at a loss for something to buy, because it followed the initial release with monthly "Adventure Pack" and "Saga" expansions in a variety of thematic cycles that continue to this day and now extend into *The Hobbit* part of the series. A "Nightmare Deck" subseries allows for more arduous play, and copies of a "Game Night Kit" are bundled for retailers.

Another card-playing option continued in 2014, courtesy of Cryptozoic Entertainment: *The Lord of the Rings: The Return of the King Deck-Building Game*. In 2003, Games Workshop continued their *Warhammer*-like tabletop battle-and-strategy system with a boxed *Return of the King* tie-in game. In 2005, the company released *The Lord of the Rings: Strategy Battle Game* to rework the series, which began in 2001. As usual, multiple supplements and "Journeybook" expansions followed the *Core Rules Manual* for this new version. A plethora of plastic and metal miniature figures also accompanied the game, as before.

The Reiner Knizia–designed *Lord of the Rings* game from Rio Grande Games added a *Battlefields* expansion in 2007. Impact Games and RoseArt both put out board games based on the film in 2004. Pressman Toy Corp. released *The Complete Trilogy—Adventure Board Game* in 2012 with a hex-tile modular board. Stern Pinball released a pinball machine based on the entire trilogy in 2003 and then rereleased it in 2009, with updates, as *The Lord of the Rings: Limited Edition*.

In 2003, Electronic Arts released a videogame for the Xbox, PlayStation 2, Nintendo GameCube, and Game Boy Advance, as well as for Windows and Mac, based on this film and *The Lord of the Rings: The Two Towers*. The game expanded on the company's previous release a year earlier and won two DICE awards in 2004. Electronic Arts continued to release (sometimes tenuous) film tie-in games, like *The Lord of the Rings: The Third Age* in 2004, *The Lord of the Rings: Tactics* and *The Lord of the Rings: Conquest* in 2009, and *The Lord of the Rings: The Battle for Middle-earth* series beginning in 2004.

More recently, Warner Bros. Interactive released *Guardians of Middle-earth* for Windows, PlayStation 3, and Xbox 360 in 2013, and even *LEGO The Lord of the Rings* for consoles and computers, that same year! In 2007, Turbine Inc. and Midway Games introduced a *World of Warcraft*–style MMORPG called *The Lord of the Rings Online* for Windows and Mac platforms. They have added multiple updates and expansions and extended the license to 2017. The game went "free to play" in 2010.

As for further films, look no further than our chapter on *The Hobbit: An Unexpected Journey* and our index entries for the next two films in that trilogy *(The Hobbit: The Desolation of Smaug* and *The Hobbit: The Battle of the Five Armies)* for the backward "prequel" continuation of the series. Just don't hold your breath for that *Silmarillion* adaptation any time soon.

TAKE UP THY SWORD!
THE SEEING STONES (MAGICAL ARTIFACTS)

The legendary Seeing Stones are large glass spheres that appear to contain swirling masses of living energy. Each stone psychically links to the others and thus can transmit and receive information from afar, including sights, sounds, and even thoughts. Using a stone requires no magical discipline, but the act can tax the user, requiring recovery through rest, even deep sleep. Use of one of the spheres can also make a person vulnerable to psychic infiltration and attack, because it links to the user's mind.

Such a stone has sorcerous construction, which grants it a radically reduced mass; thus, despite its size, its possessor does not need to employ an ogre to transport it. Even a halfling can easily lift and carry one.

Spells capable of arresting or removing magical abilities can temporarily affect the Seeing Stones. Regardless of the strength of such a spell, though, the stones' abilities always return with the rising of the sun. Few of these items remain in the world, so they are especially valuable.

THE FILM'S DESTINY

Endings aren't easy, especially with a sweeping saga of this scale and a huge cast of characters whose roles all need closure. We know that many took this film to task for its supposedly over-long parade of endings, but we can't agree. While we might quibble over the fadeout approach, the succession of final bows doesn't seem excessive at all, when this is hardly the conclusion of one film but of a three-movie epic that clocks in at more than eleven hours if you watch the extended editions. Besides, if you're as emotionally invested in the fates of all who fought Sauron by the end of this installment—as well you should be—then the series has bought every bit of goodwill it needs to justify dwelling long enough in Middle-earth to document the bittersweet passing of an age.

Both this and the previous movie juggle multiple plotlines with relative ease. This one also had to provide a conclusion that felt both triumphant and tinged with sadness. It has rousing battle sequences heretofore unseen on the silver screen, moments of joy and sorrow, a speech by a hero that gives the one at Agincourt a run for its money, and even a stunning final-credits sequence with a song scientifically designed to make even the most stoic viewer shed a tear.

This is quite simply one of the finest fantasy films ever made. Sweeping the Academy Awards might not be proof, but it's at least an indication that more than just dedicated fans noticed the accomplishment here. So ends one of the most ambitious and entertaining sword-and-sorcery sagas ever committed to film, flaws and all. We can only end by saying: Peter Jackson, you have shown your quality, sir—the very highest.

> THIS CHRISTMAS THE JOURNEY ENDS.

THIS YEAR IN GAMING

With the 2003 formation of a new company known as Great White Games, *Deadlands* designer Shane Lacy Hensley released the first edition of a new set of RPG rules known as *Savage Worlds*. Many of the core mechanics have their basis in the Origins Award–winning roleplaying game *Deadlands: The Weird West*, but much of the system is also clearly a distillation of aspects of Pinnacle's boxed miniatures game, *Deadlands: The Great Rail Wars*. Promoted as a "Fast! Furious! Fun!" alternative to many of the overly complicated RPGs on the market, it offered a generic system that could easily adapt to any genre. To accompany the release of the core rulebook, Great White also published two 144-page hardcover "Savage Settings" that same year: *Evernight: The Darkest Setting of All* (dark science-fantasy) and *50 Fathoms: High Adventure in a Drowned World* (pirate fantasy). Additional setting books, miniatures, custom dice, playing cards, and other supplemental items continue to follow to this day. The first edition of *Savage Worlds* won the 2003 Origins Gamers' Choice Award for Best Role-Playing Game.

THE CHRONICLES OF NARNIA: THE LION, THE WITCH AND THE WARDROBE

2005 • US • WALT DISNEY PICTURES / WALDEN MEDIA • 143M • COLOR • PG

SCREENPLAY: Ann Peacock, Andrew Adamson, Christopher Markus, and Stephen McFeely (based on the book by C. S. Lewis)
DIRECTOR: Andrew Adamson
PRODUCERS: Mark Johnson and Philip Steuer
CO-PRODUCER: Douglas Gresham
MUSIC: Harry Gregson-Williams
DIRECTOR OF PHOTOGRAPHY: Donald M. McAlpine
PRODUCTION DESIGNER: Roger Ford
ART DIRECTORS: Ian Gracie, Jules Cook, Karen Murphy, and Jeffrey Thorp
COSTUME DESIGNER: Isis Mussenden
CREATURE AND VISUAL CONCEPT DESIGN, ARMOUR AND WEAPONS: Richard Taylor
SPECIAL MAKEUP AND CREATURES: Howard Berger And Gregory Nicotero
STUNT COORDINATOR / SWORDMASTER: Allan Poppleton
CAST: Georgie Henley (Lucy Pevensie); Skandar Keynes (Edmund Pevensie); William Moseley (Peter Pevensie); Anna Popplewell (Susan Pevensie); Tilda Swinton (White Witch); James McAvoy (Mr. Tumnus); Jim Broadbent (Professor Kirke); Kiran Shah (Ginarrbrik); James Cosmo (Father Christmas); Judy McIntosh (Mrs. Pevensie); Elizabeth Hawthorne (Mrs. Macready); Patrick Kake (Oreius); Shane Rangi (General Otmin); Liam Neeson (Aslan); Ray Winstone (Voice of Mr. Beaver); Dawn French (Voice of Mrs. Beaver); Rupert Everett (Voice of Mr. Fox); Cameron Rhodes (Voice of Gryphon); Philip Steuer (Voice of Philip the Horse); Jim May (Voice of Vardan); Sim Evan-Jones (Voice of Wolf); Douglas Gresham (Radio Announcer); Brandon Cook (Boy on Train); Cassie Cook (Girl on Train); Morris Lupton (Train Conductor); Shelley Edwards-Bishop, Susan Haldane, and Margaret Bremner (Distraught Mothers); Jaxin Hall (Soldier); Terry Murdoch (German Pilot); Katrina Browne (Green Dryad); Lee Tuson (Rumblebuffin the Giant); Elizabeth Kirk, Felicity Hamill, Kate O'Rourke, Sonya Hitchcock, Lucy Tanner, and Tiggy Mathias (Hags); Greg Cooper, Richard King, and Russell Pickering (Fauns); Ben Barrington, Charles Williams, Vanessa Cater, and Allison Sarofim (Centaurs); Alina Phelan (Centaur Archer); Stephen Ure and Sam Lahood (Satyrs); Ajay Ratilal Navi, Bhoja Kannada, Zakiuddin Mohd. Farooque, M. Ramaswami, Prapaphorn Chansantor, Nikhom Husungnern, and Doungdieo Savangvong (Red and Black Dwarfs); Rachel Henley (Older Lucy); Mark Wells (Older Edmund); Noah Huntley (Older Peter); and Sophie Winkleman (Older Susan)

OUR STORY SO FAR

After four siblings evacuate to a professor's country home during the London bombings of World War II, they discover a mysterious old wardrobe that functions as a doorway to Narnia, a fantastic but divided land where the wintry White Witch's power has encased much of the world in ice and fear. With the arrival of the human children and their subsequent alliance with the mighty Aslan and his army, hope returns to Narnia.

> SOME JOURNEYS TAKE US FAR FROM HOME.
> SOME ADVENTURES LEAD US TO OUR DESTINY.

IT'S MAGIC

Only the most powerful beings in Narnia seem capable of wielding magic. Aslan can restore life to the lifeless with a simple breath, and the White Witch uses a powerful magical wand capable of turning flesh into stone. Using a strange green elixir, she can also forge items such as a goblet of hot chocolate or a casket of Turkish delight.

Lucy receives a healing tonic. An implication not really explored in this film suggests that the other items gifted upon the children by Father Christmas—a sword revealed later in the books to be Rhindon, a bow, a horn, a shield, and so on—are also enchanted.

THE QUEST FOR MEANING

It's no secret that C. S. Lewis wrote *The Lion, the Witch, and the Wardrobe*, as well as the rest of the books in the series, as a Christian allegory. While the 2005 feature film has somewhat whitewashed many of the elements, aspects remain. The most glaringly obvious one is Aslan as a Christ figure. He endures humiliation, torture and death—much of that caused by the sins of the sons of Adam, especially Edmund's betrayal—and then resurrects and goes forth to breathe life (the Holy Spirit) into his warriors so that they might face and defeat the forces of darkness. Some people find the black-and-white morality of the tale completely without biblical nuance, though, and others scratch their heads at Aslan's savage takedown of the White Witch (go online for some fascinating discussions about this), but Lewis clearly never set out simply to retell the Gospels in his fantastical world of Narnia. The recognizable elements are there in a Joseph Campbell *(The Hero with a Thousand Faces)* way, blended with themes, stories, and characters from Greek and Roman mythology, as well as traditional British and Irish fairytales.

WHO GOES THERE?

This was Georgie Henley's motion-picture debut. Though only 9 years old at the time—she celebrated that birthday during production—she proved a dynamic addition to the cast. Since then she's focused a lot of her energy on her education, but she had time to revisit Narnia two more times in *The Chronicles of Narnia: Prince Caspian* and *The Chronicles of Narnia: The Voyage of the Dawn Treader*, as well as play roles in the thrillers *Perfect Sisters* and *The Sisterhood of Night*.

The bulk of Skandar Keynes' rather brief acting career thus far has primarily focused on Narnia. He appeared in the first three films in the series. One ridiculously cool fact (at least to us) is that he is the great-great-great-grandson of naturalist Charles Darwin!

William "Wizzle" Moseley set his sights on acting from a very young age. His big break came with this film, in his selection from among thousands of potential Peters. Apart from the second and third installments in this series, he has also appeared in *Run, The Silent Mountain, Veil*, and the over-the-top and extremely silly *Don Cheadle Is Captain Planet* short.

Before arriving in Narnia, Anna Popplewell had already appeared in *The Little Vampire, Thunderpants,* and *Girl with a Pearl Earring*. Since allying herself with Aslan, she has played a recurring role in the TV series *Reign*.

Evil Has Reigned for 100 Years...

Starting with 1986's *Caravaggio*, Tilda Swinton has had a wide and varied acting career thanks to her exceptional talent and striking appearance. Many remember her best for her title role in the film *Orlando*, but she also appeared in *The Beach, Vanilla Sky, Constantine, The Curious Case of Benjamin Button, Moonrise Kingdom, The Zero Theorem, The Grand Budapest Hotel,* and *Doctor Strange.*

Recently, Scottish actor James McAvoy stepped into Patrick Stewart's shoes as the younger version of Professor Charles Xavier in *X-Men: First Class, X-Men: Days of Future Past,* and *X-Men: Apocalypse.* You can also find him as Leto Atreides II in the 2003 *Children of Dune* miniseries, and he appears in films like *Wanted, Arthur Christmas, Trance,* and 2015's *Victor Frankenstein.*

Jim Broadbent is one of those veteran British character-actors who needs little in the way of introduction. With a career stretching back decades and no sign of slowing down, he has lit up the screen in films like *Time Bandits, Brazil, The Borrowers, Moulin Rouge!, Hot Fuzz, Indiana Jones and the Kingdom of the Crystal Skull, Inkheart, Harry Potter and the Half-Blood Prince, Cloud Atlas,* and *Paddington.*

You can find Elizabeth Hawthorne in *The Tommyknockers, Hercules: The Legendary Journeys, The Frighteners, Xena: Warrior Princess, 30 Days of Night,* and *Underworld: Rise of the Lycans.*

Though Ray Winstone started his career in the boxing ring, many of us first saw him as Will Scarlet in the *Robin of Sherwood* series that ran from 1984 to 1986. A jobbing actor on television and in films, Winstone also appears in *King Arthur, The Departed, Beowulf, Indiana Jones and the Kingdom of the Crystal Skull, Percy Jackson & the Olympians: The Lightning Thief, Hugo, Snow White and the Huntsman,* and *Noah.*

Writer and actor Dawn French has made the world laugh for decades. On the small screen she appears in various incarnations, in *French & Saunders, The Vicar of Dibley, Murder Most Horrid, Clatterford,* and *Psychoville,* and she has also appeared in films like *The Adventures of Pinocchio, Harry Potter and the Prisoner of Azkaban,* and *Coraline.*

Rupert Everett has appeared in *Cemetery Man, The Madness of King George, Shakespeare in Love, Inspector Gadget, Shrek 2* (where he first worked with director Andrew Adamson), *Shrek the Third,* and *Stardust.*

6 DEGREES OF SORCERY

The film opens with a nighttime journey through dark clouds, similar to the opening of *Eragon.* The approaching German bombers echo the opening of the "B-17" segment of the animated feature film *Heavy Metal.* An internal and very intentional "degree of sorcery" is the imitation of the bombers depicted at the top of the film by the rock-dropping gryphons during the climactic battle. A sign in the background reads "Platform 9"; is a "3/4" just off-screen? The beautifully filmed shots of the vintage train crossing the British countryside mirror similar scenes in the *Harry Potter* films as well.

The kid-friendly zombie-film *ParaNorman* more-or-less reuses the line about the bird outside the window "pssting" at the children (there said by the character Neil). A minotaur sans clothing, looking remarkably similar to those in this film, returns to the big screen a few years later in *Your Highness* (covered elsewhere in this volume).

La Sagrada Familia, designed by Catalan architect Antoni Gaudi, inspired the queen's castle. Her throne room, however, shares design elements with the work of Sir Lawrence Alma-Tadema.

The scene in which the party hides from Father Christmas is remarkably similar to a scene in *The Lord of the Rings: The Fellowship of the Ring*, in which Frodo and company hide off the road from a Black Rider. Overall comparisons to *The Lord of the Rings* films are inevitable, considering that the majority of location shoots for both productions took place in New Zealand and both utilized the always amazing Weta Workshop for armor, weapons, props, and more.

SHATTERING THE ILLUSION

Director Andrew Adamson set out to make a movie based on his childhood memories of the *Narnia* books rather than a literal big-screen adaptation of the original text. When he revisited the book and initial script treatments, he was surprised to find certain scenes lacking details or missing altogether. His vivid imagination had created those elements, which were frequently what had made the books so impactful to him.

Working with a cast of children was both fun and challenging for everyone involved. Because tensions can run high on film shoots, Georgie Henley instituted a "potty-mouth bucket" that often filled—much of that thanks to Kiran Shah, who repeatedly slipped on the fake snow.

Much of the shooting took place in chronological order, to deal with the kids growing up. Skandar Keynes' voice changed so much that his sister came in to loop some of his lines.

About an eighth of the Paddington Station set was an accurate re-creation, expanded by CG. A British costume house shipped over all the costumes for the extras in the station. Train exteriors, shot in England, are some of the very few scenes actually shot in the UK. Exteriors of the professor's house were shot on the grounds of an abandoned manor outside of Auckland, and interiors were meticulously researched sets populated with historically accurate furniture and props, also shipped from the UK. The iconic wardrobe itself, which was constructed of fruit wood, featured inset, sculpted panels depicting scenes from Narnia, particularly story elements from the prequel book (sixth in the series), *The Magician's Nephew*. Additional nods to *The Magician's Nephew* appear on the professor's apple-shaped tobacco box.

The production could not bring live reindeer to New Zealand, for fear of bovine disease, so it required animatronic and CG versions. One of Weta's first contributions to the film was the queen's goblet and Turkish-delight casket. Note that the fish and chips offered by the Beavers are fish and wood-chips!

The real wolves used in the film had far too much fun, so digital artists had to replace their happy tails with more aggressive ones. Rumblebuffin appears only as a frozen statue in the queen's courtyard, but Douglas Gresham, Lewis's stepson, enthusiastically approved the design.

Tolkien had disapproved of the appearance of Father Christmas in the book, but Lewis had insisted. That insistence influenced Adamson's decision to ensure he appeared in the film as well.

THE BATTLE FOR NARNIA BEGINS

One sequence not appearing in the original text was the chase upon the ice floes. Adamson added it to fill what he believed was a gap in the story, and because he sought an opportunity to create an exciting and challenging scene. An elaborate hydraulic system allowed the icebergs to move independently.

Aslan's camp was constructed around the Elephant Rocks area near Oamaru on New Zealand's South Island, a location Adamson adored and found almost spiritual. The rock-and-earth ridge onto which the queen rides her sled at the start of the battle consisted of earth, rocks, and synthetic materials. The entire battlefield was cleared of sheep, fertilized, and seeded beforehand to ensure it would be a vast expanse of green at the time of shooting. A few exteriors were shot in rural Montana, but most scenes played out on stages, in the Czech Republic, and in New Zealand.

MUSIC OF THE MINSTRELS

Composer Harry Gregson-Williams has produced music for TV, films, and videogames since 1993, when he scored a TV project called *Champion Children*. He then went on to collaborate with Hans Zimmer for *The Whole Wide World* and *Smilla's Sense of Snow*, and John Powell on *Antz, Chicken Run, and Shrek*. It was on *Shrek* that director Andrew Adamson first worked with him.

When Adamson moved on to *Narnia*, he brought Gregson-Williams along, believing that he could compose a variety of themes in a number of styles reflective of the various areas of Narnia—and restrain himself from producing something too loud, dominating, and manipulative. With the assistance of the Hollywood Studio Symphony Orchestra and a choir of 150 voices, Gregson-Williams crafted a sweeping score that beautifully enhanced the childlike dream-quality to elements of the film. Along with those themes and moments, he incorporated a variety of folk instruments to accompany the children and highlight their innocence.

The score has remained in print since its release from the Walt Disney label on December 13, 2005. Fans should also consider acquiring Gregson-Williams' soundtrack to *Prince Caspian*. Be aware that *The Voyage of the Dawn Treader*, the third film in the series, features a terrific score by accomplished composer David Arnold, not Gregson-Williams.

THE SAGA CONTINUES

After the box-office success of *The Lion, the Witch and the* Wardrobe—it grossed more than $745 million worldwide—a sequel was inevitable. *The Chronicles of Narnia: Prince Caspian* came out in 2008, but for no one certain reason, *Caspian* wasn't nearly as successful as its predecessor, bringing in only $141 million in the US and $278 million worldwide. Though a moderate success, as the tenth-highest-grossing film of 2008, it made the future of the franchise uncertain. With the release of *The Chronicles of Narnia: The Voyage of the Dawn Treader* in 2010, Disney passed on distribution to 20th Century Fox. This time around, despite a tad more success worldwide, US numbers dropped significantly. In 2011, the contract Walden Media had with the Lewis estate expired, leaving the future of

THE WHITE WITCH COMETH

additional big-screen Narnia outings up in the air. A new deal with the Mark Gordon Company, announced in October 2013, might result in production of *The Silver Chair* at some point in the next few years. Clearly it's one thing for Hollywood to adapt a trilogy of books—*The Lord of the Rings*, for example—to great success and fanfare, but quite another thing to offer up seven big-budget productions . . . although Harry Potter certainly did okay for himself with eight!

> ASLAN IS ON THE MOVE

The Chronicles of Narnia books had been around for a long time before the blockbuster movies arrived. With those, in addition to various animated retellings, TV productions (be sure to seek out the ambitious BBC version from the late '80s), and the steady stream of local live-theater interpretations, the story will likely remain with us for a long time to come. The themes of family, morality, friendship, and loyalty are timeless; by exploring them through the eyes of children, we can all learn a thing or two, regardless of age.

Countless tie-in products have supported these themes and their varying interpretations, including soundtracks, toys, deluxe weapon-replicas, games, and of course books. With regard specifically to the movie, two volumes of note are executive producer Perry Moore's comprehensive *The Chronicles of Narnia—The Lion, the Witch and the Wardrobe: The Official Illustrated Movie Companion* and photographer Ian Brodie's slim but fascinating volume, *Cameras in Narnia—How The Lion, the Witch and the Wardrobe Came to Life*. Both books feature forewords by Adamson and offer insight into the production of the movie, in stylish, glossy full color. Also, fans of Narnia should all enjoy the film's deluxe DVD and Blu-ray sets.

TAKE UP THY SWORD!

THE QUEEN'S WAND (MAGIC ITEM)

This powerful magical item appears as a delicate double-ended javelin roughly three feet in length and tipped with glass or enchanted ice. Its wielder can use it as an offensive piercing weapon that deals damage equal to that of a slightly enhanced standard spear. A targeted critical strike from an opponent's weapon can destroy it. This item's most dangerous aspect is its ability to turn victims of successful attacks into stone—a form of petrification—in much the same way as a basilisk, cockatrice, or gorgon. (See those creatures for details on how to apply these effects.)

THE FILM'S DESTINY

To this writer [SAW], C. S. Lewis's *The Chronicles of Narnia* has always been the little sprawling fantasy epic that could, especially when compared to the work of Lewis's contemporary: J. R. R. Tolkien's *The Lord of the Rings* trilogy. In the special features and commentaries featured on the DVD, Adamson points out a few "flaws" with the original text, about which a number of scholars and fans likely agree with him. For example, in order to advance the action, Lewis frequently glosses over scenes, leaving gaps in the plot that fall on the reader to fill in. Adamson did a superb job of this, with suitable material for the big screen.

Overall, the film is a competently produced adventure with some technically brilliant stuff. The Weta stamp is ever present, and most of the digital work is jaw-dropping, especially Aslan.

That said, Mr. and Mrs. Beaver remain unconvincing, despite lovely vocal performances by Dawn French and Ray Winstone, and Mr. Fox and the wolves come across as cartoony—especially jarring when you see the real wolves onscreen alongside the CG versions.

Performance-wise, the film is solid and the kids all do a terrific job. There is a sense of wonder and fun about it all. The great effort Adamson and Swinton put in to make the experience enjoyable for the children clearly paid off.

At the end of the day, though, despite the glossy images, the impressive performances, the variety of cool beasts, the sprawling battles, and the superb production design, the film still seems a bit flat. You can enjoy watching it, but if given the option to watch this or one of the many other sword-and-sorcery adventures covered in this book, you might opt for one of the others first.

THIS YEAR IN GAMING

In November, *Dungeons & Dragons* finally joined the world of massively multiplayer online gaming with the launch of the open public beta test for *Dungeons & Dragons Online* (often abbreviated *DDO*). Although it was not the first time the *D&D* brand and universe appeared in a video or computer game, it was the first time the name, core concepts, monsters, and settings of the classic RPG officially made their way into a persistent MMO. Loosely based on the then-current 3.5 edition, *Dungeons & Dragons Online* (a.k.a. *Dungeons & Dragons Online: Stormreach*) was set in the Eberron campaign setting on the continent of Xen'drik, with much of the focus on the city of Stormreach. In February 2006, a few months after the start of the beta, the game officially opened to the general public. It won a few awards, including the 2005 MMORPG.COM Reader's Choice Award for Most Anticipated Game, the IGN.com Best of 2006 Award for Best Persistent World Game, and the 2006 British Academy Video Games Award for Best Multiplayer Game. In a couple nice links to the original tabletop RPG, the voices of Gary Gygax and Dave Arneson contributed. Gygax had been no stranger to voice acting, having played himself in an episode of *Futurama* a few years before. After he passed away in 2008, an in-game shrine was erected in his honor in an area of Delera's Tomb.

SOLOMON KANE

2009 • France / Czech Republic / UK
Davis-Films / Czech Anglo Productions / Wandering Star Pictures
104m • Color • R

Writer: Michael J. Bassett
Based On The Character Created By: Robert E. Howard
Director: Michael J. Bassett
Producers: Samuel Hadida and Paul Berrow
Music: Klaus Badelt
Director of Photography: Dan Laustsen
Production Designer: Ricky Eyres
Art Director: David Baxa
Costume Designer: John Bloomfield
Hair & Make-Up Designer: Paul Pattison
Special Make-Up Effects Supervisor: David Scott
Creature Designer: Patrick Tatopoulos
Special Effects Supervisor: Kamil Jaffar
Visual Effects Supervisor: Gary E. Beach
Stunt Coordinators: Mark Henson, Robert Lahoda, and Jaroslav Peterka
Sword Master: Richard Ryan
Horse Master: Romana Hajkova
Cast: James Purefoy (Solomon Kane); Pete Postlethwaite (William Crowthorn); Rachel Hurd-Wood (Meredith Crowthorn); Alice Krige (Katherine Crowthorn); Jason Flemyng (Malachi); Mackenzie Crook (Father Michael); Patrick Hurd-Wood (Samuel Crowthorn); Max Von Sydow (Josiah Kane); Mark O'Neal, Robert Orr, and Richard Ryan (Kane's Soldiers); Frantisek Deak (Cowering Guard); Christian Michael Dunkley Clark (Lieutenant Malthus); Ian Whyte (Devil's Reaper); Thomas McEnchroe (Young Monk); Andrew Whitlaw (Older Monk); Robert Russell (Abbott); James Babson (Skinhead); Marek Vasut (Tattoo); Geoff Bell (Beard); Lucas Stone (Young Solomon); Sam Roukin (Marcus Kane / Overlord); Anthony Wilks (Edward Crowthorn); Isabel Bassett (The Witch); Jeff Smith (Raider Captain); Matt Stirling (Eye Patch); Curtis Matthew (Old Man); Laura Baranik (Prisoner); Andrea Miltnerova (Old Woman Captive); Franklin Henson (Landlord); Philip Winchester (Henry Telford); Stewart Moore (Garrick); Madaleine Bassett (Young Sarah); Klara Low (Onlooker); Ryan James, Todd Kramer, Todd Benson, and Mike McGuffie (Raiders); Philip Waley (Drunk); Gordon Truefitt (Stable Master); David Listvan (Gilligan); Jiri Kraus (Smith); Tomas Tobola (Hawkstone); Beryl Nesbitt (Old Crone); Ben Steel (Fletcher); Matthew Blood Smyth (Merton); Rory McCann (McNess); Amy Huck (Prisoner); Brian Caspe (Priest, uncredited); and John Comer (Erasmus Woolman, uncredited)

ON THE MAP

The story opens somewhere in North Africa in the year 1600. A year later, we are in an abbey somewhere in England. Once Kane heads off on his journey home, he heads west, stopping at a church on "the borderlands of Somerset and Devonshire." The story concludes in the Kane ancestral seat, a cliffside castle in the civil parish of Axmouth in Devon.

OUR STORY SO FAR

Captain Solomon Kane, a bloodthirsty pirate, escapes from the clutches of a demonic servant who in turn curses his immortal soul. Seeking redemption, Kane now wanders the world as a homeless pilgrim, righting wrongs and desperately trying avoid the seduction of his former life's brutality. Unfortunately, he witnesses the slaughter of innocents along the way, so he re-embraces his savagery to rescue a kidnapped girl and avenge the deaths of those who showed him kindness.

IT'S MAGIC

Sorcery in this universe draws upon diabolical forces and is feared and punished. The film is set during a time of witch trials and deep-rooted suspicion, so users of magic hide out in dark dungeons and darker forests.

Malachi is a powerful wizard of the black arts, in league with forces outside our world. He can resurrect the dead, summon demons, control minds, and teleport.

THE QUEST FOR MEANING

This is a tale of redemption. Though writer-director Michael J. Bassett strays from the source material here and there, if there's one thing he does well, it is retaining that theme.

Kane honestly believes his soul is damned to hell after his encounter with a dark servitor, but he still wanders the world as a solitary, penitent man in search of salvation. When evil forces challenge his faith, he resorts to the only possible means of achieving any sort of justice: he turns his back on his new, clerical existence and draws his weapons once more to shed blood for justice. One wonders if Robert E. Howard was motivated by the somewhat controversial—and oft misquoted—statement from Matthew 10:34, in which Jesus spake: "I did not come to bring peace, but a sword." It describes Kane to a T. In conjunction with director John Milius's take on Howard's better-known warrior, Conan, this film suggests a consistency of approach in adaptations of Howard's characters: that the might of a weapon supersedes knowledge and understanding.

WHO GOES THERE?

James Purefoy screen-tested for the role of James Bond in *GoldenEye* and was once considered for the role of Wolverine. He was also cast in the lead role in *V for Vendetta* but left midway through production due to creative differences. He spent much of his early career on British television, as well as in the American series *The Following*. He also appears in the films *A Knight's Tale, Resident Evil, George and the Dragon, Ironclad,* and *John Carter*.

Rachel Hurd-Wood, daughter of voice-actor Philip Hurd-Wood (the voice of the alien Graske in both *Doctor Who* and *The Sarah Jane Adventures*), got her big break as Wendy Darling in director P. J. Hogan's *Peter Pan* in 2003. Though she has drifted away from acting—with more interest in a career beyond the silver screen—she has appeared in *An American Haunting, Perfume: The Story of a Murderer* (for which she was nominated for a Best Supporting Actress Saturn Award), *Dorian Gray,* and *Tomorrow, When the War Began*.

Most fans remember accomplished South African actress Alice Krige buried under extensive makeup as the Borg queen in *Star Trek: First Contact*, but she has worked rather steadily for decades, appearing in the films *Chariots of Fire*, *Ghost Story* (another memorable—and occasionally naked—role), *Sleepwalkers*, *Reign of Fire*, *Silent Hill*, *The Sorcerer's Apprentice*, and *Thor: The Dark World*. She has also appeared in a number of TV series, including *Six Feet Under*, the *Dinotopia* miniseries, *Deadwood*, and *MI-5*.

> WHEN YOU MAKE A DEAL WITH THE DEVIL, THERE WILL BE HELL TO PAY.

Jason Flemyng (son of George Flemyng, the director of *Dr. Who and the Daleks* and *Daleks' Invasion Earth: 2150 A.D.*) was bitten by the acting bug at a very young age . . . although he claims it was just a means of impressing girls. His first feature-film role was in the live-action version of *The Jungle Book*, soon followed by a steady stream of additional roles, many in genre films like *Deep Rising*, *From Hell*, *The League of Extraordinary Gentlemen* (in which he played both Dr. Jekyll and Mr. Hyde, the latter encased in a massive foam rubber suit), *Stardust*, *Clash of the Titans*, and *X-Men: First Class*. He has also appeared on TV in *The Young Indiana Jones Chronicles*, *The Quatermass Experiment*, and *Primeval*.

Patrick Hurd-Wood—recognize the surname?—is the real-life little brother of Rachel Hurd-Wood. He had a small role in *Peter Pan* and last appeared in the 2012 thriller *Blood*, apart from a couple short features.

Ian Whyte has appeared, often under makeup or inside elaborate costumes, in *AVP: Alien vs. Predator*, *Harry Potter and the Goblet of Fire*, *Dragonball: Evolution*, the 2010 *Clash of the Titans*, *Prometheus*, *1066*, and HBO's *Game of Thrones*.

There are several Robert Russells in the film industry, many of them living actors. This one has been appearing on the big and small screens since 1996's *A Young Connecticut Yankee in King Arthur's Court*, starring Michael York. He also appears in the *Dune* TV miniseries, *Doom*, *The Illusionist*, and *G.I. Joe: The Rise of Cobra*.

Many know James Babson for his role as Agent Moss in *Hellboy*. Many of his roles are relatively small. You can also find him in the films *The Shawshank Redemption*, *xXx*, *The League of Extraordinary Gentlemen*, *The Illusionist*, and *Last Knights*.

Acting-teacher Geoff Bell has played a number of small roles over the years, but as a result he has worked with some of the biggest names in the film industry: Matthew Vaughn in *Stardust*, Guy Ritchie in *RocknRolla*, and Steven Spielberg in *War Horse*.

Andrea Miltnerova appeared in *Blade II*, *EuroTrip*, and *Hellboy*.

Philip Winchester landed his first role at the age of 14 in *The Patriot*, via a local casting call in his home state of Montana. His career has continued to grow from strength to strength. He appears in the live-action version of *Thunderbirds*, in *Flyboys*, and in *The Heart of the Earth*, as well as in a number of TV roles, including in *Crusoe*, *Fringe*, *Camelot*, and *Strike Back*.

Philip Waley appeared in *Hostel* and *Hostel: Part II*.

At 6'6", Rory McCann has played a number of impressive and intimidating roles. Many of his earlier parts credited him as "goon" or "bouncer," but he soon found his way into recurring and even regular TV roles as well as roles in films. You can find him in *The Devil's Tattoo*, *Beowulf & Grendel*, *Hot Fuzz* (as the "yarp" guy), *Clash of the Titans*, *Season of the Witch*, and HBO's *Game of Thrones* (as Sandor Clegane).

Amy Huck appeared in *From Hell*, *EuroTrip*, and the 2006 remake of *The Omen*. Brian Caspe was Agent Lime in *Hellboy*.

6 DEGREES OF SORCERY

Though slightly buried in the mix, you can hear the legendary "Wilhelm scream" at the top of the film as Kane and his men advance across a bridge.

The Devil's Reaper looks mighty similar to the Nazgûl depicted in Peter Jackson's *Lord of the Rings* films.

The crucified corpses in the frozen treasure-chamber have icicles of blood similar to those seen in John Carpenter's *The Thing*.

Though the film is an original story penned by Bassett, it features a number of nods to the source material, including a reference to Kane once serving alongside Sir Francis Drake. (See Howard's poem "The One Black Stain.")

The discovery of the little girl and her initial behavior (before she reveals herself as something sinister) is akin to the discovery of Newt and her story in *Aliens*.

The demon-occupied mirrors are a nod to *Constantine*.

The coat worn by Henry Telford is the one worn by Sean Connery in *Robin Hood: Prince of Thieves*. (Both films featured costumes designed by John Bloomfield.)

Behind his grim mask, Marcus is undeniably a 17th-century version of Darth Vader from *Star Wars*: horribly disfigured when young, brought back from the brink and in service to a powerful "sorcerer," dressed in black, hidden behind a mask, and capable of manipulating others with some sort of supernatural force.

Kane's stated intention to rescue Meredith harkens back to Hawkeye's desire to find Cora in *The Last of the Mohicans*.

The great, fiery, big boss Kane battles bears some resemblance to the Balrog of *The Lord of the Rings: The Fellowship of the Ring* and even to the giant volcanic Pyrovile creatures from the 2008 *Doctor Who* story "The Fires of Pompeii."

James Purefoy's portrayal very much drew influence from Clint Eastwood's "Man with No Name" from the Sergio Leone–directed Western *Dollars* trilogy: *A Fistful of Dollars*, *For a Few Dollars More*, and *The Good, The Bad and the Ugly*.

Notable similarities, even down to costume design and the gray, rain-soaked atmosphere, exist between *Solomon Kane* and *Van Helsing*, although one was a good film while the other was a CGI-saturated train wreck (respectively). Speaking of train wrecks, another film misfire, *Jonah Hex*, also features a similar character, although the comic-book source material there is worthwhile. The basic concept—characters in a less-enlightened age taking on the forces of darkness with blade and firearm—continues to inspire films like *Hansel & Gretel: Witch Hunters* and *Abraham Lincoln: Vampire Killer*.

SHATTERING THE ILLUSION

The rights to adapt Robert E. Howard's character into film were optioned as far back as 1997. Though still strongly linked with the sword-wielding immortal Connor MacLeod of the Clan

MacLeod, Christopher Lambert was a contender for the lead role in 2001. That version of the project eventually fell apart.

Robert E. Howard fan Michael J. Bassett completed his original screenplay in August 2006, following instructions to craft an origin story that drew from the original material. James Purefoy was announced as the movie's Solomon Kane on October 1, 2007. The actor threw himself into preparing for the part by reading the Howard stories and doing historical research. Saturn Award–winner Patrick Tatopoulos's special-effects company, Tatopoulos Studios *(Stargate, Godzilla, Underworld)* handled the creatures. Production got underway in January 2008 and ran for twelve artificially rain-soaked weeks, occasionally disrupted by owls that hooted throughout the night in the Czech Republic locations. For the elaborate body-scarring and tattoos, Purefoy underwent five hours of makeup application whenever he was to go shirtless and also received stitches (real ones) in his forehead as a result of a sword-fighting mishap.

A consortium of French, British, and Czech companies produced the film with a budget totaling around $40 million. Though the title was always simply *Solomon Kane,* Bassett and company approached the producers with possible subtitles that would have given audiences a sense of the film's content and suggested the beginning of ongoing adventures. Bassett even revisited Howard's original stories, but nothing suitable presented itself. Principal photography wrapped in April 2008, but it was a full year before production was complete.

MUSIC OF THE MINSTRELS

In the summer of 2008, it was announced that multiple-award–winning German composer Klaus Badelt would score *Solomon Kane.* Fans have noted a number of similarities between this and Badelt's score for *The Time Machine,* one of his earliest and most-praised cinematic compositions.

This score features a number of Hans Zimmer–like dark chord progressions and mercifully few if no minor thirds, which other scores have played to absolute death for a few years now. It includes strings and dominating brass, along with choirs to punch up a few of the epic moments, and also features a number of authentic-sounding elements reflective of the period. A few tracks stand out, but much of the score—though competently produced—is fairly standard action-superhero fare. A track or two sound remarkably similar to some of protégé Hans Zimmer's material from *Batman Begins.* It is still great background music for your game table; however, as of this writing, an official soundtrack has not been released. For a short while, Badelt offered much of the score for download via his website, but that vanished in late 2009. Badelt's work might not often stand out as unique, but some of his scores are worth tracking down, including the aforementioned *The Time Machine, K-19: The Widowmaker, Equilibrium,* and of course his contributions to *Pirates of the Caribbean: Curse of the Black Pearl.*

THE SAGA CONTINUES

Despite a pretty wide global release in 2009, and Region 2 DVDs and Blu-rays in 2010, *Solomon Kane* didn't officially make it to the US until a late-2012 limited theatrical release, and a Blu-Ray in the summer of 2013. The movie was originally intended as the first of a trilogy,

FIGHT EVIL ... WITH EVIL.

with the second one set in Africa and presumably introducing N'Longa and Solomon's cat-headed juju staff. The third installment would have moved to the New World. Shots of Kane battling characters in a cave behind the end credits suggest a further adventure; however, the first film's poor distribution—especially in the States—and ultimate failure have likely forever shut the door on future big-screen adventures ... at least with this cast and production team.

In June 2011, Titan Books released a 304-page novelization of the film, penned by multiple-award–winning horror author, Ramsey Campbell. And if you're interested in reading more about this mysterious 17th-century demon-hunting Puritan, you simply must give Robert E. Howard's original source material a read. Different publishers have released fewer than twenty short stories, poems, and fragments. Marvel and Dark Horse have also adapted these stories into comic form over the years.

For the gamer, in 2007 Pinnacle Entertainment released the impressive *Savage World of Solomon Kane* roleplaying game using the *Savage Worlds* rules. Written by Paul "Wiggy" Wade-Williams and Shane Lacy Hensley, it continues to gain additional supplements. Paradigm Concepts published an RPG titled *Witch Hunter: The Invisible World* in 2007 that clearly owes much to the original tales, as does the witch-hunter character concept from Games Workshop's *Warhammer* universe.

TAKE UP THY SWORD!

BLACK MIRRORS (MAGICAL ARTIFACTS)

Each black mirror acts as a portal into a shadow dimension immediately adjacent to our own. In that dimension of darkness and void, twisted fire-demons and blind, humanoid, lamprey-like beasts wheel about in the dark, seeking food from extra-planar sources in the form of anything that accidentally strays into or near their world.

The glass of each mirror is actually a highly polished sheet of flexible obsidian, cursed by a necromancer on the darkest night of the year. If kept under wraps or stored in total darkness, a black mirror remains quiescent, but when illuminated in our plane of existence, it transmits the light into the dark dimension, whereupon creatures mad with hunger rush to it from their side and drag unsuspecting victims in, to quickly consume them. Anything within five feet of an activated mirror must successfully grapple these creatures to escape.

Black mirrors vary in size and thus can allow large or even colossal beasts temporary access into our dimension. For the permanent entrance of a creature from that plane through a mirror into our world, a ritualist on this side must perform a brief rite involving blood from an innocent.

Anyone who possesses a black mirror can frame it, hang it from a wall, and transport it, but as with any mirror, it is fragile. Should it shatter, it loses its interdimensional properties. While active, a black mirror even works for scrying ... if the gazer stands well away from it.

THE FILM'S DESTINY

With this film's lack of a real romantic interest and a decidedly masculine hero and plot, narrow-minded American studio-executives possibly could not determine how to market this film to tweens and teens in the US. That would explain why it languished for such a long time. Tragically, because of this and perhaps due to the movie industry's often paralyzing inability to comprehend and market to niche groups or take a niche product and sell it to wider, mainstream, movie-going crowds, American audiences remain largely in ignorance of *Solomon Kane*. The completely unfair failure of *John Carter* at the box office might also have slammed the coffin lid on this film—and certainly any possibility of a long-running franchise. As a result, a lot of people are missing out on a well-produced, well-written, and well-acted adventure that deserves its day in the sun. Though it takes a few liberties with the source material and shoehorns in a couple of cliché Hollywood "reveals" toward the end, it is very much a loving homage to those original tales and makes for a perfect companion piece, worthy of a place on the shelf alongside them.

Perhaps with a growing interest in fantasy-adventure and sword-and-sorcery entertainment via upcoming projects, there is a chance—slim but possible—that *Solomon Kane* will yet be redeemed. Wouldn't that be appropriate?

THIS YEAR IN GAMING

Dave Arneson, co-creator of *Dungeons & Dragons* with Gary Gygax, lost his two-year battle with cancer on April 7th at the age of 61. (Arneson's world of Blackmoor and his medieval-fantasy system, combined with Gygax's published medieval-wargaming set *Chainmail*, are what led to the development of the first edition.) Also in 2009 (August), Paizo Publishing launched the *Pathfinder Roleplaying Game*. This "new" game—thanks to the Open Game License—revised and extended the previously published *Dungeons & Dragons* 3.5 edition from Wizards of the Coast and went on to outsell the fourth edition of *D&D*.

HOW to TRAIN YOUR DRAGON

2010 • US
Paramount Pictures / DreamWorks Animation / Mad Hatter Entertainment / Vertigo Entertainment
98m • Color • PG

Writers: Will Davies, Dean DeBlois, Chris Sanders, and Adam F. Goldberg (uncredited)
Based On The Novel By: Cressida Cowell
Directors: Dean DeBlois and Chris Sanders
Producers: Bonnie Arnold, Michael A. Connolly, Doug Davison, Karen Foster, and Roy Lee
Music: John Powell
Production Design: Kathy Altieri
Art Director: Pierre-Olivier Vincent
Visual Effects Supervisor: Craig Ring
Special Effects / Character Technical Director: Tom Molet
Character Designers: Andy Bialk, Ricardo F. Delgado, Nicolas Marlet, Takao Noguchi, Shane Prigmore, and Tony Siruno
Dialect Coach: Jessica Drake
Cast: Jay Baruchel (Hiccup), Gerard Butler (Stoick), Craig Ferguson (Gobber), America Ferrara (Astrid), Jonah Hill (Snotlout), Christopher Mintz-Plasse (Fishlegs), T. J. Miller (Tuffnut), Kristen Wiig (Ruffnut), Robin Atkin Downes (Ack), Philip McGrade (Starkard), Kieron Elliott (Hoark the Haggard), Ashley Jensen (Phlegma the Fierce), and David Tennant (Spitelout)

ON THE MAP

We journey from the Isle of Berk, a ramshackle human stronghold, to a distant rocky island shrouded by fog and containing a volcano with a labyrinthine interior that serves as the nest of the villainous Red Death.

OUR STORY SO FAR

A father urges his young son to follow the traditional path and become a ruthless dragon fighter, but when an equally young, endearing, and legendary dragon becomes the boy's close friend and ally, the unlikely team has to find a way to bring down the biggest, baddest dragon of them all by achieving the impossible: uniting their two races in a common cause.

ALTERNATE VERSIONS

The film was released in 2D and 3D versions with no variations in the material.

IT'S MAGIC

As with *Dragonheart*, this is a movie in which dragons are the only magical element to speak of, but with such a vast scope of species and abilities, the creatures do a fine job of making up for the lack of other fantasy elements. Humans have catalogued all the ones they have encountered, describing their various forms and attack methods in a manner familiar to anyone in the RPG/gaming community, right

> ONE ADVENTURE WILL CHANGE TWO WORLDS

down to the trainees rattling off stats and strategies for dealing with the strengths and weaknesses of every dragon variant. Beyond that, this reality has no magic at all, unless of course you want to count rising above limitations, finding one's inner hero, deepening love with friends and family, and bonding with a creature in what is sure to be a lifelong partnership. But there's us getting all corny again—and that's covered more in the "Quest" section, anyway. . . .

THE QUEST FOR MEANING

A lot of themes are at play in this movie, from the superiority of intelligence and compassion over ignorance and brute force to the value in breaking down boundaries and learning to appreciate and embrace differences rather than fear them. As an antidote to many classic adventure films—including ones in this book—in which the coming-of-age thread follows the "kill monster, achieve adulthood" path, this movie has our pacifist hero befriending and forging a bond with his would-be foe and then enabling everyone, dragons and humans alike, to unite against a common enemy. That enemy, the one evil dragon, who holds all the others in thrall, is the queen-like pinnacle of that culture, with an interesting mix of cat, bat, and bee behavior.

But what the story ultimately comes down to—the love story between Hiccup and Astrid notwithstanding—is the ineffable bond between a boy and his dog . . . well, cat . . . well, dragon. You know what we mean.

Beyond that, this tale is about understanding, and finding common ground that provides a foundation for making everyone better and stronger. The revitalized, dragon-filled community of Berk at the end of the film is an uplifting symbol of hope after the stagnated version seen in the film's opening. As for where it goes from there . . . that's what sequels are for. (See **The Saga Continues**.)

WHO GOES THERE?

Jay Baruchel also appeared in the television series *Undeclared* and movies like *Almost Famous, The Rules of Attraction, Knocked Up, Tropic Thunder, Fanboys, Night at the Museum: Battle of the Smithsonian, The Sorcerer's Apprentice, This Is the End* (as a version of himself), and the 2014 *RoboCop.*

Gerard Butler had small parts in *Tomorrow Never Dies* and *Tale of the Mummy* before playing Dracula in *Dracula 2000* and Attila the Hun in the TV movie *Attila.* He also appeared in *Reign of Fire, Lara Croft Tomb Raider: The Cradle of Life, Timeline, The Phantom of the Opera, Beowulf & Grendel, 300, Gamer,* and the infamous *Movie 43.*

"It's a great day for America!" Audiences best know Craig Ferguson as the irreverent host of *The Late Late Show with Craig Ferguson,* but his career as a comic actor stretches back to appearances in television series like *Red Dwarf* and *Maybe This Time.* He was a regular on *The*

Drew Carey Show and has also lent his voice to animated shows like *Freakazoid!*, *Buzz Lightyear of Star Command*, and *The Legend of Tarzan*.

America Ferrara first appeared in movies like *Real Women Have Curves* and *The Sisterhood of the Traveling Pants* before becoming the star of the TV series *Ugly Betty*.

Jonah Hill has become a reliable goofy presence in films like *I Heart Huckabees*, *The 40 Year Old Virgin*, *Knocked Up*, *Evan Almighty*, *Superbad*, *Forgetting Sarah Marshall*, *The Invention of Lying*, *Get Him to the Greek*, *Cyrus*, *Moneyball*, the movie version of *21 Jump Street* and its sequels, *The Wolf of Wall Street*, and *The Lego Movie* (as the voice of Green Lantern!).

Christopher Mintz-Plasse is McLovin, or at least he was in his film debut, *Superbad*. He also appeared in *Role Models*, *Year One*, *Kick-Ass*, the remake of *Fright Night*, and *Kick-Ass 2*.

T. J. Miller's first film role was Hud in *Cloverfield*. He's also had parts in *Get Him to the Greek*, *Yogi Bear*, *Gulliver's Travels*, *Seeking a Friend for the End of the World*, *Transformers: Age of Extinction*, *Deadpool*, and the TV series *Silicon Valley*.

Kristen Wiig was a member of the *Saturday Night Live* cast from 2005 to 2012. She has also appeared on TV in *The Joe Schmo Show*, *The Flight of the Conchords*, *Bored to Death*, *The Looney Tunes Show*, and *Wet Hot American Summer: First Day of Camp*, and in films like *Knocked Up*, *Semi-Pro*, *Forgetting Sarah Marshall*, *Whip It*, *MacGruber*, *Date Night*, *Despicable Me*, *Paul*, *Anchorman 2: The Legend Continues*, *The Martian*, and the all-female incarnation of *Ghostbusters*.

Robin Atkin Downes has appeared in film, television, and stage productions, but animation fans and gamers know him through his extensive work as a voiceover artist. As one of the most in-demand vocal talents working today, Downes has performed in videogames based on media properties and on the franchises, like *The Lord of the Rings*, *X-Men*, *Star Wars*, *Battlestar Galactica*, *Forgotten Realms*, *Call of Duty*, *The Bard's Tale*, *EverQuest II*, *Halo 2*, *Metal Gear Solid 3*, *Prince of Persia*, *Fantastic Four*, *Quake 4*, *The Matrix*, *Rainbow Six*, *Pirates of the Caribbean*, *Gears of War*, *Mass Effect*, *Final Fantasy*, *Clash of the Titans*, *Tron*, and many, many more. He also appeared in *Buffy the Vampire Slayer*, *Babylon 5*, *Charmed*, and *Angel*, and has voiced characters in the animated TV-series *Justice League*, *Avatar: The Last Airbender*, *Star Wars: The Clone Wars*, *Batman: The Brave and the Bold*, *The Avengers: Earth's Mightiest Heroes*, *Thundercats*, and *Ben 10: Ultimate Alien*.

Ashley Jensen appeared in television series like *Eastenders*, *Extras*, and *Ugly Betty*.

We hope you don't need to be told that David Tennant was one of the most popular incarnations of the Doctor in the nearly fifty-year history of the BBC sci-fi television series *Doctor Who*. His tenure as the Tenth Doctor ran from 2005 to 2010. He's also appeared in television productions like *Blackpool*, *Casanova*, *Hamlet*, the acclaimed *Broadchurch*, and *Jessica Jones*, and films like *Jude* (sharing a scene with fellow Doctor Christopher Eccleston), *Harry Potter and the Goblet of Fire*, and the remake of *Fright Night*.

6 DEGREES OF SORCERY

We start with another village sacking, as in *Conan the Barbarian*, *The Beastmaster*, *Dragonheart*, and many others. The name Berk is a sly reference to a common British insult: generally meaning "idiot," it comes from the Cockney rhyming slang "Berkshire hunt, ----." We'll leave you to figure out that last part.

Gobber's arm attachment recalls Ash's chainsaw arm in *The Evil Dead* franchise. Stoick's hammer recalls Mjolnir, the weapon wielded by the Norse god of thunder, Thor. The people do worship or at least acknowledge gods, including Odin.

The dragons in this movie might be (fictional) living creatures, but they often behave like airplanes, in much the same way George Lucas borrowed from WWII-era dogfight footage for his spaceships in *Star Wars*. (More on that in **Shattering the Illusion**.) The auto-crossbow weapon is even controlled in the way Luke Skywalker handles the gun of the *Millennium Falcon* in that film.

Dragonheart also features a bolo weapon for tying up dragons. The dragon manual, as well as references to strategy and stats, comes straight from *Dungeons & Dragons* and the gaming world in general. *World of WarCraft* influenced some of the creature designs.

Runes in the film resemble those in *The Lord of the Rings* films. A triumphant flight above the clouds also cemented a relationship in *Superman*. If you look closely during the journey to Dragon Island, you can spot Gloria, the hippo from *Madagascar,* riding one of the dragons.

When the enormous dragon's mouth rises from the depths, it's much like the creature trying to swallow the *Falcon* in *Star Wars: The Empire Strikes Back*. We've seen hellish dragon lairs before in movies like *Dragonslayer;* at least one of the creatures in this film even walks like Vermithrax. The revelation of some of the creatures in firelight is similar to scenes in the *Alien* series. Elements of the finale echo the final showdown between Perseus and the Kraken in *Clash of the Titans,* and the fabled island at the climax of the adventure is much like many other fantasy destinations . . . perhaps even one with a skull formation and large creature dwelling on it as well . . . ?

SHATTERING THE ILLUSION

This animated feature is an adaptation of Cressida Cowell's 2003 novel, but as is often true in such cases, it veered from the book's plotline during development, particularly after Dean DeBlois and Chris Sanders—formerly of *Lilo & Stitch*—joined the production (with work already underway). Changes to the source material included the addition of a romantic angle and the alteration of Toothless's colors from green and red to the more iconic and distinctive black. Toothless's entire heritage—including his size, increased to enable Hiccup to ride him—changed for the film, with Cowell's approval.

Surely one of the most interesting choices in the making of a movie aimed a young audience, however, was to depict Hiccup sustaining a life-changing injury. The loss of Hiccup's leg mirrors Toothless's injury, further uniting the two friends and making the ending more believable. (Sure, we know: it's an animated movie. Who needs realism, right?) Whatever the rationale behind the choice, it was an unusual one and caused a bit of concern. Previews, however, proved that it was a good decision. Parents approved of the message that it helped convey, as did Cowell. Steven Spielberg provided one last key emotional element by nudging the production to make the crucial scene more reflective of the deep bond between Hiccup and Toothless, which transcended that of a master and his pet.

Star Wars isn't the only movie that can lay claim to using aerial combat footage as inspiration for key sequences (with apologies to our "6 Degrees" section). For much of the flying depicted here, animators also relied on the kind of camera angles and maneuvers seen in films of aircraft engaged in dogfights or demonstrations. Placing the virtual camera on the back or wing of Toothless also made for the best use of the 3D effect to immerse the audience in those sequences.

Though most cat owners surely recognize their pets' mannerisms in Toothless's distinctive and often disarming behavior, a mix of lizard, horse, and dog characteristics also influenced his look and disposition. His vocalizations are also a cocktail of noises, incorporating everything from cats wild and domestic to elephants—and sound designer Randy Thom.

AMC Entertainment and the Autism Society included *How to Train Your Dragon* as part of a program they launched so that children with autism could enjoy movies in theaters. "Sensory-friendly" showings had different lighting and volume, and no previews.

Although nominated for Oscars in the categories of Best Animated Feature and Best Original Score, the movie did not receive either award. It did, however, win a number of Annie Awards, including Best Animated Feature, Best Writing, and Best Character Design. Gerard Butler considers it one of the three films he's proudest to have worked on. (What are the other two? Good question.)

MUSIC OF THE MINSTRELS

John Powell's score, one of many he created for DreamWorks productions but the first he accomplished solo, mixed traditional orchestral instruments with a variety of Celtic elements intended to evoke the feel of the movie's world. Bagpipes, dulcimers, and pennywhistles joined the usual strings and horns to create a distinctive and fairly memorable soundtrack. Powell cited the score from the classic film *The Vikings,* Nordic folk music, and the works of Finnish composer Jean Sibelius, Norwegian composer Edvard Grieg, and Danish composer Carl Neilsen as influences. His Scottish heritage, which exposed him to folk music from that part of the world, also came into play. Jón "Jónsi" Þór Birgisson, an Icelandic singer who also fronts the band Sigur Rós, wrote and performed the end-credits song, "Sticks & Stones." (An animatronic-laden stage-adaptation of the film, called *How to Train Your Dragon Arena Spectacular,* which started in 2012, used another song of his, "Tornado.")

The score garnered Powell an Academy Award nomination for the first time in his career. (He didn't win; however, he did win another of those Annie Awards mentioned in **Shattering the Illusion**.) Varese Sarabande released an album of the score in March 2010.

THE SAGA CONTINUES

How to Train Your Dragon has spawned an extensive franchise and merchandising empire, including a number of other films—long and short—released or on the way, a television series, and tie-ins of every kind: tons of books, toys, action figures, plush dolls, housewares, games, and other items. It all goes back to the original book series, which concludes with a twelfth volume in the fall of 2015.

As for feature-film sequels, Dean DeBlois was the sole writer-director of 2014's *How to Train Your Dragon 2*. The third installment fell back several times, to a scheduled release date of 2018 as of this writing. According to Cressida Cowell, although the books and movies follow their own narratives, they will converge at the end of both lines.

Four mini-sequels—*Legend of the Boneknapper Dragon, Book of Dragons, Gift of the Night Fury,* and *Dawn of the Dragon Racers*—came out on DVD and Blu-ray, and the Cartoon Network debuted the *DreamWorks Dragons* animated television series, with the original voice cast, in the fall of 2012. As we conclude work on this book, a third season will move to Netflix for its run in 2015.

Activision released a tie-in videogame for the PS3, Xbox 360, Wii, and Nintendo DS in 2010. A free MMO in 3D, *School of Dragons,* debuted at Comic-Con International in 2013 for PC, iOS, and Android platforms. A number of other mobile and virtual world-themed games have been released or are in development. DreamWorks also released board games titled *Dragon Training 101* and *Terror of the Sea*. You could even enjoy the series via live shows like the aforementioned arena event featuring two dozen animatronic dragons, or an ice show (they still make those?) produced by Royal Caribbean cruises.

TAKE UP THY SWORD!

VIKING TRAINER (NON-PLAYER CHARACTER)

Descended from the author of a comprehensive and somewhat legendary guide to dragons—a valuable artifact in its own right, currently in this individual's possession—this beast of a man knows more than a thing or two about the great lizards. Large and barrel-chested, he wears his hair and long moustache in braids befitting a true Viking. A skilled blacksmith—his specialties are swords, bludgeons, armor, and dragon-slaying gear of all types—he also frequently answers calls to impart his wisdom to the youngest members of the village. These hopefuls seek to become full-fledged Vikings at an elaborate training facility of the trainer's design.

Despite the trainer's vast knowledge of dragons, many initially look upon him with a cautious eye, because previous encounters with the beasts have left him permanently scarred: he walks upon a peg-leg and has a prosthetic arm. If anything, the horrifying incident that reduced him to this state only hardened him and made him more fearless. It also gave him exciting stories to tell eager students!

The trainer is a charismatic and optimistic fellow. Many in the village are happy to call him a trusted friend as well as a skilled ally on the battlefield.

THE FILM'S DESTINY

A delightful, cute, emotionally satisfying, and surprisingly mature all-ages adventure that flips many of the genre's conventions like dragons doing barrel-rolls in midair, *How to Train Your Dragon* has one mild learning-curve issue, but only when it comes to older viewers or those not predisposed to watching full-length CGI animation. It can take a bit of getting used to. For this author [ATB], it felt like my eyes were repeatedly sliding off the screen in the first fifteen minutes or so, because I could not discern foreground from background well and focus on what was going on. But it got better, and to give credit where it's due, the excellent characterization—great vocal performances combined with expressive, nuanced visuals—overcomes the obstacles and allows you to dial in when it counts.

The ultimate triumph of the film is Toothless, a thoroughly endearing creature and the perfect analogue of every cute kitten you've ever seen on the Internet (of which there are millions) or perhaps your own pet. He's just about impossible to resist. He's also the part of the film that most rewards repeat viewings: every little head-tilt and blink distinctively defines him as a living, breathing creature with a vibrant personality. To be honest, most of the human characters pale in comparison, but a very warm father-son story arc is here as well: one that defies expectations and might break down even hardier, hardened souls who don't normally shed a tear when a movie tries to tug at their heartstrings.

This movie has the deliberate anachronistic jokes and touches that typically turn up in films of its kind, although sometimes they strain credulity. Would this sort of culture have a young girl train alongside the boys, for example? But why nitpick? It's all fantasy. Clearly in this fictional ancient realm, gender issues are not as prevalent—and why should they be?

With an ending that doesn't shy away from consequences, a fun steampunk design vibe, and some stunning landscapes and action sequences, this is that "fun for the whole family" you're always hearing about but rarely find. For now, at least, your quest is at an end.

THIS YEAR IN GAMING

After years of developers modifying the core rules (the award-winning FATE system) to make them more suitable, as well as extensive alpha and beta testing phases, Evil Hat Productions *finally released The Dresden Files Roleplaying Game* at the Origins Game Fair in late June. Based on the bestselling urban fantasy series by Jim Butcher and designed by gaming luminaries such as Genevieve Cogman, Rob Donoghue, Fred Hicks, Kenneth Hite, and Chad Underkoffler, the game comprised two large volumes, published simultaneously: *Our World* (a 272-page book detailing the factions, monsters, friends, and foes of the "Dresdenverse") and *Your Story* (a 416-page book containing all the rules for creating characters and playing the game). It won a few impressive awards, including the 2011 Gold ENie Awards for Best Writing and Best New Game, and Silver ENies for Best Production Values and Product of the Year. *The Paranet Papers*, the third volume in the series, came out in 2015. The official website offers numerous downloadable freebies, including adventures, variant rules, character sheets, and FAQs.

YOUR HIGHNESS

2011 • US • UNIVERSAL PICTURES / STUBER PRODUCTIONS • 102M • COLOR • R

WRITERS: Danny R. McBride and Ben Best
DIRECTOR: David Gordon Green
PRODUCER: Scott Stuber
MUSIC: Steve Jablonsky
DIRECTOR OF PHOTOGRAPHY: Tim Orr
PRODUCTION DESIGNER: Mark Tildesley
ART DIRECTORS: Gary Freeman, Paul Kirby, Tom McCullagh, Stuart Rose, and Dave Warren
COSTUME DESIGNER: Hazel Webb-Crozier
COSTUME ARMOR SUPERVISOR: Simon Brindle
ARMORER: Tommy Dunne
MAKEUP: Tina Earnshaw
HAIR: Nana Fischer
CAST: Danny McBride (Thadeous); James Franco (Fabious); Rasmus Hardiker (Courtney); Natalie Portman (Isabel); Toby Jones (Julie); Justin Theroux (Leezar); Zooey Deschanel (Belladonna); Charles Dance (King Tallious); Damian Lewis (Boremont); Simon Farnaby (Manious the Bold); Deobia Oparei (Thundarian); B. J. Hogg (Royal Advisor); Matyelok Gibbs, Angela Pleasence, and Anna Barry (Mothers); Amber Anderson (Maiden); Stuart Loveridge (Skinny Prisoner); John Fricker (Marteetee); Rupert Davis (Second Knight); Julian Rhind-Tutt (Warlock); Mario Torres (Great Wize Wizard); Noah Huntley (Head Knight); Ben Wright (Dastardly); Susie Kelly, Roma Tomelty, Brigid Erin Bates, Eilish Doran, and Rene Greig (Hooded Witches); Kiran Shah (Tiniest One); Simon Cohen (The Barbarian); Graham Hughes (Dwarf King); Zhaidarbek Kunguzhinov and Nurlan Altaev (Brothers Mein); David Garrick (Daronius the Swift); Caroline Grace-Cassidy (Handmaiden); Elle Liberachi (Bridesmaid); Dorian Dixon, Darren Thompson, and David Thompson (Trolls); Brian Steele (Minotaur); Ben Willbond (Ranger); Phil Holden (Dwarf Executioner); Chris Burke (Dwarf Man); Sinead Burke (Dwarf Woman); Tobias Winter (Timotay Dungeon Master); Paige Tyler (Pale-Skinned Beauty); Rhian Sugden, Amii Grove, and Madison Welch (Forest Women); Iga Wyrwal (Regina); Charles Shaughnessy (Narrator / Soul of the Maze); and Mark Byatt (Skinny Prisoner, uncredited)

ON THE MAP

The action is set in a "non-historically accurate" medieval fantasy world that, despite the presence of two moons in the sky, mirrors our own world and history.

OUR STORY SO FAR

On the day of Fabious and Belladonna's wedding, evil sorcerer Leezar kidnaps the bride, intending to impregnate her at the precise time of a fated lunar alignment to conceive a dragon that will help him seize control of the kingdom. Fabious, his brother Thadeous, and a group of warriors embark on a quest to rescue Belladonna from Leezar's clutches before he can carry out his sinister plan.

ALTERNATE VERSIONS

The R-rated version appeared on movie screens, and an extended and unrated cut was released on DVD and Blu-ray. The bulk of the edits made for the theatrical cut slightly decreased the gratuitous imagery—nudity, violence, and so on—and dialogue.

IT'S MAGIC

This film repeatedly displays two spellcasting staples of standard fantasy tabletop roleplaying: fireballs and lightning bolts, both rendered beautifully. Overall, it presents sorcery stereotypically.

Leezar is the mad wizard capable of manipulating dark, supernatural forces. His three mothers (!) are crones and also masters of magic, unleashing hell from their fingertips and teleporting from point to point in the blink of an eye.

THE QUEST FOR MEANING

Despite jealousy expressed by Thadeous towards Fabious, his infinitely superior sibling, a strong brotherly bond is ever present. Thadeous eventually expresses it via some genuinely touching bits of dialogue. In the past, tales of jealous siblings have often ended with one straying from the moral path and becoming the villain of the piece. Usually that one would then get a tragic comeuppance at the hands of the heroic relation. Here, though we begin the story with a character who very well could take that trip if properly motivated, Thadeous's self-absorbed desire to remain in the background with his fine clothes and ridiculously blended body oils precludes his potential for evil. From the beginning of the film, Fabious, despite his first-born superiority in almost every sense, expresses nothing but love for his brother, even exhibiting a naïve jealousy of Thadeous's protected lifestyle. Only through the trials and tribulations experienced together on the road do they learn to see one another in a more genuine light, as brothers sharing a strong familial bond. Heck, they even go so far as to gleefully touch tips . . . of their swords!

WHO GOES THERE?

A number of people know Danny McBride as the star of HBO's *Eastbound & Down*, co-created by *Your Highness* cowriter Ben Best. McBride has also appeared in a number of successful and not-so-successful comedies, including *Superbad*, *Pineapple Express* (with James Franco), *Tropic Thunder*, *Land of the Lost*, and *This Is the End* (as himself!).

James Franco is a versatile and award-winning actor, director, and screenwriter who seems happy to try just about anything, including comedy, drama, short films, and even daytime soap operas. While he had already appeared in a few films and TV shows, he really didn't make his mark until he appeared as misunderstood tough-guy/stoner Daniel Desario on the tragically short-lived *Freaks and Geeks*. Some of his more notable films include *Spider-Man* and its two sequels, *Flyboys*, *Pineapple Express*, *127 Hours*, *Rise of the Planet of the Apes*, *Spring Breakers*, *Oz the Great and Powerful*, and *This Is the End* (also as himself!).

Rasmus Hardiker is a British comic actor who appears on the small screen in *Saxondale*, *The Wrong Door*, *Groove High*, and *Thunderbirds Are Go*, as well as in the films *Faintheart* and *Huge*.

> THIS SPRING, PREPARE FOR THEIR EXCELLENCY.

Jerusalem-born actress Natalie Portman will, for better or worse, forever be associated with the *Star Wars* prequels. Fortunately, her Oscar and BAFTA awards for her performance in Darren Aronofsky's *Black Swan* helped her eclipse her rather wooden performance in those other motion pictures, as did her appearances before and after in *Léon: The Professional, Mars Attacks!, Zoolander, Cold Mountain, V for Vendetta, The Other Boleyn Girl, Thor, Thor: The Dark World,* and *Jane Got a Gun*.

Son of the almost legendary character-actor Freddie Jones (see *Krull*), Toby Jones has quickly grown into a versatile actor in his own right on both the big and small screens. His first feature-film appearance was in 1992's *Orlando*. He has since appeared in *Ever After: A Cinderella Story, Simon Magus, The Messenger: The Story of Joan of Arc*, a few of the *Harry Potter* films as the voice of Dobby, *Finding Neverland, The Mist, City of Ember, Frost/Nixon, Captain America: The First Avenger, Captain America: The Winter Soldier, The Hunger Games, The Hunger Games: Catching Fire,* and *Snow White and the Huntsman*. He also had a memorable television role in the *Doctor Who* episode "Amy's Choice."

Writer/producer/director/actor Justin Theroux has been busy over the past couple decades. Not only did he cowrite *Tropic Thunder* and *Iron Man 2;* he has also acted in films like *Romy and Michele's High School Reunion, American Psycho, Mulholland Dr., Zoolander, Charlie's Angels: Full Throttle,* and *Inland Empire*, and on TV in *The District, Alias, Six Feet Under*, the HBO miniseries *John Adams, Parks and Recreation*, and *The Leftovers*.

Zooey Deschanel got her start on television at the age of 17 in a TV sitcom, but she had already been indoctrinated into the entertainment industry, thanks to her mother, actress Mary Jo Deschanel *(The Right Stuff, Twin Peaks);* her father, Academy Award–nominated cinematographer Caleb Deschanel *(The Spiderwick Chronicles, Abraham Lincoln: Vampire Hunter);* and her older sister, actress Emily Deschanel *(Boogeyman, Bones)*. Zooey also appears in *Manic, Elf, The Hitchhiker's Guide to the Galaxy, Bridge to Terabithia,* and *The Happening*, as well as the TV show *New Girl*.

Veteran British thespian Charles Dance is awesome! No, seriously, a quick look at his bio reveals a nonstop string of cool roles in fantasy, science-fiction, horror, and action films and TV shows going all the way back to the mid-'70s. Do yourself a favor and check out some of his performances in movies like *For Your Eyes Only, The Golden Child, Alien³, Last Action Hero, Space Truckers, Ironclad, Underworld: Awakening,* and *Pride and Prejudice and Zombies*. On the small screen, he appears in *The Jewel in the Crown, Foyle's War, Bleak House, Strike Back,* and of course, *Game of Thrones*.

After a few roles on TV and in films throughout the '90s, British actor Damian Lewis got his big break thanks to executive producer Steven Spielberg in the HBO miniseries *Band of Brothers*, in which he played an American major. There was some concern about a British actor convincingly portraying an American, but Lewis quickly put those fears to rest, surprising even his costars with his accurate performance. If you'd like to be convinced by some of his other impressive roles, look for him in *Robinson Crusoe, Dreamcatcher, Alex Rider: Operation Stormbreaker*, and the TV series *Homeland*.

Deobia Oparaei has battled aliens in *Alien³* and *Independence Day 2,* slept on a train in *Dark City,* danced his heart out in *Moulin Rouge!,* stood up to murderous monsters in *Doom,* accompanied Captain Jack Sparrow in *Pirates of the Caribbean: On Stranger Tides,* assisted the judges in *Dredd,* and even played the *Game of Thrones*.

364 • CINEMA AND SORCERY

GET YOUR QUEST ON.

B. J. Hogg also appeared in *City of Ember,* alongside Toby Jones.

Matyelok Gibbs was Louise in *Ever After: A Cinderella Story* and Auntie Muriel Weasley in *Harry Potter and the Deathly Hallows: Part 1.*

Angela Pleasence, daughter of the late and legendary Donald Pleasence, has been acting since the mid-'60s, when she appeared on the small screen in a number of series, miniseries, and TV movies. Television roles have continued up through the present day, with appearances in *Dr. Terrible's House of Horrible, Doctor Who* (as Queen Elizabeth!), *Casualty,* and an episode of *The Sarah Jane Adventures.* She also appears in the films *From Beyond the Grave, Symptoms, The Godsend,* and *Gangs of New York.*

In addition to numerous television roles, Julian Rhind-Tutt has appeared on the big screen in *The Madness of King George, The Saint, Tomorrow Never Dies, The Trench, Lara Croft: Tomb Raider,* and *Stardust.*

Noah Huntley has journeyed into the fantastic past in the TV movie *The Mists of Avalon; The Chronicles of Narnia: The Lion, the Witch and the Wardrobe;* and *Snow White and the Huntsman.* He also battled hordes of maniacs in *28 Days Later* and explored the distant future in *Event Horizon.*

Graham Hughes appears in *Kingdom, The Libertine,* and the remake of *Clash of the Titans.*

David Garrick has dozens of stunt performances to his name, but he also had roles in *Reign of Fire, The Golden Compass,* and *Sherlock Holmes.*

Suit performer Brian Steele has been in a number of films that you've likely seen, usually buried under layers of foam latex and synthetic hair. His first role was as Harry in the *Harry and the Hendersons* TV series, a role to which he has more-or-less returned in a series of "Messin' with Sasquatch" ads for beef jerky. He also appeared in the TV series *Earth 2* and *Grimm,* and movies such as *The Relic, Men in Black II,* most of the *Underworld* films, *Hellboy, Hellboy II: The Golden Army, Blade: Trinity, Doom, Resident Evil: Extinction, Terminator Salvation,* and *Predators.*

You likely wouldn't know him from his voice as both the Soul of the Maze and the film's narrator, but Charles Shaughnessy is another of those instantly recognizable actors, mostly thanks to his long-running TV role as Maxwell Sheffield on *The Nanny.* Though he has appeared before the camera in a number of other film and television productions, a huge number of his credits have him behind the microphone, lending his versatile voice to characters in *Duckman: Private Dick / Family Man, Gargoyles, Heavy Gear: The Animated Series, The Tale of Desperaux, The Marvelous Misadventures of Flapjack,* and *Tom and Jerry: Robin Hood and His Merry Mouse.*

6 DEGREES OF SORCERY

Thadeous's mullet bears an intentional resemblance to Mel Gibson's hair in the *Lethal Weapon* films.

The throne upon which the dwarf king sits at the top of the film is the actual throne used by the High Aldwin in *Willow,* discovered in a prop warehouse.

The animated titles mirror the Frank Frazetta–illustrated opening narration of *Fire and Ice.* The severed cyclops-head is a deliberate nod to the Cyclops in *Krull.*

Belladonna is a finless copy of the mermaid Madison from *Splash* or Ariel from *The Little Mermaid*, even down to her employing a "dinglehopper" (fork) to comb her hair.

Bubo from *Clash of the Titans* clearly inspired Simon, the mechanical crow; for a while, the filmmakers even considered bringing Simon to life with similar stop-motion animation.

The royal wedding feels similar to the one depicted in *The Princess Bride* but owes more to the wedding in *Krull*, including the bride's kidnapping by sinister forces.

Boremont sports an artificial hand that looks like the mechanical gauntlet used by Ash in *Army of Darkness*.

Four different movie characters inspired Leezar: Gary Oldman's in *Bram Stoker's Dracula* (the hair), Willem Dafoe's in *Wild at Heart* (the gnarly teeth), David Bowie's in *Labyrinth* (the makeup and the rockstar persona), and Nicol Williamson's in *Excalibur* (the occasional metal headpiece)—although this author [SAW] can't help but notice similarities to Thom Christopher's Shurka from *Wizards of the Lost Kingdom*.

The elaborate spell effects behave a bit like the proton streams in *Ghostbusters*.

One can compare Leezar's tower to Isengard in *The Lord of the Rings* films.

The two moons—another salute to *Krull* and *Star Wars*—moving into conjunction echo the three suns of *The Dark Crystal*.

Tumbling down the stairs in a suit of armor, as Thadeous does, has appeared in *Bill & Ted's Excellent Adventure*.

The Great Wize Wizard is a parody of the Caterpillar from *Alice in Wonderland* or Yoda (on chronic), although the creators cite the Mystics from *The Dark Crystal* as inspiration.

The reference to jumping on the wizard's bed as kids is a nod to a "very special episode" of *Diff'rent Strokes*.

At one point, Julie actually mutters "huffle puff," a not-so-subtle reference to *Harry Potter*.

Willow and the *Indiana Jones* films influenced the coach chase; in fact, one of the Mongol warriors gets dragged behind the coach as Indy does in pretty much all of his movies.

Belladonna's capture is similar to the capture of Sunya in *Ator, The Fighting Eagle*.

The compass serves a similar function to the one in the *Pirates of the Caribbean* films.

Leezar's fish-stick dinner is a reference to the "fish-stick kitties" gag in *Cabin Boy*.

Marteetee's arena is much like Thunderdome, and various post-apocalyptic '80s rockstar warriors, including Mad Max, inspired the look of its resident gladiator Dastardly. Marteetee's colossal hand-creature is this film's take on the hydra in *Jason and the Argonauts*. A character splattered with acidic snake venom behaves a bit like the toxic waste–distorted Emil from *Robocop*.

The mud-encrusted natives are similar to the Italian cannibals in several early '80s films or even Lucio Fulci's own sword-and-sorcery romp, *Conquest* (reluctantly covered elsewhere in this volume).

The relevance of the blade being made of unicorn horn links it to the alicorn in *Legend*.

The labyrinth is a stereotypical tabletop-game dungeon, deliberately designed to look like it came right out of an '80s sword-and-sorcery film.

The Goonies partially inspired opening the door into the labyrinth with the compass.

The minotaur (sans private parts) looks as if it just stepped right out of one of the *Narnia* films.

The labyrinth and the minotaur pursuing our heroes draws from *Time Bandits*.

Isabel's playing of the pan flute to charm the minotaur is an homage to Jen's flute-playing in *The Dark Crystal*, even down to Ms. Portman's intentional "puppety" movements.

The wall of eyes is another nod to *Labyrinth*.

Shots of Thadeous standing upon rocks and swinging the Blade of Unicorn around mirror similar scenes in *Conan the Barbarian*.

Julie's deadly fall resembles the plummeting Skeksis scientist falling into the pit beneath the Dark Crystal, or Gollum's fall into Mt. Doom.

The handshake/arm-grab between Thadeous and Fabious is a nod to a similar move between Dutch and Dillon in *Predator* . . . sans the crack about pushing pencils.

SHATTERING THE ILLUSION

The movie began as the result of a film-school game played by David Green and Danny McBride, whereby one person would come up with a movie title and the other would come up with its plot. In the case of *Your Highness*, the resulting suggested plot was little more than "guy in the middle ages who smokes weed and fights dragons." The idea remained in their back pockets as a "passion project" for a decade before it saw the light of day.

A studio budget breakdown of the first draft, which featured floating ice-cities, subterranean trolls, and faeries in almost every scene, put it somewhere around the $120-million mark. With the script toned down (exclusively for budgetary reasons) the doors opened for production of a film that deliberately hearkened back to a childhood of staying up late watching trashy '80s sword-and-sorcery movies (*all* covered elsewhere in this volume). The most influential of those films, according to Green's personal top-ten list featured on Complex.com, include *The Dark Crystal; Labyrinth; Ladyhawke; Yor, the Hunter from the Future; Krull; Hawk the Slayer; The Sword & The Sorcerer* (which Green made everyone in the cast watch before the cameras started rolling); *Fire and Ice; Conan the Destroyer;* and *The NeverEnding Story*.

The creators of *Your Highness* never set out to spoof those movies. The plan was actually to make such a movie, but to bring comedy from the perspective of someone—in this case, Thadeous—who doesn't belong in the situations presented. In fact, to ensure that the cast would treat the material seriously enough, Green presented the film not as a comedy but as an action movie, prior to production. The comedy then evolved on set. For this same reason, the creators deliberately avoided casting too many comic actors, instead seeking out a number of accomplished and well-respected thespians.

The bulk of production took place in Ireland, with its abundance of impressive environments and castles. The Belfast crew was enthusiastic and extremely professional. The castle interior sets were constructed in spaces where the historical *Titanic* was built.

From the outset, Green wanted to go with as many practical effects as possible, including suits, puppets, and models. A meeting with Guillermo del Toro, who expressed his love for such traditional techniques, further cemented the idea.

Warwick Davis, first choice for the dwarf king at the top of the film, was unavailable, likely off working on a little movie about a kid named Potter. Jonah Hill was approached about playing

Marteetee, but he either didn't have the time or declined because he didn't want to appear topless.

> BEST. QUEST. EVER.

Marteetee's hand-monster was the result of a few revisions. At one point, it was a giant earthworm like an old-school *D&D* purple worm. At another, it was a monstrosity that one version of the script referred to as "Nipple-Eye." It settled on its final form when, for budgetary reasons, the arena battle moved from a subterranean cavern to a forest clearing.

Early versions of the script had the minotaur guarding Leezar's tower. A lost gag involved a magical weapon called the Hoop of Doom: a nod to the glaive in *Krull*. Alas, the idea of a sorcerous hula-hoop capable of slaying foes just didn't make a lot of sense.

Advertising company Mojo House commissioned a movie poster by fantasy-art duo Boris and Julie Bell. The resulting painting, although impressive, did not see use for any commercial purposes. Anyone interested in it can purchase prints from the artists' website.

MUSIC OF THE MINSTRELS

Like many contemporary composers, Steve Jablonsky divides his writing time among television, videogames, and motion pictures. A fan of '80s sword-and-sorcery films, he considers his score for *Your Highness* one of his best. Director David Green pushed for the inclusion of retro synthesizer sounds to emphasize the intended '80s vibe.

Varese Sarabande released the official soundtrack—twenty-four adventurous tracks—in April 2011. The score received a number of excellent reviews, with many fans applauding Jablonsky's departure from his usual bombastic work for Michael Bay's productions, such as his BMI Award–winning score for *Transformers*. Some have compared this score to the work of Hans Zimmer, particularly Zimmer's work for the *Pirates of the Caribbean* films . . . which is no surprise, because Jablonsky worked alongside Zimmer on scores for *Pearl Harbor, Hannibal, Tears of the Sun,* and others.

THE SAGA CONTINUES

Dark Horse Comics released a forty-eight-page graphic-novel prequel in March 2011, titled *Your Highness: Knight and Dazed,* written by Danny McBride and Brian Best and illustrated by Sean Phillips and Paul Peart. The book explores the events leading up to the beginning of the film, including Fabious's slaying of Leezar's cyclops and Thadeous's unlawful indiscretions while off on a diplomatic mission to the dwarf kingdom.

The production team did set things up for a sequel. To this date, the cast and crew remain open to the possibility.

TAKE UP THY SWORD!

THE BLADE OF UNICORN (MAGIC WEAPON)

The Blade of Unicorn is a real bastard of a bastard sword, imbued with powerful "unicorny" magic. It is the only weapon capable of piercing anyone temporarily granted invulnerability by the influence of the two eclipsed moons.

On its own, the blade acts as an enchanted longsword, granting mid-range bonuses to melee attacks, but if wielded against a sorcerer preparing for one whopper of an unfortunately named ritual meant to birth a dragon, it becomes something akin to the vorpal blade of ancient legend, capable of slicing through the normally impenetrable hide of any ancient and impenetrable thingy.

Anyone seeking the blade can only find it at the heart of a treacherous, trap-filled labyrinth occupied by a menacing though disturbingly amorous minotaur. Bold adventurers who brave this maze should sharpen their wits as well as their weapons . . . and remember to bring flowers and a box of chocolates.

THE FILM'S DESTINY

When the (red-band) trailer for this film first reared its head, this author [SAW] was sold! (The rating is primarily for harsher language.) I enthusiastically defended it to friends as something that touched the tabletop-gaming nerve and recalled old college RPG sessions. People offended by the use of certain words in the trailer—or by the final film, for that matter—have clearly never sat at or near a table of roleplaying gamers. Foul language, bad puns, unintentionally or unapologetically sexist jokes—most gaming gatherings should have red bands (or red boxes!) of their own.

The film on the whole is an entertaining adventure, but not without a significant number of avoidable flaws. The sex jokes get tired and repetitious, and James Franco's wavering accent—despite the suggestion that it is an intentional dig at Matthew Broderick's poor attempt in *Ladyhawke*—is distracting and likely one of the reasons he received a nomination for a Razzie for Worst Supporting Actor.

Visually, the film is stunning, with sweeping Irish vistas, castles, forests, and rolling hills often stealing the show. The costumes are also well done. Some of the visual effects—especially those dealing with magic—are flashy and perfect realizations of spells gamers grew up with.

Should you invest in the Blu-ray of the film, seek ye the bonus video titled "Shitty Moons." You won't regret its silliness.

THIS YEAR IN GAMING

Vampire: The Masquerade, the first of White Wolf's *World of Darkness* series of interconnected roleplaying games, celebrated its 20th anniversary. The company released a very limited, anniversary edition of the core rulebook, which quickly sold out a became an instant collector's item. Signed copies have sold for hundreds of dollars. Since the overwhelming success of that volume, additional *World of Darkness* core books have been published via crowdfunding and are now handled by Onyx Path Publishing, a company founded by former White Wolf creative director Richard Thomas in 2012.

BRAVE

2012 • US • WALT DISNEY PICTURES / PIXAR ANIMATION STUDIOS • 100M • COLOR • PG

SCREENPLAY: Mark Andrews, Steve Purcell, Brenda Chapman, and Irene Mecchi
STORY: Brenda Chapman
DIRECTORS: Brenda Chapman, Mark Andrews, and Steve Purcell
PRODUCER: Katherine Sarafian
MUSIC: Patrick Doyle
DIRECTORS OF PHOTOGRAPHY: Robert Anderson and Danielle Feinberg
ART DIRECTOR, CHARACTERS: Matt Nolte
ART DIRECTOR, SETS: Noah Klocek
ART DIRECTOR, SHADING: Tia W. Kratter
SUPERVISING ANIMATORS: Alan Barillaro And Steven Clay Hunter
EFFECTS SUPERVISOR: David MacCarthy
IN MEMORY OF: Steve Jobs
CAST: Kelly Macdonald (Merida), Emma Thompson (Elinor), Billy Connolly (Fergus), Julie Walters (The Witch), Robbie Coltrane (Lord Dingwall), Kevin McKidd (Lord MacGuffin / Young MacGuffin), Craig Ferguson (Lord Macintosh), Sally Kinghorn and Eilidh Fraser (Maudie), Peigi Barker (Young Merida), Steven Cree (Young Macintosh), Steve Purcell (The Crow), Callum O'Neill (Wee Dingwall), Patrick Doyle (Martin), John Ratzenberger (Gordon), and Rupert Farley, Matthew Gammie, Stephanie Farrell, Rudi Goodman, Colin Gourley, John Hasler, Jeyda Hassan, Kevin Howarth, Jamie Lee, Emma Lima, Kate Lock, Harmonie London, Gail Mackinnon, Phil Mckee, David Monteath, Alex Norton, John Kay Steel, Chris Reilly, Dean Williamson, and Joseph West (Additional Voices)
ALTERNATE TITLE: *The Bear and the Bow* (working title)

ON THE MAP

The rolling, rocky landscape of 10th-century Scotland serves as the backdrop for this adventure—especially the Callanish Stones, an ancient circle on the Isle of Lewis in the Outer Hebrides or Western Isles.

OUR STORY SO FAR

Merida, princess of a kingdom that has kept the peace among four neighboring clans, is to be betrothed to the son of one of the other three clans during a grand celebration. But the young archer has another fate in mind. In attempting to forge her own path, she endangers not only the fragile peace of her homeland but her own mother, when a spell gone awry transforms Queen Elinor into a bear. Will the same magic that tore mother and daughter asunder also mend their bond?

IT'S MAGIC

The strong magical force in Merida's Scotland might tie directly to the land and the natural world. The wisps are almost pixie-like but ethereal apparitions who seem somewhat mischievous but do not deceive or mislead: where they take you, your fate most definitely awaits. As for the witch, her cottage is a treasure trove of magical powers, from its multidimensional existence to its answering-machine cauldron with individual vials of enchanted brew serving as push buttons. Her talking crow must also be created or enchanted by similar but specific powers, because no other animals in the film, even those originally human, can speak.

In regard to the transformation spell that turns Elinor into a bear: although mending the tapestry is the solution Merida believes will undo the curse, telling her mother she loves her really seals the deal. Once again, love conquers all . . . even magic.

THE QUEST FOR MEANING

It's fitting that this book, devoted to a genre that has heavily traded in overblown male heroic archetypes, misogyny, and levels of violence suitable only for older audiences (our other animated and all-ages selections notwithstanding) should near its end with this, a beautiful film for the entire family that not only shares a genre with the likes of *Barbarian Queen II* and *Conquest* but also introduces a heroine who is as capable as any of her predecessors of embarking on a magical journey of discovery and adventure, if not more so. She handles herself physically in a world of real and illusionary perils and saves her entire kingdom with a combination of skill, determination, and strength of spirit. We would say she manages it all without a hair falling out of place, but none of them are ever really in any one place to begin with . . . and that's another meaningful part of her undeniable charm. Those curly tresses, which never calm down for a single moment, symbolize her defiance against stifling tradition and rules that impede progress. Heroes are not just those who triumph over impossible odds, but also those who challenge the status quo and lead the way to a bolder, brighter future. That Merida's ultimate victory comes through strengthening the mother-daughter bond in a genre more often concerned with fathers and sons is another bonus.

The movie signposts one of its primary themes with its very tagline: that of changing one's fate by taking control of life and not letting it pass by. It's also more complicated than that. The film neatly subverts expectations inherent in the by-now routine "Disney princess" fairytale, combines the roles of heroic prince and longing princess into a single fiery figure, and in the process gives young girls an inspirational character who can stand proudly alongside any male hero. That's not just a game-changer but a game-winner.

WHO GOES THERE?

Kelly Macdonald has appeared in *Trainspotting, Elizabeth, Finding Neverland, The Hitchhiker's Guide to the Galaxy, Nanny McPhee, No Country for Old Men,* and *Harry Potter and the Deathly Hallows: Part 2* (as Helena Ravenclaw). HBO viewers knew her as Margaret on *Boardwalk Empire*.

Emma Thompson is an accomplished Shakespearean actress of stage and screen, equally adept at drama and comedy. Famously, she often collaborated with one-time husband Kenneth Branagh. She has appeared in films like *The Tall Guy, Dead Again, Howards End, Peter's Friends, Much Ado About Nothing, The Remains of the Day, Sense and Sensibility, Treasure Planet,*

Love Actually, I Am Legend, Pirate Radio, and *Men in Black 3.* She was Sybil Trelawney in three of the *Harry Potter* films and Nanny McPhee in two movies. On television she had roles in *The Young Ones, Thompson,* and *Cheers* (as another nanny: Nanny G.).

CHANGE YOUR FATE.

Billy Connolly is a world-famous comedian who also appeared in the television series *Worzel Gummidge, Head of the Class* (taking over for departing lead Howard Hesseman in the US show's final season) and its short-lived spinoff *Billy, Pearl,* and the penultimate *Columbo* episode, "Murder with Too Many Notes." His films include *Pocahontas, Muppet Treasure Island, The Boondock Saints* and its sequel, *Timeline, Lemony Snicket's A Series of Unfortunate Events, Fido, The X-Files: I Want to Believe, Gulliver's Travels,* and *The Hobbit: The Battle of the Five Armies* (as Dain Ironfoot).

Julie Walters is a UK acting institution, with roles on stage, in television, and in films like *Educating Rita, Billy Elliot, Calendar Girls, Becoming Jane,* and *Mamma Mia!* She played the infamous censorship-crusader Mary Whitehouse in the TV movie *Filth: The Mary Whitehouse Story* and lent her voice to the animated film *Gnomeo & Juliet.* A generation of moviegoers now knows her best as Molly Weasley in the *Harry Potter* films.

Kevin McKidd had roles in films like *Trainspotting, Dog Soldiers, Hannibal Rising,* and *Percy Jackson & the Olympians: The Lightning Thief* (as Poseidon), as well as in television series like *Rome, Journeyman,* and *Grey's Anatomy.* He also provided the voice of Jezz Torrent in *Grant Theft Auto: Vice City* and Soap MacTavish in *Call of Duty: Modern Warfare 2* and *3.*

Steven Cree appeared in *John Carter, 300: Rise of an Empire,* and *Maleficent.*

Steve Purcell was a creator and writer on a plethora of *Sam and Max* videogames and also worked as an animator on the *Monkey Island* game series that partially inspired the *Pirates of the Caribbean* film franchise.

It's a proven fact: a certain generation will always remember John Ratzenberger as "fact"-spewing, know-it-all bar-regular Cliff Clavin on the hit television series *Cheers*, a character he played in five other series alongside *Cheers* cohort George "Norm" Wendt: *St. Elsewhere, The Tortellis, Wings, The Simpsons,* and *Frasier.* He also turns up in a number of films, including *Warlords of the Deep, Superman, Star Wars: The Empire Strikes Back, Motel Hell, Superman II, Outland, Ragtime, Firefox, Gandhi* (with his voice dubbed by costar Martin Sheen!), and *House II: The Second Story.* In the 1990s, he segued into largely doing voice work and became Pixar's "good-luck charm," lending his voice to every production the company has made to date. Go ahead: look them all up.

6 DEGREES OF SORCERY

The film is dedicated to the memory of Steve Jobs, Apple and Pixar co-founder. The names of Lord and Young Macintosh come from the computer (not the fruit) as a further tribute.

You can see Disney's famous mousy mascot hidden in the queen's belt. Fergus's line—"Guess who's coming to dinner!"—references the 1967 film of the same name.

Merida's affinity for archery follows in the footsteps of several recent film heroes, including Neytiri in *Avatar,* Isabel in *Your Highness,* Katniss in *The Hunger Games,* and Hawkeye in *The*

Avengers. In some versions of the classic tales, Robin Hood's Maid Marian and King Arthur's Guinevere also prove adept at hitting a target. In fact, Merida's hooded entry into the archery contest held for her hand, and her splitting another contestant's arrow, are straight out of nearly every version of the classic Robin Hood tale, including Disney's adaptation with another redhead . . . although that one was a fox.

The shriveled old witch living in a cottage in the woods—part of an oasis of classic Disney-style storytelling in the midst of a more modern movie—might remind viewers of Valerie, Miracle Max's wife in *The Princess Bride*. She serves up her wooden wares to Merida in a fashion similar to the Junk Lady making a pitch to Sarah in *Labyrinth*. Her cottage is a cornucopia of Easter-egg references to other Pixar productions: look for the Pizza Planet truck that first turned up in *Toy Story*, and a wooden doll of Sully from *Monsters, Inc.* and the upcoming *Monsters University*. The cottage also seems bigger on the inside than the outside, a trait shared by Merlin's bag in Disney's *The Sword in the Stone* and the TARDIS in *Doctor Who*. In an odd but amusing reference that doesn't quite jibe with the film's family-friendly slant, the witch mentions attending the Wicker Man festival on Summerisle, a nod to the classic but very dark 1973 horror film *The Wicker Man*.

Sticking with horror, the boys discovering the enchanted cake and becoming bears recalls another unfortunate collateral effect of a cursed pastry: the one in Stephen King's *Thinner*. Mor'du swats several warriors with a single blow as Sauron does in the prologue of *The Lord of the Rings: The Fellowship of the Ring*. When Mor'du's human spirit is released from its curse, his nod and apparent relief echo those of the king of the dead when released by Aragorn in *The Lord of the Rings: The Return of the King*. Many Disney fans have noted parallels between part of the plot of *Brave* and the 2003 animated adventure *Brother Bear*, which also featured an involuntary transformation and a quest led by lights (in that case, the aurora borealis). In a literary connection, Mark Andrews has described the Fergus-Mor'du relationship as akin to the one between Ahab and Moby Dick. As in many of our other films, green (the witch's brew) and blue (the wisps) are the colors of magic. Speaking of which, *Princess Mononoke* also has guiding spirits. And is that cauldron in the witch's cottage a "black cauldron"? No, we won't go there.

SHATTERING THE ILLUSION

Pixar's thirteenth production also marks a number of firsts for the company: its first historic setting, its first female lead—one officially granted membership in the venerable pantheon of Disney princesses, and, initially, its first female director. It's ironic, then, that controversy concerning the firing of that director, Brenda Chapman, should mar this movie. Laying bare the gender issues that still roil under the surface of the movie industry in general and the animation world in particular, Chapman's departure from the project she conceived and developed for six years is a sad footnote to an otherwise beautiful film.

When the project began, Chapman intended to pay homage to classic fairytales like those of the Brothers Grimm or Hans Christian Andersen, with a more modern family incorporated into the period setting. While trying to make a more enlightened adventure, she had no desire to spoof the genre, offering instead a heartfelt story about an independently minded princess who would make mothers less frustrated by their daughters' desire to buy princess-themed merchandise and instead see it, in this case, as an empowering choice. The first choice for Merida was actress Reese Witherspoon, but Kelly Macdonald wound up with the part when it didn't work out with Witherspoon's schedule.

Chapman's involvement came to an end in October 2010, when Mark Andrews replaced her due to "creative differences." It will surely be some time—if ever—before the full story behind the sudden change comes to light, but we can speculate. According to some theories, Disney was less than satisfied by the performance of 2009's *The Princess and the Frog*, so shortly afterward, decisionmakers fired Chapman from *Brave* and retooled the forthcoming *Rapunzel*, retitling it *Tangled* (in the hopes that it would capture a wider audience than the expected attendees: young girls). Chapman's removal from a project inspired at least partly by her relationship with her daughter might have been a move to minimize a perception of *Brave* as narrowly targeted. Chapman left Pixar shortly after the film's release and went back to former employer DreamWorks.

One of Andrews' earliest jobs in the short eighteen months he had to complete the film was to transform the setting from snow-covered Scotland to a lush green, despite the fact that years of work had created a realistic rendering of the snow. Animators went on a field trip to Scotland to research the look of the film. Although it doesn't show in detail unless freeze-framed on DVD and Blu-ray, the moss exhibits Celtic patterns that differ throughout. To render the complicated shots of Scotland's natural wonders, as well as the most dynamic hairdo yet seen in an animated film (partly influenced by previous work on the character Violet in *The Incredibles*), Pixar staffers wrote all-new software dubbed "Presto": the first change of their basic system in twenty-five years. The movie is also the first to make use of a new sound format, Dolby Atmos. It won the 2013 BAFTA for Animated Film, the 2013 Golden Globe for Best Animated Film, and the 2013 Academy Award for Best Animated Feature Film.

La Luna, a poetic, painterly short-feature with no dialogue, accompanied the film's theatrical release. It focused on a unique family business.

MUSIC OF THE MINSTRELS

Composer Patrick Doyle deserves credit for much of the authentic atmosphere that permeates the glorious landscapes of Merida's medieval Scotland. His score relies on Scottish instrumentation and traditional styles tweaked slightly for a modern audience. Two original songs, written by Alex Mandel and Mark Andrews and performed by Julie Fowlis, augment the score: "Touch the Sky" and "Into the Open Air." Birdy and Mumford & Sons provided a third song, "Learn Me Right."

In June 2012, Walt Disney Records released the soundtrack digitally and on CD. A Spanish version featured performances of "Touch the Sky" and "Into the Open Air" by Russian Red, under the titles "Volaré" and "A la luz del sol."

THE SAGA CONTINUES

As we go to press, we have no word on a sequel or any other significant expansion of Merida's story, although Internet speculation on *Brave 2* kicked in predictably fast. As part of the inevitable slew of home-video releases on disc and online, a short prequel titled *The Legend of Mor'du* filled in some background on the film's monstrous threat and adopted a different artistic style.

As for tie-ins, Random House and Disney published a junior novelization as well as a whole range of graphic-novel, story, coloring-drawing, and sticker books. DK joined in with an addition to their line of *Essential Guides,* and Chronicle released *The Art of Brave* coffee-table book. Even the short feature *La Luna* has a tie-in book from Disney Press.

You can play a *Brave*-ized version of the venerable board game, *Monopoly,* as well as a *Brave* videogame from Disney Interactive Studios on the Xbox 360, Wii, PlayStation 3, Nintendo DS, and PC platforms. Mobile players with iPhones or Android phones can get *Temple Run: Brave.*

And you didn't think a newly minted Disney princess (number eleven, in case you're counting) wouldn't have her own army of dolls, costumes, wigs, and other paraphernalia, did you? Ah, but therein lies another story, because even before that merchandise began to appear, a firestorm erupted on the Internet: Disney revealed a major redesign in Merida's look as she joined their princess pantheon. She had become notably slimmer, "sexier," unarmed, and arguably not in keeping with the very concept of the character. Chapman blamed the changes on money and marketing. Despite the comments and an online petition, Disney retained the "new look" Merida, to share space with a more faithful rendition on store shelves.

TAKE UP THY SWORD!

WITCH'S BLACKHOUSE COTTAGE (LOCATION)

On the outside, this witch's hut is nothing much to behold: a typical blackhouse cottage overgrown with grasses and moss ... but there is much more within than meets the eye. This magical dwelling is merely a shell on this plane, wherein the contents of a mirrored reality can switch in and out. Through the sorcerous manipulation of the cottage's front door, one can enter either the cluttered woodshop of an eccentric carver who specializes in animal totems (bears in particular) or the mystical lair of an ancient hag of unknown years, capable of wielding powerful magic! Both interiors exhibit physical dimensions that far exceed those of the hut's exterior, further emphasizing the door's nature as an interplanar portal.

THE FILM'S DESTINY

Brave is a brilliant new fairytale that uses an ancient landscape as a backdrop for a story with modern sensibilities, crafted by the very latest in moviemaking technology. The CG animation is beautiful, with nearly photo-realistic settings immersive in detail and grandeur, and characters who seem cartoonish only because of their deliberate design that way: they still engage an audience's emotions.

In particular, Merida's nuanced expressions create a character who feels real and endearing while exhibiting distinctly Disney-esque traits that link her to the princesses who came before her. Of course, the real star of the film is Merida's mane of unruly red hair, all 1,500 strands meticulously animated to create the perfect illusion of organic unpredictability.

All this visually entrancing spectacle wouldn't matter if the film didn't have heart, which it most certainly does. After the focus of so many tales in this genre on fathers and sons, it's wonderful to see a story in which the relationship that fuels the fairytale is that of a mother and a daughter, as they grow closer and see the world through each other's eyes. It's also a delight that Merida's greatest moment of triumph is arguably not through the wielding of a physical weapon or the defeat of a monster—though all that gets covered one way or another—but in finding the will to become a leader politically and unite kingdoms with words rather than swords. That she does so in concert with her mother, who has also learned much, is a powerful statement that should resonate not just with female moviegoers but with whole families. If you are the type to resist a film for all ages, particularly a CG-animated film [as I once was —ATB], then we urge you to think twice about it . . . and change your fate.

THIS YEAR IN GAMING

Originally released in 2009, Green Ronin Publishing's Silver ENnie Award–winning *A Song of Ice and Fire Roleplaying* returned as a revised and expanded edition in June. Given the subtitle *A Game of Thrones Edition* to tie in with the hugely successful HBO television series, the new version included updated rules, a full-length adventure titled *Peril at King's Landing*, and an attractive new cover by artist Michael Komarck, whose work has graced the covers of a number of comic books, board games, *Star Wars* novels, and *Magic: The Gathering* cards. Robert J. Schwalb (numerous *Dungeons & Dragons* 4th Edition products, *Star Wars Roleplaying Game*) and Steve Kenson *(DC Adventures, Mutants & Masterminds)* were the main writers of the core rulebook. The game is set in the pseudo-historical world of author George R. R. Martin's *A Song of Ice and Fire* series, focusing mainly on the continent of Westeros.

THE HOBBIT: AN UNEXPECTED JOURNEY

2012 • NZ/US • NEW LINE CINEMA / MGM / WINGNUT FILMS / WARNER BROS.
169M • COLOR • PG-13

SCREENPLAY: Fran Walsh, Phillipa Boyens, Peter Jackson, and Guillermo del Toro
BASED ON THE BOOK BY: J. R. R. Tolkien
DIRECTOR: Peter Jackson
SECOND UNIT DIRECTOR: Andy Serkis
PRODUCERS: Carolynne Cunningham, Zane Weiner, Fran Walsh, Peter Jackson, Philippa Boyens, and Eileen Moran
MUSIC: Howard Shore. (Featuring "Song of the Lonely Mountain," with music by Howard Shore, and lyrics and performance by Neil Finn.)
DIRECTOR OF PHOTOGRAPHY: Andrew Lesnie
MAKEUP AND HAIR DESIGN: Peter King
SPECIAL EFFECTS SUPERVISOR: Steve Ingram
VISUAL EFFECTS SUPERVISOR: Matt Aiken
SPECIAL AND VISUAL EFFECTS: Weta Workshop and Weta Digital
SPECIAL MAKEUP AND PROSTHETICS SUPERVISOR: Jason Docherty
PRODUCTION DESIGNER: Dan Hennah
SUPERVISING ART DIRECTOR: Simon Bright
COSTUME DESIGNERS: Bob Buck, Ann Maskrey, AND Richard Taylor
CONCEPTUAL DESIGNERS: John Howe, Alan Lee, AND Mike Mignola (uncredited)
TOLKIEN LANGUAGE TRANSLATOR: David Salo
STUNT COORDINATORS: Glenn Boswell, James O'Donnell, AND Paul Shapcott
ARMOR AND WEAPONS: Richard Taylor
ANIMAL TRAINERS: Mark Ford AND Chris Mcgarry
HORSE TRAINER: Les Old
HORSE DEPARTMENT COORDINATOR: Sarah Tyler
PONY SUITS: Bronwen Pattison
CAST: Ian McKellen (Gandalf), Martin Freeman (Bilbo Baggins), Richard Armitage (Thorin Oakenshield), Ken Stott (Balin), Graham McTavish (Dwalin), William Kircher (Bifur/Tom), James Nesbitt (Bofur), Stephen Hunter (Bombur), Dean O'Gorman (Fili), Aidan Turner (Kili), John Callen (Óin), Peter Hambleton (Glóin/William), Jed Brophy (Nori), Mark Hadlow (Dori/Bert), Adam Brown (Ori), Ian Holm (Old Bilbo), Elijah Wood (Frodo), Hugo Weaving (Elrond), Cate Blanchett (Galadriel), Christopher Lee (Saruman), Andy Serkis (Gollum), Sylvester McCoy (Radagast), Barry Humphries (Great Goblin), Jeffrey Thomas (Thror), Mike Mizrahi (Thrain), Lee Pace (Thranduil), Manu Bennett (Azog), Conan Stevens (Bolg), John Rawls (Yazneg), Stephen Ure (Fimbul/Grinnah), Timothy Bartlett (Master Worrywort), Bret McKenzie (Lindir), Kiran Shah (Goblin Scribe), Beneditch Cumberbatch (The Necromancer / Smaug), Glenn Boswell (Dwarf Miner), and Thomas Robins (Young Thrain)

ON THE MAP

As with the The Lord of the Rings: The Fellowship of the Ring, the adventure begins in a more-or-less linear fashion as Bilbo and his new companions travel from the Shire into the wilderness and on to the elven land of Rivendell. From there, it's in the Misty Mountains and down, down to Goblin Town before one last forest battle leads them to the high Carrock, looking across at the Lonely Mountain looming on the horizon. There is still quite a journey ahead. . . .

OUR STORY SO FAR

Sixty years before the events of *The Lord of the Rings* trilogy, the wizard Gandalf the Gray presses homebody hobbit and reluctant burglar Bilbo Baggins into service to accompany a group of dwarves in their quest to reclaim their ancestral mountain home from a malevolent dragon.

ALTERNATE VERSIONS

An aspect of this movie that has as much drama as the story itself—perhaps more—is Jackson's decision to film it in native digital 3D at a frame rate of 48fps. For those not in the know: movies have traditionally been shot at 24fps for the last hundred years or so, based on the physical limitations of celluloid, but that means very little now with the predominance of digital. Promising astonishing clarity and a far more immersive "you are there" experience, the choice led to controversy when an early ten-minute preview of *Hobbit* footage shown to exhibitors set the Internet aflame with commentary that it looked like a '70s BBC TV production or the behind-the-scenes video shot on a set rather than a film itself. Within twenty-four hours of that reaction, Warner Bros. announced that theaters would run multiple formats of the movie: a 24fps 2D version, a 24fps 3D version, and the HFR (high frame rate) 3D version. The jury is still out about whether this is the future of filmmaking. (At least one of your authors [ATB] saw no real, discernible difference in quality between the two frame rates.) Besides the release of the theatrical cut with the different formats, an extended edition with thirteen extra minutes of footage and nine hours (!) of bonus features arrived via digital download in October 2013, with 3D Blu-ray, Blu-ray, and DVD versions hitting shelves in November of the same year.

IT'S MAGIC

The rules that pertain to magic in *The Lord of the Rings* trilogy hold true here, although we see a variety of new manifestations of that magic in addition to the return of a few familiar favorite magical gambits. Gandalf's rapport with butterflies and eagles makes another appearance— Radagast has an even deeper affinity for animals and their connection to the larger world—as does a mostly similar depiction of the dimensional shift that seems to occur when one becomes invisible while wearing the One Ring. We see the shadowy form of Sauron struggling to regain his former power. The witch king of Angmar looks exactly as he did in the previous films. Perhaps most interestingly, Galadriel disappears at will when discussing Bilbo and the dwarves with Gandalf; even the wizard looks perplexed.

THE QUEST FOR MEANING

One of the key challenges from a filmmaking point of view is that the stakes are lower in this story than they are in the previous trilogy. Rather than a raging war that could claim all of Middle-earth, this is about thirteen dwarves, a hobbit, and a wizard who want to take one mountain back from one dragon. This is not to say it isn't still an epic tale—and one that influences a much larger game Gandalf is playing as he looks toward the future threat of a reconstituted Sauron. It *does* mean, however, that the thematic core of this series is at least a little different than last time.

Some aspects are the same, not least Bilbo's merciful side in action when he has the opportunity to kill Gollum—a gesture that Gandalf foreshadows when handing Bilbo his new weapon, Sting. The wizard reflects upon that moment with Frodo in *The Fellowship of the Ring*. Ultimately, Bilbo's decision sets up the entire resolution of the War of the Ring.

But if there's a primary driving idea in this film, it's Thorin's desire to reclaim his birthright. It's not about the gold or the glory: it's about belonging somewhere instead of wandering the world with no home and no purpose. As a hobbit, Bilbo is keenly aware of what home means, which is why he shares a heartfelt moment with Bofur at one point and why he embraces the quest by film's end. The film nicely structures a two-part meeting of minds and hearts between Thorin and Bilbo in the final act, when Bilbo expresses his desire to help them find a home like the one he appreciates so much, and Thorin reciprocates by embracing the unlikely hero who saved his life and kept the quest alive.

WHO GOES THERE?

Martin Freeman began his career as a reliable comedic character-actor in films like *Love Actually*, *Shaun of the Dead*, *The Hitchhiker's Guide to the Galaxy*, *Hot Fuzz*, and *The World's End*, as well as the hit television series *The Office*, but he's risen to pop-culture prominence not just here but via his role as the modern-day Dr. Watson in the BBC's *Sherlock* and via films like *Captain America: Civil War*.

Richard Armitage had an uncredited role in *Star Wars: Episode I—The Phantom Menace*, but we suspect he'd rather you remember his later work in the *North & South* TV miniseries, television shows like *Robin Hood*, *MI-5*, *Strike Back*, and *Hannibal*, and films such as *Frozen* and *Captain America: The First Avenger*.

Ken Stott appeared in *King Arthur* and was the voice of Trufflehunter in *The Chronicles of Narnia: Prince Caspian*.

Graham McTavish appeared in films like *Erik the Viking*, *Lara Croft Tomb Raider: The Cradle of Life*, *King Arthur*, and *Rambo*, and TV shows like *Highlander*, *Red Dwarf*, *Rome*, *Jekyll*, *24*, and *Outlander*. He also has a prolific voiceover career, with roles in videogames including *Quantum of Solace*, *Dragon Age: Origins*, several *Call of Duty* games, and *Star Wars: The Old Republic*. He's even the voice of Thor's evil brother Loki in the animated series *The Avengers: Earth's Mightiest Heroes*.

William Kircher had roles in television series like *Worzel Gummidge Down Under*, *The Ray Bradbury Theater*, *Shark in the Park* (we just had to put that one in), and *Xena: Warrior Princess*.

James Nesbitt did a memorable turn as a modern-day Jekyll/Hyde in the BBC TV miniseries ... well, *Jekyll*.

Stephen Hunter has had a few TV credits on shows you probably haven't seen.

Dean O'Gorman was Young Iolaus in *Young Hercules* and also appeared in *Hercules: The Legendary Journeys* (often in the same role), *Xena: Warrior Princess*, and *Farscape*.

Aidan Turner played Mitchell in the BBC series *Being Human*.

John Callen has lent his voice to the videogame *Star Wars: Knights of the Old Republic II—The Sith Lords* and the *Power Rangers Jungle Fury* TV show.

FROM THE DIRECTOR OF 'THE LORD OF THE RINGS' TRILOGY

Peter Hambleton appeared on the television series *The Strip*.

Mark Hadlow was a variety of voices in Peter Jackson's *Meet the Feebles* and had a role in the director's remake of *King Kong*. He also appeared on the TV shows *Xena: Warrior Princess* and *Jack of All Trades*.

Adam Brown also appears as Jib in *Pirates of the Caribbean: Dead Men Tell No Tales*.

Sylvester McCoy (born Percy James Patrick Kent-Smith!) is beloved worldwide by *Doctor Who* fans for his quirky (and occasionally quite dark) performance as the seventh incarnation of that long-running BBC sci-fi series' titular Time Lord. He appeared from 1987 until the show's original cancellation (they called it a hiatus) in 1989, and continues to play the role to this day in audio dramas from Big Finish. He also appeared in the 1979 film adaptation of *Dracula* and previously worked with Gandalf—Sir Ian McKellen—in a Royal Shakespeare Company production of *King Lear*, playing the Fool to McKellen's Lear.

Barry Humphries might be hidden behind a lot of CGI, but he's used to submerging himself in a character. Global audiences know him best as his alter-ego Dame Edna Everage, whom he first played in the 1960s. He has sustained that flamboyant, shrill persona in ever-increasing eye-burning wigs and ensembles on dozens of late-night talk shows, sitcoms, and series built entirely around her.

Jeffrey Thomas has appeared in *Xena: Warrior Princess*, *Hercules: The Legendary Journeys*, *Spartacus: Gods of the Arena*, and *Spartacus: War of the Damned*.

Michael Mizrahi appeared in *Hercules in the Underworld* and the TV series that followed it, *Hercules: The Legendary Journeys*.

Lee Pace turned up in *Lincoln*, *The Twilight Saga: Breaking Dawn—Part 2*, *Guardians of the Galaxy* (as Ronan), and the TV series *Halt and Catch Fire*.

Manu Bennett had roles on television shows like *BeastMaster*, *Xena: Warrior Princess*, *Spartacus: Gods of the Arena*, *Spartacus: War of the Damned*, and *Arrow*, as well as in films like *30 Days of Night* and the TV movie *Sinbad and the Minotaur* (as the heroic sea captain himself).

Conan Stevens' first role was as Marvel Comics' swamp monster, *Man-Thing*. He has also appeared in the HBO series *Game of Thrones*.

John Rawls also appeared in *30 Days of Night* and the TV series *Spartacus: War of the Damned*.

Benedict Cumberbatch might not really emerge in this series until the sequel, but he receives credit here for his brief bit as the Necromancer—and perhaps for the roar of Smaug, which he also plays via motionca-capture, *a la* Serkis's Gollum. This isn't his first matchup with Freeman, either: audiences know him best as the titular detective in the BBC's *Sherlock*. He's also storming genre entertainment with a vengeance, having appeared in *Star Trek into Darkness* as Khan, and he played scientist Stephen Hawking in a 2004 TV-movie. He was the voice of Alan Rickman in an episode of *The Simpsons,* lent his vocal talents to a BBC Radio adaptation of Neil Gaiman's *Neverwhere*, and mastered the mystic arts as the title character in *Doctor Strange*.

6 DEGREES OF SORCERY

This would be a far longer section if we tried to go through all the most obvious connections with *The Lord of the Rings* movies, but since this is a prequel and an extension of that cinematic world, we can take all of that as read, can't we? Some have noted that Azog looks a bit like the CGI zombie creatures in *I Am Legend*, but that seems a stretch when he looks far more like any of a number of Ray Harryhausen creatures given a makeover. Some of his facial expressions even echo those of Trog in *Sinbad and the Eye of the Tiger*, and he vaguely resembles Kratos from the *God of War* Playstation videogames.

As with all the previous *Rings* movies, the famous "Wilhelm scream" turns up when a goblin falls to its doom (no, not Doom—just doom) during the escape from Goblin Town. Because Gandalf cannot refer to anything outside the materials included in Saul Saentz's Tolkien film-adaptation rights, such as the *Silmarillion*, he cheekily refers to the existence of the Blue wizards but conveniently forgets their names. (Guess where those appear in Tolkien's work. Hint: it starts with an "S.")

SHATTERING THE ILLUSION

The story of the making of this long-awaited return to Middle-earth is probably as worthy of becoming a film as what Peter Jackson and company actually shot. As with *The Lord of the Rings*, there was a long road (that goes ever, ever on?) to the completed production of this version, especially if you count the number of other adaptations of Tolkien's 1937 novel that preceded this one.

Our index covers the Rankin/Bass animated version of *The Hobbit*, which many grew up with and fondly remember. The beloved children's novel also made it to a 1953 stage play and a BBC radio production. Perhaps most bizarrely, two versions of the story only recently did the rounds on YouTube and the Internet: a 1966 animated short that runs just under twelve minutes, and a 1985 Russian live-action version that lasts about seventy.

Gene Deitch and Czechoslovakian Adolf Bern, creators of the animated short, had to complete it in two years: their producer William Snyder held the rights to the story for a limited period, starting in 1964. Deitch drastically altered the story in ways that make the Jackson version look like it came straight off the page. It featured an imperiled princess and a dragon named Slag. Deitch rushed his adaptation to completion when Snyder had a unique opportunity to secure an option to the entire *Lord of the Rings* trilogy, but only if he delivered a completed film of no specific length by June 30, 1966. Miraculously, they made the deadline, but then Snyder sold off his lucrative *Rings* rights, and Deitch never saw a penny. As for the very low-budget live-action Russian production, it's a mesmerizing and often wildly altered adaptation that has its charms, if only because of its plain, simple surreality.

Once Jackson had adapted Tolkien's sweeping *Lord of the Rings* saga into one of the most successful film franchises of all time, the only thing left to do—especially given that it's the only source material left in the film-adaptation rights held by Saul Saentz (so forget that *Silmarillion* movie)—was to turn to Tolkien's first foray into Middle-earth, but it wasn't a foregone conclusion that it would happen. For one thing, a rift between Jackson and *Rings* composer Howard Shore (see **Music of the Minstrels**) meant that any prospective *Hobbit* prequel might lack the moving sound of the other movies. In addition, Jackson was embroiled in legal battles with the studio over profits from the *Rings* movies. The Tolkien estate also made the path less than smooth. After many of these issues settled out one way or another, MGM was poised to bring *The Hobbit* to the screen . . . but went into bankruptcy, costing the film its original director, Guillermo del Toro.

Jackson hadn't intended to return to the director's chair, feeling he'd be competing in some sense with his younger self. Del Toro had spent years in preproduction, writing the script and assisting in conceptualizing the creatures and other designs, but the MGM situation and other issues meant that the schedule for production kept sliding. Eventually, del Toro had to drop out in the summer of 2010. At the eleventh hour, the only way for *The Hobbit* to happen at all—without falling into the hellish limbo of turnaround—was for Jackson to put aside his longstanding misgivings and return to the director's chair in October of that year. Union issues in New Zealand and Jackson's ulcer surgery were further attempts by the dark forces to slow Bilbo's return to the big screen, but production began at long last.

When the time came to start the massive 266-day shooting schedule, cast and crew assembled once again in New Zealand, land of the previous journey to Middle-earth. Although Martin Freeman was Jackson's only choice for Bilbo, he nearly couldn't participate due to the extensive delays in development and a prior commitment as Watson for the BBC's *Sherlock* television series. Jackson adapted the shooting schedule, working on principal photography for nearly half a year without his lead actor and then breaking for about two months so Freeman could complete his work on the second season of *Sherlock*. Then Freeman arrived in New Zealand, and photography resumed. Freeman has said that while he knows others could have played the role, he had no doubt that he was well-suited for the part.

Freeman's first day on set was for the crucial meeting between Bilbo and Andy Serkis's Gollum, so Freeman found his way into the character via the film's most important sequence. Throughout the making of all three films, Freeman became noted for offering a middle finger in behind-the-scenes photographs (presumably with irony?).

Serkis graduated from just playing Gollum to working as second unit director upon completing his scene. Although he had only one sequence to shoot as Gollum, the technology far surpassed what was available when he had first played the role in the late '90s. Rather than shoot live with Freeman and then return months or a year later for motion-capture work, Serkis performed the entire sequence, with Freeman on set, for the cameras and computers simultaneously. Though the modeling preserved the look of Gollum to match that of the earlier films, it allowed for more subtlety of expression and movement.

Sylvester McCoy, known to fans around the world as the Seventh Doctor from the 1987-to-1989 seasons of *Doctor Who*, was originally a contender for the role of Bilbo in *The Lord of the Rings* trilogy. Playing opposite Ian McKellen's Gandalf as Radagast was nothing new, because the two had been in a critically acclaimed production of *King Lear* (with McKellen as Lear and McCoy as his Fool) prior to their reunion in New Zealand.

Although Ian Holm and Christopher Lee reprised their roles as Old Bilbo and Saruman respectively, they did not have to make the long trip to New Zealand this time around. Given Lee's

> **FROM THE SMALLEST BEGINNINGS COME THE GREATEST LEGENDS**

advanced age alone, there was concern that the trip might not be in his best interests. Thankfully, modern moviemaking technology made it easy to film both actors in London and integrate them into the film in post-production.

Switching to high-definition cameras and the 48fps rate meant changes in the level of detail in all aspects of the production, from the sets and costumes to the prosthetics and makeup. In the original trilogy, the prosthetic hobbit feet, designed to function like slippers fitting over the actors' feet, caused all kinds of aggravation. This time, the prosthetics were knee-length boots.

As for that frame-rate issue, the studio wanted a guarantee that a 24fps option was possible for release and would look the same as usual, but it was otherwise open to Jackson's team making the move to the new format and technology. Using specialized camera rigs that enabled the film to shoot in native digital 3D at the faster frame rate, Jackson did not let the innovation affect his approach to directing or his stylistic choices, keeping in mind that these new films had to feel as if they took place in the world of *The Lord of the Rings* movies.

As with *The Lord of the Rings* trilogy, both *Hobbit* movies were planned for shooting at the same time, in more-or-less chronological blocks, with the expectation of a pickup shoot later. During the making of the two-part saga, however, Jackson and company realized they had more story they wanted to tell, especially material from Tolkien's appendices that would further knit the new films together with the original trilogy. Petitioning the studio to finance additional shooting, the production team reworked its plans, reshaping the writing and pickup schedule to accommodate not two but three films. The original ending of the first *Hobbit* film, a climactic barrel-escape, became a crucial action sequence in the middle installment, *The Hobbit: The Desolation of Smaug*.

The Hobbit: An Unexpected Journey made it to its Wellington premiere on November 28, 2012, just two days after the last post-production work wrapped up. In 2013, production resumed for the expanded pickup schedule, which lasted about ten weeks. Video blogs continued from the set, and farewell Internet postings marked the final ever (presumably) days of shooting the series for actors like Orlando Bloom, Ian McKellen, and Martin Freeman.

Not including 2013 pickup shooting, the three *Hobbit* films cost double the budget of their *Lord of the Rings* predecessors, at more than half a billion dollars. That's a treasure even Smaug would envy.

MUSIC OF THE MINSTRELS

Key to any return to Jackson's Middle-earth was another score by Howard Shore, whose musical motifs in the original trilogy were, like other quality scores covered in this book, virtually characters in their own right. They established every aspect of the mood of that epic saga. But there was some doubt early on about Shore's return, given his falling out with the filmmaker during Jackson's project that followed *The Lord of the Rings: The Return of the King*: his remake of childhood favorite *King Kong*. He replaced Shore's work on that film with a score by James

Newton Howard. Fortunately, the rift had healed in time for Shore to journey back in time for *The Hobbit*.

Perhaps because of that tension, however, or just by the nature of the story as told in this first new film, most of Shore's work here feels a bit . . . familiar. Granted, it *should*. After all, if you're returning to the Shire or Rivendell, or reintroducing thematic material about Gollum and the One Ring, or even once again calling upon the eagles to swoop in and save the day at the last second, there's every reason to hear the same exact melodies. But that left only one area for which Shore could craft something overtly original this time: that of the company of dwarves and their desperation to reclaim Erebor, for which he composed the stirring "Misty Mountains" theme. The dwarves sing a version of it, accompanied by lyrics from Tolkien's novel, while in Bag End. Neil Finn of Crowded House and Split Enz also crafted a stunning, percussive, yet melancholy version of the song that evoked the simultaneous bitterness and determination of Thorin's band. Finn's "Song of the Lonely Mountain" serves as the accompaniment for the end titles.

WaterTower Music / Decca Records released the soundtrack in both standard and special editions, each of which consists of two discs. The soundtrack is also available through iTunes.

THE SAGA CONTINUES

The Hobbit: The Desolation of Smaug followed this film in December 2013. The third and final film of this trilogy, *The Hobbit: The Battle of the Five Armies* (originally subtitled *There and Back Again*), was released in December 2014.

This first film has the usual array of multiple-format home-video releases (covered more in "**Alternate Versions**" above), as well as a novelization. Yes, we're kidding again; it never gets old.

As with other films covered in this book, with many *Hobbit*-related items predating this movie, we're going to focus just on what came out as a result of this adaptation's arrival on our screens, including *Hobbit* editions of *Scrabble* and *Monopoly*, a "mini game" using HeroClix figures, and a variety of other licensed board, strategy, and expandable card games. Action figures, playsets, and "roleplay" toys like plastic weapons also flooded toy aisles. Miniatures enhanced Games Workshop's *Lord of the Rings Strategy Battle Game*. On the videogame front, multiple releases include free online games and Monolith Productions' *Guardians of Middle-earth* for PlayStation and Xbox.

Perhaps one of the most significant marketing developments to arise out of the *Hobbit* film series was the announcement that Lego would produce a line of building sets based not just on this movie series but also on *The Lord of the Rings* trilogy. From Bilbo's Bag End home to Helm's Deep and an astonishingly huge Tower of Orthanc, and with mini-figure versions of everyone from Gandalf to Gollum, Lego stores and participating retailers (as well as Lego's website shop) have fully stocked a rotating selection of Middle-earth sets ever since the 2012 holiday shopping season. Early on, Freeman said he owned every single set to date, but we don't know if he's kept up with it.

Even the man behind the mythology might get his day in the sun, thanks to two competing film projects in development as we conclude work on this book. *Tolkien* is a biographical film scripted by Tolkien scholar David Gleeson, and *Tolkien & Lewis* focuses on the friendship between two fantasy legends, with Simon West slated to direct. Whether the Tolkien estate will let these projects proceed (unlike a previous, similar film) remains to be seen.

TAKE UP THY SWORD!
SLED RABBITS (ANIMALS)

In most parts of the world, rabbits are small, docile mammals of little consequence, although some consider their flesh and fur valuable. In a few corners of the globe, however, one can find a much larger and at times fiercer variety that can be tamed, harnessed, and used to pull sleds at high speeds and over great distances. A coordinated team of sled rabbits can easily outpace the swiftest dire wolves, even over rough terrain, doubling or even tripling that pace across snow or ice. A sled rabbit can also put up a fight in the face of danger: it can throw a solid punch or inflict a nasty bite when cornered. Due to heightened senses, sled rabbits are extremely difficult to surprise.

THE FILM'S DESTINY

Perhaps no movie was going to live up to the expectations built by years of anticipation, and the precedent sent by one of the greatest fantasy-film trilogies ever crafted, but unfortunately, after so long, the first *Hobbit* movie comes across merely as a bittersweet reunion with a familiar world and a few beloved characters as well as a good adventure: good, but not *great*. The earlier movies made fans eager to see more and more of them, making the extended editions a true joy, but the extended edition of *An Unexpected Journey* isn't much help, except perhaps to address the much-missed emotional context of Bilbo's connection to Rivendell by restoring scenes revealed in the trailer, such as his discovery of Narsil and a heartfelt conversation with Elrond.

This is the first of Jackson's Middle-earth movies to feel in dire need of editing, but not the last: a tightly constructed two hours probably would have been best (three or four tops, if you throw in the next two films). Although we know the source material, at times it feels like he's using *The Fellowship of the Ring* as the primary template, repeating set pieces and plot beats with minor variations. Shore's repetitive music, though appropriate (see **Music of the Minstrels**), doesn't help on that score (ahem).

There are still wonderful elements here, including excellent performances across the board from all the returnees as well as Freeman, Armitage, Nesbitt, and Stott in the new group. When the time comes for you to tear up and feel something, the movie accomplishes that well enough.

Its greatest tonal weaknesses is with humor. Attempts at silly visual and verbal gags often fail to work. Some are frankly offensive. (Aren't we as a culture beyond ridiculing fat characters just for the sake of it?) As for McCoy's Radagast, he's great for the most part—and no, the bunnies aren't a problem—but someone should mention to him and Jackson that eye-crossing is not gut-busting humor. He is *not*, however, this series' Jar Jar, as some initially claimed. And when Smaug's eye opens at the end, you can't help but feel that maybe, just maybe, greatness lies ahead . . .

THE HOBBIT TRILOGY ADDENDUM

...But such was not to be. When we finished the bulk of work on this tome, only the first *Hobbit* film was out. In the intervening years, as this book trudged toward publication, the remaining two installments came and went. We were faced with a dilemma: Should we add two more chapters to the book to cover *The Hobbit: The Desolation of Smaug* and *The Hobbit: The Battle of the Five Armies* in depth, because every other Jackson Middle-earth film has a chapter of its own? Should we therefore up the total chapter count to 52, or even cut two other films to keep it at 50? We decided merely to add this addendum and cover the next two films in their index entries.

Why? Although each of *The Lord of the Rings* films is a sprawling epic of its own, with a great deal to distinguish it from the others, the three *Hobbit* movies blur together, partially because of the oppressive use of physics-defying CGI that makes everything in the once-gritty and -distinct Middle-earth look like a plastic-coated videogame cut-scene, with balloons bouncing around in place of people. There isn't much to explore thematically or otherwise in the next two installments that we don't already cover here. For us, *The Hobbit* movies prove what many feared at the first announcement that Jackson's team would try to tease another trilogy out of the source material: that it was a mistake. With two films that strain to make full runtimes out of very little, and a concluding chapter that has nothing to anchor it except one long battle sequence that can't hope to live up to similar, far more convincing engagements in *The Lord of the Rings* trilogy, *The Hobbit* movies serve as a reminder to be careful what you wish for.

THIS YEAR IN GAMING

Though founded in 2009, the crowdfunding platform for creative projects called Kickstarter didn't see much of the tabletop-gaming community until 2012. There had already been a few surprisingly successful gaming projects in the years prior, but this year, companies like Reaper Miniatures, Onyx Path, Pinnacle Entertainment, and of course Green Ronin funded projects by huge margins, showing that crowdfunding—especially in the tabletop-roleplaying community—was the future. In Reaper's case, it sought $30,000 to help fund a line of unpainted, plastic miniatures known as Bones. By the end of the thirty-day period, it had exceeded its goal by more than 11,000 percent, taking more than $3 million to the bank!

A CONCORDANCE OF SWORD-AND-SORCERY MOVIES

1924-2015

THE FOLLOWING CONCORDANCE attempts the impossible: to catalogue every sword-and-sorcery movie released from the silent era to 2015, including any alternate titles that saw distribution (more than 400 films!). Naturally this is insane, but we hope you'll find it at least nearly comprehensive, if not all-inclusive. We deliberately excluded many films included by some sources: read our introductory notes on criteria for our reasoning, with which you might or might not agree. We might have missed a few through simple human error, and we might have included a few you wouldn't consider valid in a millennium of adventuring.

We've also tried to include some soon-to-be-released films in varying stages of development or production. We could not find running times for many of them, so we could not confirm with absolute certainty that they qualified above our minimum 59-minute cut-off. With all future film projects, information often changes during the course of production, from title, release date, and people involved to, in some cases, outright cancellation. We have provided the most accurate information available as of publication. By the time you read this, some of these films might already be available in theaters, at film festivals, on home video, or online.

We expect and welcome the inevitable comments: "Why did you include _____?" "How could you leave out _____?" Just keep in mind that ultimately, this is not an intellectual treatise. We're all here to have fun.

ENTRY STRUCTURE

Each entry has this format:

Title **(Year, Countries, Languages—if not only English) Director, Details—see key below**

Description
Alternate titles appear in simple italics and reference main titles.
The 50 films featured in this book are denoted with a double dagger symbol: ‡

KEY

3D Released in 3D
AL Arthurian legend cycle
AN Animated
AN/Live Combination of animated and live-action
B&W Black-and-white
intl. International
MST3K Featured on *Mystery Science Theater 3000*
NYR Not yet released
orig. Original
Silent No spoken dialogue
TV Made for TV
TV/V Direct-to-TV, then video
V Direct-to-video (VHS or DVD)
V/TV Direct-to-video, then TV

THE MOVIES

1001 Arabian Nights **(1959, US) Jack Kinney, AN**

This is a fun animated romp for fans of the near-sighted Mr. Magoo, whose ancestor Abdul Aziz Magoo happens to be Aladdin's uncle. Aladdin is enamored with Princess Yasminda, the sultan's daughter, but the sultan's assistant, the Wicked Wazir, plans to have her and the sultan's other treasures for himself. Mr. Magoo is voiced by Jim Backus (TV's *Gilligan's Island*), the Wicked Wazir by the remarkable Hans Conried (1953's *Peter Pan*), the princess by Kathryn Grant (who was yet another princess in *The 7th Voyage of Sinbad*), and the sultan by the voice of TV's Fred Flintstone, Alan Reed.

47 Ronin **(2013, US) Carl Rinsch, 3D**

Based on the 1941 Japanese film *The 47 Ronin* (among others), this adventure, featuring Keanu Reeves (the *Bill & Ted* films, the *Matrix* trilogy) and an otherwise mostly Japanese cast, draws from the historical account of vengeful 18th-century samurai who inspired countless other versions of their exploits, collectively referred to as *Chushingura*. Although the source material regards a real-world group of ronin, this film adds fantasy elements, resulting in something of a cross between *Gladiator* and *The Lord of the Rings* series, with a dragon that looks like a more realistic rendering of *The NeverEnding Story*'s Falkor. An animated prelude teased the film. It became one of the biggest box-office failures of 2013.

7 Adventures of Sinbad, The **(2010, US) Ben Hayflick / Adam Silver, V/TV**

Adrian Sinbad, billionaire shipping magnate and Sinbad of the 21st century, must perform seven tasks to save the world from the destructive wrath of a supernatural being enraged by a sunken oil tanker. With all due respect to environmentalists, destroying the world to stop someone from destroying the world is probably not the answer. While our hero faces horrific creatures and challenges, this is definitely not your father's Sinbad. Where's Kerwin Mathews when you really need him?

7th Voyage of Sinbad, The ‡ **(1958, US) Nathan Juran**

Abelar: Tales of an Ancient Empire **(2010, US) Albert Pyun**

When the queen of Abelar finds her kingdom under attack after treasure hunters inadvertently open the tomb of vampire queen Xia, all hell breaks loose. It seems the queen's half-sister is also the half-sister of Xia. The father of one of the half-sisters can save the kingdom... maybe. Throw half-brother Aedan (played by *Hercules: The Legendary Journeys*' Kevin Sorbo), a few more half-sisters, and a daughter into the mix, and Xia will probably not be a happy camper. This film also features Michael Paré of the *BloodRayne* film series. The CGI is poorly done, but the film is not as bad as family reunions.

Abenteuer des Prinzen Achmed, Die (1931), Germany orig. title, see *Adventures of Prince Achmed, The*

Adventures of a Teenage Dragonslayer (2010, US) Andrew Lauer

A magical troll rescues 12-year-old Arthur, harrassed and labeled as a nerd by the school bully. Arthur learns he holds the secret to defeat an evil dragon. In addition to the troll, he soon has the aid of his single mom (Lea Thompson of the *Back to the Future* films) and a kind-hearted videogame master to conquer both the dragon and the evil vice-principal in a quest to save the world. See, this is why kids dread that trip to the principal's office.

Adventures of Baron Munchausen (1989, Italy/UK) Terry Gilliam

Eighteenth-century aristocrat Baron Munchausen, his crew, and a little girl embark on a wild adventure to save a town from the Turks. During their surreal adventures, they visit the moon and meet its king, played by the irrepressible Robin Williams *(Aladdin, Hook)*; a giant sea monster swallows them, Jonah-style; they dance with Venus; and ultimately they foil Death. John Neville (*Journey to the Center of the Earth*, *The X Files* TV-series) provides a beautiful interpretation of the baron. It's an amazing ride of pure imagination, adventure, and fantasy brought to you by the real wizard, director and former Monty Python member Terry Gilliam. It also features the phantasmagorical talents of Eric Idle (also of Monty Python), Oliver Reed *(Gor, Gladiator)*, Jack Purvis (*Time Bandits*, the *Star Wars* films), Jonathan Pryce *(The Brothers Grimm)*, Uma Thurman *(Pulp Fiction, Percy Jackson & the Olympians: The Lightning Thief)*, and Sting (yes, that one). Live the lies and half-truths with *The Extraordinary Adventures of Baron Munchausen* roleplaying game, originally published by Hogshead Publishing in 1998.

Adventures of Hercules II, The (1985), US DVD title, see *Hercules II*

Adventures of Prince Achmed (1931, Germany) Lotte Reiniger, AN/B&W/Silent

A flying horse transports a handsome prince to faraway lands and magical adventures, during which he meets Aladdin, battles an army of demons, and defeats an evil sorcerer and an emperor to win the love of a beautiful princess. The true magic of this silent film is its artistic creation. For silhouette animation, director Lotte Reiniger backlit black paper cutouts and photographed them frame by frame. This film is the oldest existing full-length animated film.

Aladdin (1992, US) Ron Clements / John Musker, AN

After street urchin Aladdin and his monkey Abu unexpectedly encounter Princess Jasmine in the marketplace, the evil Jafar, advisor to Jasmine's father (the sultan), jails Aladdin. Jafar plans to rule the world with a magic lamp from the Caves of Wonder. Only a "diamond in the rough"—such as Aladdin—can retrieve it. There's also the matter of winning the hand of the princess, who is legally bound to marry a prince. Robin Williams brings a genie to life in this first film of the *Aladdin* trilogy, also the first animated film promoted on the basis of a major star voicing a character. Derek Jacobi (too many credits; let's just go with *The Golden Compass*) is the magician. A series of video games for the Sega and NES systems are based on this Disney film, as well as several board- and card-game tie-ins, but all are strictly kid-friendly fare.

Aladdin 2 (1994), see *Return of Jafar, The*

Aladdin and His Magic Lamp (1968, Soviet Union, Russian) Boris Rytsarev, US title

It's your typical boy-meets-genie tale: boy finds magic lamp, frees genie trapped within, and is granted three wishes. What else would a boy wish for than to help rid the princess and her father of an evil sorcerer? It's classic.

Aladdin and His Magic Lamp (1970, France, French) Jean Image

A magician of Egypt arrives in young Aladdin's village, claiming to be his long-lost uncle and offering the boy a substantial inheritance. He endears himself to the boy, regaling him with tales of his exotic travels. Unbeknownst to Aladdin, the magician needs an innocent child to steal a highly treasured magical lamp of legend. Colors and images are rudimentary, and the delightful music takes the viewer to a simpler time. This is no Disney film, but its sweetness and simplicity are treasures.

Aladdin and the Death Lamp (2012, Canada/US) Mario Azzopardi, TV

Aladdin unintentionally frees an evil djinn from his lamp, and chaos ensues as fellow adventurers succumb to greed "that's like to die for." Aladdin, Luca, and Shifa—all orphans raised together by Khahli, a big guy with a heart—set out on a quest to quash the "let's destroy the world" plans of the djinn, by capturing an ancient magic ring and forcing the djinn back into his lamp. Unfortunately, Luca's loyalty becomes compromised, making a difficult task even harder. Sometimes you just can't catch a break ... but at least there's jewelry. Remember the old adage, "Be careful what you wish for?" Add, "Be careful how you phrase your wish." This visually satisfying film features Darren Shahlavi *(In the Name of the King: A Dungeon Siege Tale)* as Aladdin, Kandyse McClure *(Battlestar Galactica)* as Shifa, and Noam Jenkins and Eugene Clark (both from TV's *Earth: Final Conflict*) as Luca and Khahli.

Aladdin and the King of Thieves (1996, US) Tad Stones, AN/V/TV

In this last film in the animated *Aladdin* trilogy, just as Aladdin and Princess Jasmine are about to wed, forty thieves crash the wedding, seeking the powerful Hand of Midas. Aladdin learns that his long-lost father is alive. The quest to find him leads to the den of the king of thieves; it would seem Daddy's been busy. Robin Williams reprises his role as the genie, while John Rhys-Davies (the *Indiana Jones* film series, *The Lord of the Rings* trilogy) is the titular king and more.

Aladin et la lampe merveilleuse (1970), France orig. title, see *Aladdin and His Magic Lamp*

Ali Baba and the Forty Thieves (1944, US) Arthur Lubin

After the Mongols murder a Baghdad caliph, his son Ali happens upon the magic cave Sesame, where thief-leader Old Baba and forty other thieves hide. They take him in. Years later, adult prince Ali Baba, now leader of the thieves, seeks to avenge his father's death by killing his assassins and reclaiming his family's stolen kingdom. The best-known words of the Ali Baba tale have to be the very early security code, "Open Sesame." *Ali Baba and the Forty Thieves* is a roleplaying game based on the original tale, for Atari and Apple II.

Ali Baba and the Sacred Crown (1963), see *Seven Tasks of Ali Baba, The*

Amazing World (2009), see *Colour of Magic, The*

Amazons (1986, Argentina) Alejandro Sessa

Two female warriors go on a quest to retrieve a magic sword and defeat an evil wizard threatening their community of Amazon women. Ty Randolph, who plays warrior Dyala, performs all her own stunts. There are swords and sorcery but very little clothing; they probably spent all their money on swords. Just imagine a bunch of nude Xenas running around. Okay, stop! Would it surprise you that this is a Roger Corman production?

Amori di Ercole, Gli (1966), Italy orig. title, see *Hercules vs. the Hydra*

Arabian Adventure (1979, UK) Kevin Connor

How could you possibly go wrong with Christopher Lee (*The Lord of the Rings* films) as a villainous caliph who tries to trick a prince into retrieving a magic rose in exchange for marrying the caliph's daughter? An all-star cast that includes Peter Cushing *(Star Wars)*, Milo O'Shea *(Barbarella)*, Capucine *(The Pink Panther)*, and Mickey Rooney (Andy Hardy himself!), as well as a big flying-carpet battle, isn't enough to save this one. Brian Hayles (creator of the Ice Warriors for *Doctor Who*) wrote this just before his death.

Arabian Knight (1995), US re-cut version, see *Thief and the Cobbler, The*

Arabian Nights (1942, US) John Rawlins

The beautiful Scheherazade is torn between two brothers: Haroun, rightful caliph of Baghdad, and Haroun's brother, who has usurped the throne. Haroun goes into hiding with a troupe of traveling performers, including Scheherazade, who agrees to help Haroun reclaim his throne. This film features Jon Hall (Ali Baba in *Ali Baba and the Forty Thieves*) as Haroun, *The Thief of Bagdad*'s Sabu, and in the "what were they thinking?" category, the Three Stooges' Shemp Howard as Sinbad. The vibrancy of Technicolor elevates an otherwise average, yet entertaining film. If you'd care to create your *own* tales, check out the *Tales of the Arabian Nights* storytelling game originally published by West End Games in 1985, which Z-Man Games upgraded and re-released in 2009.

Arabian Nights **(1980, France/Italy, Italian) Pier Paolo Pasolini**

Instead of the traditional story of the slave girl telling tales nightly to stay alive, in this version she manipulates every man she meets. This is an erotic retelling of a select group of the *Arabian Nights* tales, enhanced by its setting in natural locations in Africa and the Middle East and by a beautiful musical score by Ennio Morricone.

Arabian Nights **(2000, US) Steve Barron, TV**

Having lost all trust in women and murdered his wife for betrayal, a psychotic sultan marries a harem girl each night and has her executed in the morning. A childhood friend of the sultan, Scheherazade, volunteers to be the next bride in hopes to cure the sultan of his madness by regaling him with wondrous stories night after night. The cast is quite remarkable, especially for a made-for-TV film. John Leguizamo (Luigi of *Super Mario Bros.*, the *Ice Age* films) shines as the genie, Rufus Sewell *(Tristan & Isolde)* brings Ali Baba to life, and Andy Serkis (better known as Gollum in *The Lord of the Rings* series) gets a rare film appearance as himself.

Arabian Nights **(2016, US) Chuck Russell, 3D/NYR**

In this 3D adaptation of the tale, a young army commander allies with Sinbad (Dwayne Johnson of *The Scorpion King* films, *Journey 2*, and *Journey 3*), Aladdin, and Ali Baba (Liam Hemsworth of *The Hunger Games* movies) to rescue Scheherazade and her kingdom from the evil sorcerer Pharotu (Anthony Hopkins of the *Thor* films). Chuck Russell of *The Scorpion King* directs.

Arabian Nights: Volume 1, the Restless One **(2015, France/Germany/Portugal/Switzerland, Portuguese) Miguel Gomes, intl. English title**

This ambitious three-part, six-hour adaptation of the *Arabian Nights* tales, set in modern-day Portugal and inspired by the country's debt crisis, begins as a documentary and then unfolds as a magical, musical farce. The film enjoyed a successful premiere at the 2015 Cannes Film Festival.

Arabian Nights: Volume 2, the Desolate One **(2015 France/Germany/Portugal/Switzerland, Portuguese) Miguel Gomes, intl. English title**

See *Arabian Nights: Volume 1, the Restless One*.

Arabian Nights: Volume 3, the Enchanted One **(2015 France/Germany/Portugal/Switzerland, Portuguese) Miguel Gomes, intl. English title**

See *Arabian Nights: Volume 1, the Restless One*.

Archer and the Sorceress, The (1981), see *Archer: Fugitive from the Empire, The*.

Archer: Fugitive from the Empire, The **(1981, US, English/German) Nicholas Corea, TV**

After Toran's mentor gives him the Heartbow, which chooses the warrior who wields it and fires grenade-like arrows, Toran sets out on a quest to avenge the destruction of his nomadic tribe and prove his innocence in the murder of his father. While seeking the wizard Lazar-Sa to help him, Toran is joined by Estra, thief and daughter of a goddess, who also seeks the wizard, for crimes against her mother. This film was a failed attempt to create a *Star Wars* sword-and-sorcery series.

Armageddon (1993), see *Warlock: The Armageddon*

Army of Darkness ‡ (1993, US) Sam Raimi

Army of Darkness: The Medieval Dead (1993), UK video title, see *Army of Darkness*

Arthur 3: The War of the Two Worlds (2010, France) Luc Besson, AN/Live

While the nefarious Maltazard (voiced by musician and actor David Bowie of *Labyrinth*) has magically enlarged himself to human size (actually seven feet) and escaped into our world to wreak havoc, Arthur (Freddie Highmore of *The Golden Compass*) remains the size of a Minimoy. With the help of Princess Selenia, her brother Betameche, and the Elixir of Life, Arthur returns to human size to battle Maltazard and thwart his evil plans. This film is based on Luc Besson's novel of the same title, with the cast reprising their roles from *Arthur and the Revenge of Maltazard*.

Arthur and the Great Adventure (2009, France) Luc Besson, UK title

After mixed reviews of *Arthur 3: The War of the Two Worlds*, that film's footage was merged with *Arthur and the Revenge of Maltazard* to create this UK theatrical release. In the US, it came out as a two-movie video set titled *Arthur and the Invisibles 2+3: The New Minimoy Adventures*.

Arthur and the Invisibles (2006, France) Luc Besson, AN/Live

Young Arthur descends into the land of the miniscule Minimoys and recovers a treasure of rubies to save his grandparents' home, unexpectedly rescuing his grandfather in the process. Evil Maltazard challenges him. To protect the Minimoys, Arthur draws a sacred sword from a stone as did the Arthur of legend. Arthur is smitten by beautiful Princess Selenia (voiced by Madonna). The cast also includes Mia Farrow *(Rosemary's Baby)* as Arthur's Granny, and the voices of musician and actor Snoop Dogg, TV personality Jimmy Fallon, and Robert De Niro *(The Godfather: Part II, Taxi Driver, Goodfellas, Stardust)* as Selenia's father, the emperor. Luc Besson directs this adaptation of his own children's books, *Arthur and the Minimoys* and *Arthur and the Forbidden City*.

Arthur and the Invisibles 2+3: The New Minimoy Adventures (2010), see *Arthur and the Great Adventure*

Arthur and the Revenge of Maltazard (2009, France) Luc Besson, AN/Live

When Arthur receives a plea for help from Princess Selenia concerning the deadly threat of the evil Maltazard, he races to her aid. Once again shrinking to the size of the tiny Minimoys, Arthur arrives too late to stop Maltazard from entering and threatening our world. Most viewers did *not* appreciate the cliffhanger ending, not resolved until the next film, *Arthur 3:*

The War of the Two Worlds. Freddy Highmore and Mia Farrow revisit their roles as Arthur and Granny. Snoop Dogg also returns, as does Jimmy Fallon as Selenia's brother, Prince Betameche. This time, musician Lou Reed is the voice of Emperor Maltazard, and Selena Gomez takes over as Princess Selenia. To promote the film, a video game with the same name was released for PlayStation 3, Xbox 360, Nintendo Wii, and PCs.

Arthur et la vengeance de Maltazard (2009), France orig. title, see *Arthur and the Revenge of Maltazard*

Arthur et les Minimoys (2006), France orig. title, see *Arthur and the Invisibles*

Arthur's Quest (1999, US) Neil Mandt, AL/TV

Merlin transports teenage King Arthur to modern-day America to save him from the evil sorceress Morgana. When Merlin returns for Arthur ten years later, the boy has forgotten where he came from and has no desire to return to the past. It rests with Merlin to prove to Arthur that he is a king who must save his kingdom before Morgana can use Excalibur to rule the world. This is an enjoyable version of the legend, for children. Zach Galligan (the *Gremlins* and *Waxwork* films, *Warlock: the Armageddon*) plays Arthur's dad, King Pendragon.

Arthur the King (1985, US/Yugoslavia) Clive Donner, AL/TV

The classic Arthurian love triangle plays out when, in an effort to save his wife Guinevere from his evil sister Morgan LeFey, Arthur sends Lancelot to Guinevere's rescue. Lancelot falls in love with Guinevere, and the rest is medieval history. With Malcolm McDowell *(A Clockwork Orange, Delgo)* as Arthur, Edward Woodward (Disney's *Aladdin*) as Merlin, and Liam Neeson *(Krull, The Chronicles of Narnia* films, Zeus in the *Clash of the Titans* remake and its sequel *Wrath of the Titans)* as the dim-witted Prince Grak, this film does not live up to the excellence of its cast.

Aslan Adam (1975, Turkey/UK, English/Greek/Turkish) Natuk Baytan

This film features a murdered king, a kidnapped queen, and a baby son and heir secreted in the woods and raised by lions. Years later, with beastly strength and claw-like appendages, the son avenges the tragedy of his parents' death. This is a film best watched as a guilty pleasure. Is this Turkey's take on *Grizzly Adams*?

As Mil e Uma Noites: Volume 1, O Inquieto (2015), Portugal orig. title, see *Arabian Nights: Volume 1, the Restless One*

As Mil e Uma Noites: Volume 2, O Desolado (2015), Portugal orig. title, see *Arabian Nights: Volume 2, the Desolate One*

As Mil e Uma Noites: Volume 3, O Encantado (2015), Portugal orig. title, see *Arabian Nights: Volume 3, the Enchanted One*

Astrópía (2008), Iceland orig. title, see *Dorks and Damsels*

Ator 2- L'invincibile Orion (1984), Italy orig. title, see *Blade Master, The*

Ator IV: The Hobgoblin (1990), intl. English title, see *Quest for the Mighty Sword*

Ator l'invincible (1983), Italy orig. title, see *Ator, the Fighting Eagle*

Ator l'invincible 2 (1984), Italy orig. title, see *Blade Master, The*

Ator, the Blade Master (1984), see *Blade Master, The*

Ator, the Fighting Eagle ‡ **(1983, Italy, Italian) Joe D'Amato**

Ator, the Iron Warrior (1987), see *Iron Warrior*

Attack of the Gryphon **(2007, US) Andrew Prowse, TV**

In a land plagued by civil war, a rival warrior-prince and princess join forces to search for a mystical weapon, the Drakonian Pike. With it, they can rid their land of a giant flying demon, the gryphon, summoned by an evil sorcerer to create destruction. This is a dismal effort in filmmaking accentuated by a substandard CGI creature. It features Sarah Douglas *(Superman, Superman II, Witchville)* as Queen Cassandra, and Andrew Pleavin (also in *Witchville*) as Prince Seth's man-at-arms.

Avalon **(1989, US) Michael J. Murphy, V**

The hero rescues the damsel in distress (because that's what heroes do), and along with the cowardly lion—make that "thief"—they set off on a quest to rescue the damsel's lover from an evil sorceress. On the way, the thief picks a golden apple ("I'll show you how to get apples"), and sinks into a swamp. They also encounter Merlin, battle zombies, and slay a dragon. *The Wizard of Oz* references suggest that you watch that truly entertaining film instead.

Avalon High **(2010, US) Stuart Gillard, AL/TV**

A quirky premise: high-school transfer-student Allie Pennington (Britt Robertson of TV's *Life Unexpected*) realizes her classmates are reincarnations of King Arthur and his court. After drawing a plastic sword, which becomes Excalibur, Allie discovers that she is King Arthur. She and her friends battle the history teacher, Mr. Moore (Steve Valentine of TV's *Crossing Jordan*), the reincarnation of the evil Mordred, with the indispensable aid of Miles, the reincarnated Merlin. The cast includes Craig Hall: Galion of *The Hobbit* films. Fans of Meg Cabot's novel, on which this film is loosely based, are less than pleased.

Avventure dell'incredible Ercole, Le (1985), Italy orig. title, see *Hercules II*

Bai fa mo nu zhuan (1993), Hong Kong orig. title, see *Bride with White Hair, The*

Bai fa mo nu zhuan II (1994), Hong Kong orig. title, see *Bride with White Hair 2, The*

Bai she chuan shuo (2011), China orig. title, see *Sorcerer and the White Snake, The*

Barbarian **(2003, US) Henry Crum, V**

Kane the Barbarian, the last great warrior-king, must restore peace to a land suffering under the reign of an evil warlord. Even four-time Mr. Universe Michael O'Hearn, a very believable hero, can't save this poorly executed *Deathstalker* "remake." Guess what? It's a Roger Corman production.

Barbarian Brothers, The (1987), intl. English title, see *Barbarians, The*

Barbarian Master (1983), US video title, see *Sword of the Barbarians, The*

Barbarian Queen **(1985, Argentina/US) Héctor Olivera**

During the Roman Empire, three young women who survive a raid on their village resolve to save those who were whisked away and enslaved. This is yet another *Deathstalker* clone, in the "so bad it's good" category. Actress Lana Clarkson, the barbarian queen herself, played a similar role in *Deathstalker*. Many enjoy this film for the nude scenes and torture, especially Clarkson on the rack.

Barbarian Queen II (1992), West Germany title, see *Barbarian Queen II: The Empress Strikes Back*

Barbarian Queen II: The Empress Strikes Back ‡ **(1992, Mexico/US) Joe Finley**

Barbarians, The ‡ **(1987, Italy/US) Ruggero Deodato**

Barbarians and Co., The (1987), Italy title, see *Barbarians, The*

Barbarian: The Last Great Warrior King (2003), Australia title, see *Barbarian*

Battle of the Dragons (1966), see *Magic Serpent, The*

Beastmaster, The ‡ **(1982, US / West Germany) Don Coscarelli**

Beastmaster 2: Through the Portal of Time **(1991, US) Sylvio Tabet**

Dar (Marc Singer of the TV series *V* and *Dragonquest*) is unceremoniously thrust into an inappropriate sci-fi story involving a time portal and a crazy brother named Arklon we never met before, played with wild-eyed embarrassment by Wings Hauser *(Vice Squad)*. He even teams up with an airheaded valley girl, Jackie (Kari Wuhrer of the *Sliders* TV-series and *Eight Legged Freaks*). Most of the movie takes place on the streets of present-day LA, and it's as bad as it sounds. Sarah Douglas *(Conan the Destroyer)* shows up to collect her check.

Beastmaster III: The Eye of Braxus **(1996, US) Gabrielle Beaumont, TV**

Dar reunites with Seth (now played by Tony Todd of the *Night of the Living Dead* remake, the *Candyman* films, and the *Final Destination* movies) and Tal (Casper Van Dien of *Starship Troopers*) to stop evil Lord Agon (David Warner of *Tron* and *Avatar*) from unleashing a creature named Braxus. Leslie-Anne Down (the *Upstairs, Downstairs* TV-series) and Olaf Pooley (*Doctor*

Who, "Inferno") provide support, but the production values are almost nonexistent. Braxus makes the Gorn from *Star Trek* look like a masterpiece in realism. Ruh has inexplicably transformed into a lion, or maybe Dar just names all his felines Ruh; he is simple like that. And it's never a good sign when a series can't decide between numbers and Roman numerals.

Beautiful Vasilisa (1939), informal literal English title, see *Vasilisa the Beautiful*

Beauty and the Beast (2005), South Africa orig. title, see *Blood of Beasts*

Beauty and the Beast (2009), see *Beauty and the Beast: A Dark Tale*

Beauty and the Beast: A Dark Tale (2009, Australia) David Lister

This is, as promised by the title, a dark re-imagining of the tale of the lovely Belle and an enchanted forest beast held responsible for the savage murders of villagers. Spoiler alert: the evil troll did it. Now go watch Walt Disney's *Beauty and the Beast*; enjoy. Lister also directed *Blood of Beasts*, a Viking retelling of *Beauty and the Beast*. Enough, David.

Beowulf (1999, UK/US) Graham Baker

In this futuristic sci-fi fantasy take on the original epic poem, Beowulf senses the "darkness" and comes to rid the Outpost of a man-eating creature, the Grendel, who has been devouring warriors. Christopher Lambert *(Greystoke: The Legend of Tarzan, Lord of the Apes*, the *Highlander* films, *Mortal Kombat)* is Beowulf.

Beowulf (2007, US) Robert Zemeckis, AN

Beowulf takes up Danish King Hrothgar's offer of rewards for the defeat of a monstrous troll, Grendel, who terrorizes Hrothgar's kingdom. The battle with Grendel is fierce, but even worse is the face-off when Mama Grendel shows up to avenge her son's death. The film features Crispin Glover as an excellent Grendel, Angelina Jolie (the *Tomb Raider* films) as Grendel's mother, Robin Wright *(The Princess Bride)* as Queen Wealthow, Anthony Hopkins *(Silence of the Lambs, Dracula, The Wolfman)* as King Hrothgar, and John Malkovich *(Eragon)* as Lord Unferth. Director Robert Zemeckis worked with Glover in *Back to the Future*. The video game *Beowulf: The Game* (voiced by the film actors) for PCs and consoles, and *Beowulf: The Movie Board Game* by Fantasy Flight Games (co-designed by Reiner Knizia and Jeff Tidball) are based on this film.

Beowulf: An IMAX 3D Experience (2007), see *Beowulf* (2007)

Beowulf & Grendel (2006, Australia/Canada/Iceland/US/UK, English/Icelandic/Latin) Sturla Gunnarsson

On behalf of Danish King Hrothgar (Stellan Skarsgard of *Thor* and of two of the *Pirates of the Caribbean* films), Beowulf leads his warriors in an epic battle against a vicious troll, Grendel, who is on a rampage, murdering villagers. But is the king truly innocent? This is an excellent retelling of the centuries-old saga, especially in the performance of Gerard Butler *(300, How to Train Your Dragon)* as Beowulf. Grendel's father is Spencer Wilding *(Wrath of the Titans,*

Eragon, TV's *Doctor Who*). Tony Curran *(Doctor Who)* and Rory McCann (the *Clash of the Titans* remake, *Solomon Kane*), also star.

Beyond Sherwood Forest (2009, Canada) Peter DeLuise, TV

This Robin Hood tale adds an element of sci-fi fantasy, with a cursed young woman who can change into a fierce dragon. The shape-shifting creature arrives through a magical *Stargate*-like passageway, and the sheriff of Nottingham captures her for use as a weapon against Robin (Robin Dunne of TV's *Sanctuary*). This film, which includes *Warlock*'s Julian Sands, features a better-than-average CGI dragon.

Big Trouble in Little China ‡ (1986, US, Cantonese/English) John Carpenter

Black Angel: The Feature Film (2016, US) Roger Christian, NYR

In 1980, *Star Wars* set designer Roger Christian convinced George Lucas to provide a modest $38,000 budget for a 25-minute short feature that would accompany screenings of *Star Wars: The Empire Strikes Back* in England, Scotland, and Australia. The epic adventure, about a knight battling the dark power of the titular commander of the demon kings, inspired later works like *Excalibur*. The short itself disappeared for decades before its rediscovery in 2011. Charging onto iTunes and YouTube by 2015, *Black Angel* captured the imagination of a new generation and gave Christian the opportunity to revisit his creation with a successfully crowdfunded feature-length adaptation. Set to start production in late 2015, the film features Rutger Hauer *(Blade Runner, Flesh+Blood, Ladyhawke)* as High Priest Sirdar, John Rhys-Davies (the *Indiana Jones* and *Lord of the Rings* films) as King Aeolus, and Laura Weissbecker *(Russian Dolls, Arena, Chinese Zodiac)* as Kyna.

Black Cauldron, The ‡ (1985, US) Ted Berman / Richard Rich, AN

Black Death (2010, Germany/UK, English/Latin) Christopher Smith

Young Osmund (Eddie Redmayne of *Elizabeth: The Golden Age* and *Hick*) joins a knight (Sean Bean from *Game of Thrones* and *The Lord of the Rings* movies) on a quest to locate a necromancer. Bean's *Game of Thrones* castmate (although they never shared any scenes) Carice van Houten and the always delightful David Warner *(Time After Time, Time Bandits, Beastmaster III: The Eye of Braxus)* also star. Smith shot this film in chronological order; judge for yourself whether that helps at all.

Blade Master, The (1984, Italy, Italian) Joe D'Amato, MST3K title: Cave Dwellers

Ator returns to help Akronas and Mila stop the evil Zor from using a nuclear bomb—sorry, Geometric Nucleus. Having rushed the making of the first Ator film to capitalize on the success of *Conan the Barbarian*, D'Amato similarly hurries the first sequel, in response to *Conan the Destroyer*. You can see the flaw in logic there. Largely improvised, with hilarious continuity and production errors, this one earns its skewering by *Mystery Science Theater 3000* in that show's third season, in which the characters call it by the title *Cave Dwellers*. It's not only one of their most famous episodes. It entertained none other than Ator himself, Miles O'Keeffe, who contacted the *MST3K* guys to obtain a copy!

Blood of Beasts (2005, South Africa / UK) David Lister, intl. English title

This retelling of the *Beauty and the Beast* tale takes place in the time of Vikings. When a beast cursed by the god Odin imprisons a king in an island castle, the king's warrior daughter, Freya, travels to the island to rescue him. A bittersweet tale unfolds. Jane March (the *Clash of the Titans* remake) stars as Freya alongside Justin Whalen *(Dungeons & Dragons)*.

BloodRayne (2005, Germany/US) Uwe Boll

Even Boll can get one right. Eighteenth-century dhampir (half-human, half-vampire) Rayne (Kristanna Loken of *In the Name of the King: A Dungeon Siege Tale*) escapes from a Romanian carnival freak show. To avenge her mother's rape at the hands of her father Kagan, king of the vampires (Ben Kingsley of *Prince of Persia: The Sands of Time*), she joins forces with two vampire-hunters, Vladimir and Sebastian. This is great fun if you accept it as exactly what it is and nothing more. Kingsley never loses his dignity. The cast also includes Will Sanderson *(In the Name of the King: A Dungeon Siege Tale)* and Billy Zane *(Journey to Promethea, Scorpion King 3)*. Michael Paré *(Abelar: Tales of an Ancient Empire)* appears in all three *BloodRayne* films, each time as a different character. This film is loosely based on the video game *BloodRayne* for PC, Xbox, GameCube, and Playstation 2.

BloodRayne 2: Deliverance (2007, Argentina/France/Germany/US), DVD title, see *BloodRayne II: Deliverance*

BloodRayne II: Deliverance (2007, Canada/Germany) Uwe Boll, Canada orig. title, V

It's the 1880s, and dhampir warrior Rayne (now played by Natassia Malthe of *In The Name of the King 2: Two Worlds*) appears in the Wild West town of Deliverance to take down vampire Billy the Kid (!) and his fanged posse. Zack Ward (Ralphie's nemesis Scut Farkus in *A Christmas Story*) is a deliciously perverse Billy the Kid, but Malthe is no Loken.

BloodRayne: The Third Reich (2010, Canada/Germany/US) Uwe Boll

Rayne (still Malthe, sigh) fights the Nazis in World War II, but she inadvertently turns an evil commandant into a powerful vampire. Now she must intervene in the plans of Dr. Mangler (Ron Howard's little brother Clint), who intends to use her blood to transform Hitler into an immortal dhampir. Boll's work often sinks pretty low, but is it really appropriate to mangle the name of one of the real world's most despicable villains for a "cute" joke?

BloodRayne: The Vampire Chronicles (2007), intl. DVD title, see *BloodRayne II: Deliverance*

Blood Reich: BloodRayne 3, The (2010), UK DVD title, see *BloodRayne: The Third Reich*

Brave ‡ (2012, US) Mark Andrews / Brenda Chapman, AN

Brendan and the Secret of Kells (2009), Ireland English title, see *Secret of Kells, The*

Bride with White Hair, The (1993, Hong Kong, Cantonese) Ronny Yu

This visually stunning Chinese sword-and-sorcery fantasy adaptation of Shakespeare's *Romeo and Juliet* follows compassionate swordsman Cho Yi-Hang, reluctant successor to the throne of the Wu-Tang clan, who falls in love with Lian, assassin for a rival evil cult. Oddities abound. Lian has the ability to morph into a white-haired killer, and incestuous conjoined twins are two of cinema's strangest villains ever.

Bride with White Hair 2, The (1993, Hong Kong, Cantonese) David Wu

Lian, feeling betrayed by her husband, Cho, has permanently morphed into an evil, white-haired witch. Meanwhile, Cho has spent ten years waiting on a mountaintop for a rare flower to bloom, which he believes will turn her hair black and stop her killing spree through the eight martial-arts clans. Lian kidnaps the bride of Cho's nephew on their wedding night to turn her against her new husband. We can probably use that rare flower right about now.

Bridges' Bride, The (1987), Philippines English title, see *Princess Bride, The*

Bridge to Terabithia (2007, US) Gabor Csupo

New girl Leslie befriends school outcast Jesse. Together they create the fantasy world of Terabithia, which they rule as queen and king. Later, the world they created helps Jesse deal with an almost unbearable tragedy. Josh Hutcherson *(Journey to the Center of the Earth, Journey 2, The Hunger Games)* as Jesse, and AnnaSophia Robb *(Charlie and the Chocolate Factory)* as Leslie show remarkable sensitivity and maturity. Jesse's father is Robert Patrick *(Terminator 2, Double Dragon)*. This is based on the Newbery Award-winning novel by Katherine Paterson and was adapted for the screen by her son, David Paterson.

Brothers Grimm, The (2005, Czech Republic / US / UK, English/French/German/ Italian) Terry Gilliam

Con artists the Brothers Grimm travel from town to town collecting folklore and pretending to perform exorcisms to protect villagers from nonexistent evil enchantments. Matt Damon (the *Bourne* films) and Heath Ledger *(A Knight's Tale, The Dark Knight)* are very believable as older brother Will (the brains) and Jake (the dreamer) when they encounter an actual magic curse that tests their courage. Jonathan Pryce (the *Pirates of the Caribbean* films) appears as ruthless nemesis General Delatombe. Director Terry Gilliam presents the fairytale material as true to the dark and gruesome source material, unlike whitewashed Disney versions.

Captain Sindbad (1963, US / West Germany) Byron Haskin

"Sindbad" returns home to find the kingdom seized by villain El Kerim, who plans to kill him. Our hero must reach the tower in which El Kerim's heart is sealed and destroy it. With the aid of a magic ring, El Kerim brings forth a variety of fantastical creatures to guard the tower and thwart Sindbad's efforts. This film is a joy for children and the young at heart: no CGI but lots of fun. Guy Williams (TV's *Zorro* and *Lost in Space*) is Sindbad. The extra "d" helped the filmmakers avoid legal complications. Amusingly, you can continue the adventures of Sindbad, with that spelling, thanks to *The Adventures of Sindbad* RPG published in 2007 by Hex Games.

Cave Dwellers (1984), US TV title, see *Blade Master, The*

***Cave of the Golden Rose, The* (1991, Italy) Lamberto Bava, intl. English title, TV**

This is an Italian fairytale of the royal families of Princess Fantaghiro and Prince Romualdo, which have been engaged in a war for centuries. When the king is challenged to a duel to end the war, he realizes his youngest daughter and expert warrior Fantaghiro, trained by the White Witch, can win the duel. Disguised as a man, she duels Romualdo, who realizes she is a beautiful woman and falls in love. This is the first part of a five-part series of TV films.

***Cave of the Golden Rose 2, The* (1992, Italy) Lamberto Bava, intl. English title, TV**

Fantaghiro and Romualdo put their wedding plans on hold when the Black Queen (*Red Sonja* herself, Brigitte Nielsen!) kidnaps Fantaghiro's father, the king. Romualdo and his army intend to save him, but the Black Queen captures Romualdo and enslaves him with a kiss. When Fantaghiro comes to his rescue, she must duel her now-amnesiac fiancé: not a great start for any marriage.

***Cave of the Golden Rose 3, The* (1993, Italy, English/Italian) Lamberto Bava, intl. English title, TV**

To avoid a prophecy declaring that a royal child will defeat him, the evil wizard Tarabas sends out his army of clay soldiers to kidnap all royal children. Fantaghiro and Romualdo must save her sisters' children. In the course of the ensuing battle, Romualdo falls into a cursed river and turns to stone. To save her beloved, Fantaghiro seeks the help of Tarabas, who falls in love with her. She must have one of those faces. Fantaghiro and Romualdo finally wed.

***Cave of the Golden Rose 4, The* (1994, Italy, English/French/Italian) Lamberto Bava, intl. English title, TV**

A black cloud devastates all life as it travels across the land. With both their castles consumed, Fantaghiro teams up with Prince Parsel to stop the horror. The wizard Tarabas joins their quest to help save Romualdo, who has been transformed into a hideous creature. The source of the curse and the cloud? None other than Tarabas's father, the evil wizard Darken.

***Cave of the Golden Rose 5, The* (1996, Italy, English/French/Italian) Lamberto Bava, intl. English title, TV**

The Black Queen captures Fantaghiro and is about to decapitate her, when Fantaghiro is transported to a parallel universe. There she discovers a villain named Nameless who—are you ready for this?—eats children. Fan consensus holds that this last installment in the series should not exist. Love might be eternal, but this is a horror. Where is Romualdo? You really don't want to know. The magic ends here.

Chasseurs de dragons (2009, France orig. title, see *Dragon Hunters*

Christmas Dragon, The (2014, US) John Lyde

Orphans are on a quest to save Christmas. This was made in Utah. And we're done.

Chronicles of Narnia, The (2005), see *Chronicles of Narnia: The Lion, the Witch and the Wardrobe*

Chronicles of Narnia: Prince Caspian, The (2008, UK/US) Andrew Adamson

Continuing the cinematic adaptation of C.S. Lewis's landmark literary fantasy saga, this first sequel brings the Pevensie children back to help the prince in his quest to wrest control of Narnia from his uncle, evil King Miraz. The story picks up 1,300 years after the first film, with all four young actors returning in the lead roles. Liam Neeson *(Schindler's List, Darkman)* returns as the voice of Aslan. *Game of Thrones*' Peter Dinklage and *Willow*'s Warwick Davis (who had roles in previous television adaptations of the Lewis books) also appear. Two scenes recorded exclusively for the tie-in video game do not appear in the film.

Chronicles of Narnia: The Lion, the Witch and the Wardrobe, The ‡ (2005, US/UK, English/German) Andrew Adamson

Chronicles of Narnia: The Voyage of the Dawn Treader, The (2010, US) Michael Apted

Just three years after their last visit, two of the Pevensie children and their cousin reunite with King Caspian, encountering slave traders and invisible Dufflepuds as they journey to save the seven Lords of Narnia. Simon Pegg voices Reepicheep (replacing Eddie Izzard), and Liam Neeson *(Star Wars: Episode I—The Phantom Menace)* returns as the voice of Aslan. The film's planned tie-in console video game was canceled, although an iPhone/iPod game was released. Original book illustrations by the late Pauline Baynes appear in the closing credits.

Clash of the Titans ‡ (1981, US) Desmond Davis

Clash of the Titans (2010, US) Louis Leterrier

Perseus (Sam Worthington of *Avatar*) resists his demigod status despite being drawn into an ancient conflict between his father, Zeus (Liam Neeson of *Arthur the King* and *Excalibur*) and Hades (Ralph Fiennes, Lord Voldemort of the *Harry Potter* films). With the help of Io (Gemma Arterton of *Quantum of Solace* and *Prince of Persia: The Sands of Time*) and Draco (Mads Mikkelsen of *Casino Royale*), Perseus embarks on a heroic quest to save the princess Andromeda from the wrath of the monstrous Kraken. This CGI-heavy remake of the 1981 Ray Harryhausen classic lacks the original's heart and soul and even seems determined to kick its source material when it's down; the insulting Bubo gag is a good example. The slithery Medusa is based almost entirely on her stop-motion predecessor, but the Kraken looks like a creepy cousin of the *Cloverfield* monster. Neeson and Fiennes reprise their roles in *Wrath of the Titans*.

Close Encounters of the Spooky Kind (1980), see *Encounters of the Spooky Kind*

Close Encounters of the Spooky Kind 2 (1980), see *Encounters of the Spooky Kind II*

Color of Magic, The (2009), US title, see *Colour of Magic, The*

Colour of Magic, The (2009, UK) Vadim Jean, TV

This adaptation of Terry Pratchett's novels *The Colour of Magic* and *The Light Fantastic* takes place on Discworld, where magic is the elemental force. The story follows the adventures of Rincewind (an inept wizard from Unseen University) and a bumbling tourist, Twofold, played by Sean Astin (*The Lord of the Rings* series). Is there a better actor to portray Death than Christopher Lee (Hammer's *Dracula*, *The Last Unicorn*, *The Lord of the Rings* films, *Season of the Witch*)? The plot of the book was adapted as a text-adventure computer game in 1986 and can be played on modern computers with an emulator. An official roleplaying-game supplement for GURPS came out in 1998, attributed to co-designers Phil Masters and Terry Pratchett.

Conan the Barbarian ‡ (1982, US) John Milius

Conan the Barbarian (2011, US) Marcus Nispel

Robert E. Howard's Cimmerian reappears in a movie that, while not strictly a remake of the 1982 classic, can't help but be compared to the film of the same name that also happens to be one of the most beloved sword-and-sorcery movies ever made. Jason Momoa *(Game of Thrones)* gives it his best as the hero, but he's no Arnold. Ron Perlman (TV's *Beauty and the Beast*, the *Hellboy* films, *In the Name of the King*, *Scorpion King 3*), Stephen Lang *(Avatar*, TV's *Terra Nova)*, and Rose McGowan, who might have been Red Sonja if that project hadn't collapsed, also star. Music is by *300*'s Tyler Bates. Despite lackluster performance, this team might still make a *Conan* sequel and a *Red Sonja* film as well.

Conan the Destroyer (1984, US) Richard Fleischer

Arnold Schwarzenegger is back in the title role. An intriguing cast consisting of Grace Jones *(A View to a Kill, Vamp)*, Olivia D'Abo (TV's *The Wonder Years, Mortal Kombat: Defenders of the Realm, Law & Order: Criminal Intent* . . . in her debut appearance here), basketball great Wilt Chamberlain, Andre the Giant *(The Princess Bride)* as the monstrous Dagoth, and Sarah Douglas *(Beastmaster 2)* as the villainous Queen Taramis can't save this one. Despite a script based on a treatment by comic-book writers Roy Thomas and Gerry Conway, this watered-down PG *Conan* misses the mark, burying plans for a third installment that would have delivered on the promise of that brooding monarch at the end of the first two movies. The next year, director Richard Fleischer and Schwarzenegger re-teamed for *Red Sonja*.

Conquest ‡ (1984, Italy/Mexico/Spain, Italian) Lucio Fulci

Corazón del guerrero, El (2000), Spain orig. title, see *Heart of the Warrior*

Corona di Ferro, La (1949), Italy orig. title, see *Iron Crown, The*

Court Jester, The (1956, US) Melvin Frank / Norman Panama

Evil King Roderick has usurped the throne of the rightful infant king. Hawkins, the baby's caretaker, poses as the new king's jester, Giacomo—"the king of jesters and jester to the king." In this complicated, zany romp of mistaken identity, Hawkins is hypnotized by the court sorceress, switches identities, is forced into a deadly joust, and is almost poisoned. All you need to remember is that "the pellet with the poison's in the vessel with the pestle, and the flagon with the dragon has the brew that is true," and that Danny Kaye (Hawkins/Giacomo) is a magnificent comedic genius.

Creature Zone (1997), Germany video title, see *Warriors of Virtue*

Crouching Tiger, Hidden Dragon (2000, China / Hong Kong / Taiwan / US, Mandarin), intl. English title, Ang Lee

The quest of warriors Yu and Li for a stolen magical jade sword, the Green Destiny, unfolds in a poignant tale of love, faith, and sacrifice. Don't look for a tiger or a dragon; they are translations of the names of characters Lo (little tiger) and Jen (delicate dragon), who share a destructive, unrequited love. The title is a Chinese proverb meaning "dangerous people hidden from view." Ang Lee directed this visually breathtaking film in the tradition of *wuxia* filmmaking. Based on *Crane—The Iron Pentalogy* by Wang Du Lu, this is the first martial-arts film nominated for an Academy Award for Best Picture. Ubisoft released a video game of the same name for Game Boy, PlayStation 2, and Xbox.

Crown and the Dragon, The (2013, US) Anne K. Black

A young woman and her aunt must recover an artifact for a royal coronation, but tragedy leads the girl, Elenn, to partner with a criminal named Aedin to complete the quest. This film features a largely unknown cast and crew. Writer-director Black has one other film to her name, *Dawn of the Dragonslayer,* and used Kickstarter to fund this project. You've been warned.

Crystal Star, The (1965), US title, see *Jack Frost*

Cudotvorni mac (1952), Yugoslavia orig. title, see *Magic Sword, The* (1952)

Curse of the Dragon Slayer (2013), see *SAGA: Curse of the Shadow*

Curse of the Ring (2006, Germany/Italy/UK/US) Uli Edel, intl. English title, TV

Based on the German epic poem *Nibelungenlied,* this is another version of the tale of Siegfried the dragon-slayer, his murder, and his wife Kriemhild's revenge. Siegfried's true love, Brunnhild, is Kristanna Loken *(BloodRayne).* Max von Sydow *(Flash Gordon, Conan the Barbarian, Citizen X, Solomon Kane),* Julian Sands *(Warlock),* and Robert Pattinson (*Harry Potter and the Goblet of Fire,* the *Twilight* films) also star.

Dai tozoku (1965), Japan orig. title, see *Lost World of Sinbad, The*

Dark Crystal, The ‡ (1982, US) Jim Henson / Frank Oz

Dark Is Rising, The (2007), see *Seeker: The Dark Is Rising, The*

Dark Kingdom: The Dragon King (2006), see *Curse of the Ring*

Dark Mist, The (1996, UK/US) Ryan Carroll

To save the world from destruction, the Lord Protector must travel through a techno-magical land to banish the threat and solve the Riddle of the Chosen. Charlton Heston's narration enriches this fantasy tale. Jay Underwood *(The Boy Who Could Fly)* is all grown up and carries the starring role. The voice of Olivia Hussey *(Quest of the Delta Knights)* also features.

Dawn of the Dragonslayer (2012, US) Anne K. Black

Will sets out on a quest to avenge the death of his father by slaying the fire-breathing dragon that killed him. While he trains under the tutelage of the tyrannical Baron Sterling (Ian Cullen of the *Doctor Who* TV story, "The Aztecs"), he falls in love with the baron's enchantress daughter, Kate. The maniacal baron comes to distrust Will and orders his men to kill him, but Will escapes. Now Will must use his skills as a paladin who can walk through dragon-fire to slay the beast and prove himself worthy of Kate.

Day the Earth Froze, The (1964, Finland / Soviet Union, Finnish) Aleksandr Ptushko, US title, *MST3K*

Finns and Soviets unite to make this movie, originally titled *Sampo*. In this adaptation of the "epic poem of Finland" *Kalevala*, Lemminkäinen faces the witch Louhi, who kidnaps his beloved Annikki, demands a Sampo, and steals the sun from the sky to force compliance. What is a Sampo? It's a magic mill that can generate all manner of precious metals, grains, and salt. Useful things, Sampos. *Mystery Science Theater 3000* covers the heavily edited English incarnation of this one in the show's fourth season, making "Sampo" an early Internet meme meaning any vital or useful device that isn't well-understood.

Deathly Hallows, The (2010), US short title, see *Harry Potter and the Deathly Hallows: Part 1*

Deathstalker (1984, Argentina/US) James Sbardellati

An ancient warrior known as the Deathstalker must collect artifacts representing the powers of creation in order to keep them from a corrupt sorcerer named Munkar. Entering a tournament that will determine Munkar's successor, the Deathstalker soon faces the evil wizard himself, with the fates of a princess and a world hanging in the balance. This is the basis for the entire *Deathstalker / Barbarian Queen* franchise, with nudity and violence galore. Schlockmaster Roger Corman executive-produced this, with Rick Hill (as the hero), *Playboy*'s Barbi Benton, and the late barbarian queen herself, Lana Clarkson, in the role that kicked off her career.

Deathstalker II (1987), see *Deathstalker II: Duel of the Titans*

Deathstalker II: Duel of the Titans ‡ (1987, Argentina/US) Jim Wynorski, V

Deathstalker III: Deathstalker and the Warriors from Hell (1989), US video title, see *Deathstalker and the Warriors from Hell*

Deathstalker IV: Match of Titans **(1991, US) Howard R. Cohen**

The *Deathstalker* saga draws to its dramatic conclusion with yet another contest of brains and brawn. As entrants fall, Agatha Christie-style, the Deathstalker must stand up for the remaining combatants, protect his latest girlfriend, and defeat an evil queen and her Stone Warriors. Rick Hill returns in the lead role due to no fan demand whatsoever, and the movie skimps on the skin and gore normally associated with the series. "Small world" note: Softcore sex-star Maria Ford, who plays Dionara, shares the screen—and so much more—with former *Deathstalker* cast member Lana Clarkson in the 1990 horror movie *The Haunting of Morella*. Do with that what you will.

Deathstalker IV: The Darkest Hour (1991), see *Deathstalker IV: Match of Titans*

Deathstalker and the Warriors from Hell **(1989, Mexico/US) Alfonso Corona, *MST3K*/V**

The man himself, now played by John Allen Nelson *(Baywatch)*, quests yet again to collect something (magic stones), protect someone (alluring Princess Carissa), and fight someone (a villainous sorcerer of the Southland and an army of undead). Corona lovingly recycles stock footage from Roger Corman's 1963 film *The Raven* here, as well as music from Corman's sci-fi epic *Battle beyond the Stars* and from Brian Eno's score in *Dune*. Thom Christopher (Hawk from *Buck Rogers in the 25th Century*) plays the wizard Troxartas and is just one of many targets mercilessly ridiculed in a seventh-season *Mystery Science Theater 3000* episode devoted to this film. "Go ahead, enjoy my area."

Deathstalker: Match of the Titans (1991), UK video title, see *Deathstalker IV: Match of Titans*

Delgo **(2008, US) Marc F. Adler / Jason Mauer, AN**

In a divided world ruled by the terrestrial Lockni and the celestial winged Nohrin, naïve yet brave teen Delgo assembles his friends to end the conflict and unite their world. In this animated tale, Freddie Prinze, Jr. *(Scooby Doo)* voices Delgo. Unfortunately, the film does not live up to the talents of a very good cast of voices, including Lou Gossett, Jr. *(Enemy Mine, The Punisher)*, Malcolm McDowell *(Arthur the King)*, Michael Clarke Duncan *(The Green Mile, The Scorpion King)*, and Monty Python alum Eric Idle *(Quest for Camelot)*. Sadly, this is the final film for both John Vernon (Dean Wormer of *Animal House*) and Anne Bancroft (Mrs. Robinson of *The Graduate*).

Devil Quest (2011), see *Season of the Witch*

Devil's Advocate, The (1982), Australia video title, see *Sorceress*

Devil's Sword, The **(1984, Indonesia, Indonesian) Ratno Timoer, intl. English title**

A nymphomaniacal crocodile-queen who abducts men to satisfy her needs angers the wrong bride-to-be when she kidnaps the groom. The bride seeks the aid of the warrior Mandala to help her search for the magic Devil's Sword. Word is that "whoever possesses the sword will rule the kingdom." There's much bloodshed as evil warriors seek the sword as well. This bizarre Indonesian sword-and-sorcery fantasy is just cheesy enough to entertain.

Djinn (2008, US) Shahin Sean Solimon

In this movie, based on ancient Middle Eastern lore, Imad must undertake a grueling journey through a black desert, battling a variety of demons, to save his true love, Amina, whisked away by an evil djinn. Shahin Sean Solimon wears all the hats in this production, as producer, director, writer, editor, and lead actor.

Dorks and Damsels (2008, Finland/Iceland/UK, Icelandic) Gunnar B. Gudmundsson, US title

When Hildur's boyfriend goes to jail, she finds a job at the local fantasy-gaming store Astropia. She really gets into the RPG scene, with the fantasy characters and even the sexy costumes. Hildur's newfound friends heroically come to her aid when her boyfriend kidnaps her. As in *Revenge of the Nerds*, the beauty falls in love with a nerd, and the moral of the story is that nerds rule.

Double Dragon (1994, US) James Yukich

Teenage brothers Billy (Scott Wolf of TV's *Party of Five*) and Jimmy Lee possess half of a magic Chinese medallion sought after by millionaire gang-leader Koga Shuko (Robert Patrick of TV's *The X-Files*), who has the other half. Although Mark Dacascos *(The Crow: Stairway to Heaven* TV-series, the "Chairman" on TV's *Iron Chef)* as Jimmy has formal martial-arts training, it doesn't change the fact that this film is a very poor adaptation of the *Double Dragon* video game. It also features Michael Berryman *(The Hills Have Eyes, The Barbarians, Beastmaster 2, Wizards of the Demon Sword)* and Vanna "I'd Like to Buy an E" White as herself.

Dragon (2006, US) Leigh Scott

To save her kingdom from destruction by an army of evil elves, Princess Vanir and two loyal subjects travel through the haunted forest of Sidhe on a diplomatic mission. They encounter a sorceress, and, as the title suggests, a powerful dragon. Thinking up a title must have taken minutes. The best part of this film might be the credit "No dragons were harmed during the making of this motion picture" (though *Dungeons & Dragons* beat them to the punch with this a few years before).

Dragon Age (2012), see *Dragon Age: Dawn of the Seeker*

Dragon Age: Dawn of the Seeker (2012, Japan/US) Fumihiko Sori, AN

A conspiracy brought on by blood mages threatens the Chantry of Andraste, a powerful religious order. The mages plan to use the beautiful dragon-hunter Cassandra, whom they have branded a traitor, to gain ultimate supremacy. It falls to Cassandra, a sword-wielding Seeker and one of the elite knights of the Chantry, to thwart them, save the Chantry, and in turn save their world. This Japanese CGI anime film is based on the popular roleplaying videogame series *Dragon Age*, by Bioware. The character animation could be better, but the full-CGI dragons are visually stunning, as is the still artwork. Also, those who have no knowledge of the videogame franchise can enjoy the film, because it provides backstory information. In 2010, Green Ronin released Set 1 of the Ennie Award-nominated *Dragon Age Dark Fantasy RPG*. Since then, Green Ronin has published a second boxed set, a *Game Master's Kit,* a book of adventures, and several additional PDF products.

DragonBlade (2008, Hong Kong, Cantonese/English/Mandarin) Antony Szetso, 3D/AN

Hung Lang, kung-fu master extraordinaire, is the go-to guy when a deadly creature attacks his town. The good news is that a weapon, the DragonBlade, will stop the threat. The bad news is that the one who finds the blade becomes subject to untold danger. (There's always a catch.) This is the first animated 3D martial-arts film and first 3D, CGI-animated Chinese feature film.

DragonBlade: The Beginning (2008), intl. DVD title, see *DragonBlade*

DragonBlade: The Legend of Lang (2005), see *DragonBlade*

Dragon Chronicles, The: Fire & Ice (2008), Australia title, see *Fire & Ice*

Dragon Crusaders (2011, US) Mark Atkins, V

Turned into hideous monsters for attacking a pirate ship, a group of Knights Templar must save the world and themselves by defeating a wizard-dragon. Actually, the knights were attempting to save a young woman on the ship, but she, unbeknownst to them, had cursed the ship and, in turn, them. So you see, no good deed goes unpunished. The cast includes Dylan Jones, Simon Lloyd-Roberts, and Iona Thonger, all featured in Atkin's film *Merlin and the War of the Dragons*.

Dragonfyre (2013, US) Kohl Glass

Who would imagine that moving out west would lead to an encounter with orcs? When John Norton, ex-Special Forces, tries to go off the grid, he must instead stand against an army of orcs that have plans to bring their dragon god to doom the world of humanity. But there's an elven princess, so John's retirement isn't all bad. This movie features Isaac C. Singleton, Jr. *(Galaxy Quest, Pirates of the Caribbean: Curse of the Black Pearl, Dragon Hunter)*.

Dragonheart ‡ (1996, Slovakia/UK/US) Rob Cohen

DragonHeart (1996), alternate spelling, see *Dragonheart*

Dragonheart 3: The Sorcerer's Curse (2015, US) Colin Teague, V

In this direct-to-video prequel to the original *Dragonheart,* wannabe knight Gareth (Julian Morris of *Valkyrie* and the *24* TV-series) bonds with a dragon named Drago (Ben Kingsley of *Ghandi, BloodRayne,* and *Prince of Persia: The Sands of Time*) who fell to Earth. As they battle a sorcerer who has designs on Drago, they learn something about bravery and friendship and … oh, you know.

Dragonheart: A New Beginning (2000, US) Doug Lefler, V

This sequel picks up after Bowen, played by Dennis Quaid *(The Right Stuff, Enemy Mine, The Day After Tomorrow),* has died. Bowen's friend Draco—the last living dragon—has left behind an egg that hatches *another* last living dragon named Drake (voiced by Robby Benson, the Beast in Disney's *Beauty and the Beast*). Orphan Geoff wants to be a knight and forms a strong bond with Drake. Together they face an oppressive new code enforced by the king's advisor Ozric, and a prophecy naming Drake's heart as a portent of doom. Drake acquires a rare power, ice-breathing (in addition to fire-breathing), and a shocking revelation recalls a heart-linking subplot from the first film. This movie is lightweight but passable.

Dragon Hunter (2008, US) Stephen Shimek

Orphaned brothers Kendrick and Darius, whose parents were killed by orcs, come from a family of dragon hunters. Older brother Kendrick protects Darius by hunting orcs that threaten their village, but when a dragon attacks the village, the brothers join forces with other hunters, including an elven princess, and travel to Ocard Castle to develop their dragon-slaying skills. There is also their mother's prophecy that a great dragon-hunter will emerge from their bloodline. Any chance it's one of her boys? Orcs, elven princess, dragon—can't you just smell "*Lord of the Rings* wannabe" all over this film?

Dragon Hunters (2009, France/Germany/Luxembourg, English/French) Guillaume Ivernel / Arthur Qwak, intl. English title, AN

The king's granddaughter enlists the aid of a powerful gentle giant, the giant's cunning partner, and their small, blue pet dragon to rid the kingdom of a ferocious, destructive dragon. This computer-animated 3D treat, based on a TV series, features a visually remarkable land of floating real-estate. A platform action video-game of the same name, for Nintendo DS, is based on the film.

Dragon Kingdom, The (2008), Japan English title, see *Forbidden Kingdom, The*

Dragonlance (2008), Germany/Italy title, see *Dragonlance: Dragons of Autumn Twilight*

Dragonlance: Dragons of Autumn Twilight (2008, US) Will Meugniot, AN/V/TV

A group of adventurers finds proof of the existence of gods when they discover a barbarian woman who possesses a magical, blue-crystal healing staff. They must band together to defeat an army of dragons invading their land. This is the first film based on the *Dragonlance* setting of *Dungeons & Dragons*. One of the most popular shared universes in fiction, *Dragonlance* was created by Laura and Tracy Hickman and expanded by Hickman and Margaret Weis into a series of gaming modules, sourcebooks, and even boardgames. The first *Dragonlance* novel, *Dragons of Autumn Twilight* by Hickman and Weis, began the *Chronicles* trilogy. In 2003, Sovereign Press (owned by Weis) began publishing new d20-based source material for *Dragonlance*, in a deal that allowed them to produce RPG materials while Wizards of the Coast retained the rights to publish novels. The cast features the voices of Michael Rosenbaum (Lex Luthor of TV's *Smallville*), Kiefer Sutherland *(Stand by Me, A Time to Kill,* TV's *24, Touch)*, Lucy Lawless (TV's *Xena: Warrior Princess, Battlestar Galactica*), and Michelle Trachtenberg (TV's *Buffy the Vampire Slayer*).

Dragon Lore: Curse of the Shadow (2013), see *SAGA: Curse of the Shadow*

Dragonquest (2009, US) Mark Atkins, V/TV

When an evil warlord unleashes a mythological beast impervious to human weapons, a young hero must complete a series of quests to awaken a dragon, defeat the beast, and save the world from destruction. Marc Singer (the *Beastmaster* films) is the old warrior mentor. How the mighty have fallen—yet he still has some decent moves with his sword. Also in the cast are Brian Thompson *(Dragonheart, Mortal Kombat: Annihilation,* the 2000 *Jason and the Argonauts)* and Jason Connery (UK TV's second *Robin Hood, Merlin: The Quest Begins*). This film has no connection to the novel of the same name by Anne McCaffrey or to the *DragonQuest* roleplaying game.

Dragons II: The Metal Ages (2005, Canada) Keith Ingham, AN/TV

In this animated sequel to *Dragons: Fire & Ice*, the two young heroes must aid a resistance leader to defeat an evil witch. Her plan? An invasion to conquer Human World and Dragon World using Shadow Dragons and an army clad in invincible armor. Michael Adamthwaite, who voices animated/anime characters in many series, reprises his role as the hero Prince Dev.

Dragon's Blood, The (1957), see *Sigfrido*

Dragons: Fire & Ice (2004, Canada) Keith Ingham, AN/TV

Prince Dev and Princess Kyra, two young warriors of rival families, arrange a duel to end a thousand-year war. When the armies of their families intercede, a common enemy rears its head, attacking both sides and abducting their kings. The young heroes join forces, along with their dragons, Targon and Aroara, to rescue their fathers and save both Human World and Dragon World. Michael Adamthwaite *(In the Name of the King: Two Worlds)* is Prince Dev in this animated tale.

Dragonslayer ‡ (1981, US) Matthew Robbins

Dragons of Camelot (2014, US) Mark L. Lester, AL

The Arthurian legend was never like this! Arthur is dead, Morgan le Fay terrorizes Camelot with her dragon trio (Khaleesi?), and the Knights of the Round Table must locate the long-in-exile Lancelot before all is lost. Mark Griffin *(Doctor Who)* is Lancelot, and Selina Giles (the *Highlander* TV-series) is Guinevere, but most of the rest of the cast won't spark any memories.

Dragons of Krull (1983) see *Krull*

Dragon Storm (2004, Germany/US) Stephen Furst, TV

Dragons transported through a meteor shower cause destruction to rival kingdoms. Instead of uniting with King Wednesbury in the face of this threat, King Fastrad takes the opportunity to overthrow him. Meanwhile, a group that includes a hunter, a warrior, and a mystic gathers to hunt down the dragons. The final, nighttime dragon-battle is quite beautiful. John Rhys-Davies (two *Indiana Jones* films, *The Lord of the Rings* series) is the devious King Fastrad. Stephen Furst (Flounder in *Animal House*, Vir of *Babylon 5)* directs.

Dragon Sword (2006), France/US TV title, see *George and the Dragon*

Dragon Trainer (2010), Italy title, see *How to Train Your Dragon*

Dragon Warriors (2015, US) Maclain Nelson / Stephen Shimek

Some people just don't take rejection well. When a princess rebuffs an evil wizard, he decides it's time to use a dragon to eliminate all demonstrations of love everywhere in the land ... as you do. Attracted by the princess's dragonfly distress-signal and the chance for wealth and romance, a gruff bounty hunter joins his marriage-minded warrior brother along with an orc and a squire to save the princess and find true love ... which we all know is almost as good as a nice MLT. With name actors like fan-favorite James Marsters (TV shows *Buffy the Vampire Slayer*, *Torchwood*, *Smallville*) as Lord Tensley, and Luke Perry *(Beverly Hills, 90210)* as Lorash—and the rest of the cast culled from other ultra-low-budget dragon flicks featured in this index, you know the quality will be top notch.

Dragonworld (1994, US) Ted Nicolaou

After the death of his parents, John lives in his grandfather's castle in Scotland. After a magical tree on the estate grants his wish for a baby dragon, Yowler, the two grow up together. Twenty years later, living alone, John is conned into "renting out" Yowler as the main attraction for the theme park Dragonworld. Yowler becomes exploited and miserable, and John needs to get him back. This is a film for children and the young at heart. Your author Scott Alan Woodard worked on animatronic effects for this film.

Dragonworld II (1999) see *Dragonworld: The Legend Continues*

Dragonworld: The Legend Continues (1999, US) Ted Nicolaou, V/TV

Young wizard John McGowan lives in the Scottish Highlands with his best bud Yowler, the last dragon on Earth. Sadly the Dark Knight, Yowler's archenemy, plans to slay the dragon to unleash the magical powers in his blood and create a dark age. Although slaying a dragon is usually a good thing, this time ... not so much. It falls to John to save his lifelong friend and the world. Put those on your "to do" list, Johnny. This negatively received film is a sequel to the original *Dragonworld* pretty much only in character names and minor details. This is the last film for Andrew Keir *(Dracula: Prince of Darkness, Daleks' Invasion Earth: 2150 A.D., Five Million Years to Earth)*, the only cast member to reprise his role.

Dungeonmaster, The (1985, US) Dave Allen / Charles Band / John Carl Buechler / Steven Ford / Peter Manoogian / Ted Nicolaou / Rosemarie Turko

Wizard Mestema doesn't have much confidence in science, so he battles programmer Paul, whose computer is transformed into a wrist device. The fate of Paul's girlfriend Gwen hangs in the balance, which should trouble *Spider-Man* fans. Paul fights through seven scenarios, one titled "Heavy Metal," each handled by a different writer-director. *Tron* inspired the film, whose title changed from *Ragewar* to take advantage of the popularity of *Dungeons & Dragons*. Richard Moll *(The Sword and the Sorcerer, Metalstorm: The Destruction of Jared-Syn,* TV's *Night Court)* is Mestema, Jeffrey Byron *(Metalstorm)* is Paul, and Leslie Wing (Queen Karis on *Hercules: The Legendary Journeys* and *Xena: Warrior Princess,* Mrs. Bolton of the *High School Musical* movies) is Gwen. Phil Fondacaro *(Star Wars: Return of the Jedi, The Black Cauldron, Willow)* also features.

Dungeons & Dragons ‡ (2000 Czech Republic / US) Courtney Solomon

Dungeons and Dragons Adventure Tale, A (2008), US subtitle, see *Dragonlance: Dragons of Autumn Twilight*

Dungeons & Dragons: The Book of Vile Darkness (2012, UK) Gerry Lively, TV

This time around, a hero infiltrates a villainous band in order to rescue his father from a mind flayer. Lively intended the debut of this film to synchronize with the release of a *Dungeons & Dragons* Fourth Edition supplement of the same name, which reintroduced an artifact that had appeared in game materials as far back as the first edition of *D&D*.

Dungeons & Dragons: The Elemental Might (2005) (Australia TV title) see *Dungeons & Dragons: Wrath of the Dragon God*

Dungeons & Dragons: Wrath of the Dragon God (2005, Germany/UK/US) Gerry Lively

A century after the original film's setting, Damodar (Bruce Payne of *Warlock III, Highlander: Endgame,* and *Dungeons & Dragons*) seeks an orb that can awaken a slumbering black dragon. He allies with a lich named Klaxx. This time, despite its low budget, the movie is surprisingly faithful to its *D&D* source, with far more accuracy in its characters, professions, spells, and monsters than the first film and with many references to *D&D* modules and other game materials. Onscreen runes are even drawn from Chaosium's *D&D* competitor, *RuneQuest*.

Dungeons of Krull, The (1983), see *Krull*

Ella Enchanted (2004, Ireland/UK/US) Tommy O'Haver

A fairy's misguided gift of obedience to Ella (Anne Hathaway of *The Princess Diaries* films and *The Dark Knight Rises*) becomes a curse. Ella must obey anyone's wishes, which becomes a horrific burden when her widowed father presents her with an unbearable stepfamily. In this modern *Cinderella* fairytale, Ella falls in love with Prince Charmont (not to be confused with Charming). Cary Elwes *(The Princess Bride, Quest for Camelot)* is evil Uncle Edgar. Monty Python alum Eric Idle narrates this tale, loosely based on the Newbery Award-winning novel by Gail Carson Levine.

Empire Strikes Back, The (1980), US short title, see *Star Wars: The Empire Strikes Back*

Enchanted (2007, US) Kevin Lima, AN/Live

Worlds collide when an evil queen magically transports the animated (in more ways than one) Princess Giselle (Amy Adams—*The Muppets*) from her fairytale world to modern-day New

York, where she is jolted into reality. Ultimately, she has to decide between the handsome prince she's left behind and the attractive lawyer in the real world. This is a tough decision, because James Marsden (the *X-Men* films, *Superman Returns*) and Patrick Dempsey (TV series *Grey's Anatomy*) play the men. The Maleficent-like queen is Susan Sarandon (*The Rocky Horror Picture Show, Thelma & Louise, Dead Man Walking* in her Oscar-winning performance). Julie Andrews, the original Mary Poppins, narrates this Disney live-action/traditional-animation/CGI hybrid fantasy musical.

Encounter of the Spooky Kind (1980), Hong Kong English title, see *Encounters of the Spooky Kind*

Encounter of the Spooky Kind II (1990), Hong Kong English title, see *Encounters of the Spooky Kind II*

Encounters of the Spooky Kind (1980, Hong Kong, Cantonese) Sammo Hung Kam-Bo

Beginning with a nightmare about ghosts, followed by a "spend a night in a crypt challenge," this martial-arts/action/comedy/horror film is quite a ride. There's a promiscuous wife, a good wizard, an evil wizard, and zombies. This cult classic popularized the "hopping corpse." Sammo Hung Kam Bo, prolific actor and pioneer of Hong Kong action films, does it all as writer, director, choreographer, and lead actor.

Encounters of the Spooky Kind II (1990, Hong Kong, Cantonese) Ricky Lau

Abao's efforts to protect his wife escalate into a supernatural battle involving an evil sorcerer and a kindhearted female ghost. Although this is another martial-arts/action/comedy/horror film choreographed by and starring Sammo Hung Kam-Bo, it's not a sequel to the 1980 *Encounters of the Spooky Kind*.

Epic (2013, US) Chris Wedge

Written by no less than six people (so you know it's going to be good), including *Hook* and *Bram Stoker's Dracula* writer James V. Hart (see?), this 3D CGI-animated extravaganza follows a young girl taken to a magical forest, world where she must join a motley collection of characters to battle the Boggan threat. Remember *Ferngully* and *Avatar*? You're ahead of the game. Loosely based on William Joyce's novel *The Leaf Men and the Brave Good Bugs*, this film features the voices of Amanda Seyfried *(Mean Girls, Red Riding Hood)*, Colin Farrell *(Minority Report,* the 2011 *Fright Night* remake), Christoph Waltz *(Inglourious Basterds, Django Unchained)*, Chris O'Dowd *(The IT Crowd* TV show, the 2010 *Gulliver's Travels)*, and Beyoncé!

Epic Hero and the Beast, The (1960), UK title, see *Sword and the Dragon, The*

Eragon (2006, Hungary/UK/US) Stefen Fangmeier

Eragon finds a dragon egg originally stolen by Princess Arya. It hatches into a dragon named Saphira. The minions of power-mad King Galbatorix, who seeks the egg (and now the dragon), kill Eragon's Uncle Garrow. Brom, a former dragon-rider, trains Eragon in magic, sword-fighting, and dragon-riding so that he might defeat Galbatorix and fulfill his destiny. This film is a poor adaptation of the best-selling children's book *Eragon* written by Christopher Paolini. The cast includes Ed Speleers *(Witchville)* as Eragon, Jeremy Irons *(Dungeons & Dragons)* as Brom, Jill Valentine (the *Resident Evil* films) as Princess Arya, John Malkovich (the 2007 *Beowulf*) as King Galbatorix, Alun Armstrong *(Krull, Sleepy Hollow)* as Uncle Garrow, and the amazing Robert Carlyle (*28 Weeks Later*, the *Once Upon a Time* TV-series) as the evil sorcerer Durza. Mega Brands released a lavishly produced tie-in boardgame that some claim is more entertaining than the film!

Ercole al centro della terra (1964), Italy orig. title, see *Hercules in the Haunted World*

Ercole e la regina di Lidia (1960), Italy orig. title, see *Hercules Unchained*

Ercole l'invincibile (1964), Italy orig. title, see *Hercules the Invincible*

Erik the Viking (1989, Sweden/UK) Terry Jones

Erik the Viking (Tim Robbins of *Howard the Duck* and *Anchorman*) and his fellow village-warriors journey to Valhalla, home of the Norse gods, to ask for an end to the Age of Ragnarok (in Norse mythology, the beginning of the end) and the return of joy. This Pythonesque tale features Monty Python veterans Terry Jones (as writer, director, and actor) and John Cleese, both of whom also play in *Monty Python and the Holy Grail*. The cast includes Mickey Rooney (Andy Hardy to one generation, the voice of Rankin/Bass's Santa Claus to another) as Erik's grandfather.

Escape from Atlantis (1997, US) Strathford Hamilton, TV

Attorney Matt Spencer is left to raise his three rebellious teens on his own. To bond with them, he charters a cruise to the Bahamas on a glorious sailboat, which turns out to be a rundown schooner. What could be a disappointing vacation becomes a fantasy adventure of a lifetime—in the Bermuda Triangle, no less. Unfortunately, the opposite is true for the film, which is not so much fantasy adventure as it is disappointing. Brian Bloom is Atlantean villain Joriath. Bloom has done extensive voice work for animated TV-series and video games: *Star Wars*, *Batman*, *G.I. Joe*, *Avengers*, *Dragon Age*, and many more.

Evil Dead 3: Army of Darkness, The (1993), UK DVD title, see *Army of Darkness*

Excalibur ‡ (1981, UK/US) John Boorman, AL

Eye of the Serpent, The (1994), US DVD title, see *Eyes of the Serpent*

Eyes of the Serpent (1994, US) Ricardo Jacques Gale

Sisters Corva and Neema fight for control of two magic swords and the accompanying ancient scrolls. While Corva lives in her father's castle with her sadomasochistic daughter, Neema and her daughter enlist the aid of great swordsman Galen to raise an army and take back the castle. This erotic sword-and-sorcery fantasy is also available in a steamier unrated version.

Fading of the Cries (2011, US) Brian Metcalf

With the help of a magic sword, Jacob defends his town from evil and saves Sarah (prolific TV-series actress Hallee Hirsh) from the personification of evil, Mathias. Together Jacob and Sarah must outrun hordes of demonic zombies to find an amulet that had belonged to Sarah's uncle. Sadly, they come to realize that sometimes the demons are within. Who better to personify evil than the voice of Chucky: Brad Dourif (also Wormtongue in the second and third *Lord of the Rings* films)?

Fantaghirò (1991), Italy orig. title, see *Cave of the Golden Rose, The*

Fantaghirò 2 (1992), Italy orig. title, see *Cave of the Golden Rose 2, The*

Fantaghirò 3 (1993), Italy orig. title, see *Cave of the Golden Rose 3, The*

Fantaghirò 4 (1994), Italy orig. title, see *Cave of the Golden Rose 4, The*

Fantaghirò 5 (1996), Italy orig. title, see *Cave of the Golden Rose 5, The*

Father Frost (1965), see *Jack Frost*

Fatiche di Ercole, Le (1959), Italy orig. title, see *Hercules* (1959)

Fellowship of the Ring, The (2001), US short title, see *Lord of the Rings: The Fellowship of the Ring, The*

Feuer und Schwert—Die Legende von Tristan und Isolde (1982), West Germany orig. title, see *Fire and Sword*

Fiore delle mille e una notte, Il (1974), Italy orig. title, see *Arabian Nights* (1980)

Fire & Ice (2008, Romania) Pitof, TV

A fire dragon severely threatens Carpia, a peaceful kingdom of knights and dragons ruled by King Augustin. The heroic princess enlists the aid of a knight errant and his mentor (John Rhys Davies of the *Indiana Jones* and *Lord of the Rings* films) to help save the kingdom. They plan to awaken an ice-breathing dragon to defeat the fire-breathing dragon. Sounds good, except for the part about then getting rid of the ice-breathing dragon. Amy Acker (TV's *Angel* and *Grimm*) as the princess, and Arnold Vosloo *(Gor, The Mummy)* as the king also feature. Pitof also directed *Catwoman*. You've been warned.

Fire & Ice: The Dragon Chronicles (2008), US long title, see *Fire & Ice*

Fire and Ice (1983, US) Ralph Bakshi, AN

In a prehistoric world, Larn seeks to avenge the destruction of his village by the glaciers of evil ice-lord Nekron's moving ice palace. When Nekron heads to the fortress Firekeep and kidnaps the princess Teegra, Larn attempts to save her. Director and co-writer Ralph Bakshi (*The Lord of the Rings* 1978) used rotoscoping, a technique of tracing over live-action movement, to create the animation. There is also some "cheeky" collaboration by fantasy/sci-fi artist Frank Frazetta.

Fire and Sword (1982, Ireland / West Germany) Veith von Fürstenberg, intl. English title

This loose retelling of the tragic, adulterous love affair between Cornish knight Tristan and Irish princess Isolde features award-winning cinematography. Christopher Waltz, Academy Award-winning actor for *Inglourious Basterds*, is Tristan. The cast also includes Peter Firth *(Lifeforce, Sword of the Valiant: The Legend of Sir Gawain and the Green Knight, The Hunt for Red October)*.

Fire Dragon Chronicles, The (2008), Germany DVD title, see *Dragon Hunter*

Flight of Dragons, The (1982, US) Arthur Rankin, Jr. / Jules Bass, AN

This last Rankin/Bass television special combines the plot from Gordon R. Dickson's 1976 novel *The Dragon and the George* with design elements from the mock 1979 history book *The Flight of Dragons*, even employing author Peter Dickinson as a character! Science threatens magic, so green wizard Carolinus stands against the evil power of red wizard Ommadon in an attempt to shield magic within its own realm. Dickinson, an everyman representing both worlds, must undertake a quest alongside a knight and a dragon ... and then things get complicated. The voice cast for this animated film features John Ritter (TV's *Three's Company*), Victor Buono (TV shows *Batman* and *Man from Atlantis*), James Earl Jones (the *Star Wars* and *Lion King* films), Harry Morgan *(M*A*S*H)*, James Gregory (TV series *Barney Miller, Beneath the Planet of the Apes*), legendary voice-over artist Paul Frees, and Don McLean of "American Pie" fame, who sings a title song.

Flower of the Arabian Nights (1980), intl. English title, see *Arabian Nights* (1980)

Forbidden Kingdom, The (2008, China/US, English/Mandarin) Rob Minkoff

In this re-imagining of the *Monkey King* fable, American teen Jason is transported to ancient China after he discovers a king's legendary fighting stick in a pawnshop. A major fan of kung fu, he joins an army of warriors to help free the captive king. This is the first film to feature both martial-arts film legends Jackie Chan *(The Myth)* and Jet Li *(The Sorcerer and the White Snake)*, each in dual (as well as duel) roles. Li is the Monkey King and the Silent Monk, while Chan is an immortal kung-fu master as a young man and, again, centuries older. This film is loosely based on the Chinese novel *Journey to the West* by Wu Cheng'en. A mini-game, *Mandolin Warrior*, is based on this film.

Fugitive from the Empire (1981), see *Archer: Fugitive from the Empire, The*

Fung wan II (2011), Hong Kong orig. title, see *Storm Warriors*

Fung wan: Hung ba tin ha (2000), Hong Kong orig. title, see *Storm Riders, The*

G2 (1999), see *G2: Mortal Conquest*

G2: Mortal Conquest (1999, Canada) Nick Rotundo

A Macedonian warrior who killed many with the sword of Alexander the Great reincarnates 200 years later to take on an evil Mongolian clan. Daniel Bernhardt (the *Mortal Kombat: Con-*

quest TV-series) is former warrior / former cop Steven Conlin. Prolific actor James Hong *(Blade Runner, Big Trouble in Little China, Kung Fu Panda)* plays Parmenion, the leader of the clan.

G2 Time Warrior (1999), see *G2: Mortal Conquest*

Gedo senki (2010), Japan orig. title, see *Tales from Earthsea*

George and the Dragon (2006, Germany/Luxembourg/UK/US) Tom Reeve

Sir George (James Purefoy of *John Carter* and TV's *The Following*) returns from the Crusades with a plan to retire from knighthood and settle down. To acquire a piece of land, he agrees to one last quest: rescuing the king's daughter, Princess Lunna, from the last fire-breathing dragon. But when he and his band of merry men find the princess, she prefers that they protect the dragon, not slay it. A light-hearted adventure loosely based on the *St. George and the Dragon* legend, this movie also features Michael Clarke Duncan *(The Green Mile)*, Paul Freeman (Belloq in *Raiders of the Lost Ark*), and Patrick Swayze *(Dirty Dancing, Road House, Ghost)*.

Ghost Hunters (1986), see *Big Trouble in Little China*

Giant Killer, The (2013), UK DVD title, see *Jack the Giant Killer* (2013)

Gli amori di Ercole (1966), see *Hercules vs. the Hydra*

Goblet of Fire, The (2005), US short title, see *Harry Potter and the Goblet of Fire*

Golden Compass, The (2007, UK/US, English/French/Icelandic/Russian) Chris Weitz

An adaptation of the first book of Philip Pullman's award-winning trilogy, *His Dark Materials*, this film takes place in a parallel world where people's souls take animal form, and "Dust" connects the entire universe of worlds, including Earth. Only one Golden Compass remains to "show all that is hidden," and only one person can interpret it. A young girl, Lyra, seeks to rescue a friend from an evil organization involved in unspeakable experimentation on children. Her quest leads to saving her world and ours. An all-star fantasy cast led by James Bond (Daniel Craig) also features Ian McKellen and Christopher Lee (both of *The Lord of the Rings* films and *The Hobbit* trilogy), Derek Jacobi *(The Secret of NIMH)*, and Freddie Highmore *(The Spiderwick Chronicles)*. A licensed boardgame published in 2007 includes components illustrated with images from the film.

Golden Voyage of Sinbad, The ‡ (1974, UK/US) Gordon Hessler

Goliath and the Dragon (1960, France/Italy, Italian) Vittorio Cottafavi, US title

Goliath must do battle with evil mythical creatures (huge bats, a monstrous dragon, three-headed dogs—you name it) to save his people from a villainous king. Goliath is actually kind of Hercules undercover, because inter-studio legalities forced a name change from the original title, *Hercules' Revenge*. Bodybuilder Marc Forest steps in as Goliath, with glorious muscles to spare, and later stars in many legitimate *Hercules* films. American actor Broderick Crawford (Oscar-winner for *All the King's Men*) plays the evil king, but oddly enough was voiced by another actor in the—wait for it—American version. Crazy, huh? This film has the ignominious honor of receiving the Golden Raspberry Award, as one of the "100 Most Enjoyable Bad Movies Ever Made."

Golok setan (1984), Indonesia orig. title, see *Devil's Sword, The*

Gor (1988, US) Fritz Kiersch

Adapted from John Norman's controversial and brazenly misogynistic *Gor* novels, this first of two *Gor* movies shot back-to-back wisely waters down the source material but also does it no favors. Meek academic Tarl Cabot is magically transported to a harsh world where he must find his inner hero and champion an enslaved people against the megalomaniacal might of Sarm, a sadistic priest-king. Large-living legendary actor Oliver Reed *(Oliver!, The Adventures of Baron Munchausen)* is Sarm, in a cast that also includes model Rebecca Ferratti, Paul L. Smith *(Popeye, Dune, Red Sonja)*, and Arnold Vosloo *(The Mummy)*. Lead actor Urbano Barberini returns with Ferratti in the sequel, *Outlaw of Gor*, but what else were they doing?

Gor II (1989), US title, see *Outlaw of Gor*

Green Destiny (2000), see *Crouching Tiger, Hidden Dragon*

Grendel (2007, US) Nick Lyon, TV

In yet another retelling of Beowulf's tale, he leads a mission to aid Danish King Hrothgar (Ben Cross of the 2009 *Star Trek*, Asylum's *Jack the Giant Killer*) by defeating the horrific Grendel terrorizing the kingdom. Word is that Hrothgar was hiding some shocking secrets. Although watchable, this film has many glaring anachronistic errors, such as modern-day crossbows (in the 6th century). Far more entertaining are *Beowulf* and especially *Beowulf and Grendel*, both featured in this index. Marina Sirtis of various *Star Trek* series and films is the queen.

Grendel Grendel Grendel (1981, Australia) Alexander Stitt, AN

Grendel narrates this unusual retelling of the *Beowulf* saga, presenting his perspective of the events as they unfold in animated form. This very well-done version tells of the tragic fate of a misunderstood creature faced with the rage of humans who show far less compassion than that of the Grendel himself. This film is based on John Gardner's novel *Grendel*. The distinctive voice of Peter Ustinov (1978's *The Thief of Baghdad, Logan's Run*) as Grendel adds a welcome level of believability.

Grimm's Snow White (2012, US) Rachel Lee Goldenberg, V

In this nontraditional version of the fairytale, after reptilian beasts brutally murder the king, the queen seeks to secure her place as sovereign by killing her beautiful stepdaughter, Snow White, who escapes into the enchanted forest. There is a dearth of dwarves, but there's an *Alice in Wonderland*-type Snow White and, oddly enough, dragons. Prince Charming is not really that charming, but then this *is* an Asylum production. You've been forewarned.

Gryphon (2007), see *Attack of the Gryphon*

Gui da gui (1980), Hong Kong orig. title, see *Encounters of the Spooky Kind II*

Gui yao gui (1990), Hong Kong orig. title, see *Encounters of the Spooky Kind*

Gunan il guerriero (1982), Italy orig. title, see *Gunan, King of the Barbarians*

Gunan, King of the Barbarians (1982, Italy) Franco Prosperi, US title

Gunan's plan to avenge the death of his parents ultimately leads to a revelation that might resonate with viewers of *The Empire Strikes Back*. The oddest swordfight moment has to be Gunan using his sword to smack an opponent on his back. It has a pointy end, you know, Gunan. Bodybuilder Pietro Torrisi *(Hercules vs. the Giant Warriors, The Sword of the Barbarians)* is Gunan, and Sabrina Siani *(Ator, The Fighting Eagle, Conquest)* is Lenni. Both star in *Throne of Fire*.

Hakuja den (1961), Japan orig. title, see *Panda and the Magic Serpent*

Half-Blood Prince, The (2009), US short title, see *Harry Potter and the Half-Blood Prince*

Hansel & Gretel: Witch Hunters (2013, Germany/US) Tommy Wirkola

This modern reinvention of the famous tale attempts to blend gore and gags, with brother and sister now all grown up as bounty hunters who travel the world hunting and killing witches (after that ugly, gingerbread-house incident years ago). This is a hybrid bid for a new series that isn't likely to take off, with Hansel played by Jeremy Renner (Hawkeye in *Thor* and *The Avengers*, Aaron Cross in *The Bourne Legacy*) and Gretel by Gemma Arterton (2010's *Clash of the Titans, Prince of Persia: The Sands of Time)*. Famke Janssen (*GoldenEye*, the *X-Men* film trilogy) is the evil Muriel, and Peter Stormare *(The Lost World: Jurassic Park, The Brothers Grimm)* is Berringer. Will Ferrell co-produces. Trying to turn the fairytale into a franchise might have been a *bad* choice.

Harry Potter and the Chamber of Secrets (2002, Germany/UK/US) Chris Columbus

This is one of only two installments of this lengthy franchise that completely qualify for this book, because it features not only a hefty dose of sorcery but a climactic battle in which Harry (Daniel Radcliffe of *The Woman in Black*) must wield the sword of Godric Gryffindor. (We include all the movies, anyway.) Voldemort (Ralph Fiennes, Hades in 2010's *Clash of the Titans*) attempts to incarnate in a young form preserved within a diary, and Harry discovers that he shares the Dark Lord's affinity for serpents. Kenneth Branagh *(Othello, Hamlet)* appears as Gilderoy Lockhart, the flamboyant and egocentric Defense Against the Dark Arts teacher for this film (a position vacated with alarming regularity). This is fun family fare like the first film but a bit flat in atmosphere.

Harry Potter and the Deathly Hallows: Part 1 (2010, UK/US) David Yates

Things get substantially darker and grayer in this first installment of a two-part adaptation of J.K. Rowling's seventh and final *Harry Potter* novel. Harry (Daniel Radcliffe) and his friends flee into the woods to hide from the growing influence of Lord Voldemort (Ralph Fiennes). Then . . . they stay there a while. And a while longer. We're a long way from the studio-bound children's movie that kicked off the series, but an air of unpleasantness—and boredom—in this penultimate entry makes one pine for the carefree days of Bertie Bott's jellybeans and whimsical Quidditch matches.

Harry Potter and the Deathly Hallows: Part 2 (2011, UK/US) David Yates

Harry (Daniel Radcliffe) and his friends chase down the last Horcruxes that contain parts of the soul of Voldemort (Ralph Fiennes). The Dark Lord holds the powerful Elder Wand, and evil is poised to spread not only through the magical realm but into the outside world of the Muggles (non-magical humans). Harry's destiny as the Chosen One is about to reach its devastating conclusion, but it's Neville (Matthew Lewis) who takes up the sword of Gryffindor to defeat the snake, Nagini. It's fascinating watching these actors grow up onscreen over eight films. Despite its flaws, this series is a landmark achievement in fantasy filmmaking.

Harry Potter and the Deathly Hallows: Part 2 3D (2011), see *Harry Potter and the Deathly Hallows: Part 2*

Harry Potter and the Goblet of Fire (2005, UK/US) Mike Newell

A magical competition held at Hogwarts, the Triwizard Tournament draws entrants from other schools around the globe. The kids are growing up and turning to pursuits other than just magic, but when Harry (Daniel Radcliffe) is selected as the fourth champion in a contest that has always included only three, the stage is set for a historic, horrific resurrection. Lord Voldemort (Ralph Fiennes) at long last returns, and war fast approaches. Robert Pattinson (the *Twilight* films), David Tennant (*Doctor Who*'s Tenth Doctor), and Brendan Gleeson *(Braveheart, 28 Days Later, Troy)* also appear in this slightly darker, action-packed installment.

Harry Potter and the Goblet of Fire: The IMAX Experience (2005), US IMAX version, see *Harry Potter and the Goblet of Fire*

Harry Potter and the Half-Blood Prince (2009, UK/US) David Yates

As the power of Voldemort (Ralph Fiennes) grows, Harry (Daniel Radcliffe) must uncover the details of the Dark Lord's insidious plan to achieve immortality. One man knows the secret of the Horcruxes: former Hogwarts teacher Horace Slughorn (Jim Broadbent of *The Chronicles of Narnia: The Lion, the Witch and the Wardrobe*)—but will he share his memories? As Ron (Rupert Grint) and Hermione (Emma Watson of *The Tale of Despereaux*) struggle with their feelings, and Harry falls for Ron's sister Ginny (Bonnie Wright of *The Philosophers*), Dumbledore (Michael Gambon of *Sleepy Hollow*) enlists Harry's aid in a quest to stop Voldemort. But Draco Malfoy (Tom Felton of *Rise of the Planet of the Apes*) has a sinister task to perform. This uneven entry in the series requires viewers to be familiar with the novel to understand some of the plot's twists and turns.

Harry Potter and the Half-Blood Prince: An IMAX Experience (2009), US IMAX version, see *Harry Potter and the Half-Blood Prince*

Harry Potter and the Order of the Phoenix (2007, UK/US) David Yates

The Ministry of Magic refuses to accept that Lord Voldemort (Ralph Fiennes) has returned. The new Defense Against the Dark Arts teacher, Dolores Umbridge (Imelda Staunton of *Citizen X*, *Twelfth Night*), stages a coup from within Hogwarts that forces Harry (Daniel Radcliffe) to lead a student rebellion. A climactic wand-battle between the heroic Order of the Phoenix and Voldemort's loyal Death Eaters is a series highlight. Helena Bonham Carter (2001's *Planet of the Apes, Corpse Bride, The King's Speech*) makes her first appearance as the maniacal Bellatrix Lestrange. More material than usual was cut between the book (the longest of the seven *Harry Potter* novels) and this adaptation, due to the book's exceptional length.

> Harry Potter and the Order of the Phoenix: The IMAX Experience (2007), see *Harry Potter and the Order of the Phoenix*
>
> Harry Potter and the Philosopher's Stone (2001), Canada/UK title, see *Harry Potter and the Sorcerer's Stone*

Harry Potter and the Prisoner of Azkaban (2004, UK/US) Alfonso Cuarón

Cuaron's stylish direction and atmospheric locations open up this previously studio-bound series and give it a newfound sense of excitement and maturity as the characters and story also come into their own. Professor Remus Lupin (David Thewlis of *Dragonheart*) has a secret best revealed in moonlight, and a dangerous escaped criminal named Sirius Black (Gary Oldman of *Rosencrantz & Guildenstern Are Dead, Quest for Camelot*, and the Christopher Nolan *Batman* trilogy) might be coming after Harry (Daniel Radcliffe). Can the kids dodge sinister Snape (Alan Rickman of *Die Hard, Galaxy Quest*, and *The Hitchhiker's Guide to the Galaxy*) and manage mischief in time? Michael Gambon *(The King's Speech)* succeeds the late Richard Harris as Dumbledore.

> Harry Potter and the Prisoner of Azkaban: The IMAX Experience (2004), US IMAX version, see *Harry Potter and the Prisoner of Azkaban*

Harry Potter and the Sorcerer's Stone (2001, UK/US) Chris Columbus, US title

In this first installment of cinema's most ambitious fantasy series of all time, young Harry (Daniel Radcliffe) learns he is a wizard and begins a journey of discovery at the mystical school called Hogwarts. Evil Lord Voldemort murdered his parents, and Harry's survival has made him famous. Could he one day defeat the Dark Lord? Harry meets friends Ron Weasley (Rupert Grint) and Hermione Granger (Emma Watson), as well as kindly half-giant Hagrid (Robbie Coltrane of *Krull, From Hell, Van Helsing*, and *Brave*), strict but loving Professor Minerva McGonagall (Maggie Smith of *The Prime of Miss Jean Brodie*, for which she won an Oscar, and 1981's *Clash of the Titans*), and Headmaster Albus Dumbledore (Richard Harris of *Camelot* and *Gladiator*). Based on the wildly successful novels by J.K. Rowling, this film was released under the original novel title *Harry Potter and the Philosopher's Stone* in the UK. The entire series of films has inspired enough licensed merchandise to circle the Earth a few dozen times, including video games for every imaginable console and a vast number of mediocre boardgames, card games, and *Clue* (*Cluedo* to our friends in the UK) variants. Surprisingly, and somewhat tragically, no licensed roleplaying game is available—a missed opportunity in that it could have helped introduce RPGs to a whole new generation of gamers.

Hawk the Slayer ‡ (1980, UK) Terry Marcel

Heart of the Warrior (2000, Spain, Spanish) Daniel Monzón, intl. English title

The life of teenage gamer Ramon takes on a surreal quality as he moves between grim reality and the allure of his fantasy world. In his dreams, he is mythic warrior Beldar, with beautiful Sonja by his side. In reality, he becomes involved in a conspiracy to assassinate a fascist leader. Ultimately Ramon's worlds collide in a shocking conclusion.

Hearts and Armour (1983, Italy/US, Italian) Giacomo Battiato, UK/US video title

During the Crusades, in the time of the Moorish invasion of Italy, a young Christian woman named Bradamante learns from a sorceress that she will fall in love with Ruggero, a Moor prince, who will then be killed by a Christian knight. The knight, Orlando, falls in love with Ruggero's sister, the Moor princess Angelica. Sadly, relationships between Moors and Christians are seriously frowned upon. Bradamante comes into possession of a magical, invincible suit of armor. The fight scenes are fierce. Blood and dismemberment haven't been this good since the Black Knight duel in *Monty Python and the Holy Grail*. Tanya Roberts *(The Beastmaster, Sheena: Queen of the Jungle)* is the beautiful Angelica. This is based on the early 16th-century Italian epic poem *Orlando furioso*.

Heavy Metal ("Den" & "Taarna" segments) (1981, Canada) Gerald Potterton, AN

This memorable animated anthology based on the magazine features two segments squarely within our genre. Richard Corben's "Den" follows a young gamer as he falls into another world, inhabits the body of a bald, muscle-bound hero, and battles an evil queen to free a princess and her kingdom. In "Taarna," a silent, scantily clad, white-haired adventuress and her winged companion face the oozing evil of a barbarian horde aided by dark and distorted technology. With a soundtrack filled with popular metal bands, voices drawn from the Second City comedy troupe, and visuals guaranteed to look better on an altered mind, *Heavy Metal* is an '80s teen-culture touchstone.

Heavy Metal 2000 (2000, Canada/Germany) Michael Coldewey / Michel Lemire, AN

Teenage Mutant Ninja Turtles co-creator Kevin Eastman spearheads this direct-to-video animated sequel to the original *Heavy Metal* animated anthology film, based on his own graphic novel, *The Melting Pot*. It features the voice of his then-wife, "scream queen" Julie Strain. Something is lacking here, as the movie focuses on a weak single narrative instead of offering multiple stories. Although it has an associated video game and a soundtrack album, this shadow of a follow-up can't hope to match the pop-culture mind-bomb that is the one true *Heavy Metal*. It also features the voices of Michael Ironside *(Scanners, Total Recall,* TV's *V: The Final Battle)* and rocker Billy Idol.

Heavy Metal F.A.K.K.2 (2000), France/Germany title, see *Heavy Metal 2000*

Hellboy (2004, US, English/Russian) Guillermo del Toro

In a final effort to save their dying cause as World War II ends, the Nazis engage in black magic, conjuring a demon before the Allies raid their camp. Dr. Broom of the Center for Paranormal Studies takes in Hellboy and raises him. Although Hellboy might have come from hell, Dr. Broom loves the hell out of him, so Hellboy becomes a defender of justice against dark forces. Wit and humor abound, especially in the performances of Ron Perlman (TV's *Beauty and the Beast*) as Hellboy, and John Hurt *(Alien,* the *Harry Potter* films, TV's *Merlin*) as Dr. Broom. *Hellboy: The Science of Evil* is a video game for PlayStation and Xbox 360 based on the character as featured in Dark Horse Comics. In 2002, Steve Jackson Games released an official roleplaying game (using the GURPS system) based on the comics.

Hellboy II: The Golden Army (2008, Germany/US) Guillermo del Toro

Prince Nuada (Luke Goss of *Witchville*) seeks to reconstruct an ancient crown to control the robotic Golden Army as he declares war on humanity. Hellboy and his team must save the world. This film transitions seamlessly from its predecessor, and it offers much to love and enjoy: swordfights, hand-to-leaf combat with a giant plant, Hellboy battling with one hand while saving a baby in the other.... Ron Perlman is enchanting, with his wit, charm, and devil-may-care attitude (so to speak) in his reprisal of the role of Hellboy. The highlight of the film is a drunken rendition of Barry Manilow's "Can't Smile without You" by Hellboy and Abe Sapien (Doug Jones, also the Silver Surfer in *Fantastic 4: Rise of the Silver Surfer*), former brilliant scientist and now brilliant aquatic life-form.

Hellboy Animated: Sword of Storms (2006, US) Phil Weinstein / Tad Stones, TV

Ancient Japanese demons of thunder and lightning, intent on dominating our world, possess a folklore professor who has accessed a forbidden scroll. Hellboy and a team of agents investigate. Raising a samurai sword sends Hellboy into a strange alternate world of Japanese legends and dangers. He's on his own, as is the professor—wherever he is—until help arrives. The voice work is perfection as Ron Perlman, Doug Jones, and Selma Blair reprise their roles as Hellboy, Abe Sapien, and Liz Sherman, respectively, from the live-action *Hellboy* films. Hellboy was just fine in those movies; this animated version is a mixed bag. But hell, it's Hellboy, so enjoy!

He-Man and She-Ra: The Secret of the Sword (1985) see *Secret of the Sword, The*

He-Man and the Masters of the Universe: The Beginning (2002, US) Gary Hartle, AN/TV

Rebooting the 1980s toy-based franchise, this cartoon retains some of the stylistic touches from the first *Masters of the Universe* series and updates it with more backstory and character development. It's all here: the grand edifice of Castle Grayskull; the cackling, bone-faced Skeletor and his monstrous minions; the struggle for control of Eternia; and the Superman-like secret-identity setup that enables brash, young Prince Adam to trade his royal countenance for the chiseled features of his muscle-bound, harness-wearing alter-ego. This feature-length premiere launched a new incarnation of the television series and the toy line, but the show lasted only two seasons.

Hercules (1959, Italy/Spain, Italian) Pietro Francisci, intl. dubbed version, *MST3K*

If you're looking for where the entire sword-and-sandal fantasy category began, here we are. While we disallow most of them—that's a whole other book—this one is a hodge-podge of the tale of Jason and the Argonauts and a number of other myths. American body-builder Steve Reeves (1961's *The Thief of Baghdad*) begins his film career with this memorable, muscular debut. Listen when the dragon roars, and you'll hear Godzilla: the American distributor owned the rights to both films. A Dell comic-book adaptation came out in the US, and RCA Victor released the soundtrack. *Mystery Science Theater 3000* gets oiled up about this one in a fifth-season episode.

Hercules ‡ (1983, Italy/US, English/Italian) Luigi Cozzi

Hercules II (1985, Italy/US) Luigi Cozzi

The Hulk—sorry, Lou Ferrigno—is back as the titular hero. This time he's questing to collect the Seven Mighty Thunderbolts of Zeus after rival gods stole them to cause havoc and generally make life miserable for everyone. Hercules must recover them from a fearsome monsters and also battle King Minos—oh, and the moon will soon crash into Earth, just to make things more interesting. It's evil science versus muscles and magic once again. There are some continuity discrepancies—including a complete dismissal of the universal origins presented in the first movie (all but ignoring Pandora's Jar), and Cassiopeia getting left in the dust—but are you honestly going to look that closely? We didn't think so. Ferrigno's wife Carla replaces Delia Boccardo as Athena, and Maria Rosaria Omaggio *(Nightmare City)* takes over from Rossana Podestà in the role of Hera.

Hercules and the Amazon Women (1994, New Zealand / US) Bill L. Norton, TV

This first in a series of movie-length adventures for Kevin Sorbo *(Kull the Conqueror)* as Hercules eventually leads to the successful series *Hercules: The Legendary Journeys* and its spinoff, *Xena: Warrior Princess*. As best man at the wedding of friend Iolaus (Michael Hurst), Herc faces a gender conflict: the women of the town have turned against the men and thrown in their lot with the goddess Hera. Anthony Quinn (*Zorba the Greek* himself) is Zeus, while Lucy Lawless appears not as Xena but as Lysia.

Hercules and the Captive Women (1961, France/Italy, Italian) Vittorio Cottafavi, *MST3K*

You have to figure that being a big hero like Hercules (Reg Park—Mr. Universe, no less, in his first outing as the demigod) means you're often tired: so many things to do, so little time to catch a nap. But Herc does his best to get some Zs while defeating the evil queen of Atlantis and battling a shape-shifter. There's also something that would have made Hitler proud about children being taken to a transformative stone drawn from the blood of Uranus (stop giggling) that turns some of its subjects into Aryan-like soldiers. The *Mystery Science Theater 3000* guys do a great job with this one in a memorable fourth-season episode. Listen for the distinctive *Creature from the Black Lagoon* theme in the cobbled-together soundtrack.

Hercules and the Queen of Lydia (1960), intl. English title, see *Hercules Unchained*

Hercules and the Ten Avengers (1965), US TV title, see *Hercules vs. the Giant Warriors*

Hercules at the Center of the Earth (1964), intl. English title, see *Hercules in the Haunted World*

Hercules Conquers Atlantis (1961), UK title, see *Hercules and the Captive Women*

Hercules in the Haunted World (1964, Italy, Italian) Mario Bava / Franco Prosperi, US title

Hercules (three-time Mr. Universe Reg Park) and his two companions undertake a dangerous quest to Hades to retrieve the Stone of Forgetfulness to . . . wait, what? Oh, yeah, to heal his love, Princess Deianira. Hercules doesn't know that her guardian, King Lico, has caused her dementia and plans to take her as his bride. The final battle involves fighting an army of flying vampire-zombies. Christopher Lee (*The Lord of the Rings* films) is King Lico. In an odd one of those "what were they thinking?" moments, another actor has dubbed over his glorious, resonant voice in the English-language version.

Hercules in the Maze of the Minotaur (1994, New Zealand / US) Josh Becker, TV

In the last of the five TV-movies that led into the *Hercules: The Legendary Journeys* series, Kevin Sorbo's Hercules has settled down with his wife Deianeira (Tawny Kitaen again) and children when he's called out of retirement to save a neighboring village from a minotaur. He journeys with his long-time friend Iolaus (Michael Hurst). Some of the best moments are of the two kicking back, recalling the glory days. Anthony Quinn *(Lawrence of Arabia)* once again plays Zeus.

Hercules in the Underworld (1994, New Zealand / US) Bill L. Norton, TV

Anthony Quinn *(Viva Zapata!)* and Tawny Kitaen *(The Perils of Gwendoline in the Land of Yik Yak)* return to lend support to Kevin Sorbo's Hercules in the fourth TV-movie go-round prior to the weekly series, *Hercules: The Legendary Journeys*. In this adventure, Herc must leave his wife Deianeira and their children and travel down to the pit of Hades, but when Deianeira thinks him dead, she might just join him. Can Hercules reunite his family, or will he lose everything he loves on this Earth? Michael Hurst (Iolaus from *Hercules and the Amazon Women, Hercules in the Maze of the Minotaur,* and the TV series) appears as Charon the boatman.

Hercules, Prisoner of Evil (1964, Italy, Italian) Antonio Margheriti, US title

Hercules (Reg Park) battles an evil sorceress who uses a magic potion to turn men into werewolf-like beasts. Hercules becomes a horrific, destructive monster under her spell, but he's unconscious much of the time, allowing Ilo, his brother, to step in and take care of business. This is very different Hercules fare set in central Asia, and not as successful a film.

Hercules' Revenge (1960), US title, see *Goliath and the Dragon*

Hercules the Avenger (1965, Italy, Italian) Maurizio Lucidi, US title

While Hercules is on a quest to save his son's soul from evil earth-goddess Gia, her son does his very best impression of an evil Hercules. If you feel you've seen this film before, it might be because of the liberal use of footage from *Hercules and the Captive Women* and *Hercules in the Haunted World*. (That's why the zombies are back.) This is the fourth and last appearance of Reg Park as Hercules.

Hercules the Invincible (1964, Italy, Italian) Alvaro Mancori / Lewis Mann

Yet again, Hercules is very much taken with a beautiful woman of royal blood, but this time he's to be pulled apart by elephants, wishbone-style. Torture, or an odd Thanksgiving ritual at the castle? Hercules shakes it off in time to fight another day. After all, he is "invincible." The big guy fights a lion and a bear. The slaying of the giant dragon is footage from *Hercules* (1958).

Hercules: The Legendary Journeys—Hercules and the Circle of Fire (1994, New Zealand / US) Doug Lefler, TV

In this third movie-pilot for *Hercules: The Legendary Journeys*, Herc (Kevin Sorbo) and Deianeira (Tawny Kitaen of *Bachelor Party* and that Whitesnake video)—not the same Deianeira played by Renée O'Connor last time—must stop the world from turning into one big ball of ice. Drawing from the myth of Prometheus, the story also features Anthony Quinn *(Last Action Hero)* in his third turn as Zeus.

Hercules: the Legendary Journeys—Hercules and the Lost Kingdom (1994, New Zealand / US) Harley Cokeliss, TV

In this second movie-length precursor to the TV show *Hercules: The Legendary Journeys*, Herc (Kevin Sorbo) helps locate Troy via a magical compass that points the way to the lost city. But finding Troy is just part one of the quest. Part two involves teaching Troy's former denizens how to reclaim their town from the Cult of the Blue Priests. Xena's future sidekick Gabrielle (Renée O'Connor) appears here as the first of two unrelated Deianeiras to grace this movie series, while Robert Trebor—a later fan favorite on the *Hercules* series, as Salmoneus—turns up here as Waylon.

Hercules Unchained (1960, France/Italy/Spain, Italian/Spanish) Pieto Francisci, US title, *MST3K*

In Steve Reeves' second and final turn as the oily hero, Hercules has to contend with rivalry between brothers who both claim the right to rule Thebes. Queen Omphale (Sylvia Lopez) derails his diplomatic mission when magical waters wipe his memory and leave him in her thrall. Lopez died from leukemia at the age of 27, shortly after completing this movie. World heavyweight boxing champion Primo Carnera makes his final film appearance as Antaeus. *Mystery Science Theater 3000* takes on this Herculean legend in a fourth-season episode, one of Joel Hodgson's two favorites and one of the first seen by one of your authors [ATB].

Hercules vs. the Giant Warriors (1965, France/Italy, Italian) Alberto De Martino

Hercules must battle a horde of superhuman bronze warriors released from a bejeweled dagger by evil sorceress Parsifae, who summons them to help her son Milo usurp the throne. When Milo captures the beautiful Princess Ate, Hercules totally loses it in a killing spree that takes some innocent lives as well. Hercules' dad Zeus gives him a brief time-out as a weak human, but our hero is restored in time to save the princess.

Hercules vs. the Hydra (1966, France/Italy), US TV title, Carlo Ludovico Bragaglia

While attempting to avenge the deaths of his wife and people, Hercules frees the princess of a besieged kingdom, battles a three-headed hydra, and receives aid from a group of Amazons whose queen transforms her former lovers into trees (giving a whole new meaning to "tree-hugger"). Muscleman and one-time Mr. Universe Mickey Hargitay is Hercules, with his then-wife and sex icon Jayne Mansfield in a dual role as Princess Deianira and the evil Amazon queen. They're mom and dad to Mariska Hargitay of the TV series *Law & Order: SVU*.

Hexer, The (2001, Poland, Polish) Marek Brodzki, intl. English title

Geralt the White Wolf is a weapons expert, a relentless warrior, a wizard, a dragon-slayer, a heroic protector, a Polish samurai, and the ultimate paladin. Whew. Protecting his world and defending its inhabitants brings him closer to his final destiny. The performance of Michael Zebrowski *(The Pianist)* as the hexer brings the character to life. This film is based on a series of Polish fantasy-adventure novels, *Wiedzmin (The Witcher)* by Andrzej Sapkowski, which has been adapted for the computer game *The Witcher*.

Highlander ‡ (1986, UK/US) Russell Mulcahy

Highlander 2 (1991), US DVD title, see *Highlander II: The Quickening*

Highlander II: The Quickening (1991, Argentina/France/UK) Russell Mulcahy

Many fans of the original *Highlander* would prefer if we didn't list this one at all. The director has even tried to fix the film with a new cut, but that's small comfort. As the plot goes: in 2024, an aging Connor (Christopher Lambert, also of *Mortal Kombat*) has saved the world from deadly radiation via an energy shield, but his youth and immortality return when he must face Immortal assassins sent from his home planet, Zeist. Wait, what? You read that right. Sean Connery (the James Bond films, *Hunt for Red October*) returns as Ramirez for no good reason, and supporting players Virginia Madsen *(Dune, Long Gone, Zombie High, Candyman)* and Michael Ironside *(Scanners, Total Recall, Kids of the Round Table)* do what they can, but no one can save this bizarre sci-fi misstep.

Highlander 3: The Final Conflict (1995), Europe title, see *Highlander III: The Final Dimension*

Highlander III: The Final Dimension (1995, Canada/France/UK) Andrew Morahan, Canada DVD title

Ignoring the second *Highlander* film entirely (thank you) while recycling most of the original (oh, well), this film finds Connor (Christopher Lambert of 1999's *Beowulf*) alone again and forced to battle a kinsman one more time. As it turns out, the Game isn't over. An Immortal sorcerer named Kane (Mario Van Peebles of *Jaws: The Revenge*) has returned to challenge Connor for the Prize. Incorporating the tried-and-true trope of re-forging a cherished weapon, and with a new love interest as well as an adopted son for Connor, this sequel tries to recapture the spirit of the first movie but fell flat at theaters as a cheap-looking retread that offered nothing new.

Highlander III: The Magician (1995), Sweden title, see *Highlander III: The Final Dimension*

Highlander III: The Sorcerer (1995), Canada orig. title, see *Highlander III: The Final Dimension*

Highlander 5: The Source (2007), UK TV title, see *Highlander: The Source*

Highlander: Endgame (2000, US) Douglas Aarniokoski

Worlds collide as Connor (Christopher Lambert of *The Sicilian*) from the previous films and his clansman Duncan (Adrian Paul of *Merlin: The Return*) from the spin-off *Highlander* TV-series unite against a corrupt Immortal named Kell, who plays the Game by his own rules. To stop this villain, it'll take two MacLeods... or will it? Bruce Payne (Damodar from the *Dungeons & Dragons* movies) is Kell, although the magical powers he exhibits in the film's trailers were apparently just for promotion and never intended for the final cut of the movie. An extended "producers' cut" available on DVD adds nearly 15 minutes to the running time and restores a lot of exposition.

Highlander: The Search for Vengeance (2007, US) Yoshiaki Kawajiri / Takuji Endo / Hiroshi Hamazki, AN/V

You thought the *Highlander* films and TV series were all over the map with continuity, but here comes an anime adventure, set in the year 2187, that features another MacLeod! Colin MacLeod adopts the surname after fighting alongside that clan, gains an Immortal mentor named Amergan, and tracks a power-mad lunatic named Marcus. Their battle rages through human history into a post-apocalyptic New York. This one has more fans than some live-action installments. The Japanese "director's cut" of the film runs 10 minutes longer than the US release.

Highlander: The Source (2007, Lithuania/UK/US) Brett Leonard

Bypassing the cinema and heading straight to the Sci-Fi Channel, this fifth installment introduces an Immortal "Source" of power that Duncan (Adrian Paul of *Storm Watch*) must find. Remember the *Highlander* bit about how "there can be only one"? This movie gives you a completely different explanation for that phrase, upending series continuity yet again. Would it kill them to be consistent just once? This was intended to be the first chapter in a new trilogy of *Highlander* TV-movies, but audience response ("They're still making *Highlander* sequels?") as well as an upcoming remake of the original film decapitated those plans.

Hobbit, The (1977, US) Arthur Rankin, Jr. / Jules Bass, AN/TV

No one raised on Rankin/Bass specials in the '70s could visualize Bilbo Baggins any other way or imagine his voice in anything other than the easygoing drawl of Orson Bean *(The Return of the King)*. From the production team that brought us perennial holiday favorites *Rudolph the Red-Nosed Reindeer* and *Frosty the Snowman*, and with animation by Topcraft (later Studio Ghibli), this Peabody Award-winning animated adaptation of the Tolkien classic—first aired around Thanksgiving—also features Hollywood film legend John Huston as Gandalf, Brother Theodore *(The Return of the King)* as a Gollum who might be madder than Andy Serkis's version, Hans Conried

430 • CINEMA AND SORCERY

(1001 Arabian Nights) as Thorin, and Thurl "You're a Mean One, Mr. Grinch" Ravenscroft. Sing along with Glenn Yarbrough (and us): "The road goes ever, ever on . . . ."

Hobbit: An Unexpected Journey, The ‡ (2012, New Zealand / US) Peter Jackson, US complete title

Hobbit: The Battle of the Five Armies, The (2014, New Zealand / US) Peter Jackson

In the final installment of this prequel trilogy, Bilbo and the dwarves find themselves in a battle beyond any they have faced before, while Gandalf must deal with the threat of the Necromancer or risk leaving Middle-earth vulnerable to a far greater evil. If you've seen *The Lord of the Rings* movies, you know how well that last part goes. If physics-defying CGI-figures bouncing across balloon rocks entertain you, this is your film. How far the saga has fallen since the heady days of the original trilogy. Your authors, at least, are thankful that the road that goes ever on stops here.

Hobbit: The Desolation of Smaug, The (2013, New Zealand / US) Peter Jackson

The journey to the Lonely Mountain ends and the battle to reclaim Erebor begins as our heroes contend with the presence of a deadly dragon, and Gandalf investigates the mysterious Necromancer. Besides the usual suspects, Orlando Bloom returns from *The Lord of the Rings* films to reprise his role as Legolas. Newcomers to the saga include Evangeline Lilly (the *Lost* TV-series) as the controversial non-Tolkien character Tauriel, Mikael Persbrandt as Beorn, Luke Evans (the 2010 *Clash of the Titans, Immortals*) as Bard, and Stephen Fry *(V for Vendetta, Sherlock Holmes: A Game of Shadows)* as the Master of Laketown. The CGI town and green-screen vistas will make you long for the stunning "bigatures" of the *Rings* films, but Smaug (voiced by Benedict Cumberbatch of the BBC's *Sherlock* and *Star Trek into Darkness*) is a relatively impressive creation . . . even if he is just a shadow of the great Vermithrax.

Hobgoblin, The (1990), intl. English title, see *Quest for the Mighty Sword*

Hogfather (2007, UK) Vadim Jean

In this adaptation of a *Discworld* novel by Terry Pratchett, who plays the Toymaker in this film, the Hogfather (Father Christmas / Santa Claus) has disappeared on the night before Hogswatch (Christmas). Death (Shakespearean actor Ian Richardson), believing the Hogfather is necessary to the importance of belief, substitutes for him, while Death's adopted granddaughter, Susan, tries to solve the mystery. The cast includes David Warner *(The Omen, Time After Time, Beastmaster III)* and Joss Ackland, who with Richardson appeared in the British TV miniseries *Tinker Tailor Soldier Spy.*

Hook (1991, US) Steven Spielberg

Contrary to his protest "I won't grow up," Peter Pan (Robin Williams of *Aladdin*) has done just that: taken the name Peter Banning, married Wendy's granddaughter, and raised a family. Now a soulless corporate type, Peter has to return to Neverland and recapture his youth when Captain Hook kidnaps Peter's children to provoke one final battle. Williams is a delightful Peter

Pan, Julia Roberts *(Mirror, Mirror)* is an almost insufferable Tinkerbell, and Dustin Hoffman *(The Graduate, Rainman)* is sheer brilliance as the villainous Captain Hook, with Bob Hoskins *(Snow White and the Huntsman)* as his first mate, Smee. Wendy? She's *Harry Potter*'s Maggie Smith. This is a delightful if melancholy continuation of the classic tale.

How to Train Your Dragon ‡ (2010, US) Dean DeBlois / Chris Sanders, AN

How to Train Your Dragon 2 (2014, US) Dean Deblois, AN

Five years after the events of the first film, Hiccup (Jay Baruchel of *This Is the End*) and the rest of the citizens of Berk face a new challenge. A newly discovered ice cave not only expands their understanding of the world in which they live but also introduces Hiccup to an enigmatic dragon-rider with a shocking secret. The entire voice cast from the original movie returns, joined by Cate Blanchett (Galadriel!) as Valka, and Djimon Hounsou *(Stargate, Gladiator, Lara Croft Tomb Raider: The Cradle of Life, Guardians of the Galaxy)* as Drago.

How to Train Your Dragon: An IMAX 3D Experience (2010), US IMAX version, see *How to Train Your Dragon*

Huntsman, The (2016, US) Cedric Nicolas-Troyan, NYR

In this sequel to *Snow White and the Huntsman*, Chris Hemsworth reprises his starring role. Other than a few additional members of the cast, like Emily Blunt *(Gulliver's Travels, The Adjustment Bureau, Looper)* and Jessica Chastain *(Corilanus, Mama, The Martian)*, we know very little information as we wrap up this book.

Ilya Muromets (1960), Soviet Union orig. title, see *Sword and the Dragon, The*

Immortals (2011, US, English/Greek) Tarsem Singh

Zeus seeks to destroy the merciless King Hyperion, who has ravaged Greece with a savage army in search of the legendary Epirius Bow, a weapon that can destroy humankind and annihilate the gods. Since the gods may not intervene in the conflicts of humans, Zeus pulls an end run and secretly selects the peasant Theseus (*Man of Steel* Superman Henry Cavill) to save humanity. On this "mission impossible," priestess Phaedra and thief Stavros accompany Theseus. Mickey Rourke *(Iron Man 2, Sin City)* is the despicable King Hyperion; Freida Pinto *(Slumdog Millionaire, Rise of the Planet of the Apes)* is Phaedra.

Immortals 3D (2011), US 3D version, see *Immortals*

In the Name of the King 2: Two Worlds (2011, Canada/Germany) Uwe Boll, Germany orig. title

Boll is back, but this time most of the name actors wisely stay away. Dolph Lundgren *(Masters of the Universe)* plays a Special Forces operative thrust back in time to the Kingdom of Ehb, where he has to defeat the two-pronged threat of the Dark Mother and Raven. Lundgren sustained an injury on the first day of shooting, and six other members of the production were hurt on the last day. Even just watching the movie might be hazardous to your health.

In the Name of the King 3: The Last Job (2014, Bulgaria/Canada) Uwe Boll, intl. English title

In his final job, American contract-killer Hazen Kaine (Dominic Purcell of the *John Doe* TV-series, the *Prison Break* TV-series, and *Straw Dogs*) inadvertently goes back in time, where he must engage in battle with a medieval army and a fire-breathing dragon to help reclaim a stolen kingdom. Only two more words here, folks: Uwe Boll.

In the Name of the King 3: The Last Mission (2014), orig. English title, see *In the Name of the King 3: The Last Job*

In the Name of the King: A Dungeon Siege Tale (2008, Canada/Germany/US) Uwe Boll

Farmer (Jason Statham of *Ghosts of Mars*) goes on a quest to avenge his son and rescue his wife from the animalistic Krugs. Let us repeat: Uwe Boll. Must we go on? All right, then: The king of crap cinema delivers a surprisingly not-entirely-awful adventure movie boasting a larger-than-average budget (for Boll) and an extraordinary cast that includes Leelee Sobieski *(Joan of Arc)*, John Rhys-Davies (the *Indiana Jones* and *Lord of the Rings* films), Ron Perlman (the *Hellboy* movies), Ray Liotta (*Goodfellas*), and Burt Reynolds *(Smokey and the Bandit, Boogie Nights)*. We can't figure it out, either. This movie is based on the *Dungeon Siege* video games, with German metal bands providing the musical score. An extended Blu-ray cut adds a half hour to its already two-plus hour running time; enjoy.

In the Name of the King: Two Worlds (2011), US title, see *In the Name of the King 2: Two Worlds*

Invincible Barbarian, The (1982), UK video title, see *Gunan, King of the Barbarians*

Iron Crown, The (1949, Italy, Italian) Alessandro Blasetti

According to 13th-century legend, a crown made from three sources—a nail in Christ's cross, kingly jewels, and the metal of a Roman emperor's sword—became famed as a symbol of justice. This film begins with a pilgrimage of crown-bearers and leads to an epic romance between an imprisoned princess and a slain king's son, who was abandoned in the woods and raised by lions. Yes, it does sound like Tarzan meets Rapunzel, only it has lots more bloodshed.

Iron Warrior (1987, Italy) Alfonso Brescia

A drastically altered Ator (Miles O'Keeffe) returns for a third adventure so off-model from the previous two films that original series director Joe D'Amato felt compelled to return for a fourth movie to correct its mistakes. (See *Quest for the Mighty Sword*.) When even D'Amato thinks you've sunk too low, that's bad. As the story goes, one velvet morning, Ator fights the evil Phaedra and her Iron Warrior, Trogar, who looks like Destro from the *G.I. Joe* cartoon. Keep your eyes peeled for the location vehicles in clear view during a gripping battle sequence. Alfonso Brescia has fifty-one directorial credits on IMDb. Sometimes you just can't make sense of this world.

Jabberwock (2011, Canada/US) Steven R. Monroe

Francis is a knight who must forge a unique weapon to defeat an equally unusual dragon that's a hybrid of dragon and insect elements: eww. Tahmoh Penikett (TV series like *Battlestar Galactica, Dollhouse,* and *Supernatural*) is Francis, and Kacey Barnfield *(Lake Placid 3, Resident Evil: Afterlife, I Spit on Your Grave 2)* is Anabel.

Jabberwock Dragon Siege (2011), UK DVD title, see *Jabberwock*

Jabberwocky (1977, UK) Terry Gilliam

A kingdom terrorized by a horrible creature chooses a meek, destitute cooper (barrel-maker)—Dennis Cooper—to slay the monster and win the hand of a lovely princess. This very black comedy with horrific incidents and wildly eccentric characters stars director Terry Gilliam's Monty Python colleague Michael Palin *(Time Bandits)*. The creature is based on the monster in the Lewis Carroll poem of the same name. Watch at your own risk, but "Beware the Jubjub bird / And shun the frumius Bandersnatch!"

Jack Frost (1966, Soviet Union, Russian) Aleksandr Rou, *MST3K*

A bizarre adaptation of a Russian fairytale, this movie follows two young lovers who must face extraordinary challenges if they are to be united. The girl suffers Cinderella-like humiliation and is then frozen by a magic staff. The boy is transformed partly into a bear and hunted by a witch's army of trees. Let's face it: this just doesn't translate well into cultures beyond its own. You have to wait a while before the title character even rears his icy head. Believe it or not, this is an annual Christmas television tradition in some parts of Europe. *Mystery Science Theater 3000* immortalizes this film in an eighth-season episode.

Jack the Giant Killer (1962, US) Nathan Juran

Evil sorcerer Pendragon plans to kidnap a beautiful princess to usurp the throne of Cornwall from her father, yet his invincible sorcery and minions of witches and wizards are no match for the farm boy who slays the giant sent to abduct her. Producer Edward Small, director Nathan H. Juran, actors Kerwin Mathews *(The Three Worlds of Gulliver)* as Jack, and Torin Thatcher (one of the most prolific stage and screen actors of the 20th century) as Pendragon were hoping to recreate their *7th Voyage of Sinbad* success. They failed but produced a relatively entertaining film based on a Cornish folktale.

Jack the Giant Killer (2013, US) Mark Atkins

This modern interpretation of the *Jack and the Beanstalk* tale has Jack encountering reptilian beasts at the top of that beanstalk instead of a giant. When these creatures threaten to destroy Jack's world, a hero is born. The anachronistic nature of the film muddies the tale, as does a giant-killer with no giant to kill. Ben Cross *(Grendel,* the 2009 *Star Trek)* features, in his "what was I thinking?" role. Do not confuse this Asylum production with Bryan Singer's *Jack the Giant Slayer.* Then again, that probably isn't possible ... or is it?

Jack the Giant Slayer **(2013, US) Bryan Singer**

In this contemporary tale, young farmer Jack inadvertently opens a passage between worlds, allowing a race of giant warriors to challenge all life on Earth. The stuff of legends has now become an unthinkable reality in which Jack must face these giants to save the world and, of course, rescue a beautiful princess. The cast includes Ewan McGregor (the *Star Wars* films), Stanley Tucci *(Captain America: The First Avenger, The Hunger Games)*, Ian McShane *(The Seeker: The Dark Is Rising)*, Bill Nighy (the *Pirates of the Caribbean* films), Warwick Davis *(Willow)*, John Kassir (the Cryptkeeper himself), and Nicolas Hoult *(About a Boy, X-Men: First Class)* as Jack.

Jadesoturi (2006), Finland orig. title, see *Jade Warrior*

Jade Warrior **(2006 China/Estonia/Finland/Netherlands, Finnish/Mandarin) Antti-Jussi Annila**

When present-day Finnish blacksmith Kai opens a mythical chest, he becomes aware of his past life as Sintai, a warrior of ancient China, and his destiny. Kai has unwittingly released an evil demon imprisoned within the chest and now must once again rid the world of this beast that threatens to enslave humankind. This film combines the mythology of the Finnish epic poem, *The Kalevala*, with Chinese martial arts.

Jajantaram Mamantaram (2003), India orig. title, see *Land of the Little People*

Jason and the Argonauts ‡ **(1963, UK/US) Don Chaffey**

Jason and the Argonauts **(2000, US) Nick Willing, TV**

Aired in two parts, this TV movie-miniseries adapts the Greek myth of Jason's quest for the Golden Fleece that inspired the 1963 Ray Harryhausen film of the same name. The charisma-free presence of Jason London *(Dazed and Confused*—that's a film credit, not his demeanor) anchors a cast that ranges from Dennis Hopper *(Easy Rider, Speed)* as Pelias to Derek Jacobi *(The Secret of NIMH*, TV's *Doctor Who)* as Phineas. Some viewers note the inclusion of a female Argonaut in this version: Atalanta (Olga Sosnovska of *Ocean's Thirteen*). Although Apollonius of Rhodes ruled out the possibility of Jason allowing a woman on board the *Argo,* other versions of the story feature her prominently.

John Carpenter's Big Trouble in Little China (1986, US), see *Big Trouble in Little China*

John Carter **(2012, US) Andrew Stanton**

Based on Edgar Rice Burroughs novels published in the early 20th century, this movie features, indeed, John Carter, an ex-Confederate soldier mysteriously transported to the planet Mars, known by the locals as Barsoom. There he can leap tall buildings in a single bound and battle hordes of enemies with ease. He becomes a reluctant hero in a conflict engineered by an ancient race known as the Therns. He also charms a sexy Xena-like scientist, befriends a race of four-armed, green-skinned desert-dwellers, and gets licked by an adorable, puppy-like dinosaur named Woola that runs faster than the Road Runner after six cups of espresso. Taylor Kitsch (Gambit from *X-Men Origins: Wolverine*) stars in the title role. The cast also includes James Purefoy *(A Knight's Tale, Solomon Kane)*, Mark Strong *(Tristan & Isolde, Sherlock Holmes, Kick-Ass, Green Lantern)*, Polly Walker (the *Clash of the Titans* remake), and Willem Dafoe *(Spider-Man)*. A few *John Carter* games have popped up over the years, including *Warriors of Mars*, designed by Gary Gygax and Brian Blume and published by TSR in 1974; Heritage Models' *John Carter Warlord of Mars*, published in 1978 and supported with its own line of 25mm miniatures; and SPI's *John Carter: Warlord of Mars* hex-and-counter boardgame released in 1979.

John Carter of Mars (2012), see *John Carter*

John Norman's Gor (1988), US complete title, see *Gor*

Journey to Promethea (2010, US) Dan Garcia, TV

A hero who leads his people out of slavery is caught and beheaded, and his people are disbanded. Before his death, he prophesies that a young warrior will lead them to a promised land, Promethea. A young farmer named Magnus is that savior. Billy Zane *(The Phantom, BloodRayne)* is the tyrannical king and does a lot of sitting and screaming.

J. R. R. Tolkien's The Lord of the Rings (1978, US) Ralph Bakshi, AN

A film that has many adherents as well as many detractors, this ambitious animated adaptation of roughly the first half of Tolkien's *Lord of the Rings* trilogy blends rotoscoped live-action footage with traditional animation to tell the tale of the One Ring and Frodo Baggins, a hobbit who must deliver it to the fires of Mount Doom. This movie features the voices of John Hurt (*Alien*, the *Harry Potter* films) and Anthony Daniels (come on—the *Star Wars* movies). Plans for a concluding film never came together, so in 1980, Rankin/Bass stepped in to provide a solution in the form of a television movie, *The Return of the King*, which followed the Rankin/Bass adaptation of *The Hobbit*. That same year, Simulations Publications, Inc. (SPI) repackaged their already popular *War of the Ring* wargame (released in 1977) with artwork from the animated film.

Justin and the Knights of Valour (2013, Spain) Manuel Sicilia, 3D/AN

Young Justin (Freddie Highmore of *The Golden Compass* and *The Spiderwick Chronicles*) dreams of becoming a knight, in a world where knights have been deposed and bureaucrats rule. His father Reginald (Alfred Molina of *Prince of Persia: The Sands of Time*), chief counsel to the queen (Olivia Williams of 2000's *Jason and the Argonauts*), prefers his son become a lawyer as well. His grandmother (Julie Walters of the *Harry Potter* films and *Mamma Mia*) regales Justin with tales of his honorable grandfather Sir Roland, the king's protector, betrayed and slain by the nefarious Sir Heraclio (Mark Strong of *Kick-Ass* and *John Carter*). Justin resolves to follow his heart and perhaps avenge his grandfather's death. The voice cast also features Rupert Everett *(The Chronicles of Narnia: The Lion, The Witch and the Wardrobe)* and Antonio Banderas (the *Zorro* and *Shrek* films).

Just Visiting (2001, France/US, English/French) Jean-Marie Poirè

An inept wizard (Malcolm McDowell of *Kids of the Round Table*) inadvertently transports a 12th-century knight (Jean Reno) to a present-day Chicago museum. It's a "fish out of water" story with heart, as the knight encounters the descendent of his former love (Christina Applegate of TV's *Married with Children* and *Anchorman*, here in a dual role) and strives to return home to his own time. In this remake of the French film *Les visiteurs*, Reno *(Leon: The Professional, Mission: Impossible, Godzilla, The Da Vinci Code)* reprises his role.

Kairyu daikessen (1966), Japan orig. title, see *Magic Serpent, The*

Kane the Barbarian (2003), see *Barbarian*

Keeper of Time, The (2004, US) Robert Crombie, V

Tim, a boy in medieval times chosen to become the ultimate wizard, must journey with his protective companions to the lair of Tor, the most evil wizard, to defeat him. If Tim, the last Keeper of Time, were to die, it would mean the death of all that is good, and evil would reign. Michael O'Hearn *(Barbarian)* gives a realistic performance as the swordsman Bullrock.

Kid in Aladdin's Palace, A (1998, US) Robert L. Levy, V

The tagline "The Kid Is Back" says it all for this sequel to *A Kid in King Arthur's Court*. Calvin Fuller (still Thomas Ian Nicholas) finds a magic lamp. An imprisoned genie sends him back in time to help Ali Baba save Aladdin from his evil brother Luxor. This children's slapstick comedy features a winged horse and a magic carpet. Rhona Mitra (Kyra in *Beowulf*, and the live-action model for Lara Croft in the interactive *Tomb Raider* videogame series) plays Scheherazade.

Kid in King Arthur's Court, A (1995, Hungary/UK/US) Michael Gottlieb, AL

A California earthquake enables teenager Calvin Fuller (Thomas Ian Nicholas of the *American Pie* films) to travel back to the time of King Arthur (Joss Ackland of *The Thief and the Cobbler, CitizenX*, and *Hogfather*). The aged king embraces this young man as the savior predicted by wizard Merlin (Ron Moody, who also played Merlin in Disney's *Unidentified Flying Oddball*) to save Camelot. Calvin trains as a knight to vanquish evil Lord Belasco (Art Malik of *John Carter*) and falls in love with young Princess Katherine. This loosely based retelling of Mark Twain's *A Connecticut Yankee in King Arthur's Court* also features Daniel Craig (the James Bond films) and a young Kate Winslet *(Titanic)*.

Kids of the Round Table (1997, Canada/US) Robert Tinnell, AL

One moment, 11-year-old Alex is regaling his friends with tales of King Arthur, which they play out with cardboard shields, aluminum-foil swords, and dirt-bike steeds. The next moment, Alex is pulling King Arthur's sword, Excalibur, from a rock with ease. Merlin (Malcolm McDowell of *O Lucky Man!* and *Just Visiting*) appears, to explain the miracle Alex has unleashed and the importance of wielding the sword responsibly. All Alex can think of is the opportunity to exact revenge on the neighborhood bully, Scar, son of Butch Scarsdale (Michael Ironside of *Starship Troopers* and *Heavy Metal 2000*).

Killing of Satan, The (1983, Philippines, English/Tagalog) Efren C. Pinon, intl. English title

Lando, an unconventional hero chosen by his dead uncle to battle the forces of evil, must rescue his wife and daughter from hell. He hones his skills against the Prince of Magic to warm up for his ultimate confrontation with Satan. Memory of the old Warner Brothers cartoons lives on in this film: a boulder flattens the uncle, yet he can still talk. Even stranger than that is the fact that Lando has actually been killed, but his uncle switches places with him through some cosmic craziness so Lando can fulfill his role as savior.

King of Kung Fu (2008), Hong Kong English title, see *Forbidden Kingdom, The*

Knights of Badassdom (2014, US) Joe Lynch

A group of live-action roleplayers brings a real demon to our world and must become true heroes to save the day. Starring Ryan Kwanten (HBO's *True Blood*), Steve Zahn *(Crimson Tide, That Thing You Do!*, HBO's *Treme)*, Peter Dinklage (HBO's *Game of Thrones*, *X-Men: Days of Future Past*), and Summer Glau (TV's *Firefly* and *Alphas*), this long-awaited film had positive buzz but a troubled road to release. The studio replaced Lynch's cut with one of its own. Time will tell (or perhaps you already know) if the director's version will ever see the light of day.

Krabat (2008, Germany, German) Marco Kreuzpaintner

Homeless and orphaned after the plague and the Thirty Years' War, a young boy, Krabat, apprentices to a mill-keeper who is actually a master of dark sorcery. Krabat befriends Tonda (Daniel Brühl of *Inglourious Basterds*), but the sorcerer brutally murders Tonda during his yearly ritual sacrifice of a boy, which keeps him young. When Krabat forms an alliance with another boy, Juro, and a girl, Kantorka, the magical adventure begins. This is based on the fantasy novel of the same name by Otfried Preussler.

Krabat and the Legend of the Satanic Mill (2008), UK title, see *Krabat*

Kriemhild's Revenge (1928), intl. English title, see *Nibelungen: Kriemhilds Rache, Die*

Krull ‡ (1983, UK) Peter Yates

Krull: Invaders of the Black Fortress (1983), see *Krull*

Kull the Conquerer (1997, Italy/US) John Nicolella

An old king killed by Kull has passed his crown to the barbarian, so the king's heirs reanimate the evil sorceress-queen Akivasha to enthrall Kull and destroy him. This is based on the Conan novel *The Hour of the Dragon* by Robert E. Howard. When Arnold Schwarzenegger refused to play Conan again, Kevin Sorbo (TV's *Hercules*) stepped in as Howard's other barbarian hero. Akivasha is a minor character from the novel, played here by Tia Carrere *(Merlin: The Return)*.

Harvey Fierstein *(Mulan, Mulan II)*, Litefoot *(Mortal Kombat: Annihilation)*, and stunt-man extraordinaire Pat Roach (the original *Clash of the Titans, Conan the Destroyer, Red Sonja,* "death by plane propeller" in *Raiders of the Lost Ark, Indiana Jones and the Temple of Doom, Indiana Jones and the Last Crusade*) also feature.

Laberinto del fauno, El (2007), Spain orig. title, see *Pan's Labyrinth*

Labors of Hercules (1959), intl. English title, see *Hercules* (1959)

Labyrinth ‡ (1986, UK/US) Jim Henson

Labyrinth of the Faun, The (2007), intl. literal English title, see *Pan's Labyrinth*

Ladro di Bagdad, Il (1961), Italy orig. title, see *Thief of Baghdad, The* (1961)

Ladyhawke (1985, US) Richard Donner

A wisecracking thief becomes the companion of an unlikely duo: a black knight who transforms into a wolf at night, and a hawk that returns to her true female human form at night. The lovers have been cursed to be forever together but separated by their mismatched shape-shifting. Perhaps love can overcome even the strongest of demonic forces? Matthew Broderick *(WarGames, Ferris Bueller's Day Off, Glory)* is the thief, Rutger Hauer *(Blade Runner, Flesh+Blood, The Hitcher, Hobo with a Shotgun)* is the knight, and Michelle Pfeiffer *(Grease 2, Scarface, Dark Shadows)* is his beloved. Leo McKern *(Help!, The Omen,* TV's *The Prisoner),* Alfred Molina *(Raiders of the Lost Ark*—"Adios, Satipo"—*Spider-Man 2, Prince of Persia: The Sands of Time),* and none other than Broderick's *WarGames* buddy, Professor Falken (a.k.a. John Wood) as the evil Bishop of Aquila also star. Although Warner Bros. lied in marketing the film as derived from an actual medieval tale, a story in *The Lais of Marie de France* bears some similarities.

Lancelot and Guinevere (1963), UK orig. title, see *Sword of Lancelot*

Land of the Little People (2003, India, English/Hindi) Soumitra Ranade

Shipwrecked, Aditya awakes on an island of tiny people. (We're talking Lilliputian, "hold in your hand" tiny.) Fearing him an evil giant at first, they eventually enlist him to battle their real problem, Jhamunda, a giant immortal shape-shifting beast with magical powers, created by army chief Singh to control the villagers. Did I mention this creature snacks on children? It seems Aditya's arrival interferes with Singh's plan to overthrow the king and marry the princess. This children's film is based on the old Hindu fable *Bakasura*.

Last Airbender, The (2010, US) M. Night Shyamalan

Teenage brother and sister Katara and Sokka (Jackson Rathbone of the *Twilight* films) discover a boy named Aang encased with a flying bison in an iceberg. Aang, the victim of an age-old war of the four nations of Air, Water, Earth, and Fire, is the long-lost Avatar, the only person able to bend the four elements. While Katara and Sokka accompany Aang on his quest to restore harmony to the four nations, others seek to find and destroy him. Dev Patel *(Slumdog*

Millionaire) is Prince Zuko, master Firebender. This film is based on the TV series *Avatar: The Last Airbender*. "Avatar" was dropped from the title to prevent confusion with James Cameron's film. This film received the ignominious honor of the Golden Raspberry Award for Worst Picture of 2011. There is a video game of the same name for Nintendo DS and Wii.

Last Unicorn, The ‡ (1982, Japan/UK/US/West Germany, English/German) Arthur Rankin, Jr. / Jules Bass, AN

Legend ‡ (1986, UK/US, English/Italian) Ridley Scott

Legend of Conan, The (2016, US) director unknown, NYR

As we wrap up work on this book, this is probably the most-anticipated new production in the genre. A follow-up to the classic 1982 film only, and featuring Arnold Schwarzenegger returning as the titular barbarian, *The Legend of Conan* is planned to feature several other actors from the original movie, with possible effects work by the wizards at WETA. There isn't any other concrete information as we go to press, and you might have seen it by now, so we can only ask . . . is it everything we hoped it would be?

Legend of Sudsakorn (2006, Thailand) Krisorn Burmamasing (a.k.a. Kaisorn Buranasing)

Raised in ancient mystic traditions by a beautiful mermaid mother, Sudsakorn—armed with his grandfather's magic staff—follows her loving guidance on a quest to find his father, a prince he's never met. Sudsakorn's bravery and use of magic powers in defeating a savage beast draw the attention of the king, who tasks him with using his powers to rid the land of evil. Accepting this challenge delays the search for his father, in a world where mystics are in great danger. This live-action/ CGI fantasy film is based on a tale from the Thai epic poem *Phra Aphai Mani* by Sunthorn Phu.

Legend of the Tsunami Warrior (2008, Thailand, Thai) Nonzee Nimibutr, US DVD title

A queen and her two daughters battle sea pirates threatening their kingdom. The story involves a magical form of Thai martial arts—*Du Lum*, or ocean sorcery—somewhat powered by fish. Yes, that is strange. The magical art, known by a poor orphan boy of a fishing village and by the evil pirate Black Raven, makes people all-powerful and allows them to breathe underwater and emit sonic screams. Throw in some pretty good swordfighting, and you have an interesting tale somewhat akin to the *Pirates of the Caribbean* films. *Somewhat*.

Legend of the White Snake (1961), see *Panda and the Magic Serpent*

Legend of Zu, The (2001), Hong Kong English title, see *Zu Warriors*

Lion Man (1975), US video title, see *Aslan Adam*

Lionman II: The Witchqueen (1979, Turkey) Mehmet Aslan

This sequel to *Aslan Adam* picks up the story with Lionman ruling his father's land. When Lionman chooses to return to his former life among the lions, leaving the throne to a friend, the sorcery of a beautiful witchqueen and the deadly attacks of his unrelenting enemy King Belisarius besieged him. Ultimately, Lionman and his companions undertake a quest to regain the throne.

Lionman and the Witchqueen (1979), UK video title, see *Lionman II: The Witchqueen*

Lion, the Witch and the Wardrobe, The (1979, UK/US) Bill Melendez, AN/TV

Four children enter a wardrobe and find themselves in Narnia, a fanciful land filled with strange creatures poised on the brink of war between the forces of the evil White Witch and the lion Aslan (*Doctor Who*'s Stephen Thorne). An Emmy Award-winning animated adaptation of the first published book in C.S. Lewis' *Chronicles of Narnia*, this TV movie is a cooperative effort from *Peanuts* television special-producer Bill Melendez and the makers of *Sesame Street*.

Little Prince and the Eight Headed Dragon (1963, Japan, Japanese) Yugo Serikawa, US title, AN

When Prince Susano's mother dies, his father tells him she has gone to another place. Bad move. To a child, a place means you can *go* there. The little prince sets off, collecting artifacts and inadvertently creating serious damage along the way. When he meets a little princess whose village is mortally endangered by an eight-headed dragon, the little prince finds his true calling. Considered an anime landmark, this film is based on a Shinto myth. It has a highly acclaimed score by Akira Ifukube, the man behind legendary *kaiju* soundtracks like *Godzilla*, *Rodan*, and *Mothra*.

Lord of the Rings, The (1978), US short title, see *J. R. R. Tolkien's The Lord of the Rings*

Lord of the Rings: The Fellowship of the Ring, The ‡ (2001, New Zealand) Peter Jackson

Lord of the Rings: The Return of the King, The ‡ (2003, New Zealand) Peter Jackson

Lord of the Rings: The Two Towers, The ‡ (2002, New Zealand) Peter Jackson

Lord Protector: The Riddle of the Chosen (1996), UK/US DVD title, see *Dark Mist, The*

Lords of Magick, The (1989, US) David Marsh

Two young wizard brothers from 10th-century England time-travel to 20th-century California to rescue Princess Lina, kidnapped by an evil sorcerer. This film features a trial for necromancy, urination on an altar, zombie swordfights, pubescent humor involving lady parts, and porn-star Ron Jeremy as a gang member. The final battle involves many spells being bandied about and ultimately the brandishing of swords. Do sorcerers really need swords?

Lost Warrior (1982), Philippines English title, see *Gunan, King of the Barbarians*

Lost World of Sinbad, The (1965, Japan, Japanese) Senkichi Taniguchi

Brave sailor Luzon (Sinbad in the American version) and his libidinous wizard friend undertake a mission to thwart the plans of an evil premier to usurp the throne and marry the daughter of an ailing king. With the help of a band of courageous rebels, they plan to free those who have been enslaved. This film combines adventure, magic, and humor—and in the "you have to see it to believe it" category, a whip dance of virgins.

Loves of Hercules, The (1966), US title, see *Hercules vs. the Hydra*

Lumaban ka, Satanas (1983), Philippines orig. title, see *Killing of Satan, The*

Maciste all'inferno (1963), Italy orig. title, see *Maciste in Hell*

Maciste in Hell (1963, Italy, Italian) Riccardo Freda

Maciste, a Herculean hero complete with greased muscles and Tarzan-like loincloth, takes a long, hard trip to hell to convince a witch who has been burned to undo a curse she has inflicted on the world. Animal lovers, avert your eyes, because on the way Maciste battles lions, tigers, and bears—oh my! Maciste is Kirk Norris, muscleman and dominant force in the Italian peplum films of the early 1960s, playing a variety of godlike heroes.

Magic Serpent, The (1966, Japan, Japanese) Tetsuya Yamauchi

When a Japanese lord is killed and his throne usurped by a villainess and his evil wizard friend, the magic bird of a benevolent wizard rescues the young prince Ikazuki. Years later, Ikazuki undertakes a quest to avenge his parents, using magic skills he has learned from a wizard mentor, who is also slain. In the ultimate battle, the good prince vies against the evil wizard, who transforms into a giant fire-breathing frog and dragon. A great deal of magic and surrealism make this film a fun ride. It is widely believed that this loose retelling of the Japanese folktale *The Tale of the Gallant Jiraiya* was an inspiration for the *Star Wars* saga.

Magic Sword, The (1952, Yugoslavia, Serbo-Croatian) Vojislav Nanovic, US title, B&W

A boy, Nebojsha, inadvertently releases the evil Bas-Celik from a barrel. Years later, he embarks on a quest to find the Magic Sword, the only weapon powerful enough to stop the Bas-Celik's reign of terror and save Nebojsha's kidnapped bride-to-be. This film is based on Serbian folktales.

Magic Sword, The ‡ (1962, US) Bert I. Gordon, *MST3K*

Magic Sword: Quest for Camelot (1998), intl. English title, see *Quest for Camelot*

Magic Voyage of Sinbad, The (1953, Soviet Union, Russian) Aleksandr Ptushko, US dubbed version, *MST3K*

Originally titled *Sadko*, this award-winning adaptation of a Russian epic tale and opera follows the adventures of a bard who travels the globe in search of a bird of happiness to bring back to his homeland. The lesson he learns is one Dorothy Gale covered earlier: sometimes happiness is best found in one's own backyard. Venice Film Festival judges lauded the lead performance of Sergei Stolyarov *(Ruslan and Ludmila)*, but the English-language version changes the hero to Sinbad and camps it up. This is the first of four Ptushko-directed movies featured in this book. Although *Mystery Science Theater 3000* features three of them (this one in a fifth-season episode), they're all well-regarded, visually distinctive fantasy films.

Magic Warriors (1997), France title, see *Warriors of Virtue*

Makai tenshô: mado-hen (1996), Japan orig. title, see *Reborn from Hell 2: Jubei's Revenge*

Makai tenshô: The Armageddon (1999), Japan orig. title, see *Reborn from Hell: Samurai Armageddon*

Maleficent (2014, US) Robert Stromberg

The *Sleeping Beauty* tale best remembered from the 1959 animated Disney classic is re-imagined and told from the perspective of the "villainous" Maleficent (Angelina Jolie of the *Lara Croft* films, *Beowulf*, and the *Kung Fu Panda* films). Now we learn about a betrayal and other events that transpire to shape a woman into an embodiment of evil. The film also explores the relationship between Maleficent and the young Princess Aurora (Elle Fanning of *The Curious Case of Benjamin Button* and *We Bought a Zoo*), who falls victim to a sleeping-curse on her 16th birthday. Vivienne Jolie-Pitt, daughter of Jolie and Brad Pitt, plays Aurora as a toddler.

Masters of the Universe (1987, US) Gary Goddard

In this movie based more on the Mattel toys than the Filmation cartoon, He-Man journeys to Earth via a Cosmic Key after arch-foe Skeletor seizes control of Castle Grayskull on Eternia. Dolph Lundgren (*Rocky IV*, *The Punisher*, *In the Name of the King 2*, both *Expendables* movies) looks the part, the naturally icy eyes of Meg Foster *(They Live)* make her a perfect Evil-Lyn, and Frank Langella *(Dracula, Superman Returns)* chews the scenery as Skeletor. *Friends'* Courteney Cox and *Star Trek: Voyager*'s Robert Duncan McNeill are unwitting teens drawn into the struggle. William Stout *(Conan* movies, *The Warrior and the Sorceress)* is the production designer. Director Gary Goddard intended to pay tribute to comic-book legend Jack Kirby's work on *Fantastic Four*, *Thor*, and the "Fourth World" mythos. Watch to the end of the credits.

Medusa against the Son of Hercules (1963, Italy/Spain, Italian) Alberto de Martino, US TV title

Perseus takes on the hydra-like Medusa, her army of stone warriors, and a treacherous dragon to avenge the death of his father King Argus and vanquish the evil Galinor, who has usurped his throne. No CGI is involved in the creation of the Medusa—only the remarkable talents of special-effects master Carlo Rambaldi *(E.T., Alien, Conan the Destroyer)*. This film retells the legend of Perseus and Medusa, later retold much better in 1981's *Clash of the Titans*. Perseus is actually a son of Hercules, which possibly links this film to the popularity of the many *Hercules* films at the time.

Meraviglie di Aladino, Le (1961), France orig. title, see *Wonders of Aladdin, The*

Merlin (1993, UK) Paul Hunt, AL

This is yet another retelling of the tale of the magical sword of Arthurian legend. This time the Lady of the Lake reincarnates as a reporter in modern times. While part of the tagline promises "a cataclysmic battle for the future," the only thing cataclysmic here is the film itself. Desmond Llewelyn (Q in the James Bond film series) is Dr. Mycroft, which is also the name of Sherlock Holmes' smarter brother. That bit of trivia is possibly more interesting than this film, which also features genre stalwarts Richard Lynch *(The Sword and the Sorcerer)* as Pendragon, and James Hong *(G2: Mortal Conquest).*

Merlin (1998), see *Merlin: The Quest Begins*

Merlin and the Book of Beasts (2010, Canada) Warren P. Sonoda, AL/TV

With a plethora of mythical beasts summoned from his magical book, the sorcerer Arkadian has taken over Camelot. King Arthur's daughter, Avlynn, engages Merlin's services in locating the sword Excalibur and winning back Camelot. James Callis (2000's *Jason and the Argonauts, Battlestar Galactica*) plays Merlin as a Welshman, which is somewhat distracting. A mishmash of Greek mythology mixed with Arthurian legend is also strange, but not as strange as King Arthur having a daughter. Look for the Dark Link reference from *The Legend of Zelda: Ocarina of Time* RPG.

Merlin and the Sword (1985), US video title, see *Arthur the King*

Merlin and the War of the Dragon Emperor (2008), UK DVD title, see *Merlin and the War of the Dragons*

Merlin and the War of the Dragons (2008, US) Mark Atkins, AL/V

Having studied under the wizard known as the Mage, Merlin (Simon Lloyd Roberts of *Dragon Crusaders*) serves King Vortigern long before the birth of Arthur and leads an army to defeat the threat of giant fire-breathing dragons. This film features Merlin's first meeting with Arthur's parents—Uther Pendragon (Dylan Jones of *The 7 Adventures of Sinbad* and *Dragon Crusaders*) and his wife Ingraine (Iona Thonger of *Dragon Crusaders*)—and Uther's eventual ascent to the throne. Jurgen Prochnow *(Das Boot, Twin Peaks: Fire Walk with Me, The Da Vinci Code)* is the Mage.

Merlin: The Magic Begins (1998), see *Merlin: The Quest Begins*

Merlin: The Quest Begins (1998, Canada/US, English/French) David Winning, AL/TV

Merlin is a young man just beginning his medieval magical gig at Arthur's side, using his skills of sorcery to end anarchy that has plagued the land. One of the greatest dangers is Merlin's evil nemesis Nimue, the Lady of the Lake. With Jason Connery (TV's *Robin Hood, Wishmaster 3: Beyond the Gates of Hell*), Sean's boy, as the young Merlin, and Deborah Moore, daughter of Roger Moore, as Nimue, there is a real strong Bond here.

Merlin: The Return (2000, UK) Paul Matthews, AL

Experimentation by scientist Joan Maxwell (Tia Carrere of *Kull the Conquerer*) with the forces on Earth that create and control magic leads to the revival of the world of King Arthur (Patrick Bergin of *Ella Enchanted*) and his knights. (Merlin had magically imprisoned Arthur's would-be assassin, the sorcerer Mordred, in a dimension of eternal darkness and placed Arthur in suspended animation.) Now it's on, as Arthur seeks to reclaim Excalibur and vanquish Mordred (Craig Sheffer of *A River Runs through It*). Although British comic actor Rik Mayall *(The Princess and the Goblin)* plays Merlin as somewhat of a bumbling, doddering, comedic fool, this is a 1,500-year-old you don't want to mess with. *Highlander*'s Adrian Paul is Lancelot.

Merlin: The True Story of Magic (1993), see *Merlin*

Mio in the Land of Faraway (1988, Norway / Soviet Union / Sweden) Vladimir Grammatikov

A genie transports a boy living an unhappy life with adoptive parents to the magical Land of Faraway, where the boy discovers his real father is king and he is actually Prince Mio. Mio and his friend JumJum undertake the task of vanquishing evil Lord Kato and freeing children he has enslaved. Based on the book *Mio, My Mio* by Astrid Lindgren *(Pippi Longstocking)*, this film incorporates many elements that could have inspired the *Harry Potter* series: a child raised by uncaring parents, an evil lord difficult to kill because of a dislodged heart and soul, a cloak of invisibility, and, of course, magic. Christian Bale of the *Batman* films is JumJum, and Christopher Lee *(The Golden Compass)* is Kato.

Mio min Mio (1988), Sweden orig. title, see *Mio in the Land of Faraway*

Mirror, Mirror (2012, US) Tarsem Singh

Snow White (now Snow), trained in the skills of martial arts by the seven dwarfs while living with them in exile, has become adept at fencing and no longer waits for "someday her prince to come." In fact, she rescues Prince Alcott. Julia Roberts, who found her Prince Charming in *Pretty Woman*, is now the evil stepmother of the young woman who takes her life and destiny into her own hands to reclaim her birthright. In this version, directed by Tarsem Singh *(Immortals)*, Snow is newcomer Lily Collins, Prince Alcott is Armie Hammer *(The Social Network)*, and the king is Sean Bean (Boromir of *The Lord of the Rings* films, Zeus in the *Percy Jackson* films). Except for a misguided puppet sequence, gazing into this *Mirror, Mirror* is far from Grimm.

Mondo di Yor, Il (1983), Italy orig. title, see *Yor, the Hunter from the Future*

Mononoke-hime (1999), Japan orig. title, see *Princess Mononoke*

Monty Python and the Holy Grail ‡ (1975, UK) Terry Gilliam / Terry Jones, AL

Monty Python's Jabberwocky (1977), see *Jabberwocky*

Morozko (1965), Soviet Union orig. title, see *Jack Frost*

Mortal Conquest (1999), UK DVD title, see *G2: Mortal Conquest*

Mortal Kombat (1995, US) Paul W.S. Anderson

An interdimensional battle is about to take place, with combatants brought to a distant island to determine the fates of their realms. *Highlander*'s Christopher Lambert leads a multinational cast. This movie weaves in references to the first and second *Mortal Kombat* video games, as well as sampled dialogue. The film's respect for the source material elicited strong support from fans, despite a mixed critical reaction. The soundtrack album from TVT was also a huge hit.

Mortal Kombat 2 (1997), see *Mortal Kombat: Annihilation*

Mortal Kombat: Annihilation (1997, US) John R. Leonetti

Adapting the *Mortal Kombat 3* video game but incorporating game references and unidentified characters to the detriment of story, this sequel features James Remar (*48 Hrs.*, *Dexter* TV-series) as Raiden (the role originated by Christopher Lambert), as well as genre vets Brian Thompson (*Dragonquest*, the *X-Files* TV-series) as Shao Kahn, and Musetta Vander (TV's *Xena: Warrior Princess*) as Sindel. Two American Gladiators duke it out in the final battle. Talisa Soto and Robin Shou reprise their roles from *Mortal Kombat* as Kitana and Liu Kang. The cast also includes Litefoot *(Kull the Conqueror)* as the shaman Nightwolf. The famous Petra temple in Jordan makes another cinematic appearance, and Ray Park (Darth Maul from *Star Wars: Episode I—The Phantom Menace*) has his first film-work playing two characters, Raptor and Tarkatan. He also serves as Remar's stunt double.

Mulan (1998, US, English/Mandarin) Tony Bancroft / Barry Cook, AN

In this retelling of a Chinese folktale, young peasant girl Mulan takes the place of her sickly father in the emperor's army. Her ancestors send a tiny dragon, Mushu, to dissuade her, but after he learns of her passion, he helps Mulan become a great warrior. This first animated Disney film to focus on an Asian heroine also features a magical musical score by Jerry Goldsmith that garnered an Academy Award nomination. The star-studded cast of voice actors includes Eddie Murphy (the *Beverly Hills Cop* films and *Shrek* movies) as Mushu, Pat Morita (*The Karate Kid* films) as the emperor, James Hong *(Merlin)* as Chi-Fu, and George Takei (*Star Trek's* Sulu) as First Ancestor. "Oh, my!"

Mulan II (2005, US) Darrell Rooney / Lynne Southerland, AN/V

In this animated sequel, as Mulan and Shang prepare to marry, the emperor assigns them to escort three princesses from a neighboring kingdom to their betrothed princes as part of an alliance to protect the fate of China. On the way, the princesses fall in love with their guards. Mulan helps them escape their fate so they can follow their hearts and marry the men they love. Love might conquer all, but it probably won't save China. Ming-Na (the *ER* TV-series) and B. D. Wong (the *Law & Order SVU* TV-series) reprise their roles as Mulan and Shang.

Mummy's Island (2006), US title, see *Legend of Sudsakorn*

My First Dragon (2010), Israel English title, see *How to Train Your Dragon*

Myth, The (2007, China / Hong Kong, Cantonese/English/Korean/Mandarin) Stanley Tong, intl. English title

Adventurous world-renowned archaeologist Jack Lee, who dreams of a past life as an ancient Chinese warrior, becomes involved in finding the mausoleum of China's first emperor. Past and present collide in this adventure of tomb raiders, immortality, and Jack's reincarnation: shades of "Indiana Jones meets Lara Croft." Irrepressible martial-arts legend Jackie Chan *(The Forbidden Kingdom)* is Jack.

Naughty Prince's Dragon Slaying, The (1963), intl. literal English title, see *Little Prince and the Eight Headed Dragon*

Neverending Story, The (1984), alternate spelling, see *NeverEnding Story, The*

NeverEnding Story, The ‡ (1984 US / West Germany) Wolfgang Peterson

NeverEnding Story II: The Next Chapter (1991, US / West Germany) George Miller

Jonathan Brandis *(seaQuest DSV)* takes on the lead role as Bastian returns to save Fantasia again. Instead of the Nothing, the wildly original "Emptiness" threatens the fanciful land. Muddled themes involving loss of memory, willingness to take a death-defying leap of faith, and the power of the heart prevent this sequel from coming close to the family-friendly charm of the original. It is loosely adapted from the second half of Michael Ende's novel. A 50th-anniversary Bugs Bunny short, "Box-Office Bunny," accompanied this film in its US theatrical release. Director George T. Miller is no relation to the *Mad Max* series' George Miller, in case you were wondering.

NeverEnding Story III (1996), see *NeverEnding Story III: Escape from Fantasia*

NeverEnding Story III: Escape from Fantasia (1996, Germany/US) Peter MacDonald

This lackluster third installment manages to wring most of the magic out of the franchise, turning it into a tepid high-school drama in which bullies not only torment Bastian (now played by Jason James Richter) but Fantasia as well. A lot of the story—now no longer based on any of Michael Ende's book—involves the Fantasians experiencing the real world, which is not a recipe for joy. There's even an obligatory trip to the mall. Funnyman Jack Black *(Ice Age,* the 2005 *King Kong,* the *Kung Fu Panda* films) makes an early film appearance. The movie's conclusion promises that the story will continue: a threat that, thankfully, has not yet been carried out.

Neverending Story III: Return to Fantasia (1996), UK title, see *NeverEnding Story III: Escape from Fantasia*

Nibelungen, Die (1925), US title, see *Nibelungen: Siegfried, Die*

Nibelungen: Kriemhilds Rache, Die (1928, Germany, German) Fritz Lang, Germany orig. title, B&W/Silent

Determined to avenge the death of Siegfried—sorry, spoilers—Kriemhild accepts a proposal of marriage as part of a plan to launch her campaign against Hagen, the man who murdered her love. It's all-out war for most of this second installment's running time, as family and foes alike fall in epic sequences of carnage that culminate in the burning of a palace. But where is the Nibelungen hoard, a treasure whose location only Hagen might know? Let's leave it at this: this story does not end well for anyone. Characters, plot threads, and themes from this seminal epic ripple through the entire genre.

***Nibelungen: Siegfried, Die* (1925, Germany, German) Fritz Lang, Germany orig. title, B&W/Silent**

Co-written and directed by Fritz Lang, with his wife Thea von Harbou as co-writer, this two-film epic silent adaptation of the 13th-century Middle High German poem *Nibelungenlied* is one of the earliest-known cinematic forays into fantasy that qualify for inclusion in this book. King Siegmund's son Siegfried forges a sword and goes off to woo Princess Kriemhild. When he bathes in dragon's blood to make himself invincible, Siegfried misses a spot. (This will come back to haunt him.) Adventures and family intrigue follow, but Kriemhild will have reason for revenge before this first installment is done. The film features a sixty-foot puppet dragon and an indelibly creepy, iconic sequence involving the image of a skull.

***Nibelungen, Teil 1—Siegfried, Die* (1966, West Germany / Yugoslavia, German) Harald Reinl**

This adaptation of the legendary tale features a Schwarzenegger-esque Uwe Beyer in the title role and alters some aspects of the original story to make things clearer for a mainstream movie-going audience. With beautiful Icelandic vistas and a less-than-convincing dragon, the film tries to replicate the sweep and majesty of Hollywood period-costume epics, and falls considerably short. It was edited together with *Die Nibelungen, Teil 2—Kriemhilds Rache* ten years later into a 110-minute omnibus version titled *Das Schwert der Nibelungen*. One thing people agree on is that Rolf Wilhelm's musical score is a minor masterpiece, available on CD from Cobra Records.

***Nibelungen, Teil 2—Kriemhilds Rache, Die* (1967, West Germany / Yugoslavia, German) Harald Reinl**

With Maria Marlow back as Kriemhild, and the lovely Karin Dor *(You Only Live Twice, The Torture Chamber of Dr. Sadism)* returning as Brunhilde, this second part of the epic adaptation also features Herbert Lom (Hammer Films' *The Phantom of the Opera*, the *Pink Panther* movies) as Etzel. As with *Teil 1—Siegfried*, the quality isn't remotely up to the standard of the 1924 Fritz Lang version but has its charms. Rolf Wilhelm's score for this installment omits strings—they ran out of money to afford the full orchestra of the first part!—but the effect serendipitously matches the story's harder edge.

Nightmare of Christmas (2007), Japan English title, see *Hogfather*

Ninja Resurrection 2: Hell's Spawn (1996), US video title see *Reborn from Hell 2: Jubei's Revenge*

***Ninjas vs. Zombies* (2008, US) Justin Timpane**

A spell to resurrect a dead friend not only brings back the friend but gives him the power to raise an army of the dead. If these guys can't right this wrong … you guessed it: zombies will rule the world. Sometimes you just can't catch a break. Now, to stop that army, seven friends use the same spell to give three of their number the power of the ninja. Why three of seven? Why ninja? Why not watch a different film? References to really good horror-genre films, from *Buffy the Vampire Slayer* to *Dawn of the Dead*, make this film almost watchable. Almost.

Ninja Zombies (2011, US) Noah Cooper

Dameon Kim has nightmares of a samurai trying to save the world from the fury of a malevolent Hell Sword, the Jigoku no Ken, that has the power to raise the dead. After finding an ancestral sword and journal, he realizes the samurai was his ancestor and the evil sword exists. Sadly, his roommate finds the Hell Sword, brings her recently dead brother back to life, and raises a clan of ninja zombies. Now it falls to Dameon and his friends to save the world. Ninjas, swords, magic, and yes, even zombies: what's not to like? Plenty. Troma's Lloyd Kaufman shows up as himself. You've been warned.

Odysseus & the Isle of Mists (2008, Canada/Romania/UK) Terry Ingram, UK orig. title

In this alternate version of *The Odyssey*, Odysseus and his crew crash upon the shore where the Sirens wait instead of bypassing it. In an especially odd circumstance, Homer is a sighted young crewmember recording the journey home from the battle of Troy. Here on the Isle of the Mists, evil queen Persephone, who desires to wed Odysseus, imprisons the crew. Odysseus longs for nothing more than to return to his wife Penelope after his twenty-year voyage. This tale turns Greek mythology upside down and inside out. Arnold Vosloo (*Gor*, the *Mummy* films) is Odysseus, and Stefanie von Pfetten *(Percy Jackson and the Olympians: The Lightning Thief)* is Persephone.

Odysseus: Voyage to the Underworld (2008), US title, see *Odysseus & the Isle of Mists*

Order of the Phoenix, The (2007, US), see *Harry Potter and the Order of the Phoenix*

Orochi the Eight-Headed Dragon (1994, Japan, Japanese) Takao Okawara, US video title

Banished from his father's kingdom after killing his twin brother, Prince Yamato needs to learn to control his overwhelming, potentially dangerous powers. He falls in love with magical priestess Oto. Together with the White Bird of Heaven that rescued him at birth, they must defeat an evil god who manifests as a giant eight-headed dragon/hydra. The prince is no slouch himself. He, too, can turn into a god ... and the throw-down is on to save the world from destruction. Japanese legends and mythology are pervasive in this film, in which the focus is not on the *kaiju* aspect of giant-monster battles—although there is that—but on Japanese sword and sorcery.

Outlaw (1989), US short title, see *Outlaw of Gor*

Outlaw of Gor (1989, US) John "Bud" Cardos, US orig. title, MST3K

This sequel that no one demanded to the first *Gor* brings back the entire cast, including wooden Urbano Barberini as unlikely hero Professor Tarl Cabot, Rebecca Ferratti as the partially clothed Talena, Nigel Chipps as the midget Hup, and Jack Palance *(Batman, City Slickers)* as the oily Xeno. Palance appeared in the final ten minutes of the previous film to set up this adventure, made easier by the fact that both movies were shot at the same time. When you get people to commit to making a *Gor* movie, you'd better make the most of it. The *Mystery Science Theater 3000* team survives this one in a fifth-season episode, "Cabot."

Pagan Queen, The (2010, Czech Republic / US) Constantin Werner

Libuse, a Slavic seeress of 8th-century Bohemia bestowed with supernatural powers, rules the land with her two beautiful sisters and an all-female army led by her friend, the Amazon Vlasta. To satisfy her people's desire for a king, Libuse weds her lover, the farmer Premysl. He allows power to overtake him. Vlasta, secretly in love with Libuse, leads her army in the Maiden War against all men. This film is based on Czech legend and German fairytales, particularly the story *The Crown of Vysehrad*.

Pagemaster, The (1994, US) Pixote Hunt / Joe Johnston, AN/Live

When young, fearful Richard Tyler (Macaulay Culkin of *Home Alone*) escapes a storm by dodging into a library, he's knocked unconscious and awakens to a wild adventure. Transformed into an animated illustration by the Pagemaster, Tyler must overcome challenges within the world of books to return to his real life. Personified book genres, represented by Patrick Stewart (Adventure), Whoopi Goldberg (Fantasy), Frank Welker (Horror), and an entire "library" of other characters—as well as the librarian Pagemaster, Mr. Dewey—help the boy find strength and courage. Leonard Nimoy does the voices of Jekyll and Hyde. The aforementioned actors are all related to various *Star Trek* projects. James Horner provides a delightful musical score. Did you catch the Mr. Dewey library reference?

Paladin: Dawn of the Dragonslayer (2012), see *Dawn of the Dragonslayer*

Paladini-storia d'armi e d'amori, I (1983), Italy orig. title, see *Hearts and Armour*

Panda and the Magic Serpent (1961, Japan, Japanese) Kazuhiko Okabe / Taiji Yabushita, US title, AN

Years after the boy Xu-Xian is forced to give up his pet snake, the snake magically transforms into the beautiful princess Bai-Niang. With the help of his panda friends and the will of Bai-Niang to remain in human form, love conquers all. Japan's first feature-length anime and first widescreen, color, animated film (very obviously inspired by Disney animation), this visually appealing adaptation of the Chinese folktale *Madame White Snake* also has pleasant musical themes.

Pan's Labyrinth (2007, Mexico/Spain/US, Spanish), intl. English title, Guillermo del Toro

This very adult, gothic fairytale set in 1944 fascist Spain tells the tale of a young girl, Ofelia, totally absorbed in stories of magical lands, only to find out she is a princess who must perform three horrific tasks to take her rightful place and be united with her father, the king. But is this fantasy world a reality or just an escape from Ofelia's harsh life? The Pale Man (Doug Jones of the *Hellboy* films), with his eyes in his palms, is one of the most disturbing creatures in film history. Writer-director Guillermo del Toro also wrote and directed the *Hellboy* films and co-wrote the 2012-2014 *Hobbit* films.

Percy Jackson & the Olympians: The Lightning Thief (2010, Canada/US, English/Turkish) Chris Columbus

Teenager Percy (Logan Lerman of *Gamer*) finds out from his best friend Grover (Brandon T. Jackson) that he is a demigod, son of the Greek god of the sea, Poseidon. When they travel with Percy's mother to Camp Half-Blood, training grounds for demigods, a minotaur attacks her, and she disappears. With Grover and a new friend, the beautiful Annabeth (Alexandra Daddario of TV's *Parenthood, White Collar*), they embark on a quest to the underworld to save Percy's mother from Hades and retrieve a stolen lightning bolt of Zeus. Very loosely based on the first book in a young-adult fantasy series of the same title by Rick Riordan, this film has an all-star cast that includes Sean Bean *(The Lord of the Rings* films, *Game of Thrones)* as Zeus, Pierce Brosnan (James Bond films) as Chiron / Mr. Brunner, Uma Thurman (*The Adventures of Baron Munchausen*, the *Kill Bill* films) as Medusa, and Kevin McKidd *(Brave)* as Poseidon. There is a RPG video game of the same name for Nintendo DS by Activision.

Percy Jackson & the Olympians: The Sea of Monsters (2013, USA) Thor Freudenthal

Back for another adventure, Percy (Logan Lerman of *The Perks of Being a Wallflower*) and his friends Grover (Brandon T. Jackson) the satyr and Annabeth (Alexandra Daddario of *Bereavement*), Athena's daughter, search for the Golden Fleece to save Camp Half-Blood from sea monsters. New to the team of young demigods are Ares' daughter Clarisse La Rue (Leven Rambin of *The Hunger Games*) and Percy's newly discovered half-brother—and very tall cyclops—Tyson (Douglas Smith of TV's *Big Love*). Another welcome addition to the cast is Nathan Fillion (TV's *Firefly* and *Castle*) as Hermes the messenger-god, appropriately a UPS courier in our world. The story is based on Rick Riordan's book *The Sea of Monsters*.

Perseo l'invincibile (1963), Italy orig. title, see *Medusa against the Son of Hercules*

Perseus against the Monsters (1963), see *Medusa against the Son of Hercules*

Perseus the Invincible (1963), literal English title, see *Medusa against the Son of Hercules*

Peter Pan (1924, US) Herbert Brenon, B&W/Silent

Peter Pan arrives at the home of the Darling family, and with a sprinkle of pixie dust, Wendy, Michael, and John fly off to Neverland for the adventure of a lifetime with the nefarious Captain Hook and his pirate crew. In this silent-film version, the title cards offer quotes from J. M. Barrie's book upon which it's based.

Peter Pan (1953, US, ASL/English) Clyde Geronomi / Wilfred Jackson / Hamilton Luske, AN

This retelling of the J. M. Barrie tale of the adventures of Never Land, with Peter Pan, Tinkerbell, the Darling children, Captain Hook (Hans Conried of 1977's *The Hobbit*), and the pirate crew, is a Walt Disney animated feature film with highly memorable iconic visual versions of the characters. Think of *Peter Pan,* and these are most likely the characters you envision.

Peter Pan **(1960, US) Vincent J. Donehue, TV**

In this magical, musical retelling of *Peter Pan* in a TV stage-production, Peter (as sung and acted by Mary Martin) makes it absolutely, perfectly clear: "I won't grow up." Cyril Ritchard deliciously plays the villainous Captain Hook. Children of the '60s carried these songs in their heads for a lifetime, remembering, "I'll never grow up, not me." Martin and Ritchard reprise their Tony Award-winning roles in this Emmy Award-winning performance.

Peter Pan **(2000, US) Glenn Casale / Gary Halvorson, TV**

This TV presentation of the *Peter Pan* tale's Broadway revival stars Olympian Cathy Rigby. It captures the dark and dangerous aspects of Neverland from the J. M. Barrie novel. Scarier and truer to the book than earlier versions, it nevertheless strays from the original story when Captain Hook's first mate, Smee, returns to the Darling nursery with the Lost Boys.

Peter Pan **(2003, Australia/UK/US) P. J. Hogan**

In this retelling of the adventures of the Darling children whisked away by the ever-young Peter Pan to Neverland, they battle the pirate crew led by Captain Hook. Jason Isaacs, best known as Lucius Malfoy of the *Harry Potter* films, is Mr. Darling as well as Captain Hook. Rachel Hurd-Wood *(Solomon Kane)* is Wendy. This might be the quintessential film-version of the J. M. Barrie tale. It presents an excellent combination of heart and high adventure.

Peter Pan in Return to Never Land (2002), Australia DVD title, see *Return to Never Land*

Pirates of Langkasuka, The (2008), Netherlands DVD title, see *Legend of the Tsunami Warrior*

Pirates of the Caribbean: At World's End **(2007, US) Gore Verbinski**

Overlong, overcomplicated, and at times painful to watch, with pure visual chaos, this "everyone and everything and ye olde kitchen sink" third chapter in the saga finds Jack (Johnny Depp of *Ed Wood* and *Donnie Brasco*) out of his mind (more than usual), Davy Jones (Bill Nighy of *The Hitchhiker's Guide to the Galaxy*) working with the East India Trading Company, and everyone sinking into a whirlpool that neatly symbolizes the out-of-control production in which it appears. Anyone rooting for the romantic leads is also out of luck, since their fortunes take a dark turn that leaves a bad taste in viewers' mouths, like sand and bad rum. Rock legend Keith Richards, Depp's template for Jack, appears as Jack's dad, Captain Teague.

Pirates of the Caribbean: Dead Man's Chest **(2006, US, English/Greek/Mandarin/Turkish) Gore Verbinski**

The first sequel in this powerhouse Disney franchise expands the world of Captain Jack Sparrow (Johnny Depp of *From Hell*) to include much more than just cursed skeletal pirates— and that's not entirely a good thing. Stunning CGI effects bring the tentacled Davy Jones (Bill Nighy of *Love Actually* and *Shaun of the Dead*) to life, but the story—intended to set up a grander mythology leading into a third installment—spirals out of control. Will (Orlando

Bloom—Legolas of *The Lord of the Rings* and *The Hobbit* films) unites with his father Bootstrap (Stellan Skarsgard of *Beowulf & Grendel*) and a mystic named Tia Dalma (Naomie Harris of *28 Days Later*), which sets up the admittedly delightful if manipulative cliffhanger ending, in which the Kraken takes Jack beneath the sea.

Pirates of the Caribbean: On Stranger Tides (2011, US, English/Spanish) Rob Marshall

Chucking almost all the continuity from the previous three films overboard, this fourth installment finds Captain Jack Sparrow (Johnny Depp of *Sleepy Hollow* and *Corpse Bride*) chasing after the Fountain of Youth, with old rival Barbossa (Geoffrey Rush of *Shakespeare in Love*, *The King's Speech*, and *Green Lantern*) in hot pursuit, having now shifted allegiance to join the imperial establishment. Depp's Jack is still a frenetic joy, as is Rush's wry Barbossa, but rather than revitalizing the series, this fourth film feels like a desperate attempt to wring more money out of a tired franchise. Other sequels are apparently on the horizon, so . . . yo ho ho! Keith Richards returns, and some other zombies appear as well.

Pirates of the Caribbean: The Curse of the Black Pearl ‡ (2003, US) Gore Verbinski

Power of J2M2, The (2003), TV title, see *Land of the Little People*

Prince Caspian (2008), intl. short English title, see *Chronicles of Narnia: Prince Caspian, The*

Prince in Wonderland (1963), see *Little Prince and the Eight Headed Dragon*

Prince of Persia (2010), US short title, see *Prince of Persia: The Sands of Time*

Prince of Persia: The Sands of Time (2010, US) Mike Newell

Fugitive prince Daston and fearless princess Tamina literally race against time to stop diabolical nobleman Sheik Amar from unleashing the power of an ancient dagger, a gift from the gods allowing its possessor to control the sands of time. Jake Gyllenhaal *(Brokeback Mountain)* is Daston, and Gemma Arterton (the *Clash of the Titans* remake) is Tamina. Alfred Molina *(Spider-Man 2, The Sorcerer's Apprentice)* also features, as Sheik Amar, as does Ben Kingsley *(Ghandi, BloodRayne)* as Dastan's uncle Nizam. Mike Newel *(Harry Potter and the Goblet of Fire)* directs. This movie is based on the *Prince of Persia* videogame franchise and co-written by the game's creator Jordan Mechner. The original 1989 game from Ubisoft Montreal was the first to use rotoscoping. (See also Ralph Bakshi's *The Lord of the Rings*.)

Princess and the Cobbler, The (1995), see *Thief and the Cobbler, The*

Princess and the Goblin, The (1994, Hungary/Japan/UK) József Gémes, AN

Princess Irene and her friend Curdie, a boy warrior, save their kingdom from being overthrown by a goblin family, with Curdie's knowledge of mining and enchanted thread, and the help of Princess Irene's magical great-great-grandmother (voiced by Claire Bloom of *Doctor Who*, "The End of Time"). This is a truly sweet film for young children, albeit slightly scary. Other voices include Joss Ackland *(The Thief and the Cobbler)*, Roy Kinnear *(Hawk the Slayer)*, and Rik Mayall *(Merlin: The Return)*. This first animated feature film from Wales is based on the 1872 fantasy novel of the same name by George MacDonald.

Princess Bride, The ‡ (1987, US) Rob Reiner

Princess Bride Story, The (1987), Japan English title, see *Princess Bride, The*

Princess Mononoke (1999, Japan, Japanese) Hayao Miyazaki, AN

Ashitaka, a young Japanese warrior seeking a cure from a deadly curse, lands in the middle of a mystical battle between forest gods and a mining colony. He encounters San, also known as Princess Mononoke, a human girl raised by a wolf deity and able to communicate with the spirits of nature. Ashitaka's efforts to establish peace are thwarted, because each side of the dispute believes he favors the other side. In this dynamic, stunning film, director Hayao Miyazaki takes animation to a highly sophisticated level.

Prince Valiant (1998, Germany/Ireland/UK) Anthony Hickox, AL

Prince Valiant, squire to Sir Gawain, now posing as the fallen knight in a case of mistaken identity, joins in a quest with Princess Ilene, whom he escorts to her fiancé so that he might retrieve the magic sword Excalibur stolen from King Arthur. Based on the comic strip created by Hal Foster in 1937, this film contains some segments of comic-book animation, with a voice-over. It features Stephen Moyer (TV's *True Blood*) as Prince Valiant, a teenage Katherine Heigl (TV's *Roswell* and *Grey's Anatomy*) as Princess Ilene, Warwick Davis (the *Harry Potter* films, *Willow*, *Labyrinth*, *The Chronicles of Narnia*), Ron Perlman (the *Hellboy* films), and Zach Galligan *(Arthur's Quest)*. Those wishing to explore the world of the titular character might wish to check out *Prince Valiant: The Storytelling Game,* released in 1989 from Chaosium. The unique system uses coin tosses to help determine task resolution.

Puen yai jon salad (2008), orig. title, see *Legend of the Tsunami Warrior*

Queen and Warrior (2000), Japan English title, see *Heart of the Warrior*

Queen of the Naked Steel (1985), Sweden video title, see *Barbarian Queen*

Queens of Langkasuka (2008), intl. English title, see *Legend of the Tsunami Warrior*

Quest for Camelot (1998, US) Frederik Du Chau, AL/AN

Young Kayley aspires to become a Knight of the Round Table like her father, who sacrifices his life to save King Arthur. When evil Ruber kidnaps Kayley's mother, Kayley embarks on a quest with a blind hermit, a bird, and a two-headed dragon to find Excalibur and save her mother, King Arthur, and Camelot. This animated film, loosely based on Vera Chapman's novel *The King's Damosel,* features a star-studded cast of voices, including Cary Elwes *(The Princess Bride),* Gary Oldman (the *Harry Potter* films), singer Celine Dion, and Pierce Brosnan (the James Bond and *Percy Jackson* movies), with John Gielgud *(Dragonheart)* as Merlin, and Eric Idle *(Monty Python and the Holy Grail)* and comedian Don Rickles as the two-headed dragon.

Quest for the Mighty Sword (1990, Italy, Italian) Joe D'Amato, Italy orig. title

D'Amato triumphantly returns to the Ator series for this fourth and final film, but this time star Miles O'Keeffe has wised up and fled to pastures new. Eric Allan Kramer, who played Thor two years earlier in *The Incredible Hulk Returns* and would one day play Little John in Mel Brooks' *Robin Hood: Men in Tights*, takes on the role of Ator's grown son: not a resumé-builder. A creature costume from *Troll 2* is frugally recycled, as is Laura Gemser of *Emanuelle* fame. D'Amato considered this *Ator III*, and some called it *Troll 3*. Either way, it's three times the tedium.

Quest of the Delta Knights (1994, US) James Dodson, MST3K/V

With a plot lifted from Robert Heinlein's *Citizen of the Galaxy*, title music repurposed from *Battle beyond the Stars*, and location shooting at a California renaissance festival, how could this not turn out to be a mind-numbing gauntlet of pain? Anachronisms abound as dignified British character-actor David Warner (Evil, from *Time Bandits*, among many other appearances in this book) gamely takes on the film's narration and two different roles, occasionally even sharing the screen with himself! Olivia Hussey *(The Dark Mist)* also appears—and oh, look: Sarah Douglas *(Attack of the Gryphon)* shows up again. *Mystery Science Theater 3000* gives this a justifiable skewering in a ninth-season episode.

Ragewar (1985), see *Dungeonmaster, The*

Rainbow Bridge (1963) see *Little Prince and the Eight Headed Dragon*

Reborn from Hell 2: Jubei's Revenge (1996, Japan, Japanese) Kazumasa Shirai

In this first film produced in the saga, with a story that picks up from the end of the prequel, *Reborn from Hell: Samurai Armageddon*—confusing, isn't it?—Jubei is (again) charged with saving the world, slaying an army of undead demons, and rescuing Princess Ohiro from an evil necromancer. This time it's a father-son thing. The same father who made Jubei a one-eyed samurai in the first place is now one of the resurrected demons. There's a warm and fuzzy moment when Jubei cradles his father's head after cutting it off; it's these memories you treasure.

Reborn from Hell: Samurai Armageddon (1999, Japan, Japanese) Kazumasa Shirai, US video title

In this prequel to *Reborn from Hell 2: Jubei's Revenge* (given that English-language title to clarify its chronological position in the saga), an evil sorcerer releases seven samurai warriors "reborn from hell" to help him conquer the world. When one-eyed samurai Jubei slays one of the demons, he realizes he's found his calling. This is an uneven adventure, but then again, there are the nude sacrificial virgins . . . *lots* of nude sacrificial virgins.

Red Sonja ‡ (1985, Netherlands/US) Richard Fleischer

Red Sword, The (2006), France DVD title, see *Tristan & Isolde* (2006)

Reign of Fire **(2002, Ireland/UK/US) Rob Bowman**

In a world in the not-too-distant future, fire-breathing dragons have devastated the Earth, and humanity struggles to survive. The British Quinn (Christian Bale of *Mio in the Land of Faraway* and the *Batman* films), who as a boy lost his mother when the siege began, meets gruff American dragonslayer Van Zan (Matthew McConaughey of *A Time to Kill*) and his group of ex-soldiers. Quinn leads a group of survivalists waiting for the dragons to die off. So far, bad plan. Van Zan believes there is only one male; kill him, and the ladies are dead meat: a new plan, worth a shot. Don't think too hard or question too much, and enjoy the action. The video game *Reign of Fire* for Game Boy, Xbox, GameCube, and PlayStation 2 is based on this film.

Return of Jafar, The **(1994, US) Toby Shelton / Tad Stones / Alan Zaslove, AN/V**

In this second film in the animated *Aladdin* trilogy, Aladdin lives a royal life and the evil Jafar, once advisor to the sultan and now an evil genie, has big-time plans of revenge against Aladdin and his friends. Add to this the betrayal of Jafar's parrot, Iago, who now cozies up to the Aladdin clan. Comedian Gilbert Gottfried voices Iago, both of whom are somewhat annoying yet entertaining.

Return of the Jedi (1983), US short title, see *Star Wars: Return of the Jedi*

Return of the King, The **(1980, US) Arthur Rankin, Jr. / Jules Bass, AN/TV**

Where there's a whip there's a way: this animated adaptation of the Tolkien saga cannily picks up where the otherwise unrelated Ralph Bakshi-produced *Lord of the Rings* animated feature film leaves off. A follow-up to Rankin/Bass's *The Hobbit*, this feature uses the same character designs as well as returning voice talents Orson Bean (as both Bilbo and Frodo Baggins), John Huston *(Battle for the Planet of the Apes)* as Gandalf, and Brother Theodore as Gollum, with the addition of Roddy McDowall (the *Planet of the Apes* films) as Samwise. For anyone who grew up with this version of the tale, no other adaptation will ever match its charm ... but its significant omissions justifiably irk dedicated Tolkien fans. The songs are infectious or annoying, depending on your point of view.

Return of the King, The (2003), US short title, see *Lord of the Rings: The Return of the King, The*

Return to Never Land (2002, Australia/Canada/US) Robin Budd / Donovan Cook, AN

In World War II London, Wendy has grown up and is the mother of Jane and Danny. When the villainous Captain Hook kidnaps Jane—believing she is Wendy—to help him capture Peter Pan, the pragmatic Jane realizes her mother's frivolous tales of Never Never Land are all too real. Even then, Peter's efforts to return Jane home will be ill-fated unless she comes to believe in the magic and power of imagination. According to Peter, "All you need is faith and trust, and a little bit of pixie dust." The cast includes the voice of Roger Rees (TV's *Cheers*, *The Scorpion King*, *Robin Hood: Men in Tights*). This is a sequel to the classic 1953 animated Disney film.

Ring of the Nibelungs (2006), Germany orig. title, see *Curse of the Ring*

Rise of the Guardians (2012, France/US) Peter Ramsey

This computer-animated 3D fantasy, inspired by William Joyce's book series, *The Guardians of Childhood*, has an edgy take on legends we've come to love. Pitch, the Nightmare King (Jude Law of the *Sherlock Holmes* films), plans to throw the world into darkness, so the Immortal Guardians band together to protect the innocence and imagination of all children. Santa, or North (Alec Baldwin of *The Hunt for Red October*), a sword-wielding warrior with a thick Russian accent, heads up a team that also includes the Easter Bunny (Hugh Jackman of the *X-Men* films); the Tooth fairy, or just "Tooth" (Isla Fisher of the *BeastMaster* TV-series); Jack Frost (Chris Pine of *Star Trek*); and the silent Sandman, a sort of legendary Harpo Marx. *Hellboy*'s Guillermo del Toro executive-produces. A video game based on the film is available for Xbox 360, PlayStation 3, and the Nintendo Wii, Wii U, DS, and 3DS.

Robin Hood: Men in Tights (1993, US) Mel Brooks

While benevolent King Richard (Patrick Stewart of *The Pagemaster* and the *X-Men* films) is busy with the Crusades, ruthless brother Prince John (comedian Richard Lewis) oppresses the populace. Meanwhile, Robin Hood (Cary Elwes of *The Princess Bride*) steals from the rich, gives to the poor, vanquishes the sheriff of Rottingham (Roger Rees of *The Scorpion King*), and rescues Maid Marian (Amy Yasbeck of *Dracula: Dead and Loving It*) with the help of his odd band of compatriots, including blind watchman Blinkin (Mark Blankfield of *Jekyll and Hyde . . . Together Again*), Will Scarlett O'Hara (Matthew Porretta, Robin himself in TV's *The New Adventures of Robin Hood*), Asneeze (composer-musician Isaac Hayes), and Asneeze's son Ahchoo (comedian Dave Chappelle). Tracey Ullman *(The Corpse Bride)* is the witch-hag Latrine, and Dom Deluise (the *Cannonball Run* films) lampoons Don Corleone as Don Giovanni. Welcome to irreverent parody as only Mel Brooks can do it. Robert Ridgely reprises his role of the hangman from *Blazing Saddles*. Another reference to that film and a reference to Brooks' *History of the World: Part I* also turn up. Not one of Brooks' best, this is still a fun ride, from misleading shadow-swordplay to a magic pill that's a Life Saver (the candy).

Ronal Barbaren (2011), Denmark orig. title, see *Ronal the Barbarian*

Ronal the Barbarian (2011, Denmark, Danish) Kresten Vestbjerg Andersen / Thorbjorn Christoffersen / Philip Einstein Lipski, 3D/AN

In this coming-of-age tale of geeky, gawky teen Ronal, growing up in a barbarian village and avoiding the quests of his muscle-bound kinsmen, he jumps into action when the evil Volcazar kidnaps his tribe. In his quest to claim a sacred sword to save his people before Volcazar can summon the beasts of hell, he gains the company of a warrior maiden, a metrosexual elf, and a sex-crazed apprentice. The voice cast of this clever take on the *Conan* films includes *Conan* veteran Sven–Ole Thorsen *(Conan the Barbarian, Conan the Destroyer)* and Brigitte Nielsen *(Red Sonja)*.

Ruslan and Ludmila (1972, Soviet Union, Russian) Aleksandr Ptushko

Dwarf sorcerer Chernomor, whose long white beard grants him incredible strength, kidnaps beautiful princess-bride Ludmila from her wedding feast. Warrior-hero Ruslan (Sergei Stolyarov of *The Magic Voyage of Sinbad*) must defeat the sorcerer to rescue his bride. The quest involves confronting a giant magical head in a thick fog to obtain a knife that he can use to cut off Chernomor's beard. This film is based on a Russian tale written as a poem by Alexander Pushkin and later repurposed as a beloved opera by Glinka.

Ruslan i Lyudmila (1972), Soviet Union orig. title, see *Ruslan and Ludmila*

Sadko (1953), Soviet Union orig. title, see *Magic Voyage of Sinbad, The*

SAGA: Curse of the Shadow (2013, US) John Lyde, V

This plucky little low-budget adventure with a bounty-hunter elf named Nemyt (the alluring Danielle Chuchran) and a quest to stop the rise of the Undead God was hard to track down, because it pops up in different sources as *Curse of the Dragon Slayer, Dragon Lore: Curse of the Shadow*, and *SAGA: The Shadow Cabal*. Pick a title, guys! As for the character names, Goth Azul and Fangtor Bloodmoon sound like they were cribbed from old RPG books, and the mermaids are named after a running gag from a *Seinfeld* episode.

SAGA: The Shadow Cabal (2013), see *SAGA: Curse of the Shadow*

Salamander (2002), Japan English title, see *Reign of Fire*

Sampo (1964), Finland orig. title, see *Day the Earth Froze, The*

Samurai Pirate (1965), Hong Kong video title, see *Lost World of Sinbad, The*

Sangraal, la spada di fuoco (1983), Italy orig. title, see *Sword of the Barbarians, The*

San wa (2007), Hong Kong orig. title, see *Myth, The*

Scorpion King, The (2002, Belgium/Germany/US) Chuck Russell

This prequel to the sequel prologue in *The Mummy Returns* features the origin and rise to power of the titular Mathayus. Aided by the beautiful sorceress Cassandra, who can predict the victories of the malevolent King Memnon, that tyrant plans to take over the ancient world. Free tribes hire assassin Mathayus to kill the sorceress, so Mathayus enlists the aid of the formidable Nubian king, Balthazar, and the horse thief Arpid. When the plan unravels, an enemy becomes an ally. Dwayne "the Rock" Johnson *(The Mummy Returns)* stars, with Michael Clarke Duncan *(Delgo)* as Balthazar, Roger Rees (TV's *Cheers* and *Warehouse 13*) as King Pheron, and Peter Facinelli (the *Twilight* films) as Prince Takmet. *The Scorpion King: Rise of the Akkadian* video game for PlayStation 2 is based on this film.

458 • Cinema and Sorcery

Scorpion King 3: Battle for Redemption, The **(2012, Thailand) Roel Reiné, V**

How the mighty have fallen. Mathayus has lost his kingdom and his wife and now hires out as an assassin. In a final effort to reclaim power, Mathayus takes a job defending the kingdom of King Horus against Horus's brother Talus and an army of ghost warriors. This film is an anachronistic, cultural mishmash. Ron Perlman (the *Hellboy* films) as King Horus is as good as ever, and Billy Zane *(The Phantom)* as Talus is as bad. Talus's comment, "I will rise like a bad idea," pretty much describes the film. The battle for redemption has failed.

Scorpion King: Rise of a Warrior, The **(2008, Germany / South Africa / US) Russell Mulcahy, V**

In this prequel to the prequel of the sequel prologue in *The Mummy Returns*, young Mathayus seeks to avenge the deaths of his father—a captain in the military corps of Black Scorpions—and later his brother at the hands of ruthless military leader and dark sorcerer Sargon, who has claimed the throne in ancient Akkad. With a band of friends, Mathayus undertakes a quest to the underworld to obtain the Sword of Damocles with which to kill Sargon, while Sargon's ally, the war-goddess/sorceress Astarte, plans to keep the enchanted sword. This battle molds Mathayus into the mighty warrior he is destined to become.

Season of the Witch **(2011, US) Dominic Sena**

Two 14th-century knights return from the Crusades to find their homeland devastated by the Black Plague. A young woman is accused of being a witch and causing the death and destruction. The knights must deliver her to a remote monastery, where the curse can be lifted. Save your sympathy for this poor misunderstood waif until the end, when a horrific force is unleashed, threatening the fate of humanity. Nicolas Cage *(National Treasure, The Sorcerer's Apprentice)* and Ron Perlman (come on—the *Hellboy* films) are the Teutonic knights, with a cameo appearance by Christopher Lee *(The Colour of Magic)* as a dying cardinal. The cast also includes Stephen Graham *(Pirates of the Carribean: On Stranger Tides)* and Claire Foy (TV's *Upstairs Downstairs*) as the troubled girl.

Secret of Kells, The **(2009, Belgium/France/Ireland) Tomm Moore / Nora Twomey, AN**

In a town in danger by marauding Vikings, Brother Adrian, a master illuminator, mentors young Brendan to complete the magical Book of Kells, which, according to legend, can turn dark into light and save his town. Brendan undertakes a dangerous quest into the woods, where woodland nymph Aisling befriends and protects him. This richly animated film, which incorporates visually stunning Celtic artwork and is accented by a sparing Celtic music score, received an Oscar nomination for Best Animated Feature. This is a fictional account of the actual Book of Kells, an illuminated Latin-manuscript Gospel book.

Secret of Moonacre, The **(2010, Australia / France / Hungary / New Zealand / UK / US) Gabor Csupo**

After the death of her father, 13-year-old Maria Merriweather (Dakota Blue Richards of *The Golden Compass*) goes to Moonacre Manor to live with her eccentric uncle. There she discovers she is the last Moon Princess and the only hope for Moonacre. She and her newfound friends must dispel an ancient curse on the magical kingdom before it disappears into the sea. Tim Curry *(The Rocky Horror Picture Show, Clue)* also stars. This film is based on the novel *The Little White Horse* by Elizabeth Goudge.

Secret of NIMH, The (1982, US) Don Bluth, AN

In an attempt to save her home and family, widowed field mouse Mrs. Brisby seeks the aid of a society of super-intelligent rats, escapees from a human scientific facility whom her late husband once aided. The wise leader of the rats gives Mrs. Brisby an amulet that gives a courageous wearer magical power. The dramatic adventure tests Brisby's courage and that of her newfound friends. This is based on the children's book *Mrs. Frisby and the Rats* by Robert C. O'Brien. It debuts (vocally, anyway) Shannen Doherty (the *Charmed* TV-series) and Wil Wheaton *(Star Trek: The Next Generation)* and also features Derek Jacobi *(I, Claudius)*, and—as Mrs. Brisby—Elizabeth Hartman *(A Patch of Blue)*, in her final film. This is Jerry Goldsmith's first animated film score, with the memorable song "Flying Dreams" sung by Paul Williams.

Secret of the Sword, The (1985, US) Ed Friedman / Lou Kachivas / Marsh Lamore / Bill Reed / Gwen Wetzler, AN

In this animated *Masters of the Universe* spin-off, He-Man goes on a quest to deliver a magic jeweled sword to the land of Etheria. While Adora, leader of the Evil Horde army, holds him captive, the sorceress of Grayskull reveals to Adora that she is He-Man's twin sister, kidnapped at birth. As Adora raises the magic sword and summons the power of Grayskull, she transforms into the princess She-Ra. This film is a compilation of the first five episodes of the *She-Ra: Princess of Power* television series but was released theatrically before the show debuted. Skeletor is Alan Oppenheimer, prolific TV actor in both live (TV's *The Six Million Dollar Man*) and animated roles. FASA released a simplified roleplaying game titled *The Masters of the Universe Roleplaying Game* this same year. L. Ross Babcock III designed it as an introductory RPG for children and families.

Seeker, The (2007, US), see *Seeker: The Dark Is Rising, The*

Seeker: The Dark Is Rising, The (2007, US) David L. Cunningham

Teenager Will Stanton (Alexander Ludwig of *Race to Witch Mountain*) discovers that he is the last of a group of immortal warriors known as The Light, who fight the forces of The Dark. Through time-travel, Will learns information that helps him face forces of incredible power. The Dark is rising, and only Will can save the world. This movie is based on Susan Cooper's book *The Dark Is Rising*, part of a five-volume series. Fans of the book consider the Americanization of the story akin to sacrilege. It features Ian McShane (2010's *The Sorcerer's Apprentice, Pirates of the Caribbean: On Stranger Tides, Snow White and the Huntsman*) and Christopher Eccleston (TV's *Doctor Who*) as The Rider, the representation of The Dark, riding on horseback to presage disaster like an evil Paul Revere.

Sette fatiche di Alì Babà, Le (1963), Italy orig. title, see *Seven Tasks of Ali Baba, The*

Sette magnifici gladiatori, I (1984), Italy orig. title, see *Seven Magnificent Gladiators, The*

Seven Curses of Lodac, The (1962), intl. English title, see *Magic Sword, The* (1962)

Seven Magnificent Gladiators, The (1984, Italy) Claudio Fragasso / Bruno Mattei

The barbarian Han forms a band of seven, and with the help of the magical Sword of Achilles seeks to vanquish an evil marauding demigod who annually terrorizes a peasant village by murdering all boys who have reached manhood. It's pretty much the *Seven Samurai,* and by extension *The Magnificent Seven,* but without all the good stuff. The cast includes Lou Ferrigno *(The Incredible Hulk, Hercules),* B-movie queen Sybil Danning (Ferrigno's co-star in *Hercules*), and Ferrigno's real-life wife Carla Ferrigno as Pandora.

Seven Tasks of Ali Baba, The (1963, Italy, Italian) Emimmo Salvi

A benevolent wizard charges Ali Baba with delivering a sacred crown to a neighboring country to free the people from an evil despot. Ali Baba and his companions are sadistically tortured for the whereabouts of the crown, which safely rests in the cave that responds to "Open Sesame." In downtime between torture sessions, a steamy sexual relationship develops with the evil one's daughter; she might well be six of those seven tasks. Rod Flash—probably not his real name—is Ali Baba . . . every well-oiled muscle of him.

Seventh Son (2015, Canada/UK/US) Sergey Bodrov

In the 18th century, Master Gregory (Jeff Bridges of *TRON, Starman,* and *Iron Man*) must train the "seventh son," a "chosen one" named Tom Ward, played by Ben Barnes *(Stardust, The Chronicles of Narnia: Prince Caspian, The Chronicles of Narnia: The Dawn Treader)* as they face the malevolence of Mother Malkin (Julianne Moore of *Boogie Nights, Children of Men,* and the remake of *Carrie*). This is very loosely based on Joseph Delaney's *Wardstone Chronicles* (*The Last Apprentice* in the US) book series.

Sfida dei giganti, La (1965), Italy orig. title, see *Hercules the Avenger*

Shadow of the Knight (1999), US video title, see *Dragonworld: The Legend Continues*

Shu shan zheng zhuan (2001), Hong Kong orig. title, see *Zu Warriors*

Siege of the Saxons (1963, UK) Nathan Juran, AL

In this seemingly alternate reality combining Arthurian and Robin Hood legends, King Arthur has a daughter who carries on, after his death at the hands of Saxon invaders. The evil Edmund of Cornwall usurps the throne and plans to marry Princess Katherine, but outlaw Robert Marshall rescues her, after which the two journey to find Merlin and save Camelot. Nathan Juran *(The 7th Voyage of Sinbad, Jack the Giant Killer)* directs.

Siegfried (1925), see *Nibelungen: Siegfried, Die*

Sigfrido (1957, Italy, Italian) Giacomo Gentilomo, Italy orig. title

This is a retelling of the tale of Siegfried, his enchanted sword, and his legendary encounter with a fire-breathing dragon, done Italian-style. See *Nibelungen: Siegfried, Die;* and *Nibelungen, Teil 1—Siegfried, Die.*

Sinbad and the Eye of the Tiger ‡ (1977, UK, Arabic/English) Sam Wanamaker

Sinbad and the Minotaur (2011, Australia) Karl Zwicky, TV

In this blend of *Arabian Nights* and Greek legends, Sinbad steals an ancient ivory scroll-case from the desert camp of the evil sorcerer Al-Jibar and escapes the camp with his crew, the scroll-case, and the kidnapped Princess Tara in tow. Scrolls in the case point the way to the treasured golden head of the Colossus of Rhodes. Pursued by Al-Jibar and his cannibal henchman, Sinbad arrives at the island to find that the treasure lies in the Labyrinth guarded by the treacherous mythical Minotaur. Manu Bennett *(The Hobbit: An Unexpected Journey)* stars as Sinbad. The cast also includes Steven Grives *(Highlander II: The Quickening).*

Sinbad at the World's End (1977), see *Sinbad and the Eye of the Tiger*

Sinbad: Beyond the Veil of Mists (2000, India/US) Evan Ricks, AN

When evil wizard Baraka threatens the island ruled by King Akron and Princess Serena, Serena enlists Sinbad's aid to journey to the depths of the sea and create a spell that can vanquish the powerful sorcerer. This movie features the voices of Brendan Fraser *(The Mummy)* as Sinbad, Mark Hamill (the *Star Wars* films) as Captain of the Guard, John Rhys-Davies (the *Indiana Jones* and *Lord of the Rings* films) as King Akron, and Leonard Nimoy (TV's *Star Trek* and *Fringe*) as Baraka, Akron, and King Chandra. This is the first feature-length animated film created solely using the technique of 3D motion-capture (animating from the movement of human actors). It is also reportedly the most expensive direct-to-video film ever.

Sinbad: Legend of the Seven Seas (2003, US, Cantonese/English/Italian) Patrick Gilmore / Tim Johnson, AN

When evil goddess of chaos Eris (Michelle Pfeiffer of *Ladyhawke* and *Batman Returns*) unjustly accuses Sinbad (Brad Pitt of the *Ocean's* films) of stealing the mystical legendary Book of Peace, his childhood friend, Prince Proteus (Joseph Fiennes of *Shakespeare in Love*), offers to sacrifice his own life while Sinbad travels to the end of the world to recover the book. Marina (Catherine Zeta-Jones of *The Legend of Zorro*), Proteus's fiancée, accompanies Sinbad on the quest. This contains very mature elements for an animated tale and combines beautifully designed 2D and 3D animation.

Sinbad of the Seven Seas (1989, Italy/US) Enzo G. Castellari / Tim Kincaid / Luigi Cozzi

Sinbad and his crew undertake a quest to retrieve four magical stones and reunite his friend Prince Ali with Ali's betrothed, Princess Alina, held captive by evil wizard Jaffar. Sinbad and his men face sword-wielding skeletons (as in Ray Harryhausen's *Jason and the Argonauts*) and a warring tribe of Amazon women. Ultimately, Sinbad stands alone to confront his demonic twin. Lou Ferrigno (with his incredible pecs) is Sinbad. Make room for this one in your "so bad it's good" file.

Sinbad: The Battle of the Dark Knights (1998, US) Alan Mehrez

A magic coin transports a young boy and his grandfather into a book and thus to the medieval world of Sinbad. They become involved in a quest to rescue a beautiful princess—why bother rescuing an ugly one?—from an evil knight. Sinbad saves not only the princess but the future of the world as well. Richard Grieco *(Almighty Thor)* is less than brilliant as Sinbad, and Mickey Rooney *(Night at the Museum)* and Dean Stockwell *(Quantum Leap)* take their careers to new lows.

Sinbad: The Fifth Voyage (2014, US) Shahin Sean Solimon

Sinbad undertakes a mission to a desert of mystical, mythical creatures to rescue the sultan's firstborn daughter, kidnapped by an evil sorcerer. Patrick Stewart (TV's *Star Trek: The Next Generation* and the subsequent films, *X-Men, Robin Hood: Men in Tights*) narrates, and director Shahin Sean Solimon of *Djinn* is Sinbad.

Sinbad: The Persian Prince (2010), UK DVD title, see *7 Adventures of Sinbad, The*

Sleeping Beauty (1959, US) Clyde Geronimi, AN

Evil witch Maleficent curses beautiful Princess Aurora by saying that Aurora will prick her finger on a spinning-wheel spindle and die before her 16th birthday. The king places his daughter in fairyland witness protection, where she receives a new identity as Briar Rose, under the charge of three fairies. But fate is just that: fate. She pricks her finger and falls into a deep sleep, awaiting true love's kiss to break the spell. Prince Philip (named after England's Prince Philip) braves the fire-breathing dragon—doesn't that look like Maleficent around the eyes?—to save . . . oops, too much information. In this last animated Disney film to use hand-inked cels, the music score is adapted from Tchaikovsky's ballet.

Snow White (2001), Canada orig. title, see *Snow White: The Fairest of Them All*

Snow White and the Huntsman (2012, US) Rupert Sanders

After a magic mirror tells evil Queen Ravenna that she needs to consume the heart of her stepdaughter to be the fairest of them all, she assigns a huntsman the task of taking Snow White into the woods and killing her. Instead, the huntsman falls in love with Snow and becomes her protector. In this dark retelling of the tale, Snow White sports a sword and shining armor, and the number of dwarfs—eight—might foretell the demise of one. Charlize Theron *(Prometheus)* is brilliant as the queen, taking evil to a new level; Chris Hemsworth *(Star Trek, Thor, The Avengers)* shines as the huntsman; and Kristen Stewart (the *Twilight* franchise) is a somewhat bland Snow White. In his final film role, Bob Hoskins *(Hook)* is the dwarf Muir. Instead of the traditional Disney names we've come to know, the dwarfs' names come from Ogham, the Celtic Tree Alphabet. Screenwriter Evan Daugherty claims the white stag is a tribute to Hayao Miyazaki's *Princess Mononoke*, which was an inspiration for this film.

Snow White and the Seven Dwarfs **(1938, US) David Hand, AN**

In this ageless film classic based on the Grimm fairytale, Snow White's wicked stepmother-queen is less than pleased when her magic mirror suggests that Snow White is the fairest one of all. Snow White escapes into the forest and takes up residence with seven pleasant dwarfs, although one is Grumpy. Eventually, the queen, disguised as an old hag, seeks out Snow White, who accepts a poison apple and becomes entombed in a glass coffin, awaiting "love's first kiss." It has to happen, because she's been singing "Someday My Prince Will Come." This first US feature-length animated film received a special Academy Award in 1938: a large statuette and seven small ones.

Snow White: The Fairest of Them All **(2001, Canada/Germany/US) Caroline Thompson, US title, TV**

This retelling of *Snow White* includes twists and turns quite different from the traditional Grimm tale. Left on an ice field with the baby Snow White after her mother dies during childbirth, her father John is granted three wishes by a nefarious genie (Clancy Brown of *Highlander*, and a recurring voice in animated TV-series like *Superman*, *Batman*, and *Justice League*). Snow's birth is a gift and a curse. John becomes king with a queen by his side, albeit the genie's wonderfully wicked sorceress sister, Elspeth (Miranda Richardson of *Sleepy Hollow* and the *Harry Potter* films). The seven dwarfs, including a female, have names after the days of the week and travel as a rainbow of colors. There's some wit and charm, with Warwick Davis *(Willow)* and Vincent Schiavelli *(Tomorrow Never Dies)* as dwarfs, but sadly a lackluster performance by Kristin Kreuk *(Smallville, Beauty and the Beast)* as Snow.

Solomon Kane ‡ **(2009, Czech Republic / France / UK, Arabic/English) Michael J. Bassett**

Son of Hercules in the Land of Darkness (1964), US TV title, see *Hercules the Invincible*

Sons of Hercules, The (1964), US video title, see *Hercules the Invincible*

Sorcerer and the White Snake, The **(2011, China / Hong Kong, Mandarin) Siu-Tung Ching, intl. English title**

In this fantasy film based on an ancient Chinese fable, young herbalist Xu Xian falls in love with and marries a beautiful woman, unaware she is the incarnation of a white demon-snake. The sorcerer-monk Fahai, who spends an inordinate amount of time battling demon temptresses, discovers the woman's true identity and battles her to save Xu Xian's soul. Jet Li *(The Forbidden Kingdom)* displays his incomparable moves as the sorcerer/monk/animal-spirit-banisher.

Sorcerer's Apprentice, The **(2002, South Africa, English/French) David Lister**

For 1,400 years, evil sorceress Morgana has failed to steal Fingall's talisman from Merlin in her attempt to conquer the world. Young Ben Clark befriends his new neighbor, the magician Milner (hmm). When both Morgana and the anagrammed Merlin realize Ben has a scar identical to that of the original staff-bearer, the game is on to save the world. Ancient magical evil threatening humanity, kid with scar drawing on newly acquired sorcery skills learned from master wizard . . . : see *Harry Potter*. Lister loves to dazzle us with his take on age-old tales and legends, but rarely successfully. Robert Davi, one of film and TV's most notable tough-guys (whose films include *Die Hard* and *License to Kill*), is Merlin/Milner. The cast also includes Kelly LeBrock *(Weird Science)* as Morgana, Byron Taylor (in yet another Milner—uh, Merlin—film, *Merlin: The Return*) as Ben, and Greg Melvill-Smith *(Blood of Beasts)*.

Sorcerer's Apprentice, The (2010, US) Jon Turtletaub

In modern-day Manhattan, sorcerer extraordinaire Balthazar Blake takes physics student Dave Stutler under his wing to train him in all ways magic, to inherit the powers of Merlin, and to thwart his evil nemesis, the wizard Maxim Horvath. Horvath plans to join forces with Morgana le Fay and raise the souls of evil sorcerers to destroy the world. The battle begins in New York. Director Jon Turtletaub and Nicolas Cage as Balthazar collaborated on the *National Treasure* films. This movie features Jay Baruchel *(How to Train Your Dragon)* in the title role, Alfred Molina *(Raiders of the Lost Ark, Spider-Man 2)* as the evil sorcerer, Toby Kebbell *(Prince of Persia: The Sands of Time, Wrath of the Titans)* as an illusionist who assists Horvath, and Alice Krige *(Reign of Fire, Solomon Kane)* as Morgana. The Nintendo DS *Sorcerer's Apprentice* video game is based on this film.

Sorcerer's Curse, The (1962), UK video title, see *Magic Sword, The* (1962)

Sorceress (1982, Mexico/US) Jack Hill

To continue his evil wizardry, Traigon must sacrifice his firstborn. Upon the birth of twin daughters and before her death at his hands, their mother leaves them with the warrior Krona to raise and train as warriors. Twenty years later, Mira and Mara are well-trained warrior-twins intent on avenging their mother's death, and Daddy Dearest is on the prowl to reclaim what's his. This film includes significant nudity and the soft-porn stylings of Pando the goat boy. Don't look for a sorceress: there isn't one. This film has the dubious honor of inclusion in the *The 50 Worst Movies Ever Made* DVD. The musical score is by James Horner *(Star Trek II: The Wrath of Khan, Glory, Titanic)*. Why, James, why?

Spiderwick Chronicles, The (2008, US) Mark Waters

Twins Jared and Simon and their sister Mallory move with their mother to the old Spiderwick Estate, given to them by their great-aunt Lucinda (Joan Plowright of *Jane Eyre, George and the Dragon*), whose father Arthur Spiderwick (David Strathairn of *Sneakers* and TV's *Alphas*) disappeared eighty years before. When Jared discovers Arthur's notes about fantastical creatures in and around the estate, he becomes a warrior committed to saving his family from the mythical dangers of the fairies, goblins, and evil ogre intent on retrieving the notebook. The performance of Freddie Highmore *(The Golden Compass)* as both twins is critically acclaimed as "the most special effect" in the film, which is based on the series of children's books by Tony DiTerlizzi and Holly Black. *The Spiderwick Chronicles* video game for Nintendo DS, Wii, Xbox 360, and PlayStation 2 is based on the film.

Spiderwick Chronicles: The IMAX Experience, The (2008), US IMAX version, see *Spiderwick Chronicles, The*

Spooky Encounters (1980), UK DVD title, see *Encounter of the Spooky Kind*

Stardust (2007, Iceland/UK/US) Matthew Vaughn

Young Tristan travels to the magical realm of Stormhold to retrieve a fallen star and win the heart of his beloved Victoria. The star is actually the beautiful Yvaine, pursued by sons of the king for her cosmic power and by an evil witch for her youth and beauty. This is a delightful, magical fairytale of good versus evil, love conquering all, and an unexpected, miraculous fate. Based on the fantasy novel *Stardust* by prolific writer Neil Gaiman *(Beowulf,* DC Comics' *Sandman)*, this winner of a Hugo Award features Robert De Niro ("You talkin' to me?"), Henry Cavill *(Tristan & Isolde, Immortals)*, Michelle Pfeiffer *(Batman Returns, Sinbad: Legend of the Seven Seas)*, Nathaniel Parker (TV's *Merlin, The Chronicles of Narnia: The Voyage of the Dawn Treader)*, and narration by Ian McKellen (*The Lord of the Rings* films).

Star Wars ‡ (1977, US) George Lucas

Star Wars IV: A New Hope (1977), US video title, see *Star Wars*

Star Wars V: The Empire Strikes Back (1980), US video title, see *Star Wars: The Empire Strikes Back*

Star Wars VI: Return of the Jedi (1983), US video title, see *Star Wars: Return of the Jedi*

Star Wars: Episode V—The Empire Strikes Back (1980), intl. English title, see *Star Wars: The Empire Strikes Back*

Star Wars: Episode VI—Return of the Jedi (1983), intl. English title, see *Star Wars: Return of the Jedi*

Star Wars: Return of the Jedi (1983, US) Richard Marquand

A new Death Star is under construction, and the Empire is poised to crush the Rebellion once and for all. The battle for freedom in the galaxy comes down to a struggle on two fronts: a tragic last conflict between father (David Prowse / James Earl Jones / Sebastian Shaw) and son (Mark Hamill), as an evil emperor (Ian McDiarmid of *Dragonslayer*, the *Star Wars* prequels, and *Sleepy Hollow*) gleefully looks on; and a war between nature and technology, as a pack of teddy bears with spears (including *Willow*'s Warwick Davis and Jack Purvis) trounces Imperial forces' superior machinery. Then everyone gathers around for a sing-a-long by the fire, as the ghosts of the departed observe. This film is heart-warming family fun.

Star Wars: The Empire Strikes Back (1980, US) Irvin Kershner

It's always darkest before the dawn. The Rebels are on the run from Imperial forces in the second and perhaps best installment of the original *Star Wars* trilogy. Luke (Mark Hamill, voice of the Joker in the animated TV *Batman* as well as a voice in *Sinbad: Beyond the Veil of Mists)* learns the ways of the Force from a Jedi legend named Yoda (Frank Oz of *Sesame Street* and *The*

Blues Brothers). Han (Harrison Ford of nearly everything in the 1980s) is turned into a Popsicle and carted away by Boba Fett (Jeremy Bulloch of TV's *Doctor Who*, "The Time Warrior"). Darth Vader has a secret.... Spoilers! The lightsaber duel between Vader and Luke is a highlight and one of swordmaster Bob Anderson's finest movie moments, in a film filled with cinematic highlights, from the snowbound AT-AT attack to the whimsical vistas of Cloud City. Vader is played by David Prowse of *A Clockwork Orange*, *Doctor Who*'s "The Time Monster," and *Jabberwocky*, but voiced by James Earl Jones (*Conan the Barbarian*, *The Flight of the Dragons*, *The Hunt for Red October*, the *Lion King* films).

St. George and the Dragon (1962), see *Magic Sword, The* (1962)

St. George and the Seven Curses (1962), see *Magic Sword, The* (1962)

Stormquest (1987, Argentina/US) Alejandro Sessa, V

The man who brought you *Amazons* one year earlier brings you the female-dominated kingdom of Kimbia, which faces rebellion from three condemned women and a renegade male faction from another realm, who seek to overthrow their evil queen. Trust us; this isn't a bold cultural statement. It's another excuse to parade barely-clad warrior women across the screen. Brent Huff also turns up in *The Perils of Gwendoline in the Land of the Yik Yak*.

Stormriders (2000), Germany DVD title, see *Storm Riders, The*

Stormriders, The (2000), UK DVD title, see *Storm Riders, The*

Storm Riders, The (2000, Hong Kong, Cantonese) Wai-keung Lau, intl. English title

After killing their fathers, evil Lord Conqueror adopts two boys, Wind and Cloud (Ekin Cheng of *Zu Warriors*, and Aaron Kwok), to raise and train as powerful warriors. Word on the street is that the young men have the power to destroy the other evil warlord, Sword Saint, whom Conqueror hopes to conquer so he can take over the world. It's the simple things in life that make you happy. When Conqueror accidentally kills his own daughter, the "take over the world" plan starts to unravel. This movie is based on the *wuxia manhua* (Chinese martial-arts comics) series *Fung Wan*. There is also a *Fung Wan Online* roleplaying game.

Storm Warriors (2011, Hong Kong, Cantonese/English) Oxide Pang Chun / Danny Pang, intl. Engish title

An evil Japanese warlord intent on obtaining the magic Dragon Bones to rule China imprisons the emperor and his warriors, one of which is Cloud. When Wind gets wind of this, he resolves to save his lifelong "brother." Unfortunately, the wicked Lord Wicked (yes, we know) convinces Wind to take the evil route, at which point he becomes Evil Wind. In this sequel to *The Storm Riders*, the same actors play Wind and Cloud. The animated opening sequence features well-known cover art of the *Fung Wan* comics on which this film is based.

Sudsakorn (2006), Thailand orig. title, see *Legend of the Tsunami Warrior*

Swan Princess, The (1994, US) Richard Rich, AN

Prince Derek and Princess Odette have spent their childhood together, but as adults the princess asks Derek to prove he loves her for who she is and not for her beauty. Hey, Derek, good luck spending your life with a conceited narcissist. When evil sorcerer Lord Rothbart attacks, he murders Odette's father, kidnaps her, and transforms her into a swan. What a foul/fowl turn of events. Okay, Derek, your move. The cast of voices includes John Cleese *(Monty Python and the Holy Grail)* as a French frog, actor-comedian Steven Wright as an old turtle named Speed (cute), and Jack Palance *(Hawk the Slayer)* as Lord Rothbart. This is no Disney film but is beloved by many who first saw it as children.

Swan Princess III, The (1998), US short title, see *Swan Princess: The Mystery of the Enchanted Treasure, The*

Swan Princess and the Secret Castle, The (1997), US DVD title, see *Swan Princess: Escape from Castle Mountain, The*

Swan Princess: Escape from Castle Mountain, The (1997, US) Richard Rich, AN

As Odette and Derek prepare to celebrate their first anniversary, villain du jour Clavius kidnaps Derek's mother, Queen Uberta. Clavius intends to rule the world using a giant orb. To thwart his plans, Odette must transform into her inner swan. This far less successful film lacks many of the likeable characters of the original.

Swan Princess: The Mystery of the Enchanted Treasure, The (1998, US) Richard Rich, US DVD title

This last time around (we hope), Odette and Derek face off with evil sorceress Zelda, who used to have a thing with the first film's bad guy, Lord Rothbart. Zelda, in an attempt to get her hands on the treasure of the Forbidden Arts, which naturally would give her absolute power, kidnaps Odette, forcing Derek to hand over the treasure or fight for his wife. Why can't she do that swan thingy now? Just watch the first film and pretend the others don't exist.

Sword and the Dragon, The (1960, Soviet Union, Russian) Aleksandr Ptushko, US title, *MST3K*

Boasting a "cast of 106,000" and based on a Russian legend, this epic follows Ilya Muromets as he drinks a healing potion and uses his restored legs to take on all manner of foes, including a wind-blowing monster called Nightingale and a pack of pagan "Tugars." There's also a climactic battle featuring a three-headed, fire-breathing *Zmey Gorynych*: that's a Slavic dragon to you and me. This severely edited version of the film, packaged by Roger Corman, features the vocal stylings of Mike Wallace (journalist / media personality) and Paul Frees *(The Hobbit, The Return of the King, Flight of Dragons)*. The *Mystery Science Theater 3000* cast mercilessly shreds it in a Season 7 episode. They're convinced it's from Finland, but they're wrong.

Sword and the Sorcerer, The ‡ (1982, US) Albert Pyun

Sword and the Sorcerer 2, The (2010), Germany DVD title, see *Abelar: Tales of an Ancient Empire*

Sword in the Stone, *The* (1963, US) Wolfgang Reitherman, AL/AN

The wizard Merlin takes young Arthur, known here as Wart, under his tutelage to train as a squire, ultimately to become the predestined king. In this Disney animated version of the legend, Merlin is an extremely forgetful old man, and his wise old owl Archimedes a much-beloved and humorous character. The battle between Merlin and the powerful witch Madame Mim is an animated-film classic, with each transforming into a series of animals. Merlin is also apparently a time-traveler, if his fashion choices are any indication. This movie features the voices of Sebastian Cabot (narrator of the *Winnie the Pooh* films and the incomparable, elegant Mr. French in TV's *Family Affair*) as Sir Ector, Karl Swenson (prolific '60s and '70s TV actor) as Merlin, and Alan Napier (Alfred of the *Batman* TV-series) as Sir Pelinore.

Sword of Ali Baba, *The* (1965, US) Virgil W. Vogel

This *Arabian Nights* tale is pretty much an exact remake of the 1944 film *Ali Baba and the Forty Thieves* already presented in this index. Footage from that movie is repurposed, including Ali Baba seeking refuge with Old Baba and the forty thieves, avenging his father's death, reuniting with his love Amara, and ultimately becoming ruler of Baghdad. Frank Puglia reprises his role as Amara's father, the evil Prince Cassim. In an odd bit of casting, Gavin MacLeod (TV's *Love Boat* captain) is Hulagu Khan, evil suitor of Amara.

Sword of Lancelot (1963, UK, English/French) Cornel Wilde, US title, AL

Lancelot, bravest of the brave and most virtuous Knight of the Round Table, is quite taken with King Arthur's beautiful bride Guinevere, to the point of engaging in a passionate, illicit romance. Think *Camelot* without the songs. Swashbuckling actor Cornel Wilde *(The Greatest Show on Earth, Gargoyles)* wears all the hats in this film, as director, co-producer, co-writer, and star, playing Sir Lancelot as the Frenchman that he is. The swordfights are exquisitely realistic, because Wilde was a champion fencer. Wilde's then-wife Jean Wallace is Guinevere.

Sword of She-Ra, The (1985), US TV title, see *Secret of the Sword, The*

Sword of the Barbarians, *The* (1983, Italy, Italian) Michele Massimo Tarantini, intl. English title

In what might be a sequel to *Gunan, King of the Barbarians*, this movie follows swordsman Sangraal, who vows to avenge the death of his wife, murdered before his eyes by evil goddess of fire Rani. He teams up with Aki, daughter of the village chieftain, and a Chinese archer to battle a wizard, monkey men, and blind cave-creatures and retrieve a mystical weapon to defeat Rani. There is also a sexual encounter with the Golden Goddess, played by Sabrina Siani *(Gunan, King of the Barbarians, Ator the Fighting Eagle, Conquest)*. Sangraal is actually the biblical name of the Holy Grail.

Sword of the Valiant (1984), US video title, see *Sword of the Valiant: The Legend of Sir Gawain and the Green Knight*

Sword of the Valiant: The Legend of Sir Gawain and the Green Knight **(1984, UK) Stephen Weeks, AL**

Squire Gawain (Miles O'Keeffe of the Ator films), knighted to answer the Green Knight's riddle and defend the king's honor, falls prey to a trick and loses the dare. The Green Knight allows young Sir Gawain a year before he must answer for his defeat. During that time, the knight travels throughout the land, experiencing life in a knightly manner and eventually solving the riddle. Could this be too little, too late? The Green Knight is Sean Connery, who was filming his parallel-universe *Bond* film, *Never Say Never Again,* at the same time.

Sword of Xanten (2006), UK title, see *Curse of the Ring*

Takeru Yamato (1994), US title, see *Orochi the Eight-Headed Dragon*

Tale of the White Serpent, The (1961), see *Panda and the Magic Serpent*

Tales from Earthsea **(2010, Japan, Japanese) Goro Miyazaki, intl. English title, AN**

In this coming-of-age tale, teenage Prince Arren travels on a long voyage with the wizard Ged to investigate strange happenings in the kingdom. Dragons have entered the human world, and the ruthless prince has killed his father. Now he seeks to defeat the evil sorcerer Cob with the help of a mysterious girl, Therru. This film is loosely based on *The Farthest Shore,* a novel in a collection of fantasy tales by Ursula K. LeGuin, who was less than pleased with this interpretation of her work. Director Goro Miyazaki, son of masterful filmmaker Hayao Miyazaki *(Princess Mononoke)* does not show the expertise evident in his father's films.

Tales of an Ancient Empire (2010), US orig. title, see *Abelar: Tales of an Ancient Empire*

Tales of Vesperia: The First Strike **(2012, Japan, Japanese) Kenta Kamei, US title, AN**

Ten years after a war between humans and demon beasts, energy known as "aer" has become a vital commodity for humanity. Young Imperial Knights Yuri and Flynn are dispatched to a town where abnormal aer activity has created an outbreak of horrific mutated beasts that threaten the population. The resolve of these young men, of the corps of knights, and of their families leads to a tragic struggle. This anime film is the prequel to the video game of the same name released by Namco Bandai Games for Xbox 360 and then PlayStation 3.

Tangled **(2010, US) Nathan Greno / Byron Howard, AN**

Naïve Rapunzel doesn't know she has been imprisoned most of her life by Mother Gothel, who has found immortality in the fountain of youth that is the girl's overflowing magic hair. Enchanted by the annual fireworks display in the distance, Rapunzel is oblivious to the fact that the king and queen from whom she was kidnapped are celebrating her birthday. Life's been good except for the imprisonment part. When Flynn Ryder, a bumbling thief but suave and sophisticated in his own mind, discovers the tower, the adventure is on with the help of his sword-wielding horse Maximus. Spunky, "brave" princess; smug, conceited prince; deliciously evil "mother"; exciting, humorous animated adventure; what's not to like? The voice cast includes Mandy Moore *(The Princess Diaries)* as Rapunzel, Zachary Levi (TV's *Chuck*) as Flynn, Donna Murphy *(Star Trek: Insurrection)* as Mother Gothel, and Ron Perlman (the *Hellboy* films) as both Stabbington brothers.

Taran and the Magic Cauldron (1985, US), see *Black Cauldron, The*

Taro the Dragon Boy (1979, Japan, Japanese) Kirirô Urayama / Peter Fernandez, intl. English title, AN

Lazy, aimless Taro is a boy who lives a carefree, singular life. A powerful wizard gives him a potion that grants him the strength of a hundred men—but only when helping others. When Taro discovers that his long-lost mother is still alive but cursed to live as a dragon, he sets off to find her and lift the curse, helping villagers along the way. This anime film, based on a Japanese folktale and the novel *Taro the Dragon Boy* by Miyoko Matsutani, is a precursor to the *Pokémon* craze.

Tatsu no ko Taro (1979), Japan orig. title, see *Taro the Dragon Boy*

Teiruzu obu vesuperia: The first strike (2012), Japan orig. title, see *Tales of Vesperia: The First Strike*

Terry Pratchett's Hogfather (2007), UK complete title, see *Hogfather*

Terry Pratchett's The Colour of Magic (2009), intl. complete title, see *Colour of Magic, The*

Thief and the Cobbler, The (1995, UK/US) Richard Williams, US video title, AN

In this *Arabian Nights* fantasy, beautiful Princess Yum Yum befriends shy, quiet cobbler Tack and saves him from an unjustified execution. The bond between the two angers Vizier Zigzag, a rhyme-speaking wizard, who plans to marry the princess and replace her father as king. A silent thief, quite by accident, provides a happy ending to this animated tale. Zigzag is the wonderfully sinister voice of Vincent Price *(The Fly, House on Haunted Hill)*. The cast also includes Donald Pleasance (Blofeld in the Bond film *You Only Live Twice,* Dr. Loomis in the *Halloween* films) as Phido the vulture, Sean Connery (the James Bond films) as Tack the cobbler, and Joss Ackland *(The Princess and the Goblin, A Kid in King Arthur's Court)* as a brigand. Because of many problems through the years and ultimately three different edited versions in existence, this film holds the record for the longest production schedule of a completed feature film, at 28 years.

Thief of Bagdad, The (1924, US) Raoul Walsh, B&W/Silent

In this *Arabian Nights* tale, rebellious thief Ahmed falls in love with the beautiful daughter of the caliph and, posing as Prince Achmed, vies for her hand in a challenge to return with the rarest treasure, competing against the prince of the Mongols, a less-than-honorable contender. Ahmed-as-Achmed encounters obstacles such as the Valley of Fire, the Valley of the Monsters, the Cavern of the Enchanted Trees, and the deadly Abode of the Winged Horse. This black-and-white silent film is visually stunning, with remarkable special effects for the 1920s. As the thief, and as a king of swashbuckling, Douglas Fairbanks rests his cinematic legacy in this true essence of a magic-carpet ride.

Thief of Bagdad, The ‡ (1940, UK) Ludwig Berger / Michael Powell / Tim Whelan

Thief of Baghdad, The (1961, France/Italy, Italian) Arthur Lubin / Bruno Vailati, US/UK title

Karim, the thief in this version, faces many obstacles to solve a riddle involving seven gates leading to a magical blue rose that will undo a sleeping-curse on his love, Princess Amina. There are many evils of biblical proportions—and even a cloak of invisibility long before *Harry Potter* was a thought. Spoiler alert! Karim finds the elusive rose, only to lose it during battle. In one of the most beautiful moments of true love, Karim hands Princess Amina a white rose, telling her it will turn blue if she loves him. She responds that it is a blue rose . . . as the white rose indeed turns blue. Steve Reeves (the *Hercules* films) is Karim.

Thief of Baghdad, The (1978, UK/France) Clive Donner, TV

In yet another retelling of the story of a clever thief helping a handsome prince overcome an evil wizard to win the affections of a beautiful princess, Roddy McDowall (the *Planet of the Apes* films) as thief Hasan is quite a pleasant aide to Prince Taj in the quest to locate the All-Seeing Eye and rescue Princess Jasmine. To do this, they must crush the evil vizier's soul, hidden in a giant egg (another Horcrux). The excellent cast includes Ian Holm (*The Lord of the Rings* films), Peter Ustinov *(Logan's Run)*, Terence Stamp *(Superman II)*, and in her first film appearance, Marina Sirtis (Deanna Troi of *Star Trek: The Next Generation*), as a harem girl.

Thief of Bagdad: An Arabian Fantasy in Technicolor, The (1940), UK title, see *Thief of Bagdad, The*

Thor (2011, US) Kenneth Branagh

The legendary Norse gods are actual beings that dwell in the far-off realm of Asgard. Brash thunder-god Thor suffers exile to Earth at the hands of his father, Odin, after igniting old tensions with the frost giants. Loki, trickster and adopted brother of Thor, plans to usurp Odin's power, while Thor defends his new human friends against the might of Loki's metallic agent, the Destroyer. This film is part of Marvel Studios' superb "Phase One" film series leading up to the 2012 superhero blockbuster, *The Avengers*. It is directed by actor Kenneth Branagh *(Othello, Hamlet, Harry Potter and the Chamber of Secrets)* and stars Chris Hemsworth *(Snow White and the Huntsman)* as Thor, Tom Hiddleston *(Henry IV, Henry V)* as Loki, Natalie Portman (the *Star Wars* prequels) as Jane Foster, Stellan Skarsgard *(Mamma Mia)* as Dr. Erik Selvig, and Anthony Hopkins *(Beowulf)* as Odin.

Thor il conquistatore (1983), Italy orig. title, see *Thor the Conqueror*

Thor: Tales of Asgard (2011, US) Sam Liu, AN/V

To prove his manhood to his father, teenage Thor sets out on a quest with his brother Loki to recover a mythical sword. After putting Asgard in danger, the rash, adventurous young god needs to become a responsible adult and accept the consequences of his actions. The lesson in this animated coming-of-age tale is much the same as in its Marvel Comics cousin, *Spider-Man*: "with great power comes great responsibility."

Thor the Conqueror (1983, Italy, Italian) Tonino Ricci, US title

After Gnut, arch-rival of Thor's father, murders Thor's parents, the sorcerer Etna, who manifests as an owl at times, takes the child under his wing (sorry). Thor becomes a great warrior, and with his newfound love, the virgin warrior Ina, undertakes a quest to find his father's magic sword and avenge his parents' death.

Thor: The Dark World (2013, US) Alan Taylor, 3D

The "god of thunder" (Chris Hemsworth) reunites with Jane Foster (Natalie Portman) and several other Earth-based friends as he faces a threat of new malevolence led by Malekith (Ninth Doctor Who Christopher Eccleston). Late reshoots added more of Tom Hiddleston's fan-favorite Loki to the proceedings than originally planned.

Throne of Fire (1986, Italy, Italian) Franco Prosperi, US video title

Morak, the son of Satan's messenger, must wed Princess Valkari (Sabrina Siani of *Gunan, King of the Barbarians* and *Sword of the Barbarians*) and sit on the Throne of Fire on the day of a solar eclipse to gain the right to rule the kingdom of Earth. Siegfried, invulnerable to all but fire, with a brief shot at the power of invisibility, flexes his well-oiled muscles in a multitude of swordfights to rescue the kidnapped princess and save the world ... but not before spending some quality time in the Well of Madness, an excellent counterpart to *The Princess Bride*'s Pit of Despair. Pietro Torrisi (credited here as Peter McCoy), who plays Siegfried, also appears in *Hercules vs the Giant Warriors*.

Throne of Fire, The (1986), UK/US video title, see *Throne of Fire*

Tiger & Dragon (2000), Germany title, see *Crouching Tiger, Hidden Dragon*

Time Bandits (1981, UK) Terry Gilliam

A band of diminutive thieves kidnaps an English lad and drags him across time and space to meet Napoleon (*The Lord of the Rings*' Ian Holm), Robin Hood (Monty Python's John Cleese), King Agamemnon (Sean Connery of *Sword of the Valiant: The Legend of Sir Gawain and the Green Knight*), and Evil himself (David Warner of *Straw Dogs, Quest of the Delta Knights,* and *Hogfather*). The cast of this surreal adventure also includes Ralph Richardson *(Dragonslayer)* as the Supreme Being, David Rappaport *(The Bride, The Wizard)*, Kenny Baker (R2-D2 of *Star Wars*), Jack Purvis *(The Dark Crystal, Labyrinth, Willow)*, and Warwick Davis *(Star Wars: Return of the Jedi, Willow)*. Python Terry Gilliam directed. Gilliam and fellow Python Michael Palin co-wrote the script. George Harrison (yes, that one) executive-produced the movie and provided the end-credits song "Dream Away."

Time Barbarians (1990, US) Joseph John Barmettler

Evil wizard Mandrak loses a hand to warrior-king Doran and then rapes and murders Doran's wife Lystra before escaping to modern-day Los Angeles using Lystra's magic amulet. Doran miraculously pulls a "sword in the stone" stunt that sends him to LA with Mandrak's severed hand, which he uses to slap the wizard around when they reunite. It's no surprise that this film is on the Worst Netflix Films list.

Trionfo di Ercole, Il (1965), Italy orig. title, see *Hercules vs. the Giant Warriors*

Tristan & Isolde (2006, Czech Republic / Germany / UK / US) Kevin Reynolds

Although the tagline sets this story "Before Romeo and Juliet . . . ," this retelling of the heart-wrenching tale of Tristan and Isolde is better compared to the Arthurian Camelot love triangle. There is a new wrinkle in the way the lovers meet: Isolde cures the dying Tristan with magical herbs, with no need for an elixir to fall in love. James Franco (the *Spider-Man* films) and Sophia Myles (TV's *Doctor Who* and *Moonlight*) as Tristan and Isolde are electrifying, while Rufus Sewell (*Dark City, Arabian Nights, A Knight's Tale*, the *Eleventh Hour* TV-series) is outstanding as King Mark. Amid much medieval pageantry and warfare, the love story shines in this "tale as old as time."

Tristan + Isolde (2006), see *Tristan & Isolde* (2006)

Tristan and Isolde (1982), US title, see *Fire and Sword*

Triumph of Hercules, The (1965), US TV title, see *Hercules vs. the Giant Warriors*

Trono di fuoco, Il (1986), Italy orig. title, see *Throne of Fire*

Two Towers, The (2002), US short title, see *Lord of the Rings: The Two Towers, The*

Unendliche Geschichte, Die (1984), West Germany orig. title, see *The NeverEnding Story*

Ursus, il terrore dei kirghisi (1964), Italy orig. title, see *Hercules, Prisoner of Evil*

Vampires vs. Hercules, The (1964), see *Hercules in the Haunted World*

Van Helsing (2004, Czech Republic / US) Stephen Sommers

Monster-hunter Van Helsing (Hugh Jackman) arrives in Transylvania to curtail Count Dracula's deranged application of Dr. Frankenstein's research to his own horrific plan. Using the original Universal films as a template, then crumpling up the template, burning it, and spreading the ashes while spitting on them, this is a big-budget misfire of terrifying proportions that liberally borrows (steals?) from the anime *Vampire Hunter D*. Still, you must agree with the *X-Men* film series' Jackman in the role: Van Helsing never looked so good. The cast includes Robbie Coltrane (Hagrid of the *Harry Potter* films) and Alun Armstrong *(Krull)*. A tie-in video game was released for PlayStation 2 and Xbox. This film clearly inspired Pinnacle Entertainment's tabletop RPG *Rippers*, which uses the *Savage Worlds* core rules.

Vasilisa Prekrasnaya (1939), Soviet Union orig. title, see *Vasilisa the Beautiful*

Vasilisa the Beautiful (1939, Soviet Union, Russian) Aleksandr Rou, intl. literal English title, B&W

Although there is a Russian fairytale of the same name, this film is based on a completely different story called "The Frog Tsarevna." It's also the first known Russian feature to incorporate fantasy in a big way. In it, three brothers seek wives, but the one who marries a frog gets the best deal. Evil serpents, magic swords, secret doors, and the wizened Baba Yaga make this an epic beyond its time, with stunning imagery that clearly inspired later films in the genre. This historic gem is well worth investigating. As of press time, a completely restored version with subtitles is available on YouTube.

Vendetta di Ercole, La (1960), Italy orig. title, see *Goliath and the Dragon*

Vengeance of Hercules (1960), US title, see *Goliath and the Dragon*

Versus ‡ (2002, Japan/US) Ryûhei Kitamura

Volkodav iz roda Serykh Psov (2007), Russia orig. title, see *Wolfhound*

Volshebnaya lampa Aladdina (1968), Soviet Union orig. title, see *Aladdin and His Magic Lamp*

Voyage of the Unicorn (2001, Canada/US) Philip Spink, TV

After the death of their wife and mother, who was an illustrator who left drawings of a mythical world, a mythology professor (Beau Bridges) and his daughters are whisked away aboard the magic ship *Unicorn* to a fantasyland in a parallel universe. A prophecy has foretold that they will save the land of the king and queen of faeries from evil trolls. The quest entails encountering the Minotaur, the Sphinx, and Medusa, while seeking a unicorn for the healing powers of its tears and a benevolent dragon also sought by the trolls. This movie is very loosely based on the novel *Voyage of the Basset* by James C. Christensen.

Wanpaku ôji no orochi taiji (1963), Japan orig. title, see *Little Prince and the Eight Headed Dragon*

Warcraft (2016, US) Duncan Jones, NYR

It's hard to believe it took this long to get a full-blown feature-film adaptation of the wildly successful MMORPG *World of Warcraft* (known affectionately as *"WoW"*) to the big screen, but now it looks like all the magical forces have aligned. The cast includes Dominic Cooper *(Mamma Mia!, Captain America: The First Avenger, Abraham Lincoln: Vampire Hunter)*, Clancy Brown *(Highlander, Starship Troopers,* the 2010 *A Nightmare on Elm Street)*, and Paula Patton *(Mission: Impossible—Ghost Protocol)*.

Warlock (1991, US) Steve Miner

Aided by sorcery, the evil Warlock (Julian Sands of *Curse of the Ring*) from the 17th century is transported to 1980s Los Angeles to escape execution. He intends to locate the Satanic Bible (the Grand Grimoire), learn the true name of God, and speak it backwards to un-create all of creation. Hot on his tail are the witch-hunter Redferne (Richard E. Grant of *Withnail & I*), who followed him through time, and the young woman Kassandra (the Beastmaster's real-life sister, Lori Singer), cursed by the Warlock with a rapid-aging spell after he murdered her roommate. Julian Sands is strangely compelling as the Warlock, a role he was born to play, while Jerry Goldsmith's musical score sets just the right mood. The video game *Warlock* for Sega Genesis and Super NES is based on this film.

Warlock: The Armageddon (1993, US) Anthony Hickox

The Warlock seeks to release the evil of his father, Satan, into the world, while two children of Druid heritage must summon powers they didn't know existed to save humanity. Five stones will unleash the evil or banish it for 600 years: toss the stones and take your chances. 'Tis like *Monopoly: The Apocalypse* edition. Once again Julian Sands is exquisitely evil as a Warlock who seems the same as the one in the first film, although this is not so much a sequel as it is a parallel adventure.

Warlock: The Magic Wizard (1991), Philippines English title, see *Warlock*

Warrior and the Sorceress, The ‡ (1984, Argentina/US) John C. Broderick

Warrior King (1984), Philippines title, see *Deathstalker*

Warriors of Tao (2005), Germany title, see *Warriors of Virtue: The Return to Tao*

Warriors of Virtue (1997, China/US) Ronny Yu

With a lame leg and an intense desire to join the high-school football team, Ryan is swept into a whirlpool that takes him to the mystical land of Tao. He arrives physically fit and is rescued by the Roos, karate-ninja humanoid kangaroos who are the Warriors of Virtue, representing the forces of good and imbued with the virtues and elements of Tao. There are also forces of evil (always are) led by the villainous sorcerer Komodo (Angus Macfadyen of 2000's *Jason and the Argonauts*). It falls to Ryan to help save the land of Tao. Ronny Yu *(The Bride with the White Hair)* directs this martial-arts film for children, in his United States debut. The cast includes Doug Jones (the *Hellboy* films) and Lee Arenberg (the *Pirates of the Caribbean* films, TV's *Once Upon a Time*). Your author Scott Alan Woodard worked on animatronic effects for this film.

Warriors of Virtue 2 (2005), US short title, see *Warriors of Virtue: The Return to Tao*

Warriors of Virtue 2: Return to Tao (2005), UK title, see *Warriors of Virtue: The Return to Tao*

Warriors of Virtue 2: The Return to Tao (2005), Canada English title, see *Warriors of Virtue: The Return to Tao*

Warriors of Virtue: The Return to Tao (2005, Australia) Michael Vickerman

In this fantasy martial-arts sequel, a new villain named Dogon rules the parallel universe of Tao. While attending a martial-arts competition in Beijing, Ryan and his friend are whisked away to

Tao to become Warriors of Virtue and once again save Tao. You'd think a mystical land filled with sorcerers and heroes wouldn't need so much saving by high-school kids from another universe, but I digress. Kevin Smith (Ares in the *Xena: Warrior Princess* and *Hercules: The Legendary Journeys* TV-series) plays Dogon. Sadly, Smith died from an accidental fall shortly after filming his scenes.

White Snake Enchantress, The (1961), intl. English title, see *Panda and the Magic Serpent*

Wiedzmin (2001), Poland orig. title, see *Hexer, The*

Willow ‡ **(1988, US) Ron Howard**

Wishmaster (1997, US) Robert Kurtzman
Introductory narration by Angus Scrimm *(Phantasm)* tells of the djinn, evil genies who grant three wishes but are then unleashed on the world to cause mayhem. Unfortunately, after Alexandra accidentally awakens a djinn from the stone in which he has been entombed, the demonic creature relentlessly forces her to make the three wishes required to release his kind into the world. Characters in the film have the names of science-fiction and horror writers and horror-film actors. Andrew Divoff (TV's *Lost*) is a deliciously evil djinn.

Wishmaster 2: Evil Never Dies (1999, US) Jack Sholder, V

Picking up from the end of the first film, this one puts a new wrinkle in the "make three wishes and all hell breaks loose" rule. This time around, the djinn must first gather a thousand souls. Released by a female art-thief in a robbery gone wrong, the djinn confesses to murder to get into prison and collect souls from the hopeless and helpless. After escaping prison, where better to collect more souls than a den of iniquity like a casino? Bet you didn't expect that. Once again playing the djinn, Andrew Divoff has perfected the menacing look.

Wishmaster 3: Beyond the Gates of Hell (2001 Canada/US) Chris Angel, V

Diana Collins (A. J. Cook of *Final Destination 2* and TV's *Criminal Minds*) inadvertently releases the evil djinn from his tomb. He cuts quite a bloody swath through her college campus to find her and elicit the needed three wishes to create hell on Earth. This time Jason Connery *(Dragonquest)* is the djinn in human form.

Wishmaster 3: Devil Stone (2001), Australia/UK DVD title, see *Wishmaster 3: Beyond the Gates of Hell*

Wishmaster 4: The Prophecy Fulfilled (2002, Canada/US) Chris Angel, US DVD title, V

In this fourth and we hope last installment of the series, the djinn is awakened by Lisa, a young woman who accepts a gift from her boyfriend's lawyer, Steven, who is in love with her. The evil djinn possesses Steven's body, but being that he's a lawyer, how could you tell? (Sorry, unprovoked attack.) Lisa's third wish creates a dilemma of epic proportions: she tells Steven (the djinn), that she wishes she could love him for who he really is. And you thought the demonic apocalypse was a problem. Michael Trucco (the *Battlestar Galactica* TV-series) is the djinn.

Witch's Curse, The (1963) see *Maciste in Hell*

Witchslayer Gretl (2012, Canada/US) Mario Azzopardi, TV

Tenacious witchslayer Hansel (Paul McGillion of *Stargate: Atlantis*) has battled surreal creatures in the magical Forest of Long Ago for many years, seeking to avenge the death of his sister, who never made it out. This new, darker version of the tale is more than twisted; we think they broke it. Spoiler alert! His sister is not only alive, but a witch herself. Shannon Doherty as Gretl is in familiar territory since her turn as a witch in TV's *Charmed*. Why isn't the title *Witchslayer Hansl*? Yeah, we dropped the *e*. You want a mystery? Where did her second *e* go? You can watch this abomination or bake a batch of gingerbread cookies; we know our vote.

Witchville (2010, US) Pearry Reginald Teo, TV

Prince Malachy returns home to find his father, the king, dead and the kingdom devastated by plague, drought, and famine. Witch-hunter Kramer informs Malachy that a coven of witches led by the Red Queen has caused the destruction. Malachy and Kramer gather a band of men to kill the evil queen, while unwittingly being hunted by her deadly enforcer, Jozefa (MyAnna Buring of the *Twilight* films). Luke Goss *(Hellboy II: The Golden Army)* is Malachy, Sarah Douglas *(Quest of the Delta Knights)* is the Red Queen, and Ed Speleers *(Eragon)* and Andrew Pleavin *(300)* are Malachy's friends Jason and Erik.

Wizards ‡ (1977, US) Ralph Bakshi, AN

Wizards of the Demon Sword (1991, US) Fred Olen Ray

Ulric, keeper of the Sword of Aktar, has been kidnapped and imprisoned, but hero Thane (Blake Bahner of *Wizards of the Lost Kingdom II*) is on it. His quest entails rescuing Ulric and Ulric's daughter, the princess, and depriving the evil wizard Lord Khoura (Lyle Waggoner of TV's *Wonder Woman*) of the Demon Sword. The one who possesses it has unlimited power. The tagline says it all: "A mystical sorceress ... a magical sword ... the adventure of a lifetime"—well, two out of three, anyway. Russ Tamblyn *(West Side Story*, TV's *Twin Peaks)* is Ulric. Writer-director Fred Olen Ray, the majority of whose films include the word "bikini" in the title, directed this film. High praise, indeed.

Wizards of the Lost Kingdom ‡ (1985, Argentina/US) Héctor Olivera

Wizards of the Lost Kingdom II (1989, US) Charles Griffith

Evil warlord-wizards have overtaken three kingdoms, and it falls to teenage wizard Tyor to use his magical powers to reclaim the Three Talismans of Creation with the help of his mentor, Caedmon of Nog, and the mighty warrior known as the Dark One (David Carradine of TV's *Kung Fu* and the *Kill Bill* films). In a scintillating scene, the dancer wife of the Dark One is lifted onto the shoulders of a guard and snaps his neck with her legs. Now that's entertainment. This film also features Lana Clarkson, partially via footage from her film *Barbarian Queen* and Carradine's *The Warrior and the Sorceress*. Put this in the "so bad it's good" category, but mostly "so bad."

Wo hu cang long (2000), Taiwan orig. title, see *Crouching Tiger, Hidden Dragon*

Wolfhound (2007, Russia, Russian) Nikolai Lebedev

This Russian Tolkien-style fantasy tells of the annihilation of the Grey Hound clan by an evil priest and his malevolent henchman, Maneater, and the revenge of an enslaved young boy who grows up to become a mighty warrior named Wolfhound. Traveling with a band of friends, including a bat and a blind sorcerer, Wolfhound escorts a princess rescued from an assassination attempt to her new husband, while seeking to avenge the death of his family and clansmen by conquering the merciless Maneater. Unbeknownst to Wolfhound, his mission is greater than his own revenge: he could save a nation. This film is based on the first novel of Maria Semyonova's tetralogy.

Wolfhound from the Tribe of Grey Dogs (2007), intl. literal title, see *Wolfhound*

Wolfhound of the Grey Dog Clan (2007), intl. long English title, see *Wolfhound*

Wonders of Aladdin, The (1961, France/Italy/US) Mario Bava / Henry Levin

This retelling of *Aladdin* presents him as somewhat of a man-child given to flights of fantasy. His mother's gift of an old lamp unexpectedly produces a genie who grants him three wishes. Aladdin and his girlfriend soon become involved in an adventure to save a prince and princess from evil plans of the grand vizier and a doddering old magician who has created malevolent life-size dolls. This might be a good time to use those three wishes. Song-and-dance actor Donald O'Connor, best known for *Singin' in the Rain,* plays Aladdin. This film is a somewhat odd choice for director Mario Bava *(Hercules in the Haunted World),* better known for the horror and giallo genres.

World of Yor, The (1983), intl. literal English title, see *Yor, the Hunter from the Future*

Wrath of the Titans (2012, Spain/US) Jonathan Liebesman

This sequel to the 2010 remake of *Clash of the Titans* has most of the cast returning to their roles. The gods lose control of the imprisoned Titans, including their leader, Kronos, who was originally imprisoned by his sons Zeus (Liam Neeson of *Batman Begins* and *The Dark Knight Rises*), Hades (Ralph Fiennes of *The Prince of Egypt* and *Red Dragon*), and Poseidon (Danny Huston—King Richard in the 2010 *Robin Hood*) in the abyss of Tartarus, an underworld dungeon. Demigod Perseus (Sam Worthington of *Terminator Salvation*) comes to the rescue when Hades and Zeus's son Ares side with Kronos.

Xin shu shan jian ke (1983), Hong Kong orig. title, see *Zu: Warriors from the Magic Mountain*

Yamato Takeru (1994), Japan orig. title, see *Orochi the Eight-Headed Dragon*

Yor (1983), UK video title, see *Yor, the Hunter from the Future*

Yor, the Hunter from the Future (1983, Italy/France/Turkey) Antonio Margheriti, US title

TV's Captain America, Reb Brown, headlines this journey into sheer lunacy as warrior Yor tries to uncover the mystery of his medallion, a trinket also worn by a goddess. It might hold the key to Yor's murky origins. Any movie with a dinosaur blood-feast, a giant bat used as a hang-glider, flying saucers, and a hero who kills innocent people can't be all bad. If you've seen *Teenage Cave Man* (featured on *Mystery Science Theater 3000*, a fate *Yor* inexplicably avoided), you're going to be way ahead on this one. Based on a comic book and originally aired in Italy as a four-part TV miniseries, this film also stars Corinne Clery *(The Story of O, Moonraker)*.

Your Highness ‡ (2011, US) David Gordon Green

Zu Mountain: New Legend of the Zu Mountain Swordsmen (1983), Hong Kong literal English title, see *Zu: Warriors from the Magic Mountain*

Zu Time Warrior (1983), intl. English dubbed version, see *Zu: Warriors from the Magic Mountain*

Zu Warriors (2001, China / Hong Kong, Cantonese/Mandarin) Tsui Hark, Finland/ Germany/US title

The legendary Zu mountain range in China, which lies between heaven and earth, is the home of the immortals of Omei, Zu's highest mountain. When the immortal demon Insomnia aspires to rule the world, Zu's leader, White Eyebrows, gathers his best warriors to draw the demon from his blood cavern and destroy the abominable threat with their mystical swords. According to director Tsui Hark, this film is neither prequel nor sequel to the 1983 film but an independent storyline. Sammo Hung Kam-Bo reprises his role as White Eyebrows.

Zu: Warriors from the Magic Mountain (1983, Hong Kong, Cantonese) Tsui Hark, Hong Kong English title

During an ancient civil war, Chinese warriors undertake a quest to a mystical mountain range in which they have 49 days to find two magical swords and kill an evil blood demon that threatens all life on Earth. The raging war feeds the demon's bloodlust for power, because he thrives on pain and suffering. Abundant swordfights create a martial-arts extravaganza against a magical backdrop. Kung-fu film master Tsui Hark, said to be inspired by the original *Star Wars* trilogy, directed this film, which features prolific Hong Kong action-film actor-director Sammo Hung Kam-Bo. It is an adaptation of the exhaustive epic fantasy novel *Warriors from Zu Mountain* by Li Show-Min.

Zwords of the Zombies (1982, Italy) Otto Fasullo

Originally released as *Zpade dei morti viventi*, this predictably gory schlockfest is a unique intersection between the Italian zombie-cannibal film renaissance and the sword-and-sorcery genre. Our burly hero (played laconically by Balordo Muscoli) and his constantly naked female companion (Sessa Spennato) fight their way through hordes of flesh-eating natives and clay-covered undead, all of which a gleefully over-the-top Cattivo Attore controls as the evil wizard Fattucchiera. The only way to dispatch these unholy creatures? "Stab-a them in-a the eye!"

INDEX OF MAIN FILMS

Symbols

7th Voyage of Sinbad, The 23

A

Army of Darkness 286
Ator, The Fighting Eagle 160

B

Barbarian Queen II: The Empress Strikes Back 281
Barbarians, The 251
Beastmaster, The 136
Big Trouble in Little China 243
Black Cauldron, The 204
Brave 383

C

Chronicles of Narnia: The Lion, the Witch and the Wardrobe, The 354
Clash of the Titans 99
Conan the Barbarian 123
Conquest 180

D

Dark Crystal, The 151
Deathstalker II 266
Dragonheart 293
Dragonslayer 107
Dungeons & Dragons 300

E

Excalibur 91

G

Golden Voyage of Sinbad, The 44

H

Hawk the Slayer 83
Hercules 173
Highlander 218
Hobbit: An Unexpected Journey, The 390
How to Train Your Dragon 368

J

Jason and the Argonauts 37

K

Krull 166

L

Labyrinth 234
Last Unicorn, The 144
Legend 225
Lord of the Rings: The Fellowship of the Ring, The 308
Lord of the Rings: The Return of the King, The 344
Lord of the Rings: The Two Towers, The 326

M

Magic Sword, The 30
Monty Python and the Holy Grail 50

N

Neverending Story, The 185

P

Pirates of the Caribbean: The Curse of the Black Pearl 336
Princess Bride, The 257

R

Red Sonja 197

S

Sinbad and the Eye of the Tiger 76
Solomon Kane 361
Star Wars 66
Sword and the Sorcerer, The 114

T

Thief of Bagdad, The 15

V

Versus 321

W

Warrior and the Sorceress, The 191
Willow 273
Wizards 59
Wizards of the Lost Kingdom 212

Y

Your Highness 375

THE AUTHORS

ARNOLD T. BLUMBERG has authored or co-authored a number of other books on film analysis and pop culture, including *Zombiemania: 80 Movies to Die For*, *The Big BIG LITTLE BOOK Book: An Overstreet Photo-Journal Guide*, and *Howe's Transcendental Toybox*. He has also designed books including *Zombiemania* and the award-winning *It Lives Again!* He is the co-owner of ATB Publishing and teaches courses in zombies, science fiction, comic books, superheroes (including the world's first course in the Marvel Cinematic Universe), and many other fun pop culture subjects at the University of Baltimore, prompting people to comment: "Where were you when *I* was in college?" Arnold has appeared in numerous zombie and horror documentaries like *Doc of the Dead*, *The 50 Best Horror Movies You've Never Seen*, and *The Walkers Among Us*, and together with producer and co-host Scott Woodard through G2V Productions, he hosts a podcast as the world renowned zombie expert known as the *Doctor of the Dead*! The team also produces podcasts on a wide array of pop culture topics, all located at G2VPodcast.com.

SCOTT ALAN WOODARD is a game designer, playwright, copywriter, and voice actor. He is the author of *The Sixth Gun Roleplaying Game* (Pinnacle Entertainment Group), and his produced dramatic work includes *War of the Elementals* (Colonial Radio Theatre), three audio dramas based on the long-running BBC series *Doctor Who*, and one play based on the classic American horror soap, *Dark Shadows* (all commercially available from Big Finish Productions). He has also won several Promax Awards for his work as a TV and radio promo producer for Warner Bros. and Disney, and he has worked as a designer, fabricator, puppeteer, and production coordinator in the movie special effects industry (look him up on IMDb!).